About Pearson

Pearson is the world's learning company, with presence across 70 countries worldwide. Our unique insights and world-class expertise comes from a long history of working closely with renowned teachers, authors and thought leaders, as a result of which, we have emerged as the preferred choice for millions of teachers and learners across the world.

We believe learning opens up opportunities, creates fulfilling careers and hence better lives. We hence collaborate with the best of minds to deliver you class-leading products, spread across the Higher Education and K12 spectrum.

Superior learning experience and improved outcomes are at the heart of everything we do. This product is the result of one such effort.

Your feedback plays a critical role in the evolution of our products and you can contact us at reachus@pearson.com. *We look forward to it.*

Fundamentals of Digital Marketing

Third Edition

Puneet Singh Bhatia

Senior Director, Axtria Inc.

Pearson

Photo Credits – Chapter Openers

Chapter 1	nmedia. Shutterstock	Chapter 7	Syda Productions. Shutterstock
Chapter 2	Dusit. Shutterstock	Chapter 8	rawpixel. 123rf.com
Chapter 3	x7vector. Shutterstock	Chapter 9	wavebreakmedia. Shutterstock
Chapter 4	123rf.com	Chapter 10	Sergey Nivens. Shutterstock
Chapter 5	peshkova. 123rf.com	Chapter 11	Rawpixel.com. Shutterstock
Chapter 6	ra2studio. Shutterstock		

Senior Manager—Product: Varun Goenka
Editor—Development: Jigyasa Bhatia
Senior Editor—Production: C. Purushothaman

ISBN 978-93-570-5961-9

First Impression, 2023

Second Impression, 2026

This edition is manufactured in India and is authorized for sale only in India, Bangladesh, Bhutan, Pakistan, Nepal, Sri Lanka and the Maldives. Circulation of this edition outside of these territories is UNAUTHORIZED.

Published by Pearson India Education Services Pvt. Ltd, CIN: U72200TN2005PTC057128.

Head Office: 1st Floor, Berger Tower, Plot No. C-001A/2, Sector 16B, Noida - 201 301, Uttar Pradesh, India.
Registered Office: 6th Floor, Tower A, Unit A and B International Tech Park, CapitaLand Chennai, 200 Feet Radial Road, Zamin Pallavaram, Old Pallavaram
Chennai – 600117, Tamil Nadu, India
Website: in.pearson.com, Email: companysecretary.india@pearson.com

Printed at : Saurabh Printers Pvt. Ltd.

॥ ਗਿਆਨੁ ਧਿਆਨੁ ਕਿਛੁ ਕਰਮੁ ਨ ਜਾਣਾ ॥

Gian Dhyaan Kich Karam Na Jaana

(Shri Guru Granth Sahib - Page 750)

I know of no bigger karma than the knowledge of truth.

Case Studies

Flipkart India: Walmart acquired Flip, grows at top clip 1

Amazon India: With the Metros in its pocket, 'Apni Dukan' Amazon to wow the heartland 52

Google India: Your Voice can Command Everything 83

Facebook (Meta): Indians don't text, they 'WhatsApp' 128

Twitter India: Working towards zero rifts and monetization 169

Times Internet: The Voice of Indian News 216

Linkedin India: Transitioning from Networking to Advertising 260

MakeMyTrip India: Recovering from the Pandemic 295

Info Edge India: Betting on Investments for Growth 366

One97 Communication: India's Go-To Payment Partner from Starbucks to Paan walas 397

Contents

Preface to the Third Edition xv
Preface to the First Edition xvii
Acknowledgements xxi
About the Author xxiii

UNIT I BASICS OF DIGITAL MARKETING

Chapter 1 Introduction to Digital Marketing 1
Evolution of Digital Marketing 4
From Traditional to Modern Marketing 5
Rise of the Internet: The Dotcom Era 7
Post Dotcom: Creation of Internet Business Models 8
Growth of 'E' Concepts: from E-Business to Advanced E-Commerce 11
Digital—The Next Wave of Marketing 17
Digital Marketing: An Introduction 19
Emergence of Digital Marketing as a Tool 20
Media Consumption Drivers for New Marketing Environment 22
Digital Marketing Channels: Types and Business Models 23
Digital Marketing Applications and Benefits 28
Internet Marketing: Underlying Technology and Frameworks 30
Internet Basics—Internet/Intranet/Extranet/Portals 31
Understanding Web and Wireless Technologies 31
Reshaping Interactions: Individuals/Businesses/Non-Profit 33
Opportunities and Challenges to Internet Marketing 36
Digital Marketing Framework 37
Delivering Enhanced Customer Value 38
Market Opportunity Analysis and Digital Services Development 40
ASCOR Digital Marketing Framework 41
Application of Digital Marketing 44
Critical Success Factors for Digital Marketing 48
Chapter Summary 49
Review Questions 49
Digital Application Exercises 50

Chapter 2 Digital Marketing Models Creation **52**

Factors Impacting Digital Marketplace 54

From Brick and Mortar to Bricks and Clicks 54

Growth of Interactive Platforms 56

The New Network Economy 59

From Marketspaces to Marketplaces 60

Changing Sales and Customer Service Patterns 62

Value Chain Digitization 64

Understanding Value Chain Functions 65

Key Value Chain Process: A Basic Understanding 66

Value Chain Elaboration: A Case of Journal Publishing 67

Emergence of Digitized Value Chain 69

Digital Marketing Business Models 71

Understanding Digital Value Elements 71

Digital Value-Led Marketing Approach 74

Digital Marketing Models Creation 75

Application of Digital Marketing Models 78

Chapter Summary 81

Review Questions 81

Digital Application Exercises 82

Chapter 3 The Consumer for Digital Marketing **83**

Consumer Behavior on the Internet 85

Evolution of Consumer Behavior Models 86

Impact of Digital Technology on Consumer Behavior 89

Attributes of Online Buying Behavior 92

Influence of the Web Experience 94

Introduction to Data Driven Marketing 95

What is Data-Driven Digital Marketing? 95

Basic Data Types 96

Understanding Data-Driven Analytics 97

Data-Driven Digital Marketing Strategy 97

Examples of Data-Driven Marketing Implementation 99

Marketing Intelligence from User's Online Data 100

Managing Consumer Demand 102

Understanding Consumer Demands 102

Demand-Led Product Development Process 105

Brand Building on the Web 107

Customer Identity and Privacy Management 110

Understanding Customer Identity 110

Understanding Customer Data Privacy 111

Developing Customer Identity: The Importance of Cookies 112

What are Website Cookies? 112

What are website cookies used for? 112

What are the different types of website cookies? 113

What are consent management platforms? 114

Impact of Demise of Third-Party Cookies on Marketers & Advertisers 114

Strategy for Future 115

Web-Tracking Audits and Forecasting 115

Integrated Marketing Communications (IMC) 117

Basics of Integrated Marketing Communications (IMC) 117

Channels for Integrated Marketing Communications 119

Four Pillars of the IMC Construct 121

Impact of Digital Channels on IMC 123

Practical Exercise 124

Executing Consumer Analysis 124

Chapter Summary 125

Review Questions 126

Digital Application Exercises 127

UNIT II DIGITAL MARKETING STRATEGY DEVELOPMENT

Chapter 4 Digital Marketing Assessment Phase **128**

Elements of the Assessment Phase 130

Marketing Strategy and its Digital Shifts 130

The Assessment Phase Elements 134

Macro-Micro Environment Analysis 136

Marketing Situation Analysis 138

Digital Marketing Internal Assessment 141

Analyzing Present Offerings Mix 141

Marketing Mix Analysis 146

Internal Resource Mapping 149

Core Competencies Analysis 151

Digital Marketing Objectives Planning 153

Digital Presence Analysis 153

Digital Presence Analysis Matrix 156

Digital Marketing Objectives Development 158
Digital Marketing Objectives Review 164
Practical Exercise 165
Market or Industry Trend Assessment 165
Chapter Summary 166
Review Questions 167
Digital Application Exercises 168

Chapter 5 Digital Marketing Strategy Definition **169**
Digital Marketing Strategy Groundwork 171
Understanding Digital Business Strategy 171
Emerging Digital Business Structures 175
Digital Core Competency Alignment 179
Customer Development Strategy (STP 2.0 Framework) 184
Defining the Digital Marketing Mix 192
Offering Mix for Digital 192
Digital Pricing Models 196
Channels of Purchase—Reaching the E-Consumer 199
Managing Promotional Channels 201
Developing the Extended Ps- People, Process, Programs, and Performance 203
Digital Marketing Strategy Roadmap 204
Developing Digital Marketing Strategy Roadmap 204
The 6S Digital Marketing Implementation Strategy 207
PLC Concept—Marketing across the Product Life Cycle 209
Practical Exercise 211
Executing Competitive Research 211
Chapter Summary 213
Review Questions 214
Digital Application Exercises 214

UNIT III DIGITAL MARKETING PLANNING AND SETUP

Chapter 6 Digital Marketing Communications and Channel Mix **216**
Digital Marketing Planning Development 217
The Media Planning Shift to Digital 218
Understanding Digital Media Planning Terminology 220
Digital Media Planning Stages 223
Investment Analysis and Planning for Marketing RoI 231

Designing the Communication Mix 233
Marketing Communications: from Mass Market to Mass Customized 234
Steps to Creating Marketing Communications Strategy 236
Developing Communications Messaging 239
Communication Mix across Digital Channels 241
Introduction to Digital Marketing Channels 243
Intent-Based Marketing (Search Marketing) 243
Brand-Based Marketing (Display Marketing) 247
Community-Based Marketing (Social Media Marketing) 250
Partner, Direct, Content, and Platform-Based Marketing Channels 252
Practical Exercise 255
Establishing Earned Media Presence 255
Chapter Summary 256
Review Questions 257
Digital Application Exercises 258
Chapter 7 Digital Marketing Operations Set-up **260**
Understanding Digital Marketing Conversion 262
Basics of Lead Generation and Conversion Marketing 263
Lead Nurturing and Lead Scoring Concepts 265
Setting up for Conversion: from Web-Page to Landing Page 268
Lead Management across Channels—Owned, Earned, and Paid 271
Basics of Web Development and Management 273
Pre-Planning for Web Development 273
Website Development Stages 276
Developing Site Diagrams and Wireframes 278
Website Content Development and Management 279
User Experience, Usability, and Service Quality Elements 282
Understanding Elements of User Experience 282
Implementation of Interaction Design 285
Understanding Web Usability and Evaluation 286
Measuring Service Quality Elements 288
Practical Exercise 290
Developing Owned Media Presence 290
Chapter Summary 291
Review Questions 292
Digital Application Exercises 293

UNIT IV DIGITAL MARKETING EXECUTION

Chapter 8 Digital Marketing Campaign Management **295**

Basic Elements of Digital Campaigns 297

Basic Elements of Digital Campaign Management 297

Campaign Planning and Budgeting 299

Campaign Set-up and Launch 301

Campaign Monitoring to Reconciliation 303

Implementing Intent-Based Campaigns (Search Execution) 305

Search Campaign Planning Basics 305

SEM Campaign Set-up and Execution 308

SEO Basics and Management 319

Implementing Brand-Based Campaigns (Display Execution) 327

Display Campaign Management Basics 328

Emerging Data-Driven Display Models (Programmatic and RTB) 337

Rich Media Ad Campaign Management 342

Campaign Execution for Emerging Marketing Models 344

Content Marketing (Cornerstone of Emerging Marketing Models) 345

Community-Based Campaigns (Social Media Execution) 347

Campaigns for Partner, Communication, and Platform-Based Marketing 349

Campaign Analytics and Marketing RoI 352

Basics of Web Analytics 352

Understanding KPIs 353

Introduction to Google Analytics 353

Web Analytics 2.0: Developing a Marketing Analytics Framework 355

Marketing Implementation RoI 356

Digital Marketing Refinement Phase 358

Practical Exercise 360

Executing Paid Promotions 360

Chapter Summary 362

Review Questions 363

Digital Application Exercises 364

Chapter 9 Digital Marketing Execution Elements **366**

Managing Digital Marketing Revenue 368

Digital Revenue Generation Models 368

Customer Loyalty Management in the Digital Era 370

Rise of Relationship Marketing: Turning Loyalists to Advocates 372

Driving Advocates through Customer Experience 374

Managing Service Delivery and Payment 376
Understanding Electronic Payment Systems 376
Emerging Digital Payments Solutions 378
Managing Digital e-Services (Setting up Digital Services Unit) 381
Selling through Cybermediaries 383
Managing Digital Implementation Challenges 385
Understanding E-commerce Implementation Challenges 386
Internal Challenges: Business and Infrastructure 387
External Challenges: Legal and Compliance 389
Consumer-Specific Security, Privacy, Ethical, and Social Challenges 391
Practical Exercise 393
Executing Marketing Analytics 393
Chapter Summary 394
Review Questions 395
Digital Application Exercises 396

UNIT V DIGITAL BUSINESS—PRESENT AND FUTURE

Chapter 10 Digital Business–Landscape & Emerging Areas **397**
Digital Marketing Landscape 399
Conceptualising the Digital Marketing Landscape 399
Digital Marketing Technology/Tools Landscape 402
Key Digital Advertising Trends in India 404
India Digital Marketing/Advertising Tools Landscape 406
Digital Marketing—Emerging Trends and Concepts 406
Big Data & IoT- Data Technologies Impacting Marketing 411
B2B and SMB–Segments Based Digital Marketing 413
SoLoMo-The Next level of Hyperlocal Marketing 415
Emerging Web 3.0 Trends 417
Blockchain Technology 417
Metaverse 419
Digital Payments 422
Audio-Social Marketing 423
Chapter Summary 424

Chapter 11 A Career in Digital Marketing **425**
Emerging Opportunities for Digital Marketing Professionals 426
The Changing Role of CMOs in Organizations 426

Building a Career in Digital Marketing *427*
Chapter Summary 431
Bibliography 1 *433*
Bibliography 2 *466*
Index *473*

Preface to the Third Edition

Five years have passed in a blink! And still the feeling of a new edition is the same as launching it for the first time.

I can completely recollect a similar time in 2017 when I was penning the first edition of this title. Little did I know, I would be on its third version in less than 5 years. Also, what I never imagined is how digital marketing as a subject will need to straddle across two multiple verses (web 2.0 and web 3.0) in the quest of a new identity.

Today, on one hand, as marketers we are worried about how web 2.0 concepts like data-driven marketing, customer identity and privacy, omnichannel marketing, etc. will evolve. On the other hand, we need to rapidly gain a foothold across emerging web 3.0 areas (Metaverse, Blockchain, Digital Payments, Audio-social Marketing, Artificial Intelligence) and review their impact on the existing marketing concepts and practices.

The third edition of the *Fundamentals of Digital Marketing* aims at establishing the first steps towards laying the foundational bridge from Web 2.0 to Web 3.0. This will help marketers grasp the changing facets of this transition and gauge the potential impact for professionals looking to implement these trending areas. Personally, it is both thrilling and a coincidence that the third edition of this text runs parallelly to the emergence of Web 3.0 itself!

Throughout these past five years, I have received many endearing reviews from readers. Your interactions have both propelled and inspired me on this journey to share the most exciting observations and learnings in a simple and lucid way.

Fundamentals of Digital Marketing, 3e, aims to expand upon the last two editions to include the emerging concepts across both Web 2.0 and Web 3.0 worlds along with the revision of the previous sections as per latest changes in the digital marketing ecosystem:

- Introduction to **Web 3.0 concepts** and in-depth coverage of key trends including **Blockchain Technology, Metaverse, Artificial Intelligence and Machine Learning (AI-ML), Digital Payments** and **Audio-Social Marketing** to review their impact on the digital marketing landscape
- Complete revision of the **Case Studies**, considering where the top Indian digital marketing firms stand across the digital marketing ecosystem as compared to the last five years
- Inclusion of a new section on **Introduction to Data Driven Marketing** to understand its impact on digital marketing
- Coverage of a new section on emerging concepts of **Customer Identity and Privacy Management**, which are becoming critical with the rise of customer-centricity over marketing funnel
- Review of **Digital Marketing Technology/Tools Landscape** and **Key Digital Advertising Trends** in India
- Mapping changes in digital marketing careers through an advanced **T-Shaped Growth Marketer Model**

I firmly believe that additions and updates to this edition will help both new learners and established marketers develop sound concepts and excel across all types of industrial and functional digital marketing implementations.

My gratitude goes out to Varun Goenka for his constant support since the beginning to present the best possible editions of this book. Great thanks to Jigyasa Bhatia and Anindita Malhotra for their incredible efforts in pulling the third edition together with the highest levels of editorial accuracy.

I look forward to an enthusiastic reception to this edition and future interactions (especially on LinkedIn and www.fodm.in) from each of you. Also, please share any inputs or feedback with the Pearson or directly with me. One-on-one conversations with my readers are what I cherish most as a writer and digital marketing professional. I hope to keep inspiring, and in turn, be enthused by the heights each of you reach in your professional, academic and entrepreneurial ventures.

Puneet Singh Bhatia

Preface to the First Edition

Digital marketing is all about the challenge of balancing both the sides of the marketing wheel while walking tightrope on the rim. On one side lies any marketer's owned media (websites, apps, social media pages) while the other represents the ever-changing demands and perceptions of his target customer. And this is just the start of the balancing act; one which extends across an advertiser and a publisher's needs, between CPM (Cost per mile) and CPC (Cost per click) and extends to measuring data and managing privacy concerns. The list is endless and so are the solutions available in the market.

It is these complexities and choices that make digital marketing unique and render a distinct flavor to this field of study. This book aims at helping both digital marketing enthusiasts and practitioners discern such nuances to make informed decisions right from digital marketing environment assessment and strategy development to marketing operations till refinement.

One of the key endeavors of authoring this title was to develop a textbook on Digital Marketing in India which starts from base zero and explains the key fundamentals to those new to the subject. This book will act as a primer not only for management students but also media professionals, marketing managers, brand marketers, budding entrepreneurs and even individuals looking to create a personal brand online and understand the basics of digital marketing concepts, tools, and techniques from grounds-up.

So why should you consider this text for academic, corporate, or personal needs? While there are many international texts available on multiple constituent areas of digital marketing like search, social, display, mobile, video marketing, etc., a need was felt for an India-specific standard text which lays the foundation for the genesis of digital marketing, explains the transition from traditional 'E-marketing' to 'Digital Marketing' and presents an integrated digital marketing framework to move step by step towards creating a digital presence, and finally benefitting from it.

Fundamentals of Digital Marketing provides unique features along the following lines:

- *Outlines the move from 'E-marketing' to 'Digital Marketing'*: This is one of the first marketing titles in India which moves beyond the 'E-marketing' plank to cover the new digital paradigm which is in essence a movement from:
  - (a) 'Traditional Channels' marketing to purely 'Digital Channels' marketing
  - (b) 'Supply Orientation' marketing to 'Personalized Consumer' marketing
  - (c) 'Product or Service' marketing to 'Digitized (Hybrid) Offerings' marketing
- *Underlines a practically-oriented digital marketing model (ASCOR Framework)*: This is one of the first Indian marketing texts which has a 'Digital Marketing' specific Framework: ASCOR (Assessment, Strategy, Channel and Communication, Operations and Refinement) that forms the backbone for the entire ecosystem of digital marketing activities and concepts.

- *Provides a detailed orientation to Digital Transformation*: To understand 'digital' as a concept and establish its importance for marketing, in the beginning of the textbook itself (Chapter 2) we have provided an extensive orientation to 'digital transformation' to help students/ business owners/entrepreneurs realize how they can best digitize any traditional business at hand through 'Digital Marketing Models' and identify key 'Digital Value Elements'.
- *Showcases industry deployable frameworks*: This title has been written in a manner which would help readers to deploy digital marketing concepts across each aspect of their industry, and be realistically ready to market each product digitally.
- *Details concepts through topical Case Studies of Indian businesses*: Each chapter starts with a case study on a prominent India-born or global India-based business, traverses through the company's growth in digital marketing, key challenges faced and lessons the reader can learn from their business story.
- *Includes Digital Application exercises on Indian brands*: At the end of each chapter, application exercises on key digital marketing concepts (pertaining to each chapter) have been provided, for students to self-assess their concepts and also apply them to brands which they have seen around/grown with in India since the last decade.
- *Devotes a complete chapter to careers in digital marketing*: The last chapter of the book is devoted specifically to the kind of jobs available in the market and how to approach those career tracks. Once the reader has mastered the concepts in all preceding chapters, he/she would know exactly the areas where he can look to be employed across digital marketing.

Coming to the structure of the book, this book has been covered across eleven chapters which form a part of five core units as follows:

- UNIT I (Basics of Digital Marketing): The first part introduces the reader to the basics of digital marketing, its underlying technologies and frameworks and establishes the ASCOR digital marketing framework. It further delves into defining the concepts of value chain digitization and digital marketing models creation. It also touches upon consumer behavior aspects for digital marketing including consumer demand management and Integrated Marketing Communications (IMC) for digital platforms.
- UNIT II (Digital Marketing Strategy Development): This part begins with an elaboration of the Assessment stage of ASCOR Framework which covers the Ecosystem for Digital Marketing, key elements of Digital Marketing Assessment and Digital Marketing Objectives Planning. It is followed by an exploration of the Digital Marketing Strategy stage which includes developing an understanding of the Digital Marketing Mix elements and a deep-dive into the 6S Digital Marketing Implementation Stages.
- UNIT III (Digital Marketing Planning and Setup): In the third part we cover the planning and setup stages of the ASCOR Framework including Digital Marketing Communications and Channel Mix and Digital Marketing Operations Setup. It starts with the coverage of Digital Media Planning stages and provides an introduction to all key digital marketing channels. Apart from this it also covers the basics of conversion marketing, web development and management along with developing an understanding of User Experience, Usability and Service Quality Elements.

- UNIT IV (Digital Marketing Execution): The fourth part drills deep into the basic elements of digital campaigns and their execution across all key Digital Marketing Types (Search, Display, Social, Partner, Direct, Content, Platform marketing). It completes the ASCOR Framework stages with coverage of Digital Marketing Measurement and Refinement. This part concludes with a full chapter on Digital Marketing Execution Elements including Digital Marketing Revenue, Service Delivery & Payment, Security & Privacy Concerns, Legal and Ethical Issues.
- UNIT V (Digital Business-Present & Future): This last part sheds light on key present and future aspects of Digital Marketing starting with the latest trends in digital business to covering the rise of E-commerce along-with discussing emerging digital business models. The book ends with a dedicated chapter on emerging career opportunities for digital professionals which will help readers of the book decide on career tracks they could follow being digital marketing professionals.

This book comprises insights gained from my years of corporate work experience and industry interactions with clients/workmates across multiple sectors, domains and geographies, which I have aimed to transform into practical and actionable frameworks and models. The title has been authored keeping in mind the needs of students, faculty, corporates, entrepreneurs and individuals who want to master the core concepts of digital marketing. I believe the title will best equip readers to begin a career in digital marketing and use the concepts as a launchpad to venture into specific channels, platforms and techniques as they discover them during their digital marketing careers.

And as is beautifully put in the parting words of the iconic and inspiring Pixar animation 'Ratatouille', I hope that with the knowledge gained from this book, you don't just 'Inspire Others' but regularly 'Surprise Yourself' in the true moments of exhilaration this journey presents!

We, at Pearson, wish you all the best for these digital expeditions.

Puneet Singh Bhatia

Acknowledgements

Among the many endeavors of marketing is to make its way into one's subconscious. And that is what this field of study probably did to me through mediums unknown and ways unsaid. The thrill of being able to reach out and influence even strangers through the written word and associated imagery is probably one of the most lucrative aspects of a marketing career (the ability to make a real dent in sales for business being the other).

It is between these traverses that one finds the inspiration and influence to write a book on marketing. And in this journey there are many who inspire you with their passionate conversations and those who make it real with their practical insights. From those who let marketing run breathlessly to those who let it tiptoe with a strict bridle, a marketer gets shaped through interactions across such multiple extremes. And it is these exchanges that have manifested themselves in the form of the text laid out in front of you right now.

From academic influences including Prof. Simran Singh (Simran Singh & Associates) who *taught me the basics of Retail Marketing at NIFT, Delhi to Prof. Ramesh Kumar (IIM Bangalore)* who reiterated the fact that each word in Marketing had a meaning (to quote one of his most popular comments 'There is a difference between Marketing and English and you should know when you are speaking what!') to corporate gumption exemplified by Ganesh Venkataraman (AVP, Cognizant Technology Solutions), I have both been impressed and blessed to be associated with media, marketing and digital professionals who have shaped my understanding of the subject and brought me closer to viewing it through the lens of a regular observer (which has been my attempt in writing this book).

From ideation to the ink on this page there are special mentions which I have for Pearson India team whose support has been highly instrumental in bringing forth this book. I would like to thank Varun Goenka for believing in my idea and the need for a comprehensive India specific title on Digital Marketing. A big word of thanks to Jubi Borkakoti for making sure that not only do we have the best edited text at hand but also supporting introduction of new ideas and features and for the relentless hours of discussions, at times on just a single image or an inverted comma. My gratitude also goes out to Priyankita Dey and Anumeet Kaur from the Rights and Permissions team at Pearson for their painstaking work on obtaining the rights for each image along-with Neha Nupur and team for all her efforts on the marketing of the title. I am also deeply thankful to Vikram Singh (DGM Product & Senior Managing Editor, Pearson) for providing me this opportunity to convert and present my experiences in the form of this title.

And finally coming to those who lay right to the major share of my gratitude: Family. My biggest indebtedness to my parents, especially to mom who taught me how to burn the brightest even when situations seemed tough- her strength and wisdom will always be the backbone for each of my endeavours. I also owe a lot to the endless technical and data related discussions with my brother (Avneet Bhatia) and content related feedbacks from my partner (Manpreet Kaur) both of whom have been my constant support throughout this extensive undertaking.

My final acknowledgment to the light of my life, my daughter Aarza, who lovingly (and unknowingly) gifted a lot of her hours which went into the making of this title for which I am obligated forever.

I hope that this edition provides you (the reader) the most simple yet practical way of learning digital marketing concepts from scratch and really helps in developing your knowledge to emerge as a strong digital marketing professional in future. Request each of you to share feedback and suggestions on topics you would like to extend or change in the book and I would try my best to include the same in forthcoming editions.

Thanks again for providing an opportunity for us to learn this wonderful and emerging area together.

Puneet Singh Bhatia

About the Author

Puneet Singh Bhatia is a digital marketing professional with over 18 years of experience. He has been conferred with '100 Most Influential Marketing Tech Leaders' award by the CMO Council and World Marketing Congress in 2016 followed by the '100 Most Innovative Marketing Tech Leaders' award in 2018 and 'Marketing Mavericks' title in 2021. Puneet has authored two books with the title 'Fundamentals of Digital Marketing' turning an Amazon #1 Bestseller.

After completing his MBA from IIM Bangalore, Mr Bhatia has led industry-transforming digital marketing projects. His interest areas include tracing the shifts in digital marketing landscape especially in upcoming areas including data-driven marketing, experiential marketing, digital story-telling, marketing automation, etc. During his corporate stint, he has been responsible for creating marketing strategies, developing digital domain and process transformation frameworks, and executing thought leadership in multiple positions he has held at Patni Computers (now Capgemini), Cognizant Technology Solutions and Axtria Inc. At present, he's Senior Director in Axtria, one of the fastest growing Big Data and Decision sciences company serving global clients across sales and marketing functions.

Mr Bhatia has provided marketing consulting, operations and delivery services for prestigious international and Indian clients including Google, Viacom, RTL Group, Wiley, The New York Times, Apple, Twitter, Reliance, The Hindu, The Hindustan Times, Anand Bazaar Patrika, etc.

The author has participated in multiple campus conclaves, corporate workshops and digital enablement seminars across prominent Indian colleges, corporate and public institutions. He has conducted both faculty and student interaction sessions across prominent Indian colleges and is also on the advisory board for digital marketing across multiple MBA colleges guiding them on their digital initiatives and curriculum development.

About the Author

CHAPTER 1

UNIT I BASICS OF DIGITAL MARKETING

Introduction to Digital Marketing

LEARNING OBJECTIVES

After studying this chapter, you will be able to:

- Explain the evolution of digital marketing
- Define digital marketing and differentiate it from traditional 'e-models' like e-business and e-commerce
- Outline the underlying technology and frameworks within which digital marketing operates and gain an understanding of digital transformation models
- Describe the structure of digital marketing, opportunities, applications, business modes and challenges
- Understand key components and application of ASCOR Digital Marketing Framework across multiple stakeholder scenarios

CASE STUDY Flipkart India: *Walmart acquired Flip, grows at top clip*

From Indian to international, from elusive customers to inclusive hyperlocal growth, from spiralling revenues to leading the ecommerce pack, Flipkart has shown tremendous growth since its inception in 2007.

To get a perspective on the changes in Flipkart, let us first map some interesting statistics on India's e-commerce market. A 2015 Flipkart case study by IBEF (see Bibliography for details) pointed to an anticipated valuation of US$100 billion by 2020. However, the figures by the end of 2020 stood at only around US$46.2 billion—only almost half the projected number. Despite this, the overall market grew by a tremendous clip of around 150 per cent since 2015, which shows the robustness and growing demand for the online retailing industry. Let us also underpin the next set of anticipated numbers which pegs Indian E-commerce market to grow to US$ 85.5 billion by 2025.

While Flipkart was the Bellwether Online Retail Firm in 2014 (surpassing Snapdeal and Jabong), the challenge of retaining the 'No.1' position in the Indian e-commerce market was hard. Flipkart clocked paltry revenue growth and negative profit growth figures in FY2016 and 2017 (Figure 1.1). The month of October 2016 was make or break, with Flipkart facing continuous losses and stagnant sales growth. This tipping point was mounting over the past few years with Flipkart losing customers and revenue to Amazon, primarily due to Amazon's aggressive investments in experience, payments, storage and logistics.

Facts & Figures

Standalone Financials of Flipkart India **Figures in ₹bn**

Year	FY14	FY15	FY16	FY17	FY18
Revenue (₹ billion)	28.4	95.3	131.7	155.6	216.5
Revenue growth (%)	140.6	70.1	27.6	15.3	39.1
Profit (₹ billion)	–4.0	–8.3	–5.4	–2.4	–20.6
Profit growth (%)	207.6	107.5	–53.7	–55.5	758.0

Figure 1.1

Source: Annual report of Flipkart India Private Limited for the year 2021–22.

Till 2017, Flipkart had raised US$1400 million from investors, but due to impending challenges (specific to Amazon's aggressive investments), the owners of Flipkart sold their majority stake to Walmart in 2018 for US$16 billion (one of the biggest deals in the e-commerce history). This deal allowed Walmart to jump straight into a small but rapidly growing Indian e-commerce market with about a 100 million customers at the time.

The three focus entities for Walmart in 2018 were Flipkart (Core e-commerce), Myntra (Fashion e-commerce) and PhonePe (Payments App). While all three entities have shown tremendous growth in the retail sphere of their core businesses, Flipkart expanded into other areas like Flipkart Wholesale (B2B), Flipkart Health+ (healthcare), Cleartrip (Online Travel Aggregator), and Shopsy (social commerce). In an interesting new precedent for India, in July 2020 Flipkart acquired its parent company Walmart's loss-making B2B wholesale franchise 'Best Price'—an attempt to consolidate its operations with the launch of its own service, 'Flipkart Wholesale'.

Walmart acquired Flipkart in 2018. Post-acquisition, Walmart proved to be a 'good partner' for the company. With Walmart's second round investment of US$1.2 billion,

Flipkart's market valuation grew from US$21 billion in 2018 to US$24.9 billion in 2020. The acquisition supported both Walmart and Flipkart with their revenue and growth goals.

Over the last seven years, there have been huge changes in the functioning of Flipkart. Post acquisition, the company's performance has been credit-worthy. On almost all fronts, apart from the total number of sellers, Flipkart has been ahead of its competitors. Future projections for Flipkart are bright, with the Business Insider group estimating Flipkart's e-commerce gross sales for 2023 to be higher than that of Amazon India (US$14.9 billion vs. US$11.7 billion).

Company	Flipkart
Founded In	2007 (Walmart acquired Flipkart in 2018)
India Headquarters	Bengaluru
Parent Company	Walmart Inc.
Number of Sellers	375K+
Number of Users	350 Mn+
Number of Unique Products	150 Mn+
Market Share in 2020	31.9%
Revenue FY20	$4.6 Bn

Figure 1.2 Flipkart's Statistics in FY 2020
Source: Annual Report of Flipkart India Private Limited for 2020

Key statistics that reflect Flipkart's performance enhancement are as follows:

(a) During 2021 festive sales, Flipkart retail arms (Myntra and Flipkart) emerged as the leader in gross merchandise value (GMV), capturing 62 per cent of the market share. Flipkart has cracked the code to festive sales that the company seems to continue using for its future growth.

(b) Between January and November 2021, Flipkart recorded more competitive Google Play impressions compared to Amazon India on the Google Play Store. This is attributed to the growth of its platform Shopsy, which directly competes with the likes of Meesho and DealShare, popular social commerce platforms in India.

(c) During 2021 festive sales, Flipkart was perceived as the best platform for customer satisfaction and topped the brand equity score with 9.7.

(d) Walmart is investing heavily in online payment systems and the supply chain through PhonePe, which will help in Flipkart's ability to execute omnichannel commerce.

(e) Flipkart struck a deal with Adani Logistics Limited to build a 534,000-square-foot warehouse and data centre. The deal is expected to help Walmart gain a bigger fulfilment presence in India.

(f) By September 2020, Flipkart had onboarded 50,000 additional kiranas in preparation for its annual "Big Billion Days" sale across India's festival shopping season.

(g) Apart from this, innovations like Flipkart's introduction of 'Hagglebot', which lets consumers bargain through voice shopping will help differentiate itself and make its e-commerce platform more attractive.

In 2021, Flipkart also invested a large amount in digital marketing, which worked effectively for this brand. With the targeted campaign of "India's Fashion Capital", Flipkart India has changed its outlook and opted for fashion as its key marketing pivot. This strategy has made Flipkart touch new milestones and increased awareness multifold. Even during the COVID-19 pandemic, Flipkart saw a nearly 50 per cent increase in new users right after initial pandemic lockdowns. The platform also experienced a 35 per cent increase in onboarded sellers during 2020, compared to the previous year.

Other players like the Tata Group's recent launch of a super app called Tata Neu to noise-up its e-commerce presence, after its acquisition of popular e-commerce apps—BigBasket and 1mg. The Reliance Group, on the other hand, is rapidly expanding its ecommerce platform JioMart, and has made multiple investments in 2022—the most important one being Dunzo, a quick commerce platform.

With newer players emerging by the day, in the next few years it will be interesting to witness how Walmart-Flipkart tries to maintain its leader position in the Indian market and hit solid revenues to extend its lead in the wake of formidable competitors like Amazon India, Reliance Jio and Tata Group.

EVOLUTION OF DIGITAL MARKETING

Marketing as a discipline has undergone radical changes over the past few decades. Since 1450, when Gutenberg's printing press began its operation, leading to mass production of flyers and brochures, till the present time when automated posting of online advertisements has become very common, marketing has kept up incredibly well with changing technology. Along with shifts like customers' social orientations towards buying and the humongous information available at hand to compare multiple products and brands, 'modern marketing,' a phrase coined recently, has emerged steadily marking a new phase.

To understand how and why the original marketing concept and its orientations have shifted, let us go through the various stages of evolution termed as 'Marketing Eras'—

- **Trade era:** products were handmade; hence supply was limited
- **Production era:** products were mass produced and consumers focused on features like low cost and availability

- **Product era:** focus moved from quantity to quality and consumers laid more emphasis on quality, performance, and innovative features
- **Sales era:** with increasing competition companies were compelled to emphasize on aggressive selling and promotion, commoditization of products, leading to saturation of consumer demand
- **Marketing era:** marketing emerged as a practice as consumers started demanding better products; differentiators like pricing, distribution, and promotion became important
- **Relationship era:** customers started getting valued to build a long-term orientation
- **Digital era:** also called the social/mobile era, the focus is on real-time and social exchange-based marketing where communication and social interactions play a prime role

From Traditional to Modern Marketing

To appreciate the evolution of marketing through its history, we need to first understand how marketing as a discipline was applied in a traditional sense to its modern avatar.

The classic definition of marketing according to AMA (The American Marketing Association) *is 'the activity, set of institutions, and processes for creating, communicating, delivering,* and exchanging offerings that have value for customers, clients, partners, and society at large.'

If we elaborate this definition to compare and contrast traditional marketing activities with how they are being managed in the modern sense, we will see that technology has played a big part in this transition.

Premise of Traditional Marketing

Traditional marketing, by definition, includes platforms and techniques which were used as one-way communication tool rather than interactive ones. Four such historically important tools are listed below.

- Print marketing (newspapers/magazines/direct mailers/catalogues) provided daily news, classifieds, local and interest-based dailies/periodicals/flyers which were monetized through promotions and local advertisements
- Broadcasting (television/radio) provided entertainment, knowledge, and live events, primarily supported by television advertisements
- Home marketing (billboards) has had great impact over decades in terms of influencing consumers
- One-to-one marketing (telemarketing) had been effective though expensive

Factors Impacting the Shift from Traditional to Modern Marketing

Traditional marketing techniques (more prevalent prior to the 1990s, before interactive technology started making its impact) focused on elements which in the present age have undergone significant shifts (for comparative estimate between traditional and modern marketing areas, see Table 1.1). Key reasons for such shifts include:

Table 1.1 Comparison of Modern Marketing Scoring over Traditional Techniques

Area of Comparison	Traditional Marketing	Modern Marketing
(a) Interactivity	Customer has no choice in receiving messages of his interest	All channels have certain interactivity
(b) Engagement	Difficult to track results and impact of marketing	Focus is on customer satisfaction and building a relationship
(c) Agility	Delivery though physical channels takes larger fulfillment time	Efficiency in terms of 'agility of service' is much higher
(d) Conversions	Closer to product awareness and interest stages	Activities targeted to more towards 'end of the funnel' relating them with consumption
(e) Personalization	Mass marketing techniques with low personal touch	High potential to customize offerings for each customer
(f) Brand imagery	Difficult to build brand imagery because of platform limitations	With rich media/video gaining prominence strong imagery is possible
(g) Social involvement	Not able to involve social integration features	Ability to socialize and build trust by leveraging social networks

- Power shift from business to consumer attributed to availability of a wide variety of product choices and saturation of key categories
- Growing amount of communication channels leading to clutter and brands moving away from mass marketing to customized online marketing
- Consumers' preference for interactive rather than traditional medium like newspapers, magazines, TV, which had a one-way information flow
- Need to validate marketing with product and service recommendations from trusted group of influencers/social interactions
- Need for comparison of product benefits to make informed decisions (multiple messages need to be heard, understood, and trusted upon by target segment)
- Higher interaction with products and more avenues for such interactions facilitating holistic messaging rather than the traditional practice of one-off marketing
- The emergence of marketing as a discovery-led immersive exercise for an individual/group rather than forced messages targeted to large audiences

Advent of Modern Marketing Techniques

Modern marketing involves the following platforms and techniques:

- **Search marketing:** using search technology towards marketing
- **Online advertising:** placing ads across websites/digital platforms

- **E-mail marketing:** sharing commercial messages with people
- **Social media marketing:** using social media platforms/networks for marketing
- **E-commerce:** selling/trading goods and services on any online platform
- **Digital on traditional mediums:** integrating digital technologies with traditional marketing mediums to improve interactivity (set-top box for TV can be integrated with internet-enabled features to support digital sales)

Although modern marketing is surging ahead, traditional marketing methods have their own importance while targeting niche customers and high-end groups who are more used to personalized and value-added targeting.

Rise of the Internet: The Dotcom Era

The transition from traditional to modern marketing has occurred over a period of time on the basis of fundamental technological changes impacting marketing. Most of them, undoubtedly, have been the invention of the internet and its wide application to business marketing. The concept of internet which began with development of electronic computers in the 1950s in United States impacted the basic manner in which information would be stored and distributed globally through the concepts of communication protocols and internet networking (wherein multiple separate networks could be joined to a network of networks).

More important were the advancements which led to the creation of e-mail and World Wide Web (WWW), which brought out the power and influence of the internet and related it to common man's needs for communication and information. E-mail started in 1965 as a way for multiple users of a time-sharing mainframe computer to communicate with each other. In 1989, Tim Berners-Lee, a scientist at CERN, with his invention of the World Wide Web ensured that the practical application of this technology would be made available to all. This followed by the inventions of web browsers like Mosaic and Netscape, made sure that sitting in any corner of the world one would be able to access data and receive information from any other part of the globe. It liberated the way information would be shared and marketing would be promoted in the coming years.

World Wide Web Leading to an Explosion of Information Share

The invention of the internet led to a large-scale economic boom that never witnessed before. The evolution of WWW brought the development of HTTP (Hypertext Transfer Protocol) which is the foundation of data communication for the World Wide Web. HTTP functions as a request–response protocol in the client–server computing model. Typically for any particular data to appear on any web page, a request is placed by the client to the server using an HTTP protocol. For example, a web browser like Netscape could be the client and a music player running on a computer can be the server.

Emergence of Websites and the Concept of URL

World Wide Web started facilitating the display of text and images through websites which were a set of static web pages containing information useful for their target audience.

A website is typically hosted on at least one web server and is accessible through an internet address known as the Uniform Resource Locator or the URL. All the websites together constitute what we call the World Wide Web. Websites contain web pages which are typically documents in plain text with specified formatting instructions of Hypertext Markup Language (HTML).

Dotcom Era and the Phenomenon of Modern Marketing

Modern marketing began to create and use web pages to build virtual information centers for their products and brands primarily for information dissemination and also to become the first movers to adapt technology as a part of their marketing activities. In that period, the entire scale of activities and reach of internet for marketing was still not well established, even difficult to envision. A unique phenomenon that occurred with the rise of WWW related to what we call the dotcom era or more popularly referred to as the Dotcom Bubble.

With websites started to be developed at a rapid scale, each individual/firm would need to create a unique name or URL which would become the address for its online venture. Dotcom (*.com*), the last part of the url and a short form for commerce, indicated that the companies were engaged in internet commerce. As it became clearer to companies, investors, and speculators that internet was going to be the next biggest medium for selling and marketing, several companies started setting up virtual shops in the hope that a large part of their business would start functioning online through these websites.

This led to multiple initial public offerings (IPOs) in succession wherein businesses were throwing huge sums of money on a relatively new medium for which they had little knowledge and no experience. The valuations of these companies were based on nothing more than just business ideas scribbled on a piece of paper. The basic principle was that investors did not want to lose out on a chance to be a part of the gold rush, even when they had no understanding of how or by when these investments would turn into a profit.

On 11 March 2000, Nasdaq, the key stock index for Wall Street witnessed a tumble of technology shares' valuation, following which the net worth of a large of number of dotcom companies started to fall rapidly. Nasdaq experienced big falls as the business community realized that most of these technology companies were merely bubbles waiting to burst and blew away billions of dollars with them. This led to the era which we now commonly know as the dotcom bust, post which a lot of companies understood that digital was to play a supportive role in marketing and sales would primarily be driven through physical models, a thought that would eventually change in the subsequent decade.

Throughout this mayhem, the biggest positive takeaway was that digital marketing as it is known to be today got defined and established. Many interesting business ideas came forth, which a decade later, would flourish to actually become internet behemoths.

Post Dotcom: Creation of Internet Business Models

As discussed in the last section, even while the dotcom bubble was taking technology stocks down, a lot of positives were being registered on the internet timeline. In 1995, Amazon.com bookstore had appeared; Netscape IPO was launched; and Sergey Brin and Larry Page were planning the future Google. Microsoft Internet Explorer appeared in 1996 and Hotmail came up as the first web e-mail site whereby internet started to impact the daily lives of its consumers laying the foundation of business to consumer (B2C) as a prominent online business model.

By 1997, people in the United States were looking at more than one million sites on their screens and blogging as an activity was beginning to attain prominence. The next year saw Mozilla come up with an open-source browser and Google answer more than 10,000 search queries a day. All of these were positive and stable milestones which saw internet take its baby steps in an environment of huge frenzy and over-hyped expectations.

The emergence of Microsoft as the most dominant browser along with AOL's purchase of Netscape were activities at the peak of the dotcom bubble which had significant impact post 2000, with Microsoft and Google dominating the technology landscape. The biggest impact at this point of time was the emergence of search as a broad area of research where rapid strides led to the expansion of web as a critical marketing platform and Google as its most dominating player.

Growth and Impact of Search Technologies

The biggest impact which internet had on marketing can be clearly attributed to the rise of search technologies. The main aim of a search engine is to organize the internet and provide a coherent structure for easy access to information on specific keywords. Research on search computing had began as early as 1990 with the launch of WebCrawler, the first full-text web search engine, in 1994. Before WebCrawler only web pages were searched and this was the first search engine which was 'all-text' crawler based and allowed users to search for any word on any web page. Also in 1994, Lycos was launched and it became the first major commercial endeavor of its kind.

The following years saw the emergence of a lot of competing search engines including Excite, Infoseek, Inktomi, Altavista, Yahoo, the last two becoming industry leaders in web directories and web search engines respectively. Around 2001, Google with its proprietary 'Relevancy Ranking' approach was close to disrupting the search engine business and, in the process, went on to create a commercial engine which made it the center of internet activity. Google's Page Rank patent was not only a technological revolution but also a business innovation which changed the way marketing could be approached and profitable business models developed on the internet. The impact of search technology is pivotal to digital marketing and would be discussed in later chapters in detail.

Post 2000, there have been multiple other technological advances, apart from search, which have impacted businesses run on the internet. Key ones of those include impact of file-sharing technology, integration of communication services, growth of design—user interface (UI) technologies, and emergence of social collaboration tools. We would touch upon a few of these in detail to understand their right impact on the growth of digital marketing.

The Advent of Web 3.0

With the emergence of multiple technology streams beyond the dot-com era, it is important to trace how the nature of the web has transformed over the years and how it has impacted internet commerce and marketing.

The term Web 2.0, which was coined by Darcy DiNucci in 1999, was popularized by Tim O'Reilly at the O'Reilly Media Conference in 2004. It came to signify the cumulative changes in how webpages were made and built from their earlier avatar pre-dot-com era. Web 1.0 came to be known as the era in which a vast majority of users simply acted as consumers of content and content creators themselves were very few (according to Cormode, G. and Krishnamurthy, B. 2008)[1].

The previous two versions of the internet (Web 1.0 and Web 2.0) supported access to information and interactivity. But they had their limitations too. In the Web 1.0 version, it was difficult for users to find relevant information as there wasn't any algorithm to sift internet pages. Even though Web 2.0 had technical advancements over its previous version, it had issues like information overload, risk of security breaches (like fake IDs), spamming, forgeries, etc.

Web 3.0 is the next-generation technology that promises to integrate the vast amount of data on the Internet to make it more valuable for users. It is driven by a semantic web employing a machine-based understanding of data, with the objective of developing a more intelligent and connected web experience.

Web 3.0 is the future Internet where a user will have control over their own data, identity, and destiny. Also sometimes styled as Web 3, the term Web 3.0 was coined by Ethereum co-founder Gavin Wood. This future of the World Wide Web is based on Blockchain Technology for providing better security, privacy, and scalability to the users. Highlights that make Web 3 better than Web 1.0 and Web 2.0 include:

1. **Artificial Intelligence:** Web 3.0 at the core involves combining artificial intelligence and natural language processing to make computers understand and process words intelligently like humans do. This will help provide faster and more accurate results.
2. **Semantic Web:** The evolution of Web 3.0 involves the semantic web, which will improve the process of generating and sharing content by understanding the meaning of words, rather than processing it through numbers or keywords.
3. **Connectivity:** Connectivity in Web 3.0 will be highly effective because of semantic metadata. Content and information will be more accessible across applications and with a growing number of commonplace devices connected to the internet, it will provide a better user experience leveraging all available information.
4. **3D Graphics:** Extensive use of three-dimensional design in websites and services including computer games, e-commerce, etc.

[1] Cormode, G. & Krishnamurthy, B. (2008). Key differences between Web 1.0 and Web 2.0. First Monday, 13(6). https://doi.org/10.5210/fm.v13i6.2125

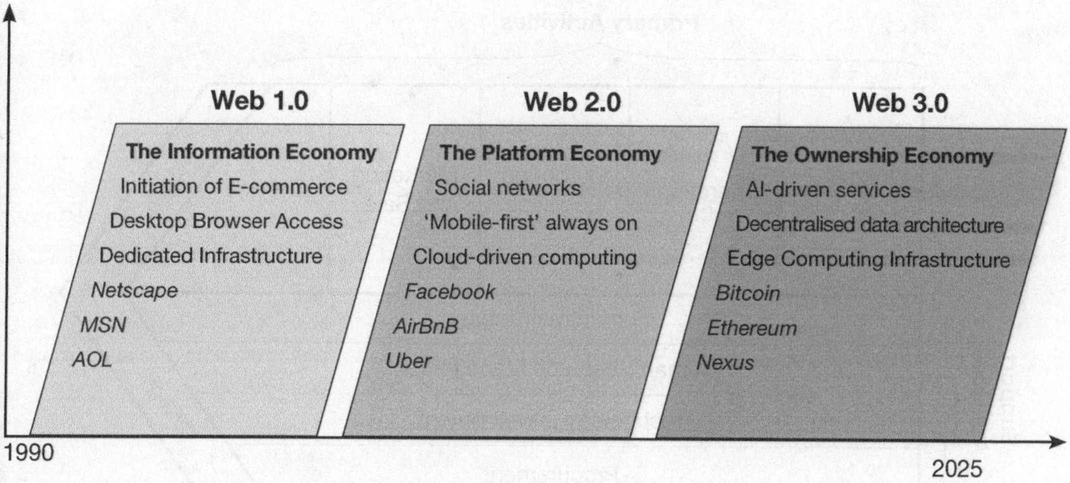

Figure 1.3 The Evolution of the Web

5. **Blockchain:** Blockchain technology will help protect and encrypt user data, ensuring that large companies do not make use of them in an unethical manner.
6. **Decentralised:** Data networks will be decentralised and users will be able to maintain ownership over their data and digital assets.

Growth of 'E' Concepts: from E-Business to Advanced E-Commerce

The rapid rise of internet and its effects on business at large can only be appreciated once we understand the influence, extent, and impact of multiple technologies at the business value chain level. A value chain is a chain of activities that a firm operating in a specific industry performs in order to deliver a valuable product or service for the market.

Essentially, as defined by Michael Porter in his understanding of value chains, there are five key primary activities, (as listed below), performed by any firm towards reaching its goals of value and revenue creation.

(a) **Inbound Logistics** includes relationships with suppliers and all the activities required to receive, store, and disseminate inputs.

(b) **Operations** refers to all the activities required to transform inputs into outputs (products and services).

(c) **Outbound Logistics** includes all the activities required to collect, store, and distribute the output.

(d) **Marketing and Sales** refers to activities that inform buyers about products and services, induce them to purchase, and facilitate their purchases.

(e) **Service** includes all the activities required to have the product or service work effectively for the buyer after it is sold and delivered.

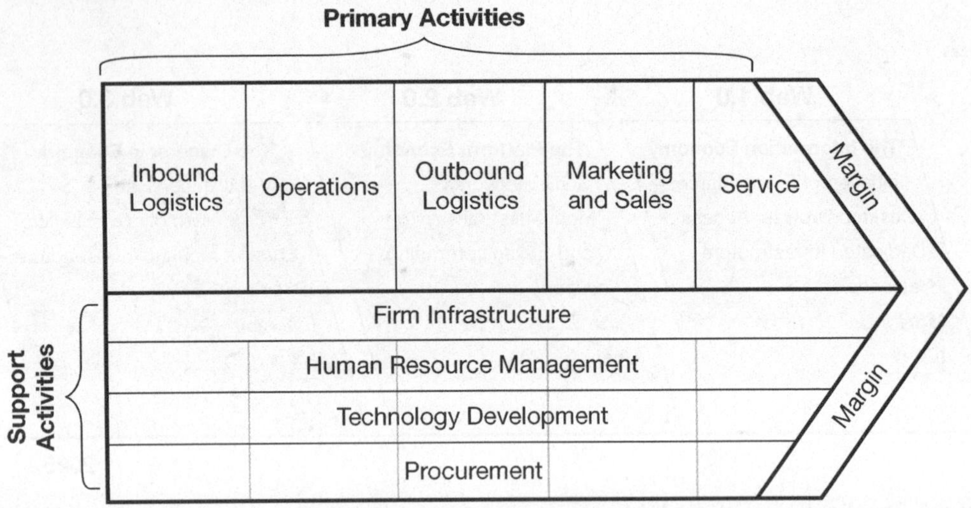

Figure 1.4 Value Chain Processes

Source: Michael E. Porter (1985: 11–15).

To understand and trace the impact of technology on these stages, it is imperative to map the processes enhanced by technology across each of them (see Fig. 1.4). This would also help us appreciate the differences in the definitions of terms such as e-business, e-commerce, e-marketing, online marketing, or the most recently coined term, digital marketing. In all these cases, 'E' stands for 'Electronic Networks' and describes the application of electronic network technology—including internet and electronic data interchange (EDI)—to improve and change business processes.

The reason for application of Porter's Value Chain model is that it explains in a single consolidated view, the coverage of each of the e-models and why they are essentially different even though they are used interchangeably in multiple contexts across business discussions and texts. That said, there are variations in the way these concepts have been explained across various standard marketing primers and one would benefit from taking this explanation as an instance of such attempts.

Understanding E-Models

To understand what each e-model encompasses, we would need to map the key physical process areas as described in Porter's model and understand the extent and coverage of technology on each of them in a holistic manner. To understand, let us take an example of the most ubiquitous internet term 'e-business' whose impact covers each of the four process areas outlined in Fig. 1.5 to appreciate how it impacted business in general and became the pioneer of future e-models.

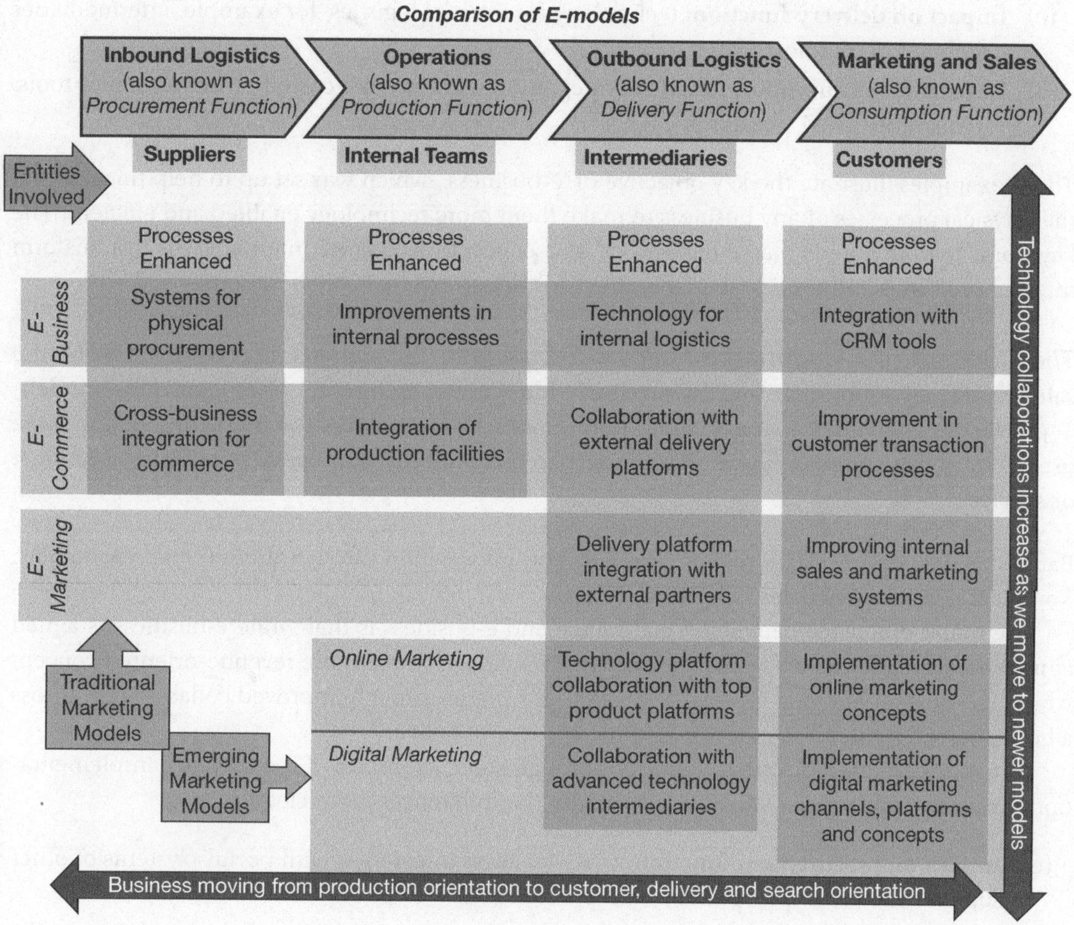

Figure 1.5 Comparison of E-models Mapped to Porter's Business Value Chain

E-business The term 'e-business' was coined by IBM's marketing and internet teams in 1996 and was looked at as a key differentiated market offering. It involved application of information and communication technologies (ICT) to support all the physical processes and activities of any business looking to go virtual.

Here are some examples of the kind of processes that impact across the value chain which form the basis of any e-business model.

(a) **Impact on procurement function:** management of physical procurement through IT, for example, Supply Chain System

(b) **Impact on production function:** improvements in internal production or resourcing, for example, production/knowledge portal

(c) **Impact on delivery function:** technology for internal logistics, for example, intermediaries collaboration portal

(d) **Impact on consumption function:** integration with internal customer management tools, for example, CRM platforms

These examples illustrate the key objective of 'e-business,' which was set up to help transition of the physical processes of any business to make them more technology enabled and efficient. The key point to note here is that 'e-commerce' as a concept has a more internal focus to transform internal processes and tools and enable them for better external collaborations.

The Concept of E-commerce Follows E-business E-commerce is considered to be the sales aspect of e-business and involves a wide variety of internet-based business models. Typically, an e-commerce strategy incorporates various elements of the marketing mix to drive users to a website or an online marketplace (like Ebay) for the purpose of purchasing a product or service.

Baourakis defines it as: 'The trading of goods and information through the internet' (Baourakis, Kourgiantakis, and Migdalas, 2002).

The major difference between e-commerce and e-business is that while e-business is aimed at improvements in efficiency and productivity, e-commerce is a more revenue-oriented concept which focusses on bridging internal and external systems through improved collaboration across all commerce-oriented functions, from procurement to delivery.

As in the case of 'E-business,' let us go through some examples of e-commerce implementation across the value chain which would clarify the differences more clearly.

(e) **Impact on procurement function:** cross-business integration with portals/systems of other suppliers, for example, portal-based procurement

(f) **Impact on production function:** integration of common production facilities, for example, value added production chains

(g) **Impact on delivery function:** collaboration with external delivery platforms for example, web-based marketplaces

(h) **Impact on consumption function:** improvement in transaction/sales/payment-focused processes, for example, customer payment platform

As can be seen above, e-commerce has a stronger orientation towards technology investments for commerce and better collaboration with the internal–external tools to carry out the sales process.

As can be seen in Table 1.2, e-commerce in India had started with the launch of IndiaMART in 1996, almost during the same time as the rise of the dotcom era. The recent growth in e-commerce had started with the rise of Flipkart in 2007 by two ex-Amazon employees which gave Indian customers the first taste of how orders, placed through a website, can be fulfilled efficiently, in time, and of the expected quality. (A detailed case on Flipkart and its unique growth characteristics is covered in the beginning of this chapter.)

Table 1.2 A Timeline for the Development of E-commerce Globally

1979: Michael Aldrich demonstrates the first online shopping system.
1981: Thomson Holidays, UK, is the first business-to-business online shopping system installed.
1982: Minitel was introduced across the nation in France by France Télécom and was used for online ordering.
1984: Gateshead SIS/Tesco is the first B2C online shopping system and Mrs Snowball, aged 72, is the first online home shopper.
1984: In April 1984, CompuServe launches the electronic mall in the USA and Canada. It is the first comprehensive electronic commerce service.
1992: 'Book Stacks Unlimited' in Cleveland opens a commercial sales website (www.books.com) selling books online with credit card processing.
1994: Netscape releases the 'Navigator' browser in October under the code name Mozilla. Netscape 1.0 is introduced in the late 1994 with SSL encryption that made transactions secure.
1994: Ipswitch IMail Server becomes the first software available online for sale and immediate download via a partnership between Ipswitch, Inc. and Open Market.
1994: 'Ten Summoner's Tales' by Sting becomes the first secure online purchase.
1995: Jeff Bezos launches Amazon.com and the first commercial-free 24-hour, internet-only radio stations, Radio HK and NetRadio, started it broadcasting. Dell and Cisco begin to aggressively use the internet for commercial transactions. eBay is founded by a computer programmer Pierre Omidyar as Auction Web.
1996: IndiaMART, a B2B marketplace was established in India.
1996: ECPlaza, a B2B marketplace was established in Korea.
1998: Electronic postal stamps can be purchased and downloaded for printing from the web.
1999: Alibaba Group is established in China. Business.com was sold for $7.5 million to e-companies, which was purchased in 1997 for $149,000. The peer-to-peer file sharing software Napster was launched
2000: The dotcom bust
2001: Alibaba.com achieved profitability in December 2001.
2002: eBay acquires PayPal for $1.5 billion. Niche retail companies like Wayfair and Netshops are founded with the concept of selling products through several targeted domains, rather than a central portal.
2003: Amazon.com posts its first yearly profit.
2004: DHgate.com, China's first online B2B transaction platform is established, forcing other B2B sites to move away from the 'yellow pages' model.

(Continued)

Table 1.3 *(Conitnued)*

2007: Business.com was acquired by R.H. Donnelley for $345 million.
2009: Zappos.com was acquired by Amazon.com for $928 million. Retail Convergence, an operator of private sale website RueLaLa.com, was acquired by GSI Commerce for $180 million, plus up to $170 million in earn-out payments based on the performance through 2012.
2010: Groupon reportedly rejects a $6 billion offer from Google. Instead, the group buying websites went ahead with an IPO on 4 November 2011. It was the largest IPO since Google.
2011: Quidsi.com, the parent company of Diapers.com, was acquired by Amazon.com for $500 million in cash plus $45 million in debt and other obligations. GSI Commerce, a company specializing in creating, developing and running online shopping sites for brick and mortar businesses, was acquired by eBay for $2.4 billion.
2012: US ecommerce and the online retail sales was projected to reach $226 billion, an increase of 12 per cent over 2011.
2014: Overstock.com processes over $1 million in bitcoin sales. India's e-commerce industry is estimated to have grown more than 30 per cent from a year earlier to $12.6 billion in 2013.

Difference between E-Business and E-Commerce

While some use e-commerce and e-business interchangeably, they are distinct concepts. In e-commerce, information and communications technology (ICT) is used in inter-business or inter-organizational transactions (transactions between and among firms/organizations) and in B2C transactions (transactions between firms/organizations and individuals).

In e-business, on the other hand, ICT is used to enhance one's business. It includes any process that a business organization (either a for-profit, governmental, or non-profit entity) conducts over a computer-mediated network. Apart from the above-mentioned processes, from procurement to sales, e-business can also include enhancement of internal management processes like employee services, training, internal information-sharing, video-conferencing, and recruitment which help improve internal productivity.

Moving ahead from business and commerce, the most commonly used marketing term to denote any form of internet operations is e-marketing. By definition, e-marketing involves utilization of electronic medium to perform marketing activities and achieve the desired marketing objectives for an organization. *This term is typically misused for e-business and e-commerce and, as per proper definition, should also be used to denote and represent marketing-related activities.*

The focus of e-marketing is to facilitate the transition of physical marketing and sales-based activities to a more automated, technology supported system which can drive the product discovery process. Two examples which make the concept of e-marketing clearer include:

(a) Delivery of products/services through collaborations with external partners, for example, logistics platform implementation

(b) Improvement of internal sales and marketing systems for stronger customer connect, for example, loyalty automation platforms

Before we move on to explain 'Online Marketing,' we should understand how it differs from e-marketing. Typically (as shown in Fig.1.5), e-marketing has a broader coverage which includes not only online/internet marketing aspects but also more enterprise-specific marketing areas like e-CRM, digital customer data, which gives it a broader scope than both of them. This is also the reason why in the e-models comparison diagram, e-marketing has been shown in the traditional bucket along with e-business and e-commerce.

The Concept of Online/Internet Marketing Online/Internet marketing started with reference to the internet and e-mail-based aspects of physical marketing and went on to grow and represent activities aimed at transitioning all marketing activities to web and online platforms—most primary of them being web-portals, e-mails, and blogs.

Along with the transition to web, the other most crucial characteristic of online marketing was the collaborations which started developing with other top platforms/websites holding inventory for commerce including Amazon/E-bay. These collaborations formed the basis of the growth of online marketing to its present avatar called digital marketing whose mainstay is deep technology and multi-platform marketing engagement.

Digital—The Next Wave of Marketing

The growth of online marketing and proliferation of new media platforms and communication channels have led to the evolution of marketing to its present form most commonly known as digital marketing.

Digital marketing if explained on the lines on the Porter Value Chain concept would include consumer and data-based technology implementations which aim at introducing and integrating newer technologies for a more data-oriented highly targeted marketing which is personalized for every consumer.

Key examples which bring forth the power of digital marketing in the context of the Porter model include:

(a) Delivery function: Collaboration with advanced technology intermediaries, for example, Marketing Automation Tools for Lead Generation/Reverse Auction Platforms

(b) Consumption function: Implementation of digital marketing platforms, channels, and concepts, for example, Search Marketing, Display Advertising, Social Media Marketing, etc.

While in the above section we have made introductions to key e-concepts and the basics of online and digital marketing, before we delve deeper into defining digital marketing, its types, models, and applications, it is imperative to also spend some time to understand the basis behind digital becoming so important to companies globally and how it has become a broad subject of study.

Definition of Digital and What It Means for Business

Digital by definition involves storing and transferring data in machine-readable language by conversion into binary values of 'zero' and 'one.' It involves a shift from the way data, be it audio, video, and images, was stored in the traditional mode (analog) to the manner in which it is presently stored in the digital world.

For business verticals of all types, moving to digital helps improve efficiency of operations and support transfer of more data at lower costs and bandwidths. It also optimizes the move to paperless processes, improves data procurement and delivery functions, and helps better integration with end-consumer technologies to enhance customer interaction and service.

To understand how digital is transforming overall stakeholder interactions, let us look at Fig. 1.6 which showcases transformation elements for each of the four key stakeholders—suppliers, internal teams, intermediaries, and customers across the Porter value chain model, as discussed in the preceding sections.

For each of the process functions related to each stakeholder (Procurement, Production, Delivery, and Consumption), Fig. 1.6 showcases transformation elements across three key transformation types:

(a) **Automation:** includes automation of various functions to enable faster and cheaper ways of performing key business activities

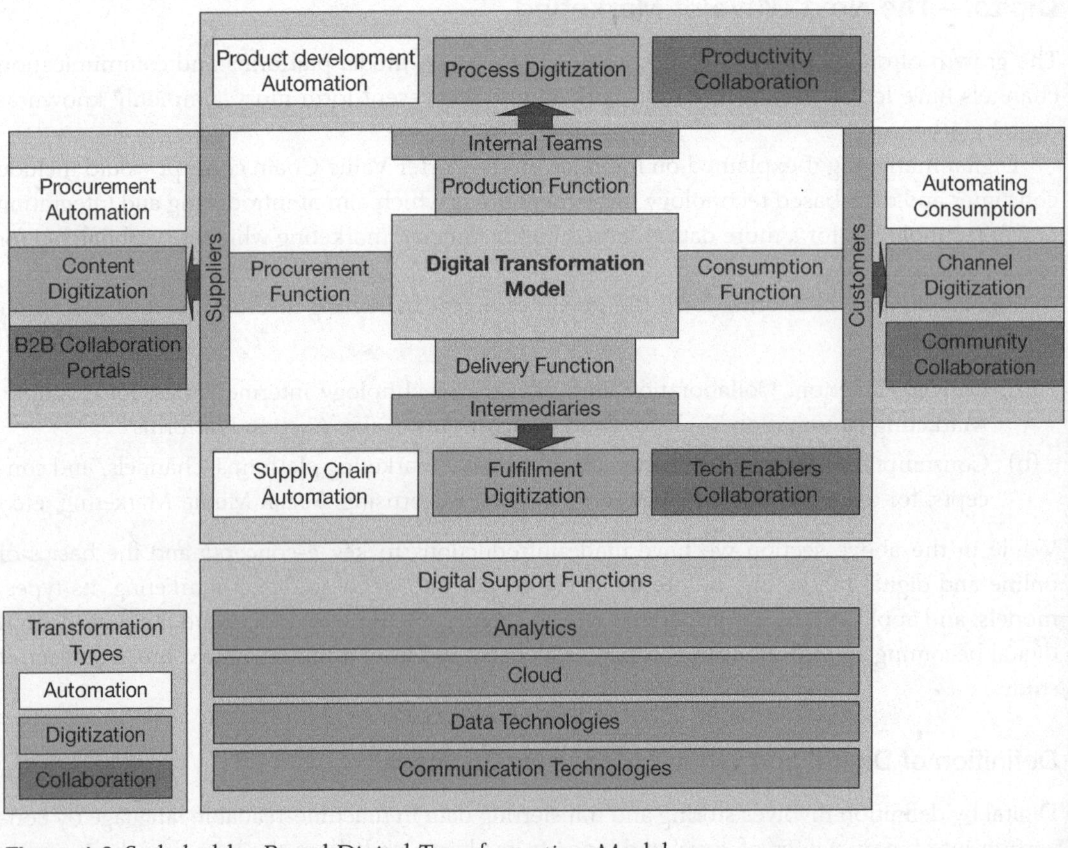

Figure 1.6 Stakeholder-Based Digital Transformation Model

(b) **Digitization:** involves conversion of physical assets and processes to port them on digital platforms to be utilized by stakeholders and delivered to customers

(c) **Collaboration**: helps integrate and share knowledge through a set of tools and practices to provide customers with a multi-channel digital experience.

Apart from the above elements, other digital support functions, which are essential to digital transformation, include analytics, cloud (infrastructure), data management, and communication-related technologies. This underlying technology stack is crucial to any successful digital implementation and will be discussed in greater detail in the later chapters.

Digital marketing typically corresponds to consumption function, wherein the main scope of this book lies. The importance of explaining digital transformation elements (before we cover digital marketing in detail) is to help visualize it as a part of the overall digital transformation strategy. Before we move further that since the scope of digital marketing itself has expanded tremendously, this textbook aims to cover digital marketing strategies in depth, while touching upon other digital transformation elements, as and when they seem important in relation to digital marketing itself.

DIGITAL MARKETING: AN INTRODUCTION

As seen in the Digital Transformation Model (Fig. 1.6), the extent of technologies and collaborations across digital marketing are much more pronounced than all the other e-concepts put together which outlines the essential difference and its rising prominence.

The definition of digital marketing according to IDM (Institute of Direct and Digital Marketing) includes *'the management and execution of marketing using electronic media such as the web, email, interactive TV, wireless media in conjunction with digital data about customers characteristics and behavior.'*

The unique differentiators from the definition are explained below.

(a) Digital marketing involves reaching out to potential customers through a set of interactive, intuitive, and advanced electronic devices and platforms which go beyond the normal web and e-mail to include mobiles, PDAs, interactive TV, applications, social media, which were earlier not common to marketing online through 'e' models. This explosion of platforms and devices has been possible due to rapid growth in mobile technologies and successive innovations which have made instruments like smartphones available in the hands of large audiences with readily accessible information.

(b) Application of marketing to consumer interaction touchpoints that integrate digital data about customers and their behaviors in a manner which was not extracted and targeted earlier. This has resulted in a whole new ecosystem of advanced technologies to target each valued customer customized with messages and promotions specific to their needs and intent.

(c) Introduction of interactive communication channels like search, display advertising, social media, etc., which have a strong combination of pull–push marketing rather than the earlier models which were primarily of push marketing nature. (In the next section, we shall detail the differences between the two types of models—pull/push and how this affects the way in which digital marketing creates a difference.)

(d) Incorporation of a variety of technological advances in communication, social integration, machine learning algorithms along-with their application to multiple devices and platforms, all of which have made it possible for digital to carve itself as an established area of marketing.

The key reasons as to why digital scores over other traditional forms of marketing include:

(a) **Audience targeting:** Helps to know which audience to target and why, with specific pre-designed messages suited to their specific problems and needs.
(b) **Cost leverage:** Digital mediums can be the most cost effective for messaging across a larger audience, which was the key reason in the first place for marketers to adopt them.
(c) **Actionable reporting:** The kind of quantitative customer segment data and qualitative feedback obtained here is far more authentic and actionable.
(d) **Location-based messaging:** No other type of marketing can develop and target personalized, location-based messages for customers as per their specific interests.
(e) **Quicker funnel fulfillment:** The covering of marketing funnel from awareness to action can be fulfilled much quicker after the customer has shown the first intent.
(f) **Multi-channel reach:** Digital marketing integrates data, communication, and messaging across multiple platforms, making it the best form of integrated marketing.
(g) **Instant customer interaction:** With customer interaction and service tightly integrated, it is the first time that marketers can interact in real-time to understand and support the problems faced by first-time or their most engaged users.

In the next section, we shall discuss the reasons behind the rise of digital as a prominent marketing tool, its types, and key applications and benefits.

Emergence of Digital Marketing as a Tool

Why has digital become so important and prominent lately and how does it matter to practitioners of marketing?

To understand and appreciate the rapid rise of digital marketing over its preceding concepts, it would help to gain an understanding of how the marketing function has changed over the years in terms of the most important parameter—*customer interaction*.

We define customer interaction as the manner in which any potential lead or customer gets to know or interacts with any product or service with the intention of gaining information or to respond to the marketer's goal of considering him/her as a consumer and finally convincing the latter to buy its products. This leads us to a key question as to *what does a consumer really look for from marketing?*

Any consumer, in a reactive or proactive mode, is typically looking to obtain information on any specific area of interest. He/she might not be looking at a product or a service itself but information which would solve any one of the problems at hand. He might also be just curious to gain knowledge on any subject (academic or general interest) or might just generally want to know what is happening currently around his neighborhood, city, or the world at large.

In the traditional form of marketing, the information to be delivered to consumers was decided, selected, or created by a group of media experts who took the decision of what knowledge would be circulated, printed, or broadcasted (in the relevant examples of newspaper, magazines, radio, and TV), which format it would be shared, and at what price would it be delivered. The consumer was more of a passive receptor of information and while in certain feedback columns or radio programs he could raise some questions. He was essentially gaining information and knowledge pre-curated for him and packaged with advertisements and promotions which he had no control over and maybe not much interested either.

The difference which successive marketing concepts kept bringing about till the present digital marketing era relate most to the manner in which the power of consumer choice has shifted from being a tame receptor to an active seeker of information. And, it is in this active seeking of information process that the heart of digital marketing lies. With this understanding, we would now put forth the two most important concepts which define and differentiate digital marketing—Pull and Push marketing.

Pull and Push Marketing

Any type of customer interaction with any digital media can be most simply be divided into two types depending upon where the contact is initiated:

(a) **Medium-initiated contact (Push marketing):** This is the traditional type of marketing where marketing messages are packaged with information pre-configured for a particular set of users. Take the example of a newspaper, which typically is current information packaged across different verticals like politics, economics, sports, etc., and packaged along with large ad columns which bring in the revenue (along with the classifieds). In contrast, let us understand what pull marketing entails.

(b) **Consumer-initiated contact (Pull marketing):** Pull marketing involves a consumer placing his intent and specific interest for a particular type of information and being offered that information along with relevant marketing messages suited to his intent, query, or profile-based interests. In the same example of a newspaper, as above, consider that the company decides to provide information in a way that each article of the newspaper is tagged and categorized based on multiple criteria to be searched upon a digital platform. In this case, when a consumer makes a specific search for a piece of content and chooses matching information/news, promotions are sent based on his profile preferences, real-time location, and the topic of the article he found interested in reading. This would then become be an example of pull marketing.

Based on key characteristic of these two types of marketing, the development of new digital platforms can be explained and understood. *Digital marketing includes all those techniques and concepts that utilize the intent (pull-based) action of the consumer to market products and services (in a push-based manner) which would be most needed, relevant, and of interest to him/her.*

Let us understand a few key types of digital marketing areas to see how digital technologies have been built around the combinations of pull–push marketing concepts:

(a) **Search marketing:** Search was one of the most pioneering pull–push marketing concepts which involved providing a technology platform to consumers to help them express their intent towards finding a particular piece of information and building a push marketing-based business around that search. (We would cover this particular topic and its technologies in detail in subsequent chapters and sections).

(b) **Display advertising:** Similar to print advertisements, display advertising was built on pulling data from consumers' readership interests on any particular website wherein display ads were pushed next to the content being read for consumers to interact, click, and buy on landing pages created for this action.

(c) **Social media marketing:** With the power of social networks coming to internet-based platforms, a marketer could not only use the information pulled from customer intent but also from the intent of his social networks which would be marketed back to him in the form of sponsored and native advertisements.

Media Consumption Drivers for New Marketing Environment

With the understanding of the pull–push concept, one would naturally tend to think about the key drivers behind this change in marketing to digital platforms and the reasons for shifting consumption patterns:

(a) **Emergence of internet** as discussed in the previous sections was one of the biggest factors of the transition to digital marketing. With growing availability of the internet, it became possible to access data and information as and when required.

(b) **Rise of millennial generation** or Generation Y (those born during the 1980s and early 1990s) with their differing attitudes and aspirations and also the rapid rise of social networking and collaboration concepts has led to the acceptance of digital as a major buying platform. It has grown tremendously to a level that certain product categories now are being bought only through digital channels.

(c) **Technology advancements in devices** and investments in hardware, infrastructure, location positioning and device memory, have brought forth convenient and feature-rich platforms like mobile, PDAs, tablets, etc., whose computational power and storage options have made it possible to execute research, personal interactions, and commerce, all on the go.

(d) **Advancements in design/UI** is becoming crucial. With Apple bringing design to the fore and ease of access becoming important by the day, digital has the fillip over other traditional platforms in being a slicker, more user-friendly platform where brand experiences can be felt and shared in their tangible and intangible forms not possible earlier.

(e) **Consumerism/rising global economies** in the context of emerging nations since the past two decades and with the rise of discretionary income across many work sectors, it has become easier for a large middle-class population to consume smartphones and tablets at prices never thought before. Also, with the rise in education levels and increasing accessibility, the effect of digital is reaching far and wide to even smaller towns and cities, thus increasing the consumer net rapidly.

Digital Marketing Channels: Types and Business Models

Before we to understand the digital marketing types, it is important to realize the difference between the concepts of digital media and digital marketing which sometimes are used interchangeably but are distinct from each other. Digital marketing, typically, refers to the electronic channels through which marketing is performed while digital media includes the process of digitization of media content (text, audio, video) to be transmitted over internet or online platforms. Typically, digital media/content is placed over multiple digital channels to achieve the objectives of marketing.

Digital Marketing Types Explained through REAN Marketing Engagement Framework

To explain digital marketing types, we first need to develop an understanding of the historic marketing funnel models and use one of them as a base to explain how different digital marketing types cater to each of the marketing funnel stages of that model. A marketing funnel model also referred to as a 'purchase funnel,' 'customer funnel,' or 'sales funnel' aims to put a structure to explain how a marketer or consumer goes through the various stages of marketing and consumption to finally purchase any product or service online.

One of the earliest models, which is still the most prevalent is the AIDA model which when expanded stands for Awareness, Interest, Desire, and Action stages. There are depicted in a trickle–down funnel-type diagram and showcase how a marketer induces awareness, generates interest for his product, creates a desire or impulse to buy, and finally, takes the customer through the action of purchasing the product or service. This model was introduced in 1893 by Addison Richards, an advertising agent from New York City, who wrote an advertisement for his business containing virtually all steps from the AIDA model, but without hierarchically ordering the individual elements.

Following this model, there have been numerous iterations and improvements based on the changing demands and functions of marketing and the addition of new digital marketing elements. The one we have used here as a base to explain the multiple digital marketing types is the REAN (Reach Engage Activate Nurture) model developed in 2006 by Xavier Blanc. We have added a Plan Stage before the four stages (to include the set of activities which involve planning and creation of the marketing material) and termed it as the 'Marketing Funnel' view. To explain the concepts further and understand the corresponding impact and involvement on the consumption side, we have also created a mirror funnel called the 'Consumer Funnel' which replicates the stages of the marketing funnel to look at consumer inputs and impact on the marketing cycle across each of the stages, which also impacts the overall digital marketing types deployed at each stage.

Explanation of Marketing and Consumer Funnel Stages

'Marketing Funnel' as depicted in Fig. 1.7 consists of four REAN model stages (including the additional added stage of Plan) which can be described as:

(a) **Plan:** Develop marketing plan, content strategy, and branding material which would be used to conduct marketing across the following funnel stages.

(b) **Reach:** Involves the set of activities to raise prospect's attention to marketer's brand product or service. (This is the stage where prospects are created.)

(c) **Engage:** The gradual, typically multi-channel set of activities needed to engage the prospects developed during the 'Reach' stage (This is the stage where leads are generated.)

(d) **Activate:** The activities needed for prospects to take the actions marketers want them to take. (This is the stage which relates to final converts or those who purchase.)

(e) **Nurture:** The activities needed to nurture the customer relationship created in the activation stage. (This is the stage which relates to creation of loyalists.)

With digital marketing providing a strong platform for consumers to proactively show their intent and interest towards a product, service, or brand, we felt it imperative to move beyond the regular 'Marketing Funnel' model to also add the 'Consumer Funnel' to it to help understand key interaction points which would form a base to describe the major digital marketing types.

Interaction Points of Marketing and Consumer Funnel Stages

(a) **Interaction Point A (PLAN-INTENT):** Involves integration of marketer's activities related to planning and consumer activities related to pre-marketing intent (towards brands, products, and services even before they have been exposed to any type of marketing). Typically by collating consumer intent-based activities, marketers can plan better for the search keywords they would invest in, customer support to be provided during the marketing cycle, and type of interest-based portals, aggregator sites, blogs etc., that, their target customer segments are specifically interested in.

(b) **Interaction Point B (REACH-AWARENESS):** This is the first stage of digital marketing activities wherein marketers typically invest in the most basic marketing activities like publishing content on major platforms, social sites, and most prominent interest portals/blogs. On the consumer side, this is the 'Passive Interaction' stage wherein the consumer initially discovers the marketing message but is not actively looking to interact and purchase. Investment areas for marketers here include Search Marketing (SEO/SEM/PPC), Display Advertising, Site Sponsorships, Affiliate Marketing, Social Sites Promotion, etc., which we will discuss in detail below.

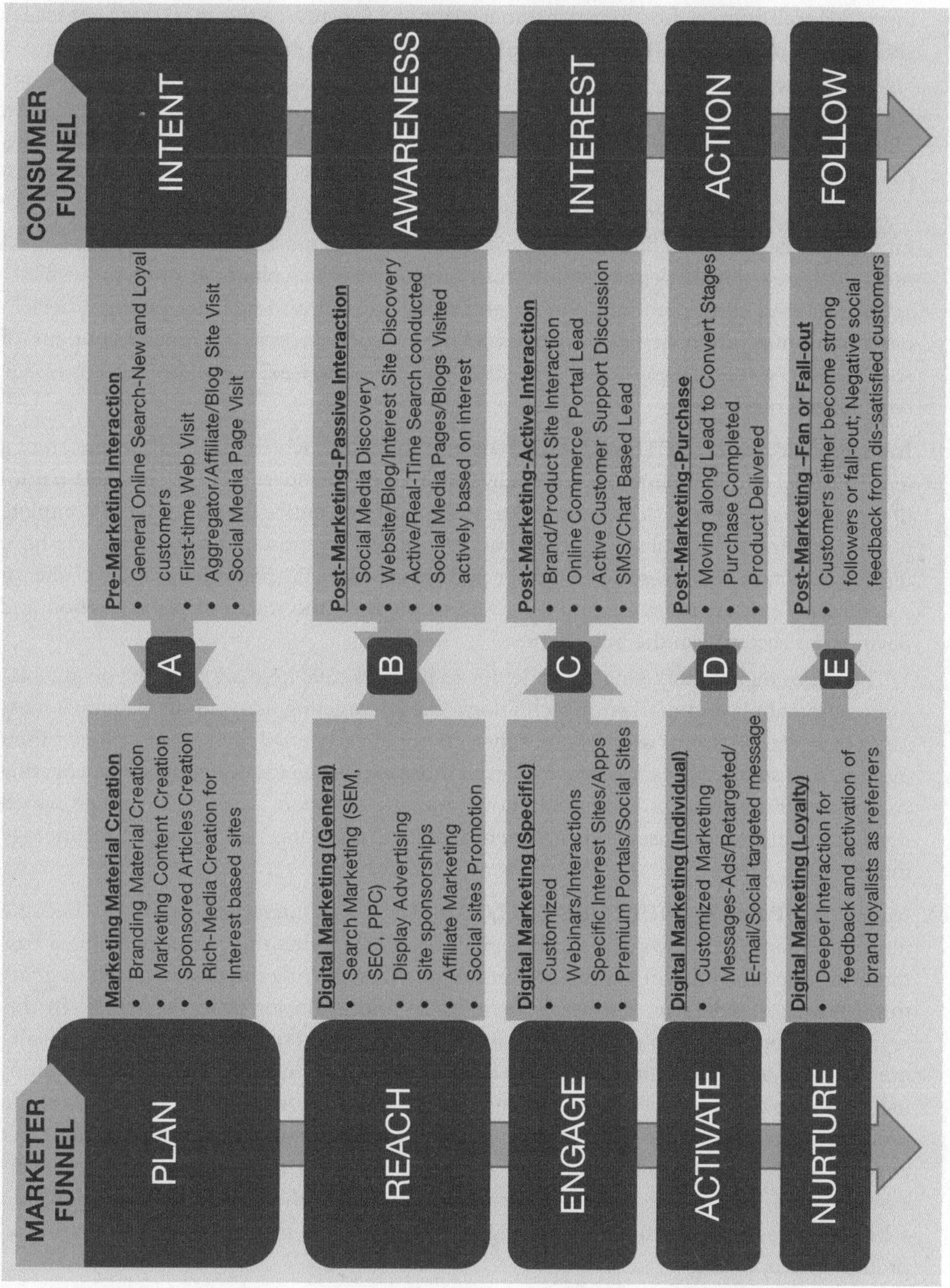

Figure 1.7 Digital Marketing Areas and Activities Explained through REAN Marketing Engagement Framework

(c) **Interaction Point C (ENGAGE-INTEREST):** This next stage involves marketers realizing a general interest for their consumer segment for any of the marketing messages shared and investing further in the marketing funnel to convert this 'interest' into a 'lead'. The consumer in this stage shows an 'active interest' in the marketing message which is tailored according to his needs and also starts to take part in active online and offline discussions and brand/product site visits to know more about the product for a purchase.

Marketing activities here are the ones closer to consumer interests, specific to his communication devices, and directed at times when he/she is most willing to indulge. Digital marketing areas for marketers include customized webinars/collaterals on main website/specific interest sites, premium portals, and social sites. It also includes personal device-based communication like personalized SMSes, e-mail messages, targeted coupons of special interest, etc. Marketing at this stage could be more expensive on a per message basis for the marketer.

(d) **Interaction Point D (ACTIVATE-ACTION):** In this stage, which involves conversion of a lead to a final purchase, marketers are fully aware of the prospect planning to buy a particular product/service and their main task is to support and entice the customer to complete the last mile so that a sale is registered at their end. The consumer side, which we have termed as 'action,' involves the consumer picking up a specific platform, brand website, or e-commerce site for purchase and following through all the stages of plan selection and payment to accomplish the buy action.

The major digital marketing types deployed by marketers here are those involving a lot more automation and marketing technology like re-targeting ads and offers, native messages on social platforms used by consumer, personalized e-mail messages to convert their interest, and so on. This stage becomes even more expensive for the marketer as targeting can be as advanced as providing 20 known parameters about a particular profile which involves inclusion and usage of high-end analytics, big data, and advanced technology intrusions.

(e) **Interaction Point E (NURTURE-FOLLOW):** This final interaction point has become most important these days as it has been well established that the cost of retaining a customer is much lower than getting new customers (considering the cost involved in going through and spending on the whole cycle again and again for new customers). In this regard, marketers have to make sure that they invest in enterprise-wide customer loyalty management and interaction systems to not only keep the customer excited on a continual basis, but also to know and rectify any negative feedback he/she might have on the product or the experience of it. On the consumer side, the greater aim for the marketer is to make the satisfied client become a long-term fan of the product. Such consumers become a part of the brand's-clan/community, rather than falling-out, develop into a brand ambassador themselves to bring in new followers through word-of-mouth and product-championing.

With a good understanding into marketing and customer models, we are now in a position to understand better the key digital marketing types (as mentioned in the earlier section) which form the underlying basis for all digital marketing activities:

(a) Intent-based marketing (search marketing)
(b) Brand marketing (display/digital advertising)
(c) Content marketing (website, blog, native content)
(d) Community-based marketing (social media, business communities)
(e) Partner marketing (affiliate marketing, sponsorships, PR)
(f) Communication channel marketing (e-mail, messaging, SMS)
(g) Platform-based marketing (mobile, video, out-of-home, media platforms (surface), kiosks, in-apps)

Table 1.3 gives a quick peek into the different classifications of digital marketing. We will go in depth to understand and distinguish the various types and examples of digital marketing, as described earlier, in the following sections.

Table 1.3 Digital Marketing Types Explained

Digital Marketing Type	Explanation
(a) Intent-based marketing	Marketing through messages placed in conjunction with information obtained on search engine queries
(b) Brand marketing	Utilizing advertising across websites and digital media formats for marketing
(c) Content marketing	Using story-based elements to share marketing messages in a targeted fashion
(d) Community-based marketing	Utilizing social communities, networks, and platforms to conduct marketing
(e) Partner marketing	Includes involvement of affiliates, third party sites for marketing; also includes sponsorship and PR activities
(f) Communication channel marketing	Involves marketing on all communication lead platforms; this is a more recent and upcoming digital marketing area
(g) Platform-based marketing	Using new platforms and digitized traditional platforms to integrate marketing in the device and medium itself

Understanding Digital Marketing Business Models

Moving forward let us look at the key digital marketing business model types deployed for marketers to earn revenue from their investments across various digital media types described earlier.

BUSINESS MODELS	EXPLANATION	KEY TYPES	EXAMPLES	FULFILLMENT TYPE
Advertising-based revenue models	Fees from advertisers in exchange for advertisements	CPA, CPM, CPC	Yahoo	Online websites/ portals; interest blogs, mobile sites, and apps
Subscription-based revenue models	Fees from subscribers in exchange for access to content or services	Portal subscription, information-based subscription, service subscription	WSJ.com consumer reports.org	Web portals, info-educational websites; premium services sites
Commerce-based revenue models (Direct sales)	Direct revenue from sales happening through commerce sites and portals	Pay-per content	Amazon; Flipkart; iTunes	E-commerce sites; product websites, mobile sites and, apps
Transaction fee/ affiliate/market-pace-based revenue models	Fees (commissions) for enabling or executing a *transaction or for* business referrals	Pay-per referral	My points	E-commerce sites; content websites; mobile sites and, apps
Social collaboration based revenue models	Pull-through revenue from leads generated through social media sits and interest blogs	Pay-per lead	Facebook; WhatsApp	Social media sites; portals; interest blogs; messaging services

Figure 1.8 Digital Business Model Types

Largely, there are five different types of digital marketing business models which are further classified into sub-types based on transaction and application. These are—advertising, subscription, commerce, transaction fee, and social collaboration-based revenue models. Their key definitions, sub-types, and examples are discussed in Fig. 1.8. It should also be noted here that the fulfillment of these models is done through a variety of platforms and channels, most suited to each business model.

Next we move to understand key digital marketing applications and the benefits they provide to marketers at large. The true extent and reach of these applications will be understood once we have gone through the whole book and become familiar with the various ways how digital marketing is applied across multiple industries.

Digital Marketing Applications and Benefits

Digital marketing has become indispensable for almost all types of businesses, organizations, and, if we dare say, to even individuals. There is not a day in present times, when we at a personal, professional or societal level do not interact or are not affected by digital marketing. From the time we open WhatsApp in the morning to check messages from our social groups to the time we hit the first search on Google, to looking at the latest scoreboard on our smartphone cricketing app, we are interacting with digital media applications and being affected by digital marketing all the while.

The key applications for marketers utilizing digital marketing channels and platforms would include:

(a) **Enhancement of revenues:** The most pertinent application of all business models is the potential to increase revenue beyond present numbers and digital does so in multiple ways. From top-branded product manufacturers to local small and medium businesses, all are embracing the power of digital to get enhanced revenues and move from just a physical sales model to an omnipresent sales channel where the biggest orders can come in at times and from locations not even known to the marketing manager.

(b) **Brand presence amplification:** Marketing done only across traditional channels is typically time consuming and requires a large effort to gather new prospect base. Digital marketing helps reach out to newer target segments in a much lesser time-span and amplify brand presence multiple times over.

(c) **Support information-seeking and customer validation exercise:** Digital marketing's biggest application for marketers is its impact across multiple channels to support the customer gather information, compare competing products, and validate his purchase decision through comments and thoughts from multiple online sources which he was not able to gather in the physical world.

(d) **Develop customized forms of consumption (like applications and social pages for targeted communities):** One of the most interesting aspect of digital application is towards creation of targeted low-cost apps, social media pages, and curated articles on interest blogs and platforms, which provide a way to not only personalize information but also how it is accessed with utmost ease by the target segment in which the marketer wants to engage.

(e) **Mixing multiple digital channels and online-offline media:** With newer innovations like integration of Twitter with e-commerce companies to place orders in e-carts by inclusion of special hashtags in their tweets, marketers are utilizing multiple digital media platforms and integrating online–offline media to help customers complete the purchase cycle, on whichever medium, channel or platform they are present. These growing integrations we believe will impact even the most physical of industries like agriculture and healthcare in ways never thought of before.

(f) **Instant response generation mechanism to negative customer feedback:** We have seen a lot of instances wherein brands have not only been able to identify when customers are not feeling good about certain products and experiences on offer but have also been able to avert huge losses and save face in the outcry of key issues important to them both on the product and brand side. In some instances, digital media has even led to companies take back stocks worth millions of their wares to maintain customer trust and brand integrity.

There are multiple such applications which we have seen across industries and client interactions on digital platforms which can be shared here. We would be going through a lot more examples in the book as we move forward to chapters which detail each media and the use of technology towards making digital media such a huge part of the marketing mix these days.

Key benefits of digital marketing include:

(a) Provides a level-playing field be it a small or large business
(b) Much cheaper to run campaigns, collaborate, and analyze insights
(c) Helps to reach out to customers in real time based on their latest actions
(d) Easier to measure effectiveness of a campaign or a marketing message
(e) Viral effect includes ability of a strong concept to reach the mass market instantly
(f) Provides greater engagement with the use of imagery, content, information, customer support, and personalization
(g) Utilizes multiple technologies and collaborative platforms available to harness the power of big data and internet reach
(h) Acts as a medium to understand customer segments and their actions better
(i) Helps understand customer intent across multi-channel platforms
(j) Utilizes the power of social networks to reach out to multiple users in a trusted environment
(k) Integrates traditional campaigns to extend the reach of branding to its longest possible tail
(l) Change marketing messaging based upon latest feedback or acceptance to campaigns
(m) Make collaboration, feedback, and continued engagement with the brand possible in online–offline mode

INTERNET MARKETING: UNDERLYING TECHNOLOGY AND FRAMEWORKS

With an initial understanding of digital marketing, its types, and basic models, it is important to understand the technology behind how digital marketing is set up and delivered. In this next section, we would be taking off from where we left in the first section on the understanding of internet and its growth pre- and post- dotcom era. We would look at the basic internet terminologies used across the industry and the differences between internet, intranet, extranet, and portals. We would then touch base on the commercial beginnings of web and wireless technologies and the basic internet models–B2B, B2C, C2C.

Finally, this chapter would also touch upon the basic infrastructure needed to set up digital marketing functionally and also the key opportunities and challenges to internet marketing.

Internet Basics—Internet/Intranet/Extranet/Portals

As we discussed in the initial section, internet by definition is a global system of interconnected computer networks where millions of private, public, academic, business, and government networks worldwide connect with each other to share massive amounts of information, resources, and services.

Intranet and extranets, which have similar functionality and set-up as internet, are concepts that differ in terms of their usage—intranet being an internal only network while extranet being a network set-up to be accessed by a select set of external users only. An intranet is a local network that uses internet technologies and creates a localized version of the internet that would only be used by the members of a corporation with authorized access to share data on the network. On the other hand, extranet can be looked at as an extension of the company's intranet. Stakeholders can have specific access areas based on the type of interaction and collaboration set up for each of them.

The key difference between intranet and extranet is that if the intranet network is connected to the internet, the intranet will reside behind a firewall and, if it allows access from the internet, it will be termed an extranet. A portal in common internet parlance is called a web portal which is a specifically designed web page that brings together information from many sources in a uniform way. The same context can be applied to intranet and extranet where portals are developed as in the web version which provides links to different sites and pages that the specific set of users might need to access to accomplish their jobs.

Portals as a concept and terminology is very common in internet parlance and is used to describe sites which have been developed on specific business interest topics or verticals like business, government, culture, entertainment, etc. As a portal brings together and aggregates content from a number of systems or servers, maintaining and profitably running a portal is always a much more intensive exercise than developing and running a few pages.

Understanding Web and Wireless Technologies

Having discussed portals, we move on to the most basic type of portal which in common parlance is called a website, visited by all of us on almost a daily basis. With a basic understanding of website in the earlier section, let us get into a more detailed understanding of web technologies and its concepts.

At the basic level, web technologies involve a combination of multi-tier infrastructure stacks which put together help deliver the data and content requested through any specific web browser. As discussed earlier in the book, any user, who visits a webpage from any internet-connected platform or device, will place a request by typing in a URL into the browser which then sends a request to the back-end server.

Client–Server Model

The most important concept which forms the basis of web technologies relates to how a request is placed and information packets are sent back to the receiver. Typically, when any of us log on

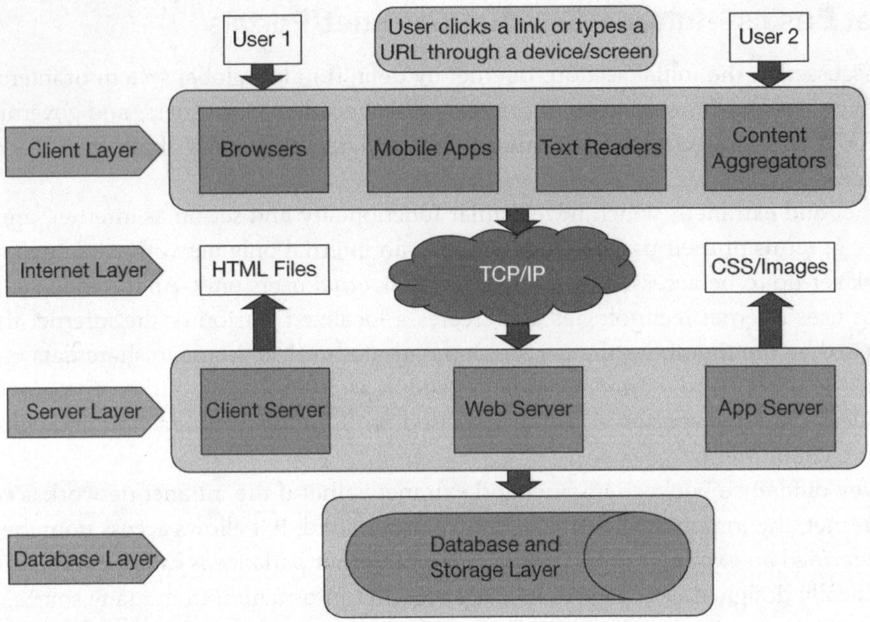

Figure 1.9 Understanding Web Technology Layers

to the internet, we are basically accessing what in web terminology is termed as a 'client.' Clients are the devices that request and render web content. The request is typically executed from any device into a browser, mobile application, text reader, content aggregator. This layer is called the Client layer as shown in Fig. 1.9.

On the other side of the Client layer is the Server layer. Servers are applications that deliver web content or services to clients. There is a layer in between client and server called the Internet layer which facilitates the request from a client device and fulfillment by a server. Typically, when a browser makes a request, the URL passes it to a DNS (Domain Name Server) which translates the URL to an IP address. The browser then uses this IP address to locate the host's server and send a request for the content.

In Fig. 1.9, the Server layer is differentiated into a Web Server, App Server, and Data Server, all of which process requests specific to them. Based on the type of files requested, the Server layer shares static or dynamic content like HTML files, CSS/Images, and other dynamic content through the network. There is also a final database layer below where all the information is stored. The difference between the various servers is that while the Client Server is the presentation layer and contains the presentation logic, the Web and the App Server layers contain the Business and Data Access logic responsible for computing the business logics of the web application.

Wireless Networks

Wireless by definition is the transfer of information between two or more points that are not connected by an electrical conductor. The Wireless Local Area Network (WLAN) serves the same purpose as the wired one which is to link a group of computers, the main benefit being that it is generally easier, faster, and cheaper to set up. Wireless communication has become important for the digital age as it can cover various types of fixed, mobile, and portable applications (which are crucial to present-day marketing communications) like cellular phones, personal digital assistants (PDAs), SMS, GPS, Wi-Fi, Bluetooth, satellite, and broadcast television among others.

Behind wireless networks is the Radio Frequency (RF) technology, a frequency with a unique ability for long-range communication associated with radio wave propagation. The cornerstone of a wireless network is a device known as an access point (AP). The primary job of an access point is to broadcast a wireless signal that computers can detect and 'tune' into. Typically, to connect to an access point and join a wireless network, computers must be equipped with wireless network adapters or can be made wireless-capable through the use of an add-on adapter.

Mobile as the Most Important Wireless Technology for Marketing

The biggest impact wireless technologies have had on marketing is the commercialization of telecom networks for which this generation is also sometimes referred to as the smartphone generation. Marketing through a wireless device, mostly referred to as mobile marketing, provides multiple advantages of an easy-to-carry computing device, location-based promotion, personalization, multiple communication channels, etc., which are difficult to achieve with any fixed line or communication device.

The way wireless technologies have rapidly entered our lives and the credible advancements in design and functionality since the creation of iPhones by Apple have led to a simultaneous marketing revolution in which all types of customers with an affordable investment can utilize the benefit of marketing communications targeted at them which they can receive and respond to instantly.

Also with the emerging concept of marketing applications, each brand can now hope and establish a one-to-one connect with each customer to know their product preferences, periods of interaction, promotion likeability, instant feedback, and sharing recommendations with their social groups similar to word-of-mouth in the offline world. Also this unique combination of online and offline marketing is being deployed and integrated in a manner never attempted before because of the possibilities opened up by wireless networks.

Reshaping Interactions: Individuals/Businesses/Non-Profit

When we look at how business transactions take place in digital marketing and the interactions between different entity types, we traditionally classify them with acronyms like B2B (Business to Business), B2C (Business to Consumer), and C2C (Consumer to Consumer also termed as

Peer to Peer). These terms for long have been very helpful in categorizing specific groups of sellers and buyers to analyze their unique interactions and businesses likewise.

But as we move forward and embrace the complex digital world and its multiple channels of interactions, we would see a change in the manner various entities interact and produce business possibilities not envisaged earlier. And there is also a distinct shift in terms of the end objectives of different businesses which is reshaping and usurping old interactions. With earlier business interactions focusing mostly on revenue and brand building, there are new sets of individuals, small and medium businesses, and even non-profit organizations which though might be small and local in nature, are run professionally and have in turn devised digital models which are completely new in nature. The biggest example of this is Wikipedia which started out as an online encyclopedia and positioned itself to provide the most accurate expert crowd-sourced definitions while running on a donation model, has been quite unique in inception, marketing, and the iconic status that it has obtained.

Fig. 1.10 showcases key digital business entities and multiple interactions which have developed over the past few years as digital businesses and concepts. The most common business models have mostly been referred to as interactions between large brands and other large businesses termed as B2B (business to business) and also the same businesses targeting individuals which are called B2C (Business to Consumer).

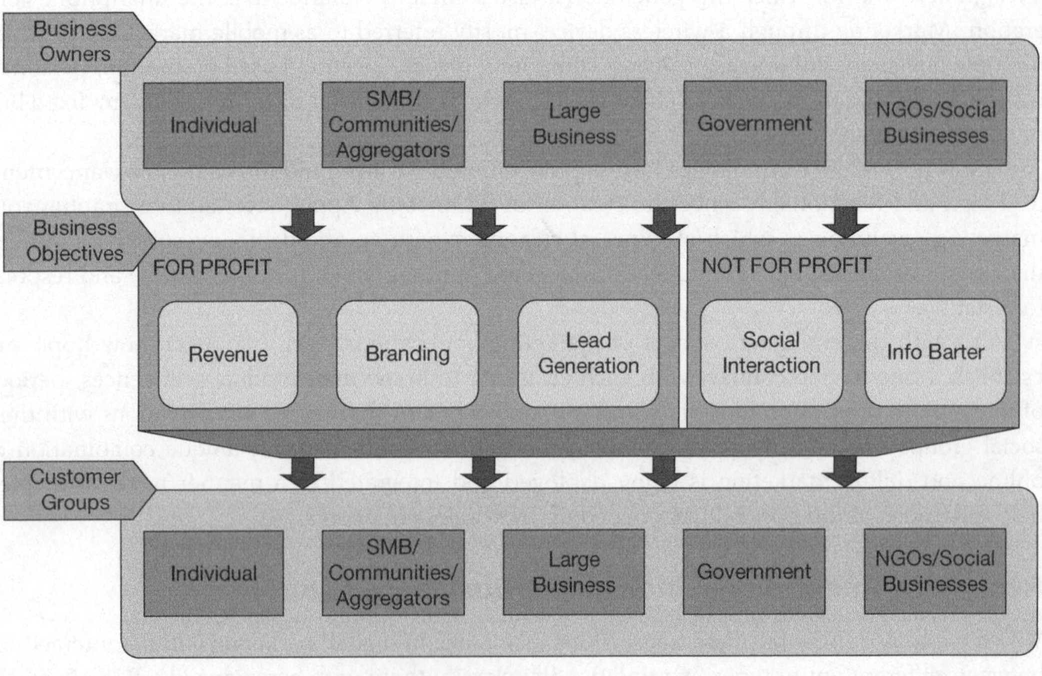

Figure 1.10 Types of Digital Business Interactions

As businesses appeared to grow, we saw addition of two new business groups—government and non-governmental organizations (NGOs). With the advent of digital marketing, there have been two new categories which have emerged strongly—the individual as the business owner (who can create, market, and deliver goods over internet-based channels all by himself) and the SMBs (Small and Medium Business Groups) which could either be standalone businesses or groups of entities/people/aggregators and even rural/home-maker communities who can combine together to execute businesses and deliver profits as smaller organizations. SMB organizations have become a strong target for online marketing companies developing new platforms and providing them advice to help them establish online and also sell their goods for incremental revenues.

In the middle layer of Fig.1.10, we have divided the key business objectives for each type of business interaction into two main buckets—'For Profit' and 'Not for Profit' objectives. 'For Profit' objectives include the three most important outcomes businesses are measured against—the primary one of course being revenue, and the two other as secondary objectives related to an established or newly launched product/service. For an established service, a goal which does not have revenue generation as a primary objective could have an objective like developing new leads to build newer customers for the same product/service. For a newly launched product/service, the key objective would be to increase branding/visibility so that the product starts fetching revenue in future.

The second bucket, which is 'Not-for-profit,' can relate to any of the five business groups. However, it would definitely be more pertinent to the NGO/social business and government categories as a lot of their interactions are oriented towards launching products/services/schemes geared towards two key objectives—social interaction and information barter. Both social interaction and information barter have the sole purpose of creating and catering to social groups to exchange information and sometimes products/services (as in the case of government organizations) for the betterment of society or some special interest groups.

The interaction mesh at the top of the customer groups layer showcases how the present digital era provides opportunities for almost any type of group or business entity (be it a single individual work-from-home or a subsidiary of a government arm) to market, sell, or develop stronger social ties with any other customer groups without the intensive effort which was needed to be put in earlier times.

To understand the impact of these multiple business interactions better, here are some examples:

(a) **Individual to individual:** Key examples are one-to-one ecommerce and Peer to Peer (P2P) data sharing on websites

(b) **Individual to SMBs:** Traditional home-made products delivered to small businesses to market and re-sell to big conglomerates

(c) **Individual to NGO:** Professional services to create blogs and promotional material for NGO social events

(d) **SMB to individual:** Many SMBs are professionally deploying Google Advertising to sell to individual customers and customize services specifically to their tastes

(e) **SMB to SMB:** Certain small concerns are in the business of providing value addition to raw products to refine them for use by other small and medium enterprises

(f) **Large business to individuals:** Large brands are using real-time advertising techniques to target high-end customers on e-commerce sites based on their previous cart buys and favored product categories

(g) **Large businesses to social enterprises:** Many companies are promoting social causes like health and environment by supporting social concerns and groups wherein the cause is also in line with their product and brand philosophies

(h) **Government to government:** There are interesting cases in which different central government departments market their policies to state governments to influence them on investing in key sectors for both commercial and social causes

(i) **NGO to consumer:** In multiple instances, NGOs these days are reaching out to customers through mobile messages to involve them in promoting their causes like event-related marathons, donations, and even buying socially relevant products

Opportunities and Challenges to Internet Marketing

Internet Marketing Opportunities

Marketing on the internet has opened up a plethora of opportunities for traditional marketers to utilize multiple mediums and channels:

(a) **Reaching out to new set of prospects and leads:** Internet marketing opens up opportunities to identify and target new segments apart from the present customer set

(b) **Improving customer connect:** The plethora of channels from which customers can obtain information about the brand and product are helping to improve brand credibility

(c) **Increasing availability:** With increased avenues to buy products on the go from different devices and avenues, customers now have multiple options to buy products

(d) **Multiple pricing options**: With intermediaries being cut out of the equation and with reduced warehousing costs, most products online are available with plans and options at prices and discounts which were not available before.

(e) **Reaching international markets**: The technology behind internet marketing enables a major category of products and services to be available online without incurring extra costs in establishing presence at a physical level

Challenges to Internet Marketing

The biggest challenge in introducing and establishing internet marketing in any new organization has six key aspects to it (see Fig. 1.11).

Figure 1.11 Internet Marketing Challenges

(a) **Investment**: Getting the firm to invest in IT is the biggest challenge for marketers as marketing has always been looked at as more of a cost center
(b) **Adoption**: Once investment is finalized and agreed upon, a clear strategy has to be adopted by each of the key company divisions specific to their objectives
(c) **Resource**: The next important step is the realization of an expert resource set to be hired or groomed internally to execute marketing efforts on the internet
(d) **Training**: Providing the right kind of training and establishing key deliverables which support the firm's business objectives is essential
(e) **Integration**: Once marketing is operational one of the biggest challenges is to integrate its various functions across departments and end channels
(f) **Establishing RoI (Return on Investment)**: Finally, the most difficult of tasks is to establish a cause and effect for each of the marketing activities so that the management is convinced of its outcomes and also develops a consistent reporting for follow-up actions

DIGITAL MARKETING FRAMEWORK

In sections 1 and 2, we looked at the evolution of marketing and the basics of digital marketing as a field of study. With Section 3, we understood the key underlying technologies behind internet marketing and how internet has reshaped business interactions across the ecosystem and the challenges it poses for implementation.

In this last section of the chapter, we will build upon our basic understanding of digital marketing as detailed in Section 2 to build a digital marketing framework which would form the basis of developing a digital marketing strategy and executing it to achieve the desired objectives. To reach there, we need to start developing the concept with the end goal in mind—which is 'Enhancing Customer Value.' But what is this value we talk about and how do we ascertain that we are deciphering it correctly for our intended customer segment?

The next two sub-sections will form a basic grounding to help us understand concepts like OVP (Online Value Proposition), Market Opportunity Analysis, and Digital Services Development, which would form the core pillars of the ASCOR Digital Marketing Framework (the core strategic framework for this text and ensuing chapters).

Delivering Enhanced Customer Value

The core of any marketing activity is to ascertain that the customer has a specific need and is looking to a solution to meet that need. That solution could be a product, a service, a piece of information and even an online advice forum. Meeting that need is the core job of marketing and in the same breadth, meeting that need through any of the digital channels provides the base for digital marketing.

Understanding Problem-Value Mapping

Before defining the terms Customer Value and OVP (Online value proposition), let us understand the root where all marketing and, in a larger sense, all business endeavors begin, and which explains the 'customer problem.' In simplest terms, a customer problem is a set of issues which a customer might face while performing any activity or going through a process. It could be even a simple act of buying grocery or requiring a house for rent. Every activity which is accomplished by a customer can typically have one or more problems associated with it. Each of these problems give rise to what we call in marketing terms as customer needs which translate into opportunities for marketers to service through present products or create new product/service categories accordingly.

Philip Kotler, the marketing guru in his book (*Marketing Management*, 14th edition), defines needs into multiple categories which can broadly be bucketed as 'stated needs' (those which the customer knows and expresses) and 'unstated needs' (those which a customer does not express and might not even know that they exist). From Kotler's text, we have picked three other kinds of needs to be included in the unstated needs bucket—'delight needs' (those which offer the customer higher satisfaction than he would normally expect), 'secret needs' (those which the customer will never state but secretly wish for), and 'efficiency needs' (those which will help the customers execute any activity/task in a much quicker, convenient, and efficient manner) to bring to light the opportunities which marketers can capture if they are able to correctly identify a customer problem and service their arising needs.

With this understanding of customer problem and his needs, let us look at Fig. 1.12 to establish the mapping between customer problem and his needs with the OVP concept developed to respond to those needs. Fig. 1.12 showcases the two sides of marketing and product, service or

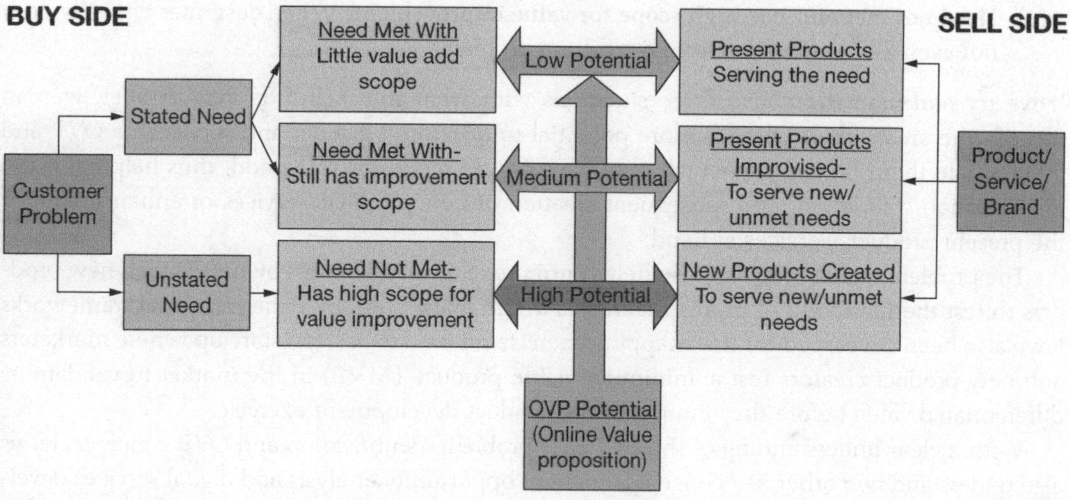

Figure 1.12 Mapping Customer Problem to Online Value Proposition (OVP) Potential

brand—the Buy side and the Sell side. For each business transaction to occur, there has to be a mapping between the left and right sides and only when the Sell side is able to identify the right kind of needs and service them with an appropriate kind of product/service does a business transaction occur.

With a clear understanding of 'customer problem,' let us understand what we mean by 'value' which would lead us to define the concept of OVP. The term value for a customer would be any kind of tangible or intangible (or a mix of both) enhancement which a customer experiences while interacting with any product or service in comparison to similar products/services which he has used/interacted with earlier.

The term value is more experiential in nature and relates to the extent to which a customer finds any new additions worthwhile/differentiated or of an enhanced use for him which helps ease the present process/manner in which he deals with the specific problem at hand. Since the term value can mean differently to different clients in different circumstances, it is very important to know the potential for offering such a value online, which will finally decide whether the customer will pay for that additional value or not. This identification is termed as knowing the OVP which has to be created for each customer segment depending upon the known/unknown 'customer problem' at hand and helping them solve it.

Let us go back to the earlier definition of the two kinds of needs (stated and unstated) to map them to ultimate fulfillment which will help clarify the concept. Any need stated or unstated by a customer will typically lead to three conditions:

(a) **Need met with:** When customers' needs are met with at a more or less satisfactory to good level and there is little scope of a value add

(b) **Need met with but still has improvement scope:** When customers' needs are being met but there is a clear and stated improvement scope which marketers can decipher through customer connect/feedback or dedicated focus group

(c) **Need not met and has high scope for value improvement:** When customer typically does not even know of his needs and resulting problems

If we try and map the above three situations with what the 'Sell Side' has to offer, we can identify the areas where there is more potential to develop a distinct and serviceable OVP and differentiate them from those which only have a little scope for value-add, thus helping in the identification, validation, and subsequent creation of new products/services or enhancement of the present products/services at hand.

The problem–value mapping also helps entrepreneurs and business owners launch new products to test the feasibility of product launches in the market. Many entrepreneurial frameworks have also been developed for this mapping exercise referred to as 'lean start-up' where marketers and new product creators test a 'minimum viable product' (MVP) in the market to validate its differentiated value before they jump into the product development exercise.

With a clear understanding of the customer problem identification and OVP concepts, let us also understand two other key concepts—market opportunity analysis and digital services development as they are the next two key steps before any customer would logically move ahead in the value chain.

Market Opportunity Analysis and Digital Services Development

With an understanding of the concepts of customer problem and OVP, we have already been able to identify digital opportunity. But for large businesses investing into new product development or entrepreneurs choosing a new area to enter, this opportunity needs to be refined and developed further before companies understand the overall revenue potential and market-share they can tap into.

Before firms even start to think of executing a digital marketing strategy (to be discussed in greater detail through the next section on ASCOR Digital Marketing Framework), it is essential for companies to conduct a Market Opportunity Analysis to clearly identify a market segment (which is ready to consume their products/services) and a viable revenue mode towards adoption of those products/services. Digital Services Development has also become an important step as products and services need to be oriented or developed from scratch to suit the digital marketplace and its consumption pattern. A round-up of the strategies needed for Market Opportunity Analysis will be explained when we detail the Assessment Phase of the ASCOR Digital Marketing Framework.

The Digital Services Development concept has recently become quite important (and also relates to the Digital Transformation exercise most of the firms are getting involved with) to support creation and implementation of traditional and digital products for selling on newer platforms. Few important strategies which companies need to take care of include:

(a) Converting present traditional products to digital formats for digital consumption
(b) Looking at avenues to create new digital/virtual avatars of present physical products
(c) Understanding the impact and pressure digital marketing is placing on the whole backend value chain to help provide efficiencies which have actually differentiated digital services

in the first place. (This will also be covered in detail in Chapter 2 when we will discuss the impact of digital on the product value chain.)

(d) Defining strategies for procurement, production, fulfillment, and channel digitization, all of which are integral to creation of new digital offerings. (This has been covered earlier in detail in the section on digital transformation.)

(e) It is also important to realize aspects related to storing of digital products on cloud platforms, the way they are searched and retrieved, how their metadata is managed, and how they are rendered onto multiple platforms, devices, applications (all of this would be covered in multiple chapters later).

With this understanding, we are now in a better position to discuss the ASCOR Digital Marketing Framework and recognize the key aspects and their application to multiple digital marketing use-cases.

ASCOR Digital Marketing Framework

For any type of company to move into digital marketing, be it a traditional firm with more physical products and services mix or one that has transformed itself to a large degree to tweak its products for the internet generation, there needs to be an underlying framework which helps to map the process and its progress. To help large and SMB firms, as well as individual marketers, we have devised a methodical phase-wise plan which we call the 'ASCOR' Digital Marketing Framework where ASCOR is an acronym standing for the five phases:

(a) Assessment phase
(b) Strategy phase
(c) Channel and communication plan
(d) Digital marketing operations
(e) Refinement phase

Let us understand each of the phases with the help of Fig.1.13. We would go through an in-depth understanding of each of the phases and execution activities involved in the subsequent chapters of the book.

(a) **Phase 1-Assessment:** The first phase involves any firm's or individual's assessment and analysis of their present external/internal marketplace environment to ascertain that they have clearly assessed their current digital presence to develop high-level digital marketing objectives and review criteria. This stage involves executing all the necessary market research to assess present market trends impacting them.

Key activities involved in the assessment stage include-

- **External analysis**: It refers to the analysis of macro-micro environment (entities which surround and influence the firm, its products, operations, and opportunities) and market situation analysis (includes market and competition analysis, specific to the industry where the firm and its product are operating).

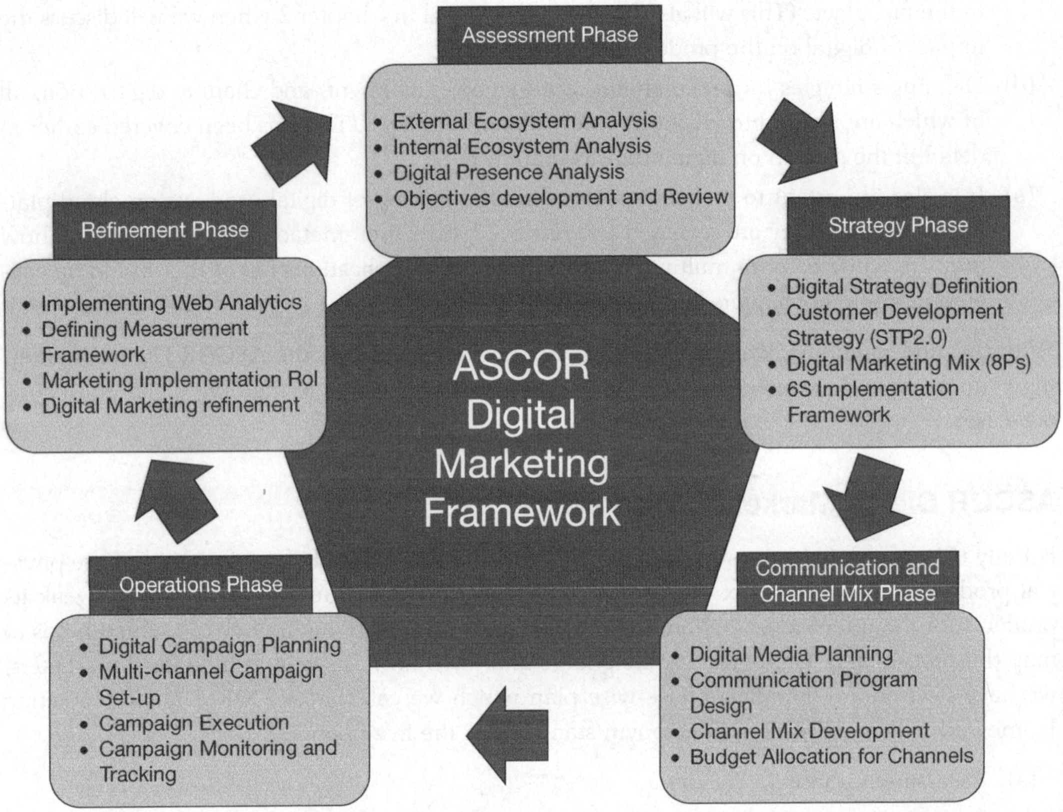

Figure 1.13 ASCOR Digital Marketing Framework Phases

- **Internal analysis:** It involves an analysis of factors which are internal to a company and within their control to influence their goal setting and create successful and realistic digital marketing objectives. It includes four main areas of analysis- offerings mix, marketing mix, resources mix and competencies mix.
- **Digital presence analysis:** It is a 2×2 matrix which helps firms identify their present digital state through a combined analysis of external and internal factors. There are four key digital presence states depending upon the present 'extent of digital presence' of any firm and its 'market standing' with respect to direct competition in their specific industry segment and market category.
- **Objectives development and review:** It involves setting of high-level digital marketing objectives based upon the specific digital state in which the firm is present. The review stage consists of activities that involve monitoring, evaluating, and controlling marketing activities continuously.

(b) **Phase 2-Strategy:** The second phase involves creating the digital marketing strategy roadmap in line with traditional marketing strategy and objectives. Key stages include-

- **Digital strategy definition:** It defines business strategy for firms going digital, their impact factors and emerging business structures. It also involves alignment of firm's core competencies to changing value function shifts to develop appropriate OVPs.
- **Customer development strategy (STP2.0):** It includes revisions to classic STP (Segmenting, Targeting and Positioning) activities to develop a revised STP2.0 version for digital. This helps to form the base for creating the customer development strategy.
- **Digital marketing mix (8Ps):** It involves looking at the classic 4Ps (Product, Price, Place, Promotion) with a digital view and also developing the new set of 4Ps for modern marketing (People, Process, Programs, and Performance).
- **6S Digital marketing implementation framework:** The final stage involves developing the 6S (Scoping, Shadow, Set-up, Stability, Scale-up, and Spectrum) digital marketing implementation framework for executing the strategy elements.

(c) **Phase 3-Communication and Channel Mix:** This stage involves a more in-depth communication and channel mix plan creation for each of the marketing objectives

Key activities include

- **Digital media planning:** It involves developing the strategy towards creating a digital media plan post the digital strategy definition exercise from the last phase to determine the communication and channel mix for specific brand offerings, taking into consideration the present product lifecycle and digital presence stage.
- **Communication program design:** It details out seven steps to create an overall communications strategy and helps create an implementation plan towards developing the communication message and its orientation for specific end objectives.
- **Channel mix development:** It lays out the nature of each channel and the type of communication which can be targeted through the particular channel to meet a specific communication objective. It also involves looking at the positives of one channel over the other for specific marketing objectives and strategies.
- **Budget allocation for channel mix:** It involves utilizing the four key methods commonly used for budget allocation to ensure that appropriate emphasis is given to each channel depending on the communication objectives and the nature of returns expected from each of the channels in the overall mix.

(d) **Phase 4-Digital Marketing Operations:** This is the deployment stage for digital operations and involves the actual planning, implementation, monitoring, and optimization of campaigns during the media flight dates so that marketers obtain the maximum impact for their investments during the campaign run period.

Key activities include

- **Digital campaign planning:** It involves activities performed towards planning the campaign before it starts and aligning the resources, tools, and key activities. It starts with developing the campaign objectives which would include developing a high-level brief of the product, the type of segments to be targeted, targeted message, overall flight dates (run-time), and the final tangible output desired in terms of response rates, website visits/leads, or conversions.

- **Multi-channel campaign set-up:** It refers to the actual operations work for setting up the campaign across multiple channels and begins with developing a campaign calendar and getting it approved internally before sharing with execution teams for implementation.
- **Campaign execution:** It involves all the activities performed by campaign managers right from the time they make the campaign 'Go-Live.' Typical representative parameters (which we would learn more in the upcoming chapters too) include Bid, Geo, Targeting, Networks, Devices, Languages, Ad Extensions, Advanced Settings, etc.
- **Campaign monitoring and tracking:** During the implementation of the campaign, marketers start receiving daily and weekly data points and extensive metrics so that all data captured can be effectively analyzed and monitored.

(e) **Phase 5-Refinement**: This is the final stage of digital marketing wherein marketers and the campaign team analyze overall RoI for the effort and investments, create reports and analytics dashboard, and refine present strategies for further digital marketing activities, based on customer response and collated data.

Key activities include

- **Implementing web analytics:** Traditionally, web analytics helped evaluate website performance, but the emerging Web 2.0 world involves analytics activities like multiple-outcome analysis, site testing, understanding customer and competition, etc.
- **Defining measurement framework:** It involves developing a marketing measurement framework that helps generate quantitative and qualitative analytics for all three digital media types (owned, earned, and paid).
- **Marketing implementation RoI:** It involves developing a RoI model which calculates key expense areas for spend across all marketing channels and overall marketing impact for the firm.
- **Digital marketing refinement:** As a final step, the overall digital marketing strategy is refined using a five-step model of Define, Measure, Analyze, Action, and Improve or Eliminate to ensure that the campaigns are run most effectively in future executions.

Application of Digital Marketing

With a deeper understanding of the ASCOR Digital Marketing Framework, it would make it much clearer to apply specific stakeholder-based scenarios to understand how digital marketing can be applied by individuals, SMB (small and medium businesses), and large companies as per their needs and end outcomes. The examples here are representative of situations and projects which digital marketing companies face and execute on a daily basis. All the scenarios have been run across the ASCOR stages and a quick view of Table 1.4 will give a basic grounding in the first chapter itself of the kind of cases we will go through in the rest of the book to apply our knowledge to real-life digital marketing situations.

Table 1.4 Application Examples of ASCOR Framework Applied to Multiple Stakeholders Cases

Business Type	Digital Marketing Use-Case	Phase 1-Assessment	Phase 2-Strategy	Phase 3-Channel & Communication	Phase 4-Operations	Phase 5-Refinement
		• External Ecosystem Analysis • Internal Ecosystem Analysis • Digital Presence Analysis • Objectives Development & Review	• Digital Strategy Definition • Customer Development Strategy (STP2.0) • Digital Marketing Mix (8Ps) • 6S Implementation Framework	• Digital Media Planning • Communication Program Design • Channel Mix Development • Budget Allocation for Channels	• Digital Campaign Planning • Multi-channel Campaign Set-up • Campaign Execution • Campaign Monitoring and Tracking	• Implementing Web Analytics • Defining Measurement Framework • Marketing Implementation RoI • Digital Marketing Refinement
Individual						
	A local orthopedic wants to build his reputation online	• Assess potential to develop online brand • Compare present standing among similar doctors • Study visit patterns for doctor websites	• Define unique value creation elements • Develop OVP built on repute & experience • Define brand-building elements	• Develop Content and Intent based marketing mix • Plan for blog, website, SEO, SEM creation	• Developing content & marketing material • Website/Blog Launch; marketing initiated on search engines • Customer Queries handled with Chat	• Review web visits and marketing reports • Analyze improvement in service enquiries and patient visits • Refine marketing tactics regularly

(Continued)

Table 1.4 (*Conitnued*)

Business Type	Digital Marketing Use-Case	Phase 1-Assessment	Phase 2-Strategy	Phase 3-Channel & Communication	Phase 4-Operations	Phase 5-Refinement
	A Digital Media manager wants to setup online consulting services	• Assess need for digital media consulting services • Study online consumption pattern • Map present vendors with such service set	• Target professional communities marketing as key • Create Marketing Ps with OVP focus on unique consulting services & execution	• Develop Content, Intent, Brand and Community based marketing mix • Professional agency to develop consulting & brand building content	• Execute SEO, SEM, Marketing on Professional Blogs & Consulting Stories • PR as communication tool to target professional groups	• Review consulting leads and conversions from online investments • Analyze RoI for clients engaged in services • Refine brand & offering elements regularly
SMB						
	A home-based handicrafts developer wants to increase sales through online platforms	• Map online buy propensity • Compare competitor presence online • Search Marketing Platforms for handmade products	• Create Online Sales elements mix • Develop set of high-selling product lines with OVP such as material, location, history or fashion	• Develop brand story through blogs/social • Create online e-commerce store • Use search and display channels for sales	• Run campaigns on fashion sites, blogs • Track & Optimize Keywords & images for brand impact • Solicit Product feedback	• Review RoI on investment in multiple channels • Gather customer data for e-mail connect • Use Product Feedback as Testimonials

	A medium business owner wants to build a pan- India brand for toy products	• Map brand strength online competitors • Conduct brand STP Analysis • Define objectives and roadmap for branding activities	• Define Branding elements mix • Create distinct online channel development strategy to be executed phase-wise	• Develop brand identity through blogs, PR and a commerce site • Create omni-channel messaging plan	• Drive brand imagery through Rich-media advertising, social media pages and engaging viral videos • Monitor and measure campaign outcomes	• Review overall brand connect through fans, followers on social media and websites • Connect further with coupons/ loyalty parenting newsletters
Large Business						
	An erstwhile top product is struggling for sales &wants to go online for revenue	• Map customer attitude to brand • Market/ competitive analysis to know changing trends • Define digital marketing objectives	• Developing revised 4Ps to support new digital strategy • Creating OVP in terms of increasingproduct appeal to target segment	• Target loyal offline customer base on online platforms • Develop new audiences through content marketing & social channels	• Drive retargeting and target customer media blasts for repeat exposure • Measure conversion and new customer funnel interactions	• Improve post-sales connect and service through communities and e-mail connect • Target friends of present customers to improve perception
	A large brand strong on web platform wants to position its brand as mobile first	• Understand present mobile environment for similar brands • Define need for a mobile first strategy- location marketing, branding, sales, etc	• Defining mobile strategy elements • Create mobile value proposition which is design led, app-specific & marketed as mobile first	• Engage in mobile platform – WAP and APP based marketing • Develop more imagery based content including rich media & messaging features	• Develop video, blog and ad based campaigns • Facilitate transition from web to mobile with early bird coupon based offers	• Review positioning shift in terms of number of customer who have shifted to mobile first • Promote multi-channel shift to other mobile devices and sites

Critical Success Factors for Digital Marketing

With a basic understanding of the digital marketing framework and scenario-based applications, let us summarize the chapter with an understanding of the most differentiating elements of digital marketing and those key elements which make it successful.

Digital marketing, by definition, cannot change the physical attributes of the product but in reality it does much more to make it more marketable than competitive. The essence of digital marketing lies in the strong understanding that marketers and campaign managers have of the product/service and how they can weave a credible story around the brand, improve its imagery, and create a compelling story around it, elements which are difficult to create in a physical world. With the use of testimonials, customer reviews, positive social feedback, and product championing by top adopters, marketers are able to influence key buyer groups and create a positioning in their mind which adds tremendously to a positive marketing influence.

To appreciate the key differentiating factors better, we have developed a '6i Model' which represents six key elements that in a combined manner help create a compelling reason for any product/service to be marketed online and investments made in this area.

(a) **Intent-based:** The biggest differentiator and a critical success factor for digital marketing is the actionable information obtained from visitors and customers each time they get involved in searching for a product online which helps in the backward integration of the overall product development cycle making it the most effective medium to gain information on customer preferences and unstated needs.

(b) **Interactive:** The power of interaction which digital marketing provides in terms of response, action (impression/click), and voluntary sharing of personal information, enables marketers to engage audiences in multiple ways and keep them hooked to the product/service/brand specifically on the medium or platform they like the most.

(c) **Immersive:** With digital communication created to appeal to our senses with strong design, aesthetics, cultural connotations, and a cosmopolitan appeal, these days, immersive elements can be built through ads, video content, picture sharing, and story-telling sites like Instagram and Pinterest. These novel ways of providing truly immersive experiences can go even beyond real-life interactions at times.

(d) **Immediate:** The biggest differential which digital provides is the immediacy to the customer, wherein he/she can browse a product from a smartphone fashion app at even odd hours at night and go ahead to buy such a product. Browsing patterns at even brand websites show how much convenience matters to today's generation. Such elements were never available to marketers before.

(e) **Interesting:** The multiple ways in which contests are being run for brands, sweepstakes organized, fashion experts roped in for chats, webinars conducted, brand imagery shared through viral-cartoon videos and product information shared virally through humorous videos, clearly testify how interesting digital marketing can be and how this has been a real differentiator for fans and new customers alike to click a brand or product.

(f) **Informative:** Success factors which have been really key to digital marketing, include the possibility to develop targeted content, share information across multiple vertical channels, and provide brand credibility and trust in the most effective manner. On the customer side, the possibility to get 'word-of- click' information through social feedback of friends on their real-time usage of the product and interaction avenues like brand experts on the website has truly re-defined what information can achieve, much to the help of marketers and their marketing efforts.

CHAPTER SUMMARY

- **Part 1:** We learnt about the evolution of digital marketing, how it grew from the traditional to the modern era, passing the pre- and post- dotcom phases. We realized the role of the internet in supporting the internet-based business models and the differences between Web 1.0 and 2.0. The above sections also provided an in-depth understanding and differences between the often confusing 'E' concepts and lead to an understanding of the core concept of digital through the digital transformation model.
- **Part 2:** The section began with providing the basic definition of digital marketing, 'push/pull' marketing concepts and the key media consumption drivers. The key digital marketing channels were explained with the help of the REAN model as a base and also the interaction detailing funnels from both the marketer and consumer sides. Finally, digital marketing business models, their applications and benefits were also explained in great detail.
- **Part 3:** Helped develop an understanding of the internet marketing principles and its basics (internet/intranet/extranet and portals) and explained the underlying web and wireless technology essentials. The reshaping of interaction between various business groups (individuals, SMB's, large businesses, government and NGO's) was also elaborated upon. This section also shed light on opportunities and challenges to the internet marketing arena.
- **Part 4:** This final section helped establish concepts like OVP, market opportunity analysis, and digital services development. The foundation of ASCOR digital marketing framework was developed, its concepts explained, and its application for key business stakeholders were discussed. Finally, we learnt about the critical success factors for digital marketing and an underlying '6i' framework to explain the key differentiators better.

REVIEW QUESTIONS

1. Which factors are responsible for the transition of Traditional Marketing to Modern Marketing?
2. How does modern marketing score over traditional marketing techniques?

3. What are the key areas of comparison between Web 1.0 and Web 2.0?
4. What are the differences between e-commerce, e-business, and e-marketing?
5. Can you explain the three-key transformation elements of the Stakeholder Based-Digital Transformation Model?
6. In which way is digital marketing better than its traditional counterparts?
7. What are the key drivers for the shift of media consumption to digital platforms?
8. Can you explain the Consumer Funnel Stages as explained through the REAN Marketing Engagement Framework?
9. What are the seven key digital marketing types which form the underlying basis of all digital marketing activities?
10. Please share examples of key Digital Business Model Types along with their examples.
11. What are the key applications for marketers utilizing digital marketing channels and platforms?
12. Can you explain five key benefits of digital marketing?
13. What are the five key types of digital business interactions?
14. Can you compare the key internet marketing opportunities to key challenges?
15. Can you explain the concepts of Customer Value and OVP (Online Value Proposition)?
16. What are some of the important strategies which companies need to take care for Digital Services Development?
17. What are the five key phases of ASCOR Digital Marketing Framework? Choose any one of the phases and expand on its key activities.
18. Explain the six key elements of the '6i model' that in a combined manner help create a compelling reason for any product/service to be marketed online.

DIGITAL APPLICATION EXERCISES

1. Take the example of transformation of UTI Bank to Axis Bank. How did the company shift from a traditional model to modern marketing? What were the key elements behind the shift?
2. Choose any Indian company which you believe has not still transformed itself to a digital model. Apply the three key transformation elements of the Digital Transformation Model (Automation, Digitization and Collaboration) to showcase how it can transform the best in its present business environment.
3. Compare the REAN Marketing Funnel Stages for a consumer purchasing a Samsung mobile. Are there any key observations gleaned during the exercise?
4. Select any product category and share your thoughts on any one of the seven key digital marketing types which you feel typically impacts you the most from a digital marketing standpoint.
5. Can you share the example of an Indian brand/product that runs on three or more business models as shared in the digital business model types?

6. Can you think of any recent product/service you have used where the mapping between Customer Value and its OVP is not well established? In your opinion, what could be the reasons?
7. Think of any government institution in India and provide in detail the five stages of ASCOR Digital Marketing. Look for a similar institution or website in US/Europe and point out the differences.
8. Suppose you want to market a premier brand of any health ingredient (fruit, herb, spice). How would you apply the '6i' model to market it?

CHAPTER 2

Digital Marketing Models Creation

LEARNING OBJECTIVES

After studying this chapter, you will be able to:

- Explain the evolution of bricks and clicks model, the shift from a marketplace to a marketspace model, and emergence of interactive platforms
- Describe the concept of value chain functions and importance of transaction cost concept
- Understand digital marketing business models elucidating on the six core digital value elements and how they can be used to generate customer value

CASE STUDY Amazon India: *With the Metros in its pocket, 'Apni Dukan' Amazon to wow the heartland*

Since its inception, Amazon India has grown in every aspect, be it the number of sellers or platform users. Amazon's headquarters committed an investment of US$6.5 billion to capitalize on the huge potential of India's e-commerce market. It goes without saying that Amazon India has successfully established itself in this market space. As of 2020, the user base of Amazon India grew up to 100 million, which is quite impressive for a company that has grown in India from scratch in less than 10 years. Even sellers on Amazon have gained more trust in the brand, and by December 2021, Amazon had over 10 lakh registered sellers on its platform.

Amazon India has gained this success by appealing to its audience's emotions, most of whom were not used to the concept of online shopping. With its campaign *'Apni Dukan'* (your own shop!) and the heart-warming storylines in its advertisements, it gained the trust of

Indian shoppers. Amazon made deliveries faster, designed an algorithm to detect fraudulent sellers and increased the credibility of its platform. Amazon India also slimmed down their application version to become more compatible and deal with Indian internet challenges. They kept their product prices affordable to suit the needs of Indians and make them loyal advocates.

Another reason behind the success of Amazon India's platform is the diversified approach followed post 2015. From 2016, Amazon India expanded their reach to different industries which contributed well to its e-commerce business. These initiatives include inroads through Amazon Prime (online streaming platform), Alexa (virtual assistant), Kindle (e-reader), Amazon Food (food delivery), and Amazon Pay (online payment platform). Each initiative targeted a different Indian audience segment. For instance, Amazon Prime targeted the youth, Alexa caught the fancy of the upper class, while Amazon Pay had its eyes on the middle-class segment. These strategies contributed to Amazon India's rapid and strong growth. Further, its focus on customer service and strength in 'returns and refunds', hit the baseline in its quest to become a customer favourite.

Amazon India faces tough competition from other e-commerce companies such as *Walmart-owned Flipkart. Amazon's presence is less in smaller towns and it majorly relies* on metro cities for sales. Apart from this, Amazon is also not too keen to grow inorganically through acquisitions, whereas its competitors rely on acquisitions for growth.

Amazon is trying to counter competition by using various strategies:

- Amazon has added the option of viewing its website in Hindi, as well as other visual aids to make shopping easier for Indian consumers.
- In its bid to grow into the Indian heartland, Amazon also acquired Perpule, a startup that specialises in helping *'kirana'* (meaning local in Hindi) stores move online.
- Amazon India has also expanded its popular "I Have Space" program, which handles last-mile delivery by partnering with local shop owners and providing them with pickup and delivery services for customers within 2-4 kms of the store. As of March 2021, the program covered 12,500 stores across 180 cities, up from 2,500 stores when it launched in 2015.

Table 2.1 E-commerce Scorecard for FY 2021

	FY 2020		FY 2021	
	Revenue	Profit/Loss	Revenue	Profit/Loss
Amazon Wholesale	3,384	–132	3,131	46
Amazon Seller Services	10,847	–5,849	16,200	–4,748

Figures in ₹crores

Source: Annual report of Amazon Retail India Private Limited for the year 2021–22

- The firm has also enhanced its focus on its two key brands: Amazon Pay and Amazon Prime, to expand them further and tap higher market share.

Recently, Amazon India took a cue from Flipkart to acquire its first 'Social Commerce' start-up in India. GlowRoad (with DealShare, CityMall, and YouTube-owned Simsim as competitors), allows suppliers to sell their items to end customers via resellers in over 20,000 pin codes across 2,000 locations. Resellers, who are often housewives, temporary workers, or students, help the company target Tier-II and III markets. GlowRoad will support Amazon India in its mission to help millions of creators, homemakers, students, and small business owners increase their business in India. This acquisition will also aid the company's goal of digitising 10 million businesses by 2025.

While all the above initiatives are helping Amazon India stay course, stronger market penetration and revenue growth strategies will further help it to get past competitors and be the leader in both mind and market share.

FACTORS IMPACTING DIGITAL MARKETPLACE

In the last chapter, we learnt about the evolution of digital marketing and the underlying technology frameworks responsible for the growth of multiple digital marketing models on the internet platform. In this chapter, we will underline key marketplace factors behind the development of digital marketing, how value chains get revised, and the impact of digital value shifts across business models.

This first section focuses on how factors like increase of interactivity, revised relationships between multiple business groups, emergence of network economy and surfacing of customer experience at the core have been responsible for fueling the growth and sustenance of digital marketing. It is important to understand these trends and functions as they are not only a direct byproduct of the growth of internet technology, but also includes efforts made by different types of businesses and leaders to give meaningful shape to that growth and give digital marketing its right place in the sun.

From Brick and Mortar to Bricks and Clicks

The most commonly used terminology to describe a shift of any business from a pure physical presence to any part of it being executed online is referred to as a shift from brick and mortar to bricks and clicks model. "Brick and Mortar," as the phrase implies, refers to a company possessing physical assets like buildings, production facilities, or retail stores for their operations. To put some interesting literary connotation, this term was originally used by Charles Dickens in *Little Dorrit*.

In contrast, "Bricks and Clicks," describes a business model where a company integrates both offline (bricks) and online (clicks) presences, including all post-internet actions. Apart from these, many other terminologies and combinations of the words bricks, clicks, mortar, and even flips (physical catalogs) have also been used in business to describe the multiple states where a business might fall in.

Brick and Mortar only companies, in the present context, are referred to as firms which either by their very nature have a high physical component, for example, agriculture, or are present in locations where their prime customer can only interact with them offline, for instance, a small and medium-sized business (SMB) in a small town, or those which have still not transformed themselves to shift online and are essentially lagging behind.

Brick and Click companies also vary in terms of the online component they have embraced. Some might have just begun their web journey and have a basic website only (or a classified listing in, say, Just Dial, the top Indian listings website), or might be a bit more advanced, are selling only a small portion of their products online (like on eBay or Amazon), or might have adopted full digitization (as in full-fledged e-commerce businesses like MakeMyTrip for travel bookings or Myntra as a fashion destination portal).

According to a 2012 Booz & Company Digitization study, where the consulting firm came up with a digitization index for Europe, financial services, automotive, and computers and electronics were the three top sectors having greater than 50 per cent digitization while hotels, restaurants and construction companies were found to be the least digitized (see Fig. 2.1).

If we study the methodology behind the calculations for this study, we will find four dimensions on which the extent of digital presence was measured:

- *Input:* The extent of involvement of digital processes in the procurement stage of business, including data points regarding the use of computer networks as well as electronic transmissions suitable for automatic order processing.

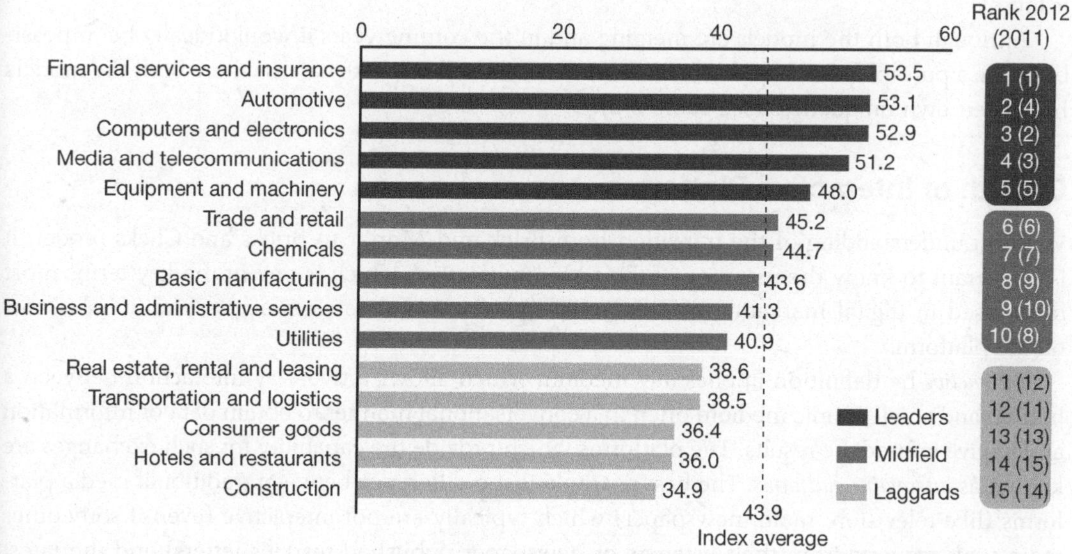

Figure 2.1 Industry Digitization Index (2012)

- *Processing:* The degree to which processes are integrated, both internally and with external partners. The internal integration sub-factors include data points regarding the existence and use of digital technologies such as enterprise resource planning (ERP) and customer relationship management (CRM), as well as the use and purpose of internal information sharing among different organizational functions. External integration comprises activities such as electronic data interchange or supply chain management.
- *Output:* The importance of digital processes in the sales function, including the use of computer networks, as well as electronic transmission of data suitable for automatic sales processing.
- *Infrastructure:* The sophistication of the underlying IT technology, focusing on the presence and use of computers and computer networks (wired and wireless), as well as the presence and type of connection to the internet, including the use of fixed and mobile broadband or other fixed connections such as cable or leased lines.

From the definition and index explanations, as described in the preceding paragraphs, we need to understand that though going digital is critical, beneficial, and relevant for almost all companies today, it is not that a company would want to operate online only and forego the offline channel completely. On the contrary, we are seeing increasing examples in the context of Indian e-commerce, specifically of companies who had scaled up big-time online, scaling down to open physical stores later, either because of low-online penetration or customer mindset and buying pattern which have not yet evolved fully.

A good case in point for the above trend is the story of Firstcry.com, one of the earlier and bigger online baby-care stores, which has planned to increase its online store presence to 400 stores by the end of 2017 from its existing operational 30 stores. This is primarily to increase their penetration into the untapped markets where the presence of physical baby products stores is low.

Although both the models are merging and in the coming years it would ideally be impossible to be a pure-play Brick and Mortar firm; there are still some key areas where both the models have their own uniqueness (see Table 2.2).

Growth of Interactive Platforms

With an understanding of the transition from Brick and Mortar to Bricks and Clicks model, it is important to know the meaning of the term "interactive" which is one of the key terms most often used in digital marketing to differentiate products and services across traditional versus online platforms.

Interactive by definition implies any medium which allows a two-way interaction between a human and an electronic medium often in a conversational manner to obtain data or information and to give immediate results. The platforms which provide the capability for such exchanges are known as *interactive platforms.* The best example is the difference between traditional media platforms (like television, radio, newspaper) which typically are not interactive (even if sometimes radio took requests from their listeners or newspaper published reader's letters) and the latest digital platforms like personal computer, mobile, kiosk, gaming consoles, etc., which enable

Table 2.2 Uniqueness of Each Model—Brick and Mortar versus Bricks and Clicks

Area of Comparison	Brick and Mortar	Bricks and Clicks
(a) Customer Interaction	High personalization—customer can touch and feel the product	Feature richness—real-time product, price, and variety comparison possible
(b) Inventory Management	Higher control—products can be better managed on a smaller scale	Virtual logistics—time and cost for procurement can be huge savings
(c) Brand Presence	Local visibility—traditional shops have great local brand presence	Multi-brand offering—opportunity to provide multiple brands in one visit
(d) Relationships	Store trust—through regular interactions higher trust is built	Personalization—with advanced analytics high personal touch possible
(e) Expert Assistance	Salesperson as guide—salesperson acts as the expert	Information as guide—data and social feedback provide expert knowledge
(f) Brand Imagery	High touch—all brand elements can be exhibited in store	Rich interface—possibility of giving global imagery to local products

interaction of data either between individuals or between human and a machine through the electronic medium.

Impact and Importance of Interactive Platforms

The development of interactive platforms started primarily (as explained in the first chapter) with the growth of the web and applications built on it like chat, e-mail, comments section, etc. Users for the first time got the option to share a thought, put a comment, or send a piece of information, and in return be able to interact in real-time with another person, an expert or an automated robot to get an almost instant (or rather very quick) response to the communication or query (see Fig. 2.2).

Let us understand the key types of interactions supported by interactive platforms which help digital marketers reach their goals more effectively.

(a) **Information-seeking interactions:** The biggest impact of any interactive platform is to help a customer seek answers and gain information towards his needs and problems, an activity which can also be directed to match the query with relevant products and services. This is precisely what search marketing does and that is why it is still the most effective and widely used digital marketing channel.

(b) **Problem-solving interactions:** The next level of interaction is when the customer and marketer have a real-time ability to conduct a one-to-one discussion to listen and provide

Impact of Interactive Platforms

- Give customer a chance to voice opinions
- Pose queries and discuss with experts in real-time
- Help marketers get instant feedback on their communications
- Ability to reach out in a personalized manner and tell stories about their brands

Importance of Interactive Platforms

- One-way communication is good for sales but is the biggest barrier to marketing
- Customers need to communicate with trusted communities and experts before buying
- Marketers can get instant feedback on their communications
- Multiple contacts can be developed and channels can be nurtured
- Customers can become involved in co-creation process

Figure 2.2 Impact and Importance of Interactive Platforms

solutions to the problems a customer is facing while interacting with a product or service. Such interactions which started as more of casual chats between strangers in chat rooms have advanced to become interactive tools, that B2B and B2C companies have built in as a standard feature on their website, giving them huge returns thereof.

(c) **Community interactions**: The next level of interactions utilize the effect of networks in a manner never imagined. Multiple sites with collaboration/group-creation features or niche areas, broad-based social networking sites like Facebook, in-game group interactions (which are immersive in nature) are examples where several like-minded people are able to share information and marketers can benefit out of those interactions and market their brand to an actively involved audience.

(d) **Activity/promotions-based interactions**: One of the most interesting kind of interactions which marketers have used very effectively is to conduct activities and events-based interactions like contests for online participation. Customers are made to interact with key elements of the product/service/brand to help promote its attributes and usefulness; At the same time, customers are kept highly engrossed; and lured with the possibility of interesting returns, rewards, rebates, improved social status, etc.

(e) **Expert opinion interactions:** Apart from general query-based interactions, interactive platforms have also given marketers a chance to showcase expert knowledge and opinions about their products/services through designated product experts who are available online. This has helped brands retain their edge over competition and at the same time help the customer throughout the marketing funnel activities.

(f) **Feedback eliciting interactions**: The best way to elicit direct and pertinent feedback for a brand and its products is through mini-feedback forms or quick post-buy surveys which are not time consuming or intrusive. Interactive platforms have helped brands get responses to the various attributes of sales and marketing through such tools.

The growth and proliferation of interactive platforms thus have given power to both customers and marketers to understand, influence, and accomplish their objectives in ways which were never possible before with one-way traditional communication channels.

The New Network Economy

In the last section we saw the importance of community interactions and how they have impacted the growth of digital marketing. This section will help us appreciate how the phenomenon of network economy has evolved on the internet and taken shapes and forms which have helped the concept grow and become widely prevalent in present times.

The Network Economy Phenomenon

The concept of network economy involves value being added to products and services through social networks operating on a large or global scale. This is in contrast to the economies of the industrial era wherein a single firm was responsible for providing all the intellectual property behind a product or an idea.

The core principle behind this economy is termed as the "network effect." The concept states that a product displays positive network effects when increasing usage by a user augments the product's value for other users (and sometimes all users). The best example to understand network effect can be seen in the way Facebook grew through social connections and each of us found more value from the product only if we had our friends, relatives, and contacts join in and keep sustaining that value.

The effects we describe here are known as "positive externalities," wherein an externality is any situation in which the welfare of an individual is affected by the actions of other individuals, without a mutually agreed-upon compensation. We make a case for the word "externalities" as there could be situations termed as negative network externalities too, where more users make a product less valuable (more commonly referred to as network congestion).

Evolution of Network Effects

Network effects was first studied in the context of long-distance telephony in the early 1970s (one of the earliest papers on the topic is Rohlfs, 1974). Today, they are widely recognized as a critical aspect of the industrial organization of IT industry and are prevalent in a wide variety of sectors, including software, microprocessors, telecommunications, e-commerce, and electronic marketplaces. Empirical evidence of network effects has been found in product categories as diverse as spreadsheets (Brynjolfsson and Kemerer, 1996), databases (Gandal, 1995), networking equipment (Forman, 2001), and DVD players (Dranove and Gandal, 2003).

Types of Network Effects

Network effects can be classified on the basis of cause and effect relationships of the networks in hand. Key classifications include:

(a) **Direct network effects** where increase in usage of a particular good or service leads to a direct increase in value and subsequent adoption for other users. The most common example is the telecom industry where increased adoption of a mobile network raises the value for other users joining the network as this might reduce the costs, allowing more services, and facilitating better investments for research by the company operating the network. This clearly describes the direct network effect.

(b) **Indirect network effects** where increase in the usage of one product or service augments the value of a complimentary product or service which in turn raises the value of the original product. A good example here is the increase in adoption of external hard drives, compatible with laptops or other computing devices. The more laptops are sold, the more hard drives would be adopted or sold (as they gather more value to act as storage devices for increased content storage needs), thus increasing the use of laptops as a home-computing device.

(c) **Two-sided network effects** where increase in the usage by one set of users increases the value of a complementary product to another set of users distinct from the first set and vice versa. One good example of this type is the development of video games on gaming consoles. Developers charge a price for developing these games for which users pay. As the network of users who play the game increases, the value of the developers who develop it rises, and in turn, the game has better developers, hence increasing the value for the players.

(d) **Local network effects** where the micro-structure of the networks influences how much network effects matter to each group. In this case, the value increase that a particular good typically witnesses with the number of increased users does not have impact on the growth, of say its two subset groups, whose usage might depend on each other's presence in the network. The best example is instant messaging.

Impact of Networks on Digital Marketing

With different types of dependencies and value-based outcomes based on the kind of network effect involved in any particular case, the impact on how network effects are utilized by various sectors, has a profound impact on their growth. With social channels and networks being a key component of the growth and perpetuity of major digital marketing efforts, it is evident that these impacts need to be traced by marketers so that companies which have grown through positive network impacts are not hit by sudden negative network effects, which can take a huge toll on brand standing, imagery, and trust. Although these concepts look more related to product development, they are equally important for marketers as the overall value which a network derives from a product directly determines the lock-in period and impact of various regular and viral campaigns exposed to customers.

From Marketspaces to Marketplaces

With the development of network economies and the possibilities to build and propagate services online, traditional marketers have shifted their marketing and sales efforts from a marketplace to a marketspace model.

A *marketplace* (from its most generic definition) is a regular gathering of people for purchase and sale of provisions, livestock, and other goods. In other words, marketplace is the physical equivalent of what marketers term as the offline model where buyer and seller transactions occur in specific designated places without the use of any electronic communications or software. Over centuries, this has been the mainstay of business and commerce for all types of products and services.

The *marketspace* concept, on the other hand, is a recent one which involves information and communication-based electronic exchange environment, where goods and services instead of being sold only physically are marketed through an online space that facilitates bi-directional commerce (as also explained earlier through the concepts of interactive platforms in the second section of this chapter).

The role of the marketspace is to match buyers and sellers whose contexts have sufficient similarity; if the product being requested and offered has a high degree of match and the buyer and seller can come to an agreement on price, location, and timing, then a successful match can be made that will culminate in a transaction. Typical examples of these are Ebay, Amazon, and a multitude of other e-commerce sites which run on the marketspace model, where apart from their own products and brands being sold, they also act as a platform for other smaller and niche brands to sell at designated prices and deliver goods at their end. This helps bigger e-commerce sites manage warehousing and delivery at almost negligible costs and concentrate more on marketing and brand-building efforts.

The term marketspace was introduced by Jeffrey Rayport and John J. Sviokla in 1994 in their article "Managing in the Marketspace" that appeared in *Harvard Business Review*. In the article, the authors distinguished between electronic and conventional markets. In a marketspace, information and/or physical goods are exchanged, and transactions take place through computers and networks. The three most distinct concepts which define a marketplace transaction include:

(a) Content of the transaction
(b) Context in which the transaction takes place
(c) Infrastructure that enables the transaction to occur

In the *Harvard Business Review* article, Jeffery and John have shared multiple examples to explain how the value creation exercise differs between a marketplace and a marketspace. It shares that in a marketplace, the three differentiating concepts of content, context, and infrastructure are all combined as an entity to provide the experience, while in a marketspace the marketer can utilize and build upon each of the three components as unique differentiators by themselves which individually can build unique differences difficult to replicate otherwise.

With the concept of marketspace having moved ahead leaps and bounds with the growth of online and emerging digital concepts, the classification of uniqueness on the lines of content, context, and infrastructure still holds quite valid. If we take the mobile application as the latest example of the marketspace model, we realize that most firms and brands developing mobile applications for marketing are looking at digitized content as a differentiator, the availability of information, simple interface, and superior design as the context, and cloud-based mobile networks as providing uniqueness on the infrastructure plank.

These days, the concepts of the marketspace model have grown to such advanced levels that with social concepts like hashtags (#) in Twitter, marketers can break down and use each piece of intangible information or context related to a product as searchable metadata. Such hashtags, if searched in Twitter, would lead to thousands of relevant articles, real-time information, and commerce-led links through which customers these days can even place orders in their e-carts on e-commerce sites like Amazon and get their needs fulfilled through a connection of online networks—ideas which couldn't even be thought of a few years back.

In the upcoming sections, there will be a mention of multiple such instances where content, context, and infrastructure play a vital role in differentiating a product, service, or a brand which would help extend the concept of marketspace even further. Ideally, companies with the right mix of marketplaces and marketspaces would be the ones to succeed the most and it is for digital marketing to take the lead and integrate the two, with the efforts surely being led by the marketspace models.

Changing Sales and Customer Service Patterns

With the impact of multiple forces on the way, customers are receiving information and conducting business through marketspaces and distinct shifts have occurred in the way sales and customer service are structured in the internet age. Typically, the role of sales, which was considered to be an activity related to pushing a product onto the target segment, has changed in many ways with the introduction and integration of digital marketing techniques.

Changing Sales Function in the Digital World

In the traditional sense, a job of a salesperson was quite clear. He had to collect a few product samples in the morning, move out to his designated territory, have a look at the list of retailers (in the case of B2B) or customer home addresses (in B2C), visit them, and showcase the power of their products and services. When radio, television, and out-of home portals started developing concept of marketing (which primarily was to entice the customer towards a certain brand), the sales function was supported by the instant connect which had already been developed between the customer and the brand.

With the onset of online marketing and the present digital era, the sales channel too has changed its ways with the following trends:

(a) **Information accessible to customer:** Earlier, sales used to rule and had an information arbitrage, knowledge of comparative prices, and a stranglehold of the supply chain in his area which was not available to the customer. But with the rise of multiple buying options on the internet and the amount of information available through websites, blogs, sales collateral, dedicated product portals, and social reviews, the job of a salesperson has become tougher in terms of being up-to-date on what his consumer might be knowing and to have clear differentiating points.

(b) **Changing pattern of communication channels:** While still a large part of the marketing budget flows through the traditional media channels like TV, newspaper, magazines, etc., the influencing channels at the end of the funnel are increasingly shifting online which makes it imperative for sales to follow its unique customer set on multiple digital channels and be able to put strong conversion techniques for those who already are brand champions and would be most willing to convert their interest into real sales.

(c) **Deriving meaning and utilizing huge sets of customer data:** Once sales has the requisite data from multiple marketing efforts both online and offline (along with CRM data of loyal customers), the most important task for them is to chaff out the true set of customers they should concentrate for their sales activities and the kind of sales communication to send out to those who may have visited the brand's website, or looked at a product video, made a sales enquiry, or have even left the cart at the last step. It is a time where sales and marketing have to collaborate rapidly to convert a customer's product search lest they lose out the opportunity to a more alert competitor.

(d) **Knowledge of changing platforms and tools for sales:** Earlier the job of a salesperson was more on managing the intangibles and personal influence, which now is changing rapidly. A mature and effective sales manager now has to reskill himself with the knowledge of the latest sales and marketing tools and technology available in the market and guide his/her sales-force teams accordingly. The biggest challenge is to know which technology is the best to deploy a willing customer to make the next sale.

With these trends, the sales function would do best not to put up an artificial face in front of the customer and understand that being transparent is the key to success in present times. They need to utilize story-telling elements, converse with content which is compelling and thoroughly analyzed, engage in a consultative, educational mode, and be available to service customer queries in a real-time mode to really convert deals they wish to. As shared earlier, it is the context which salespeople bring to the deal which will be the key differentiator between win or loss in these modern times.

Impact of digital on customer service patterns

Customer service is typically defined as a series of activities designed to enhance the level of customer satisfaction. The concept traditionally included services which were provided at the time of buying or after sales has taken place. But increasingly in today's world with every competitor trying to snatch customers away and build their own communities, customer service elements have become equally crucial in the pre-buy "awareness" stage so that marketers are in constant loop of how they can provide customer satisfaction even in the early funnel stages.

The most pertinent example of this changing function is the support a customer might be expecting while he/she is searching for your product category. Suppose he/she clicked on a marketing newsletter where he got to know of your brand, or paid a visit to your website, or filled a form for an engaging video, or checked out your social page on Facebook. These would be signs of getting right into action to support his/her search process and maybe share a personal e-mail enquiring if he/she might need any assistance with the product, maybe even share some interesting trivia or trending news on core elements of your product. This is possible in the digital era and according to McKinsey (as shown in one of their surveys), a pure digital journey

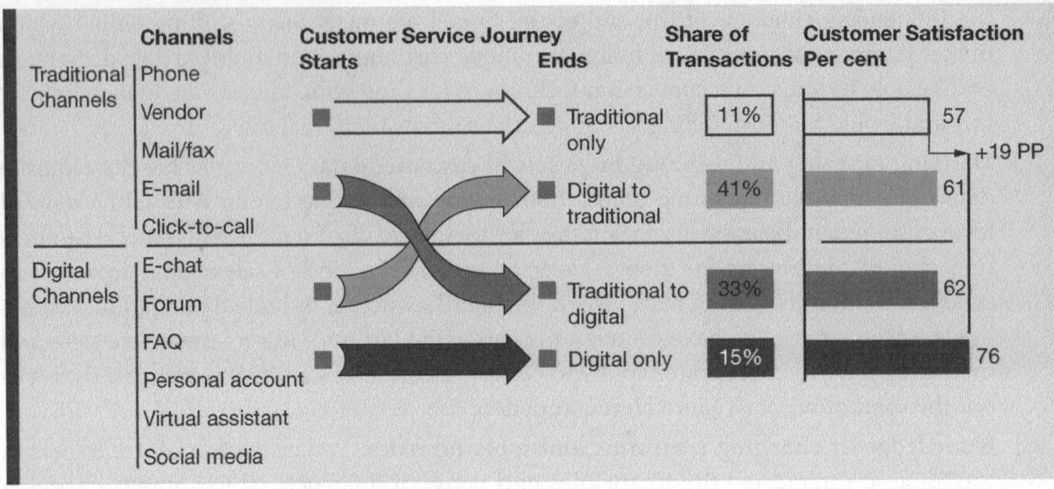

Figure 2.3 McKinsey's e-Care Survey on Customer Satisfaction

has the potential to drive higher customer satisfaction across all stages of the customer journey (see Fig. 2.3).

The objective of the survey was to understand if digitization had any impact on providing higher customer care. McKinsey structured its e-Care Survey around 11 touchpoints grouped into two categories—traditional channels (such as phone, vendor, mail/fax, email, and click-to-call) and digital channels leveraging digital platforms (e.g., e-chat, forums, FAQs, personal accounts, virtual assistants, and social media).

The key differentiating factor for customer satisfaction was to understand service elements across the customer journey touchpoints from start to finish. There were four key journeys identified—traditional only, traditional to digital, digital to digital, and digital only. As is shown in the corresponding line graph, customer satisfaction was higher for digital only journey which is a clear indicator of the impact of digital.

In this first section of the chapter, we identified multiple factors which have and are continually impacting what was known as the traditional marketplace. In the next section, we would concentrate on the impending shifts in the value chain brought about by this changing landscape and how companies are revising their relationships with key stakeholders (suppliers/partners) to remain relevant to the customer and tweak or even in cases disrupt their business models accordingly.

VALUE CHAIN DIGITIZATION

In the last chapter, we learnt about the stakeholder-based 'digital transformation model' to understand how various elements affect the interactions of a firm with their suppliers and intermediaries, and how internal processes can yield necessary transformation elements for customer satisfaction.

Starting with elements of the same model, we would start to map out key value chain elements, focusing on key process functions like procurement, production, and delivery. Instead of the consumption function, here we would concentrate on a new function called the expert function, which would emphasize on new-age intermediaries who bring their expert knowledge, reduce transaction cost (explained later), and develop new value-led models. We would also take up the case of journal publishing to elaborate its generic value chain process steps and contrast it with revised value chain elements brought about with the help of intermediaries.

Understanding Value Chain Functions

A value chain is defined as a chain of activities that a firm operating in a specific industry performs in order to deliver a valuable product or service for the market. To go through the concept in depth let us look at the revised Porter's model (see Fig. 2.4), we went through in the last chapter.

Figure 2.4 represents a high-level view of the key elements of production any business entity would have to go through to supply goods and services to any type of customer. The business entities and customer types mentioned here span across individual business owners/customers, SMBs (Small and Medium Businesses), large businesses, government divisions, and NGOs (Non-governmental Organizations). The production element has four distinct "Interaction Functions" related to four types of stakeholders.

(a) **Procurement function:** Related to all activities for procuring raw material and other types of input content (for services) from multiple supplier sets

(b) **Production function:** Involves the set of processes towards creating or in certain cases assembling new products and services to be sold to multiple customer groups

(c) **Delivery function:** Involves the set of activities geared towards warehousing, delivering, and ensuring final consumption at the customer's end

(d) **Expert function:** Relates to expert activities or services provided by multiple intermediaries or as we call them here "expert partners" who can bring down operational costs

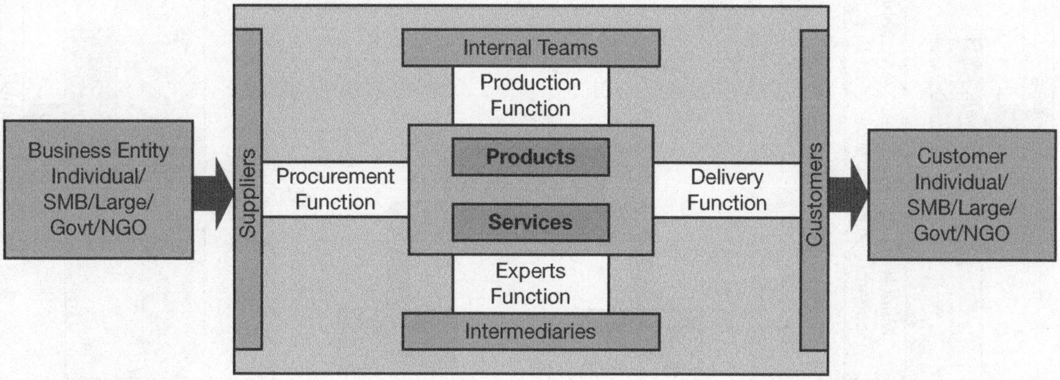

Figure 2.4 Key Value Chain Functions

and provide higher value across the process through their expert knowledge in multiple sub-activity areas and processes

The key takeaway from this representation is to give a better idea of how key value chain processes are structured along the four functions and how in the modern digital age, the fourth function is providing efficiencies to help generate new "value it should be 'value-driven' driven" business models for business entities.

Key Value Chain Process: A Basic Understanding

With key value chain functions defined, let us move on to get a basic understanding of the key processes across each of the procurement, production, and delivery functions, and also look at the impact of the expert function and how intermediaries provide value across the value chain.

Figure 2.5 showcases key value chain processes across procurement, production, and delivery functions. Below is a detailed understanding of each of these processes:

(a) Procurement function processes

- *Market research:* involves activities related to researching the market for the best suppliers, quality supplies, and optimum prices
- *Procure supplies:* includes steps for procurement like collaborating with vendors, making an order, and paying for the supplies
- *Warehouse supplies:* involves executing a quality check on supplies procured, raising red flags for bad supplies, and storing supplies in warehouses either managed by business or leased firms across production locations

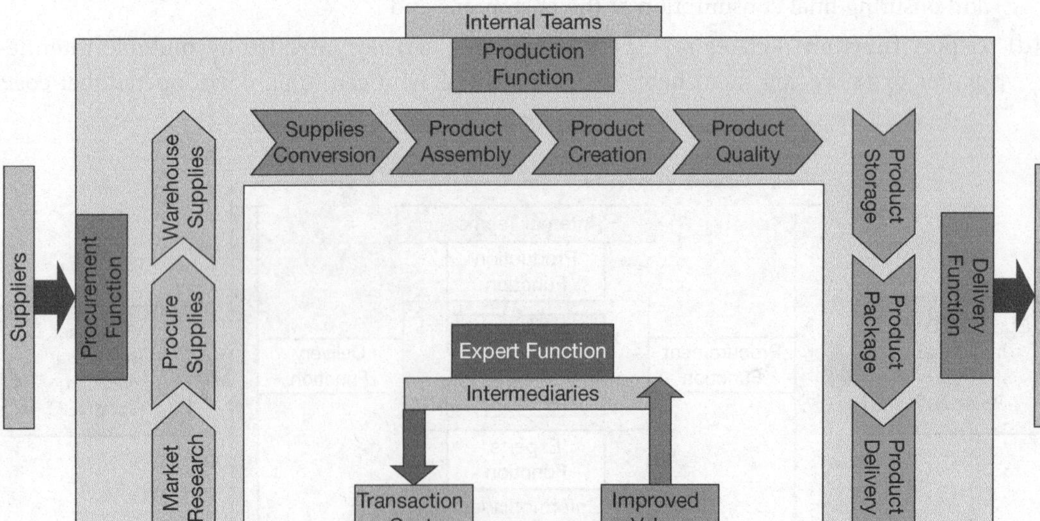

Figure 2.5 Key Value Chain Functions

(b) **Production function processes**

- *Supplies conversion:* involves conversion of supplies into readily usable raw material which would be put in an assembly line for production
- *Product assembly:* aligning all raw materials, people, and machinery in line for production. In the case of services, it would involve putting in place all the necessary tools for production purposes
- *Product creation:* actual production process takes place and the final product is created
- *Product quality:* involves a quality review of the final product before storage; products not following quality norms are sent back for revision

(c) **Delivery function processes**

- *Product storage:* involves storage-related activities across multiple locations for-client fulfillment
- *Product package:* activities related to packaging the product as per customer demand and requirements and making them ready for shipping
- Product delivery: activities related to final delivery and distribution according to client demands and market potential; delivery could be online or offline or a mix of both

Transaction Cost Concept for Expert Function

With the knowledge of the basic process steps across the value chain, we now move to an understanding of the impact of expert functions and how they provide value to the overall chain. Towards this we first need to understand the concept of transaction cost.

Transaction cost by definition is the cost incurred in making an economic exchange. Now, every transaction that we see happening across a value chain process will involve some specific cost. These transaction costs typically add friction to commerce. *Expert functions* are the intermediaries which while acting as experts across different areas of the value chain, help reduce this cost and provide most value to the process. We would look at a detailed example in the next section wherein transaction cost reduction concept is applied to the journal publishing value chain. This example would help explain how these intermediaries reduce economic friction and add tremendous value not only for them but also for the overall value chain.

Value Chain Elaboration: A Case of Journal Publishing

With an understanding of the basic value chain functions and key process areas across them, we would apply the concepts to a specific example to see how the value chain is laid out for that product and how the concept of transaction cost helps reduce friction and develop a revised value chain with the help of expert intermediaries.

The example we choose here is of journal publishing which is interesting in the way that although the final product is in a physical form, the content pertains to it being disaggregated into service-led models (we would take a closer look at this in the next section).

In line with the value chain function and processes as elaborated in the last section, here we explain the key process steps (see Fig. 2.6) for journal publishing (physical form).

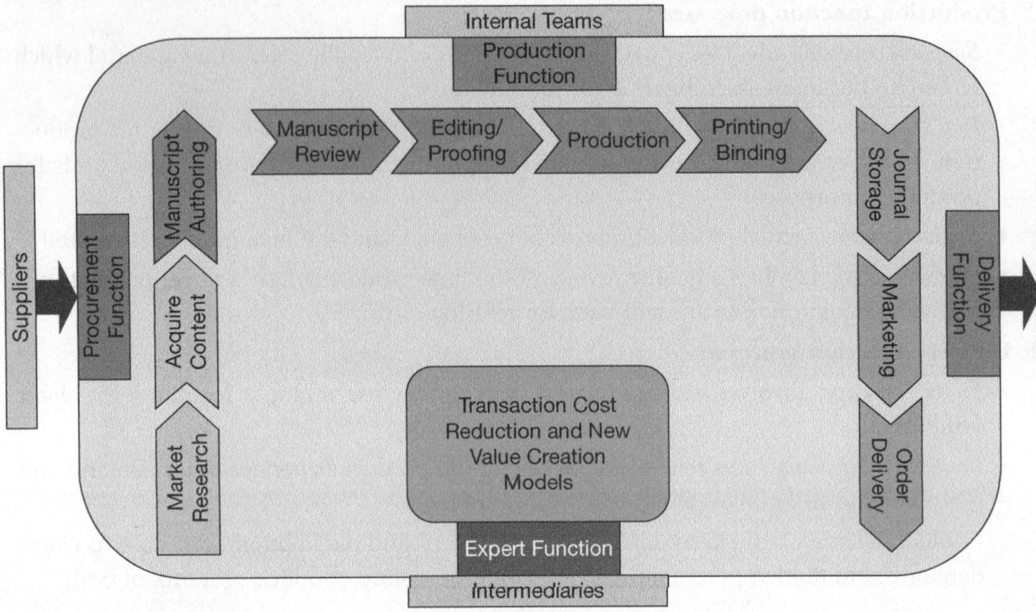

Figure 2.6 Journal Publishing Value Chain

The key process functions are described below:

(a) **Procurement function**

- *Market research:* involves activities related to research on trending topics, top authors in each area, subjects which readers would want to read most, and the market where certain kind of content needs to be published
- *Acquire content:* involves journals opening up for submissions in specific areas and obtaining solicited and unsolicited manuscripts. Journals can also acquire historic content for reference or re-publishing

(b) **Production function**

- *Manuscript authoring:* involves activities related to authoring of major titles using various content pieces sourced to create compelling pieces of content
- *Manuscript review:* consists of activities related to reviewing articles once they have been written to check quality benchmarks before it goes to the editorial and proof-reading team
- *Editing/proofing:* includes editing and approving a piece of content and proofreading it so that the content can be published
- *Production:* involves collating the final content, sourcing images and diagrams, executing design and layout, and developing the blueprint for printing
- *Printing/binding:* involves physical printing of pages and binding into a journal format to be shipped to multiple locations

(c) **Delivery function**

- *Journal storage:* refers to activities related to storage of the journal in boxes in designated warehouses situated near fulfillment locations from where it is to be delivered, based on demand
- *Marketing activities:* involves demand creation and promotion, both of which impact sales and final delivery effort
- *Order delivery:* includes the final steps of reaching the individual subscriber, library owner, corporate researcher, and order execution

Role of the Expert Function

As discussed in the previous sections, expert functions are those which help reduce transaction costs and create a digitized value chain which lends itself to creating more business models and subsequently (as we see in the last section of the chapter) create more digital marketing models.

Emergence of Digitized Value Chain

With an understanding of the value chain process steps for a generic journal publishing value chain, let us look at how multiple and digital expert functions help revise the value chain to create a completely refined and agile 'Digitized Value Chain' which opens up the possibility of creating newer digital marketing models (which we will cover in the next section).

Looking at Fig. 2.7, we can see the original journal value chain depicted in the same manner as in Fig. 2.6. The two new inner layers here pertain to:

(a) **Oval layer:** located next to the generic value chain, this layer contains ovals which stream out from the central expert function. The arrows moving out to each of the ovals are actually individual digital value elements which are associated with each process of the outer value chain and help reduce the transaction cost for that process step (the impact of each of these ovals is covered process by process in this section).

(b) **Inner digitized value chain:** the inner value chain processes, which have been reduced to just four steps instead of 10, (as was in the original chain), showcase how digital can help create a more agile value chain which has lesser friction than before, hence, provides more value creation possibilities both for the firm and the customer.

We will now go through each of the key process steps which we had drawn out in the generic value chain earlier to assess the impact of expert function ovals on each of them and also understand how some of the circled process activities in the original chain are disappearing (since they are not core to the firm), leading to a more compact inner digitized value chain.

Let us discuss the impact on each of the 10 process steps.

(a) **Process 1** Market research (retained): Since market research and estimation is a core activity for a journal, it has been retained as one of the four core steps of the digitized

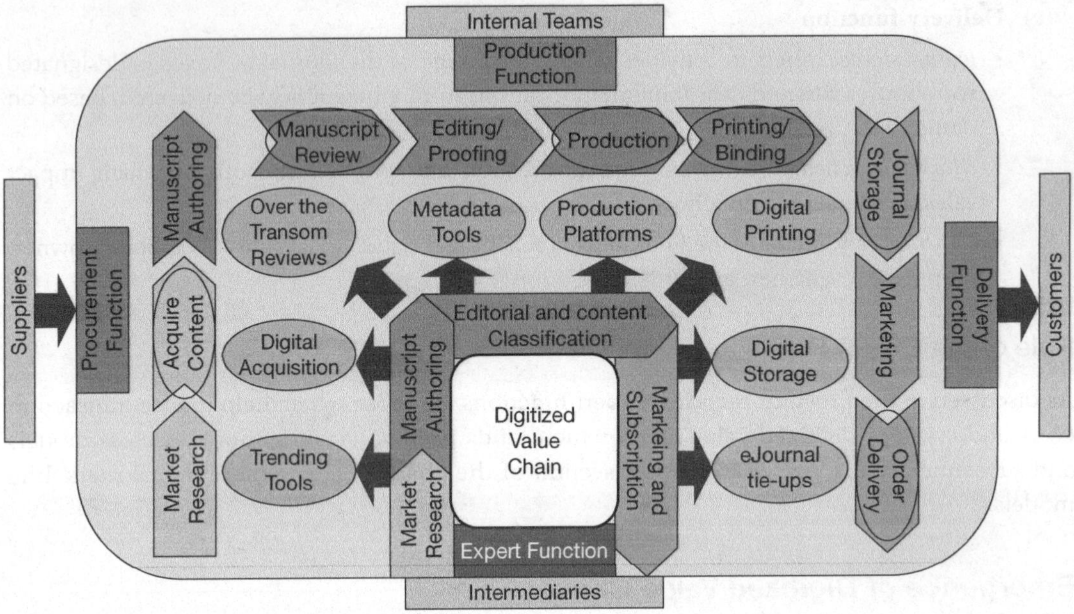

Figure 2.7 Digital Journal Publishing Chain

value chain. Here we see an oval on 'Trending Tools' which shows how multiple tools for gauging market trends (on useful and sellable titles) can help companies decide on which titles and authors to publish.

(b) **Process 2** Acquire content (disappearing): The oval next to the Acquire Content stage, shows how the whole manuscript acquisition process is going digital, wherein digital tools are being deployed to manage the activities of submission, validity check, author rankings, title acquisition, and rejections.

(c) **Process 3** Manuscript authoring (retained): This is a critical process which is the core competency for any publisher and needs to be retained in-house though several advanced tools have come up to support the authoring process in a digital manner (impact of which we would observe in the next chapter wherein new business models are being generated through content classification and metadata management).

(d) **Process 4** Manuscript review (disappearing): This stage, which involves managing submission reviews and checking content in a detailed manner for context, accuracy, and relevance, is taken over by external experts which is referred to as 'Over the Transom' reviews, which help manage submissions on publisher's site and save cost and time with their expertise in specific subjects and usage of multiple digitized tools.

(e) **Process 5** Editing/proofing (retained): With editing and content proofing being critical steps in manuscript publishing, this process forms an integral part of the digitized value chain with an addition of content classification. The ability to classify content (as we would also see in the next section) with the use of metadata and classification tools has helped support the digitization process tremendously, in turn creating newer digital marketing models.

(f) **Process 6, 7, 8** Production, printing, and storage (disappearing): With the advent of digital production and printing platforms and tools, and with the growth of digital storage, these three process activities (which are not core to the firm) are being combined and given off to expert intermediaries, hence, find no representation in the digitized value chain.

(g) **Process 9, 10** Marketing (retained), delivery (disappearing): With marketing gaining prominence and search-based discovery getting more important than delivery of the journal itself, this function is retained in the revised value chain along with addition of subscription-based platforms and applications which are supporting most of the traditional marketing activities. Many firms rather than investing in fulfillment are tying up with multiple e-journal and vertical platforms which have more investments in developing customer facing tools for digital delivery.

With the concepts discussed in this section, we see the transformation of older value chains into digital chains supported by expert intermediaries. In the next section, we would look at how this digitally transformed value chain provides opportunities for firms to disaggregate and re-bundle their products and services and how in turn multiple digital marketing models are created to service these emerging consumer needs.

DIGITAL MARKETING BUSINESS MODELS

From the last section we learnt how reduction of transaction costs across the value chain has helped create the new digitized value chain. We are aware that a product or service sold on any digital platform provides some additional value due to which customers prefer to buy from these new channels. We term this congregation of unique elements as 'value elements.' In this section, we would be gaining an understanding of these key digital value elements, their drivers, and how digital marketing business models are developed and deployed.

Understanding Digital Value Elements

Value elements essentially are the set of key differentiators which when used individually or in conjunction with each other provide a unique compelling proposition for any customer to buy a product from online rather than physical channels. In Fig. 2.8, we will showcase how a combination of physical goods and services along with the value elements (discussed in detail) provide an unique 'Digital Value.'

Let us go through each of the value elements in detail.

(a) **Convenience:** The foremost value which any digital business will provide a customer is to make it more convenient for the him/her to search, catalogue, select, order, and receive goods or services than to do the same in the physical environment. This applies both to

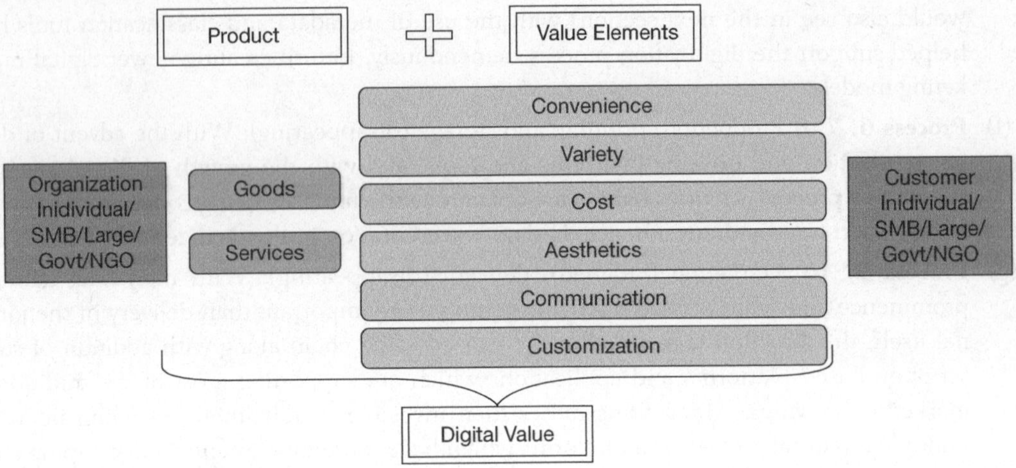

Figure 2.8 Digital Value Elements

B2B and B2C types of businesses. In B2B, investments made by the organization towards a procurement automation tool or process digitization or a collaboration platform for delivery would be part of initiatives to help develop products and services in a more efficient and convenient manner for the customer.

(b) **Variety:** The next important factor is the variety of products and services which can be put on display across dedicated websites and commerce portals, and the sheer amount of information which can be shared for each of the available elements. On the services side, this capability becomes even more pronounced as organizations have the capability of creating a variety of sub-services using modules of high-level services. The key feature here is the quick computational power of online medium, which is able to pre-classify products and services and provide customers the ability to quickly search across multiple offerings and pick and choose the best one suited to their needs.

Here we should also mention the striking advantages of the 'Long-Tail' concept wherein physical stores lack the warehousing capabilities to store the large per cent of stock keeping units (SKUs) that are not bestsellers, while online platform provides the best medium to sell SKUs which are not bought as regularly but might fetch heavy premiums when sold. This concept was coined by Chris Anderson in 2004 and since then has widely been looked at as a differentiator for products sold online.

(c) **Cost:** Involves the ability to manage costs by either utilizing efficient expert intermediaries (as seen in the last section) or bypassing multiple levels of middlemen who add to the costs of the final products. The biggest example is cost efficiencies shared by e-commerce companies which are setting up their own procurement and logistics arms to bring costs down for customers.

Another related concept is how multiple pricing models can be built across products and services depending upon customer proximity, loyalty, buying propensity, purchase frequency, etc., and how these models can be developed utilizing vast amounts of customer interaction data available across all digital touchpoints including websites, mobile applications, CRM, salesforce data, etc. Also, with multiple price-comparison sites springing up, cost arbitrage, and the knowledge of products available at discount helps customers get a much better deal especially on the B2C side where they have low influencing power.

(d) **Aesthetics**: It is one of the most novel differentiators which is not given much attention during online value creation discussions. Aesthetics include an array of tangible and intangible value-enhancing components like product design, overall styling of medium, channel and message, impact of subtle imagery, etc., all of which contribute a great extent towards the packaging of even average products and showcasing them online in a highly stylized manner. Popular examples would include Instagram and Pinterest platforms both of which have been curated in a compelling manner with high design factors which tremendously influence present-day urban values, seeking customers for whom packaging matters as much as, if not more than the product and content itself.

(e) **Communication:** A broad value differentiator, communication can go on a long way to provide digital value which normally cannot be generated for a product sold offline. Communication these days would not only include the message shared with the customer while marketing but also includes ways in which online marketers can track the customer across all stages of their online purchase and influence them with the right kind of messaging. For example, at the stage where a customer is about to decide on buying a particular product but is not sure, an expert discussion if provided by the brand might relieve customers of any doubts. Another example would be the integration of positive social comments or customer success stories, which if communicated at the right time and in the right manner, go a long way to develop customer trust and propel them towards making the final purchase.

(f) **Customization:** Out of the six digital value addition elements, customization is probably the one which is being largely discussed and still has a lot of room for improvement. Customization typically means identifying key customer segments, developing their personas (key traits, buying patterns, goals, skills, attitudes, etc.), and being able to deliver the exact experience which even a single customer might be looking out for, provided it makes investment sense.

The present level of customization possibilities reached by marketers are focused only around retargeting online advertisements to visitors who might have checked out specific products on certain sites so that they are enticed to click those advertisements and finish their purchase. With high amount of investments going towards developing tools across areas like advertisement technology, consumer data management, sentiment analysis, etc., there is still a long way to go before a company is rightly able to identify the customer's needs for a specific product, service, and is able to offer him/her a compelling proposition based on initial intent itself, to provide a product which would be most suited to his/her needs.

Digital Value-Led Marketing Approach

With an understanding of the key value elements which differentiate sales of products and services in an offline or online mode, let us extend these concepts by applying them to the same example—journal publishing—which we were discussing in the earlier section for easy reference.

Laying down the key digital value aspects on all of the six differentiating value elements, we can see how any journal publisher can make use of these pointers towards improving his/her present marketing approach and activities (see Fig. 2.9).

Following Fig. 2.9, let us go through the various digital value drivers related to the marketing of an academic journal.

(a) **Convenience:** Academic journals had already made the journey from physical titles, (which were shipped across the world to multiple locations), to uploaded scanned copies on various e-subscribed journals for universities. But when new technologies to render content on multiple digital platforms came across, educational publishers started making use of content available on multiple platforms and devices. This, along with the industry's move to open access models, has led to real-time access of e-journals possible, not only for researchers and students but also for those who earlier could not access them because of price constraints.

(b) **Variety:** It includes the possibility of indexing and classifying multiple articles across a journal based on context and also providing multiple access options with the recent advancements in search technologies. We would cover the impact of classification of data in the latter part of this section in detail to see how metadata tools and technologies (which provide context to multiple pieces of content) have increased the number of

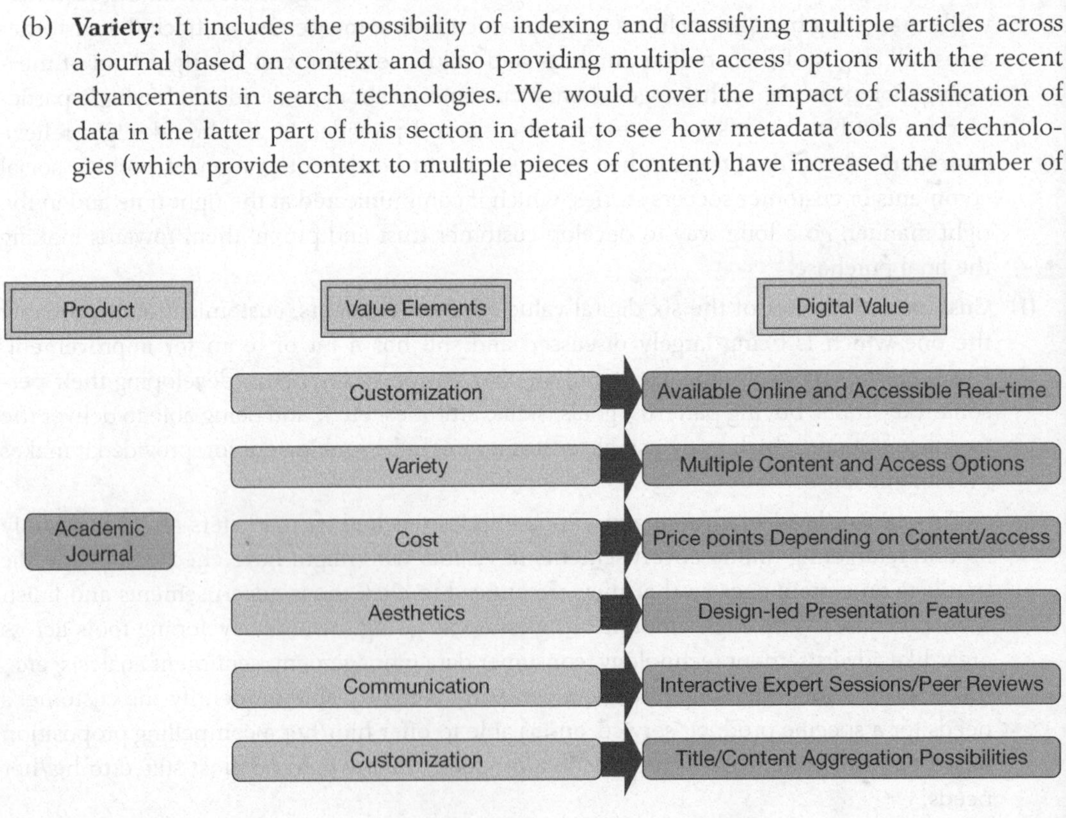

Figure 2.9 Digital Value Marketing Approach—Journal Publishing

content pieces which can be generated and sold in real-time, thus tremendously impacting the variety offered by e-journals.

(c) **Cost:** Even five years back, journals were costly, particularly the printed subscriptions. Though open-access models are still not in vogue, with new disruptive models in place (and students adopting digital platforms in a big way), the mode of accessing journals and the price universities and international students (who demand a low-cost model) are willing to pay is changing drastically. Journals now have to decide between which titles to share for free, which premium ones to keep in print, which ones to sell through generic aggregators, and which content to sell as upmarket packages based on advanced research.

(d) **Aesthetics**: If any young scholar were to go back 20 years in time and try to remember the look and feel of books which were available through university kiosk systems and libraries, he/she would probably think of them as reverse sci-fi, in terms of the dull interfaces and unappealing fonts those digital interfaces presented. In present times, where a student wants to access his book though an iPad app, he/she looks for ease of interface, moving across chapters intuitively, and seeing diagrams in an interactive fashion even sometimes linking them to educational videos. These examples show the vast changes marketers have to execute to sell the content.

(e) **Communication:** With each journal being heavily marketed to make it stand out against competition in the market, content ceases to be the only differentiator. Instead communication of that content and its value becomes critical for adoption. Authors these days not only have to maintain their own websites, but also have to make easily comprehensible interactive content like videos and webinars readily available to customers. Also, peer and expert reviews are being showcased as part of improving connection with customers and building trust with them. When an industry expert or a peer markets a product, it is seen as a sign of the journal being more credible. These days even Facebook, LinkedIn, and Twitter are being widely used to reach out to new customers and help loyal customers be engaged regularly.

(f) **Customization**: Finally, customers these days are not looking at buying full-text articles which they do not have time to go through. Rather they are looking towards publishers to provide mind-maps or break down the content into chunks which can be easily grasped and used. This customization is not only helping publishers look at content in a different manner but also improve monetization abilities and venues for long-tail consumption in a manner they could never have attempted earlier. This is also possible with the coming up of a much larger ecosystem of apps, content aggregators, and vertical portals, which we will cover at the end of this section.

Digital Marketing Models Creation

With an understanding of how key digital value elements impact the manner in which new marketing models are generated and utilized, the following sections would extend the exam-

Figure 2.10 The Traditional Marketing Approach

ple of journal publishing to see how new business models are developed combining a couple of value elements and how digital marketing acts as the key behind supporting these new models.

We start with Fig. 2.10 taking a hypothetical example of a journal of digital marketing, aiming to develop new digital business models by using a combination of the digital value elements discussed in the last section.

In the traditional model, typically a journal has a set of articles which are sold as a booklet published quarterly or monthly, and shared through a subscription model in a physical or an accessible e-journal mode (mostly sold as library subscriptions).

The customer for this journal, once subscribed to it, can only view the journal as a single piece of content with multiple articles strung together. With this model, the issue has always been that it lacks the possibility of a customer (in this case a university student) being able to search and aggregate content based on his/her specific needs and pay only for the content he/she intends to use rather than paying a high price upfront for a mix of articles which he/she might never even consume.

With this problem at hand, we applied the digital value elements concept to see how the utilization of some of these value elements can help journal publishers develop new business models which are led by consumer needs and driven by digital marketing.

In Fig. 2.11, we showcase the interactions between the publisher and the individual with an addition of a content layer in between. Now, rather than looking at the journal as a single piece of product, we have divided it into its key content elements which are the articles (for simplification we assume in this example that this journal only has three articles).

For each of the articles in the middle layer, we will try to apply the digital value elements of variety and customization to see how we can create multiple content types and business models to service these content needs. If we look at the content composition of any academic journal article and break it down further, we will see distinct content classification types including:

(a) *Author:* Each article has one or more authors tagged to them who might have written multiple papers or articles for this journal
(b) *Subject:* Subject is the full text of the article broken down into logical sections which can be consumed based upon each title header and its body in a combined manner
(c) *Context:* Context involves looking at the background/summary for which this article might be useful to read, helping readers know, (even before they spend their time reading), whether they have found the right article that matches with their problem area

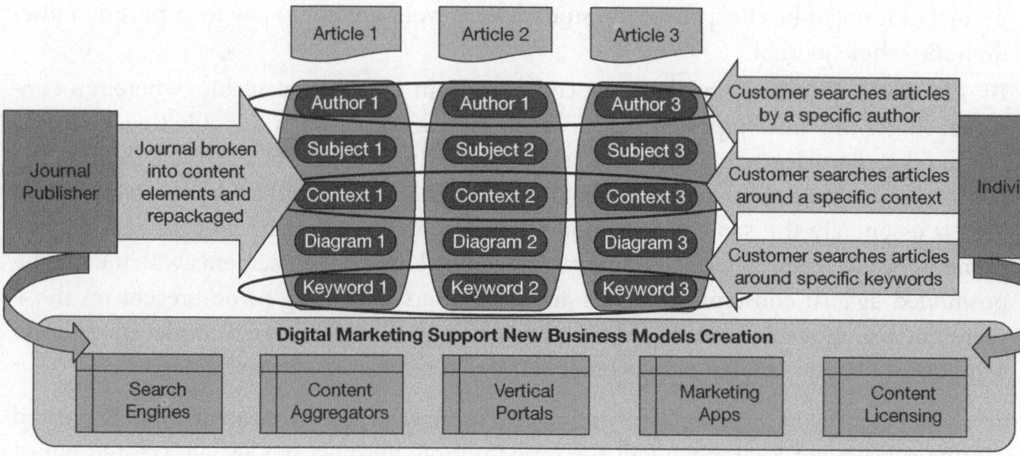

Figure 2.11 Digital Value Elements (Classification and Aggregation)-Led Marketing

(d) *Diagram/Frameworks:* Includes non-text based data which can be searched separately or made use of just by themselves towards elaboration of any other research work

(e) *Keywords:* Finally, all set of content today can be classified as a set of relevant keywords so that a user with just one word or phrase or an aggregation of words is able to search and find the right paragraph in minimum time

Let us now see how using the concepts of *variety* (which in this case relates to *classifying* a piece of content and converting it into various usable forms) and *customization* (relates to looking at a customer query and aggregating content based on his/her requirements) will help generate new business models. With content divided in the five-point manner (author, subject, context, diagrams, keywords), we can provide any consumer the possibility to search, aggregate, and buy content in the following manner (few examples):

(a) **By author name:** Users searching for a particular topic, say, for example, knowledge on 'Evolution of Search Algorithms for Digital Marketing' can punch in this phrase in an advanced search-box (specifically created to support content classification) and thereby obtain a list of authors who have written papers/articles on these topics. The users can go ahead and buy only the articles related to these authors and this search topic rather than paying for all articles.

(b) **By context:** Because multiple contexts can be provided to each title/section combination and the overall article content itself (in the form of a summary), numerous possibilities can be generated for a customer to search for his specific context (which could be a need to know how search technologies are built on legacy databases). If content is well *classified* and has the ability to *aggregate*, it becomes possible to provide the specific paragraphs or text (which have a relevance for the consumer context) and integrate them into a package for which the customer can be charged separately. The price for such customization might be higher than a per-article price (as there is additional customization being provided here), but it might be cheaper for the student who would prefer to pay for a portion rather than the whole journal.

(c) **By keywords:** This is by far the most common form of search available, wherein a consumer shares the most important keywords he is looking out for and is able to get a listing of top related articles across the whole set of present and historical journals available (the consumer would be able to see a summary related to that keyword for each search result). This is essentially the same search model which was pioneered by Google and became immensely successful in terms of intent and display-based advertisements which could be positioned against consumer searches and advertisers paying up to be present on those premium search results (we would be going through Google's search model in detail in subsequent chapters during our coverage on search marketing and technologies).

With the few instances of 'classification and aggregation value-based' content models created earlier, in the subsequent section we will see how multiple business models are created out of this identified customer need for content search and how digital marketing supports these value shifts to create new opportunities.

Application of Digital Marketing Models

The new content models discussed in the earlier section showcase opportunities generated through a mix of digital value elements. Most of the times, the organization in consideration (like the example here of the academic journal publisher,) might not be in the best position to put forth and develop all emerging business models possible, because of multiple factors of investment, new opportunity assessment, management readiness, etc.

But in the emerging digital world there are a lot of entrepreneurs picking up such niche expert areas and acting as intermediaries to create a market for themselves. Fig. 2.12 showcases a few of those including Search Engines, Content Aggregators, Vertical Portals, Marketing Applications, and Content Licensors. The digital marketing opportunity arising through these intermediary models and the customer value arising from their execution are also shared in the diagram.

Let us go through each of the models in detail.

(a) **Search engines:** These are entities which provide search-related function and map customer searched content to pre-classified content.

Digital marketing opportunity: A classic example is the route Google took on marrying search intent to provide a listing of weblinks which would serve that search need best and get advertisers and individual companies to sponsor against those results. But this opportunity is not only limited to Google. Search as a concept has opened up doors on how matching a query to an outcome can help create profitable business models and higher consumer satisfaction. The *search marketing concept* will also be discussed in detail in the later chapters.

In this case, consumers who search on Google or even on other websites can be either brought to the journal's main website/affiliate sites or be guided directly to articles/sections

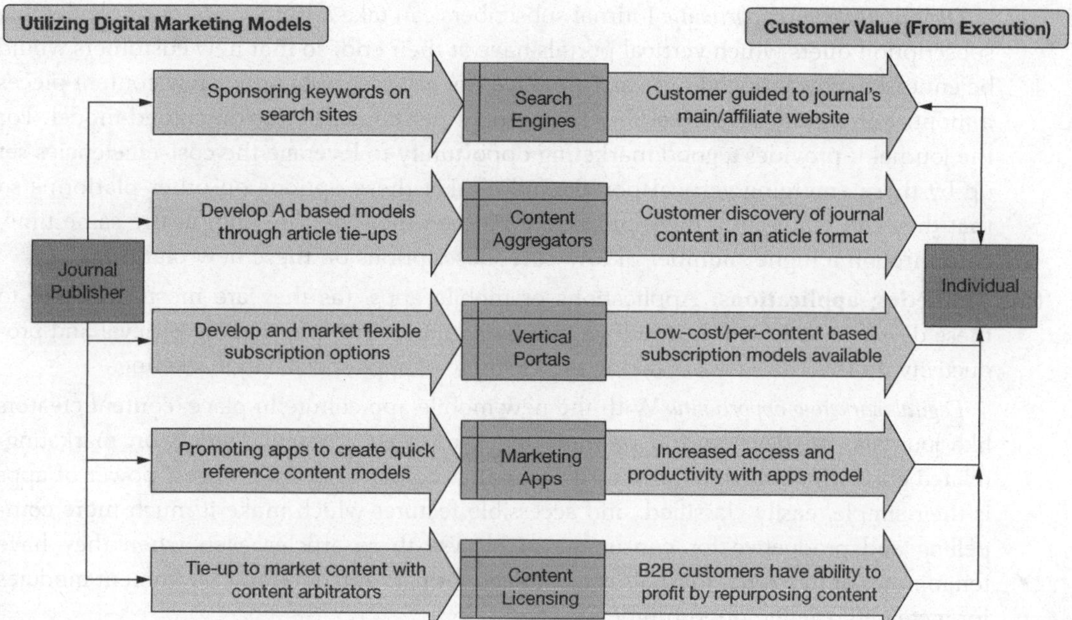

Figure 2.12 Application of Digital Marketing Models

that contain the data which they might need. The publisher can then apply pay-per content or pay-per view-type of business models to this activity.

(b) **Content aggregators:** These are companies/websites which aggregate content pieces from various sources and provide them in the form of curated articles in a highly classified format.

Digital marketing opportunity: The opportunity to share content with content aggregators comes from the fact that these aggregators are typically well known and well marketed to the general audience. A journal which supplies content or articles to such an aggregator could benefit from the advertising revenue created through display advertisements showcased along with content in a contextual manner, so that when the reader clicks the advertisement, he/she is sent to the advertiser's site and the journal can benefit from this model with an advertiser fee cut. This is called the *display advertising model* and will be discussed in detail in the later chapters. The consumer in this case will benefit from discovering the content in the form of an engaging article which he might not be able to discover otherwise. After reading through the article if he finds it interesting, he can click the article link to go to the journal website and become a regular reader/subscriber to the journal.

(c) **Vertical portals**: Niche content companies which focus only on a particular vertical, (like in this case only marketing-related articles), will provide news, views, articles, forums, social networking features dedicated to that particular subject area.

Digital marketing opportunity: Journal subscribers can take advantage of multiple flexible subscription offers which vertical portals have at their end, so that new customers would be enticed to pay a much lower first-time fee (for say accessing only a few content pieces a month) or would have an ability to pay on a per-content view/download model. For the journal it provides a good marketing opportunity to leverage the cost-efficiencies set up by these emerging vertical portals and market these options on other platforms so that they can maintain a high-end positioning on their website and, at the same time, earn through a higher number of low-cost subscriptions on these new platforms.

(d) **Marketing applications:** Applications or mobile apps, (as they are mostly referred to these days), provide simple, intuitive interfaces to improve information retrieval and productivity. In this case, we are taking the example of apps specific to marketing.

Digital marketing opportunity: With the new mobile app culture in place, content creators like journals can develop and promote quick reference content models on marketing-related apps which already have a substantial customer base. The biggest power of apps is their simple, easily classified, and accessible features which make it much more compelling and productive for consumers to browse these articles even when they have ten minutes of free time. Journals can use such formats and develop easy content modules for increased revenue opportunities.

(e) **Content licensing:** Includes models wherein content (which might be owned or tied-up with) is leased or licensed further to other websites, to create other content-based offerings or packages, a portion of which is then paid back to original content producers.

Digital marketing opportunity: Journal publishers can market multiple content licensing tie-ups with other books, instructional material creators through content arbitrators who deal with collecting and licensing content to other business owners for a cut of the pie. This example pertains more to B2B customers who can make use of the proprietary content/research which has already been conducted/developed and can pay a license fee either to use this content in their new work/publications or get rights to reprint the content for other content models. The power of this model is that content can be made available for further research in a manner which is both accessible to new companies and profitable to the ones who have invested in it earlier. With the examples of the models shared earlier and the applications of marketing which can be explored for each of them, we see how companies utilizing the digital platform can make use of its specific value elements and drive new businesses by using multiple digital marketing applications which previously were not available to them. What makes all of this possible is the entire ecosystem of technology, entrepreneurs, customer value focus, and the knowledge of digital marketing opportunities available to multiple businesses in today's time.

CHAPTER SUMMARY

- **Part 1:** We started learning the concepts of Brick and Mortar companies and how they are evolving to Bricks and Clicks models, and understood the uniqueness of each of them. We then looked at the growth of interactive platforms and understood the six types of new interactions supported by these platforms. This was followed by an understanding of the four types of network effects and the shift from a marketplace to a marketspace model. Finally, we went through the reasons behind the changing sales function and the impact of the digital world on customer service patterns.
- **Part 2:** This section began with an understanding of key value chain functions (procurement, production, delivery, and expert functions) and how production has to manage interactions with each of them. We then laid down key value chain functions and understood the important concept of transaction cost. This was followed by an elaboration of each process step of the value chain through an example of journal publishing wherein we saw how expert intermediaries are helping journal publishing firms to digitize their value chain through transaction cost reduction at each step, finally creating a much more efficient and value-driven digital value chain.
- **Part 3:** In the last part we developed an understanding of the six core digital value elements which any industry can utilize to create new online business models. We then applied these value elements to the journal industry, and utilizing variety and communication elements, we showcased how new business models (supported by digital marketing) can be generated based upon customer demand to access and consume content in the manner most preferred by them. In the last section, we got an understanding of how customer value is generated by applying multiple digital marketing models successfully across identified business propositions.

REVIEW QUESTIONS

1. Can you describe the difference between Brick and Mortar and Brick and Click models?
2. Can you share four dimensions on which the extent of digital presence can be measured?
3. Can you describe any three unique elements of the Brick and Mortar and Brick and Click models separately?
4. What do we mean by impact and importance of Interactive Platforms? What are the key types of interactions supported by Interactive Platforms?
5. What is the meaning of Network Effects? Explain the four key types of network effects?
6. Explain the difference between marketplaces and marketspaces.

7. What are the ways in which the traditional sales function is changing in the digital world?
8. Can you explain the concept of value chain? Please elucidate on the concept with the example of any industry.
9. What are the four distinct Interaction Functions of the production element of value chain functions?
10. What do we understand by the concept of transaction cost?
11. What do we mean by digital value elements? Can you explain in brief the six digital value elements?
12. Can you apply the Digital Value Marketing Approach to journal publishing as explained in the chapter?
13. From the example of journal book publishing, explain the application of three key digital marketing models.

DIGITAL APPLICATION EXERCISES

1. Pick up an industry of your choice in India and discuss the four dimensions of digital presence for that industry at large.
2. Expand on the example of Firstcry.com in the chapter to detail the shift from a Brick and Mortar to a Brick and Click model.
3. Can you provide an example for each of the six types of interactions supported by interactive platforms?
4. Pick any one of the four key types of Network Effects and apply it to an online brand to explain the concept.
5. Take the example of Shopclues.com to detail the differences between marketspaces and marketplaces.
6. Visit the website CarDekho.com and contrast the sales function of the auto market on the ground from that on the digital platform.
7. Study the website Quickr.com and share the key initiatives it has taken over the years to differentiate itself on the six key digital value elements.

CHAPTER 3

The Consumer for Digital Marketing

LEARNING OBJECTIVES

After studying this chapter, you will be able to:

- Explain the evolution of consumer behavior models, key attributes of online buying behavior and the impact of digital technology on buying patterns
- Understand consumer demand patterns and the ways these can be analyzed online through web-tracking audits and forecasting
- Describe integrated marketing communications, the channels, and basic constructs of such communication

CASE STUDY Google India: *Your Voice can Command Everything*

Technology giant Google has always seen India as the biggest market for their business and invested hugely in the Indian marketplace. Today, Google India has taken its place in almost every Indian household, and CEO Sundar Pichai is working on making life even better for Indians. Since its inception Google India experienced constant growth and offered the best possible online solutions to every member of Indian society - be it the government, companies, or individuals.

Google India has kept its focus on artificial intelligence (AI), YouTube, cloud services, and launching a payment service for Indian users. As per Statista, Google India hit a revenue of INR 72.4 billion in 2017, INR 93.37 billion in 2018, INR 41.47 billion in 2019, INR 55.94 billion in 2020, and INR 63.86 billion in 2021, which could be termed as variable performance. The 'Digitisation policy' adopted by the Indian government proved to be a great benefit and paved the way for Google India to reach every corner of the Indian society.

Google India used AI and machine learning capabilities to build online classrooms with better language compatibility, which helped schools and teachers tremendously during the COVID-19 pandemic. With this initiative, Google India took two important steps: First, they expanded their reach to the semi-urban and rural populations, and second, they helped create meaningful change and impact within Indian society by offering education to rural children. Google even pledged to invest US$10 billion on the digital transformation in India which will involve affordable internet access, building digital products/services, empowering local businesses and leveraging AI for rural economies.

Google India also leveraged their Google Assistant service to cater to the different Indian languages. Campaigns like "Bolne se Sab Hoga" (with the objective of empowering users to access internet in their own language), were able to create massive awareness on how voice search can turn around every Indian's life by providing access in one's own language.

Apart from AI, Google India also worked hard on its cloud services and took various steps in this direction. From big collaborations to exceptional service delivery, Google Cloud established its position as one of the largest and fastest growing players in the cloud market in India (among Amazon and Microsoft). The reason behind this success is their collaborations *with Reliance Jio, Bharti Airtel, RBL Bank, Wipro, and some other major companies.* As per Bikram Singh Bedi, the MD of Google Cloud India, Google Cloud India's presence accelerated because of the onset of the pandemic. More Indian businesses invested in cloud infrastructure, tools, and software, especially in the automation, manufacturing, and education sectors. In Jan 2022, Google invested in 20 Indian startups that are a part of Google Accelerator's 6th cohort. This program has benefitted 20 Indian startups through its three months equity-free accelerator program to provide mentorship and support (based on challenges outlined by each startup).

Google also never took its focus off from its most prominent platform: YouTube. Google India accelerated the growth of YouTube through YouTube Shorts (a short video-sharing platform that limits pieces to 60 seconds in length). Although it has not been very long since Shorts was launched, its growth is impressive in the Indian marketplace. Additionally, Google India has strived to become a key service provider for the Indian government as well. From Google AI (for education advancement) to CoWIN App (COVID-19 vaccination registration portal), Google India never missed an opportunity to help the Indian government.

Google India's multiple undertakings have helped them grab a 99.66% share (as of May 2021) in the mobile search engine market, although Amazon India has started taking control of over 20% of India's digital marketing spend (US$2.54 billion in 2021). Google Pay also holds the second position in the UPI market (PhonePe being the leader). As of December 2021, Google Pay executed INR 3.03 crore's worth of transactions in India.

It has not always been easy-going for Google India, since they have faced antitrust cases in the past globally. Google has been accused of using its dominating position in the market for news aggregation services for a long time. It has been regularly accused of power imbalance in terms of leveraging publisher content to earn advertising revenue while denying fair share to publishers who created it in the first place. (Digital News Publishers ...

vs Alphabet Inc. And Others on 7 January, 2022, see Bibliography 2 for details). In India, Google had issues surrounding compliance with IT regulations in 2021, but CEO Sundar Pichai navigated the situation by making sure they adhered to all new regulations of the Indian government.

Despite the above mentioned legal issues, the growth of Google India has been clearly visible to users due to its diversified approach. Looking at its growth trend, it is expected that Google India will rule the Indian market both in erstwhile Digital Advertising and in emerging fields like Cloud Computing, Education, Artificial Intelligence, Digital Payments, etc. for the coming years.

CONSUMER BEHAVIOR ON THE INTERNET

Consumer behavior and related studies have formed an integral part of marketing as it is crucial to understand the motivations and factors which lead to a consumer buying any specific brand over another and choosing certain websites, platforms, and channels over and over again for purchases. In this chapter, we shall go through the impact and influence of digital technology to understand how consumer demand can be anticipated and managed with available online data, how traces of consumer footprint can be tracked, and a fully customized marketing program can be developed.

First, it is important to understand the difference between two terms which are often confused and substituted for each other—the consumer and customer. In marketing parlance, the term customer refers to the purchaser of the product whereas consumer refers to the end user of the product or service. The simplest example relates to baby products wherein a mother is the customer while the actual consumer is the baby for whom the product has been bought. In several cases, the consumer can also act as a customer, when he/she is singularly involved in searching, evaluating, and buying the product, and finally consuming it.

Why is this distinction between the two definitions important? It is because of the different strategies which need be applied by brands to know whom to exactly market and who is the influencer (also termed as advocate) to buy the product on behalf of the consumer. In a lot of cases, the consumer would leave the selection process to the customer and it is actually customer behavior which marketers need to track and comprehend to target all marketing activities towards him/her.

For ease of understanding and non-repetition, marketers typically use the word 'consumer behavior' while making a holistic consumer targeting strategy as it encompasses all intermediaries and influencers who might affect the purchase decision. Let us begin this chapter with an understanding of the evolution of consumer behavior models to see how this field has developed and is impacting the way marketers absorb and analyze consumer behavior.

EVOLUTION OF CONSUMER BEHAVIOR MODELS

In the section on Chapter 1 titled "Digital Marketing Channels—Types and Business Models," we had looked at the key stages of the consumer funnel which any consumer would typically go through before finally buying a product. These stages (intent, awareness, interest, action, and follow), describe the journey of the customer from an initial thought to sealing the purchase.

But even before all of this occurs, a marketer has to be completely clear and focused on which consumer segments he/she is planning to target the product portfolio and which consumer segments are the most important for the product. And, to do that successfully, he/she needs to understand the basic concepts of consumer behavior and how it varies across the emerging digital channels.

According to 'Schiffman and Kanuk', the leading authority on Consumer behavior, this marketing field is defined as "the behavior that consumers display in searching for, purchasing, using, evaluating and disposing of products and services that they expect will satisfy their needs." It would be important here to understand that it is not only the consumer's personal thoughts and dispositions which matter during product selection but also the influences and interplay of external forces like people, ideas, environment (social, political, and economic), which impact a consumer's mindset towards a particular product interaction.

Over the years, there have been multiple models developed by different researchers to explain consumer behavior process and factors impacting it. Traditional consumer behavior models, which were developed, drew their origins from varied disciplines (see Table 3.1).

Although the above models explained a generalist view of how consumer behavior works, they were limited in their approach, composition, and lacked a broader perspective. This led to the development of the modern consumer behavior models, the most influential of which included 'The Howard Sheth Model of Buying Behavior,' 'The Nicosia Model,' and the 'Engel, Blackwell, and Miniard (EBM)' Model.

Table 3.1 Traditional Consumer Behavior Models

Traditional Models	Definition
Economic Model	Believes that man being self-interested, makes decisions based upon his ability to maximize utility while expending minimum effort
Learning Model	Marketers develop association of products with strong drivers and cues which lead to positive reinforcement through learning
Psychological Model	Based on concepts of psychology, this view believes that behavior is subject to instinctive forces or drives which act outside conscious thoughts. The biggest contribution to this model has been the theories of Sigmund Freud with his concepts of Id, Super Ego, and Ego
Sociological Model	This model believes that an individual is part of an institution called society which influences his thoughts and actions and he, in turn, also influences society

The Howard Sheth model was pivotal in bringing forth the 'Theory of Buyer Behavior' which provided "a sophisticated integration of various social, psychological, and marketing influences on consumer choice into a coherent sequence of information processing." The model though revolutionary in its approach and construct was quite complex and included variables which were not too well defined and difficult to measure. For this reason, it underwent improvements in the form of new models, the most applied among them being the EBM model which we would discuss in detail (see Fig. 3.1).

The 'Engel, Blackwell and Miniard (EBM)' Model encompasses all types of need-satisfying behavior for a consumer, including a wide range of influencing factors and different types of problem-solving processes. This model has been influential since it has undergone multiple revisions and has included works of other researchers too.

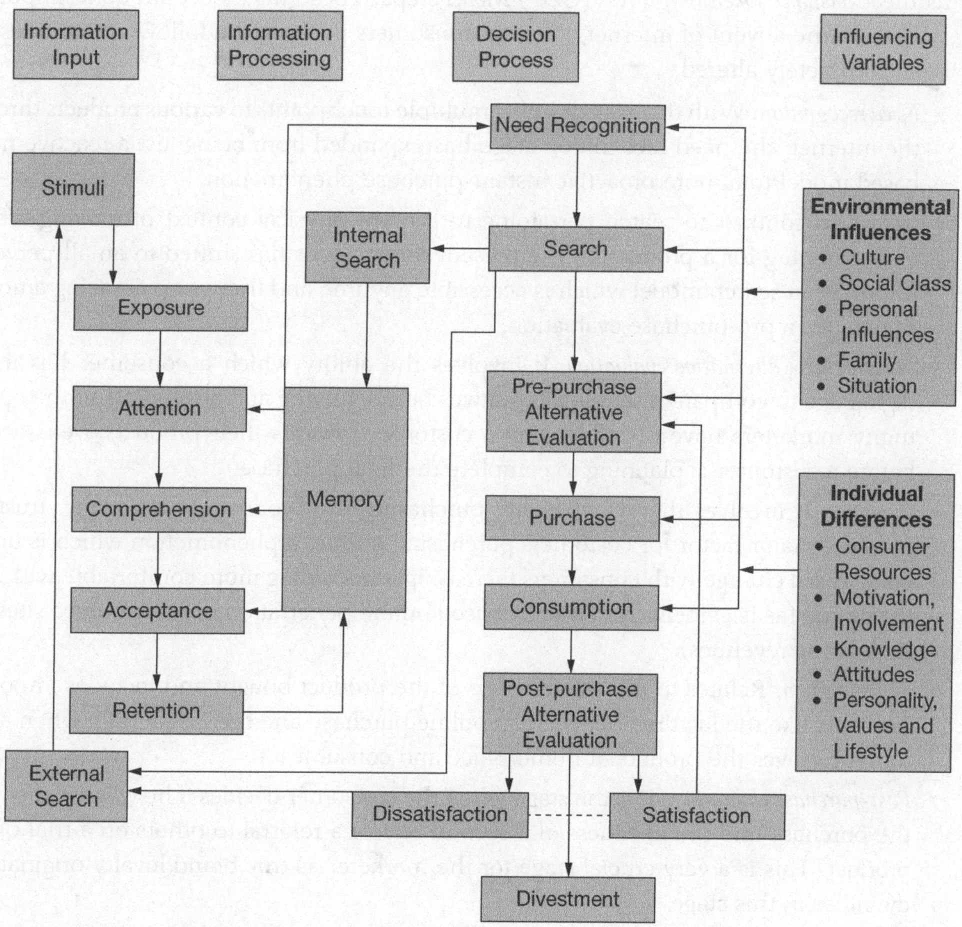

Figure 3.1 The 'Engel, Blackwell, and Miniard (EBM)' Model

The model consists of four key stages:

(a) **Information input stage:** This stage includes all the inputs and stimuli from marketing (like advertisements in television, radio, newspapers, internet, word of mouth, etc.) and non-marketing sources which form the basis for information processing in the next stage. The stage also includes additional external information search which the consumer conducts, especially when not enough information is available from memory or when post- purchase dissonance occurs.

(b) **Information processing stage:** The information processing stage is similar to the consumer funnel, discussed in the beginning of this section, which involves the consumer getting exposed to the marketing message, paying attention to it, comprehending its intent, proactively or subliminally accepting it, and retaining in memory to make a decision the next time he/she is exposed to a similar message.

(c) **Decision process stage:** Involves the following key stages which are commonly looked at as the *Consumer Decision Process (CDP) Model* steps. These have become quite important since with the advent of internet, the way consumers perform the following activities has been completely altered.

- *Need recognition*: With the availability of multiple touchpoints to various products through the internet, the need recognition stage has expanded from being just a reactive need-based model to a more proactive instant-purchase phenomenon.
- *Search:* In contrast to search pertaining to a more physical context of moving around and searching for a product, in the present times, focus has shifted to an all-pervasive information search model which is accessible anytime and throws up amazing amounts of data for a pre-purchase evaluation.
- *Pre-purchase alternative evaluation:* It involves the ability which a consumer has in the digital age to compare multiple alternatives before buying and also points to the opportunity marketers have of influencing a customer towards their product, even seconds before a customer is planning to complete the final purchase.
- *Purchase:* It involves the act of finally purchasing the product. Traditionally, trust has played a major factor for customers purchasing online, a phenomenon which is undergoing rapid change with consumers increasingly becoming more comfortable with buying online (as is evident from the increased online penetration of e-commerce sites and their rising revenues).
- *Consumption*: Relates to the actual usage of the product bought and includes important concepts like the lag time between an online purchase and the actual time when a customer receives the product at home/office and consumes it.
- *Post-purchase evaluation:* It is the stage when the consumer decides if he was satisfied with the purchase and the likeliness of a second buy or a referral to others on a trial of that product. This is a very crucial stage for the marketer as true brand loyalty originates or dwindles in this stage.

- *Divestment:* The final stage of the CDP model involves the consumer divesting the product which is not dependent on the purchase channel or buy pattern.

(d) **Variables influencing the decision process**: Includes two broad categories—
- *Environmental influences:* It includes factors like culture, social classes, personal influences, family, and other situations which impact a consumer's decision process throughout the CDP stages.
- *Individual differences:* This includes more individual-driven factors which differentiate one kind of consumer from another, based on factors like consumer resources, motivation and involvement, knowledge, attitudes, personality, values, and lifestyle all of which could have a huge impact on a consumer's final decision towards a product or service.

With an understanding of the evolution of consumer behavior and key models which have shaped it over the years, we move forward to understand the impact digital technologies have had on decisions and motivations of online buyers and how the internet has impacted consumer behavior and changed the marketing landscape.

Impact of Digital Technology on Consumer Behavior

Before we move ahead to understand the impact of digital on consumer behavior, it is important to know the difference between a regular consumer and one who is online. What are the characteristics which separate these two types of consumers and why is it useful for marketers to give importance to digital consumers?

A digital consumer has the following characteristics which differentiates him/her from the traditional (offline) consumer and helps support the marketer's cause.

(a) **Higher potential for profiling**: Technology now provides the possibility to map each move of the online customer, resulting in a much higher potential to gather data points on consumer's profile like location, number of visits, type of products bought, time spent on different webpages, product browsing history (before final buy), etc., typically adding to the overall information on specific customer sets.

(b) **Development of consumer personas**: The concept of consumer personas has become quite crucial and is widely applied across the advertising and marketing industry in present times. It refers to creating fictional characters to represent specific customer segments and their needs. Consumer personas help marketers understand the kind of products and services which can be targeted to specific personality groups wherein their behavior towards purchase has already been tested and measured and products are specifically developed to target to their tastes and likings.

(c) **Possibility to gather unsolicited feedback**: With online customers sharing comments and reviews across multiple social networking sites and with advanced tools being developed to analyze consumer sentiment through text analytics, marketers are now endowed with tools which can help them gather feedback in an unsolicited manner to understand the real preferences and attitudes of customers towards products which cannot be gauged even through well-organized focus groups.

(d) **Availability of real-time expert/peer influence:** Digital customers who in their offline avatar have high difficulty to gather opinions and views of experts and friends, can obtain these in a much more directed fashion online and marketers can influence consumer decisions through investments in content marketing and targeted messaging even during the last-mile steps of a consumer who is about to convert a purchase.

(e) **Use online data to target loyal offline customers:** With digital channels, there is a high possibility to gather preferences and attitudes of consumers who might already be loyal customers in the offline world. With marketers now having the ability to track and map their traditionally loyal customers and gather online data, they can use this knowledge to provide customized experiences to customers who are buying products in real stores.

Knowing that online customers are distinctly important to marketers, let us see how marketers are using multiple online elements to influence their CDP (Consumer Decision Process), and thus, getting more leverage. Let's discuss a classic example of buying a pair of branded jeans, an activity which is quite normal in the traditional marketing world but one which has added a lot of consumer-influencing elements to it with the advent of online channels.

In Fig. 3.2, we see how a particular consumer in the traditional world would be influenced while purchasing a pair of jeans. We have divided the influences into two types—passive and active. *Passive influences* are those on which the consumer does not have much control and he receives them in an unsolicited manner, though he might be influenced by them. *Active influences*, on the other hand, are the ones which a consumer actively seeks out while he/she is evaluating or finalizing a purchase.

In Fig. 3.2, we see how the traditional marketing model could impact the CDP in a limited manner only and there were not many opportunities that the marketer had to influence consumer behavior and make it favorable for his/her set of products and services.

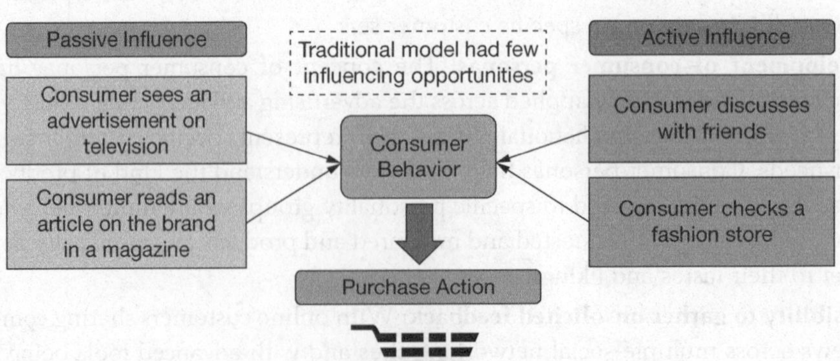

Figure 3.2 Traditional Areas Impacting CDP (Consumer Decision Process)

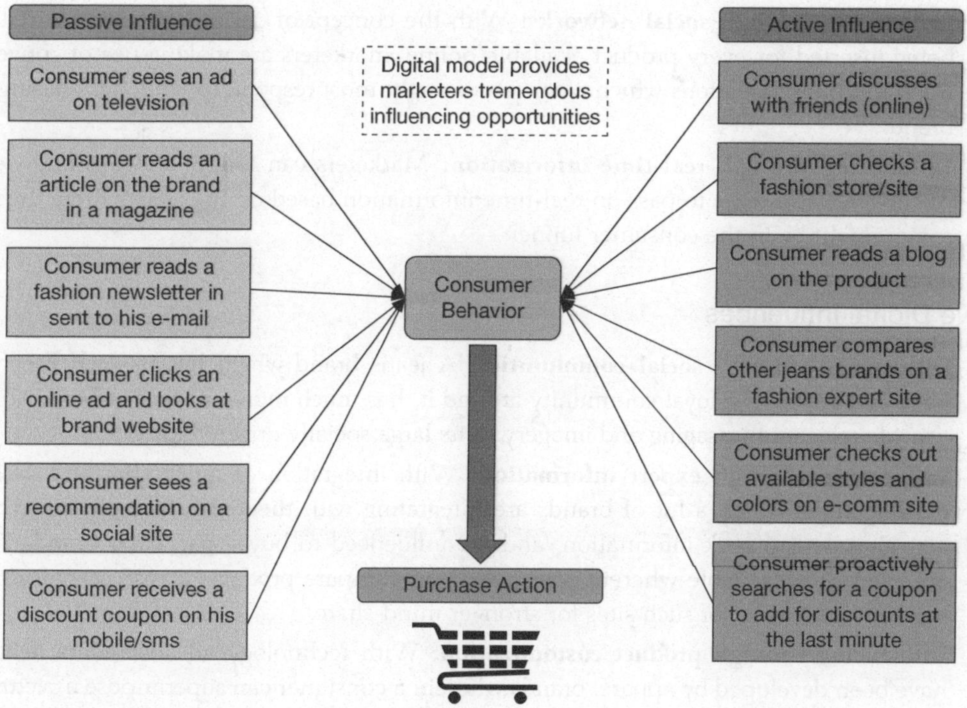

Figure 3.3 Impact of Digital Technology on CDP (Consumer Decision Process)

In contrast, if we look at the impact of digital technologies (see Fig. 3.3) on CDP , we shall see addition of multiple marketing channels which the marketer now has at his/her disposal to impact a consumer's behavior and attitude towards his/her brands. Some of these passive and active influences brought about by digital technology can be explained as below.

Passive Digital Influences

(a) **Influencing through more marketing channels:** With digital technology providing far more targeting options, marketers can use a mix like search marketing, native content, e-mail communication, affiliate marketing, etc., which were not available traditionally.

(b) **Influencing through customized content:** Marketers, with their knowledge of consumer personas and individual data from previous buys of an individual, have the ability to target through the use of customized content. Such content may be based on consumer's background, buying behavior, and even, in certain cases, cultural and social affiliations which could be very powerful.

(c) **Influencing through targeted/re-targeted advertising:** By knowing the set of customers who have visited the brand page/e-commerce listing, for example, of a particular jeans brand, one can set a retargeting campaign to try and influence conversions in the next couple of days for customers who showed an interest but did not follow thereafter.

(d) **Influencing through social networks:** With the concept of customer recommendations being inserted for every product available online, marketers are making use of conversations and online relations which a consumer might most respond to while purchasing the brand.

(e) **Influencing through real-time information:** Marketers can follow and use knowledge of customer locations to pass on real-time information based on the stage where the customer might be in the consumer funnel.

Active Digital Influences

(a) **Influencing through social communities:** A jeans brand which has its own Facebook page and has built a loyal community around it, has much more chances of being able to provide relevant messaging and imagery to its large socially driven audience.

(b) **Influencing through expert information:** With integration of quick chat and 'fashion guru' features which a lot of brands are integrating with their websites, consumers can actively interact, seek information, and get influenced to buy a particular brand. There are even sites available wherein consumers can compare products across categories and marketers can sponsor such sites for stronger mind-share.

(c) **Influencing through product customization:** With technology advancements, features have been developed by apparel brands wherein a consumer can superimpose a picture to see how he/she would look in a particular jean's style and colour, thus giving a high level of personalized touch to the buying experience.

(d) **Influencing through data-driven promotions:** Marketers can also avail of the knowledge of their traditional customers to offer them discounts at the last mile-stage of product purchase, which is only possible with the use of extensive technology.

Attributes of Online Buying Behavior

With a good understanding of the impact of digital technology, let us now study the key attributes of online buying behavior and what motivates customers to buy online.

In Chapter 2 we had looked at the key value elements which create 'digital value' for any online buying. Those included convenience, variety, cost, aesthetics, communication, and customization. Lewis and Lewis (1997) in their studies have spotted five different kinds of web users:

(a) **Directed information-seekers**: These users look for information about specific products. Their intention is not to buy but to search for information.

(b) **Undirected information-seekers:** These users regularly browse and scan websites by following hyperlinks. They are referred to as 'surfers' because they look around the websites to find something interesting.

(c) **Directed buyers:** These users visit a website with the intention to buy products online. They search specific products and make the transaction.

(d) **Entertainment seekers:** These users visit websites that offer entertainment features, such as quizzes, puzzles, and multi-player games.

(e) **Bargain hunters:** This type of users search for special offers such as free samples or discounts.

This classification helps us realize that although we might see a large number of visits to certain websites, it is also very important to understand the behaviors and motives of key consumer segments visiting those sites which will eventually determine the success or failure of the business. To understand better how to guide potential consumers who are always present at the top of the consumer funnel and do not trickle to the conversion stage, we would need to understand important influencing factors or attributes which any online marketing activity must offer to be a success.

The three key attributes identified across major studies done in this area include:

(a) **Price:** Price is one of the earlier attributes for online buying. It has priority even before convenience since for a long time buying online was not possible because of the unavailability of broadband and the absence of the plastic card culture—considerations which still hold true in developing counties like India. It has been studied that consumers started going to internet primarily to compare prices and see if cheaper versions of the product they intended to buy were available online. With a multitude of price comparison sites available today and several e-commerce companies leveraging logistics-based savings, price has definitely become the key attribute for online buying. It has also been responsible for another much talked-about online trend, impulsive buying, wherein shoppers who become quite comfortable with online buying do not even check prices and at times overpay for products and services they might not have even tried to look at earlier. This unanticipated trend though has proved to be quite useful for marketers.

(b) **Trust:** Monsuwe et al (in 2004) had concluded that because internet was a new way of shopping, initially it was looked at as being risky by consumers. This was primarily because of the absence of a salesperson who was their major source of trust, as well as because of the worry of payments going through and goods (once paid for) reaching the consumer in delayed time. But companies like Amazon (globally) and Flipkart (in India) changed this perception to their advantage trying to assure customers that online could also stand for trust. This was possible through relentless pursuit of perfection across all areas of the consumer purchase lifecycle, from secure buying to warehousing, to final delivery, replicating this experience over and over. Flipkart even went to the extent of providing the 'Cash on Delivery' feature to show how the medium can be trusted in nations which had never trusted online buying. Initiatives like these have led to trust becoming one of the key attributes of online buying.

(c) **Convenience**: This much discussed attribute truly has been the bedrock of online buying, with customers taking advantage of being able to shop from wherever they like, at a time most suited to them and in a way which requires just a few clicks. With companies nowadays even looking to supply essentials like grocery and fruits through mobile applications, online companies have completely redefined the concept of convenience to include categories and services which could not have even been envisioned before.

These days, the growth and sustenance of online buying is attributed not just to the above basic factors but also to constant innovations and efficiencies built in supply chain structures, wherein pure online retailers are even looking at opening up offline spaces to provide maximum coverage and convenience to their buyers, to supply products in a day with guarantee. In the next sections, we would look at the key building blocks through which online companies are developing such experiences for customers to keep them hooked onto this medium.

Influence of the Web Experience

According to Hofacher (2001), the information that is presented on a website is processed by the human mind in five separate stages—exposure; attention; comprehensions and perception; yielding and acceptance; and retention. These are also the same stages as put forth in the EBM model (see Fig. 3.1). Let us understand how these five stages are crucial to developing web experience online and how firms are integrating these elements into their web presence (we can also see that these stages mirror the consumer funnel stages 'Intent, Awareness, Interest, Action, and Follow' as described in Chapter 1).

(a) **Exposure:** The content must be presented for a long time in order to be processed by the user. The user might not process messages that quickly disappear off the screen or words that cannot be read easily.

(b) **Attention:** People have a tendency to give attention to things related to their expectations and needs. Attention is influenced by the visual appeal of the information presented on a website. Users notice things that move or are bright and loud.

(c) **Comprehensions and perception:** The terms 'comprehension' and 'perception' are related to the process of understanding and observing an element and connecting with the information stored in our memories. When users look at a picture or a word they automatically relate this information with the information stored in their minds.

(d) **Yielding and acceptance:** The information must be up to date and truthful in order to be accepted by the users. Users may not accept the content of the website if it does not seem convincing.

(e) **Retention:** The term 'retention' refers to the extent to which the information of the website will be remembered by the user. It is accepted that information from a website that is well organized will be easier to remember.

According to these five characteristics, websites should be developed to cover, if not all, most of these aspects so as to gain the attention of the visitor. Let us now look at the key building blocks of web experience as showcased in Fig. 3.4.

The building blocks and the factors mentioned herewith were a result of the review of 48 academic papers in the area of consumer behavior authored by Efthymios Constantinides for the Emerald Group Publishing. The research came up with three key classifications under which the following factors have been bucketed:

Functionality factors		Psychological factors	Content factors	
Usability	**Interactivity**	**Trust**	**Aesthetics**	**Marketing Mix**
Convenience	Customer service/after sales	Transaction security	Design	Communication
Site navigation	Interaction with company personnel	Customer data misuse	Presentation quality	Product
Information architecture	Customization	Customer data safety	Design elements	Fulfillment
Ordering/payment process	Network effects	Uncertainty reducing elements	Style/atmosphere	Price
Search facilities and process		Guarantees/return policies		Promotion
Site speed				Characteristics
Findability/accessibility				

Figure 3.4 The Building Blocks of Web Experience

(a) **Functionality factors:** Factors enhancing online experience by presenting the virtual client with a good functioning, easy-to-explore, fast, and interactive website. Functionality includes elements of 'Usability' and 'Interactivity'.

(b) **Psychological factors:** Websites must communicate integrity and credibility in order to persuade customers to stop exploring them and interacting online. Psychological factors play a crucial role in helping online customers unfamiliar with the vendor or with online transactions overcome fears of fraud and doubts regarding the trustworthiness of the website and vendor.

(c) **Content factors:** Factors referring to creative and marketing mix-related elements of the website. These factors exercise a direct and crucial influence on the web experience. They are divided in two sub-categories 'Aesthetics' and 'Marketing Mix.'

We would go through details of some of these impact factors in the later chapters, but for now it would be important to understand how multiple factors help influence the web experience and how consumer's reaction to it would decide the fate of related marketing activities. The key here is to realize that deciding the right combination of web experience elements is not an easy task. The specific buying conditions, customer's experience and needs can shift the importance among different elements as influencers of the buying process.

INTRODUCTION TO DATA DRIVEN MARKETING

What is Data-Driven Digital Marketing?

While data has always been leveraged by brands and marketing teams towards achieving their goals, the role of data has been secondary when compared to marketing channels and tactics. Traditionally, marketing has been product focused and not customer oriented. This meant that the nature of data collected and deployed for marketing programs was related mostly to post-channel implementations. Pre-implementation, the only kind of data for planning was collected through market surveys and focus groups (which was highly qualitative in nature providing lesser insights).

With the growing usage of mobile and the ability to collect large volumes of data points (generally referred to as big-data), marketers today are now in a position to collect and leverage customer-driven events and actions data (for not just outbound campaigns but for inbound customer interactions as well). With this understanding, we can define data-driven marketing as the strategy developed by marketers to proactively leverage large amounts of customer data (across sources) to optimize audience development, media buying and brand communications. Data-driven marketing techniques support marketers to:

(a) Build audience personas and understand journey interactions
(b) Contextualize and personalize each customer's experience
(c) Develop dynamic and real-time segments for targeting
(d) Measure and improve marketing implementations in agile manner
(e) Apply Artificial Intelligence (AI) models across campaigns

Data-driven marketing strategy is next generation in nature as it sets high-level expectations among clients and customers in terms of improving service and increasing the relevance of marketing offers. The present usage of data-driven marketing leverages CRM software as the starting point to gather promotional interactions data. CRM software propels data-driven marketing strategy and lends support to the growth of marketing automation tools. Data-driven marketing strategy is based on three key types of data which we will discuss below.

Basic Data Types

With an understanding of the data-driven marketing concept, let us look at the way in which data across sources is classified:

(a) **First-Party Data:** Data which is collected by a company from its own offline or online sources. It includes all user information collected across multiple owned properties, tools and channels e.g., website, mobile app, CRM, marketing automation, point of sale, surveys, etc. This type of data can be used by companies to create personalized experiences for users through better segmentation. First-party data offers the highest level of reliability, accuracy, and confidentiality as it comes through a firm's owned sources.

(b) **Second Party Data:** Data that is owned by the business partner of a company willing to trade data. This kind of data is not owned by a company. A partner company can collect this data through their sources including websites, social media, surveys, etc. and barter it with other companies. With the help of second party data, digital marketers can have control over what data they exchange with partners. Second party data is utilized by marketers to predict behaviours, reach new audiences and build better relationships with visitors.

(c) **Third Party Data:** Third party data is the data received from paid external sources and is not the original data collected by a company. Providers of this type of data usually gather a large database, categorize it on various grounds and then sell it to the companies in need. This type of data lacks accuracy but serves the needs of various business verticals. Typical example includes buying verified email data for email marketing purposes.

Understanding Data-Driven Analytics

When marketers choose to deploy data-driven digital marketing, it is essential to build a strategy on the basis of data analysis and interpretation. Data-driven analytics is an approach whereby a company analyzes user data to draw conclusions and formulate a goal-oriented strategy. Data analytics helps organizations to transform their businesses using innovative ideas to formulate better decision making.

Let us understand the types of data analytics that are shaping business decisions today:

(a) **Predictive Data Analytics:** Predictive data analytics is the most commonly used data analysis technique. This type of analytics requires historical data to analyze trends and develop a model to predict recurrence. For instance, a digital marketer can make predictive data analysis to determine how closely the conversion rates of a Facebook campaign relate to target income brackets or interests.

(b) **Prescriptive Data Analytics:** In prescriptive data analysis, AI and Big Data are used to predict outcomes or plan future actions. With the help of prescriptive data analysis, companies are able to formulate future oriented data-driven analytics.

(c) **Diagnostic Data Analytics:** In diagnostic data analytics, past data is analyzed to understand the cause of an event that has already happened. Data mining, correlation, data discovery, and drill-down techniques are used in this type of analysis. Through diagnostic data analytics, marketers can discover and alert any potential issues in the future.

(d) **Descriptive Data Analytics:** With descriptive data analytics, marketers can summarize large datasets for describing progress to shareholders. This kind of data analysis constitutes a reporting system (also known as dashboard). Strategies from this analysis can help track success and failure of a company.

Data-driven decision-making is formulated with the help of above analytical techniques. However, before making such a decision, it is important to know the goals and sources for collecting data. Sources of data collection can be feedback forms, social media, or different databases. Post data collection, cleaning and data organization is essential to remove any incorrect or incomplete data before organizing into small groups. Statistical analysis then helps draw correct data-driven decisions.

Data-Driven Digital Marketing Strategy

Formulating a data-driven marketing strategy requires better understanding of customer requirements and data management tools. A digital marketer can easily collect user data from various sources but the goal of collecting that data is to utilize it to make a sale. Key data-driven digital marketing strategies that are adopted by marketers include:

(a) **Personalization strategy:** Personalization is the best strategy for gaining audience attention. Most marketers use sophisticated algorithms and big data to understand crucial details about customer needs. This allows marketers to reach new audiences, predict behaviour, improve targeting, and create better relationships with customers. Personalization strategy is typically used for advertising and real-time support use cases.

Marketers also use demographic data to personalize marketing campaigns for better return on investment (RoI). To personalize customer experience, brands can collect data including information about devices, interactive channels, time of the day when customers engage the most, etc.

(b) **Cross-channel Advertising:** Marketers use data to increase reach and promote their brands across multiple channels. With the help of omnichannel marketing, marketers are able to send consistent and aligned messages that can reach a wider audience at the right time. Cross-channel advertising and marketing can be difficult to execute if proper data tools are not utilized. With the help of organized data processes, marketers can reduce repetitive work and concentrate on marketing analysis for higher productivity.

(c) **Data-Driven Campaigns:** Data-driven campaigns are based on extensive customer data which helps select desired audience. Accurate data-based predictions help marketers utilize specific segment information to optimize campaign performance. Data-driven marketing campaigns help marketers deliver personalized, highly targeted, and effective campaigns to targeted audience. Below are the right steps to set up data-driven marketing campaigns:

- **Define goals:** No marketing campaign can be formulated and executed without defining goals. To build data-driven campaigns, a marketer needs to build data-specific goals. These goals could be boosting sales, driving website traffic, improving customer satisfaction, increasing brand awareness, etc. Goals should be relevant, measurable, achievable and time-bound for them to be effective.
- **Understand target audience:** A marketer needs to narrow down the audience group and segment batch or real-time audiences to run effective campaigns. Segmentation can be executed based on demographics, value, behaviour and motivations of the audience. Be specific and choose audiences based on business rules/advanced models for better targeting.
- **Right usage of data:** As campaigns are going to be data-driven in future, making use of relevant and accurate data is very important. For choosing the right data, a marketer should know the relevance and accuracy of data that was collected for past customers across multiple sources (sales history data, customer service data, website visitor data, or completed customer surveys). Organize data on a data management platform (DMP) and select most appropriate fields to develop the marketing campaign.
- **Choose appropriate marketing channels:** The next step is to choose the marketing channels on which a campaign would be run. These channels can be social media sites, company blog, email, television, pay-per-click ads, billboards, and radio commercials. Evaluate all potential channels in context of audience behaviours or any other demographics on which the campaign is targeted.
- **Deliver contextual content:** Design marketing content and implement it across selected channels. Messages should ideally be personalized and based on buying journey stages. Optimizing content as per customer journey will encourage selected audience to move to the next part of the journey.
- **Track campaign performance:** Data-driven marketing campaigns require continuous performance tracking. Marketers need to spend considerable time deciding specific

metrics and analyzing each metric on regular basis. Through such insights, a marketer can develop efficient campaigns by eliminating ad waste and identifying patterns to optimize content strategy.

Examples of Data-Driven Marketing Implementation

Data-driven digital marketing strategies are being heavily adopted by marketers today. Brands have now started leveraging disparate data in a highly structured way to gain better consumer reach and connect. Here are a few examples of real-life data-driven marketing strategy deployments that were successful in attracting more customers resulting in higher revenues:

(a) **Demographic data usage by GreenPal:** GreenPal, a lawn care service-provider company marketed their new product to customers using extensive demographic data available to them. Before this campaign, GreenPal used to run an AdWords (Google search tool) campaign in the metro Nashville area and were trying to improve conversions by using contextual information about users. Through data-driven marketing, the brand was able to analyze multiple publicly available datasets and found that homeowners in East Nashville were more price-sensitive as compared to other demographics in the same area.

With the analysis, GreenPal decided to target Zip codes for East Nashville neighbourhoods and specific ads were carried out using keywords like "cheapest lawn care solution in Nashville". This ad campaign was successful, and the brand saw more than 200% lift in click-through rate and 30% in conversion rates. This campaign showed that a company can achieve better conversions if its marketing campaign is backed by extensive analysis.

(b) **Correlating food data with political leanings by GrubHub:** GrubHub is a food ordering application that has a wide base of customer data and their food preferences. GrubHub gets revenue through partnerships with a variety of publishers who use their food data to create advertisements that feel real and natural. As a step to expand these partnerships, GrubHub conducted a survey where customers were asked about their food preferences along-with their preference for a political party in the US.

The survey was an attempt to expand their partnerships with political publishers. Grubhub achieved great results which helped them translate their data to secure new partnerships. The attempt also helped the company expand their native advertising base and earn better revenue from different publishers.

(c) **Self-Esteem data usage by Activia:** Activia is a probiotic yogurt company that launched a marketing campaign "It Starts Inside" in February 2017. The motive of this campaign was to spark conversations around helping women reach their full potential. The company wanted to make women rise above their distracting thoughts and self-esteem issues. This campaign was based on a study conducted by a partner research firm, Global Web index. Under this study, it was found that 80% of women under the age of 25-55 view themselves as their own worst critic.

Activia decided to launch this data-driven marketing campaign that featured interviews with women talking about experiences where they were in self-doubt. It was a successful campaign as the company tried to know real problems their customers faced in everyday life. This emotion-based campaign helped Activia build empathy and change the perception of their customers impactfully.

Marketing Intelligence from User's Online Data

This final section of the first part focuses on how to gather marketing intelligence through user's online data and the key application areas to benefit from those insights.

Consumer behavior data typically resides across multiple repositories and platforms and marketers need appropriate tools and technologies to gather, integrate, and analyze that data. This field, typically termed as web analytics across the marketing fraternity, includes concepts drawn from large software implementation areas like data warehousing (relates to data storage methodologies and structures), business intelligence (methodologies to generate business insight from data), and advanced analytics (much more in vogue these days and relates to advanced statistical analysis conducted to develop complex co-relations between multiple sets of data often in real-time). Although web analytics is the core terminology that is used to mention any exercise towards gathering market intelligence online, these days usage of terms like big-data is also quite prevalent as it pertains to combining large sets of data to gather insights not only from online data sources but through a logical combination of online and offline data.

Let us go through the key stages to understand how marketing intelligence is derived from these multiple sets of data (see Fig. 3.5).

(a) **Stage 1—Online data collation:** To explain this stage, we would use key concepts of owned, earned, and paid media (introduced by Forrester Research Group and used widely these days to classify interactive media) and the type of user data they generate:

- *Owned media data*: Owned media refers to all the channels that a brand controls. This includes data gathered from user/visitor activity to company's prime online properties be it their website, blog, social media page, or mobile applications.
- *Earned media data*: Earned media refers to coverage obtained and customers converted through non-owned media channels which are mostly social in nature. Data here would be about customers who post online comments, share viral videos, re-tweet companies, Twitter posts, etc.

Paid media data: includes consumer data derived from actions users perform on multiple paid channels which the brand uses for their marketing activities. This includes data on visitors clicking a display ad or a search ad put up next to Google search. It would also include third party audience data collated from other companies generally known as data-management platforms (an emerging concept in online marketing, which we would cover in detail in later chapters).

(b) **Stage 2—Consumer data repository creation:** This stage involves collating all the data obtained from the first stage and integrating it into a consumer data repository. Once

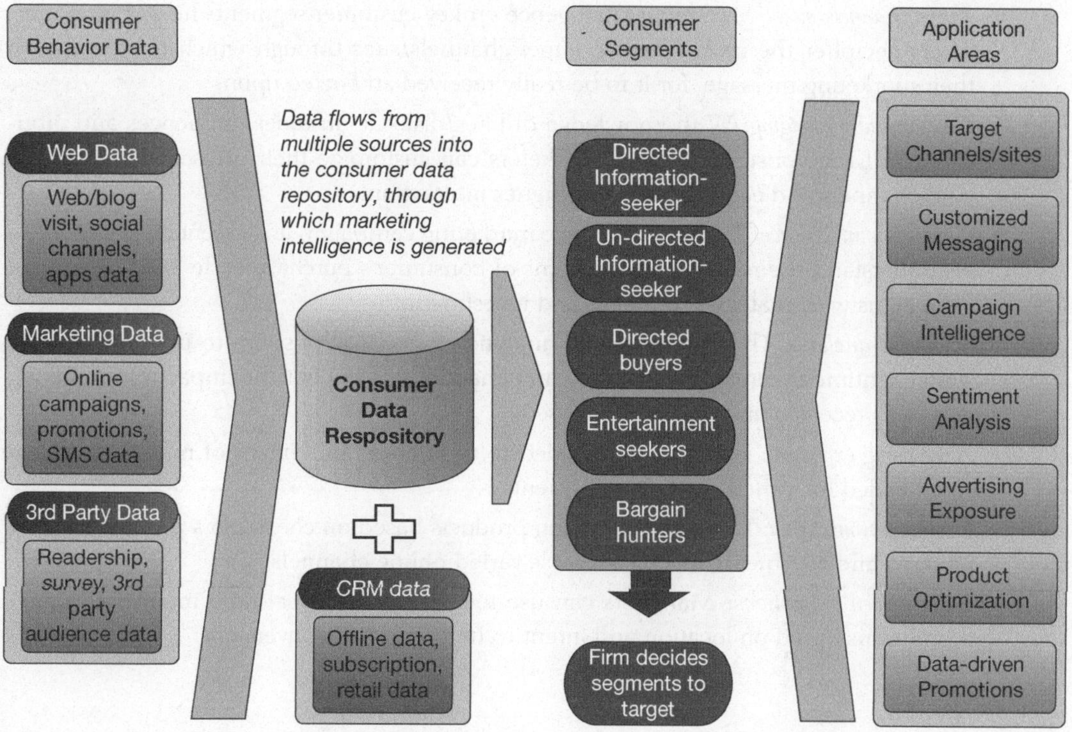

Figure 3.5 Marketing Intelligence through User Data

that is accomplished and duplicate data is refined/cleansed (for accuracy and quality), this dataset is compared and merged with offline datasets which consists of traditional databases, customer relationship management (CRM) lists, product/service subscription, retail, events and promotions, etc. With a combination of all these data sets, the firm is in a position to identify each customer individually and build customer segments and personas related to their area of products and operations.

(c) **Stage 3—Consumer segments development:** Following stage two, in this stage, consumer segments are formed along the lines as already discussed in the section titled 'Attributes of Online Buying Behavior.' This segmentation helps understand the nature of customers who are interacting with the brand in its various online forms and their attitudes towards these interactions. Once these segments are built, it is much easier for firms to decide which products to target to a particular nature of customers, at what price bands, and across which channels.

(d) **Stage 4—Application areas identification:** Finally, with the customer target segment decided, marketers can use all the consumer data and intelligence from their previous interactions to apply it to improve their digital marketing initiatives and optimize campaigns in the most effective manner. Key application examples of this marketing intelligence include:

- *Target channels/sites*: Marketing intelligence on key customer segments helps brand marketers decipher the most effective target channels/sites through which they can push their marketing message, for it to be really received and acted upon.
- *Customized messaging*: With knowledge of likes/dislikes, attitudes, influences and motivations of key consumer groups, marketers can customize their messages both across paid channels and earned media for higher interaction.
- *Campaign intelligence*: To run an effective marketing campaign, it is essential that marketers understand the routines and patterns of consumer's purchase cycle and align/target campaigns with matched resources and investments.
- *Sentiment analysis*: Through advanced analytics tools, it is possible to understand consumer sentiment across any property and channel to decipher the impact of marketing messages received and products browsed.
- *Advertising exposure*: Helps marketers decide the nature and extent of marketing exposure needed for varied consumer segments.
- *Product optimization*: Involves optimizing products based on consumer's previous buying patterns and comments/feedback across varied online channels.
- *Data-driven promotions*: Marketers can use technology in a real-time manner to target promotions based on location and intent to help improve conversions.

MANAGING CONSUMER DEMAND

With an understanding of consumer behavior and its changing patterns and influences, in this second part of the chapter we shall concentrate on what consumer demand means, how we can gauge it, the factors impacting demand and how marketers can interpret and manage changing consumer demands to integrate them into the product development lifecycle.

Understanding Consumer Demands

Before we start to focus on the forces that impact consumer demand let us get an insight into the concept of demand itself and how it varies from traditional to online marketing mediums.

The concept of demand (which originated from the field of economics) is the utility for a good or service of an economic agent, relative to his/her income. Though the definition seems loaded, simply translated in marketing terms it refers to the want for a commodity backed by the ability and willingness to pay for it.

Consumer demand as a term is generally used to denote the overall demand for a product or a service in the market. It can also be seen in two different ways—individual demand and market demand, wherein individual demand is the quantity a consumer would buy at a given price, while market demand would be the total demand of all buyers together at a given price in a given period of time.

In Chapter 1, section titled 'Delivering Enhanced Customer Value,' we had touched upon the concepts of Online Value Proposition (OVP) and seen how different types of needs (stated and unstated) can lead to new/improved products/services to be developed. The concept of consumer demand moves parallel to that of needs and wants. There are mainly eight types of demand patterns which have to be taken into consideration by marketing teams:

(a) **Negative demand:** consumers dislike the product and may even pay a price to avoid it
(b) **Non-existent demand:** consumers may be unaware or uninterested in the product
(c) **Latent demand:** consumers may share a strong need that cannot be satisfied by an existing product
(d) **Declining demand**: consumers begin to buy the product less frequently or do not buy at all
(e) **Irregular demand**: consumer purchases vary on a seasonal, monthly, weekly, daily, or even hourly basis
(f) **Full demand:** consumers are adequately buying all products available in the marketplace
(g) **Overfull demand:** more consumers would like to buy the product than can be satisfied
(h) **Unwholesome demand:** consumers may be attracted to products that have undesirable social consequences

With an understanding of key demand pattern types, we would now look at the key factors impacting consumer demand.

The primary factors impacting consumer demand can be classified into four broad areas (see Fig. 3.6):

(a) **Consumer factors:** This area refers to factors impacting a typical consumer of the product at hand. Key consumer factors cover the extent/type of consumer need, his income level,

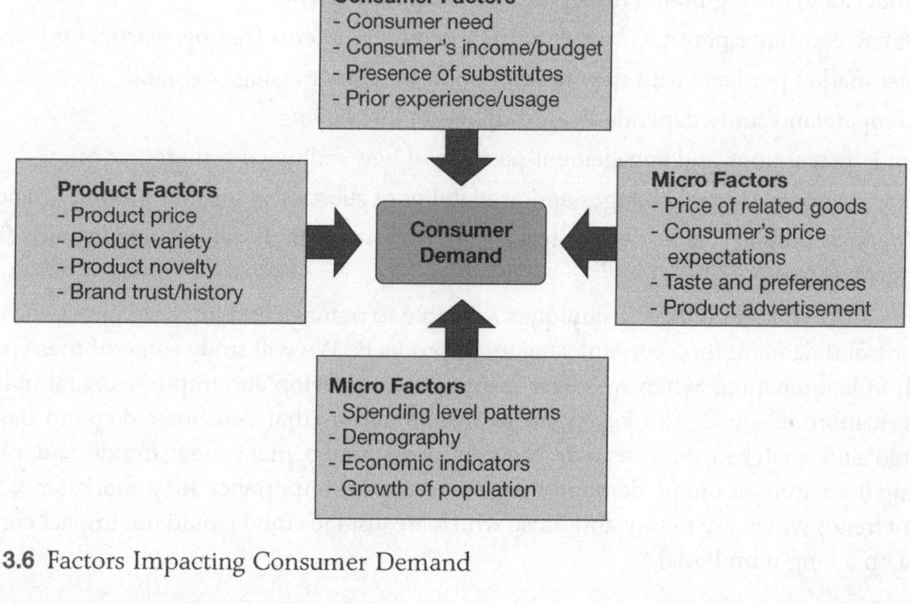

Figure 3.6 Factors Impacting Consumer Demand

historical budget to spend on that category, presence of substitutes available which the consumer can buy, and his prior experience with the use of that product or brand and views/opinions he/she holds of it.

(b) **Product factors:** This category includes product/brand-specific factors that impact a consumer's choice for it. The price of product and its variants is a key determining factor here followed by product variety (including availability) as also its novelty/desirability factor along with the overall trust a brand exudes through its communication, history, or imagery.

(c) **Micro-factors:** Involves other factors which are crucial and can be impacted by marketers one way or the other. Key micro-factors include the price of related goods (in competition with the product/brand, wherein marketers can compare and match prices with their nearest competitor to improve demand), consumer expectations of increase/decrease of prices in the near future, specific tastes and preferences of an audience/regional area, and other aspects like product advertisement or channels of marketing.

(d) **Macro-factors:** Involves ecosystem factors which actually define key consumer segments and typically cannot be impacted by marketers. Macro-factors include overall spending patterns of consumer segments, the demography they belong to, key economic indicators (to gauge the growth of that sector itself), population growth and other such macro-economic indicators.

With an understanding of these impact factors, it is also important to know how digital marketers can gauge these changing consumer demand patterns. Typically, any marketer who wants to manage and direct consumer demand for higher profits needs to:

(a) Conduct regular demand analysis along with online sales channel partners
(b) Measure audience activity on various digital sales channels
(c) Understand buying preferences/patterns of digital audiences
(d) Define consumer personas based on their demand patterns (timing/seasonality)
(e) Test-market products with new promotional strategies to gauge demand
(f) Compare and study dependencies of offline/online buying
(g) Study perceptions and engagement patterns of new online customers
(h) Assess impact of price changes and availability of substitutes for that product/brand
(i) Conduct usability and design tests (multivariate A/B Tests) to understand channel attractiveness

We have earlier shared multiple techniques available to manage and improve target consumer's perception and demand for a certain category of products. We will study some of these pointers in depth in later chapters when we cover techniques to develop and improve digital marketing to make it more effective. The key point to realize here is that consumer demand has to be monitored and analyzed on a regular basis as there are so many new trends and variables impacting the nature of online demand that it is of utmost importance for a marketer to realize and chaff trends which are to stay and those which are just fads (and would not impact consumer demand on a long-term basis).

Demand-Led Product Development Process

With an understanding of consumer demand and its patterns, we realize how important it is for marketers to continually understand and incorporate consumer demand to service them in the most productive manner. Although product improvements based on feedback are a historical given, there is a whole new wave of demand-led product development which aims at drawing inferences from the nature of demand emerging across multiple channels and platforms and making them as a starting point for inputs related to the product development process.

Marketers have traditionally relied on superior product attributes, thoughtful communication, advertising, and other public relations platforms to create a demand for their product. The typical feedback they gathered from multiple channels post sale was limited to the number of stock keeping units (SKUs) sold in a region or territory, which was the singular indicator to know which kind of products a particular population liked and which specific variants were bought more. What this approach lacked was a kind of qualitative indicator which could help marketers know about the following details:

(a) The kind of experience people had
(b) How they went about searching for the product
(c) Which features in their view differentiated the products from competition
(d) The nature of demand behind the purchase: was it for a specific occasion; was there a context to the purchase; what kind of specific keywords a customer used while searching for the product; what was the scale of customer satisfaction post purchase; and so on

A lot of these questions, though may have been touched upon or gathered through offline responses, customer surveys, salesperson feedback, and focus groups, there never existed a structured way to get such responses and insights in the traditional world. The online world with technology by its side, opened up multiple ways to not just gather split-second responses but also provide a mechanism to store them for future analysis to build demand-led marketing strategies.

The biggest example of this was the proliferation of search technologies wherein consumers for the first time had an option to write plain text in a searchbox indicating his/her need or in economic terms putting up a very specific demand for marketers to cater to. This was the start of *Search Engine Marketing (SEM)* as one of the most prominent digital marketing tools (which we will cover in greater depth in the later chapters). SEM with its advanced algorithms was able to match a consumer's intent and match it to a marketer's product to create an instantaneous-demand-driven fulfillment process which had never been envisioned before.

To understand this search demand driven marketing, we would need to briefly introduce the concept of *keyword* which forms the core of this most successful form of digital marketing. Keywords in digital marketing terminology are "words or phrases typed in a search engine by potential consumers which showcase their intent and a corresponding demand signal for any marketer". The way keywords are written, their sequencing and structural composition with the use of semantic algorithms and tools, gives marketers lots of insights to comprehend and reason out whether a particular product is being demanded by the consumer and whether it makes sense to market a particular product based on that query.

It is believed that Yahoo! first made available targeted keyword advertising to its customers. In 1996, Chip Royce , head of online marketing for InterZine Productions of Boca Raton, Florida, approached Yahoo!'s sales agent (Flycast Communications) suggesting ads around keyword results to provide a more effective, targeted advertising within Yahoo!'s search results. Yahoo! obliged placing targeted ad banners when the keyword "Golf" was searched by Yahoo! users. Yahoo! later turned this opportunity into a formal marketing program for its entire customer base and promoted this in a July 1996 article in the *Internet World* magazine.

The example of journal publishing (showcased at length in Chapter 2) is a good example of how consumer demand and intent can be determined much more accurately in the online world and how marketers can analyze the aggregate of these cues to develop products on which consumers are more willing to spend, thus impacting the whole product development process itself. With multiple keyword analysis techniques like keyword occurrence analysis, seasonality and usage statistic, topic-based relationships and other qualitative and quantitative techniques, marketers now have real-time tools to judge demand patterns even at a daily or hourly level.

For creating scholarly articles (as already shared in Chapter 2, section titled "Digital Marketing Models Creation"), a journal publisher today has the wherewithal to access the entire keyword set which their target consumer (student community) would have typed or queried and with the help of a keyword planner, can easily classify demand for a specific type of content to develop multiple pricing models based upon the more sought after keywords and related content.

This search/intent-based model is just one of the examples of how marketers can gauge demand through online channels to model and market their products accordingly. The other ways in which marketers can gain substantial insights on consumer demand include consumer feedback through comments, social media mentions, product purchase analysis, Facebook page likes, etc. Marketers are applying multiple demand analysis techniques to the data gathered through these online consumer interactions:

(a) **Consumer feedback/comments:** One of the more relied ways in which consumer comments across various websites, e-commerce forums, review sites, blogs, etc., is collated and consumer sentiment towards a particular product is analyzed.

(b) **Social media mentions:** Community development tools are becoming crucial to gauge trending factors which influence communities as a whole rather than just individuals. For example, analyzing Twitter mentions are becoming crucial for brands to gauge whether their products are in demand (being conversed) or falling out of favour.

(c) **Product purchase analysis:** With large amounts of historic product purchase data trends available through APIs (Application Programming Interfaces) shared by top online merchants, it has become important to keep a tab on the purchase analysis for specific regions and markets.

(d) **Facebook page likes:** We are taking a specific example of Facebook (the top social networking site in the world) which has become the barometer for brands to test their followership and not only get reactions from them on new product launches, but also involve them in new product creation. These days through crowd sourcing (gathering thoughts from a large crowd for business applications), new ideas can be developed and tested with top influencers (top 2 per cent of the intended audience) to forecast future demand and potential acceptance of new.

The example mentioned earlier shows the wide extent of data available to online marketers to gauge demand in a much more scientific fashion and apply elements of this knowledge gathered to various aspects of product development, be it, product research, feature creation, pricing, marketing, and online/offline fulfillment. We would look at multiple examples in the next set of chapters on how consumer insights, if researched well, can be really crucial, particularly for the success of newly launched products.

Brand Building on the Web

In this section, we would understand the actions marketers take to develop brands on the web which consumers can relate to, lend their trust, and be swayed by them over an extended term. A *brand* according to classic marketing definition is the "name, term, design, symbol, slogan, packaging, or any other mix of such elements that identifies one seller's product distinct from those of other sellers". Brands are typically known to provide value through these elements which are far beyond just the product or service. Below are the six main criteria for choosing *brand elements* which any firm can use to build a brand:

(a) **Memorable:** It should be easily recognized and have a top-of-the-mind recall.
(b) **Meaningful:** It should be descriptive, credible, and suggestive of the corresponding category. Elements with rich visuals and strong verbal imagery make stronger impact.
(c) **Likeable:** It must be aesthetically appealing or pleasing. For certain categories, it is important that brand exudes fun and is interesting to the consumer segment.
(d) **Transferable:** It should be transferable across product categories, geographical boundaries, and cultures. A great example here is Coca-Cola and McDonalds.
(e) **Adaptable:** It should have an ability to synchronize with changing consumer perceptions and preferences, be flexible, and should have an ability to be updated easily.
(f) **Protectable:** It should be legally and competitively protectable.

With an understanding of brand and key criteria impacting brand elements, let us understand the concept of customer-based brand equity and how it is crucial in building brand presence on the web. *Brand equity* is a phrase used in the marketing industry which describes "the value of having a well-known brand name and its ensuing benefits". The valuation of brand equity can include a number of factors like changing market share, profit margins, consumer recognition of logos and other visual elements, brand language associations made by consumers, consumers' perceptions of quality, and other relevant brand values.

To relate brand development to consumer behavior and build the right kind of experiences in the customer's mind such as positive thoughts, feelings, beliefs, opinions, perceptions, etc., Kevin Lane Keller, a marketing professor at the Tuck School of Business at Dartmouth College, developed the Customer-Based Brand Equity (CBBE) Model. This model is built on the premise

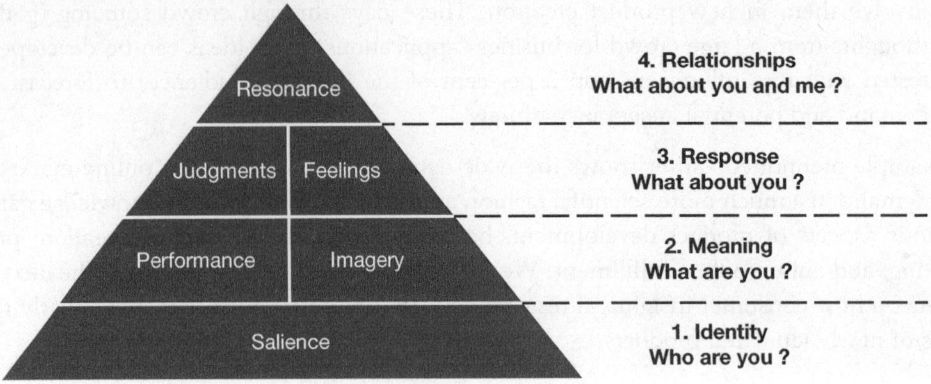

Figure 3.7 Keller's CBBE Brand Equity Model.

that when you have strong brand equity, your customers will buy more from you; they will recommend you to other people; they will be more loyal, and you are less likely to lose them to competitors.

The four steps in the Keller's CBBE model (see Fig. 3.7) contain the six building blocks that must be in place along with specific questions which need to be answered at each stage to develop a successful brand. Let us look at each of the six building blocks across the pyramid:

(a) **Salience dimension** includes creating brand salience or 'awareness,' to make the brand stand out so that customers recognize it.

(b) **Performance dimension** defines how well a firm's product meets its customer's needs. According to the model, performance consists of five categories—primary characteristics and features; product reliability, durability, and serviceability; service effectiveness, efficiency, and empathy; style and design; and price.

(c) **Imagery dimension** refers to how well a brand meets its customer's needs on a social and psychological level.

(d) **Judgment dimension** refers to judgments made by customers about a brand and these fall into four key categories:

- *Quality*: Customers judge a product or brand based on its actual and perceived quality.
- *Credibility*: Customers judge credibility using three dimensions—expertise (which includes innovation), trustworthiness, and likeability.
- *Consideration*: Customers judge how relevant the product is to their unique needs.
- *Superiority*: Customers assess how superior the brand is, in comparison to competitor's brands.

(e) **Feeling dimension:** A brand can evoke feelings directly, but customers also respond emotionally to how a brand makes them feel about themselves. According to the model, there are six positive brand feelings—warmth, fun, excitement, security, social approval, and self-respect.

(f) **Resonance dimension:** Brand resonance is the most difficult and desirable element for a marketer as it relates to consumers' feeling of a deep psychological bond with the brand. Brand resonance is divided into four key categories:

- *Behavioral loyalty*: This includes regular, repeat purchases.
- *Attitudinal attachment*: Refers to the love customers show towards a brand, and the product they buy, which is considered as a special purchase.
- *Sense of community*: Customers feel a sense of community with people associated to the brand.
- *Active engagement*: This is the strongest example of brand loyalty. Customers are actively engaged with the brand, even when they are not purchasing or consuming it. This could include joining a club related to the brand; participating in online chats, marketing rallies, or events; following the brand on social media; or taking part in other, outside activities.

With this understanding of how a successful brand can be developed for each product, let us look at a structured mechanism to build *web-specific components* of a brand. A lot of the techniques mentioned here have been drawn from strategy and tactics marketers are using extensively these days to build their brand online. These steps include:

(a) **Knowing the online audience:** The first and most important step is the ability to differentiate online specific audience from the traditional segment, understand their needs and how they approach buying a product of the same brand online. Take the case of the sports shoe brand Nike. Though it might seem that the audience who buy a pair of Nike shoes online would be the same as the one buying it from a nearby physical store, there would be genuine differences in the way each of them approach these channels.

Nike being a premium brand, it is highly likely that a typical online Nike consumer would be a loyalist of the brand or possess a good knowledge of the attributes of the product, or have researched well about the brand; hence, there are good chances for him/her to have even shared thoughts on previous shoe models bought on social platforms. So, it becomes imperative for brands promoting online to:

- *Develop a listening strategy*: This means being present on prominent listening posts to know where customers spend their time online.
- *Understanding audience segments*: Involves utilizing analytics to track and understand consumer segments as a part of consumer/market research.
- *Analyze social sentiment*: Even before developing brand attributes on the web, it would be helpful to understand present consumer sentiment by gathering customer feedback though text-analysis tools.

(b) **Developing brand elements specific to the audience:** In the next stage, once marketers have a clearer idea of online customers and their habits, brands need to extend their profile to add elements which differentiate them online. These parameters include:

- *Engaging web presence*: Any brand, even if it is an influential one offline, needs to replicate and transfer its core brand values to develop online presences and destinations in the form of websites, blogs, affiliate sites, social pages, etc., which catch the fancy of online customers and engage them best. Important elements include site layout, usability features, product imagery, expert content, compelling design, etc.
- *Online reputation/partnerships*: As important it is to develop a brand's own channels, it is crucial to make relationships with other top brands, trusted sites, and e-commerce channels to build the brand. These techniques are referred to as relationship marketing.
- *Order fulfillment strategies*: As in the second layer of CBBE model described earlier, along with imagery, performance is crucial; so the brand needs to build and test its complete back-end support model to ensure that it can fully support the online promises made and reputation earned.

(c) **Web communication strategies to build the brand:** Once the brand elements have been developed, brand messaging and marketing strategies become crucial to get online customers to try the product and get hooked to purchasing it online. Depending on business objectives and how strongly the brand is already positioned in the minds of the intended online customers, marketers can go out for a big-bang communication strategy launch or develop a selective-multiple burst strategy on influential channels which the audience visits regularly.

(d) **Reinforcing brand values and attributes**: Once consumers have started interacting and purchasing the brand online, it is crucial to develop strategies to keep customers engaged and make the brand relevant and interesting. Brand values can be reinforced through regular connect with customers on social channels, through contests, promotions, loyalty based discounts, exclusive club memberships, etc., which keep the customer involved with the brand.

(e) **Converting loyalists to brand advocates:** Finally, as in the last stage of the CBBE model, it is important that engaged consumers be converted to brand advocates, wherein their aspirations are aligned to the brand and they are influenced to promote the brand through product reviews, brand mentions among their communities, writing positions for brand's blogs, and in certain cases, being invited to discussions on new product development to make them feel a part of product creation. Such brand inclusions done in an exclusive manner would help the brand achieve cult status and display unique elements which would be difficult to copy.

CUSTOMER IDENTITY AND PRIVACY MANAGEMENT

Understanding Customer Identity

Digital customers are essentially billions of users that are quite different from each other. The challenge for digital marketers is to identify each of them uniquely for campaign targeting. Customer identity, also referred to as 'digital identity' is a set of data that uniquely identifies each user across the digital landscape. Digital identity allows users to get identified for brands to leverage their promotions.

An important question which should be answered first: 'Is digital identification important for both users and marketers?' The answer is yes. For individuals, digital identification enables them to make secure payments or access services in exchange for their data. For digital marketers, customer identity helps marketers personalize each interaction and track distinct user behaviour.

There are numerous ways through which the digital identity of an individual can be ascertained. Currently, marketers generally drop pixels on a customer's device to track a user. With such pixels, the device ID of users can be tracked across websites, mobile sites and applications which helps develop a single view of an individual along-with providing information of their behaviour. Login and authentication features on any website or platform help to correctly identify a user.

The digital identity of a user is carried across their journey (websites, mobile apps, social media platforms, search engine platforms, etc). In this section, we will understand how brands develop customer identity through cookies. But tracking private information like user behaviour, browser and device ID, etc. creates concern among users related to their fundamental right to privacy. Before we deep-dive the topic from marketer's standpoint, let us first go through the various regulations which are in place to preserve customer data privacy across marketing environments.

Understanding Customer Data Privacy

Customer data helps enterprises improve their engagement and it is the responsibility of businesses to manage and protect this data. With an understanding of customer identification tactics, concerns for customer data privacy are growing among users. Due to these data privacy concerns, various data protection regulations have been created by the regulators, the most important among them being:

(a) **General Data Protection Regulation (GDPR):** General Data Protection Regulation (GDPR) is a comprehensive set of regulations that state that different types of personal data information require different levels of protection which means sensitive records are subject to a higher level of protection. As per this regulation, every business has to take consent for collecting any personal data from users.

Businesses need to define data usage objectives clearly while collecting the data and it should not be used for another purpose apart from those objectives. Each individual has the right to object on or correct their data. Users also possess the right to get notified if their personal data is breached in any manner. Any non-compliance with this regulation attracts penalties and fines.

(b) **California Consumer Protection Act (CCPA):** The California Consumer Protection Act is majorly focused on consumer privacy rights and regulates individual data. It is enforced by the Attorney General of the State of California and provides appropriate rights to a consumer to know what personal data is collected and sold for what purpose. Consumers can request deletion of data and choose which data can be collected or sold. In case of any data breach and privacy failure, consumers have the right to sue a company. In such cases, companies can be penalized up to $7500 per violation.

(c) **Brazilian General Data Protection Act (LGPD):** The Brazilian General Data Protection Act (LGPD) came into effect in 2020 and replaced existing legislation with a general legislation. This act regulates both public and private sectors. LGPD act aims to protect personal data to strengthen Brazil's economy. It regulates the data of an organization (small business or a multinational company) which collects personal information of users.

As per this act, entities subject to LGPD have to appoint a Data Protection Officer (DPO) who will in-turn be regulated by Autoridade Nacional de Proteção de Dados (ANPD), Brazil's data protection authority. It is the duty of companies to maintain security of personal data and notify potential data breaches to ANPD. Consumers have the right to know the purpose of data collection, requesting transfer or alternating their data. Any non-compliance with this law can lead to a penalty of 2% of total annual company revenues or up to $50 million Brazilian Reals.

In the next section, we will look deeper at developing customer identity and the concept of cookies which is key to understanding data collection and web tracking mechanisms.

DEVELOPING CUSTOMER IDENTITY: THE IMPORTANCE OF COOKIES

What are Website Cookies?

Website cookies are small bits of text that are downloaded to consumer browsers as they surf the web. The purpose of cookies is to identify users and record information about their website visits & activities. It helps web developers provide a more personal and convenient visit the next time they arrive (knowing the preference of each customer through their past visits). HTTP cookies, web cookies, and browser cookies are other names for website cookies used in the industry.

Website cookies have data that gets created by web servers upon any user connection. Cookies are labelled with a unique ID specifying the user and their computer device. Cookies get exchanged between a network server and computer device of the user which allows the server to read the ID and provide information that is specific to that individual user.

What are website cookies used for?

Usage of website cookies include following purposes:

(a) Recording interactions of the users
(b) Storing user data (especially in case of e-commerce websites)
(c) Retargeting advertisements
(d) Saving website interaction preferences of users
(e) Authenticating users

Website cookies record interactions and information about a user (including their preference). For instance, when a user selects a preferred language on a website, website cookies record this information and the next time a user visits the website, the server reads the cookies and displays the preferred language.

Website cookies are relevant to website owners to help identify user interaction and improve experience. While for advertisers, website cookies help provide targeted content to each individual based on their past visits.

What are the different types of website cookies?

Different types of cookies are useful for tracking a visitor's behaviour and identity.

(a) **Session Cookies:** Before understanding session cookies, it is important to understand the concept of web sessions. Web sessions include all interactions that a user has with an individual website within a given time frame. Session cookies are temporary bits of text that get stored in the memory of the browser (only when it is open). When a browser gets closed, they get automatically deleted from the browser's history. This offers a lower security risk to users.

(b) **Persistent Cookies:** Persistent cookies are used for a longer period of time and the issuer tags an expiration date to them. These cookies remain stored in the web browser even if the browser is closed. When a user revisits the website that created these persistent cookies, data returns to the issuer. Persistent cookies track all the activities that are executed over more than one site. Generally, these types of cookies are used by social media platforms.

When a user chooses "Remember Me" while logging-in to the platform, persistent cookies are created which store login details on a browser. These cookies however impose a greater security risk to a user because they are stored for a longer time period as compared to session cookies.

(c) **First-party Cookies:** First-party cookies are created by the website on which a user is visiting. Such kinds of cookies are usually safe as long as a user is browsing reputed websites. First-party cookies are important for any website because without them, a user will not be able to purchase more than one item in a single transaction. Disabling first party cookies will not allow a user to add more items to the cart.

(d) **Third-party Cookies:** Third-party cookies are created by entities that a user is not visiting (for example a third-party advertisement on a website). These cookies collect information about the behaviour and preferences of a user on the visiting website, post which it is passed on to the entity that actually created those third-party cookies. Generally, these cookies are used by advertisers.

For instance, when a user looks for a handbag on a website, third-party cookies on the visiting website collect information and pass it to the advertisers. Through this mechanism, a user can see the exact handbag advertisement on other websites or social media platforms (during retargeting). This type of cookie is highly important for digital marketers and advertisers to provide a better user experience and generate leads using partner websites.

In the next section, we will discuss points of difference between first-party and third-party cookies.

Difference between First-party Cookies and Third-party Cookies

Points of Comparison	First-party Cookies	Third-party Cookies
Origination	Originated by the main domain that a user visited. It is set by publishers to the website using JavaScript code	Originated by third-party servers on a publisher's websites. It is not owned by the main domain that the user visited
Availability	Available on the main domain website only	Available across all websites that can load third-party server codes
Web browser support	All web browsers support first-party cookies but users have an option to block these cookies	Earlier supported by all web browsers but now these are being blocked from multiple browsers due to privacy concerns

What are consent management platforms?

Consent management platforms (CMP) are platforms mostly used by marketers to manage cookie consent requirement. These systems allow site visitors to know details about the cookie consent users have given to the website. CMP systems need to store user consent data which is guided by law. These tools can also manage content regulations such as GDPR, LGPD, and CCPA. For cookie consent management, there are various industry tools like Osano Consent Manager, Quantcast Choice, Piwik Pro Consent Manager, Cookiebot, and TrustArc Cookie Consent Manager.

Impact of Demise of Third-Party Cookies on Marketers & Advertisers

Third-party cookies are essential for digital marketers and advertisers to track user behaviour. But it creates major privacy concerns for users. Due to this, third-party cookies are being phased out by top players like Google and Apple. The demise of third-party cookies will have a major impact on marketers and advertisers:

(a) **Inability to track user behaviour:** With third-party cookies, digital marketers and advertisers are able to track user behaviour. But with their demise, marketers and advertisers will be unable to track users and offer the right product to them based on their data. This will ultimately lead to a decrease in lead generation activity.

(b) **Difficulty in establishing user identity:** Establishing user identity will become difficult with the demise of third-party cookies. Advertisers who are typically able to identify a user with the help of these cookies will find a big challenge of stitching user data points and events.

(c) **Inability to retarget ads:** With the demise of third-party cookies, marketers will be unable to retarget users based on their previous internet behaviour. Presently through third-party cookies, digital marketers can target ads to users as per their previous and current behaviour.

Strategy for Future

The demise of third-party cookies is a matter of concern but companies don't necessarily need to revamp their entire marketing strategy to tackle this change. Google has announced an initiative called 'Privacy Sandbox' that will replace the lacunae of third-party cookie availability. The Privacy Sandbox will block invasive tracking techniques but marketers can still use other collaborative initiatives to map users while maintaining their privacy. The future of website cookies will include:

(a) **New Browser Tracking Techniques:** The Privacy Sandbox initiative by Google will help retain individual user data in the browser (which will not be controlled and sold to advertising agencies). With this change, Google claims that they will be able to control user privacy along-with offering personalized ads to users.

Another technique is called the Federated Learning of Cohorts (FLoC). This technology will collect user data and group it. This organized data will be shared with advertising companies in aggregate fashion rather than sharing individual profiles. Google claims that with this technology, targeted ads can be permitted but with control over data.

For now, Google's claim on these new alternatives is not considered as a true alternative for marketers. Brand marketers and advertising agencies are also formulating their own strategies which might not leverage these Google options.

(b) **Leveraging First-party Cookies:** First-party cookies are not going to be part of this ban and will still be allowed to collect user's data. First-party cookies will be most important as per the upcoming 'Privacy Sandbox' initiative by Google. However, marketers need to find out newer tactics to leverage first party data for better interaction to earn the trust of website visitors (ex. contextual advertising).

(c) **Identity-Based Tracking:** With identity-based tracking, every user will be given an advertising ID based on unchanging traits like email addresses. Advertisers can identify and track these email addresses using this specific ID. With this tracking, it will be easier for marketers and advertisers to offer targeted ads similar to that of cookie-based system. This seems to be the most viable alternative for future user tracking.

Web-Tracking Audits and Forecasting

In the earlier section, we learnt the steps to build a brand on the web and how multiple elements go on to influence the target consumer. We also learnt how engaging web presence is crucial for brands to make a lasting impact and maintain the trust factor. In this section, we would look at the importance of regularly tracking a firm's web presence in relation to consumer activities to know whether the performance is going as per target. Based on the consumer behavior analyzed through such web audits, future demand patterns are forecasted accordingly.

A *web-tracking audit* implies using web visitor tracking tools to analyze visit behavior on a website. Any web-tracking process typically involves a code that tracks each user's visit pattern and with the resulting data on consumer behavior helps provide targeted content and experiences that make the website and the brand experience more personal and interactive.

Need for Web-Tracking Audits

Web-tracking audits began more with a business context of understanding a website visitor's behavior to gather his intentions and browsing pattern, but with growing times, it has also been linked tightly with consumer privacy. Since the past four–five years, several legislations have been issued to safeguard a consumer's privacy where web data in the form of cookies is being gathered without the knowledge of the user. Typically, web-tracking audits are important for the following reasons:

(a) **Improve consumer interaction:** With the knowledge of consumer types, their demographics, time spent, pages accessed, features used, brands can take better decisions and improve profitability through more accurate demand analysis.

(b) **Understand consumer preferences:** With data on site search performed by customers, marketers can accurately decide which content is best suited for consumer's interest, which products are most sought after, and how the navigation of the site should be improvized.

(c) **Develop successful campaigns:** With strong web-tracking tools, content websites can earn by executing well laid-out campaigns where an ad network tracks user behavior and serves the most relevant ads to visitors to generate advertising revenue.

(d) **Improve site performance:** If the website has excess tags from old and redundant programs, the website load time increases and web page downloads slow down. Web-tracking audits help to keep most optimal site performance so that customers do not leave the website due to performance issues.

(e) **Track consumer data leakage:** With third-party codes being used on websites, a data-aggregator might collect useful information on customers and sell it to competition or other sites causing a breach of privacy. A quality website-tracking audit identifies such trackers, their sources, purposes, privacy risk levels to decide which ones to continue.

The Web-Tracking System

Web tracking is done by looking and combining data collected through these cookies and other sources like flash trackers, server logs, and web beacons. These set of cookies contain trackers which run on the browser and keep collecting every piece of information by observing the web browser session of each consumer. A web-tracking tool typically analyses these trackers to understand relevant consumer behavior and at the same time manage a list of approved vendors who can place their cookies (third party trackers) onto the website. This helps manage data integrity and also prevent loss of consumer data to other aggregators and competitors. Apart from that this exercise also gathers information towards forecasting consumer demand.

INTEGRATED MARKETING COMMUNICATIONS (IMC)

With an understanding of consumer demand, the impact of its patterns on product development, and the basics of web tracking, we move towards the final section of this chapter which discusses integration and application of consistent brand messaging across both traditional and non-traditional marketing channels through an understanding of the fundamentals of Integrated Marketing Communications (IMC).

Basics of Integrated Marketing Communications (IMC)

In 1989, IMC was formally conceptualized and introduced in Northwestern University. The first definition of IMC (according to Schultz and Kitchen Schultz et al, 1993) was used in a survey conducted in 1991 by Northwestern University in cooperation with the American Association of Advertising Agencies (4As) and the Association of National Advertisers in the United States. The definition of IMC used in this research was: "IMC is a concept of marketing communications planning that recognizes the added value of a comprehensive plan that evaluates the strategic roles of a variety of communications disciplines (for example, general advertising, direct response, sales promotion, and public relations) and combines these disciplines to provide clarity, consistency, and maximum communications impact."

The *Journal of Integrated Marketing Communication* from the Medill School of Journalism at Northwestern University which is dedicated to research in this area describes IMC as "a strategic marketing process specifically designed to ensure that all messaging and communication strategies are unified across all channels and are centered around the customer." The concept involves leveraging the strength of each separate communication channel to achieve a stronger combined impact than is possible by a single channel. The concept is closely related to consumer's ability to absorb messaging from each medium and takes into account limitations of each medium to cover them up with others.

The concept of IMC evolved in the 1980s, when most companies in US were set up as departments that conducted their operations as separate profit centers. With a need to go global and still manage the communication, branding, and cultural elements, it became important to integrate messaging across all channels to make them consistent so that the customer across all countries could see one view and image of the product and there could be better synergies not only in promotion but also in the manner distinct product features are built.

Historically, communication elements like advertising, public relations, sales promotion, etc., were planned and developed, as well as implemented and measured separately. The key issue in implementing IMC was how to bring across key elements in a coherent manner which not only leverages synergies but also makes communication comprehensible to the customer as a whole. With new digital channels coming forth and with the changing forms and technology developments behind them, Mulhern, in 2009, suggested using a set of axioms about relevance, exposure, timing, behavioral response, and other precepts of media planning. But these are still not as developed and this field keeps on evolving even to this day.

According to Tom, Duncan; Caywood, Clarke (1996), the following trends and changes have been the key factors behind the adoption of integrated marketing communication:

(a) **Decreasing message impact and credibility:** Consumers are becoming callous to commercial messages to the extent that it is increasingly difficult for a single message to have an effect.

(b) **Decreasing cost of using databases:** The dramatic reduction of storage and retrieval costs, coupled with the increased sophistication of audience segmentation has provided marketers with more effective ways to reach target audiences.

(c) **Increasing client expertise:** Clients now are not only pushing their agencies to be more cost effective, but are also realizing that television might not be always the primary advertising medium for consumers.

(d) **Increasing mergers and acquisitions of agencies:** Many top public relations firms and advertising agencies became partners or were partnered with other communication firms. These mergers allowed for more creativity and the expansion of communication from advertising to other disciplines, such as event planning and promotion.

(e) **Increasing mass media costs:** While database costs were falling, increases in mass media cost per thousand impressions (CPMs), especially television, prompted marketers to look at a mix of other channels too which would be relatively less expensive.

(f) **Increasing media and audience fragmentation:** With increase in radio, television stations (especially cable), and magazines, media was getting fragmented, thus increasing the competition for consumer's attention. Also, with the use of computers and sophisticated research methods, companies were able to target specific segments and geographic audiences more accurately.

(g) **Increasing global marketing:** There was a rapid influx in advertising competition from foreign countries. Companies quickly realized that even if they did not conduct business outside their own country, they were now competing in a global marketplace.

(h) **Increased number of competitive products:** With increasing number of new products being launched in the market, marketers needed to look at newer communication models to strengthen their brands against competition.

With an understanding of the factors that led to the rise of IMC, let us now understand the key channels for Integrated Marketing Communications.

Channels for Integrated Marketing Communications

The key difference between traditional marketing and the integrated marketing concept as discussed in the definitions in last section relates to IMC being an audience-driven business process. This essentially means while firms develop business plans, the audience or targeted consumer becomes central to the planning process and the main driving force for all key decisions.

The difference between traditional marketing communication approaches and the IMC audience-driven approach has been summarized in the paper on 'Revisiting the IMC Construct' by Jerry Kliatchko (see Table 3.2).

With an understanding of these differences, let us now look at the key channels which can be included as a part of IMC depending upon how firms want to develop their marketing communications strategy:

(a) **Advertising:** It includes *broadcasting/mass advertising* (print, internet advertising, radio, television commercials) and *outdoor advertising* (billboards, street furniture, stadiums, rest areas, subway advertising, taxis, transit).

Table 3.2 Difference between Traditional Communication and IMC Approaches

	Traditional Marketing Communication Approach	Integrated Marketing Communication Approach
1	Mass marketing and mass communication mindset	One-to-one marketing approaches
2	Transactional model of marketing	Relational model of marketing
3	Product-focused marketing strategies	Consumer-focused marketing strategies
4	Marketing to a consumer with similar traits	Marketing on the basis of behavioral differences between consumers
5	Focus on outputs of marketing communication	Focus on outcomes
6	Customer acquisition emphasis	Customer retention emphasis
7	Intuition feel-based marketing	Fact-based marketing
8	Covers only the 4Ps (product, price, place, promotion)	Includes the extended four Cs (consumer, consumer costs, convenience, communication)
9	Traditional media mindset	Multiple, relevant, interactive, digital contact point
10	Bombarding audience with messages	Building personalized relationships

(b) **Sales promotion:** Contests, coupons, product samples (freebies), premiums, prizes, refunds/rebates, special events, bonus packs, loyalty programs, sales materials (sell sheets, brochures, presentations), installation, customer help, returns and repairs, billing. On the trade side they include trade allowances, POP displays, training programs, trade shows, co-op advertising, etc.

(c) **Public relations:** includes special events, interviews, conference speeches, industry awards, press conferences, testimonials, news releases, publicity stunts, community involvement, charity involvement, and events.

(d) **Direct marketing:** refers to direct mail, telemarketing, catalogs, shopping channels, internet sales, emails, text messaging, websites, online display ads, fliers, catalog distribution, promotional letters, outdoor advertising, telemarketing, coupons, direct mail, direct selling, grassroots/community marketing, mobile.

(e) **Digital/internet marketing:** This being the latest addition to IMC includes all the digital marketing and communication channels which we would be looking at in this book. These include all the channels as shared in Chapter 1 (Section 'Digital Marketing Applications and Benefits'):

- Intent-based marketing (search marketing)
- Brand marketing (display/digital advertising—banner ads, rich media ads, online classified ads, email ads, mobile advertising)
- Content marketing (website, blog, native content)
- Community-based marketing (social media, business platforms)
- Partner marketing (affiliate marketing, sponsorships, PR)
- Communication channel marketing (e-mail, messaging, sms)
- Platform-based marketing (mobile, video, out-of-home, media platforms (Surface), kiosks, In-apps)

It is primarily the addition of digital/internet marketing and communication channels which has brought about the value differentiators of customer centricity and audience-driven inputs to the overall IMC process. Since this textbook is about digital marketing, we would be looking at multiple examples of integration of digital components to the overall communication mix in the subsequent chapters which would help understand how these elements cover up the limitations of traditional media and provide avenues for a stronger one-to-one consumer connect.

Since IMC primarily deals with leveraging the strong characteristics of each key communication medium and strengthening the limitations with newer communication channels, it would be important to know the key advantages and limitations of major media types (see Table 3.3) as shared by Philip Kotler in *Marketing Management* (Millennium Edition). This would also help us realize the need to for additional digital channels to upend the traditional ones for enhanced communication impact.

Table 3.3 Profiles of Major Media Types

Medium	Advantages	Limitations
Newspapers	Flexibility; timeliness; good local market coverage; broad acceptance; high believability	Short life; poor reproduction quality; small "pass-along" audience
Television	Combines sight, sound, and motion; appealing to senses; high attention; high reach	High absolute cost; high clutter; fleeting exposure; less audience selectivity
Direct mail	Audience selectivity; flexibility; no ad competition within the same medium; personalization	Relatively high cost; "junk mail" image
Radio	Mass-use; high geographic and demographic selectivity; low cost	Audio presentation only; lower attention than television; non-standardized rate structures; fleeting exposure
Magazines	High geographic and demographic selectivity; credibility and prestige; high-quality reproduction; long-life	Low ad purchase lead time; some waste circulation; no guarantee of position
Outdoor	Flexibility; high repeat exposure; low-cost; low competition	Limited audience selectivity; creative limitations
Yellow Pages	Excellent local coverage; high believability; wide reach; low-cost	High competition; long ad purchase lead time; creative limitations
Newsletters	Very high selectivity; full control; interactive opportunities; relative low costs	Costs could run away
Telephone	Many users; opportunity to give a personal touch	Relative high cost unless volunteers are used
Internet	High selectivity; interactive possibilities; relatively low cost	Relatively new media with a low number of users in some countries

Four Pillars of the IMC Construct

IMC as an emerging paradigm has been studied in a number of ways and through multiple approaches. One of the first consolidated studies was done by Jerry Kliatchko in 2005 (further revisions made to it in 2008) wherein he proposed the four pillars of IMC and viewed IMC as an evolving developmental process. His work is important as it provides the much-needed understanding and a theoretical context to this otherwise applied process. The four elements of IMC as defined by Kliatchko (2008) include stakeholders, content, channels, and results. Let us understand them in more detail through content aggregated from multiple papers by Kliatchko (the text below has been picked up as direct excerpts from those papers):

(a) **Stakeholders:** The term 'stakeholders' refers to all relevant publics or multiple markets with which the firm interacts. The term 'publics' include both external and internal audiences. External audiences may refer to customers, consumers, prospects, intermediaries, and other entities outside the organization, while internal audiences consist of those within the organization, such as employees, managers, etc.

Managing the external markets in IMC pre-supposes that the entire process of developing an integrated brand communication program places the target market at the core of the business process so as to effectively address their needs and wants and establish long-term and profitable relationships with them (Kliatchko 2005).

(b) **Content:** The development of content in IMC flows from a deep knowledge and understanding of multiple markets that an IMC program is intended to address. Understanding consumers beyond traditional marketing descriptors, such as demographic and psychographic data is essential (Schulz and Schulz 2004). An appreciation of consumer understanding gives rise to consumer insights and the discovery of the consumer "sweet spot"—the perfect connection between the brand and the customer (Fortini Campbell 1992)—that ultimately leads to the creation of compelling content.

Content in IMC may be differentiated between messages and incentives. Messages refer to brand concepts, ideas or associations, and all other values or perceptions that marketers transmit to customers, while incentives are short-term offers or rewards to consumers for having done something of value to the firm and consumer (Schultz and Schultz 2004).

(c) **Channel:** There are two main determinants to consider in deciding which marketing or brand communication channel to utilize in preparing an integrated media plan: relevance and preference (Schultz and Schultz 2004). Contrary to a common misconception that media planning in the era of IMC implies 'ambushing' consumers at all possible points of contact for maximum exposure, the IMC planning approach deliberately takes on the consumer's perspective in deciding which channels would be the most effective in reaching target audiences.

By conducting a brand contact audit of consumers, as well as examining the consumer's 'path to purchase,' marketers could determine which contact points or channels are relevant to them and which they prefer as sources of information about a company and its brands. The brand contact audit may also aid marketers in determining how consumers would want to communicate and interact with the company in return.

(d) **Results:** Measuring results of marketing communications programs against set objectives has always been the norm for business organizations. However, unlike the traditional attitudinally-based models of measuring effectiveness that focus on evaluating communication effects (for example, brand recall or awareness) and outputs (for example, what media placements were bought), the IMC approach measures behavorial responses (for example, actual purchases made by consumers and prospects) and outcomes (for example, financial returns in terms of income flows from consumers) (Schultz and Walters 1997).

At the heart of IMC, therefore, is the drive for accountability, that is, IMC programs must be accountable for business results. This is done through a process of customer valuation and by estimating return-on-customer-investments, or ROCI (that is predicted incremental sales achieved by investing in specific customers), which are then verified and evaluated at certain points over time, to track the effectiveness of IMC programs (Kliatchko 2005). Schultz and Schultz (2005) further explain that measuring IMC programs follows the predictive modeling approach that focuses on customers that generate returns for the brand, and estimating the impact and effect that a variety of brand marketing investments might have on the program.

IMPACT OF DIGITAL CHANNELS ON IMC

With an understanding of the four pillars of IMC, let us look at the impact integration of digital channels had on overall marketing communications:

(a) **Intent-based marketing (search marketing):** With the incorporation of search-based marketing communication, not only do firms get to know the top keywords which are important to their customer set with regards to the products they aim to sell, but it is also the most credible medium to take customers from an intent to the consumption stage in the least possible time.

(b) **Brand marketing (display/digital advertising):** With display having the power to track all online customer actions and send them targeted messages based upon each marketing-funnel stage interaction, this form of advertising extends a creative and immersive angle to other integrated communication channels.

(c) **Content marketing (website, blog, native content)**: Digital content as also in the case of traditional content is a powerful addition to the marketer's communication armoury and with the emerging usage of native content and advertorials, it becomes crucial to have a strong online content marketing strategy for each campaign.

(d) **Community-based marketing (social media, business platforms):** With digital community channels providing a quick, responsive, and immediately accessible word-of-mouth option, it has grained a lot of prominence in improving brand trust and letting consumers know that similar people also have a preference for the product they are about to purchase.

(e) **Partner marketing (affiliate marketing, sponsorships, PR)**: With the need for communication extending to multiple destination sites, instead of just one portal, partner marketing helps the overall IMC program reach out to customers with varied interests on the online destinations they like to visit.

(f) **Communication channel marketing (e-mail, messaging, sms):** Through details collected from traditional visits and feedback forms, companies now have options to pursue personal data for permission-based marketing, wherein communications are guided by seeking customer permissions rather than pushing the product onto the consumer. Online offers are being integrated with offline purchases, through offers, coupons, location-based marketing, contests, and other successful techniques.

(g) **Platform-based marketing (mobile, video, media platforms kiosks, In-apps):** Finally, with new technology platforms being developed and adopted, there are tremendous possibilities to improve reach, extend branding, customized interaction, all of which form the core of IMC exercise.

PRACTICAL EXERCISE

Executing Consumer Analysis

Key Objective To develop an understanding of consumer trends and gather insights into the consumer mindset with the help of available internet tools.

Project Brief Imagine that you are working in a team looking to launch a new smartphone in India and you need to gather insights on Indian audience, types for smartphones, feature preferences, usage patterns, etc. Which online websites or platforms would you use to conduct the research and gain relevant insights across target audience? Please visit those resources and share a report on your consumer insights or observations in your class.

Execution Let us look at some of the websites or platforms you could use to gauge specific consumer insights.

(a) **Searching Articles on Consumer Preference:** As a first step, you should start searching both Indian and global websites that regularly publish multiple articles on consumer preferences and trends across multiple age, demographic, and psychographic segments across geographies. An example of one such website is https://www.nielsen.com/in/en.html that publishes articles on consumer insights.

(b) **Reviewing Trend-Watching Websites:** The next step includes following and searching for trends across multiple trend-watching websites. Some example includes:

- www.jwtintelligence.com
- www.trendhunter.com
- www.psfk.com

(c) **Following Google Alerts:** Apart from searching the web, the best way to gather information is to setup specific alerts in the form of RSS feeds to your email inbox. Google Alerts is a great way to specify keywords and get daily consumer insights in the form of trending articles delivered in your inbox.

(d) **Executing Consumer Surveys:** One of the best ways to gather consumer insight is to execute specific surveys (most of them for free) with your target audience segment. Most commonly used survey tools include:
- Survey Monkey
- Typeform
- Google Forms
- Google Survey
- AYTM

(e) **Reviewing Quora questions and answers:** One of the best ways of gauging the questions on top of consumers' mind in your segment and their thoughts across areas related to your product or service is to go through Quora questions and answers.

(f) **Finding Influencers in an Industry:** Influencers are important audience set to know across any research category. Key influencers can be reached for a partnership to gather their insights or pay them for marketing a brand. Key tools for finding influencers include Klout, Kred, PeerIndex, etc.

(g) **Social Media Channels:** Social media platforms are a great way to interact with your followers and members of your Facebook or LinkedIn groups to gather insights from them across multiple topics and interest areas. You could also utilize the social media audience from groups created by your college or company for research purposes. Facebook audience insights is a great too to classify regional audiences based on their age, demographic, interests, education, relationship status, work, etc.

(h) **Following Industry Association Reports:** Multiple industry reports related to consumer insights and trends are shared on a yearly basis by top consulting firms, agencies, marketing associations, etc. These reports gather the pulse of Indian and global audience across multiple industry segments, technology, and process areas, and can be used as a useful barometer of consumer preferences.

Researching consumer trends across digital and online platforms is crucial towards forming an integrated view of any consumer segment for any specific product or category. This exercise along with gathering market and brand insights will help digital marketers place their bets on the right action areas that are most useful for digital campaign execution. Once you have completed the consumer insights research exercise, please have the document reviewed by your faculty or teammates for any comments and feedback.

CHAPTER SUMMARY

- **Part 1:** We learnt about the basic concepts of consumer behavior and the evolution of consumer behavior models, especially the EBM model and its four key stages. We also looked at the impact of digital on Consumer Decision Process (CDP) in an active and passive manner. This was followed by an understanding of the key attributes of online buying behavior and the building blocks of an effective web experience. We also looked at utilizing market intelligence to gather customer data to build segments and resulting marketing application areas.

- **Part 2:** In the second part, we looked at the eight types of demand patterns and key factors impacting consumer demand. This was followed by an understanding of demand-led product development process. We then looked at the Keller's CBBE Brand Equity Model to understand the six brand equity elements and the five-step process to building a brand on the web followed by an understanding of web-tracking audits and demand forecasting.
- **Part 3:** In the final part, we introduced the concept of IMC, its history, and key factors behind its adoption. This was followed by looking at the differences between traditional communication and IMC Approaches and the four pillars of IMC construct. At the end, we also learned about the impact of digital channels on IMC and how they have enhanced its concept and utility.

REVIEW QUESTIONS

1. What is consumer behavior? Can you describe the four traditional consumer behavior models?
2. Explain the four key stages of "Engel, Blackwell and Miniard (EBM)" Model in detail.
3. Name some of the characteristics that differentiate a digital consumer from a traditional (offline) consumer.
4. Can you compare passive and active digital influences stating at least two examples for each?
5. According to Lewis and Lewis, what are the five different kinds of web users as discussed in the chapter?
6. Explain the five stages during which information that is presented on a website is processed by the human mind?
7. Describe the key stages by which marketing intelligence is derived from multiple user data sets.
8. What is consumer demand? Which eight types of demand patterns need to be taken into consideration by marketers?
9. Explain in detail the four factors impacting consumer demand.
10. What is a brand? What are the six main criteria for choosing brand elements which can be used by a firm for brand building?
11. What are web-tracking audits? Why are they important?
12. How did the Integrated Marketing Communications (IMC) concept emerge? What trends and changes have resulted in the adoption of integrated marketing communication?
13. Explain at least five key differences between Traditional Communication and IMC Approaches.
14. Share the advantages and limitations of any four major media types.
15. Explain the four key pillars of the IMC construct.
16. State five distinct impacts of digital on Integrated Marketing Communications.

DIGITAL APPLICATION EXERCISES

1. Take the example of Oyo Rooms to explain the four key stages of "Engel, Blackwell and Miniard (EBM)" Model.
2. From the five different kinds of web users in the chapter, what kind of web user would you identify yourself as and why?
3. Uber is a classic example of one of the most modern consumer-oriented apps. Can you describe the five stages how any user might process the interactions with the app across the five interaction stages?
4. Can you think of eight different Indian brands representing each of the eight types of consumer demand patterns?
5. Zomato has developed itself into an iconic brand name in India with high recall. Visit Zomato.com and lay out the key criteria of the six brand elements you feel they have used to develop their brand building activities.
6. Pickup BigBasket.com as an example to discuss key differences between traditional competition and IMC approaches.
7. If you were to build a digital brand from scratch, which category would it be and why? Share your approach to develop the four key pillars of IMC construct for that digital brand.

CHAPTER 4

UNIT II DIGITAL MARKETING STRATEGY DEVELOPMENT

Digital Marketing Assessment Phase

LEARNING OBJECTIVES

After studying this chapter, you will be able to:

- Establish the need for a shift from traditional to digital marketing strategy and understand the key elements of the Assessment Phase of ASCOR Digital Marketing Framework
- Explain the four key internal analysis elements and application of underlying frameworks to support their analysis
- Underline the need for digital presence and explain how external and internal analysis components can help firms develop their high-level digital marketing objectives
- Apply a marketing review framework to monitor, control and revise digital marketing objectives

CASE STUDY Facebook (Meta): *Indians don't text, they 'WhatsApp'*

India has always been one of the biggest markets for Facebook (now Meta), especially because of the sheer number of people using this website. The growth of Facebook India is clearly visible in the fact that as of May 2021, Facebook held a 77.58 per cent market share in the Indian social media market. The company reported gross advertising revenues of ₹9,326 crore in FY21, which is an astounding rise of 314% from the last two years (₹2,254 crore). However, over the last 5 years, Facebook India has also faced immense challenges in the Indian market from the acquisition of WhatsApp, to facing privacy concern cases, etc. Regardless, the company is fighting strong to stay relevant with its services in the Indian marketplace.

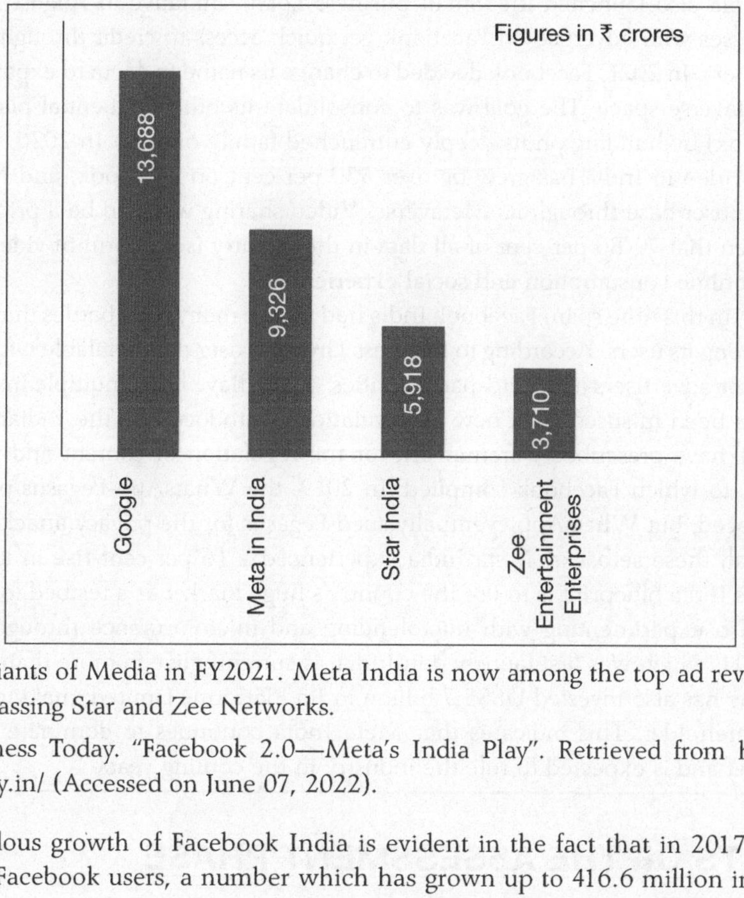

Figure 4.1 Giants of Media in FY2021. Meta India is now among the top ad revenue earners, surpassing Star and Zee Networks.

Source: Business Today. "Facebook 2.0—Meta's India Play". Retrieved from https://www.businesstoday.in/ (Accessed on June 07, 2022).

The tremendous growth of Facebook India is evident in the fact that in 2017, there were 241 million Facebook users, a number which has grown up to 416.6 million in 2021, indicating that Facebook has deeply penetrated the Indian market. One major reason for this is the availability of better internet facilities and hence, an increased number of internet users when compared to 2017. The second biggest reason is the explosive growth of WhatsApp and Instagram, which were acquired by Facebook in 2012 and 2014 respectively.

India has over 487.5 million WhatsApp users, which has largely contributed to Facebook India's growth. Instagram too has made huge progress in India due to Facebook's focus on influencer marketing as a growth strategy pivot. In 2021, Instagram Reels were introduced, and it took the platform to next level. The reason behind this growth is also attributed to the ban of Tik Tok (Instagram's biggest competitor) in India.

The 'advertising earning model' set in place by the global giant played a very important role in its success. 'Facebook for Business' has helped many sellers advertise their products on Facebook and carry out direct sales activities. Through this initiative, many physical sellers became associated with Facebook India, which in-turn increased overall Facebook users. Not only small businesses, but content creators and influencers today are also earning well through the trio of Facebook, WhatsApp, and Instagram platforms. In addition to this,

Facebook India also launched the 'Small Business Loans' initiative in August 2021, to help small businesses who advertise on Facebook get quick access to credit through independent lending partners. In 2021, Facebook decided to change its name to Meta to expand its horizon into the Metaverse space. The goal was to consolidate its other influential platforms (apart from Facebook) by building on its deeply entrenched family of apps. In 2020, viewership of live gaming video in India has grew by over 530 per cent on Facebook, and Meta plans to tap the same user base through its Metaverse. Video sharing will also be a priority for Meta in India, given that 70-80 per cent of all data in the country is the form of video, which also drives most online consumption and social experiences.

However, in this time span, Facebook India had to face many legal battles that have created concerns among its users. According to Business Line, the user data available with Facebook is a goldmine for advertisers and third-party entities. There have been multiple instances where this data has been misused. The new IT regulations introduced by the Indian government in June 2021 have prescribed a framework for the regulation of content and prevention of data privacy, to which Facebook complied. In 2019, the WhatsApp-Pegasus privacy breach scandal surfaced, but WhatsApp eventually sued Pegasus for the privacy attack.

Despite all these setbacks, Meta India experienced a 16 per cent rise in its revenues in FY21. Meta's India blueprint is to use the country's huge market as a testbed for future products. It is also experimenting with microlending and microinsurance through WhatsApp. Express Wi-Fi, which was first launched in India, is currently live in more than 20 countries. The company has also invested US$5.7 billion in Jio Platforms Limited, making it the largest minority shareholder. This indicates that Meta India continues to dominate India's social media market and is expected to rule the industry in the coming years.

ELEMENTS OF THE ASSESSMENT PHASE

In the first part on Introduction on Digital Marketing, we learnt about the evolution of internet technologies driving digital marketing, its value chain, and business models, along with the impact of consumer behavior on digital marketing.

This next part on Digital Marketing Strategy Development and the following two parts on Digital Marketing Planning and Set-up and Digital Marketing Implementation would focus on the implementation aspects of the ASCOR Digital Marketing Framework as shared in the end section of Chapter 1. The ASCOR Digital Marketing framework which forms the core for all digital marketing activities and implementations has five key phases, and this chapter would look at developing a basic understanding of the first phase which would help us build up our knowledge for the subsequent phases in the next chapters.

Marketing Strategy and its Digital Shifts

In Chapter 1 Section titled, 'Digital Marketing Framework', we had laid out the core elements of the ASCOR Digital Marketing Framework at a high level. Let us first establish the need for the framework, before we go further into the first phase and its elements.

Typically, any framework by design supports and helps build the core elements for any strategy implementation. In the case of marketing, the need for a well-developed and thought-out strategy becomes all the more crucial considering the multitude of channels through which customers can be influenced and the impact of changing consumption patterns. Be it traditional marketing or its present-day digital form, marketing heads of firms have always had limited budgets wherein they were expected to lay out a well-structured marketing plan to support and enhance sales and consumer-connect activities. In this section, we would look at the basics of marketing strategy and how marketing plans have been developed traditionally.

Marketing strategy, by definition, has the goal of increasing sales and achieving sustainable competitive advantage. Typically, this is differentiated from sales strategy as marketing aims at a 'Pull Strategy' wherein the intention is to create a strong positive disposition towards the brand through the use of regular marketing tactics, while sales strategies deal more with setting up plans to sell (and even exceed) targeted volumes of a product in a certain defined period.

Generally, marketing strategies are initiated as a part of the strategic planning for an organization which includes setting up the vision (long-term objective) and mission (shorter term tactical objectives) for each of the organization's key product/service divisions. Peter Drucker, who is best known as the 'founder of modern management' shares that while developing the corporate strategy, each firm needs to ask and develop answers to questions like "What is our business? Who is the customer? What is the value to the customer? What should our business be?", etc. The marketing process as defined by Philip Kotler (1999) includes:

(a) **Analyzing marketing opportunities**: According to Kotler, a marketer's initial task is to identify potential long-run opportunities given the company's market experience and core competencies.

(b) **Developing marketing strategies:** In this step, the marketer prepares a positioning strategy for each new and existing product based on its progress through the life cycle, makes decisions about product lines and branding, and designs and markets its services.

(c) **Planning marketing programs:** It involves transforming marketing strategy into marketing programs and making basic decisions on marketing expenditures, marketing mix, and allocation.

- The first decision is the level of marketing expenditures needed
- The second relates to dividing the total marketing budget among various tools in the marketing mix—Product, Price, Place, Promotion
- The third is how to allocate marketing budget to various products, channels, promotion media, and sales areas

(d) **Managing the marketing effort:** This stage involves organizing the firm's marketing resources to implement and control the marketing plan through feedback and control.

With a basic understanding of marketing strategy and planning process, we can now better appreciate the need for a structured digital marketing framework to understand and lay down in specific terms, the key objectives of digital marketing, the controls needed to execute it, and the processes to put in place to measure the outcome and refine original plans.

The ASCOR digital marketing framework has been developed specifically to guide practitioners of digital marketing to develop and manage it as a predictable process rather than view it as an art on which we have no control.

The key differences in marketing strategy/framework creation traditionally and with the advent of digital media include:

(a) **Knowledge of customer preferences:** With advanced analytics on consumer preferences and interactions with brands now available to marketers, it is easier to know and include value-drivers much earlier into the marketing planning process.

(b) **Leveraging traditional brand presence:** What traditional marketing lacked is the leverage it could obtain and pass on to other channels which were typically distinct in nature. With digital marketing, the right mix of influence can be gathered and built into digital marketing planning in a selective manner.

(c) **Reactive to predictive approach:** Traditional marketing plans like newspaper, radio, and television had no means to know individual segment-based consumption patterns and preferences. Data, though available, could not be used to develop predictive models of planning, which is much more possible now.

(d) **Disintermediation of value chains/life cycles:** With multiple intermediaries and new value-trapping entities in the fray, traditional value chains have been drastically altered, thus shifting the marketing objectives themselves which have to become more and more aligned directly to the consumer rather than leaving that job to intermediaries.

(e) **Impact of prosumerization**: Prosumerization involves emergence of low-overhead start-ups which are competing with capital intensive incumbents. With these new start-ups using technology to their advantage, more novel marketing techniques are being planned by traditional firms which involve lower budgets with higher customer impact.

(f) **Brand to channel attribute alignment:** An interesting aspect of digital marketing channels is the way brand attributes can be aligned to a particular marketing medium, making it much more impactful to spend larger marketing budgets on those and similar mediums rather than allocating them proportionately across a mix. A good example of this could be the way a professional camera brand can tie-up with a photo-sharing social site like Instagram and make use of the aesthetic and immersive elements of that single channel to sell its range of high-end cameras. Such media channels and brand alignments could not even be thought of earlier.

(g) **Unique digital-connect concepts:** With the proliferation of short-text messaging, and concepts like trending topics and viral marketing, it is now possible for new brands to build a name and brand presence in less time with unique marketing short bursts. Planning for these kinds of marketing tactics is emerging as a completely new area.

(h) **Follow-the-customer model (attribution concepts):** The most interesting change which marketing has brought about is the possibility to track each consumer's purchase pattern on the internet and relate it to a particular influence, reason, or combination of events (attribution phenomenon). This not only helps the marketer to intervene and influence the consumer while he/she is purchasing actively but also makes pitches, provide discounts, etc., when they are plainly browsing, thus influencing them to a discovery-led purchase.

The Need for Digital Strategy

We now have an understanding of key differences and the specific impact brought about by digital channels and their influence on marketing strategies and planning. While developing a strategy framework for digital marketing one has to look into a whole set of unique elements. Also, equally pertinent is the fact that however much resources and attention firms across the globe pay to digital strategy, it still has to be aligned to and serve the needs of traditional marketing.

Let us see the scenarios below to understand how digital strategy supports and extends traditional marketing strategy (see Fig. 4.2).

In Fig. 4.2, we have taken up three general scenarios to see how a thorough understanding and development of digital strategy can support marketers to enhance the output of their overall marketing spend.

(a) **Scenario 1**: A well-established brand with a product/service which is doing quite well with traditional marketing channels but can leverage digital for further brand impact, enhanced revenues, and a global reach. There is also a good possibility for the brand to test niche and premium products with its audience segments, which it might not normally be able to accomplish because of the high costs of traditional marketing channels like television and print advertising.

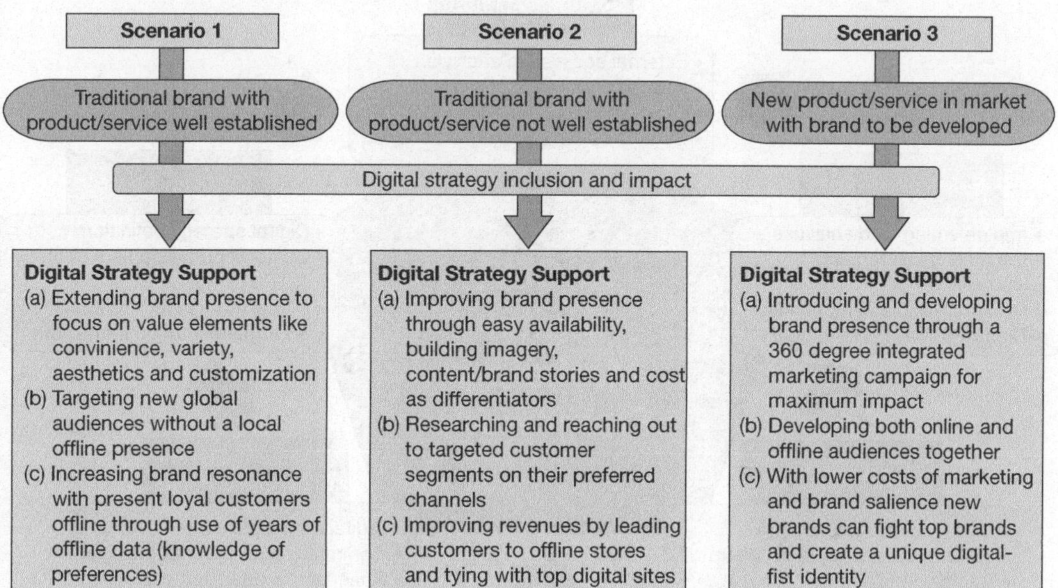

Figure 4.2 Scenarios for Digital Strategy Inclusion to Traditional Marketing

(b) **Scenario 2**: A brand which has been present offline for a long time, but is more of a contender and might not be doing that well as compared to competition in its category. This brand can make use of digital platforms to create a strong identity among certain identified target groups and can also leverage digital partners and channels to improve sales and online presence.

(c) **Scenario 3**: Takes a look at how a new product/service can avail of a digital-first strategy to launch itself in the market. Typically, new product developments are riskier and brands these days are utilizing social and owned media platforms to gather responses to their launches, introducing themselves with more willing audiences (the influencer group) to get their feedback and improvize products before a big-bang launch.

With the above examples, it is evident that not only is digital strategy crucial for marketers going forward, they would need a thorough framework to structure their approach and make sure they are moving in a well laid-out fashion to achieve their traditional as well as digital objectives.

The Assessment Phase Elements

With an introduction already made to the ASCOR Digital Marketing Framework (Chapter 1), in this section, we would start with elaboration of its first phase—The Assessment Phase. Before we start to dwell deeper we are sharing below the ASCOR framework base diagram (Fig. 4.3) for a recap of what we understood in Chapter 1.

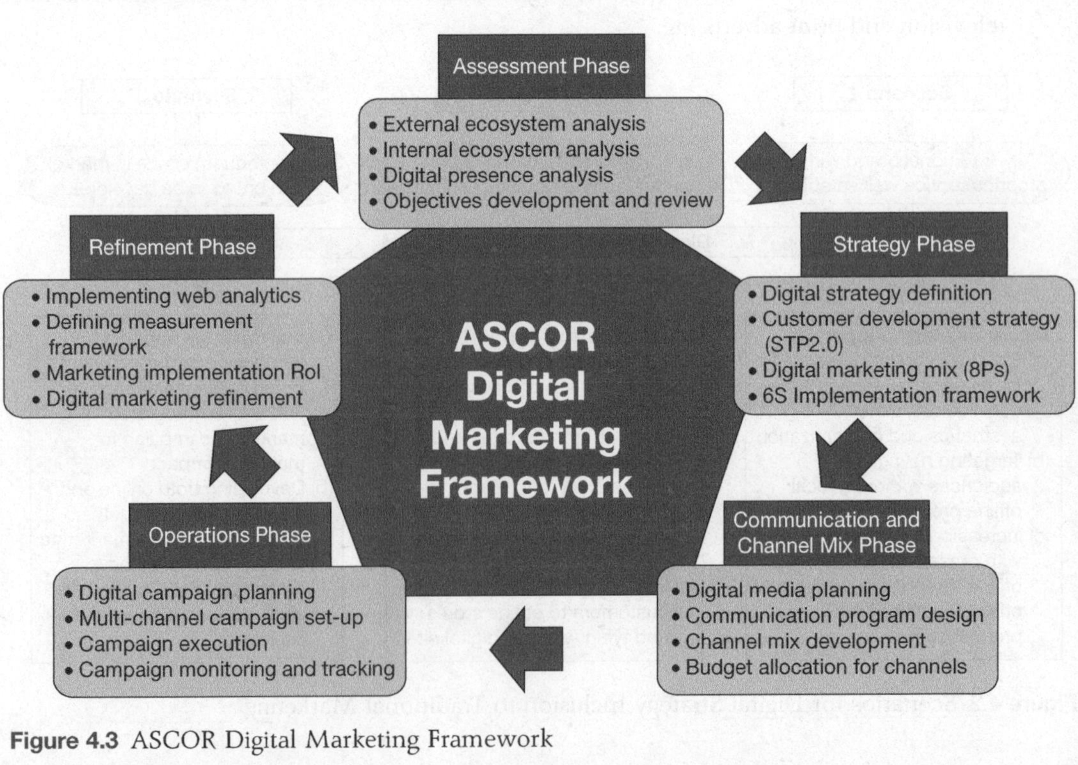

Figure 4.3 ASCOR Digital Marketing Framework

Understanding the Assessment Phase

The assessment phase is the first of the five phases of ASCOR Digital Marketing Framework and also the starting point for any digital marketing plan. It involves an initial analysis of the internal and external environment to define and develop digital marketing objectives for the firm or individual.

The assessment phase can be divided into four key elements (See Fig. 4.4) based on the nature and interaction of all forces impacting digital marketing objectives development:

(a) **External analysis:** Includes the analysis of *macro-micro environment* (entities which surround and influence the firm, its products, operations, and opportunities) and *market situation analysis* (referring to market and competition analysis, specific to the industry where the firm and its product are operating).

(b) **Internal analysis:** Involves an analysis of factors which are internal to a company and within their control to influence their goal setting and create successful and realistic digital marketing objectives. It includes four main analysis areas—offerings mix, marketing mix, resources mix, and competencies mix.

(c) **Digital presence analysis:** It is a 2 × 2 matrix which helps firms identify their present digital state through a combined analysis of external and internal factors.

(d) **Objectives development and review:** Involves setting high-level digital marketing objectives based upon the specific digital state in which the firm is present. The review stage consists of activities that involves monitoring, evaluating, and controlling marketing activities continuously.

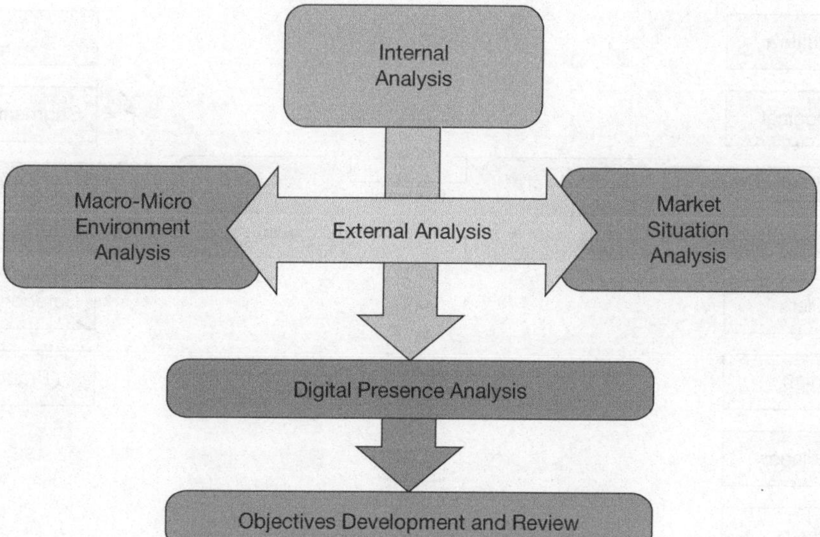

Figure 4.4 Key Assessment Phase Elements

Macro-Micro Environment Analysis

With a basic understanding of key assessment phase elements in the last section, let us understand the first element of the external analysis which is the macro-micro environment analysis. The next section focuses on the second element named as market situation analysis.

To begin, we first need to gain a broader understanding of all the elements which encompass the external analysis of the assessment phase.

Understanding Macro-Micro Environments

The terms macro and micro environments are classic marketing environment terminologies used to bunch and analyze key factors that impact a firm's ability to build and maintain a profitable business and relationship with customers. A macro environment, by definition, includes variables and factors outside the business which have a positive or negative influence on the growth and continued existence of the business (Le Roux et al.1999). The four key elements of macro environment (also termed as PEST) include political, economic, socio-cultural, and technological factors (see Fig. 4.5). Apart from these, researches have included other allied elements too like legal, demographic, and even natural forces as a part of macro environments. The four key elements of macro environment and their impact are described below.

(a) **Political:** The most pertinent example of political forces and world events impacting and propelling the growth of one of the top personal marketing firms is that of Twitter. Twitter,

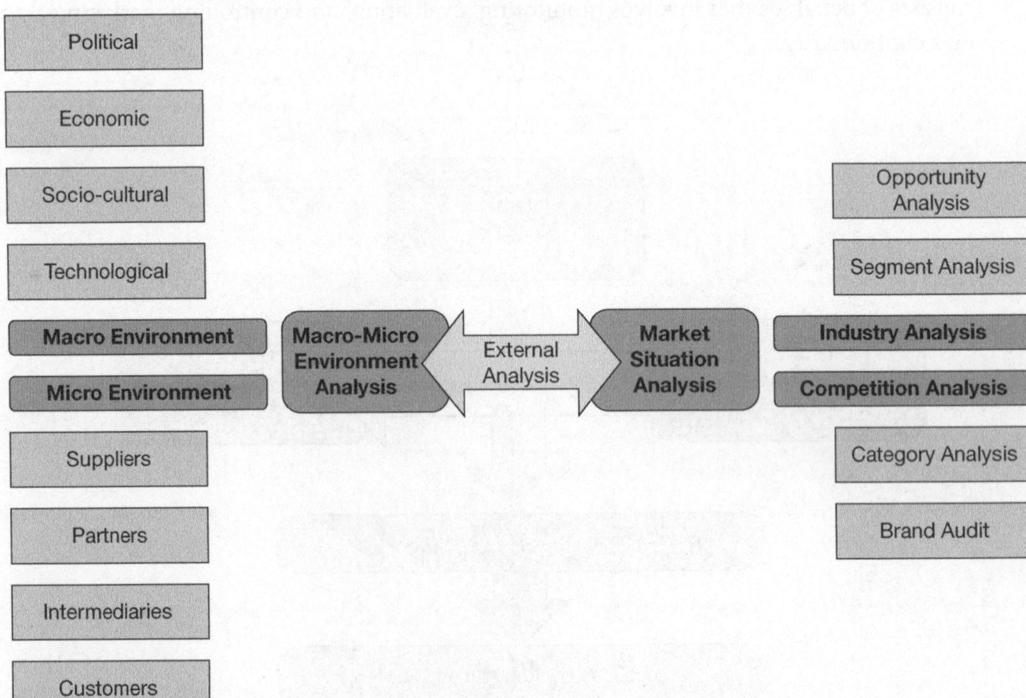

Figure 4.5 Elaborating External Analysis Elements

which began as a short form (micro) publishing site (aimed at consumers and organizations who are allowed to share 140 character-only messages), got a big boost when protesters and political activists started using the platform to share views and opinions to mobilize political events and even liberation movements in certain cases.

The example goes on to showcase how political events in any country or region impact the business environment which is so crucial for any firm to incubate and propagate. Around the world there have been multiple cases wherein business-friendly leaders and regimes have led to the creation of an entrepreneurial environment which has rapidly fueled the growth of firms. A related example in the Indian context was the rise of Special Economic Zones (SEZ) in India during the time Information Technology (IT) software outsourcing (as a concept) was on the rise; a time when a political will to set-up SEZs (and promote entrepreneurs take up land and build establishments at much cheaper prices) helped mushroom multiple organizations in a short period.

(b) **Economic:** Typically, key indicators like economic growth rate, per capita income, interest rates, inflation have impacted a firm's growth in a particular country or region. With increasing globalization, impact of FDI (Foreign Direct Investment), presence of Venture Capitalists, and with the recent phenomenon of Seed Accelerators and Hackathons (technology/coding events), there has been a surge of interest and support for technology companies where initial funding is crucial for incubation and growth. A large part of the e-commerce growth story in India has also been attributed to these developments and the presence of a sound financial ecosystem.

(c) **Socio-cultural:** This factor deals with the social and cultural values, morals, ethics, and to say the least, the overall structure and thought on which society runs and does commerce. As shared in Chapter 3 on consumer behavior and its impact on marketing, it becomes crucial for marketers to not only have a strong understanding of the cultural factors that affect their buying behavior but also understand which concepts customers would most easily adopt and the ones that need a lot of effort towards brand building and customer conditioning.

(d) **Technological:** With technology playing a crucial role in advancing marketing in the digital era, this is one of the most important macro factors (along with customer data availability) for marketers these days. It is crucial not only to have knowledge of key technology and automation tools which drive and impact marketing but to also keep up with the changing trends of each of the digital marketing elements like search algorithms, advertising technologies, launch of new operating systems, cloud platforms, competitive mobile app features, etc. Only through an integrated use of technology with other marketing elements can a firm hope to succeed digitally these days.

With an understanding of key macro environment factors, let us look at the major micro environment impact factors now. Micro environment factors include those entities which directly impact the firm and its growth prospects and are closer to the company's ecosystem than the macro factors. If we recollect, similar factors have also been covered at length in Chapter 1, section titled Digital: the Next Wave of Marketing, wherein we studied the Stakeholder-Based Digital Transformation Model. Let us have a look at them.

(a) **Suppliers**: The definition of suppliers in the digital context is quite different from its traditional manufacturing definition wherein suppliers provided raw materials and the firm would have to go through the whole process of procurement, warehousing, production, delivery, and marketing. With digital products and market ecosystem (as also shared through the Journal Publishing extended example in Chapter 2), the definition of suppliers has altered dramatically. If information becomes the final product/service, the nature of information aggregation, conversion and sales can be a much simplified process wherein the only value a firm adds is enhancing or providing structure to a suppliers' content and sell it to a pre-built audience online. Through technology we see the lines between supplier, producer, and seller diminish and marketers make use of these changing trends to create high-value customized products.

(b) **Partners:** Typically, partners were firms which tied up with each other to make use of the specific strengths of each of them. The definition though remains the same, the nature of such partnerships has changed in that nowadays it is not the production or delivery expertise which might be shared but more often companies are co-creating go-to-market (GTM) plans by pooling in resources and most importantly customer data. There is also a big trend of data management companies which are aggregating and providing third-party data to firms on key potential customers (who might have an interest in a brand online but have still not converted).

(c) **Intermediaries:** This third category of players differ from partners as they are firms which run independently but provide value-differentiation and reduce transaction costs (market friction elements as also discussed in Chapter 2 on value chain models) for firms across any vertical. The best example is of a large number of logistics and last-mile fulfillment companies which have sprung up in India in the past two years to cater to the explosive growth witnessed by larger e-commerce companies like Flipkart and Amazon.

(d) **Customers:** Finally, we come to the most crucial of the micro environment elements which are the customers themselves. As shared in detail in Chapter 3 also, identification of correct customer segments and building relation with those segments through multiple channels, platforms, and activities will be the key to any successful digital marketing implementation. Customer interactions and the awareness of the most effective touchpoints enhancing those interactions are thus the key to any firm's digital growth story.

Marketing Situation Analysis

In this section, we will look at the second element of External Analysis. This includes analyzing two key components:

(a) **Industry analysis:** involves conducting market research to analyze key industry trends related to marketer's product/service on digital platforms.

(b) **Competition analysis:** includes researching direct and indirect competitors to compare a marketer's product portfolio. It also helps assess the leverage digital marketing can provide to a brand's objective of positioning itself online.

Application of Market Research

To begin understanding how we analyze these two elements—industry and competition—we need to go through a few basics of the vast field of study called market research, which is defined as an organized effort to gather information about target markets or customers. Market research is not only important to understand and analyze the present market situation, but as we would see in the next chapter, it also provides qualitative and quantitative tools and frameworks which help create and validate the overall business and marketing strategies too.

For this section, we need to be familiar with two basic kinds of market research:

(a) **Primary research:** consists of a collection of original primary data collected from the field by the researcher using questionnaires, focus group discussions, interviews, etc.

(b) **Secondary research:** involves the summary, collation and synthesis of existing research available from multiple sources like research papers, previous experiments, articles, etc.

These days with the amount of data available and being generated in large amounts even at an hourly basis, market research matched with statistics is an emerging field across businesses. Even more than traditional marketing, digital marketing relies on sound data-driven market research to understand its present industry and competitive environment, hence it is crucial for any marketer to be aware of basic market research techniques if they want to be present online and operate successfully.

With a basic introduction to market research, let us look at the key market situation components discussed earlier to understand the analysis that goes behind them.

Industry analysis

The two key elements behind an industry analysis includes:

(a) **Market segment analysis:** Let us suppose, a firm XYZ plans to launch a new mobile phone in the market. Even before it starts to develop a product, the firm needs to conduct enough research to understand the market segment and its data points. This includes:
- Market data on the primary and secondary industry segments they would operate in (which in this case would be telecom hardware and mid-range smartphone category)
- Key customer segments to target online (includes gender, demographic, psychographic differences)
- Top partner and intermediary firms to tie up with online, to market the products
- Key market trends, industry compliances, digital platform presence, etc.
- Primary research conducted by firm (surveys, focus groups, interviews)
- Secondary research consisting of analyst reports, surveys, industry association reports, mergers and acquisitions, consumer social mentions, major blogs, etc.

(b) **Opportunity analysis:** Apart from research on industry and specific market segment, the firm would also need a market opportunity sizing exercise with the help of the following research data:

- Total market size for the category (including all types of mobile phones)
- Growth of particular market segment in the past two to three years (specific segment includes smartphone mobile category)
- Sales growth of mid-range smartphone segments on all digital channels
- Comparison on price points and ranges of similar mid-range smartphones
- International sales figures for similar smartphones across key geographies

With support of the data collected through market research on areas similar as above, XYZ should be able to perform analysis to make decisions on the following questions:

- What is the market they can capture with the launch of their new mobile in short and long term?
- What sales target should they plan for the initial period of the launch phase?
- What key customer segments would be most open to purchasing their product?
- What level of growth can they expect with the launch of their smartphone?
- Which key stakeholders would they need to partner with to grow their sales on digital platforms?
- Which platforms would be the best suited to market their products to?

By gathering such segment and industry-based market research and analysis of data points, firms like XYZ can answer a lot of similar market assessment questions. What is not included in the above coverage though is an analysis of the competition and intangible factors relating to branding and product imagery for which we would need to conduct the second component of the Market Situation Analysis which is Competition Analysis.

Competition analysis

After a high-level industry and segment analysis, let us get down to category-level analysis where a product's standing with respect to direct and indirect competition and its brand positioning should be studied through a brand audit. The key elements of competition analysis include:

(a) **Category analysis:** This element of competition analysis maps the specific category of product (which in our present example is the mid-range smartphone category) to understand key competitors and defining elements which would make the product stand apart in the wake of competition. Key elements of the category analysis include:

- Number of competitors in the specific product category
- Presence of competitors in the specific market (years of presence)
- Top competitive players in the category for firm XYZ
- Competitor profiling, including top product analysis, and depth and breadth of product line
- Entrenchment of key competitors across target customer segment

- Key customer segments served, market share, and growth rate
- Competitors' digital marketing spend, promotional mix, and budgets

(b) **Brand audit:** It involves conducting an analysis of key brand attributes against competing brands to realize intangible factors like brand value, imagery, perception, and other unique value elements which differentiate it in the market and would make it stand out in its category. A brand audit would typically include:

- Comparison of brand attributes and positioning
- Key brand values and unique selling proposition
- Brand communication voice and related cultural attributes
- Benefits-based comparison of brand usage output
- Perception of target consumer segment of the brand in comparison with other competing products in the category

With all the factors collated through category competition analysis and brand audit elements as above, the XYZ firm discussed above would be able to uniquely position its mid-range smartphone across specifically targeted customer segments by countering competition and positioning its brand in the most appealing manner.

With an understanding of the key components of external analysis and their unique elements, in the next section we would go through a detailed analysis of key internal analysis elements, which together combined, can provide any marketer with the best set of data to form their digital marketing objectives and plan for an appropriate budget to achieve desired RoI (Return on Investment) over short and long-term periods.

DIGITAL MARKETING INTERNAL ASSESSMENT

The outcome of external assessment as elaborated in the previous section is for any digital marketer to gather market research data relating to how the four key external environment factors—macro, micro, industry, and competition, impact initial assessment. As we move forward to understand internal assessment elements, we should keep in mind that any assessment related to internal strengths and competencies in the upcoming internal assessment section should be made comparative to the external environment elements, as an analysis in isolation might not help marketers gain a complete and accurate perspective of their internal situation and strengths.

Analyzing Present Offerings Mix

Internal analysis involves looking at key elements which are typically in control of the firm and which they can improve/alter to suit to changing external circumstances and macro–micro factors. For our present understanding, we have divided this section on lines of these four elements to have a detailed look at how each of them can be assessed through the use of common industry frameworks unique to each element (see Fig. 4.6).

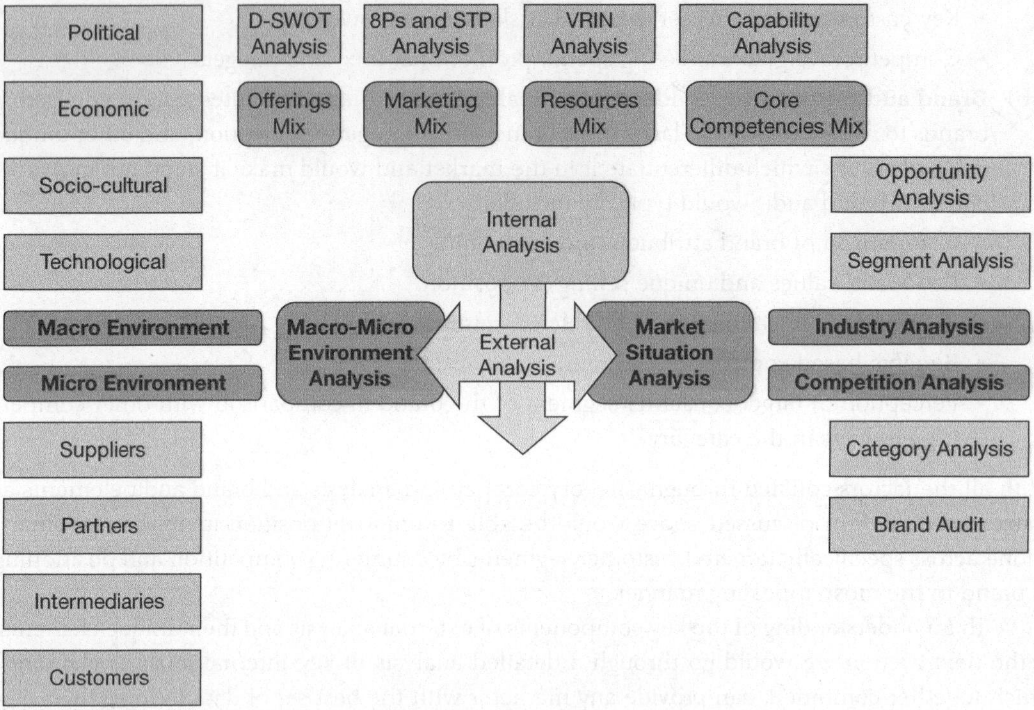

Figure 4.6 Elaborating Internal Analysis Elements

Offerings and Marketing Mix

The first two of the four elements, relate to any firm's analysis of present offerings at hand and how well they are able to analyze and compare the marketing mix of segmentation, targeting, and positioning (STP) to establish themselves online. Offerings here refer to the mix of product and services as a cohesive set rather than as segregated units. A firm would first need to assess the key attributes and marketability of its products and services before deciding who and how to market it.

Typically, most of this analysis is done before even developing the product as a part of the product strategy. But here we would be looking at it more in the context of marketing to gather enough market research and information to develop a product strategy as part of the next ASCOR marketing stage.

When we talk about analyzing the offerings mix from the perspective of a product and marketing mix, we would typically come across a scenario wherein a set of products are already present and well known in the offline world. So how does it differ when we plan to market the same in the online world? A few pointers are listed below.

(a) **Products are virtual in the digital world**: The way products are marketed and presented in the digital world lends itself far more virtual elements than when compared to the same products in the real world dangling from the shelves. So even a bar of normal soap has to have those subtle intangible elements to it, since the real positives of the offline world, the touch, smell, and experience are missing.

(b) **Nature of target audience differs:** Audiences buying the same product online would typically be more aware and open to checking our product features and elements. With such an audience set, the way brand imagery has to be built has to have unique online elements which marketers need to master.

(c) **Brand switching is quite high:** A unique characteristic of online marketing is the easy availability of information and product variety which make it much easier to offset brand loyalty and encourage switching even on the basis of a few price points.

(d) **Digital requires different communication elements**: Although communication developed for TVCs (Television Commercials) still rules the integrated communications mix, marketers have realized the impact of developing digital/social/e-mail based campaigns which have to be much different for the product to standout for this unique audience.

(e) **Products in control of intermediaries/aggregators**: With customers online buying a lot more from top e-commerce/aggregation sites and even low-cost intermediaries, product manufacturers and brand owners sometimes have little influence on packing, delivery, and branding aspects which is a unique challenge.

To ensure that marketers are able to understand these differences and make them count, both during the first stage of setting up the offerings mix and second stage of deciding the STP, we have shared below the concept of a D-SWOT which means a Digital SWOT.

Traditionally, a SWOT (Strengths, Weaknesses, Opportunities, and Threats) framework is used to analyze the market position of a product/service in relation to its direct competition. With an addition of the letter D, we have tried to improvize on the base framework to make sure that all of the four analyses on Strengths, Weaknesses, Opportunities, and Threats are done with a digital lens and should include only those traditional elements which actually are a strength in the online space and not generic strengths pertaining only to offline presence.

To take an example, there might be a case where an established offline brand does not have any presence online, so its strengths against competition should be weighed on a scale which gives due importance of this fact. Also, for executing a D- SWOT, we should also consider and include key transferable attributes from offline to online, which should not be ignored as they add to the strengths of a product being marketed online. The biggest example of this would be intangible elements like brand recognition or trust, which an offline brand carries with it when it goes online. Similarly, a brand with a bad reputation offline would carry its spin-off to the online world, which should be a part of the enlisted Weaknesses in D-SWOT.

Understanding D-SWOT Analysis

A SWOT analysis is the most commonly used planning method to evaluate strengths, weaknesses, opportunities, and threats for a product, place, industry, or person and also forms the perfect bridge between comparing internal factors (strengths and weaknesses) to external factors

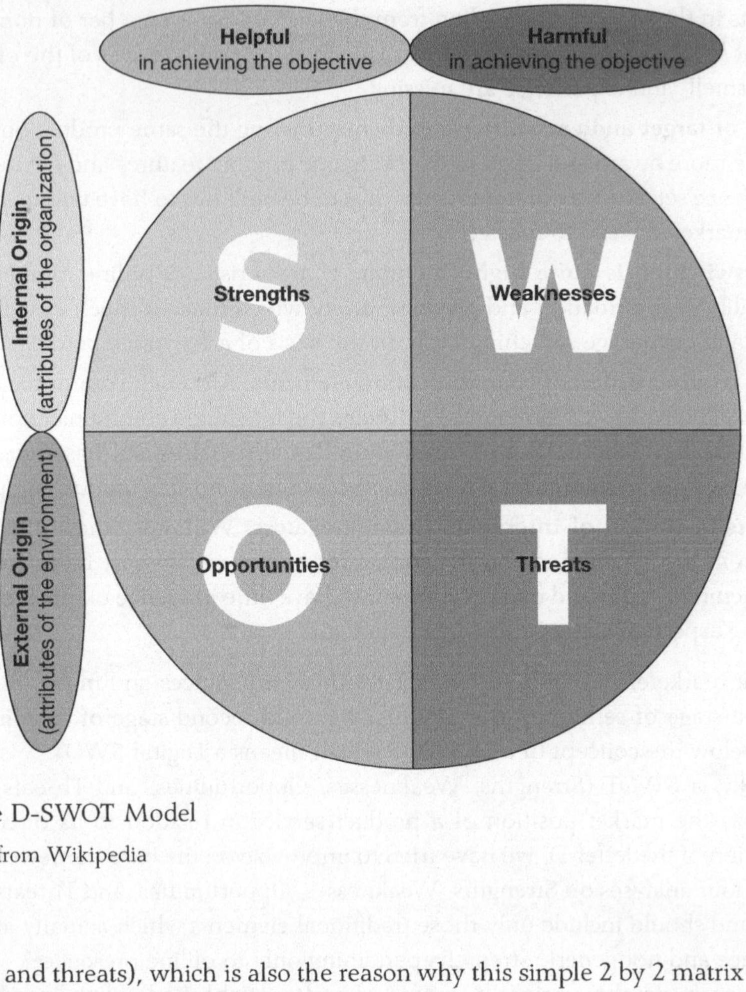

Figure 4.7 The D-SWOT Model

Source: Adapted from Wikipedia

(opportunities and threats), which is also the reason why this simple 2 by 2 matrix has been used so extensively and to great effect (see Fig. 4.7).

The key elements of the D-SWOT model include:

(a) **Strengths:** Key characteristics or attributes which give a firm and its digital offerings an advantage over competition. Depending upon the product, industry, and earlier inroads into the digital space, strengths would vary not only across product lines but also for each product individually, and should be studied accordingly. Given below are the most common examples of areas which would be termed as strengths for any firm looking to compete and grow on digital platforms.

- Strong and stable media presence: highly visited website, social media page, well-admired blog, a micro-blogging strategy, etc.
- Well-etched brands with high recall
- Strong customer satisfaction and feedback on social media
- Trust among partners and intermediaries, strategic tie-ups

- Intellectual capability to build unique products in line with changing trends
- Strong execution and leadership teams
- Consumer-centric design and communication
- Ability to influence policy and attention of internal and external investors
- High adoption of technology as an intrinsic differentiator
- History of profitable collaborations and online acquisitions
- Well set-up revenue models and regular identification of new growth models
- Increasing geographic presence and a wide affiliate network

(b) **Weaknesses:** Characteristics or attributes that place the business and its product portfolio at a disadvantage relative to others. Similar to strengths identification, as above, it is crucial to get as many data points to identify and term a characteristic as a weakness since a lot of future decisions of the company would depend on this analysis.

- Low or very negligible historical online presence
- Online Value Proposition not uniquely defined
- A product/brand portfolio which is not among the top three in their segments
- Low margins as compared to peers
- Lack of integration to mobile and other growing online platforms and channels
- Content, website structure, and communication which is not customer-centric
- Not looked at as a genuine and trusted partner by other online intermediaries
- Poor on-service delivery and execution strategy
- Low advocacy and public relations skills
- Resource planning and internal process organization not optimally managed

(c) **Opportunities:** These are the market-facing elements which companies can internally plan for and exploit once they understand key digital market trends and landscape changes which would impact their specific industry and products. The timing of opportunity assessment and its modelling is typically quite crucial so that the company can differentiate between fads (short term trends) and changes which are going to shape the industry in the long term. We have identified a few of them below.

- Consumer adoption of mobile communications and increased online penetration
- Increasing per capita income and improving economic indicators
- Adoption of new technologies which increase user experience
- Rise of multilingual technologies and content publishing in native languages
- Availability of expert technology workforce at affordable salaries

(d) **Threats:** These are again external environment-driven elements which can impact the functioning and growth of a firm. Companies need to anticipate key threats on a regular basis since without it, emerging disruptions in the market could cause firms and even specific brands to lose their allure and slip away from customer recall altogether. Key threats which should be taken care of (specifically relating to digital growth) include:

- Presence in a highly competitive segment with slow growth rate
- Declining average selling prices due to impact of innovation and technology
- Firm not attuned to changing industry and segment trends and losing initiative
- Inability to scale up in a sector through acquisitions and inorganic growth
- New laws or regulations in the market inhibiting growth

Apart from the general examples shared above, there would be specific Digital SWOT areas (depending upon the industry, sector, nature of competition, prior digital inroads, company's financial strength, online growth propensity), which the company needs to think through for a complete assessment of its offerings and their suitability for a digital launch and growth. Marketers would be advised to thoroughly scan each element of their external interaction with a focus on internal strengths and weaknesses to assess feasible growth potential and develop the right target offerings mix specific to digital.

Marketing Mix Analysis

With the application of D-SWOT for the offerings mix analysis, the next step in the internal analysis involves a marketing mix analysis specifically for digital platforms. A typical marketing mix analysis looks at the four classic Ps of Product, Price, Place, and Promotion along with an STP (Segmenting, Targeting, and Positioning) analysis. With the growth witnessed across online platforms a new set of four more Ps have been added specifically for digital marketing including People, Process, Programs,and Performance. Let us look at these 8Ps and STP concepts to understand how to analyze the marketing mix from a digital perspective.

Marketing Mix and the 8Ps

The term marketing mix was initially developed by Neil Borden who first starting using the phrase in 1949. He started teaching the term after an associate, James Culliton, described the role of the marketing manager in 1948 as a *mixer of ingredients*, "one who sometimes follows recipes prepared by others, sometimes prepares his own recipe as he goes along, sometimes adapts a recipe from immediately available ingredients, and at other times, invents new ingredients no one else has tried."

This is also the reason why we have used the word mix to name the four key components of the internal analysis, as we believe that like marketing mix it is a mix of offerings, resources, and competencies, which are specifically chosen and carefully implemented depending upon the situation at hand and the company's position relative to it.

The marketing mix concept relies on 4Ps as its key constituent (Product, Price, Place, and Promotion) and E. Jerome McCarthy (McCarthy1960) was the first person to suggest these four Ps. But with the advent of holistic marketing concept and the growth of online platforms, four more Ps have been added to the list, including People, Process, Programs,and Performance (Kotler). In this section, we would understand only the basic definitions of these 8 Ps. The strategic elements and applications of these 8Ps would be discussed in detail in the next chapter as a part of the ASCOR Strategy Phase.

Let us understand the definitions of the 8Ps of marketing mix as below:

(a) **Product**: A product is an item that satisfies what a consumer demands. Products can either be physically tangible (which can be handled and felt) or in the form of intangible services (without a physical presence). As discussed earlier, most products which are sold online assume a service orientation to them as a customer cannot touch and feel them and it is the service elements only that can differentiate a product from its online competition.

(b) **Price:** Simply put, it is the amount a customer pays for the product. But if we go deeper into the multiple considerations that go into pricing a product or service, we would see that pricing involves a lot of analysis and careful consideration of which price brackets would be suitable for a particular segment of consumers. And with the impact of cloud and pay-per content-based emerging digital models, pricing has become an even more crucial element in a highly competitive, per transaction-driven online environment.

(c) **Place:** It refers to the provision of the product where the customer finally accesses it. This element has also assumed prime importance with changing retailing trends wherein, earlier, customers used to visit the stores but in present times, online deliveries are being done at every possible location where the customer wants to receive the product. In the next chapter, we would also go deeper into the key business considerations which product placement brings up in terms of an impact on distribution and related logistics efforts.

(d) **Promotion:** It includes the type of communication which a firm uses to sell its products and services across multiple purchase channels. In a traditional marketing world, it was typically referred to the set of media and marketing activities but as we have seen in the last chapter, integrated market communications has had a major impact on how new digital channels, (based on the strengths and the potential impact they have on the customer receiving that promotion), are being utilized to communicate. Chapter 6 will cover the whole gamut of digital channels and communication techniques in detail.

(e) **People:** This is the first of the new set of 4 Ps representing modern marketing. According to Kotler, 'People' reflect internal marketing and the fact that employees are critical to marketing success. Also, it places an emphasis on looking at consumers more deeply than just looking at them as bodies consuming products and services. Essentially, it relates to the need of deep-set consumer data which helps understand the influencer community to market specifically to key digital personas.

(f) **Process**: It includes the creativity, discipline, and structure brought to marketing management in terms of a planned marketing and campaign process. It reflects the manner in which marketing as a discipline is changing from its traditional avatar (where objectives were not clearly defined and executed) to a much more process-driven and structured approach using technology and automation tools to drive efficiencies.

(g) **Programs**: It relates to consumer-directed activities which a firm organizes. This involves the set of all traditional and digital marketing activities which the marketer would run in parallel where each one would leverage the other to execute an integrated marketing program.

(h) **Performance:** The final addition to the 4 Ps is Performance which relates to capturing and measuring the range of possible outcome measures that have financial and non-financial implications (profitability as well as brand and customer equity) and those beyond the company itself (social responsibility, legal, ethical, and community related). It essentially means planning for and exhibiting not only business performance but also being seen as a company that has an impact on environment and society as a whole.

With an understanding of the 8Ps, we now have an idea about the key points of analysis which a company should undertake to see how they are presently performing and make specific adjustments when they enter the digital marketing arena. Specific implementation strategies related to each of these 8Ps would be discussed as we go through the rest of the ASCOR Digital Marketing framework elements.

We would now take a look at the second aspect of marketing mix which is the development of STP (Segmenting, Targeting, and Positioning) strategies post the 4P development.

Understanding STP Basics

STP is an acronym for three key marketing development and application concepts and stands for Segmenting, Targeting, and Positioning. The STP process demonstrates links between the overall market and how a company chooses to compete in that market. It is sometimes referred to as a process with segmentation being conducted first, followed by selection of one or more target markets, and finally, the implementation of market positioning. Let us understand each of the three concepts in more detail.

(a) **Segmentation:** It is defined as the process of splitting a market into smaller groups with similar product needs or identifiable characteristics, for the purpose of selecting appropriate target markets. Typical segmentation categories include demographic segmentation (age, income, marital status, education, family size, gender, occupation, geographical location, social status etc.), psychographic segmentation (brand preferences, price sensitivity, hobbies, lifestyle, service preferences, peer influence, etc.), and behavioral segmentation, also covered in detail in Chapter 3 (purchase history, shopping pattern and preferences, internet usage, information sources, etc.). With the use of technology and pattern recognition possible with digital marketing, the field of segmentation is getting sophisticated by the day which makes its application even more pertinent.

(b) **Targeting**: It refers to an organization's proactive selection of a suitable market segment (or segments) with the intention of heavily focusing the firm's marketing offers and activities towards this group of related consumers. Typically, if the marketer understands the customer segments deeply, he/she would be in a much better position to have a differentiated and focused targeting strategy depending on their key exhibited characteristics. In the present world of multiple audience segments across channels, it also becomes crucial for marketers to decide which channels to invest more and make efforts to be one-up on competition.

(c) **Positioning:** It is the target market's perception of the product's key benefits and features, related to the offerings of competitive products. Positioning exercise typically involves understanding target consumers, analyzing market/competition, and defining the competitive advantage and relevant attributes to successfully communicate and deliver the chosen position. The positioning a marketer decides for his/her brand should be strongly differentiated, credible while communicating, and should be relevant to the audience in terms of providing the perceived benefit over and above competition.

The concepts of STP and their execution are core to developing the overall digital marketing mix strategy and we would understand the application of these concepts in more depth in the next chapter on digital strategy formulation.

Let us now move on to the third key element of internal analysis—the resources mix.

Internal Resource Mapping

With an understanding of *offerings and market mix* elements, we would look at the third key element of internal analysis—Resource Mapping. A resource is defined as a source or supply from which benefit is derived or produced. Resources for any organization could be classified as follows (including tangible and intangible elements):

(a) **Input-driven resources:** materials, energy, natural resources

(b) **Economic resources:** land, capital, infrastructure

(c) **Human resources:** employees, contractors, third parties

(d) **Technology resources:** information, communication, storage systems

(e) **Intellectual resources:** brand capital, intellectual property, patents, and trademarks

(f) **Partner/intermediary resources:** resources which can be leveraged with the support of strong partners, specific associations/alliances, and tie-ups with key intermediary firms

In marketing, as in the case of other businesses, companies can utilize a mix of any of these elements at the right time to deliver outputs based on changing situations and trends. It is with the support of these resources that firms can create unique differentiators in the marketplace as compared to competition. For digital marketing, specifically, some of the intangible elements like brand capital and differentiated marketing techniques could act as crucial resources which can be leveraged quite effectively to make an impact. Some of these elements form a part of the competency mix, which is the last element we would cover for internal analysis.

With an understanding of basic resource elements and types, let us now see, how a company can benchmark its resources to know which of them are more strategic than others and which of them would stand the test of competition more effectively. To conduct this benchmarking exercise, we can make use of a popular framework which companies have applied to develop the best resource mix available for deployment. It is known as the VRIN Framework.

The VRIN Framework (Valuable, Rare, Inimitable, Non-Substitutable) derives its roots from the RBV (Resource-Based View) of viewing the firm and, in turn, developing its approach strategy. RBV theory postulates the firm to be a bundle of resources including assets, capabilities, organizational processes, firm's attributes, information, and knowledge. It believes that the firm can utilize a mix of these resources taking an inside-out approach as the starting point of the analysis of the internal environment of any organization.

The VRIN model originated from the thought that all the resources that an organization has, may not have strategic relevance. Only certain of those resources are capable of being an input to a value-creating strategy which will put the organization in a position of competitive advantage.

According to the VRIN model (Barney 1991), a firm should display four key attributes and only if these conditions hold can the firm sustain above average returns. These four elements are described as:

(a) **Valuable**: A resource must enable a firm to employ a value-creating strategy, by either outperforming its competitors or reducing its own weaknesses. Relevant in this perspective is that the transformation costs associated with the investment in the resource cannot be higher than the discounted future rents that flow out of the value-creating strategy.

(b) **Rare**: Resources drive competitive advantage only when they are relatively scarce. While a resource does not need to be unique to only one firm, it must not be widely available. The exact amount of rareness will vary by situation, but it must be uncommon enough to give a distinct advantage to the firms that have it. When comparing the rarity of a resource, it is essential to include not only current competitors but also other firms who could possibly enter the industry in future.

(c) **Inimitable:** A resource is termed to be inimitable, if it is controlled by only one firm. A resource can provide sustainable competitive advantage only if competitors are not able to duplicate this asset perfectly and lack the capability to obtain them. The best example in this case would be the development of intellectual property which the company has trademarked and is tough to replicate.

(d) **Non-substitutable:** Even if a resource is rare, potentially value-creating and imperfectly imitable, an equally important aspect is lack of substitutability. If competitors are able to counter the firm's value-creating strategy with a substitute, prices are driven down to really low levels which make the resulting economic profits negligible.

The VRIN characteristics mentioned are individually necessary, but not sufficient conditions for a sustained competitive advantage. Within the framework of the resource-based view, the chain is as strong as its weakest link and therefore requires the resource to display each of the four characteristics to be a possible source of a sustainable competitive advantage.

Most of the elements of the VRIN model are factors which if rigorously applied by companies to their resource set would result in unique differentiators also termed as internal competencies (which would be discussed in more detail as the last of the internal analysis elements). It is essential that the VRIN framework is iteratively applied to each of the key identified resources across key competitors so that a firm can keep perfecting their resource advantage and to bring it to a level which would be really difficult to imitate or substitute by any competitor.

With this understanding, let us move on to the last element of *internal analysis*.

Core Competencies Analysis

The development of core competencies falls in perfect order as the fourth element of internal analysis where present offerings have been developed, marketing mix defined, and internal resources analyzed for competitiveness. The outcome from the third component of internal analysis typically yields in identification of key capabilities of a firm from its resource set. But there is a difference between resources and capabilities which we shall address now.

Differences between Resources and Capabilities

Amit and Schoemaker (1993) made a key distinction of the encompassing construct called 'resources' and divided it into resources and capabilities. Resources are a stock of available factors that are owned or controlled by the organization, and capabilities are an organization's capacity to deploy resources.

Understanding Competitive Advantage and Core Competencies It is important to understand the reason for conducting a competency analysis which is primarily to gain competitive advantage. Competitive advantage occurs when an organization acquires or develops an attribute or combination of attributes that allows it to outperform its competitors. A competitive advantage can be attained if the current strategy is value-creating, and not currently being implemented by present or possible future competitors.

Although a competitive advantage has the ability to become sustainable, this is not necessarily the case. A competitive advantage is sustainable when the efforts by competitors to render the advantage have ceased. When the imitative actions come to an end without disrupting the firm's competitive advantage, the firm's strategy can be called sustainable. For a firm to manage sustainable competitive advantage over time, it needs to sustain its core competencies. Let us delve deeper to understand this concept.

Core competency as a management concept was introduced by C.K. Prahalad, Julian Kriviak, and Gary Hamel. It can be defined as a harmonized combination of multiple resources and skills that distinguish a firm in the marketplace. In their book *Competing for the Future*, Hamel and Prahalad suggested that business leaders view their organizations as a portfolio of competencies which should be shared across business units rather than being retained by small business units for their own benefit. A competency according to them is built and sustained over time and is a bundle of skills rather than a unique skill. It is this integration of skills that define a core competence.

A core competency, thus, is a bundle of skills that enable an organization to provide particular benefits to customers. Its not a product or service in itself rather it helps build such new offerings.

According to the authors, there are three tests to identify core competencies of a firm:

(a) **Relevance:** The competence must give the customer something that strongly influences him/her to choose a firm's product or service. If it does not, then it has no effect on competitive position and is not a core competence.

(b) **Difficulty of imitation**: The core competence should be difficult to imitate. This allows the firm to provide products that are better than competition. And, through continuous work to improve these skills, a company's competitive position can be sustained.

(c) **Breadth of application**: It should be something that opens up a good number of potential markets. If it only opens up a few small, niche markets, then success in these markets will not be enough to sustain significant growth.

Let us look at a few examples of how top companies develop unique core competencies and make use of them to develop new and even more differentiated offerings. The nearest example which would come to anyone's mind of the top two most innovative, classy, and yet differentiated companies in today's time is of Google and Apple. If we compare both, we would see a quite differentiated set of core competencies though each of them have targeted similar customers in the same period in history.

For Google, here are some of the key core competencies which it has developed over the years through a mix of skills and capabilities across product, design, marketing, technology, etc.

(a) **Search accuracy:** With its patented algorithms which could conduct millions of searches with much higher accuracy than competition, this was its first-mover advantage, a competency which it has still retained to its present day.

(b) **Design simplicity:** With just a plain textbox at the center, and much superior design across all of its digital products, design has been crucial to Google's success.

(c) **Querying speed**: The investment in setting up huge and expensive servers to make sure that search results appear the fastest on a click has been a very strong competency.

(d) **Aesthetic branding:** With a recognizable and vibrant logo to succinctly laid corporate values, to its hiring and employee care policies, Google has established itself as a brand with a great recall, owing much to its product set which is highly consumer centric.

(e) **Guided navigation concept:** When Google came across, it brought unique concepts like superior and guided web navigation, a competency mix which had never been thought of earlier. Also, the testing and execution of these concepts is what made the biggest difference as consumers could now expect flawless performance regularly.

(f) **Free of cost services:** With Google's market strategies of charging advertisers rather than consumers for its services, its pricing model has helped it gain prominent mindshare across a wide set of customers, a move which improved the positioning of its other consumer products too.

Similar to Google, Apple also had a first mover advantage in launching premium-end technology products which had no earlier precedence in their respective industries. Let us look at some of their evident core competencies.

(a) **Product innovation:** With the launch of industry-changing products across areas like computing, music, telecom, movies, graphics, Apple has showcased a unique approach to product innovation as its core competency.

(b) **User experience**: With design and user ease as its founding philosophies, Apple showed how superior user experience in itself can be a core competency for firms.

(c) **Technology competence**: Apart from product, incremental innovation in multiple technology areas and trade-marketing has been a unique differentiator.

(d) **Brand marketing:** The whole aura and unique marketing prowess displayed by Steve Jobs helped build a brand which marketed itself through credible word-of-mouth.

(e) **Premium positioning**: As opposed to Google, Apple's products have adopted the premium pricing strategy, a move which not only helped develop it as a premium category product but also became a core competency which was hard to emulate.

In both of the above examples we see that there are some distinct overlaps of key competency areas; it is actually the development, execution, and continuous enhancement of these unique skills which sustains competitive advantage and makes the 'core competency' difficult to imitate. With Google's multiple changes to its search algorithm throughout the year and with Apple's regular product launches, software upgrades, and new version launches of its operating systems, both the companies are able to maintain their distinct competitive elements.

With a knowledge of the concept of core-competencies emerging from a firm's resources to capabilities development towards building a set of differentiated skills, according to Hamel and Prahlad, a company needs to keep evaluating its core competencies by answering some of the questions below:

(a) Do customer's benefits revolve around these core competencies?

(b) How long could we dominate our business if we didn't control this competency?

(c) Does it provide access to multiple growth markets and help in developing new products and services?

(d) What future opportunities would we lose without it?

In this section, we have understood the concept of core competencies and their importance in developing truly differentiated businesses. It is crucial, as we have seen here, to identify and nurture core competencies in a strategic manner and also align digital marketing activities to portray these strengths and expertise areas uniquely for customer connect.

DIGITAL MARKETING OBJECTIVES PLANNING

With an understanding of the external and internal analysis components and their impact on the overall market and growth assessment, let us see how to conduct a *digital presence analysis* and define key digital marketing objectives through the *Objectives Planning exercise*.

Digital Presence Analysis

The external and internal analysis conducted in the last first two parts of this chapter is to support a company with all the necessary data points towards developing the right digital marketing objectives to serve the business needs and goals of the firm. For any large and established firm, these days, it's almost a foregone conclusion that they have to be present on key digital platforms not just for sales growth but also to keep up with emerging competition across the globe. But for a large set of companies which are small to medium businesses and even for individual,

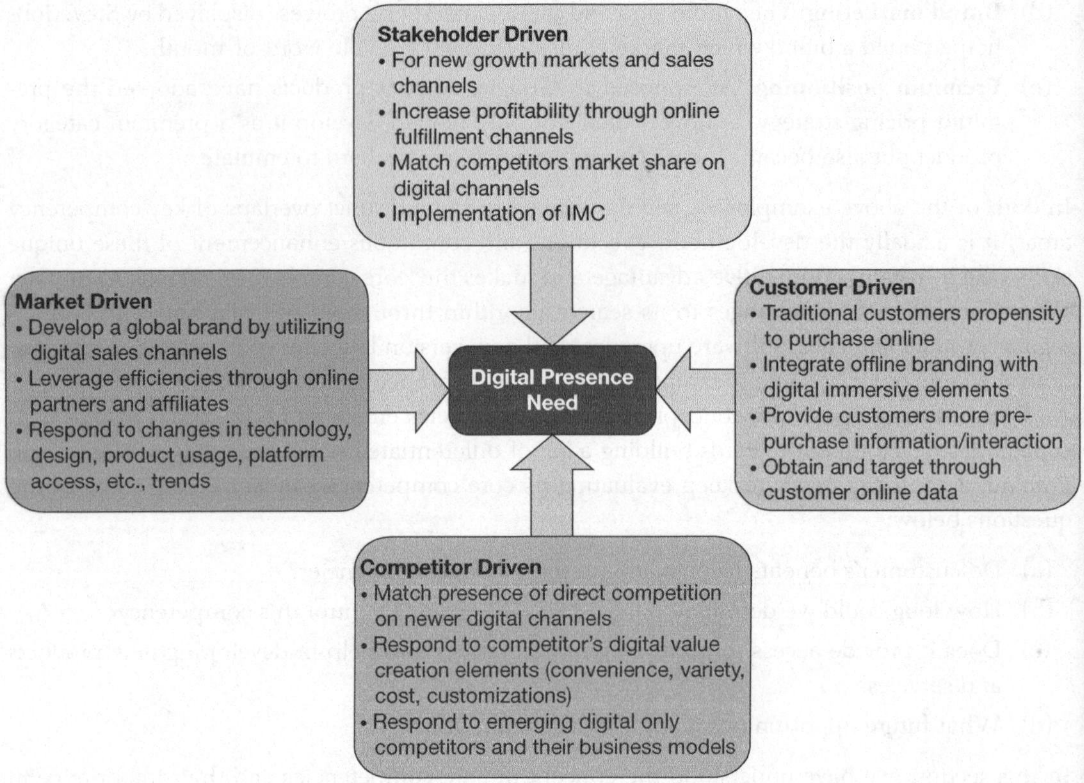

Figure 4.8 The Need for Digital Presence

government, NGO segments, they might still be in the contemplation stage of the kind of digital presence that is required for them to be competitive and how much of their budgets should be allocated to each digital marketing activity.

Fig. 4.8 showcases the four key drivers for any firm to consider its presence on digital platforms.

(a) **Stakeholder-driven needs:** It includes factors which are business/stakeholder-driven which necessitates a firm to move its product portfolio online.

- New growth markets and sales channels: Firms, year-on-year have pressures to meet increasing sales and other financial targets and also to move into newer growth markets.
- Increasing profitability through online fulfillment channels: With the help of digital fulfillment channels and reduction of intermediaries in the value chain, firms can reduce costs by shifting some percentage of their portfolio online.
- Matching competitor's market share on digital channels: Many a times, a stakeholder urges to match a rising competitor's growth; this results in the firm's move to develop newer digital channels.

- Implementation of IMC: With the growing need to utilize each key marketing channel for its benefit, presence on digital channels become imperative from an IMC (Integrated Marketing Communication) standpoint.

(b) **Market-driven needs:** As discussed in the last part on 'External Analysis' components, the external or market environment has a huge role to play in driving firms online. Key market-driven factors include:

- Developing a global brand by utilizing digital sales channels: With mature economies stagnating, there is a need for marketers to develop a global brand for higher sales and visibility through digital channel implementation.
- Leveraging efficiencies through online partners and affiliates: Through online partner and affiliate integration, many traditional companies have been able to leverage digital growth, without setting up their operations online.
- Responding to changes in technology, design, product usage, platform access, etc. trends: There are multiple other market-driven trends related to improved technologies, design implementations, product usage, new platform development trends, which necessitate the shift to digital channels.

(c) **Customer-driven needs:** The most immediate and relevant trends driving brands online are posed by customers themselves in the way their consumption patterns evolve. Key trends which are impacting firms in this area include:

- Traditional customer's propensity to purchase online: With most loyal customers who used to buy through traditional channels slowly embracing the digital revolution, it is important for brands to develop an integrated marketing strategy.
- Integrating offline branding with digital immersive elements: A lot of brand marketers understand the need to make use of the unique immersive elements which digital channels offer to traditional brands.
- Obtaining and targeting through customer online data: Marketers these days cannot miss the opportunities of obtaining deep personal data through all digital channels, integrating them and utilizing those online personas productively.

(d) **Competitor-driven needs:** Finally, it is competition too which drives brands to move towards digital channels. Key competitive factors include:

- Matching presence of direct competition on newer digital channels: With direct competitors moving online it becomes imperative for all types of companies to be present online for growth and mindshare capture.
- Responding to competitor's digital value creation elements (convenience, variety, cost, customization): As discussed in Chapter 2 section on Digital Value Elements, companies need to map and respond to new values being created by competition which in an integrated manner provides unique differentiation to customers.
- Responding to emerging digital only competitors and their business models: A new crop of digital intermediaries and apps is replacing a company's marketplace position and being digital is the only way firms can counter their moves and develop their present business models to suit digital channels.

Apart from the factors shared here, there are traditional firms which have already proactively placed themselves on the digital landscape to protect their market share and also leverage incremental revenues in the process. These companies have already analyzed the benefits of being digital and also reaped major benefits in terms of initial recall, better knowhow of digital technologies, stronger partnerships, and enhanced branding which is also impacting traditional sales objectives.

In the next section, we have shared a DPA (Digital Presence Analysis) Matrix which helps companies assess the extent of their digital presence to decide which digital marketing objectives they need to create and ensure that they develop related marketing strategies to implement and achieve those objectives.

Digital Presence Analysis Matrix

Before we discuss the topic of Digital Marketing Objectives creation, it is important for us to know how companies can decide the kind of objectives they should formulate which, in turn, depends on their extent of digital presence.

Digital presence is defined as the relative extent to which a company is present on digital channels in comparison to direct competition, based on comparison of key competitive factors. The data for such comparitive factors would typically be derived from a mix of external and internal factors (data points collected during the internal and external assessment stages described in the first two parts of this chapter).

Given below are some of the general factors which can be compared by a firm to its competition (similar to the VRIN framework shared in the earlier section) to judge their digital presence (see Fig. 4.9). It has to be noted that the comparison is a subjective one for the firm, as they would need to decide which key competitors would they want to compare themselves against, the chosen factors for comparison, and the veracity/validity of the data researched.

Key Competitive Comparision Factors

- Digital market share
- Digital channels presence
- Quality of web properties
- Digital sales
- Channel profitability
- Total digital customers
- Digital partner Tie-ups
- Daily purchases (overall including affiliates/partners)
- Social media followers
- Daily social mentions
- Comparision sites and analyst reviews
- Digital marketing spend RoI
- Brand perception and engagement
- Brand sentiment analysis
- Online value proposition
- Core competency analysis

Figure 4.9 Competitive Comparison Factors for Digital Presence

Post the analysis, once a firm has a broader assessment of where it stands in comparison to competition it would benefit from the DPA (Digital Presence Analysis) Matrix which is introduced next. This matrix would help provide the base for developing Digital Marketing objectives in the next section of this chapter.

The Digital Presence Analysis is a 2 × 2 matrix, which has been developed across two axes—Extent of Digital Presence and Market Standing wrt (with respect to) Competition. It has been developed with the earlier competitive comparison as the base and introduces four key states (in the form of matrices and a fifth state related to a new launch) through which the extent of digital presence of a firm can be established and used for digital marketing applications.

In the DPA Matrix (see Fig. 4.10), the X Axis is the Extent of Digital Presence, beginning from the left corner and depicting firms which are only traditionally led and without any inroads onto digital channels. As we move to the right, the extent of digital presence in the firm is the strongest. We have to remember that this extent of digital presence is relative to a specific firm within a particular industry section in relation to its direct competition and is not in any way absolute in nature (since the purpose is a classification and not arriving at a specific digital presence percentage figure).

In a similar manner, the Y axis is the firm's Market Standing w.r.t. Competition, which on the bottom corner depicts a firm which is either a market laggard in its specific industry sector (with regards to direct competition) or is a newly launched company. As we move up on the Y axis, the

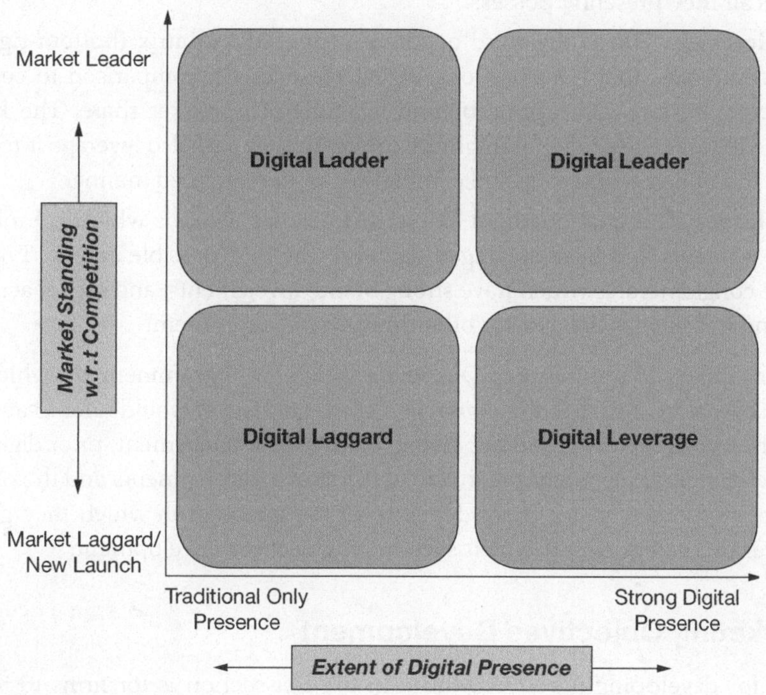

Figure 4.10 Digital Presence Analysis Matrix

highest point shows that the firm is a relative market leader in its particular segment with respect to its direct competition. As in the previous case, this is also absolute in nature.

Now let us understand the four key digital states which can also be called DLs (the initials of the fourth and the fifth one related to New Launch all begin by the letters D & L):

(a) **Digital laggard:** This is the first quadrant of the DPA Matrix (bottom-left) which relates to firms which have no or minimal digital presence and are lagging their respective market/industry segment wrt to direct competitors. The key characteristics of the digital laggard state is that the product/offerings mix for such firms mostly have an offline presence and the business/stakeholders have not made much (or half-hearted) efforts to be present on digital channels. This may or may not be the reason for them lagging wrt competition but surely these firms would need maximum planning and effort to start moving to digital platforms once they decide the need to do so.

(b) **Digital ladder:** The second quadrant of the DPA Matrix (top-left) would be the second state of the DPA matrix, wherein firms themselves are in a much better shape wrt competition (as they are market leaders across some key products), but they still do not have substantial digital presence. Since they typically would have a strong brand and a loyal customer set with good sales (as they are market leaders), it would be much easier for them (as compared to digital laggards) to start climbing the digital ladder, and in many ways for some products, they might already be present on digital platforms in a decent manner and can easily move up their digital presence with the investment potential and brand recall they presently possess.

(c) **Digital leverage:** This is the third quadrant of the DPA Matrix (bottom-right) and represents companies that have a strong digital presence (in comparison to competition in their sector) but are still lagging behind in terms of a market share. The key for them would be to utilize their digital might to grow it further and also leverage it to gain market share in the offline world to tackle completion in an integrated manner.

(d) **Digital leader:** The final quadrant (top-right) belongs to firms which are market leaders in their segments and have leveraged digital to the best possible extent. Typically, these are large conglomerates which have strong brand, investments, and digital acumen behind them, and it is always difficult for other firms to outsmart them.

With an understanding of the four key DLs, there is one more prominent DL which completes the DPA Matrix Analysis which is the digital launch. *Digital launch* would refer to any firm which is newly launched in its segment, and depending upon their management, prior digital expertise, and their entry segment, they might fall in any of the above four segments and the objectives and strategy development exercise for them depends on the quadrant in which they get launched. We would cover this category in the next section on objectives development.

Digital Marketing Objectives Development

The intention for developing the DPA Matrix in the last section is for firms to identify their digital presence, strengths, and weaknesses towards developing high-level Digital Marketing

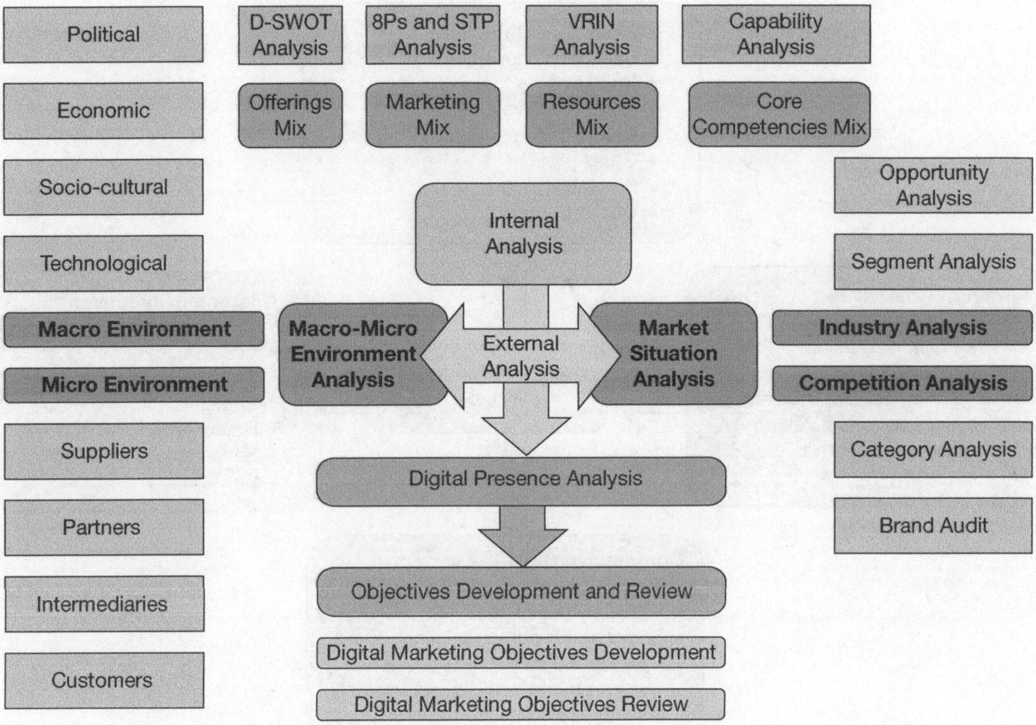

Figure 4.11 Assessment Elements Elaboration

Objectives. Typically, these objectives, set on a yearly basis, during the yearly marketing plan creation are followed, reviewed, and revised even at a weekly level to ensure that firms are on track.

In this section, we shall move on to the last element of the Assessment Phase which is the Digital Marketing Objectives Development.

In Fig. 4.11, we can see that after covering the elements of external and internal analysis, we have gained sufficient data to help firms analyze their present digital state. In this section, we shall look at elaborating the last element of the assessment stage which involves developing digital marketing objectives and a framework to review these high-end objectives on a regular basis.

SMART Objectives Creation

Objectives creation as an exercise has to be clear, rigorous, and at the same time,achievable in the time-frame it has been set to achieve. The most widely used framework across management circles for objectives creation is commonly attributed to Peter Drucker in his "management by objectives" concept which is also termed as the SMART criteria. The first known use of the term occurs in the November 1981 issue of *Management Review* by George T. Doran which elaborates this acronym as follows:

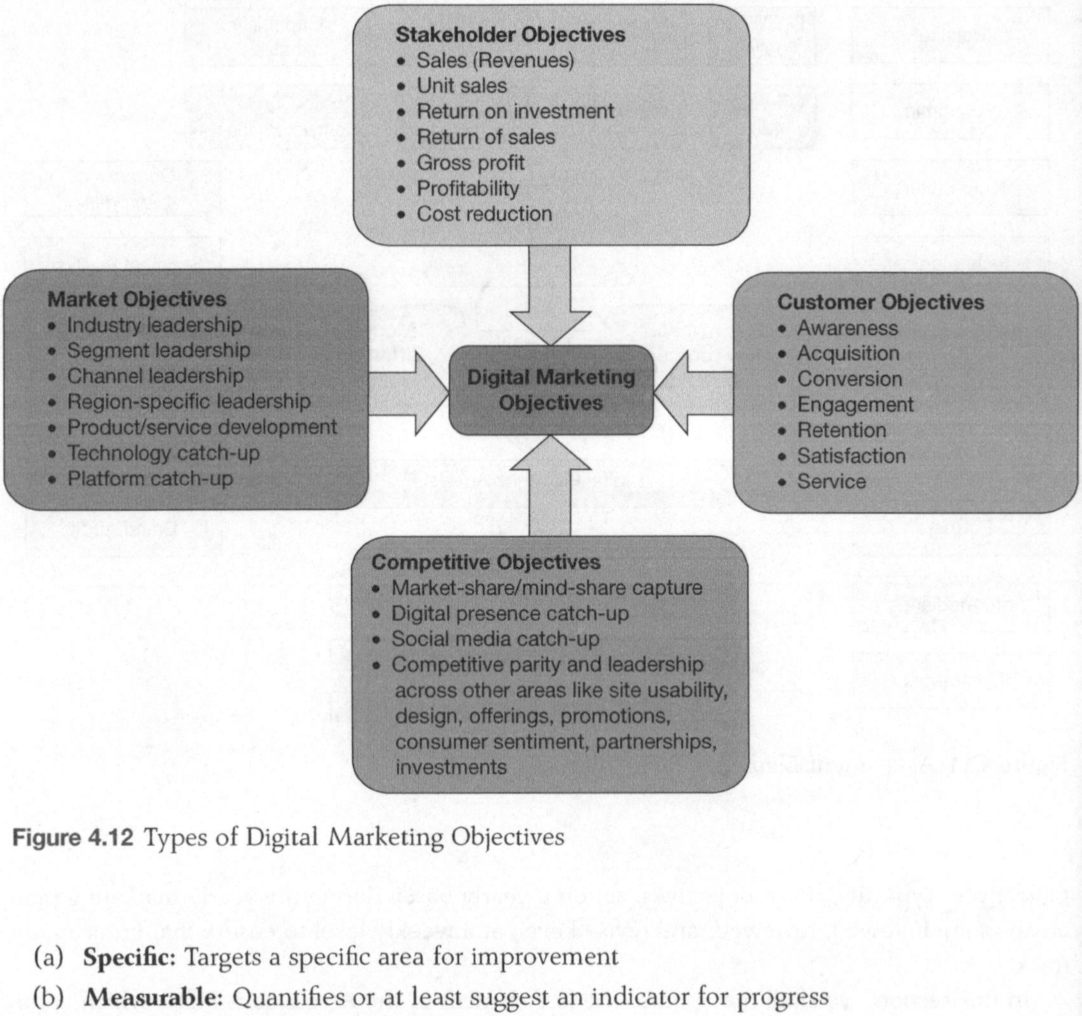

Figure 4.12 Types of Digital Marketing Objectives

(a) **Specific:** Targets a specific area for improvement

(b) **Measurable:** Quantifies or at least suggest an indicator for progress

(c) **Assignable:** Specifies who will do it

(d) **Realistic:** States what results can realistically be achieved, given the available resources

(e) **Time-related:** Specifies when the results can be achieved

With an introduction to the SMART criteria as above, let us now understand the key types of digital marketing objectives, which firms set for themselves as depicted in Fig. 4.12. It has to be kept in mind that the high-level objectives shared and discussed below do not cover the objective setting and review for the other ASCOR stages and only involves the initial objective-setting exercise.

Fig. 4.12 has the same four entities as shared earlier and lists the key objectives which the firm can set against each of them.

(a) **Stakeholder-based objectives:** These typically are objectives related to financial performance of a firm's marketing operations. The most prominent of them include:

- Sales (revenues): Overall digital revenue objectives for the firm and key brands
- Unit sales: Relates to objectives of selling certain units across key channels
- Return on investment: Measures performance against key investment areas
- Return on sales: Measures firm's operational efficiency calculated as = *Net Income (Before Interest and Tax) divided by Sales*
- Gross profit: Defined as company's residual profit calculated as = *Revenue after selling a product or service minus its cost of goods sold*
- Net profit: Calculated as *Sales Revenue Minus Total Costs*
- Cost reduction: Objectives for reducing cost by being present on digital channels

(b) **Market-based objectives:** These objectives are to be developed in relation to the specific market, category, or region where the brand operates. Important ones include:
- Industry/segment leadership: Leadership across a specific industry or segment
- Channel leadership: Leadership across a specific channel of sales
- Regional leadership: Leadership across a specific region of operation
- Product/service development: *Develop a product* or service on digital channels
- Technology catch-up: Match company's technology to important external technology shifts/trends
- New platform catch-up: Develop firm's operations across new/emerging platforms in the market

(c) **Customer-based objectives:** These objectives relate to developing target customer segments and marketing profitably to them. Key sample objectives include:
- Awareness: Objectives related to improving awareness on digital channels
- Acquisition: Develop targets for new online customer acquisition related to a particular segment, demographic, or consumption type
- Conversion: Related to increase of conversion rate or increase in sales order rate, average value of sales order or sales order increase for a particular segment
- Engagement: Intangible element relating to increase in engagement levels
- Retention: Objectives for new online customer retention, increase in repeat purchase, percentage of customers utilizing loyalty points or coupons for further purchases
- Satisfaction: Improvement of consumer satisfaction rates including turnaround time, first-time complaint resolution, average handling time for customer call
- Service: Improvement in overall service, fulfillment, customization factors
- Credibility: Develop objectives for building credibility, improving trust, etc.

(d) **Competition-based objectives:** Involves objectives set to counter or pre-empt direct competition to remain one-up in comparison. Key objectives in this area include:
- Market-share/Mind-share capture: Objectives related to increasing market share against competition or improving mind share of a brand across a segment
- Digital presence catch-up: Involves set of combined objectives to catch up to the digital presence of a competitor who is the market leader in the same segment

- Social media catch-up: Objectives to develop similar social mentions, fans, engagement, posting rates, positive sentiment as top competitors
- Competitive parity and leadership across other areas like site usability, design, offerings, promotions, partnerships: Includes objectives for catching up with key competitors and gaining leadership position in other competitive areas

With a listing of typical objectives across four key entities, we would now see how firms across the four digital states (as discussed in the last section) can set up objectives based on their digital presence and market share to rise to a level better than where they are at present.

(a) **Digital laggard:** Some of the digital objectives which firms in this state typically set are:
- Stakeholder objectives:
  - Increase overall digital revenue by 30 per cent in the next three years
  - Double per piece sales of their product across mid-tier segment X
- Market objectives:
  - Develop entry strategies for getting to third position in the largest digital market segment for firm's product (choosing the top offline product)
- Customer objectives:
  - Improving awareness of brand across top three digital channels for the product by at least 50 per cent more than present
  - Increase brand engagement rates by 30 per cent for key products across channels and e-commerce platforms where the brand is already present
- Competitive objectives:
  - Increase overall market share by 5 per cent across all combined digital channels where competition is present

(b) **Digital ladder:** Typical digital objectives for this state include:
- Stakeholder objectives:
  - Transfer 20 per cent of present offline sales to digital channels with minimum 25 per cent profitability
  - Set up a global online sales channel for an established brand offline with sales target of ₹10 lakh in the first six months
- Market objectives:
  - Already a segment leader in offline sales, the objective is to develop presence across two online channels to gather a market leader position in the next one year alongwith improving margins by 10 percentage points
- Customer objectives:
  - Support transition of 30 per cent of present offline loyal customers to present digital channels in the next two years
  - Improving re-purchase levels of new customers across all digital channels by 20 per cent within three months of the first buy

- Competitive objectives:
    - ➤ Develop online partnerships with at least five major online only e-commerce players to improve digital sales by 20 per cent

(c) **Digital leverage:** Key business objectives for firms in this digital state include:

- Stakeholder objectives:
    - ➤ Improve return on investment by 10 per cent in the next one year
    - ➤ Increase gross profit margin for top two channels by at least 20 per cent
- Market objectives:
    - ➤ Replicate success elements across a particular channel (where the brand is already leveraged) to a new upcoming channel to reach leadership
- Customer objectives:
    - ➤ Improve site conversions on an average by 2.5 per cent across top three firm-owned digital channels
    - ➤ Develop an emerging digital channel to obtain 20 per cent of all revenues from it in the next two years
- Competitive objectives:
    - ➤ Develop social media presence across key social channels to create a fan base of 1 million in the next two years and engagement rates of more than 20 per cent through posts and positive sentiment comments each month

(d) **Digital leader:** With the firm already in a leading digital position, here are the typical objectives developed in this state:

- Stakeholder objectives:
    - ➤ Reduce operational costs by 10 per cent by utilizing marketing automation
    - ➤ Increase net profit across 30–44 years age segment, the most growing segment, by 20 per cent
- Market objectives:
    - ➤ Increase revenue by at least 10 per cent across key digital channels by investing in new technology and automation platforms
- Customer objectives:
    - ➤ Improve CSAT (Customer Satisfaction Rates) across all top digital channels by 5 per cent in the next six months
    - ➤ Increase credibility of conversations by improving FCR (First time call resolutions) by 10 per cent in the next three months
- Competitive objectives:
    - ➤ Improvization of site design and user-experience-related factors to increase web visits by new prospects by 20 per cent and average site engagement time by 20 minutes per customer in the next six months

The *digital launch* stage in which a new brand launch could relate to any of the four states depending on firm's management, prior digital expertise, entry segment, investment figures, etc., the digital objectives would be similar to the state in which they are launched. If very low digital impetus is present and the firm has low brand recognition and market share in their target segment, then the objectives will be similar to the digital laggard state. If the same low market share brand is launched with a strong digital investment, its key objectives would be set similar to the digital leverage state.

Important thing to note here is that at this stage we are not defining the strategy which each firm should adopt depending on their digital state but only the high-level digital marketing objectives which they should develop. Other secondary or tactical objectives for each sub-stage would be developed once the strategy has been finalized for the firm respective to the situation at hand. This would be discussed in detail in the next chapter on strategy development.

For now, let us only be concerned about the creation of these digital objectives, as shared in the last section, and how firms can review these objectives once they are set. The review for each of the tactical objectives across the conversion funnel specific to target customer segments and digital channels would also be taken up in upcoming chapters.

Digital Marketing Objectives Review

Post setting up the high-level digital objectives, a firm in one of the digital presence states, also needs to create in a parallel a sound 'digital objectives review plan' and adhere by it on a regular basis to measure progress. A typical *marketing objectives review* consists of activities that involve monitoring, evaluating, and controlling marketing activities continuously. According to Philip Kotler, there are four types of marketing controls needed by companies to monitor and review their marketing activities:

(a) Annual plan control
(b) Profitability control
(c) Efficiency control
(d) Strategic control

Let us understand these four control types specifically for digital marketing objectives:

(a) **Annual plan control:** It involves reviews to ensure that firms achieve the targets set for sales, market share, and other such financial goals set up across the key digital channels. This is conducted through a four-step management by objectives process which includes:
- Setting monthly or quarterly goals
- Monitoring the digital performance
- Determining causes for key performance deviations
- Develop rectifying actions to be back on course

(b) **Profitability control:** It involves understanding the digital channels where the company is making profits and those where it is losing out. Profitability is measured across products, territories, customer segments, and business to business (B2B) channels. The company has to follow similar profitability models as it does for traditional sales to ensure that they are not investing in assets and platforms which are not profitable.

(c) **Efficiency control:** Post annual plan and profitability control, marketers have a much better idea on how best they can improve spending and allocate resources and efforts to channels which might yield them more efficient results. This would include performing a rigorous financial analysis, optimally re-allocating budgets, measuring channel and communication efficiencies, and revising promotional budgets.

(d) **Strategic control:** It involves periodically re-assessing a firm's strategic approach through market effectiveness reviews, strategic re-orientation, operation efficiency analysis, and digital marketing audits across all key products and markets.

Apart from these high-level objectives review, we would also see in the upcoming chapters how firms are involved with tactical, campaign, and sub-process specific reviews at each small stage of the digital marketing process, thus, supporting the overall marketing objectives.

PRACTICAL EXERCISE

Market or Industry Trend Assessment

Key Objective To assess the latest trends across a specific market or industry for single or multiple product categories by researching global as well as Indian websites and reports.

Project Brief You are the brand manager for a leading international FMCG firm (with a multi-product category portfolio) planning an entry into India. Thus, you are required to research the latest market trends across FMCG categories to decide on the best product-mix for your brand's launch.

Which websites or reports would you utilize to gather the ecosystem trends to assess market potential and audience receptiveness for the products? Please review the top research sources and share an analysis based on observed market or FMCG industry insights.

Execution Following are some of the prominent methods to gauge the overall market and specific industry insights:

(a) **Reviewing Overall Market Trends:** Understanding the key global and Indian trends impacting the market landscape is crucial to execute market analysis. One of the best sources to regularly review key areas impacting the ecosystem is to follow latest "Google Trends" and "Think with Google" blogs as they provide the finest research and opinion pieces on key market trends. Google News shares comprehensive, up-to-date news coverage, aggregated from sources across the world, while Think with Google not only provides global insights but also India specific articles, infographics, and analysis on a month-on-month basis.

(b) **Searching Key Industry Statistics:** Apart from qualitative analysis, a marketing team also needs quantitative inputs to qualify their analysis and create market projections for each brand. Some of the key websites that offer relevant and up-to-date graphs and statistics include www.Statista.com and www.DazeInfo.com.

(c) **Following Global Industry Trends:** There are several great resources on the internet, and they provide excellent industry reports that you may scan for industry insights on specific product categories. Some of the prominent ones include:

- GfK Insights Blog
- Mintel Blog
- GlobalWebIndex
- Experian
- WARC

(d) **Gauging India-Specific Trends:** Apart from global blogs, there are some very useful websites on India-specific trends that provide latest information and regular reports on Indian market trends. Here are some of the best websites to follow for your research:

- www.ibef.org
- www.nasscom.in
- www.economictimes.com
- www.euromonitor.com/india
- www.octaneresearch.in

(e) **Reviewing Reports of Top Consulting Firms:** Another important source of changing market trends can be found in regular trend reports published by top consulting firms such as KPMG, Deloitte, Accenture, PWC, and EY. These reports are published quite regularly and they highlight India specific insights across multiple areas including digital marketing, technology, media, consumer behavior, platforms, etc.

(f) **Keeping track of top Indian Publications:** Lastly, publications like the BusinessWorld come up with their regular edition of the BW Marketing Whitebook, which is a compendium of overall digital and marketing statistics in India providing a detailed analysis of emerging trends across the Indian marketing landscape.

Developing a view of the Indian digital and marketing ecosystem and changing trends is crucial for digital marketers to have a broader understanding of not only newer areas impacting the marketing arena, but also the way traditional approaches are changing their course. This market assessment exercise is crucial to gain prowess in developing a comprehensive idea of the changing digital marketing landscape. It is important to share your market insights research with other students or fellow marketers to review how they attempt an ecosystem analysis for similar products or markets with varying insights.

CHAPTER SUMMARY

- **Part 1:** We started with developing a basic understanding of marketing strategy and looked at scenarios which impact traditional firms to develop digital specific strategies. Next, we looked at key assessment phase elements, including external, internal, and digital presence analysis along with objectives, definition, and review. The final two sections of Part 1 detailed the two key Assessment Phase elements of Macro-Micro Environment Analysis and Market Situation Analysis to understand their underlying components and the type of research and market analysis involved.

- **Part 2:** The section detailed the four key internal analysis elements and application of underlying frameworks to support their analysis. We had a look at how a customized D-SWOT framework and the 8Ps+STP Analysis help to develop the offerings and marketing mix. Further, we understood the development of VRIN Framework which helps compare the resource mix of a firm as a competitive advantage. Finally, through the examples of Google and Apple, we saw how firms can identify and develop their core competencies through a mix of skills and capabilities across product, design, marketing, and technology.
- **Part 3**: In this last part of the chapter, we looked at the four key areas which drive the need for a digital presence (stakeholder, market, customer, competition) and how external and internal analysis components, once researched and analyzed (in the earlier part), can help firms understand to which of the four key digital presence states they presently belong, and help them develop their high-level digital marketing objectives accordingly. Finally, we also covered how a digital firm can apply a marketing review framework to regularly monitor, control, and revise their digital marketing objectives.

REVIEW QUESTIONS

1. Explain five key differences in marketing strategy which occurred with the advent of digital media.
2. Compare and contrast three different scenarios in the chapter which showcase how digital strategy supports and extends traditional marketing strategy.
3. Explain at a high level the four key elements of the ASCOR Assessment Phase.
4. What is PEST? Describe these four key elements of Macro Environment Analysis.
5. What are the key micro-environment impact factors? Explain the factors in detail.
6. Explain the two key components of Market Situation Analysis and their key elements in detail.
7. What are the four major types of Internal Analysis of the ASCOR Assessment Phase? Explain two of them in detail.
8. What is D-SWOT? Explain the key elements of D-SWOT model in detail.
9. What are the 8Ps of Marketing Mix analysis? Name the 8Ps and explain five of them in detail.
10. How would you classify resources for any organization? Explain in detail the VRIN Model.
11. Explain the concept of Core Competency. Mention the three tests through which the core competencies of a firm can be identified. Explain the concept using the example of Google/Apple.
12. Which are the four key drivers for any firm to consider its presence on digital platforms? Explain any one of them in detail.
13. What do we mean by Digital Presence. Name at least six Competitive Comparison Factors for Digital Presence.

14. Explain the Digital Presence Analysis Matrix. Describe the four key Digital States of the Matrix.
15. Explain the SMART Objectives acronym for Digital Marketing Objective Development? Take up one of the four Digital Marketing Objectives Types to detail typical Objectives.
16. Which are the four types of marketing controls needed by companies to monitor and review their marketing activities as per Philip Kotler (*Marketing Management*, Millennium Edition)? Please explain two of them.

DIGITAL APPLICATION EXERCISES

1. Think of any traditional Indian brand and map it to any one of the three scenarios for Digital Strategy Inclusion. Lay out all the ways in which digital strategy can support marketers to enhance the output of their overall marketing spend.
2. Develop a Macro-Micro Environment analysis for any traditional industry sector moving to digital platforms like Healthtech, Fintech, 3D Manufacturing, etc.
3. Analyze the emerging Home Food Delivery sector in India by picking up few of the top brands (FRSH, Joocy, Inner Chef, etc.) visiting their websites and applying the Market Situation Analysis for them.
4. SimpliLearn.com is one of the top online educational learning sites today. Execute a D-SWOT analysis to compare it with its key competitors in the marketplace.
5. Apply the 8Ps of Marketing Mix analysis to MobiKwik, one of India's top mobile payments firm. Explain the key initiatives they have taken to implement four more Ps for their digital marketing post India's demonetization exercise.
6. Visit Micromaxinfo.com, one of India's top mobile brands and apply the VRIN model to describe the key resources which provide a strategic digital advantage.
7. Pick up any SMB local firm around you (a bakery, local garage shop, kirana store) to contemplate and share the key digital drivers for the firm to be present on digital platforms (owned, earned or paid).
8. Search online for three firms from any three different sectors in India and based on your analysis decide where they would lie on the Digital Presence Analysis Matrix.
9. Pick up any one of the four digital states to explain how companies can set up objectives based on their digital presence and market share.

CHAPTER 5

Digital Marketing Strategy Definition

LEARNING OBJECTIVES

After studying this chapter, you will be able to:

- Understand the key concepts of developing strategy for digital business and the emerging business structures
- Analyze the core competencies of a firm and how they can be aligned with changing value functions to redefine a firm's OVP (Online Value Proposition)
- Understand the customer development strategy and concepts of STP2.0 Framework
- Define the digital marketing mix and the 4 extended Ps of Digital Marketing
- Plan the digital marketing strategy roadmap, its four key stages and their elements
- Understand the 6S Digital Marketing Implementation Stages and PLC (Product Life Cycle) Stages in the context of Digital Marketing

CASE STUDY Twitter India: *Working towards zero rifts and monetization*

US-based social media giant Twitter entered the Indian market in 2006 and has been growing ever since. Twitter has always seen India as one of the biggest social media markets for their business and has tried various strategies to reach the Indian masses.

As per Statista, Twitter India had 6.83 million users in 2017, and this number has increased subsequently with every passing year. As of 2021, Twitter India had 25.77 million users (4 times the number of users in 2017). The company has been successful in grabbing market share across Tier II and Tier III city users. As for supporting Indian marketers, Twitter India managed to attain a sharp decrease in cost per engagement (which is what advertisers would pay) by taking it down by 86 per cent, which means that advertisers are getting far more return on investment (ROI) and impact with their limited budgets.

Setting aside their user growth trends, Twitter India can still widen its reach when it comes to grabbing market share. As of April 2019, Twitter India held 2.2 per cent share of the social media market. Twitter faces competition from popular social media platforms because of their strong branding, easy-to-follow features, and quick loading of images and videos.

In 2017, Twitter launched 'Twitter Lite' to make its application more compatible with smartphones, which performed well in the Indian marketplace and strengthened their user base. Higher traction was also observed across cricket, political, and entertainment sections. Twitter India also collaborated with Vodafone India to offer live cricket updates to users. This 'T20 cricket' strategy worked well for Twitter India. They also partnered with Cricbuzz and ESPN Cricinfo to make further inroads into the Indian market. In 2021, Twitter India collaborated with Snapchat and Daily Hunt to increase their user base. The execution involved partner apps introducing a dedicated tab called 'Twitter Moments India' to showcase curated tweets pertaining to news and other events. Additionally, they also signed 16 new partners in the digital content space (e.g., Bloomberg, BuzzFeed, etc.) to bring in premium live content.

In 2020, Twitter witnessed dramatic growth, possibly because of the COVID-19 pandemic. It brought global features like Topics and Twitter Fleets to the Indian market. Topics lets visitors follow specific subjects of their interest and allows them to see additional content on these subjects on their timeline. Fleets are self-disappearing tweets that vanish in 24 hours and do not have retweets, public comments, or even likes. India was among the first markets after Brazil to get the new feature. After it was run for a year in Aug 2021, curtains were put to the service because the tool wasn't as widely used as the company hoped.

In early 2021, Indian social media saw a massive outrage due to the farmer's protest. In the light of this, the Indian government issued new IT regulations that every social media platform had to comply with to continue their operations in India. Although apprehensive at first, Twitter India complied and adhered to the regulations to operate in the Indian market. They are also improving their relations with the government through their support for 'Made in India' and other start-up initiatives.

Twitter is generally used as a medium for news, and every top news story breaks out on Twitter first. Today, Indians share both news and outrage on Twitter and it requires minimal time to get trending on the platform. It is expected that Twitter India will grow more in the upcoming years, with Statista forecasts indicating that Twitter India users will grow up to 43.53 million by 2025. However, this will be possible only if Twitter India ends its regular strife with the Indian Government and works towards achieving a cordial, synchronised working relationship with them. It also needs to work a lot more to strengthen its monetisation models to get a larger pie of the Indian media's promotional spend.

DIGITAL MARKETING STRATEGY GROUNDWORK

In this second chapter on Digital Marketing Strategy Development, we would apply the concepts learnt in the last chapter on Digital Market Assessment Phase to develop an understanding of how marketers can use the information collected in the first ASCOR Framework Phase to develop its digital marketing mix and program.

In the first part of this chapter, we will develop a basic background of the most applied strategy models historically and the way digital strategy is shaping up with the intrusion of new marketplace disruptors. We will then look at the way in which firms that plan to develop digital market strategies and create relevant Online Value Propositions (OVPs) should develop their core competencies online. The last section of this part mentions about the process of digital strategy creation by delving deeper into the concepts of customer development strategy and segmentation, targeting, and positioning (STP) elements.

Understanding Digital Business Strategy

Strategy and strategic thinking have been one of the most prominent and widely used terminologies in the management context, though their origins go back to war times and involve developing a high-level plan to achieve one or more goals under conditions of uncertainty.

By uncertainty in the business context, we mean the set of those conditions and factors which impact the company in its external environment and cause them to allocate and think through their overall plan of action in light of their internal resources and capabilities. This concept is even more applicable (as we shall see across this chapter) since the impacts of the digital medium on marketing strategy have been immense, varied, and not easy to map and attribute. For this reason, let us first understand the basics of business strategy as defined in the texts on strategic management to understand its digital nature, and finally, create a roadmap for digital marketing strategy.

Strategic management, by definition, involves the formulation and implementation of major goals and initiatives taken by a company's top management on behalf of owners, based on consideration of resources and an assessment of the internal and external environments in which the organization competes. If we read through it carefully, we have actually covered most of the important stand-out elements of this definition in the last chapter. Let us understand some of the key concepts and frameworks which drive and define strategic management.

The concepts of strategy started to be applied to businesses around the 1960s when senior executives were experiencing increasing difficulty in coordinating decisions and maintaining control of companies that were growing in size and complexity. Before that period, strategy was looked upon more as corporate planning and financial budgeting rather than developing long-term strategies to ensure corporate survival and growth.

By the mid-1960s most large US and European companies had developed corporate planning departments. The 1970s saw an emphasis on diversification and portfolio planning. The 1980s and 1990s were characterized by a focus on core competencies and the development of less analytic, more people-oriented approaches to management. The biggest change though which happened was the shift from a product focus to marketing focus and how the customer became the driving force behind business decisions.

Although there is much literature available on strategy as a concept and how it can be applied, we would look at those concepts and frameworks which relate to digital more closely and would support a firm's digital marketing strategies. Two of the most widely used strategy frameworks (which have also been covered in the earlier chapters) include the SWOT Model and Michael Porter's Value Chain analysis. Porter who is considered to be the leading authority on competitive strategy has contributed to multiple strategy frameworks including:

(a) **Modern portfolio theory:** Talks about corporation as a portfolio of business units, with each unit plotted graphically based on market share and industry growth rate.
(b) **Porter's Five Force analysis:** A framework for analyzing the profitability of industries and how those profits are divided among the participants. The framework involves the bargaining power of buyers and suppliers, threat of new entrants, availability of substitute products, and the competitive rivalry of firms in the industry.
(c) **Porter's generic strategies:** Porter shared that there are three generic strategies—cost leadership, differentiation, and focus—and a company must choose only one of these three or risk wasting precious resources.

Students of basic marketing texts would have gone through these concepts as they have been applied as standard marketing frameworks for years now. Though most of Porter's aforementioned strategies still hold true and are relevant to this day, we believe that with the trends impacting a firm on the digital front, each of the major impact elements—stakeholder, market, customer, and competitor (discussed in the last chapter on Digital Presence Analysis)—is causing formulation of additional frameworks specific to digital marketing.

To develop some of these digital-specific frameworks, we would be using Porter's key concepts of market share, market growth, and competitive differentiation to help firms map disruptive elements and track emerging digital business structures. For example, in developing the 'Digital Presence Analysis Matrix' in Chapter 4, we have already included the concept of market share to extend it to businesses moving towards the digital platform. The deeper we go into further sections, the more we would realize how in the digital world firms need to not only manage and map market leaders and challengers but also guard themselves against low-cost innovators who have been able to completely usurp the traditional business strategies of firms.

Digital Factors Impacting Business Strategy

To understand and provide the context on the factors impacting a firm's strategy development for digital platforms, we would use the same mix of Digital Presence Drivers—stakeholder, market, customer, and competitor.

In Fig. 5.1, the intent is to compare and contrast how sub-elements of each key external factor have been impacted by digital strategy and have changed over the years in a highly customer-driven direction.

(a) **Stakeholder-driven factors:** It includes impact of factors which are most important to stakeholders and how they are being measured differently across digital businesses. Key example areas include:

- *Revenue targets → Customer acquisition targets:* For traditional businesses, it has always been revenue targets which held topmost importance, but with revenue on the digital front being directly related to how much is paid per prospect for acquisition (and the final revenue obtained per conversion), customer acquisition targets have become far more important to measure than just revenue.
- *Firm investment driven → Funding driven:* Even a decade ago, firms typically used to invest their cash surplus into newer investments, but now with the rise of low-cost cloud-based business models and much higher prevalence of investor-funded projects, the way business sustenance and growth is measured has altered in a big way.

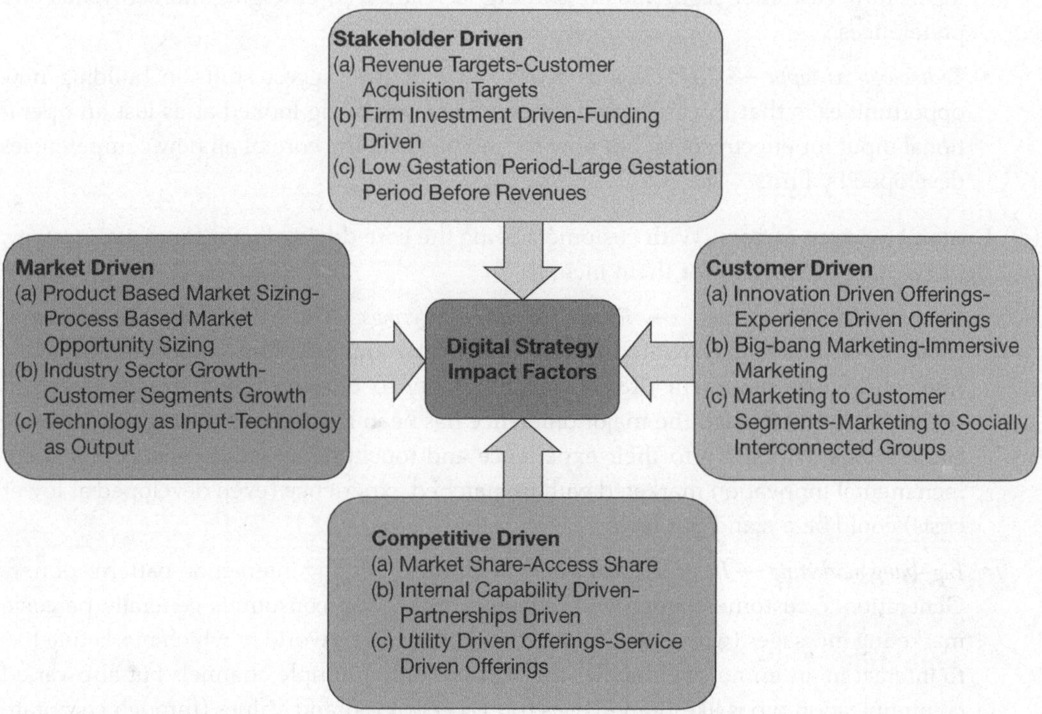

Figure 5.1 Digital Strategy Impact Factors

- *Low gestation period → Large gestation period before revenues*: In continuation with the impact of funding, there is also a complete shift in the way new firms and their investor communities look at business returns. In earlier times, stakeholders offered low gestation periods for incubation and new products were expected to yield revenues much quicker as it was the firm's own money at stake, but now we see examples of new-age digital firms like Facebook and Twitter which took a long time before they yielded any viable revenues.

(b) **Market-driven factors:** The overall structure of digital markets, its operations, and changing trends lend itself to factors which are quite unique to this space.

- *Product-based market sizing → Process-based opportunity sizing:* One of the bigger differences between how market opportunities are identified and developed in offline and digital mode is how a product starts to morph itself into service elements with newer digital offerings created by picking process-flow-related issues and converting the opportunities into service-oriented products. We would take a deeper look into this in the next two sections.
- *Industry sector growth → Customer segments growth*: Earlier marketers used to look at their presence across multiple industry segments and their market share and growth in them. This is now changing rapidly with firms following their consumer set and looking at how customer segments are shifting in relation to emerging market trends and preferences.
- *Technology as input → Technology as output*: One of the biggest shifts in building new opportunities is that in earlier times technology was being looked at as just an operational input for effectiveness, but now technology is at the core of all new competencies developed by firms.

(c) **Customer-driven factors:** With customers being the core driving factor for digital strategy, the key change elements for them include:

- *Innovation-driven offerings → Experience-driven offerings:* The emphasis on customer centricity was normally related to how much investment a firm could pump into its research and development (R&D) and the ability to develop innovative products. In the digital world though the major difference has been that consumers care much more about elements relating to their experience and touchpoints with products. For them incremental innovation marketed with unmatched experience (even developed at lower costs) could be a stand-out factor.
- *Big–bang marketing → Immersive marketing:* With the emerging interaction patterns of new Generation Y customers along with changes in the way consumers generally perceive marketing messages (with a bit of skepticism), we are in a world in which marketing has to interact in an immersive manner through not only multiple channels but also varied communication types like Brand Pages (on Facebook), Brand Values (through corporate blog), Brand Imagery (through Twitter posts), Brand Connect (through e-mail), and should relate at a much personal level than before.

- *Marketing to customer segments → Marketing to socially interconnected groups:* On the same lines as the factor shared earlier, marketers of the present times need to understand their consumers not just as a segment, but also as a socially active and interconnected group to which word-of-mouth matters much more than before. This is because of the democratic platforms being made available through technology and the openness of people to share their experiences and connect with others in public and private forums. Companies need to take care of this social aspect while still trying to market to a consumer individually.

(d) **Competitor-driven factors:** With a new breed of competitors, aggregators, value-chain-breaking intermediaries giving strong competition to traditional business structures, here are some key ways in which marketers should view their digital presence with respect to fancied and digital only competitors:

- *Market share → Access share:* Companies which are used to measuring only market share growth need to orient themselves to measure 'access share,' which involves looking at the kind and number of consumers they have at hand across related segments in the digital world. This directly translates into a firm's 'Digital Clout' which includes the ability to to target dynamic audiences in real time and know where they would likely be present and receive firm's messages rather than look at static audience numbers as firms had been used to traditionally.
- *Internal capability-driven → Partnerships-driven:* The major force which firms need to harness on the digital platform is that of allied partners through both horizontal and vertical integration for their specific sets of products and services. With it being impossible to have a presence across multitude consumer interaction platforms, this will be the key differentiator for firms eyeing a digital platform.
- *Utility-driven offerings → Service-driven offerings:* As shared in the earlier part of this section on strategy orientation (changing from product to marketing focus), firms need to tie in the Digital Value Elements as discussed in Chapter 2, since it is service differentiation that will make a firm standout across digital competition and not just the given basic utility- driven features.

Emerging Digital Business Structures

Having attained an understanding of how business strategy evolved and which key factors impact strategy development on digital platforms, in this section we shall look into emerging digital business structures (in line with the impacts of the factors shared in the last section).

For any business to succeed, the major pre-requisite (as is said in business terms) is to achieve RoI (Return on Investment) in line with the company's expectations. Defining RoI and strategic intent for any company operating in a particular industry sector would typically involve thinking through key questions which the management needs to decide in the best interest of the shareholders. Some of these include:

(a) Where does the organization intend to be in the long and short term? What kind of growth is it looking to chase?
(b) What business is the organization in and does it want to stay there? Is the organization averse to risk or open to venturing into uncharted markets and segments?
(c) What is the set-up of the company in terms of ownership (public, private, investor-driven), management, company's philosophy (vision, mission), core building blocks?
(d) Does the company have the necessary investments, resources, and capabilities to meet its desired objectives and the pace of growth it envisions?
(e) What kind of an image would the company want to develop for itself—aggressive, stable, customer-centric, innovative, values-driven? (Incidentally, it has been seen that it is difficult to change an image which is once set in the mind of the consumer. So a company which is seen as a very stable company with standard set of products offline, would find it quite difficult to change that perception and suddenly position itself digitally)
(f) What kind OVP, (as discussed in the earlier chapters), would the company target?
(g) What core competencies does it retain and how adaptable should the company be to develop newer competencies when it sees its market share being taken away?

A lot of these and many other questions need to be posed by a firm which is planning to compete on digital platforms, so that not only does it understand what is achievable but also makes its customers follow them with the launch of their new digital initiatives and forays. We will try to address some of these important points in this chapter. But first, let us look at the kind of new digital business structures which are evolving and challenging top firms and what strategies the different-natured players are targeting while approaching the same customer and revenue pie. To understand this we have developed a market structure based Return on Investment (RoI) model which we shall discuss here.

As discussed earlier, a company's RoI is the key criteria for it to determine its performance. In Fig. 5.2, we have used the key elements of an RoI calculation which relates to:

(a) The investments a firm is willing to put into its operations (as X axis and classified as Minimal, Requisite, and Strategic), depicting the risk profile of any firm for digital operations.

(b) The type of returns and subsequent growth expected (as Y axis and classified as Nominal, Decent, and Industry-Leading), depicting targeted growth and expectations.

By plotting different types of firms and their digital objectives across the two axes of investment and growth, we see multiple types of digital business structures operating in the digital market

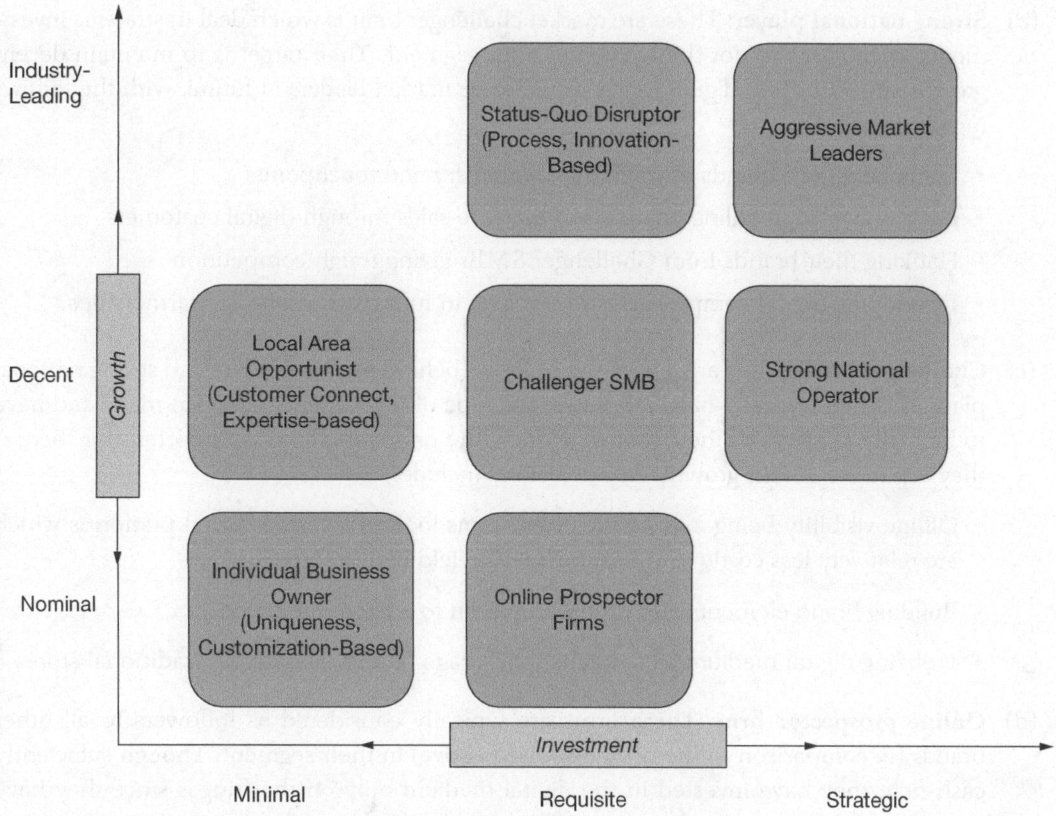

Figure 5.2 RoI-based Digital Market Structure Development

and at times even usurping a firm's offline operations. Let us understand them in a bit more detail (we have removed the top-left and bottom-right boxes as they correspond to unrealistic investments and growth equations).

(a) **Aggressive market leader:** These are typical big-weight players with strong and stable portfolio of brands and huge investments at hand. Their prime goals of being on digital platforms include:

- Developing and nurturing key brands on digital platforms
- Maintaining loyal customers to support their online buys
- Getting newer online customers from top competitors
- Developing real-time communication and customer intimacy points

(b) **Strong national player**: These are market challenger brands which deal in strategic investments since they are not the leaders in their segment. Their target is to maintain decent growth and with their digital forays aspire to be market leaders in future, with the following objectives:

- Enhancing their brands through digital imagery and touchpoints
- Developing more online channels to increase sales through digital customers
- Flanking their brands from Challenger SMBs giving tough competition
- Developing digital competencies to leverage in future, for example, partnerships

(c) **Challenger SMB:** They are a third set of firms (behind market leaders and strong national players) which typically have a limit on the type of investments they can make and have to be really strategic in their spends. Hence, the online medium is important for them if they aspire for decent growth. Key objectives include:

- Offline visibility being a key issue, these firms look to leverage digital platforms which are relatively less costly to manage and can yield high returns
- Building brand elements and promoting them to a larger audience
- Utilizing digital medium as a means to leverage offline sales across traditional stores

(d) **Online prospector firm**: These firms are typically considered as followers to all other brands (in comparison to the ones discussed above) in their segment. Though sufficiently cash-rich, they have invested in the digital medium only on the fringes since they have not realized the strategic advantages of being online. In many cases, it is their proprietors who either are not knowledgeable of the benefits of going digital or have not deployed a vendor with enough expertise to be able to leverage the digital medium in a strategic manner.

(e) **Status quo disruptor:** These set of firms do not have huge investments behind them but are being developed by a smart generation of new entrepreneurs who have strong backing behind them and innovative ideas to disrupt and challenge the status quo of market leaders and strong national players. They aim for industry-leading growth in the digital part of their segment and are slowly becoming market leaders in their own right in terms of valuations and market capitalization.

Few examples of such firms in India include Flipkart (Online Retailer), Makemytrip (Online Bookings), and Big Basket (Online Grocery delivery). The ways they use digital medium include:

- They are one-of the first-movers in their category with unique digital core competencies in terms of market, process and customer value understanding
- Strong on technology deployment and data-driven business modelling
- Have target segments who are digital natives and hold their loyalty
- Develop online partnerships and reduce intermediary costs efficiently

(f) **Local area opportunist:** These are firms at a regional level which have minimal resources to spend online but loyal regional audiences whom they want to serve online and, in the process set themselves up for better growth across other regions of the country. Key characteristics of these firms include:
- Strong recall and customer connect with regional/local audience who are loyalists to the brand and would support them on their digital journeys
- Strong regional expertise which can be taken to other markets and even internationally, if they are able to create a distinct online image
- Utilize only a few key owned channels and emphasize largely on earned media since that can be executed with much less investment

(g) **Individual business owner:** This is the last type of business entity and most ubiquitous online. Presently, there are millions of individual business owners who leverage internet as a model to set up their own web pages, blogs, e-commerce sites, consulting services, professional services, social media groups, subscription-based products, etc., even with the minimal resources and budgets they have at hand. Most of them typically anticipate nominal growth, though some of them also make it to the big league with their unique concepts. Key characteristics of this entity includes:
- Unique concepts developed online through personal abilities and skills
- Have only one or two owned media but are part of all related online communities through which they can sell and build communities
- Possess strong knowledge of their consumer segment and provide a clear offerings set, which gives them the biggest leverage over other firms

Depending upon a firm's appetite for growth and investment resources available at hand, it needs to look at where it is presently positioned in the above matrix and identify its competitors in the digital platform. Brands which are already industry leaders and challengers offline, need to develop strategies to counter the Status quo Disruptors, Challenger SMBs, Local Area Opportunists, and other purely digital aggregators and unique concept providers to maintain their fort and be relevant.

In the next section, we would be sharing strategies on how firms need to identify credible trends which are making an impact in the marketplace and customer's minds to make sure they counter such disruptors through Core Competency Alignment (CCA) to manage and provide a better OVP at every stage of their product development.

Digital Core Competency Alignment

In Chapter 4 we had discussed in detail on how firm's can understand their core competency mix through internal capability analysis (see section titled 'Core Competencies Analysis' in Chapter 4) and also saw the examples of Google and Apple to understand how core competencies would differ across competitors. In this section, we shall understand how companies which have different business structures/objectives (specifically those which are transitioning from offline to a major online presence) need to regularly map the changing OVP for their customer set to align core competencies to revised industry/sector/competitive value propositions.

Let us look at Fig. 5.3 to understand concepts like Value Shift Functions (VSF) and Core Competency Alignment (CCA).

While developing an understanding of the concept of OVP in Chapter 1 under the section titled 'Delivering Enhanced Customer Value,' we had looked at how new firms and those entering newer segments can understand customer's stated and unstated needs to come up with a value proposition which satisfies customer's specific problem areas. For mature players though, once the market for a product is developed, market challengers and new competitors entering the market bring forth new value propositions which established brands either have to match

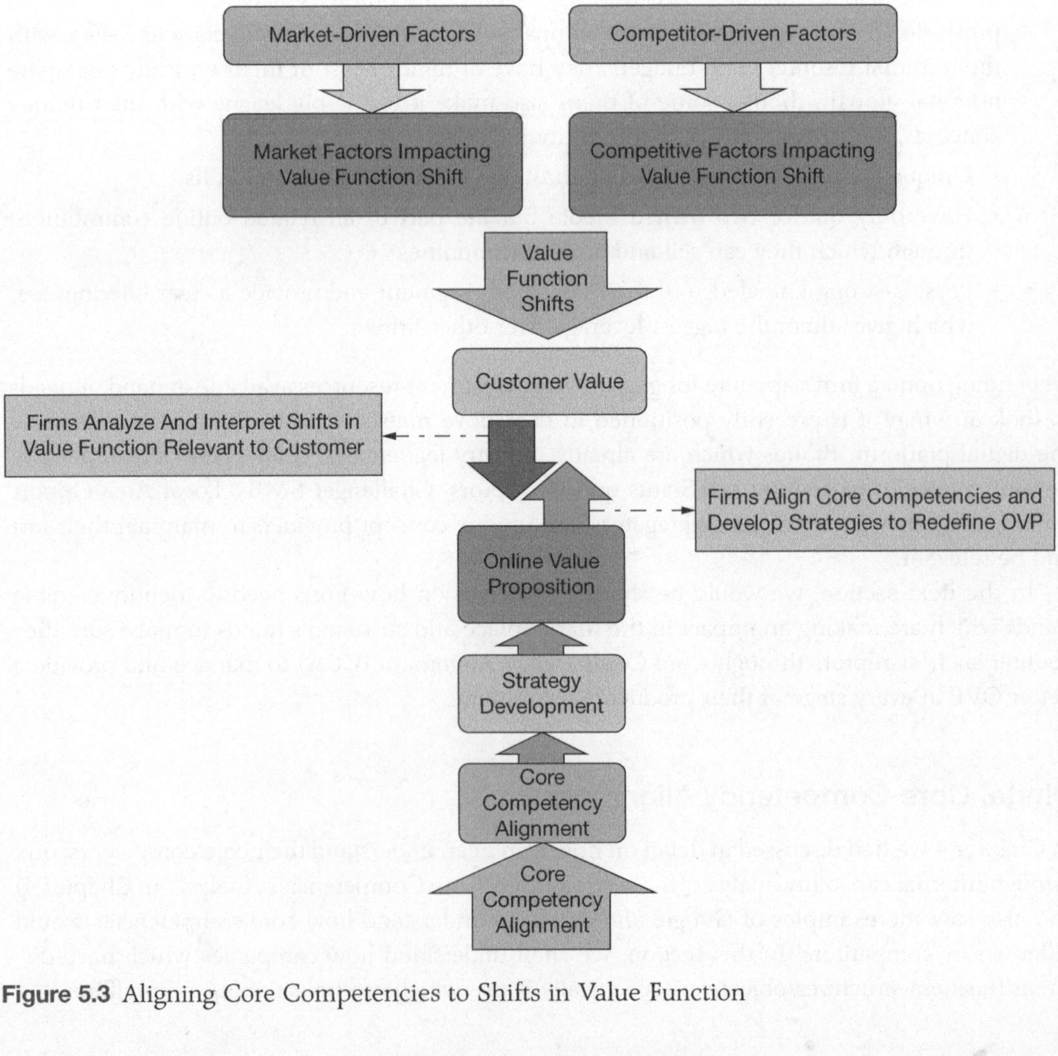

Figure 5.3 Aligning Core Competencies to Shifts in Value Function

or create new set of value additions to keep differentiating and maintaining the brand position they enjoy.

Apart from competition, there are also market factors like changes in customer preferences, product consumption pattern shifts, technology intervention, reduced component costs, changing tariff structures, government regulations and compliances, etc., which can impact the way 'value' within the industry shifts from one set of players to another. Together, these market and competitor-driven factors shift the earlier value which was being provided to the customer to create a new set of value functions. We term these as 'Value Function Shifts.'

The concept of CCA relates to the response which any specific firm of a particular industry will develop to match and compete in the wake of the multiple value shifts caused in its sector. Here, we need to understand that CCA is not about a firm changing its core competencies, but instead aligning them to changing industry value function shifts so that they are able to use their core strengths and enhance them in the best possible manner to changing environment and competitive forces.

As we can see in Fig. 5.3, once the firm has aligned and developed a new set of core competencies based on emerging market structures, it can define its overall strategy accordingly to create/refine its set of OVPs to match the changes in customer value and achieve its short and long-term objectives.

For a better understanding of the concepts shared earlier, we have taken an example of one of the rising and most value generating industries of present time, the telecom sector, to look at how multiple changes in the market and competitive factors have caused value function shifts (driven mostly by individual brands) and impacted overall customer value in the industry.

We chose the telecom industry and smartphone sector specifically as that is where we see online and digital platforms playing a large role in causing value shifts and being the key differentiators for the industry. For understanding the concepts of CCA, we have taken the example of a fictitious local brand to explain how it could have responded to changes in the industry caused by global and national players to align its core competencies of being a regional brand with the knowledge of local/mass segments to differentiate itself in the market and later be a major player in the segment (once the hardware/equipment manufacturing costs, internet access costs, etc., come down).

Figure 5.4 expands on all the key stages depicted in Fig. 5.3. At the top are illustrated the major market and competitive factors which impact customer value and cause value function shifts. The arrows below them correspond to individual value shift functions (which can either be market or competition driven or driven by a combination of both). In the following customer value layer depicted through a five-stage example of the top five mobile brands (across the past decade), we will see how customer value functions for the entire global industry shift.

The CCA exercise is depicted in the bottom two layers wherein the last layer of arrows showcase CCAs (which competitors across the industry execute in response to the changing value shift functions) and the layer above that provides an example of a local brand and the specific alignments it would need to make to its core competencies, to respond to and grow in the light

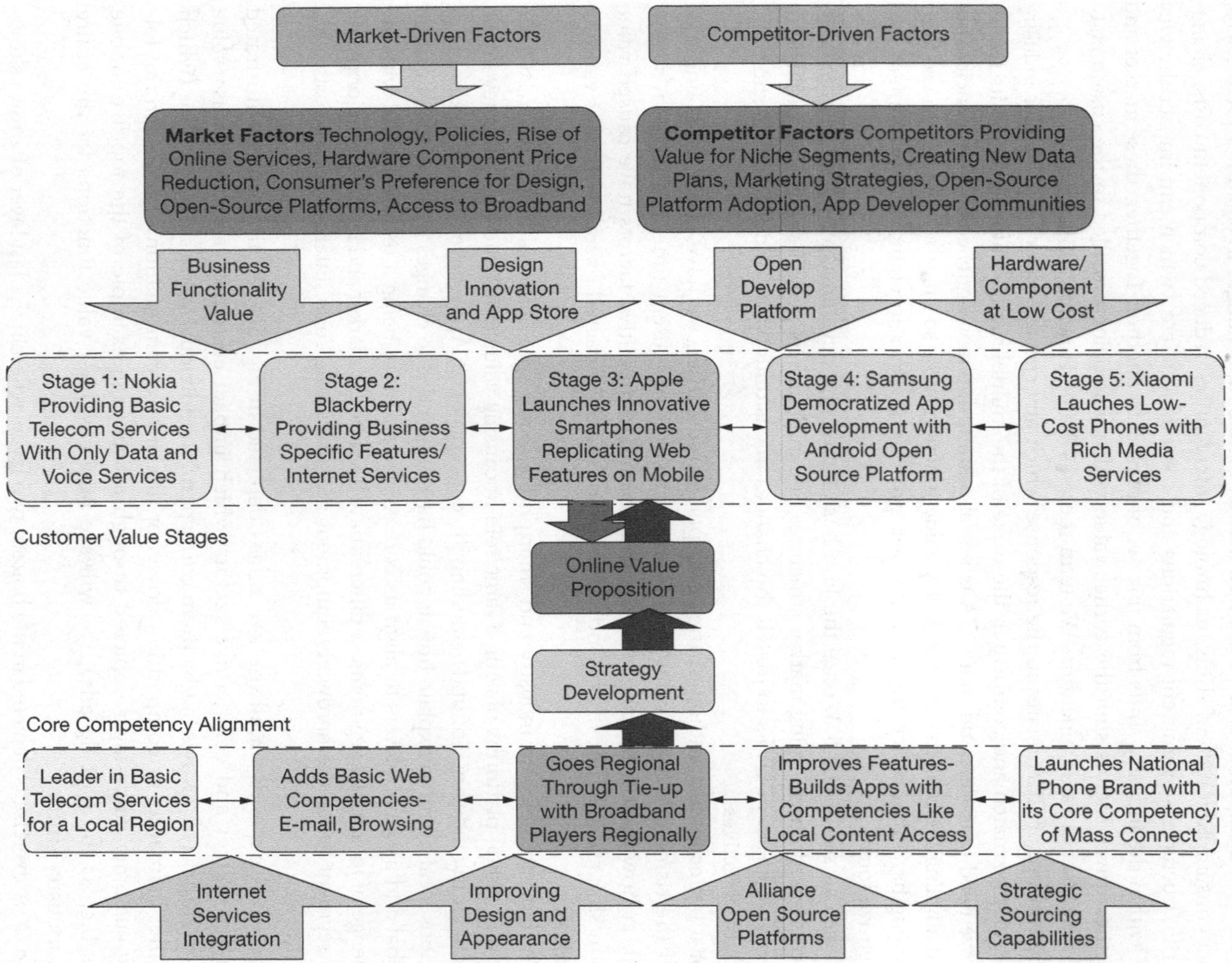

Figure 5.4 Applying Core Competencies Alignment Concepts to Telecom Industry

of competition across each of the five customer value stages. Let us go through each of these five value-shifts and CCA response stages in more details below.

(a) **Stage 1**

- Showcase brand: Nokia
- Value function: first-mover advantage and top recall as a mobile manufacturer
- Customer value: Nokia started with basic telecom services (including voice and data). With limited broadband development in this period, there was no specific OVP developed for the industry
- Industry alignment: very few local players had forayed into this sector
- Local brand CCA alignment: we take the example of a local manufacturer which starts to replicate basic voice and data services specific to a local region only

(b) **Stage 2**

- Showcase brand: Blackberry
- Value function: first brand to offer business functionality and features
- Customer value: one of the first brands to provide online convergence to support push e-mail, internet faxing, and web browsing as OVPs
- Industry alignment: other mobile companies started to integrate internet services as a part of their core offerings
- Local brand CCA alignment: local brand follows industry leaders to integrate e-mails and web-browsing based on the bandwidth provided in its local region

(c) **Stage 3**

- Showcase brand: Apple
- Value function: market altering innovations like Design/App Store/Touch, etc.
- Customer value: a game changer in the premium category, iPhones integrated online features through its app store, and replicated web experience on mobile
- Industry alignment: with iPhone, basic standards of mobile development improved, for example, user experience, app platform, visual interfaces, etc.
- Local brand CCA alignment: local brand goes regional with advanced online features and tie-ups with regional broadband players for service variety

(d) **Stage 4**

- Showcase brand: Samsung
- Value function: adoption of open source and developer community set-up
- Customer value: Samsung democratized app development with android open source platform and offered cheaper app packages for larger online access

- Industry alignment: mobile companies started expanding on android platform wherein they could get mass audiences with lower investment outlays
- Local brand CCA alignment: local brand makes use of open source to build local apps utilizing its competency in working with local content and developers

(e) **Stage 5**

- Showcase brand: Xiaomi
- Value function: one of the leading brands makes use of hardware and component cost reduction which has brought down smartphone rates
- Customer value: providing phones at lower cost with rich media services
- Industry alignment: mobile companies started to develop low-cost phones through strategic integration with global suppliers and investor funding
- Local brand CCA alignment: local brand becomes a national phone brand by extending its core competency of mass connect and developing low-cost smartphones for this segment with astute national marketing

Here, the telecom industry and the local mobile manufacturer follow key value function shifts in the market and act proactively to align their core competencies accordingly to come up with compelling OVPs to provide customer value and grow to a national level.

This example showcases how various business structures (as shared in the last section) need to keep tab of the changing and emerging business structures to map value shifts and differentiate their business model and core competencies accordingly. The key here is for the firm to have a clear view of their customer set, the meaning of incremental value to them, and how they would like to receive services from known and new brands.

The next section focuses precisely at this area of identifying the right customer through the application of STP marketing techniques to the digital world and then developing the right OVP through careful analysis of value functions and core-competency alignment.

Customer Development Strategy (STP 2.0 Framework)

With an understanding in the last section on how firms can align their core competencies to suit and serve changing customer value functions, we would look at the most important element of digital strategy which is defining and developing the target customer. We would examine how the classic functions of STP (discussed earlier in Chapter 4, section titled 'Marketing Mix Analysis Share') have evolved to STP 2.0 and the elements which constitute its formation.

As understood in the earlier sections on 'Consumer Behavior' and 'Managing Consumer Demand' in Chapter 3, the key characteristics of digital platforms is that they provide firms with not just a broad-based segmentation of their customers, but gives the ability (through technology) to narrow those segments into like-minded customer groups, business-oriented customer personas, and the knowledge and identification of customers at an individual level.

Angus Jenkinson in his essay 'Beyond Segmentation'(*Journal of Targeting, Measurement and Analysis for Marketing*), presents his views on how a 'grouping' approach on segmenting customers helps create 'customer communities' or clusters which support creation and preservation of loyalty within these groups, thus helping firms target micro-communities within the broader segments which used to be defined traditionally.

This chapter aims at developing the next advanced level of STP which we term as STP2.0 Framework and discusses new approaches to all the three elements of segmenting, targeting, and positioning. It involves looking at how concrete customer action data (derived through analytics) and knowledge of customer's buying intent and final action (through search and conversion keywords and data) can help marketers develop highly refined target segments, and position them through personal communication and channels which could never be deployed earlier because such data was never available in the first place.

This refined STP Version 2.0 is depicted in Fig. 5.5 which showcases a new approach to developing each of the three components. The framework has been developed keeping in mind the latest approaches to market segment creation, consumer, and buyer persona development, mapping the consumer journey in real time and creating multiple positioning strategies to target customers uniquely across each of the consumer funnel stages through a mix of channel and communication approaches.

We would like to state here that with advances in technology, both quantitative and qualitative data is being accessed, interlinked, and applied in multiple ways by companies and it is not possible to cover all of those newer techniques and advancements in detail here. The intent of the framework is to provide a base on top of which marketers can use data from multiple channels to feed information, refine their segments, and position themselves real time in the most customized fashion.

At a broad level, STP 2.0 Framework differs primarily from traditional STP as follows:

(a) **Segmentation 2.0:** The key difference between traditional and online segmentation relates to the kind of data that was available, collected, and the manner in which segments were developed. All these three aspects differ primarily with the online channels, as not just basic demographic, psychographic, and behavioral data but also data at each customer transaction level can be analyzed with sophisticated technologies to yield highly refined and actionable audience clusters.

(b) **Targeting 2.0:** Earlier, once the customer segments were created, marketers had limited options to choose from the segment mix and even media planning for traditional channels only allowed targeting to such broad-based classifications. Targeting 2.0, on the other hand, deploys the concept of user personas which involves defining audience clusters and making use of more authoritative and quantitative data available across multiple online elements.

(c) **Positioning 2.0:** With digital marketing providing the possibility of understanding audiences at an individual level (for each of the chosen target clusters) and segregating them across the marketing funnel, marketers have the power to position differential, customized messages in real time across each of the funnel stages depending upon the customer type and conversion metrics being targeted for that channel.

To understand STP2.0 Framework, we would need to understand the analysis behind each of the three key elements in Fig. 5.5:

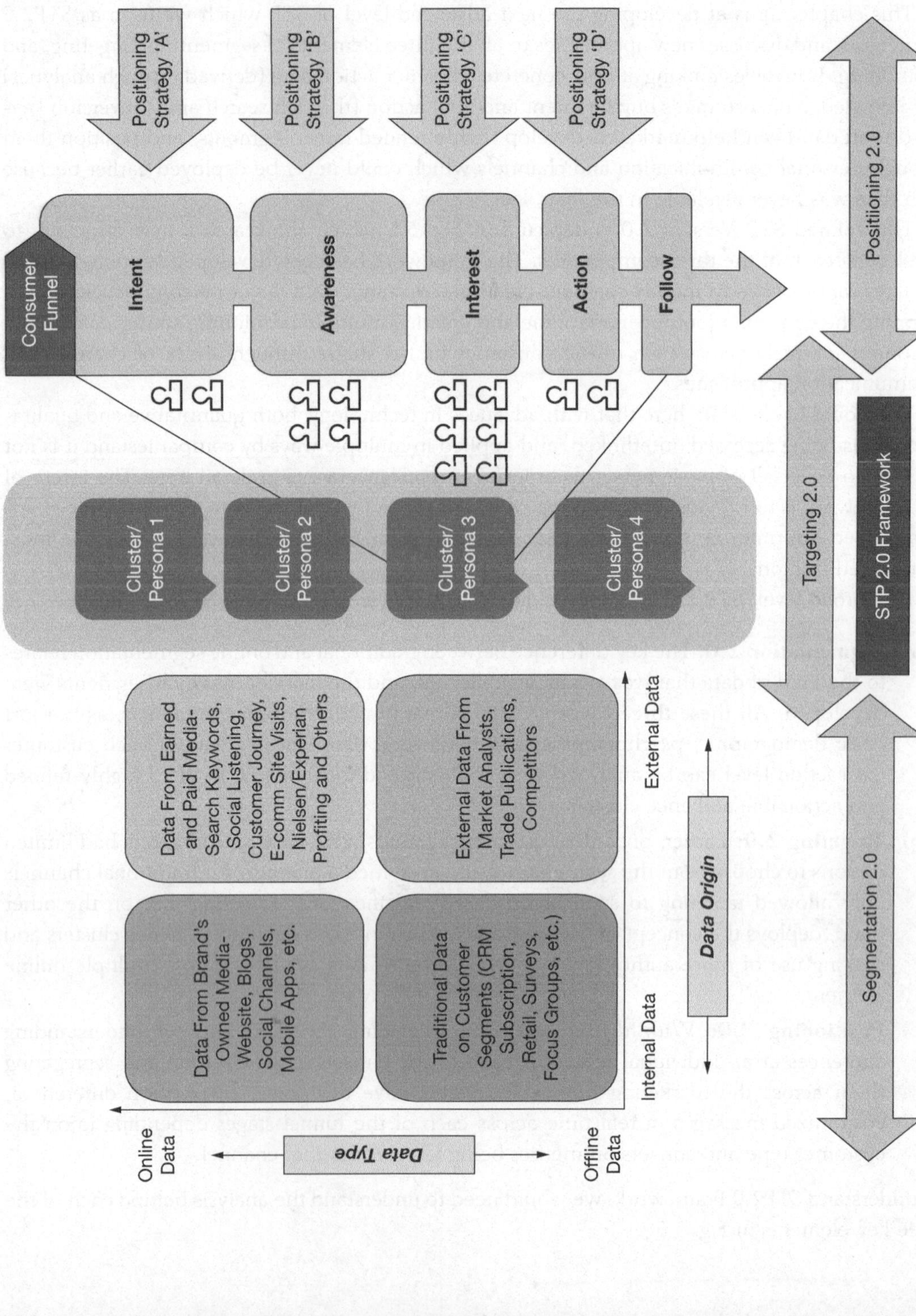

Figure 5.5 Elements of STP2.0 Framework

(a) **Data segmentation matrix** (Segmentation 2.0): To understand the kind of extended customer transaction data which can be used to develop segments in present times, we have developed a data segmentation matrix with data origin (across X axis) and data type (across Y axis), mapping all data collated across internal/external or offline/online generated data. The four quadrants which emerge from this matrix include:

- *Traditional data:* Involves data sets which are internal to the company and derived from traditional (non-online) data sources. These include company's CRM/internal systems data, subscription/retail sales transaction data, and other qualitative data like customer surveys, focus groups, interviews, etc.
- *External data:* Includes other offline data collated from external sources like market analysts, trade publications, competitor, and third-party data, etc.
- *Data from brand's owned media:* Includes all data collated online from firms' owned properties only. Examples include websites, microsites, blogs, social channel pages, mobile apps, etc.
- *Data from earned and paid media:* Takes stock of all other customer transaction-related online data channels (earned and paid media), which could range from search keywords, social listening data, transaction data from customer's journey across the funnel stages, e-commerce site visits, etc.

The data segmentation matrix provides an easy-to-classify framework for all data which can be collated across online and offline presences to integrate it and develop clarified, meaningful, and actionable segments which customers can further target.

Traditionally, consumer segments were generated using key variables of demographic, psychographic, and behavioral data, but with the present set of advanced online and transactional data available, market segmentation has turned into a highly sophisticated and data-intensive exercise. With companies like Nielsen, Experian devising customized segmentation techniques for different clients based on their needs, firms can make use of such predefined microsegments to discover which segments are best suited and most probable to respond to marketing efforts targeted to them. To share an example of how Nielsen segmentation system helps customers customize their segmentation exercise, let us look at Fig. 5.6 which provides a screenshot of one of the segmentation types—Nielsen PRIZM, based on consumer lifestyles, shopping behaviors, and media preferences.

Apart from this, Nielsen also has other segmentation types available for firms as products like Nielsen P$YCLE (identifies households by financial behavior and wealth), Nielsen ConneXions (segments based on consumer technology usage and behaviors), Find MyBest Segments, etc., which provides firms with interactive tools that they can slice and dice to arrive at top segments most suited to their market and product strategy. For effective segmentation, the five key aspects which firms should always keep in mind (according to Philip Kotler, *Marketing Management*, millennium edition) include:

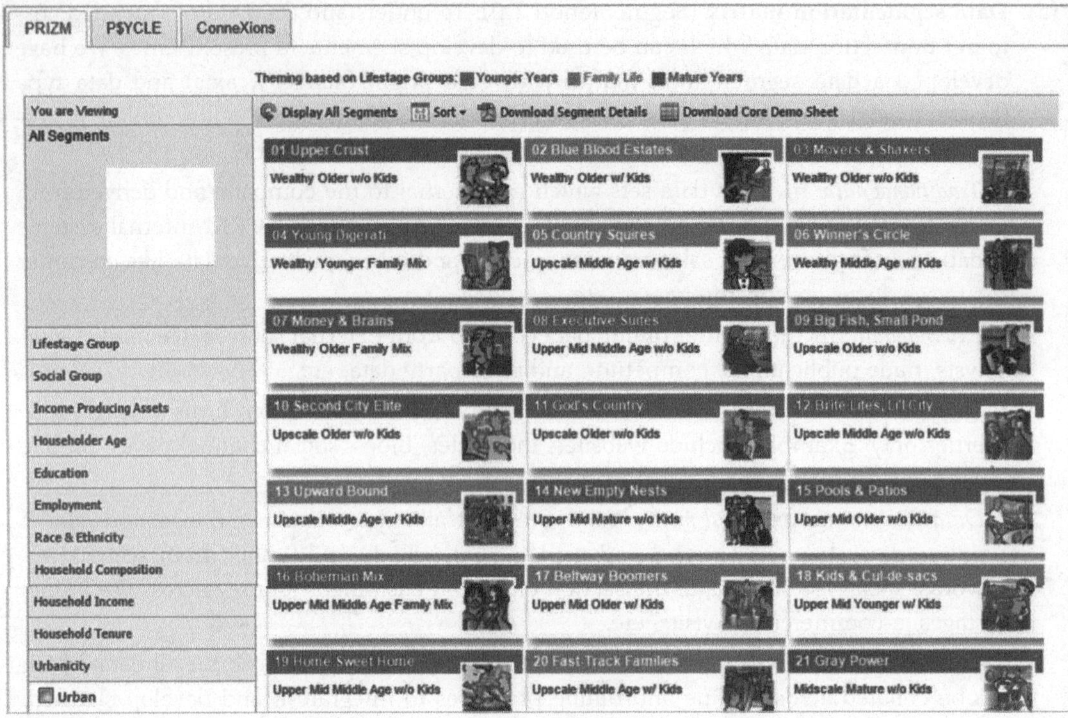

Figure 5.6 Nielsen's PRIZM Segmentation Framework

Source: Michael King, 'Personas for SEO in 2012 (PubCon)', 16 October 2012, https://www.slideshare.net/, accessed on 27 February 2017 at 8.49pm.

- Measurable: The size, purchasing power, and characteristics of the segments should be measurable.
- Substantial: Segments should be large and profitable enough to serve. A segment should be the largest possible homogeneous group worth going after with a tailored marketing program.
- Accessible: The segments can be reached and served effectively.
- Differentiable: Segments are conceptually distinguishable and respond differently to different marketing mixes. If two segments respond identically to a particular offer, they do not constitute separate segments.
- Actionable: Effective programs can be formulated for attracting and serving the segments.

The second element of the STP2.0 Framework discusses the concept of clustering and persona development to target the set of buyer groups that a company choses to serve.

(b) **Clustering and persona creation** (Targeting 2.0): By definition, 'User Personas' is a representation of the goals and behaviors of a hypothesized group of users. Persona development as an exercise involves building archetypes of the members of a target audience to create reliable and realistic representations of them. The chosen segments are referred to as clusters since their members share a common set of needs and display similar buying characteristics which the brand has willingly chosen to target. Persona creation has become common for large marketing companies and there are multiple ways in which marketers can attempt to create them depending on the information available and specific outputs companies are seeking through the exercise.

Once a firm has a clear idea of the high-level demographic, psychographic, and behavioral variables it wants to include as a part of its segmentation strategy, it would look at analyzing some of the following key factors stated below, to finalize its target segments and develop representative personas related to each segment:

- Segment size and growth
- Company's strategic direction
- Product mix and product life cycle stage
- Competitor's market strategy
- Emerging marketplace and consumer trends

With marketing activity increasingly moving away from addressing broad segments to targeting microsegments, it becomes imperative for firms to develop these target clusters in the form of individual personas which are well defined with all their characteristics well understood, at a level akin to understanding an individual's personality. Persona creation typically helps in the development of customized marketing material, optimized websites, responsive landing pages, consumer funnel-based web navigation and features, etc. Personas are different from segmentation as they help marketers target different content to consumers coming with varied goals to the website. How marketers position that content across the consumer funnel though would be covered in Positioning 2.0 section.

For 'Persona Development' exercise, let us look at the kind of research a firm would need to further refine its chosen segments and understand their characteristics.

- **Target segment identification:** To begin with persona development, firms must have identified multiple segments/clusters for which they would want to develop detailed personas. The initial inputs towards building personas would be basic demographic data, along with a clear assessment of the needs and pain points which drive them. At this stage, it would really help to know (through earlier available data) typical interactions and perceptions of identified segments with the brand, their value expectation from product/service, and specific engagement needs of the segments.
- **Understanding values, behaviors, and interests:** The next stage involves going deeper into customer's purchase patterns, their motivations and driving factors, key sources of influence, their role in decision making, specific interest areas related to a firm's product set, common values they exhibit during their interactions and other such information. For companies launching new products, it would also hold good for firms to research competitor's customers to understand their behaviors and buying motivations.

- **Research site analytics, search keywords, social media listening:** The biggest advantage which digital channels provide is the capability to gain insights from multiple consumer touchpoints and channels to understand interactions and consumer preferences across all the funnel stages right from intent to credible historic purchase patterns. With previous reporting available through site analytics, providing details on the sites referred, content consumed, keywords searched, social interactions undertaken, etc., firms can now overlay and use all this data to understand and extract chunks of micro-text and develop personas in ways which were not traditionally possible.
- **Qualitative data-audience interviews/focus groups/affinity mapping:** Once basic historical research and quantitative inputs have been mapped, firms also conduct multiple qualitative assessment techniques including specific segment interviews, focus groups, use-case scenario development, affinity mapping, etc., to graft finer elements of the personas. Affinity mapping, which involves taking representatives from different teams and brainstorming on persona-building exercise, is specifically useful, as it binds together the experience of multiple stakeholders to arrive at more actionable personas.

With this research conducted through the steps mentioned here, firms can start to develop identified user persona in the following manner:

- *Naming the persona*: A persona should have a name so that it feels like a real person. It is generally suggested to have between three to seven personas for relevance and practicality of the exercise.
- *Developing the persona*: Apart from name, other sections could include:
  - ➤ Demographic details like age, education, income, job, role, company;
  - ➤ Persona's goals and challenges, pain-points, motivations, values, and fears;
  - ➤ Type of product experiences they desire, main sources of information/influences;
  - ➤ A day in the life of the persona, key activities they perform online;
  - ➤ Types of sites visited, social media usage, content preference, etc.
- *Refining the persona*: Once a profile has been created, it is repeatedly put to test to check what holds true and valid for that persona and whether it really represents the needs of that group (from their viewpoint) post which it is refined accordingly.

Companies that create personas regularly have developed pre-built templates which are specific to their objectives of identifying and targeting only those customer profiles which are most profitable to them in the long run.

The third and last element of the STP 2.0 Framework involves positioning the brand across multiple funnel stages where the customer is present across the marketing funnel.

(c) **Positioning across consumer funnel scenarios (Positioning 2.0):** Once marketers have identified key customer segments and developed personas to target, they need to develop messages and actions to complete the objectives set for each of the customer interaction stages. In this aspect, it is important to develop an appreciation of customer journeys across the funnel stages to understand the specific positioning which firms need to develop. A customer journey involves the path a customer must take in order to fulfill a particular need or goal. Personas are typically developed by marketers in order to know the customers better to help fulfill their goal across the funnel stages. The typical flow of actions from ascertaining the need to its fulfillment follows the path:

CUSTOMER JOURNEY (Need Definition across Funnel Stages) →**PERSONA CREATION** → **POSITIONING**(Need Fulfillment for each Cluster/Individual)

Let us look at examples of positioning for identified personas and their customer journeys across a firm's key product site through application of consumer funnel stages:

(a) **Intent:** In the first stage of the funnel, a typical example could be:

CUSTOMER JOURNEY—Customer has heard of a brand a lot and has visited the site for the first time by searching Google with a specific set of keywords. There is no specific need which the customer intends to fulfill at present.

PERSONA CREATION—A persona by the name 'Curious Customer' is developed for this segment of new consumers enquiring about the brand with no specific intention to buy on their first visit to the brand site.

POSITIONING—Marketer's task is to make the experience of a prospect's first landing on the firm's website an impactful and experiential one where he/she gets to take away a positive opinion of the brand and its imagery.

(b) **Awareness:** Typical example includes:

CUSTOMER JOURNEY—Customer has interacted with the brand and looked through two–three key pages of the website, identified brand's social media page, discovered and read a couple of articles on its blog. There is passive interest shown by customer which points to a possibility of converting it into a lead.

PERSONA CREATION—A persona by the name 'Passive Prospect' is developed for this segment of new consumers who have shown more than just intent to touch-base with the brand, though still at a passive level.

POSITIONING—A marketer would want to make sure that the design, layout, first-touch content on the site, blogs, social channels is developed in a way that positively showcases the core attributes and brand values. Positioning here should focus on more emotional aspects to develop consumer connect.

(c) **Interest:** To cite an example:

CUSTOMER JOURNEY—Customer shows active interest in the brand and has a definite need which he/she wants to fulfill, hence, spends considerable time on the brand site, performs searches, views demos, fills enquiry forms, etc.

PERSONA CREATION— A persona by the name 'Active Lead' is developed for this segment of new/returning consumers who like the brand and are close to the conversion stage, provided their clarifications have been well addressed.

POSITIONING—With a prolonged sales cycle for consumers at this stage, marketers need to position their messages in an informative manner and focus on functional aspects so that consumers know the value of the brand.

(d) **Action:** An example of this stage:

CUSTOMER JOURNEY—Customer has conducted all the necessary research and comparison with competitors and is completely sure that he/she wants to buy a product from the marketer.

PERSONA CREATION—A persona by the name 'Last Mile Purchaser' is developed for this segment of new/returning consumer whose main objective is the ease with which he/she can conduct transactions most efficiently.

POSITIONING—Marketer's task is to optimize the site heavily around not just getting the new visitor to place an order, but also increasing the average order size of the returning customer by reinstating post-purchase benefits.

(e) **Follow:** A typical example would be:

CUSTOMER JOURNEY—Customer has become a strong supporter of the brand or has fallen out to another competitor. The needs of both kind of groups are completely opposite and need to be devised accordingly.

PERSONA CREATION—A persona by the name 'Brand Loyalist' or 'Brand Estranged' can be developed for these two distinct segments. The interaction objectives of the estranged group would have to be re-assessed.

POSITIONING—Marketer's task is to make stronger post-purchase connection with loyalists to further develop them as brand referees and for those who have fallen out, they need to devise a completely new positioning strategy.

With the above examples we learn that the objectives of each firm should follow the customer journey across funnel stages and position accordingly. In the next section, we shall look at how marketers develop their strategic positioning for customers across the funnel with the help of traditional 4Ps and the extended Ps.

DEFINING THE DIGITAL MARKETING MIX

In the last part of the chapter, we established an understanding of the business strategy for digital marketing and its structures along with doing the groundwork for CCA and customer development through implementation of STP2.0. In this section, we shall look at how marketers need to map changes which the digital landscape has brought to the 4Ps of Product, Price, Place, and Promotion along with the introduction of four other Ps—People, Process, Programs, and Performance.

Offering Mix for Digital

In this section, we shall deal with the first P of the marketing mix known as Product. Typically, when we talk about a product, the coinage also relates to a service or a brand. The case of digital is more complex, since the regular traditional distinctions between each of these terms (product, service, brand) begin to diffuse not only because of the elements which the digital medium lends to it but also how marketers are actively mixing components of one into the other to make it a wholesome value enhancing unit which we can call as the 'Offering mix.'

A key feature of a product or service in the offline world is that they can be a commodity, or as we say non-branded enough, but still sell on the basis of local availability and the 'reach factor,' where they are available in nearby stores and do not have to bear the costs of being on a digital channel, marketing themselves, and delivering to a location. This brings us to the fact that any product or service which is being sold online and across digital channels needs to be reasonably differentiated and have so-called 'brand attributes' or elements attached to them, to differentiate from competition and be seen in the first place.

A product can be classified as consisting two key components—tangible and intangible. Tangible components are described as the ones which can be physically seen while the intangible parts might not be directly visible but their impact is felt and perceived by the customer. A service is also considered to be a product category which is intangible in nature.

An offering on the digital platform differs from its traditional form primarily in the way it develops and integrates the intangible or service aspects to it. These services can either be developed as new digital products (along with the main product line) or be an extension to the physical product itself to make it easier for the customer to access, interact, and ultimately, purchase the main product. Philip Kotler (*Marketing Management*, 14th edition) has shared five states of service mix components that can be built around a product.

Figure 5.7 showcases the five states of an offering mix, which starts with a pure tangible product with no service element and ends as being a pure service with no product component. The offering mix of any firm can be classified across any of these five states depending upon the extent of tangible products and intangible service elements which are a part of it. Let us understand them as follows:

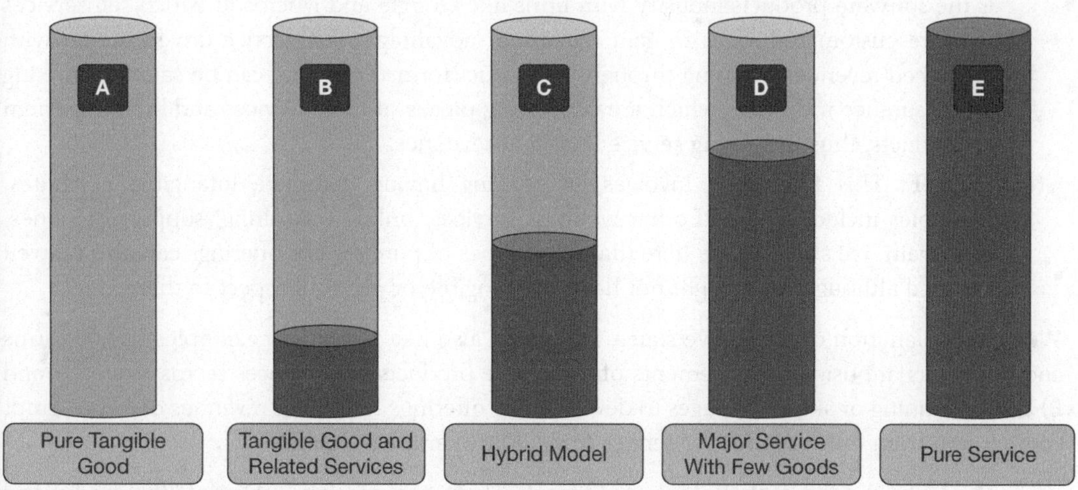

Figure 5.7 Offering Mix (Product-Service) States

(a) **State A:** Firms in this state have a mix of only tangible products which are primarily physical in form and mostly commodity in nature. Examples could be sugar, steel, a basic accessory, etc. Most of these products might have a generic brand name but do not exhibit the characteristics of a brand or its experiential elements. Although there is scope to differentiate, but without a service element, consumers are not able to build a connection to a product. Pure tangible goods are typically not geared enough for the digital platform.

(b) **State B:** It involves tangible goods which have a decent service element to them. Examples include mobiles, automobiles, furniture, etc., which in their base state are tangible products, but addition of digital value elements (aesthetics, customization, convenience, etc.) provides a service experience to the target customer. Most of the products sold through e-commerce sites would fall in this state, where the product is sold mostly in the physical form, but with good amount of intangible elements like information, history, positive customer references, demo videos, etc., built around it.

(c) **State C:** This is a unique state in which the offering has an equal mix of product and service elements built into it. Key examples would relate to hospitality services like theme parks (which sell a service and also merchandise), restaurants (where food is tangible and service is the intangible part), etc. Even firms like Apple and Samsung which are built and marketed as products but have strong technology-based service elements around them can come in this category. There are only a few firms who can deliver an offering mix in this state as they need to have strong product and service elements in their portfolio which is often hard to achieve and sustain.

(d) **State D:** In this state, the intangible part forms the core service, while the tangible part is built as a support element. This includes typical examples like air travel where additional services or supporting goods like snacks and drinks are sold, but increasingly we are seeing service-oriented companies moving to a productized format wherein each of their key features and processes are being broken down and sold as a product in itself. Point in case is the software products industry with firms like Google and Microsoft which sell services that are customized so as to gain maximum advantage of a service-driven model with enhanced revenues accruing through its product form. The same can be said for banking and insurance industries which are converting pieces of their services and branding them as products, thus increasing service lines and revenues.

(e) **State E**: This final state involves an offering having complete intangible attributes. Examples include Spa and other wellness services, online consulting, support helplines, etc. Again, we should state here that these types of pure service offerings can also be well branded although they might not have any tangible or physical aspect to them.

With an explanation of the above states, we would also like to take up examples of how firms and marketers are using base elements of their pure products and services (across states A and E) and combining or skipping stages to develop new offerings for higher revenues or to pre-empt competition from other product or service firms. Key examples include:

(a) **Products changing their form to digital**: There are specific industries like media and broadcasting which easily lend to a complete change of their form to digital products.

Books, music, movies, TV content, etc., all have the ability to move directly from a physical to a digital product stage with large associated service elements. Other examples could include a hardboard games manufacturer, for instance, converting the whole concept of the Monopoly board-game to a digital game format for new revenues.

(b) **Products picking up a perceived benefit to convert into a service**: Nike which is the top global manufacturer of footwear, took one of its key elements 'performance' to launch iPhone Apps which provide services as a neat extension of the brand and its core values and in turn, also helps earn additional revenues.

(c) **Products converting content into new products:** Traditional information product companies are looking at strong disruptions to their models as a part of which they are creating customized products for key user segments, utilizing content as a differentiating factor.

(d) **Products converting a particular feature into a service**: Zappos is a well-known example of how a particular product element (like in this case, customization of shoes) can be taken up to develop a unique set of service elements around it, which become so differentiating as to the product itself being seen as a service. A similar example is Starbucks which built its reputation on strong service elements while delivering a rather commodity product like coffee.

(e) **Services picking up a sub-process to market as a product**: Messaging, which was always looked at as a free service to be provided to consumers (in reference to Google and Facebook for their e-mail and social media products) was picked up by WhatsApp and tweaked to build a product which helped in individual and group messaging, with an yearly subscription charge. This goes to show how sub-processes can be picked up and developed into mass offerings.

(f) **Services converting an expected service to a unique product**: The classic example here is of Geek-Squad (the post-purchase service arm of Best Buy) which was so well developed and branded into a desirable product for which customers pay yearly charges for support and maintenance services which they might not even need. A similar example on the e-commerce side, is how companies have started introducing paid services like 'Online Delivery in a Day' for extra charge which customers are delighted to pay for as an extra.

(g) **Service firms creating content-based service lines:** An example of this kind would include management institutes conducting soft skills trainings for corporates apart from their academic programs, thus utilizing the content they produce in-house through one service to create other sets of services.

(h) **Service firms using intangible elements like social networks to provide new services:** One of the best examples in this category include LinkedIn which has started providing paid services to customers to connect and send messages to other members in the social network. This is a good example to showcase how intangible digital elements, if identified and crafted well, can be used to generate incremental revenues on newer platforms with the same customer set.

With multiple examples shared, as above, on how marketers are disrupting and combining various tangible and intangible elements to create multiple product-service offerings, brands should also take care that it is not just in the creation of new products and services that business survives but how well the offering mix is differentiated and sustainable. As shared in Chapter 3 in the section titled 'Brand Building on the Web,' firms should look at developing the six brand elements (Memorable, Meaningful, Likeable, Transferrable, Adaptable, and Protectable) to their mix to achieve their digital objectives and keep differentiating.

Next we would look at the second "P" of the marketing mix which is Pricing. Pricing has a crucial impact on how offerings which have been created fare in the market and how successful companies execute their business strategies and revenue objectives.

Digital Pricing Models

Pricing by definition is the process of determining what a company will receive in exchange for its product or service. Pricing products and services for digital sales has changed in quite a many ways from how it was done traditionally. Key trends which have impacted this shift include:

(a) **Reduction of intermediaries through digital channels:** The two key reasons as to why people buy products online are convenience and cost. Also marketers are adopting and selling across digital channels as they see a chance to reduce intermediaries and provide the same product at attractive/competitive prices to more people than they are being able to do so presently through traditional channels.

(b) **Knowledge of customer buying habits and propensity:** Helps create cluster/persona-specific and channel-specific pricing. Also products can be sold at a higher price with more value-added services to support individualized needs.

(c) **Economic pressures and possibility of instant price comparisons online**: With economy paying a large role in price pressures and with internet medium providing the possibility of on-the-spot price comparisons, brands can no longer be complacent, as customers have a clear idea of both the competitor's quote and firm's product being sold on a discounting site, both of which would demand the marketer to be highly aware.

(d) **Ability for consumers to set and negotiate online prices**: With sites like Ebay where customers can take part in online auctions and also with concepts like 'Buy and sell' platforms where customers can barter products at self-set prices, a large part of the pricing control is going into the hands of the customers themselves.

(e) **Concept of 'Free Services'**: The most prominent impact of online marketing is the way businesses are built these days with consumers wanting to test products and services for free before firms can start charging. In the case of online content and service, they are being run mostly through accompanying ad-models rather than a rate-card itself.

(f) **Customer's demand for payment elasticity**: Most of today's youth who want to consume products and services instantly, need easy payment options being offered to them in terms of extended payment installments which impacts the way products and services should be priced and marketed.

(g) **Possibility of content modularity and digitization:** With a large category of products like information, books, music, entertainment, games, etc., easily lending themselves a digital format, which can be customized and sold as modules, marketers need to develop accurate and predictive pricing models to make most use of it.

(h) **Possibility of innovative business models:** With new forms of digital models emerging, marketers must utilize these trends to make revenue in varied and novel ways. Examples include—In-Game payment, App Subscription, Donation, Pay As you wish, affiliate sales, etc.

With the impact of the above trends, there has been a distinct shift in how companies today are managing their pricing for key products and services. Let us look at a typical process of developing a pricing model which companies have been following traditionally (developed by providing a digital context to 'Setting the Price' model shared in *Marketing Management*, 14th edition, by Philip Kotler).

(a) **Selecting the pricing objective**: Firms should look at their digital strategy and decide what offering mix (products and services) they would want to take online and the kind of revenue, market share, and profit objectives they aim with their presence. This would also depend on the type of channels being chosen, the kind of customer segments targeted, and how those services can be priced with regards to audience consumption patterns on those channels and sites.

(b) **Determining demand**: Generally, there is an inverse relationship between price and demand and companies need to be careful of how they price different product categories and lines. The economics behind developing demand curves and their price elasticity (responsiveness of quantity demanded to a change in its price) is not being covered in detail here as it is an extensive area of study in itself. Firms going digital typically have a lot more data and more sophisticated ways to test changes in demand based on price and large firms deploy proper statistical techniques to arrive at varied pricing depending on the kind of site, audience, landing page, and even the day and time they are selling their multi-portfolio products.

(c) **Estimating costs:** As it is important to develop pricing techniques, in the same manner, firms need to develop accurate cost models and apply them to each pricing scenario to be sure that they are profitable enough. With internet, though it seems that overheads should be lower because of reduction of intermediaries, there are other technology and infrastructure costs like website maintenance, server set-up, online security, partnership development costs which have to be borne if companies need to accurately estimate their fixed and overhead costs.

(d) **Analyzing competitor's costs, prices, and offers:** Since digital is a very price-sensitive medium and customers have access to even historic data points on each product's price, it becomes crucial to build models which will not only predict and preempt key competitors' price moves on their websites, but also make sure that for the multiple product categories being sold on e-commerce sites, the firms' products are competitive enough and are not losing out to bigger discounts or bundling options.

(e) **Selecting a pricing method:** This stage involves the actual exercise of choosing different pricing models. We have further shared traditional pricing techniques and the ones which are being followed more commonly in the digital space.

(f) **Setting the final price**: Once all the above factors have been considered, the final price is reached by including factors like impact of other marketing activities, company-specific pricing policies, impact of pricing on other parties, etc. The digital world offers marketers much more flexibility in adapting their prices since the medium itself is amenable to quick changes, which was not the case with physical pricing, where changing and labelling pricing could take days if not months. Also, a major impact on digital pricing comes in the form of promotions and deals which are very common to online landscape and whose impact we would see in the 'fourth P' on Promotions.

Traditionally, the following pricing methods have been deployed by companies:

(a) **Mark-up pricing:** This is one of the most basic pricing techniques in which a standard mark-up is added to the production cost. This method typically works only if the marked-up price brings in expected level of sales.

(b) **Target return:** The firm determines the price that yields its target rate of return on investment.

(c) **Perceived value:** Involves basing the price on customer's perceived value. It is made up of a host of inputs like buyer's image of product performance, channel deliverables, warranty quality, customer support, etc.

(d) **Value pricing:** Includes charging customers a fairly low price for a high-quality offering to win loyalty and become a low-cost producer without sacrificing quality.

(e) **Going rate:** It is where the firm bases its price largely on competitor's pricing.

With new digital structures in place, pricing models are being developed to serve these emerging business models apart from the ones shared above.

(a) **Comparative pricing**: Similar to 'going rate', this type of pricing not only compares competitor prices, but also varies itself in relation to data on customer visits, their loyalty, influence of the channel, e-commerce site on which it is being sold, customer sentiment across social networks, keyword searches, etc.

(b) **Ad supported model:** This is one of the core models on which digital business was developed wherein instead of charging the consumer, businesses and advertisers were charged for placing ads across most read content, or keywords searched in Google, or against reviews they liked across a social network. We would get into the dynamics of how advertisers are priced in the later chapters in detail.

(c) **Subscription model**: With a large part of content being available in digital format, and customer's problems being broken down into sub-processes and serviced through quick-reference applications (for example, mobile apps), there has been a surge of interesting subscription-based models where customers are paying for packages of information, entertainment, education, etc., on a time-bound fixed price basis.

(d) **Pay-per content/use model**: It is now possible to charge customers for each content piece and even on the usage time for that content as digital medium can provide all of this information on a real-time basis to marketers.

(e) **Auction type:** With multiple models being developed using auction techniques, this pricing technique has been democratized for consumers with such ease on digital platforms that it deserves to be a digital-led pricing model.

(f) **Last minute pricing**: Possible only in online mode; either you can increase prices in case of high demand-low supply (online airline prices) or you can reduce prices in case of low-demand and high supply (for example, unsold event tickets on the day of the event).

(g) **Customized pricing/cart-based pricing**: For loyal customers, who buy regularly from a site or a platform, digital technology can help marketers calculate discounts, provide bundling offers, share free coupons on regularly bought items as a part of their pricing strategy.

With the above discussion on most prevalent digital pricing models, let us see how some of them are being applied to the five digital offering states:

(a) **State A (pure tangible good):** Goods sold through e-commerce, auction, and branded sites; typically comparative, mark-up, auction pricing are applied here.

(b) **State B (tangible good and related services):** Bundling popular offline product with online services (Newspaper with its digital edition); this is generally a subscription model which can also include perceived value or customized pricing models.

(c) **State C (hybrid model):** Products like B2B Information have an equal services aspect, wherein specific pieces of information can be segregated and provided in a customized manner to higher paying or niche segments. The most common pricing models for information being sold in such a modular fashion include subscription pricing, price per content, and price per usage.

(d) **State D (major service with few goods):** Typical examples include productized service companies which essentially sell services in the form of products like Google or Microsoft. Target return and comparative pricing are typically applied here.

(e) **State E (pure service):** Online industry mostly started out with content, networks, and sharing as its core models (for example, blogs, curated news sites, aggregators, social networking sites, etc.) which did not charge initially but developed delighted and loyal customers. They were then typically charged through advertising, subscription, and pay per content/use model. Most prominent examples include YouTube, Facebook, Twitter, which are mostly ad-supported apart from other models like LinkedIn, WhatsApp, Wikipedia which go either the subscription or donation way.

Channels of Purchase—Reaching the E-Consumer

Moving to the third P which is known as Place, we will see how channels of purchase are critical to a firm and how companies can make sure that their products and services are present at the right places where their e-Consumers would be looking for them.

A key distinction has to be made here to understand the difference between Place and the next P which is Promotion. By channels of purchase, we mean only those channels through which final ordering and fulfillment happens while channels which are utilized for promotion (like search engines, e-mail, display ads, social media, etc.) and are more of a conduit to the final purchase (will be covered in the Promotions section).

With this understanding, we will first look at the basic classification of channel ownership across direct and indirect sales channels and also across sales effort orientation which could be push-based (more transactional) or pull-based (more informative/engaging). We should note that the matrix developed here as an example pertains more to marketing of products than services.

Typically, channels of purchase are divided into two types:

(a) Direct sales channels—where a producer and ultimate consumer directly deal with each other. These channels are typically owned and controlled by firms themselves.
(b) Indirect sales channels—when there are indirect intermediaries between the producer and consumer. Third party companies typically have more control of these channels.

In Fig. 5.8, we have created a matrix between channel ownership and sales orientation. By sales orientation, we imply the effort of sales and marketing activities and its direction. As discussed in Chapter 1 in the section titled 'Emergence of Digital as a Marketing Tool,' push and pull marketing differ in the way products and services are sold to the e-consumer. While push marketing has a more sales mindset in which firms set an inventory target to be sold in a particular period, pull marketing has a more information-oriented focus in which the customers

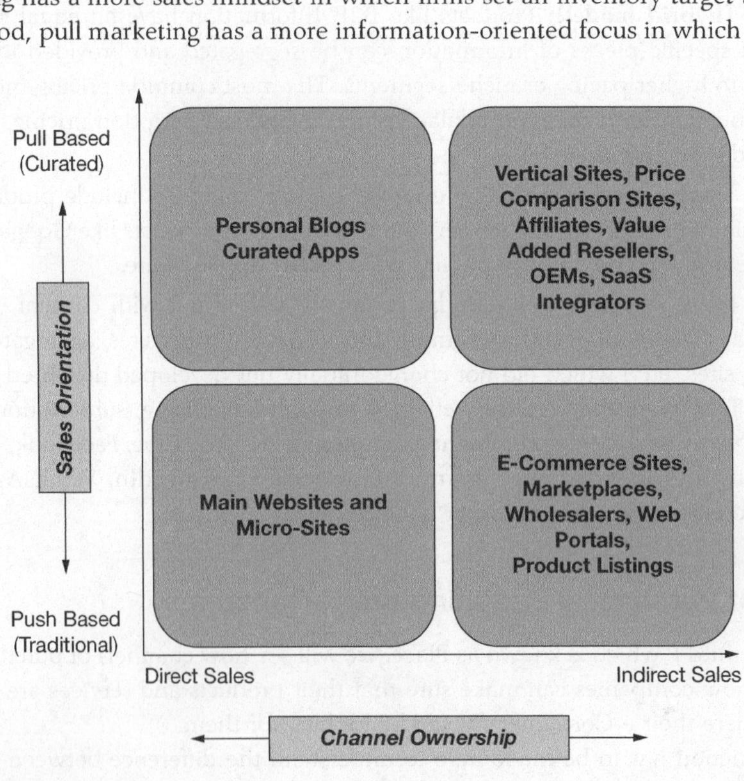

Figure 5.8 Channel Ownership—Sales Orientation Matrix

are made to engage with the channel through customized and curated content (which can be hosted either on direct or indirect sales channels). Some of the key examples of each of these matrix quadrants include:

(a) **Direct push channels:** Involve branded websites and microsites which are developed and controlled by the firm, through which firms make a direct sale to customers.

(b) **Direct pull channels:** Include content-based channels like blogs and, the more recent phenomenon of mobile apps specific to a particular business process, developed in a well guided and curated manner to make it simple and engaging for customers to buy.

(c) **Indirect push channels:** This quadrant typically contributes the most to online sales and includes highly popular e-commerce sites, marketplaces, wholesalers who have set up online presences, web portals which offer widgets to firms to sell their products, product listing sites which help market the firm and list its products, etc., among others.

(d) **Indirect pull channels:** These are channels which have high engagement rates with custom audiences and provide value beyond the push-based channels. These include vertical sites (like car sales only sites), price comparison sites, affiliates (who sell products on behalf of a firm for a commission), value-added resellers (who provide services wrapped around a firm's product to deliver a more complete solution to customers), Other Equipment Manufacturers (OEMs) who resell a firm's product under their own name and branding (for example, Salesforce announced its AppExchange OEM Edition in 2006), SaaS Integrators (system integrators who provide end-to-end solutions by integrating a firm's product with others and make their revenues through services rather than product resale, for example, Bluewolf).

With an understanding of the channels of purchase, we now move on to the last of the four main Ps, which is Promotion. Promotion is what determines the extent and quality of traffic to come to direct and indirect sales channels.

Managing Promotional Channels

As discussed in the last section, promotional channels are those which help marketers position and promote their products across customer funnel stages so that they finally purchase products on the aforementioned channels of purchase. This said, we should actually look at all of the channels of final purchase shared above as promotional channels since they too contribute to increasing awareness, generating interest, and managing engagement for a consumer to fulfill marketing objectives across the funnel.

Promotional channels form the core of digital marketing and the key types of channels and communication methods would be covered in detail in the next chapter. For the present section, we will make an introduction to some of the most important online promotion channels through the use of the key marketing funnel stages (as shared in the REAN Marketing Engagement Framework in Chapter 1). We would be covering here the key stages of Reach, Engage, and Activate, which include the most important promotional channels.

Figure 5.9 Promotional Channels across Key Marketing Funnel Stages

In Fig.5.9, we have divided the key promotional channels across three major marketing funnel stages of Reach, Engage, and Activate. We will have a quick look at major types of promotions covered across these channels and will cover key channels in depth later.

(a) **Reach**—As we have seen before, Reach involves the set of promotional activities to raise prospects' attention to marketer's brand product or service. Key promotional areas include:

- **Search engine marketing:** Part of intent-based marketing channels, it includes areas like search engine marketing/pay per click, search engine optimization.
- **Display marketing:** Classified as a part of brand marketing, it includes banner ads, sponsorships, rich media ads, video ads, among others.
- **E-mail marketing:** Forms a part of direct message marketing and includes personal messages shared via e-mail, sms, newsletters, etc.
- **Affiliate marketing:** Part of the partner marketing channel, it includes promotions shared as a part of affiliate sales efforts.
- **Social media sites:** Part of community-based marketing areas, it includes social media, collaboration, networking platforms.

(b) **Engage:** Involves the set of activities needed to engage prospects developed during the Reach stage. Key areas include:

- **Content marketing:** Includes all content and information-related areas through which marketers promote their products and services, as well as, web content development, blog management, native content, webinars, playbooks, etc.
- **Public relations:** Oriented typically towards media, key areas include newsletters, online magazines, link-building on sites, etc.
- **Special interest marketing:** Involves activities related to developing specialized content and building networks through vertical and special interest sites.
- **Viral marketing:** Refers to videos, social messages, articles on buzzing topics created as sharable content for people to share brand values in an entertaining manner.
- **Gamification**: Involves techniques in which brand marketing is done by deploying gaming in non-game contexts where users are given prizes, discounts, and coupons for engagement and product trials.

(c) **Activate:** Includes activities to convert leads and make prospects take other actions which marketers want them to. Key areas include:
- **Interest-based marketing:** Involves promotion to customers who have interacted with a product on any of the online sales channel through personal messaging or giving them offers/discounts/coupons for real-time conversions.
- **Social targeting:** Includes sharing targeted messages to leads on social platforms; for example, Twitter tying up with Amazon to support consumers buy a product on Amazon using a Twitter message.
- **Retargeting**: Involves all sets of promotional activities to re-target ads (images and content) specifically for products which they left abandoned in website carts.
- **Response marketing:** Covers all activities which help respond to specific consumer queries while prospects are at the last stage of buying. It includes automated chats, sending response mails/SMSes to queries, social media responses, etc.
- **Custom recommendations:** Involves sending direct promotions to consumers on related products/recommendations associated to what they have already bought.

With an understanding of the classic four Ps, we would now move to understand the set of extended 4Ps including People, Process, Programs, and Performance in the next section.

Developing the Extended Ps- People, Process, Programs, and Performance

With the growing proliferation of marketing channels, techniques and technologies being deployed, the 4Ps suggested by McCarthy have been added with four more Ps which should be considered by marketers while creating their marketing mix plans and strategies. Below, we would go through them in detail:

(a) **People**: Involves developing online teams with a mix of digital marketing expertise, technology know-how, multi-channel experience, knowledge of automation tools, and most of all, target customer insights. It also involves how to look at customers with all their human impulses and desires to know what would entice them most towards marketing efforts both on the content and creative side.

(b) **Processes:** Involves developing a rigorous process-driven marketing organization which lays down clear steps to understand and identify target customer clusters, develop thought-through and tightly integrated supplier-customer processes and manage campaigns as a series of processes with clearly aligned goals parallel to consumer funnel activities, with ways and means to refine them as needed.

(c) **Programs:** It is defined as the entire set of consumer-driven programs which are run in a holistic manner online and offline to meet a firm's marketing objectives. It also includes all the multi-channel initiatives which are taken across traditional and new platforms to make sure that customers at all stages, be it targets, prospects, or leads are touched upon and impacted in a 360-degree manner.

(d) **Performance:** The final P relates to setting up systems and ways to measure performance and desired output at each stage of the marketing activity, through well-defined metrics and KPIs (Key Performance Indicators). Performance evaluation should touch all of the other Ps to continually refine the offering mix, related pricing offered, performance of various channels of purchase, and the extent of impact brought about by various promotional set-ups.

With a knowledge of these extended Ps, (specifically developed to cater to the changing demands of today's digital marketing activities), we are now in a position to understand how the strategy for a Digital Marketing Program can be developed, how firms (depending upon the digital and Product Lifecycle stage they are in) can make use of the '6S Strategy Roadmap' to plan their journey and successfully conduct digital marketing programs. In the next part, we shall look into all of these in more detail.

DIGITAL MARKETING STRATEGY ROADMAP

In the first two parts of this chapter, we showcased a basic understanding of the factors to be considered by any firm while developing a strategy for digital. In this section, we would use the concepts developed on digital business structures, competency alignment, STP2.0, and the 8 Ps to look at how firms can create a digital marketing implementation strategy for their needs depending upon their digital state and presence of products across the product lifecycle.

It should be noted here, that this is the last part of the two chapters on digital marketing strategy development and we have till now covered most of the inputs we need to develop a digital marketing strategy roadmap. The next chapter would take on the concepts of digital marketing strategy shared here to develop digital marketing planning, operations, and set-up. Understanding this part and its applications is thus crucial for marketers and students as it will form the base for the rest of the planning and implementation-related chapters.

Developing Digital Marketing Strategy Roadmap

In this chapter, the overall objective was to show how a digital marketing strategy can be developed and the stages which would go into building the roadmap. In this section, we would take a closer look at the four stages of this roadmap.

Figure 5.10 enlists the four key stages of developing a digital marketing strategy roadmap. These four stages constitute the key steps required to develop the second phase of the ASCOR framework, which is the strategy phase:

(a) **Business strategy for digital**: Involves developing the overall strategy and direction for any firm planning to move to the digital platform

(b) **Customer development strategy:** Includes strategy elements to identify and define target customer segments and position product marketing and experience accordingly

(c) **Digital marketing mix strategy:** Includes the 8 marketing Ps to develop the marketing mix

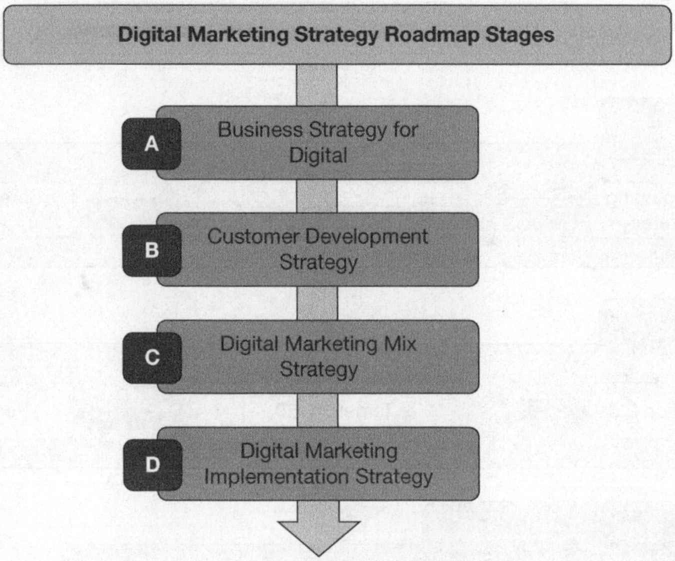

Figure 5.10 Digital Marketing Strategy Roadmap Stages

(d) **Digital marketing implementation strategy**: Includes the 6S of digital marketing implementation strategy for each product depending on its presence across product life cycle stage

With this understanding of the digital marketing strategy roadmap stages, let us look at key elements which constitute it in more detail.

Figure 5.11 showcases the key elements of all four strategy roadmap stages. The first three stages A, B, and C have already been covered in detail in the first two sections and we would cover them briefly over here. The final Stage D on digital marketing implementation strategy would be covered in the next section.

The digital marketing strategy roadmap stages include:

(a) **Business strategy for digital**: As discussed in the first section, firms need to develop the following elements as a part of their overall business strategy for the digital platform:

- **Factors impacting digital strategy**: Involves firms understanding the impact of digital presence drivers—stakeholder, market, customer, and competitor to define the overall business strategy intent for going digital
- **Firms strategic intent**: Includes analysis of the business structure of the firm, type of investments they are willing to put to their digital operations, and the kind of returns and growth they are expecting from digital channels
- **Core competency alignment**: Involves firms analyzing and interpreting shifts in the value function of their industry relative to their customer and aligning core competencies accordingly to develop the most appropriate OVP

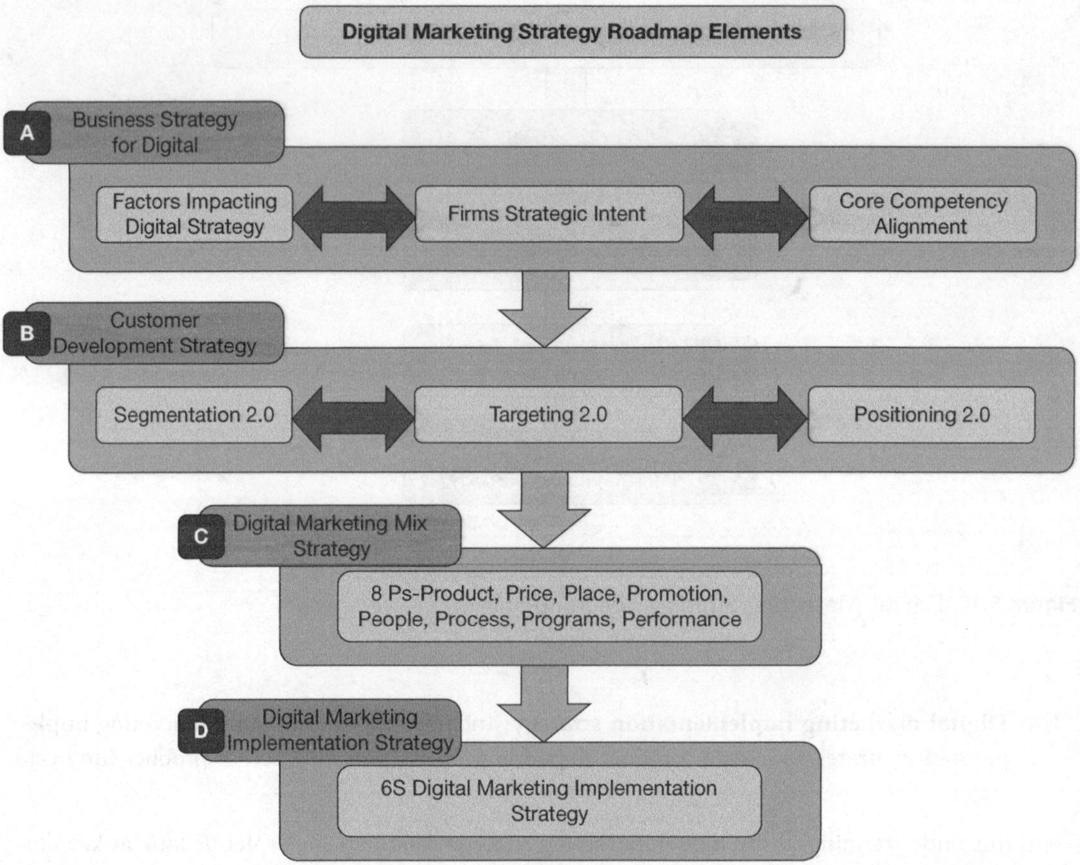

Figure 5.11 Digital Marketing Strategy Roadmap Elements

(b) **Customer development strategy:** Includes activities for understanding key customer segments, creating clusters, and developing personas of the type of segments which the firm would target and develop the positioning towards customers' need fulfillment

- **Segmentation 2.0:** Involves usage of sophisticated technologies to yield highly refined and actionable audience clusters for market segmentation
- **Targeting 2.0:** Involves development of user personas to understand the goals and behaviors of the group of users which the firm would like to target
- **Positioning 2.0:** Refers to the set of activities, which the firm will develop to respond to the needs of each customer segment across their marketing funnel journeys

(c) **Digital marketing mix strategy:** Involves development of the 8Ps of the Marketing Mix:

- **Classic 4Ps:** Include the most widely used marketing mix of product offering, pricing models, channels of purchase, and promotional mix
- **Extended 4Ps:** Include the extended Ps—People, Process, Programs, Performance

(d) **Digital marketing implementation strategy:** Involves development of 6S digital implementation strategy roadmap which we will cover in detail in the next section. This would also include looking at each product's presence across the product lifecycle stage and developing strategies accordingly.

The 6S Digital Marketing Implementation Strategy

Once a firm has done the groundwork for digital marketing strategy development, the last stage involves developing an implementation strategy for chosen customer segments and marketing mix to chart the strategy for firm's digital growth. To develop this implementation strategy, we have developed a '6S Framework' which has been developed using the 'Digital Presence Analysis Matrix' (discussed earlier Chapter 4) as its base.

To understand the key elements of the 6S Framework as developed in Fig. 5.12, we have taken the same X and Y axis in the matrix diagram as the 'Digital Presence Analysis (DPA) Matrix.' To recap the DPA, it is a matrix which talks about four digital states in which a firm can be present depending on the extent of its digital presence and its market standing with regards to competition in the same segment.

To develop the 6S implementation stages, as we can see in Fig. 5.12, the matrix has been divided into six distinct columns which represent the gradual journey of a firm which has no digital presence (as shown in extreme left through the DS1 Column) to the stage where it is present across multiple digital channels and platforms (shown as DS6 Column in Extreme Right). Each of these six digital implementation stages combined, form the 6S Framework. We have to note

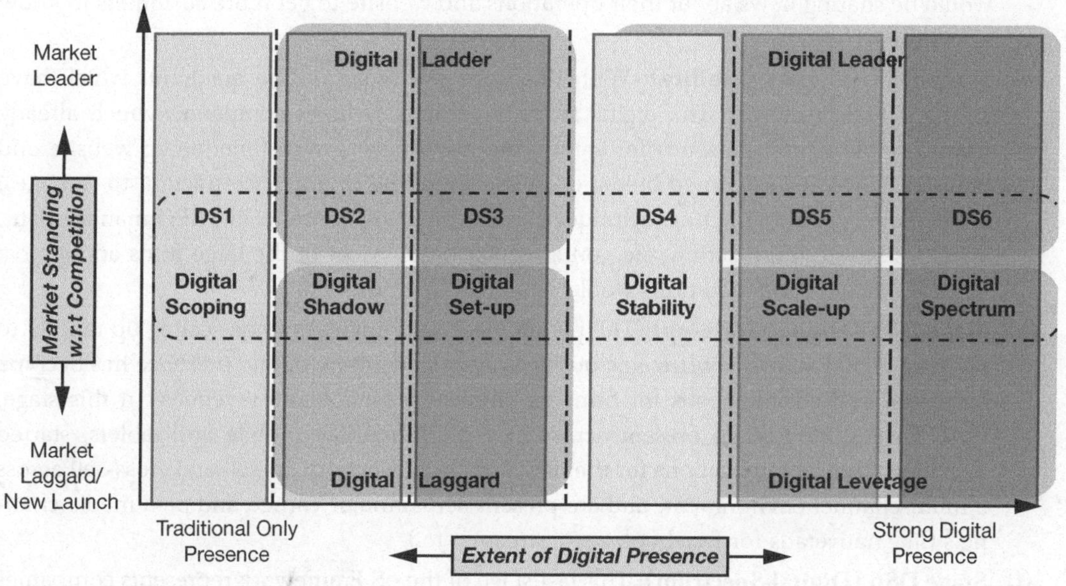

Figure 5.12 6S Digital Marketing Implementation Stages

here that apart from DS1, all the other five progressive columns cut across at least two quadrants, which means that any particular stage covers all types of companies for that digital presence, be they a market laggard or market leader. We detail the 6S stages as follows:

(a) **Stage DS1 (Digital Scoping):** This stage includes firms which are purely traditional and have no presence at all on any digital channels. They essentially are either in a denial state or have been considering digital for some time, thus weighing their options to know how and which channels would be the best to engage for a start. Such type of firms typically include the SMB (small and medium business) segment or individuals who have not realized the power of the digital platform or are doing so well with their offline presence that they do not intend to go digital in the near future.

(b) **Stage DS2 (Digital Shadow):** This next stage is covered with companies which have taken their first steps towards being digital in the form of getting their names to be a part of product listing sites or placing basic information on their presence up on Google Maps/Places. They might also have created limited presence on earned media (social channels like Facebook or account on Twitter) which is almost like a shadow to their well-developed offline operations. Firms in this stage still have not realized the importance of developing owned media presence online.

(c) **Stage DS3 (Digital Set-up):** The third column represents firms which have definitely realized the importance of an online set-up to their offline operations and are willing to spend effort and budget in developing the appropriate channels to compete and climb the digital ladder. Firms here have developed their first websites (owned media presence) and would also have set-up campaigns through paid media channels (particularly SEM, Display). They would also have a stable Facebook page (might not be highly active) on which they would be sharing news about their operations and website to get more customers to know about them.

(d) **Stage DS4 (Digital Stability):** With this stage, we move on the quadrants which have strong digital presences. The digital stability column includes companies which already have a stable digital presence for some time now; have a well-functioning website and blog; presence across earned media channels (resulting in audience traction to website); are deploying paid marketing techniques; and even using concepts like SEO management, analytics-based optimization, etc., on a regular basis. Most of the large firms and almost all new digitally launched firms would definitely be in this stage.

(e) **Stage DS5 (Digital Scale-up):** The penultimate state involves firms scaling up rapidly to leverage digital across key strategic business areas and where online presence has become as crucial and advantageous for firms as physical presence and revenues. In this stage, firms have started to be present across new platforms like mobile and tablets, started developing native applications for the new platforms, begin to up-sell and cross-sell across a multi-channel environment, and are present across major earned and paid media channels (like native ads for Facebook news stream, etc.).

(f) **Stage DS6 (Digital Spectrum):** This last stage of the 6S Framework represents companies which are digital-first in nature and where most of the digital activities and campaigns are well orchestrated with clarity of desired outcomes. These companies can also be referred to be digital leaders and have covered the whole spectrum of advanced digital marketing activities like retargeting, content optimization, funnel-stage specific response marketing, analytics-driven customized recommendations, etc. The biggest players in this segment leverage digital in multiple ways to increase offline sales too.

With an understanding of the 6S Framework, let us see how firms can make use of the digital marketing implementation strategies depending upon the stage where they are present:

(a) With a knowledge of the stage in which the firm is present they can devise specific implementation strategies for their digital state depending upon their business objectives and the kind of digital leverage they need

(b) Helps know the type of channels and strategies firms can deploy for their set of chosen target audience clusters and help them understand and establish their need to be online and the extent to which they really need to invest for incremental RoI

(c) Provides insights on how they can model their marketing mix in the best possible manner to put forth offerings with the pricing structure and promotions specific to the digital stage where the firm's products or services might be

(d) Helps firms map their competitor's presence across these six stages to assess where they need to invest further or alter their digital marketing strategy to be present on platforms and embrace newer concepts and media presences in quick-time

For developing the 6S digital marketing implementation framework, there is one more key element which firms need to definitely look at to develop a successful digital marketing strategy roadmap. This is the presence of firms' products across the PLC (product lifecycle stages) which determines whether the product is in its introductory stage, growth, or decline phase. This along-with factors like digital presence extent and product's standing in the market (as discussed in the matrix above) provide the best direction to a firm on how they can develop strategies for each of their product categories and product lines specific to the target audience.

We would look at understanding the PLC concept and its key stages in the next section of this part, analysis of which is crucial for the firm to finalize its implementation strategy.

PLC Concept—Marketing across the Product Life Cycle

In this final section of the chapter, would understand a key concept related to Product development and used across multiple business and industry functions. Applied to the marketing context, it is also called product life cycle management and involves the process of managing the entire life cycle of a product from inception, through engineering design and manufacture, to service and disposal of manufactured products.

The importance of understanding PLC in the context of digital marketing involves marketers having a knowledge of the life cycle stage in which each of their products in the portfolio lie, so that they can develop specific implementation strategies in accordance with the 6S digital presence state as shared in the last section.

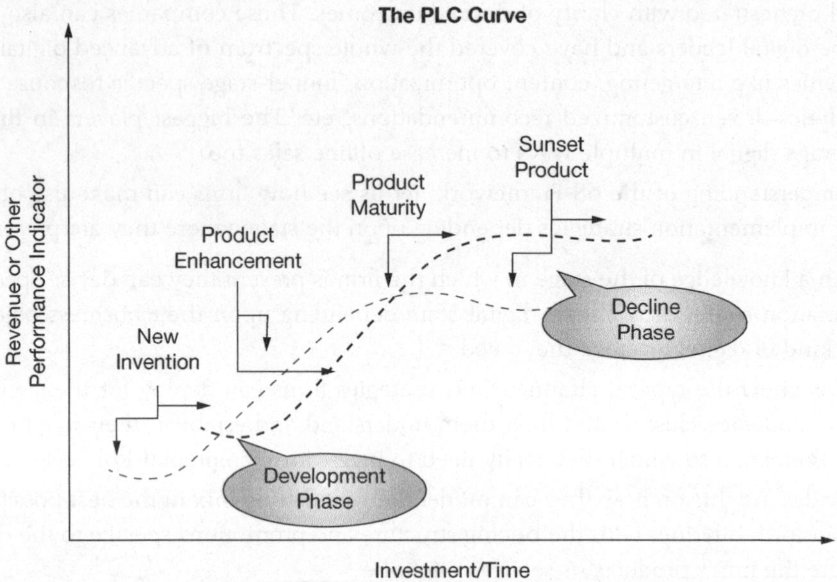

Figure 5.13 Understanding PLC Phases
Source: Captives in India, http://survey.nasscom.in, accessed in February 2017

To get into more detail, let us first view the key phases of the PLC curve.

In Fig. 5.13, the growth stages of any two generic products (two curves as shown) have been plotted across the axes of investment/time (key lifecycle stages can be extended with higher investments) and revenue growth (or other performance indicators like market share/profitability etc). We would detail out each of the four phases here:

(a) **Product launch/development phase:** Refers to the period when a new product is launched in the market or an old product is repositioned in the market with a new variant or completely new positioning to a similar or new audience segment.

(b) **Product growth/enhancement phase:** This is the stage where the product grows in stature and it's in the most flourishing state. Most of the products typically touch their highest revenue and market share during this phase, although that can be prolonged to the next stage of product maturity too.

(c) **Product maturity phase/decline phase:** In this phase, the product starts to decline, its features are being perceived as generic, and there are other competitors which have arrived to take over the value function and develop compelling value propositions.

(d) **Product sunset phase/termination phase:** This last and final phase involves a gradual termination of the product wherein it is either pulled out of the portfolio or is put aside to market a similar brand in the portfolio which has attributes well suited to changing consumption patterns and tastes of the new target audience.

An understanding of the PLC stages helps marketers know where a particular product might lie in the present market environment and help the firm create relevant implementation strategies depending on their present state. Key examples of how PLC helps devise digital marketing implementation strategies across each of the four stages include:

(a) **Development phase:** For a product in the development or launch stage, firms need to invest a lot more in driving visibility and initial awareness. Digital channels like search, display, e-mail, and viral marketing could help drive and support offline initiatives. Firms here should put more efforts to developing paid and owned media.

(b) **Enhancement phase:** Products in the growth stage need to put more focus on earned media so that customers engage with the product at a deeper level and become loyalists/advocates who would not leave the brand even through its decline.

(c) **Decline phase:** In this phase, the product has lost the sheen and excitement it once had with its target customers and too much of newer investments into growing the channels might not help. Instead, focusing investments on key customer groups which have been loyal to the brand would make sense, so that they keep the brand afloat. A more content and emotive brand communication focus would help here.

(d) **Termination phase:** This is where the product category or key product-lines are finally terminated and the cycle of new product development starts to replace those.

With an understanding of the key PLC stages and the type of digital marketing most suited to them, in the next chapter, we will study key digital marketing channels and communication types through which marketers can implement their digital marketing strategies across the 6S stages (with knowledge of the PLC Phase) specific to each product.

PRACTICAL EXERCISE

Executing Competitive Research

Key Objective To gain practical know-how of the best way to execute competitive research for an already existing or to be launched product in the market.

Project Brief Your company plans to launch a new air purifier in the market and wants you to develop a competitive research on the products of existing competitor(s) products and their perception in the market.

How would you start gathering competitive trends in the category to understand the performance of various competing brands? Execute a digital analysis based on the inputs provided in this section along-with an offline research of the key competitors in the market.

Execution Here are some of the top resource categories for executing a competitive research for this exercise:

(a) **Gathering Latest News on Competition:** First and foremost, marketers should start gathering and analysing top news and feeds on key competitors for their product category with the help of Google News/Google Alerts/Feedly and any other RSS aggregator tools. This would help gain an understanding of the latest activities and initiatives across the brand's competitive environment.

(b) **Searching Audience Set:** As a next step, you should try and understand key demographic or psychographic trends of related audience set for the product category. Google Display Planner is a great tool to analyze multiple audience sets and the type of publisher sites they visit for any specific category of product.

(c) **Comparing Competitive Website Traffic:** The next key step involves gathering a stronghold on traffic analysis across competitive websites to review key traffic sources, volumes, patterns, time spent on key pages, etc. Multiple industry tools can help marketers execute a strategic analysis of competitive websites among them include:

- Alexa
- SimilarWeb
- Compete
- Website Informer
- BuiltWith

(d) **Social Media Listening on Competing Brands:** Apart from website traffic trends, it is crucial to understand what each competitor is talking about in the market and how they are positioning consumer interactions and content for their brands. Social media listening sites help make sense of key message trends for each competing brand. Some of the top websites for competitive social media listening include:

- www.socialmention.com
- www.brand24.com
- www.RivalIQ.com
- www.Talkwalker.com
- www.brandwatch.com
- www.Buzzsumo.com

(e) **Keyword Analysis on Consumer Intent:** Understanding consumer intent while they search for a competing brand provides important clues on what consumers find most useful about a brand while they search for a specific category and their key intent. Major keyword analysis tools that help map competitive keywords include:

- SEMrush
- Google Keyword Planner
- Ahrefs
- Websonfs.com
- Raven Tools

(f) **Other Competitive Benchmarking Tools:** The market also has a lot of unique tool categories that can help marketers map the competitive landscape through varied benchmarking features. Some of the prominent ones include Track Maven, Google Analytics

(Benchmarking Data), Google Ad Preview and Diagnosis Tool, Facebook 'Pages to Watch', and MOAT.

Competitive benchmarking is a crucial exercise for digital planning, and brand managers need to select the most appropriate set of tools to compare their brands based on product categories and competitive set. Inputs from any competitive research exercise should be integrated with both consumer and market trend analysis to gain a complete picture of the market situation for most efficient strategy formulation. After completion of this exercise, do try and map your competitive research document with similar consumer and market assessment exercises to share common findings and emerging patterns that could impact any digital marketing strategy formulation exercise.

CHAPTER SUMMARY

- **Part 1:** In the first section, we started with the key concepts of developing strategy for digital business, which acts *as the groundwork to develop the digital* marketing strategy roadmap. We looked at the type of impact factors and emerging business structures for digital. This was followed by a detailed understanding of how firms planning to go digital should align their core competencies to changing value function shifts and strategies to redefine OVP. The part ends with a thorough look into the elements of customer development including the revised STP2.0 (Segmenting, Targeting, Positioning) Framework and how with the help of advanced technologies marketers can position their offerings across the funnel stages.
- **Part 2:** This part covered the classic 4Ps of marketing mix (Product, Price, Place, Promotion) along with extending them to the new 4Ps of People, Process, Programs, and Performance. We started with understanding the five offering (product-service) mix states and how firms across these are developing digital offerings. This was followed by an understanding of how pricing models on digital platforms have changed from traditional ones. We then looked at the key 'Channels of Purchase' and learnt *the type of* 'Promotional Channels' deployed for each of the marketer funnel stages. Finally, we had a quick look at the definitions and impact of the four new digital Ps.
- **Part 3:** The last part of the chapter focused on developing the digital marketing strategy roadmap and its four key stages. We learnt how the elements of business strategy, consumer development strategy, digital marketing mix and implementation strategy combine to form the overall strategy roadmap and how the groundwork for these stages (shown in the first two parts) helps create the roadmap. We looked at the 6S (Scoping, Shadow, Set-up, Stability, Scale-up, and Spectrum) Digital Marketing Implementation Strategy Framework and its stages to see how firms present in each of these stages can implement a digital presence in a gradual fashion. Finally, we also looked at the concept of Product Life Cycle (PLC) and how firm's products present in each of the four phases would have differing digital marketing strategies.

REVIEW QUESTIONS

1. Explain the four Digital Strategy Impact factors. Pick up any one of the four drivers to compare and contrast the sub-elements of one of these external factors to understand how they have been impacted by digital interventions.
2. Explain the RoI-based Digital Market Structure Development model. Discuss briefly, the seven types of Digital Business structures.
3. Explain the concept of Core Competency Alignment and its five key stages in detail.
4. What is STP 2.0 Framework? How does it differ from the traditional STP model?
5. Explain in detail either of the three STP 2.0 elements:
   (a) Data Segmentation Matrix (Segmentation 2.0)
   (b) Clustering and Persona Creation (Targeting 2.0)
   (c) Positioning across Consumer Funnel Scenarios (Positioning 2.0)
6. Explain the concept of Positioning 2.0 through the process of persona creation across each of the five consumer funnel stages.
7. What do we mean by an offering mix for digital? Explain the five stages of an offering mix across product-service states.
8. What are some of the key trends which have impacted the shift of pricing products and services from traditional to digital?
9. With new digital structures in place, name some pricing models which are being developed to serve these emerging business models.
10. What do we mean by channels of purchase? Share your understanding of the Channel Ownership-Sales Orientation Matrix in detail.
11. What are promotional channels? Name the key promotional channels across key marketing funnel stages and explain the channels across any one of the funnel stages in detail.
12. Explain the four key stages of the Digital Marketing Strategy Roadmap.
13. What is the 6S Framework for Digital Marketing Implementation Strategy? Explain the six implementation stages in detail.
14. What is the PLC concept? Describe the 4 key stages of the PLC curve as discussed in the chapter.
15. Share few examples of how PLC helps devise Digital Marketing Implementation strategies across each of its four stages.

DIGITAL APPLICATION EXERCISES

1. Pick up any of the top Indian FMCG companies (Uniliver, P&G, ITC, Patanjali, etc.) and scan their online website to understand their business direction. Which of the four digital strategy impact factors do you feel has attributed the most to their digital roadmap in the past few years? Compare and contrast on the lines discussed in the chapter.
2. Choose any FMCG product category in India (soap, shampoo, juices, etc.) and

explain the five key stages through any five brands in that product category similar to the telecom example shared in the chapter.

3. For the chosen FMCG company (in the first digital application exercise question) choose any of the food/beverage brands you like the most to develop and describe the STP 2.0 Framework model for that brand.
4. For online travel booking site Cleartrip.com, choose any one of the five consumer funnel stages and create a persona and positioning for that funnel stage.
5. Visit Jet Airways.com as an example to study the aviation offering mix model. Out of the five stages which one do you feel applies most to it and why?
6. Share any Indian online business which deploys three different pricing models to garner online revenue?
7. Intex Technologies is an India-bred consumer electronics company which steadily grew across product categories with the rise of the Indian online marketplace. Visit Intex.in and pick up any single product category which Intex sells (mobiles, LED, consumer durables, etc.) and research the type of channels it sells through by applying the Sales Orientation Matrix.
8. Research and make a list of all promotional channels on which Flipkart.com promotes itself. Then segregate that list across the three key funnel stages as per the chapter.
9. Patanjali Ayurved has started its journey to become the biggest FMCG brand in India (www.patanjaliayurved.net). Devise a complete digital marketing implementation strategy for the brand utilizing the stages of the 6S Framework as shared in the chapter.

UNIT III DIGITAL MARKETING PLANNING AND SETUP

CHAPTER 6

Digital Marketing Communications and Channel Mix

LEARNING OBJECTIVES

After studying this chapter, you will be able to:

- Explain the terminology and concepts for developing web-specific media plans
- Classify promotional channels across paid,owned, and earned media and analyze digital marketing investments for RoI
- Describe the activities that shape the communication mix across different digital marketing channels and learn how to develop and deliver communications message across them
- Analyze the functions, advantages and applications of the seven important types of digital marketing channels

CASE STUDY Times Internet: *The voice of Indian news*

Ever since 2000, the mode of news delivery to audiences has changed a lot and so has the Times Internet Limited (TIL) group. From delivering news digitally to offering entertainment platforms, TIL experienced impressive growth in most of their key divisions over the last five years. As per the Times Internet Annual Report 2021, though the group has faced challenges, online advertising income surged 26 per cent to ₹621.27 crore, while net losses narrowed 79 per cent down to ₹40.53 crore from ₹196 crore.

Times Internet has maintained good engagement levels because of two key contributing factors: first is the Indian digitalization policy and second being the COVID-19 pandemic. Since the past 5 years, Indian media companies have focused on digitalization where the huge trend has been Indians looking for news updates online. Times of India is still the ruling English newspaper in the Indian media market and during the pandemic, they were able to increase their digital reach. Even (NBT) NavBharat Times and (ET) The Economic Times witnessed subsequent growth in these years. Times Internet launched 'Times Fact Check' as an initiative to detect manipulated and fake news prevailing on the Internet. This strategy has made this platform more reliable and trustworthy for users.

Since their inception, the Times Internet group had also made some big bets by acquiring major platforms like MagicBricks (2006), Gaana (2010), Cricbuzz (2014), and Gradeup (2014). As smartphone penetration has steadily increased since 2017, all these platforms gained a lot of engagement and users, which ultimately helped Times Internet grow. Cricbuzz is the most popular application in India for getting cricket updates. In 2019, over 118 million people used Cricbuzz for latest updates. Times Internet group also made a huge bet on Gaana.com, which crossed 100 million monthly users in March 2019. Times Internet-owned Gradeup saw a 200% growth in their student-base in FY 2019. Much of this growth can be attributed to the fact that Gradeup launched online classrooms which turned out to be a booster for them (engagement increased 4 times as compared to recorded lectures).

In addition to all these bets, the Times Internet group also added newer platforms, which include Times Prime (2018), ETimes (2018), ET Prime (2018), and MX player (2019). In 2020, MX Player was launched and it gained over 275 million active users worldwide. In a short span of time, MX Player has become the top OTT platform in India and in 2021, it had 175 million active users. TIL has partnered with Twitter to ensure that the best content from its leading online publications is available on the social network. This has helped to not just delight audiences, but also to ensure that advertising partners align with Twitter's Amplify sponsorship program.

The reason for Times Internet's success is the diversified approach that this group had adopted, be it sports, entertainment, news, education, personal finance, food, or real estate. The company is investing in transactional and subscription businesses like Dineout (restaurant reservation app), Times Prime (exclusive membership program), ETMoney (personal finance platform), etc. for ARPU (Average Revenue Per Unit) uplift and continued growth along with investment in technology and R&D. In the next two years, the group expects to continue investing across multiple new and existing businesses.

DIGITAL MARKETING PLANNING DEVELOPMENT

In the last two chapters (4 and 5), we looked at the first two phases of the ASCOR Digital Marketing Framework to cover the external/internal assessment and strategy development stages. The next step involves understanding how digital marketing plans are created and specifically how the communications mix is developed.

This chapter will commence with an understanding of traditional media planning concepts that cover marketer's promotional activities on offline media, how those concepts translate to the digital side and the meaning of media planning on online platforms. We will then cover the basic stages of digital marketing planning, its success criteria, and evaluation. This will be followed by two sections specifically on designing communication strategy and discussing this further through examples of key digital marketing channels.

The Media Planning Shift to Digital

To develop an understanding of the third phase of ASCOR Framework Communication and Channel Plan, we need to first understand the basics of media planning as has been conducted in its traditional sense. Media planning by definition is the task of allocating promotional budgets to multiple media channels/platforms to communicate a product's presence, differentiators, and values. Traditionally for marketers, this has been a crucial exercise and mostly conducted in collaboration with an agency which works on behalf of the company and gets a commission for handling all media buying, placement, and execution activities. Let us look at some of the traditional definitions which form a part of media planning exercise and how these key concepts are being redefined with the coming of digital channels.

(a) **Media channel:** It is the medium/platform through which brands communicate their message to target audiences. Typical traditional media used for promotions include television, radio, newspaper, magazine, outdoor, while digital channels would include company's website, third party sites, social media sites, blogs, apps, etc.

(b) **Media vehicle**: It includes the specific methods used by companies to deliver the communication message, for example, advertisements placed in a TV or a radio program. In the case of digital, an example would be ads in the news-stream of a Facebook user or ads inserted within Twitter stream for a popular hashtag by a particular brand. Another example could be a sponsorship ad inserted in a set of personalized e-mails sent to users.

(c) **Media audience**: The target audience which consumes a particular communication message placed onto a channel. For example, in the case of TV it would be the specific audience watching a particular program in which the advertisement is placed, while in the case of online media, it could be just the audience which is watching a particular ad placed for him/her even on a single landing page of a website.

(d) **Media schedule**: In traditional media planning, specific insertion dates or time periods (parts of the day in case of broadcasting) were chosen to share promotions. In the case of digital media, companies can even go to the extent of accurately identifying the exact decision making (even to the last minute) which makes media scheduling exercise highly targeted and real-time.

(e) **Media budget**: Earlier, firms needed to only think of allocating a part of their revenues to marketing on defined channels. With digital channels, marketers need to think and invest

Table 6.1 Key Differences in Media Planning (Offline vs Digital)

Key Trend	Offline Media Planning	Digital Media Planning
(a) Focus on vehicle than creative	Earlier media planners used to worry more on having the best creative	A shift towards placing the ad in the right channel and vehicle to be more visible
(b) Focus on context rather than message	Ad message was considered to drive the brand	Context of placement is prime not the copy
(c) Focus on brand stories rather than repeat views on a channel	Output based solely on strength of repeat messaging on a channel	Target messages integrated across multiple channels in the form of stories
(d) Focus on influencer-based social sharing of content rather than push marketing	Content on all traditional media was pushed onto customer	Customer creates content and shares it socially while media tracks them
(e) Focus on native content rather than placement external to vehicle	Advertising had slots separated from programing	Blurring of spots and content with more ads turning native

in multiple other factors like market research, customer profile development, testing strategies, costs of tracking and monitoring, purchasing analytical products, etc.

(f) **Media delivery**: Finally, there are concepts of media delivery like reach, frequency, impressions, etc., which have differing connotations and strategies in the online world, which will be covered in broader detail in Chapter 8 on Digital Marketing Execution.

With an understanding of the key media planning terminologies, let us study the differences between media planning on digital channels versus traditional ones (see Table 6.1).

As is evident, the old rules of media planning, channel selection, and messaging for communication are changing with tremendous pace. These shifts are bringing about new execution realities on digital channels as opposed to the traditional ones.

Figure 6.1 discusses the impact of digital channels on media planning exercise. We have taken the example of advertising here to discuss key impacts on this type of promotion.

(a) **Marketing shift (from outbound to inbound):** According to Comscore, 3 in 10 ads are never seen by their target audiences. Consumer's response to traditional advertising is changing from a one-time per-chance click to inclusive marketing. Advertisements should tell a unique story and not just try to sell.

(b) **Pricing shift (from premium to targeted):** Earlier, advertising prices on traditional media used to be premium as there were only a few media channels. With digital media and the advent of automated tools for buying, marketers now have the option to differentiate inventory to increase yield through private trading desks and other tools.

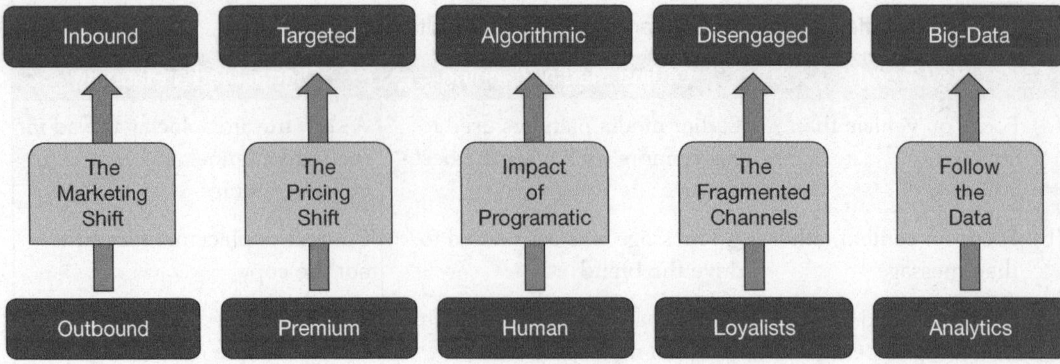

Figure 6.1 Digital Channels Impacting Media Planning

(c) **Impact of programmatic (from human to algorithmic):**Programatic marketing is the practice of implementing an automated set of business rules to efficiently target a firm's most valuable customers and prospects with personalized ads.

(d) **Fragmented channels (from loyalists to disengaged):** Media is becoming increasingly fragmented with most consumers assuming greater control of how, when, and where they consume content. This trend is forcing companies to seek out new strategies and adapt to the new landscape.

(e) **Follow the data (from analytics to big data):** Advertisers need to manage inputs and feedback not only across traditional channels but also a plethora of data across multiple new channels to be able to gauge impact. Media companies need to move from just channel analytics to analysing the big data available to increase value and remain competitive.

With an understanding of the basic media planning concepts and trends impacting them on digital platforms, let us get well-versed with media planning terminologies across traditional media and the ones most widely applied to digital media planning.

Understanding Digital Media Planning Terminology

To understand basic terminologies of a digital media plan, we have to first study the key concepts which have been used for developing traditional media plans. The two key considerations for a media planner while selecting a particular media for any type of promotion include:

(a) **Effectiveness of media channel:** Media planner has to ascertain which media channels would be best for higher *reach* and *response*.

(b) **ROI of communication/promotion on that media:** The other key factor is the anticipated return on investment (RoI) from the media promotions. RoI depends on *cost*, *frequency*, and *revenue* potential of executed promotions.

To understand the concepts of media planning better, we will apply the key terminologies of reach, response, cost, and frequency to the three most common media channels—newspaper, broadcast media, and online (web), and see how these concepts map. We should note here that we have not considered revenue in the comparison table as revenue attribution for newspaper and broadcast-based promotions is not directly attributable as is possible online.

Figure 6.1 takes us through the application of key media planning concepts as applied to the specific media. We would not go into detail to explain how each of these concepts are applied but rather share key concepts which are common to any media plan as explained below.

(a) **Reach**: refers to the total number of potential audience exposed to media during the plan time period at least once. Reach does not take into account the total audience who actually see the promotion but it only gives an indication of the universe of people who can be reached with the media among the client's target audience segment. For example, for a media plan targeting two million men in the 25–39 age bracket, a reach of 50 means that 50 per cent (1 million) of the target audience will be potentially exposed to some of the media vehicles in the media plan.

(b) **Response:** includes the actual audience who actually read, viewed, or made a web visit and performed an action which is related and is important for marketer's promotion.

(c) **Relevance/impact:** involves looking at the relevance or context of a particular promotion in relation to the media vehicles chosen.

(d) **Timing and scheduling**: relates to decisions taken by a firm for its specific set of products to determine the period for promotions run and the way they would be scheduled for maximum impact. A typical example is advertising wherein a media planner can choose from one of the following allocation strategies:

- **Continuous:** involves even exposures throughout a given period.
- **Concentration:** refers to taking a specific period and spending the entire budget.
- **Fighting:** refers to alternate periods of high and no advertising.
- **Pulsing:** involves low advertising all the year round and heavy advertising for peak periods

(e) **Cost:** includes the basis on which costs are calculated to communicate different types of promotions. Digital media is typically bought as cost per million impressions (CPMs).

(f) **Frequency:** It involves the number of times a particular promotion is exposed to a person during the media plan. Frequency can be multiple exposures across the same medium or single exposures across multiple media for the same individual.

(g) **Media plan RoI:** It refers to the overall RoI which a marketer would achieve based on the total amount spent on a particular media plan across all the media channels and promotions combined. This takes into account the revenue generated through final conversions, following the funnel stages from impressions to clicks to leads to purchases.

With an understanding of key media planning terminologies, let us study the digital-specific terminologies to gain a better appreciation of how concepts like reach, frequency, cost, and RoI are calculated for digital and how marketers can make use of these concepts to further understand basic digital media planning stages.

Media Plan Concepts	Newspaper (Vehicle as Single Page)	Broadcasting (Vehicle as Single Program)	Online (Web) (Vehicle as Single Web Page)
Channel Effectiveness			
Reach	**Measured as circulation** (Average gross distribution unclaimed copes)	**Measured as target audience** (% of Target audience exposed to a media vehicle)	**Measured as total web audience** (Total of all audiences across web pages)
Response	**Measured as readership** (Circulation* % of homes receiving* read claims)	**Measured as viewership** (% of target audience who actually viewed the program)	**Measured as total web visits** (Audiences which visited any of the web pages in a period)
Promotion Effectiveness			
Cost	**Measured as price per column inch** (Per Page)	**Measured as cost of GRPs** (% Who Watched a Program)	**Measured as CPM** (Cost Per Million Impressions)
Frequency	**Measured as pass-along rate.** (One ad can be viewed by many people)	**Measured as multiple views per person.** (Does not double-count exposures)	**Measured as total impressions.** (Each multiple view counts as an impression)

Figure 6.2 Understanding Media Plan Concepts

Key Digital Planning Concepts

In line with the terminologies shared in the last column of Fig. 6.2, let us understand the key concepts of digital planning and their calculations. The following terminologies relate more to advertising-specific promotions and channels. These concepts form the base of developing digital campaigns and we would look at the application of these concepts in greater details in Chapter 8 on Digital Marketing Execution, when we discuss how campaigns are created and implemented.

(a) **Web visits:** A visit refers to a visitor's session on all the firm's product sites within a particular period of time. During the session, the user might view multiple pages but the overall session is counted as a single one.

(b) **Page visits:** Involves the number of people visiting a particular page of the firm's website. This could be the homepage or a landing page specifically created to channel pre-defined consumer actions across the funnel.

(c) **Unique visitors:** Refers to the number of unique individuals that visit a website within a specific timeframe. The two methods to track unique visitors include tracking cookies or unique IP addresses.

(d) **Impressions:** The most important concept for digital buying, impressions relate particularly to display ads placed on multiple webpages and are the sum total of responses from a web server to a page request from the user browser. Impressions are calculated as *Reach * Frequency (number of people reached (X) number of times they saw an ad across media vehicles)* and are measured in an automated fashion by designated servers. It should be noted that even in the same web session, if a user lands on a particular page twice, it would be counted as two impressions instead of one.

(e) **Page views:** The total number of unique pages viewed by a person in a particular session would be the page views for that session.

(f) **Clicks:** The opportunity for a user to download another file by clicking an advertisement, as recorded by the server. After impressions count, this is the next stage in the conversion funnel for advertising.

(g) **Click-through:** The action of following a link within an advertisement or editorial to another website or another page or frame within the website.

(h) **CPM (cost-per-thousand)**: Refers the cost of serving 1000 impressions. Almost all of the digital media buys are executed using this metric.

(i) **CPC (cost per click)**: Cost of advertising based on the number of clicks received.

(j) **CPA (cost per action)**: Cost of advertising based on a visitor taking a specifically designed action in response to an ad. Actions could include sales transaction, customer acquisition, or a click.

With the understanding of these key digital media terminologies, in the next section, let us study in detail how a digital media plan is developed and key stages constituting it.

Digital Media Planning Stages

Planning for digital media buying is as complex an exercise for marketers as is buying for offline media, the simple reason being the fragmentation and nature of digital media channels. The digital platform, as we know from earlier chapters, can be divided into three key types—paid, earned, and owned media. The key difference in planning media for digital channels from traditional offline planning is the presence of owned media. Firms in the earlier era had no possibility of owning media and the only form of owned media they could use was the digital signage on top of their office buildings or large ads on the distribution vehicles they owned.

With the advent of the digital platform, a brand's most credible marketing channel is supposed to be its website and blog, where you hear directly from the brand owners on their products and services and where communication is mostly in the form of content-based marketing. Let us classify the variety of promotional channels available to marketers on the digital platform.

In Fig. 6.3, we have classified key promotional types and their respective channels to understand the type of communications brand marketers can choose to execute through the three major types of digital media—paid, earned, and owned. As we can see, traditional marketers

Digital Media Classification / Promotions Type	Paid Media	Earned Media	Owned Media
Intent Marketing	*Search Marketing*		
Brand Marketing	*Advertising*		
Content Marketing	*Native Content*		*Website, Blog Content, Videos, Webinars*
Community Marketing	*Social Media Ads*	*Social Media Posts*	*Community Platform*
Partner Marketing	*Affiliate marketing, PR, Editorial Partnerships*		
Direct Marketing	*E-Mail, SMS*	*Inbound Calls, Customer Comments*	*Direct Response, Chat*
Platform Marketing	*In-game, Kiosk Ads*		*Mobile Apps*

Figure 6.3 Digital Media Classification of Promotion Types

now have extended options to develop and market on owned media properties and garner earned media (with minimal investment on social channels)—options, which they could not even think of earlier. It has to be kept in mind though (as also covered in Chapter 3, section titled 'Four Pillars of the IMC Construct') that with such large options available, marketers should think in a strategic manner on how to integrate both the media for maximum impact in an integrated 360-degree manner and not in a disjointed fashion. To help them with planning their digital media buys, we now share the key 'digital media planning' stages which marketers should follow to manage the extensive channel types and communication choices available. Figure 6.4 reveals the four key digital media planning stages discussed herewith.

Determine the Media Planning Strategy

The first step towards creating a digital media plan is to determine what the brand wants to communicate and which channel mix is the best to promote given the budget allocation for the product portfolio and the timelines it has set to achieve its desired objects. The best place for marketers to obtain information for their planning would come from the digital marketing roadmap (see Chapter 5, section titled, 'Developing the Digital Marketing Strategy Roadmap'), which provides marketers with necessary research on the offering mix and its lifecycle stage, specified target audience, and their presence in the funnel along with the company's strategic intent.

The digital media planning objectives for a firm could be multiple depending on the overall product portfolio and the needs of each separate product. There are typically four core elements, a mix of which can be used by media planners on digital platform (apart from the offline

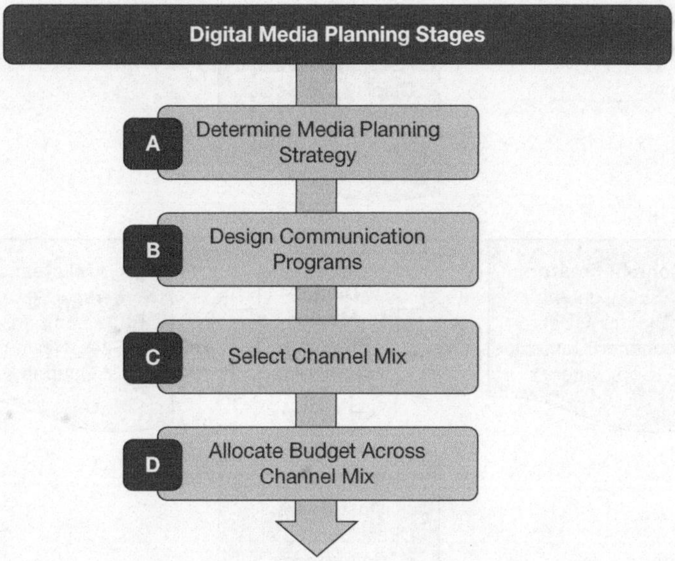

Figure 6.4 Digital Media Planning Stages

elements) to develop a strategy specific to each product. These include—channels, affiliates, content creators, and customers.

In Fig. 6.5, we have mentioned four core elements which digital marketers can mix to create specific media plans based on the requirements of each product and the promotional budget available.

(a) **Channels**: includes general digital marketing communication channels like search engines, display sites, social media communities, e-mail, and other media platforms like mobile, video marketing, etc., to which a promotional budget is paid.

(b) **Affiliates**: involves developing a partner network in the same business, industry, similar product theme start-ups to obtain leads and conversion prospects at an agreed price. It includes vertical sites, price comparison portals, reward/loyalty sites, coupon sites, and other referral sites.

(c) **Content creators**: Firms can utilize content as one of the core elements and pay content producers to generate compelling content for SEO blogs, websites for converting targeted leads. Firms, in present times, are driving their content strategy in a lean manner through crowdsourcing and curating relevant user-generated content.

(d) **Customers**: Apart from allocating budget to the top three elements, the fourth mix involves using direct customers and their influencers as a channel, wherein consumers are either paid for their loyalty in the form of points or given discounts for trails and even freebies or coupons for writing reviews or giving product feedback, thus making them further advocates or influencers for the brand.

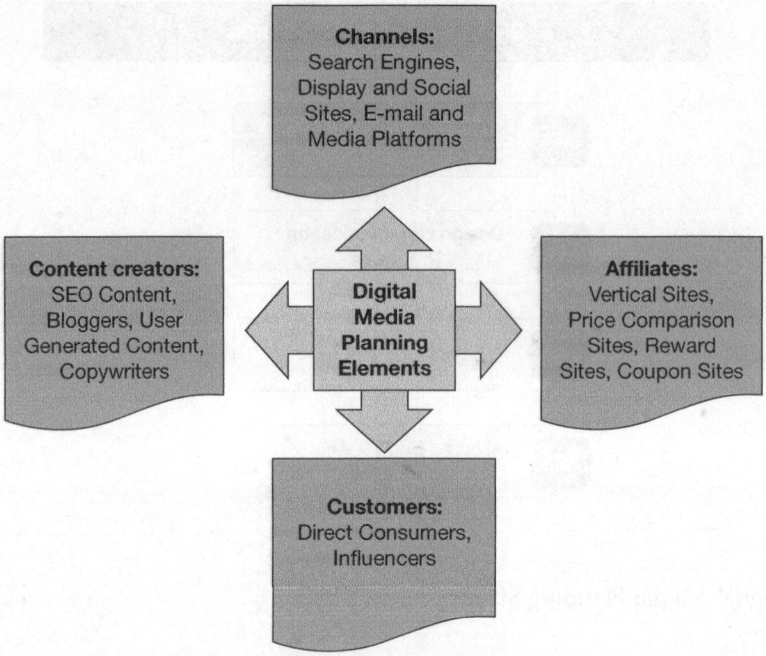

Figure 6.5 Core Elements of Digital Media Planning

Design Communications Program

With an understanding of how digital media planning-mix strategy is created, the next stage is to decide the types of communications message to be designed for specific objectives of each product. The two basic tasks of marketing communications are message creation and message dissemination. We would cover this in detail in 'Designing the Communication Mix,' the next part of this chapter.

Select Channel Mix

The third stage of digital media planning involves selecting the digital channel mix most suited for a firm's product, depending upon which stage it is present in one of the 6S Digital Implementation stages, as discussed in Chapter 5 earlier. To develop the channel mix, let us revisit the 6S Framework and group the six stages into three groups, depending on their present state and implementation objectives.

In Fig. 6.6, the six stages of digital marketing implementation have been grouped into three buckets to chart their channel mix strategies (as the firm grows from digital scoping to digital spectrum stage) for the specific product at hand. This is explained below.

(a) **Launch stage:** Involves the firm (product) in its launch stage where it chooses specific media mix to generate awareness and initial enquiries.

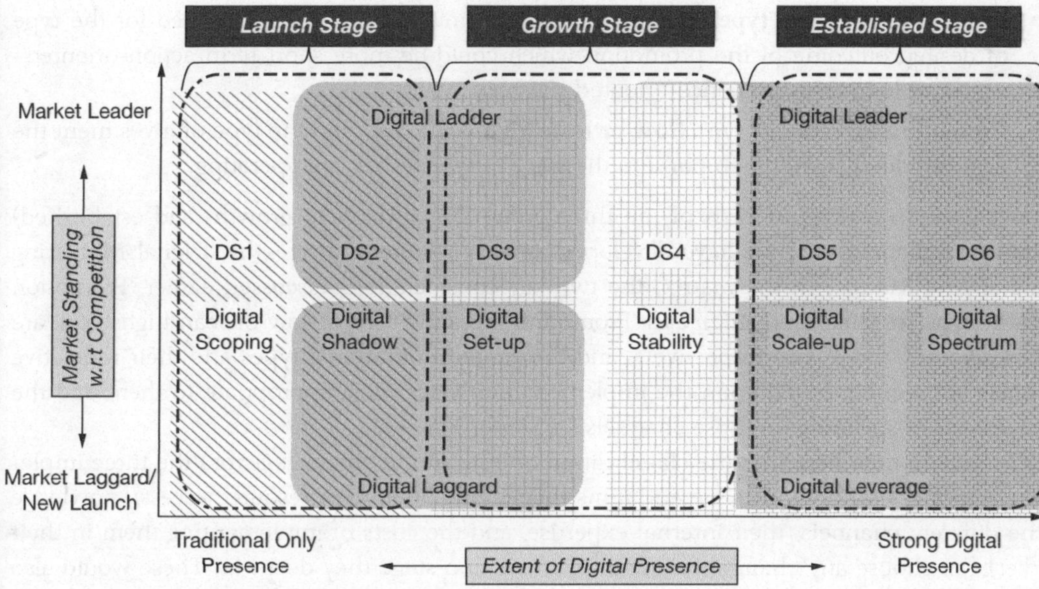

Figure 6.6 6S Digital Marketing Implementation Groups

(b) **Growth stage:** The firm (product) is already established and needs channels which would help convert prospects to confirmed leads to convert further into sales.

(c) **Established stage:** In this stage, the product is already stable and known and looks to guard its position and scale-up to become a leader across all possible channels.

For each of the above three group stages, depending on the specific product objectives, different channels are deployed and integrated. The first and most credible step for a firm is to decide on the channel mix (where it should start spending its budget), develop its owned channels like websites and blogs, and study the analytics of visitors and their actions on these owned channels to get a fair idea of their customer's credible intent through actions on these channels. Apart from this, while selecting a specific channel mix, other types of considerations could also include:

- *Mass media vs selective audience* communication needs
- *Expert vs social impact* communication needs
- *Implicit vs highly engaging (responsive)* communication needs
- *New product launch vs existing product* communication needs
- *Attention-seeking vs credibility-enhancing* communication needs

Once the firm has grouped its product portfolio across the three group stages, it can look at multiple channels across the promotional mix to decide on its final channel mix for execution. The two key considerations which would help firms decide their channel mix include:

- **Promotion outcome type (organic/inorganic)**: involves assessing the need for the type of desired outcome of the promotion which could be more short-term/action-oriented–*organic* or long-term/influence-oriented–*inorganic.*
- **Promotion investment type (low or lean/high cost):** includes the type of investment the firm (product) is willing to put into the stage in which they are operating.

To help firms (products) in each of the three group stages (launch, growth, and established) decide their channel mix, we have developed an easy-to-refer matrix—the 'Digital Marketing Channel Mix Matrix'. In the matrix, the two key considerations discussed earlier 'Promotion outcome type (organic/inorganic)' and 'Promotion investment type (low or lean/high cost)' are placed across X and Y axis respectively, and the varied promotional types and their respective channels are plotted, based upon the implementation stage most appropriate to them and the relative costs of spending on those channels.

We have to note here that the classification of each of the channels across the three implementation stages is only indicative and firms (depending upon their resource access/knowledge of the different channels, their internal expertise, and the costs of implementing them in their market) can choose any channel in any implementation stage they deem fit. These would also change depending upon specific marketing needs of the firm (product) which could emerge as a part of the overall marketing plan implementation.

In Fig. 6.7, let us look at each group implementation stage to understand the multiple channel mix that can be selected for digital media execution and reasons for the same. We would get into the details of each of the channels later in this chapter.

Launch Stage The key objectives of firms (products) in the launch stage is to create awareness for their product/service, generate traffic/prospects, build customer database, and develop a better connect through compelling content and organic engagement. An example of typical channel mix across digital media would be:

- *Owned media channels:* include SEO (website/blog); community platforms for partners/affiliates
- *Earned media channels:* include social media (free posts); inbound customer care
- *Paid media channels:* which, besides other options, include Display, PR (general articles), SEM (long-tail keywords), SMS for connect, affiliate marketing (generally higher commissions are paid as brands are not yet established with customers)

Growth Stage The firm (product) in this stage has been growing, and has established better brand awareness, customer connect, and partner relationships. With growing clout and revenues, it should go aggressive for spending on channels (more CPC, CPA models) to gather higher targeted and interested customers, develop stronger co-branded content, incentivize influencers, and give more discounts to customers for higher lead conversions. An example of channel mix for this stage would be:

- *Owned media channels:* include customer pull through mobile apps development; customer knowledge-focused content development (tutorials/ videos)

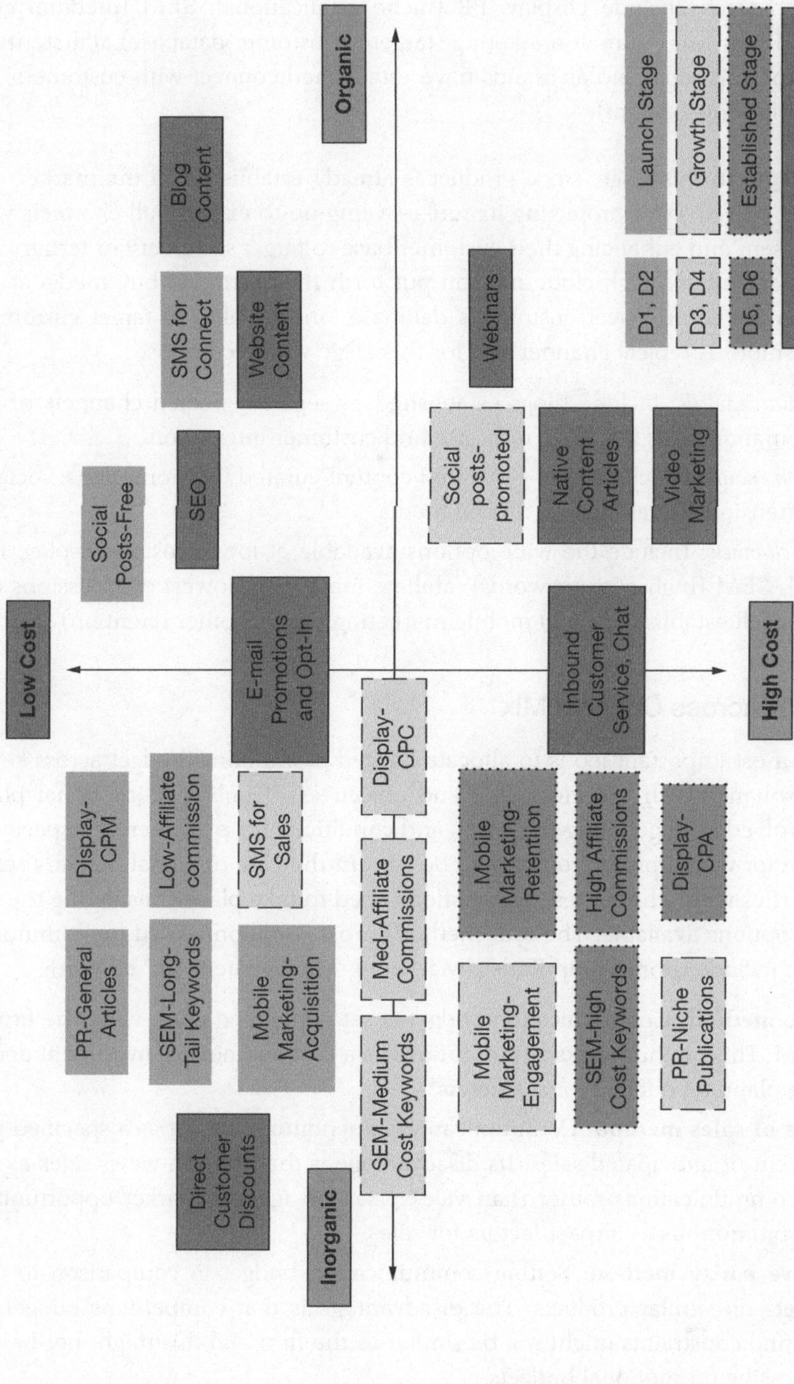

Figure 6.7 Digital Marketing Channel Mix Matrix

- *Earned media channels:* include comments and feedback on affiliate and third party sites; increasing reach to vertical specific social media platforms
- *Paid media channels:* include Display, PR (niche publications), SEM (medium cost keywords), SMS for sales, e-mail marketing (targeted customer database),affiliate marketing (medium commissions paid as brands have established connect with customers), mobile marketing (for engagement).

Established Stage In this stage, since product is already established in the market, the firm will have two key objectives of protecting its turf—scaling up to exist on all channels where its customers are present and enhancing their customer base to target secondary or tertiary customers. Firms in this stage have high clout and can put forth their terms to buy media at cheaper prices, exercise larger control over customer's database, and be able to target customers in a multi-channel fashion. A typical channel mix for this stage would comprise:

- *Owned media channels:* include blogs established as separate owned channels of engagement; automation tools for direct response and customer interaction
- *Earned media channels:* include user-generated content curated for promotions; social media channel extensions developed on owned media
- *Paid media channels:* Include the wide options available at lower costs—Display, PR (firm controlled), SEM (high-cost keywords), affiliate marketing (lowest commissions are paid as brand is well established), and mobile marketing (for customer retention)

Allocate Budget across Channel Mix

Media planner's most important job is to allocate limited promotional budget across key digital channels in consonance with the messaging and objectives of online promotional platforms. They are also involved in negotiating the terms and conditions for placement on specific media and also the time for which promotions would be run. In the case of digital media, there could be a lot many parties with whom these negotiations need to take place considering the number of channels and options available. The four methods most commonly used for communication budget allocation include (from Philip Kotler, Marketing Management 14th edition):

(a) **Affordable method:** Communication budget is set depending upon what the firm thinks it can afford. This method looks at promotions as a cost and not an investment and makes long-range planning difficult for marketers.

(b) **Percentage of sales method:** Communication expenditures are set as a specified percentage of current or anticipated sales. Its disadvantage is that it again views sales as a determiner of communications rather than vice versa and ignores market opportunities and aggressive promotions as impact factors for sales.

(c) **Competitive parity method:** Setting communication budget in comparison to competitive budgets on similar products. The disadvantage is that competitor's budget factors, resources, and constraints might not be similar to the firm and this might not be the best way of assessing promotional budgets.

(d) **Objective and task method:** Here marketers develop communication budgets by defining specific objectives, determining the tasks for executing those objectives, and estimating the costs of performing those tasks. The sum of all these costs is taken as communication budget. The advantage that this method has over others is that it involves managers taking a clear view of their objectives and laying forth proper grounds for a calculated approach to budgets, taking into consideration all the assumptions, thus, making it more scientific.

The key considerations which marketers should keep in mind for budget allocation include:

- The implementation stage with respect to the 6S Implementation Framework
- The business model (B2B/B2C), (paid, free initially), (advertising/subscription), etc.
- The type of investment, self-funded, and marketing media budget allocations
- Growth imperatives as put forth by promoters and stakeholders
- Prior experience of channel implementations and knowledge of intricacies involved
- Prior partnerships across key channels/affiliate types that can be leveraged

In the next section, let us study how a Digital Media Plan is measured, what are the key success criteria, and which are the most relevant evaluation parameters.

Investment Analysis and Planning for Marketing RoI

With an understanding of the development of digital media planning stages, we will now look at the ways in which firms can analyze their digital marketing investments and plan for better RoI from their digital media planning exercise by applying marketing metrics.

According to Lenskold Group (a leading authority on Marketing RoI development), the sole mission of any firm's marketing program is to help maximize company's profits. RoI development and management involves taking stock of the promotional budget at hand and the priorities for allocating budget in the most profitable manner. According to Lenskold, RoI can typically be calculated as:

$$\text{ROI} = \{(\text{Net Present Value of Profits \& Expenses}) - \text{Investment}\}/\text{Investment}$$

'Investment' here represents the marketing expense and the 'Net Present Value of Profits and Expenses' represents the resulting flow of profits and expenses, with future cashflow discounted back to reflect the time value of money. RoI can be measured at an overall business level, the department level, and even at the marketing campaign level. Here, we would be looking more into the RoI at an overall business level, and metrics related to specific campaigns would be discussed in Chapter 8 on 'Digital Marketing Execution.'

The three key components of the RoI equation which can be used to measure and plan marketing initiatives include:

(a) **Customer Lifetime Value (CLV):** It represents the net present value of profit from the stream of customer transactions resulting from the investment. RoI improves as CLV increases.

(b) **Total number of customers:** It is generated from marketing investment. RoI improves as total number of customers increase, provided the CLV per customer is greater than the marketing expense per customer.

(c) **Marketing expense:** Includes the total investment made with the expectation of generating a return.

With this understanding of the broader concept of RoI, we would now look at developing a plan for marketing RoI. The Marketo Group (one of the top digital marketing product companies) has devised a three-step process to plan for marketing RoI.

(a) **Establishing targets and RoI estimates**: The first objective for any marketer includes definition of their digital planning objectives and identification of measurable metrics for the chosen goals of their specific product portfolio and respective presence across marketing funnel. The basic RoI model for any type of marketing activity should capture the following metrics:

- Incremental sales generated
- Revenue per sale
- Gross margin percentage
- Total marketing and sales investments

All the RoI estimates set should have best case, worst case, and risk scenarios included so that for each outcome, the marketer is already planned.

(b) **Designing measurable programs:** All the programs developed should be measurable. The marketer should exactly know what he is going to measure for the specific channel, timing of measurement, and the way the program will be measured.

(c) **Marketing improvement decisions:** Involves marketers focusing not just on data which is measurable but which improves company profitability. This means marketers should focus beyond 'what is' to 'what if.'

To support the Marketing RoI initiatives, Marketo in their 'Definitive Guide to Marketing Metrics and Analytics' have shared a framework for measurement which discusses multiple metrics that a firm can track including revenue, margin, profit, cash flow, RoI, shareholder value across three key categories—*business performance metrics and KPIs, diagnostic metrics, and leading indicators.* Typical areas of metrics, put up against this framework, are discussed below.

In Fig. 6.8, three key types of metric areas—*revenue, marketing program performance, and profit per customer* have been placed against the framework to identify most important metrics for a firm.

To share the importance of the right metrics for each marketing program, the Marketo report has picked up one of the three key metric areas—the revenue metric—to place it along the revenue cycle (aligned to general marketing funnel), to define and explain the four key 'metrics that really matter' for a marketer and where critical insight can be gained in measuring and optimizing marketer's aggregate impact on revenue. These include *flow (lead generation), balance (lead counts), conversion, and velocity.*

		Business Performance Metrics and KPIs Past: How Did We Do?	**Diagnostic Metrics** Present: What Is Working?	**Leading Indicators** Future: How Will We Be Doing?
Revenue Metrics	*Aggregate Impact on Company Revenue*	• Lead Generation Versus Targets • Cycle Time	• Conversion Rate Versus Trend or Benchmark	• Size of Prospect Database Size • Marketing Contribution Forecast
Marketing Program Performance Metrics	*Incremental Contribution of Individual Marketing Programs*	• Investment • Pipeline Contribution • Program Roi	• Response Rates • Lift Over Control Group	• Expected Contribution Forecast
Profit Per Customer	*Lifetime Value of an Incremental Customer*	• Average Selling Price	• Investment to Acquire a Customer • Marginal Cost to Serve	• Retention Rates • Products Per Customer • Net Promoter Scores

Figure 6.8 Right Metrics Summary by Marketo

Source: Definitive Guide to Marketing Metrics and Analytics, https://cdn2.hubspot.net, © Marketo, accessed in February 2017

Figure 6.9 gives a good picture of the kind of questions to be asked for evaluating and measuring each of the four metrics and also related examples. Apart from revenue metrics, a company can develop metrics across multiple other areas of the program, including channel returns, product performance, sales effectiveness, customer profitability, brand performance, among others. It is typically advised that marketers pick up a few specific areas of measurement across their marketing programs and funnel activities and focus on the quality of metrics rather than quantity to assess their present operations and effectiveness. Also, it is crucial that other key aspects of marketing implementation like people, process, technology, etc., are also aligned to RoI analysis activities to achieve the most impactful results from the exercise.

DESIGNING THE COMMUNICATION MIX

With an understanding of the basics and investment (RoI) analysis for digital media planning, we get to the point where all of the research we have done till now and the objectives set in prior chapters will reach the intended audience for the first time. At this stage, the communications mix aims at designing the specific message to be targeted to chosen audience, the format and manner in which the marketer would want the audience to receive it. In the next and final part, once we have dwelled upon the basic communication concepts, we would get into a deeper understanding of the kind of channels which marketers have at their disposal for executing the communication and the ones which are most beneficial for a certain kind of promotions mix.

Metric	Questions it Will Answer	Examples
Flow (Lead Generation)	How many people entered each stage in a given period? Are these trending up or down?	How many new prospects were created last month, and how many marketing qualified leads did we pass last week?
Balance (Lead Counts)	How many people are in each pipeline stage? How many accounts? How does that vary by lead type? Are the balances going up or down over time?	How many active prospects do I have – since the size of my target prospect database is a key leading indicator of future success?
Conversation	What is the conversion ratio from stage to stage? Which types of leads have the best conversion rate?	Which (if any) of my conversion rates are trending up or down?
Velocity	What is the average "revenue cycle" time? How does it break down by stage?	Do certain types of leads move faster through the pipeline? How is their speed changing over time?

Figure 6.9 Right Metrics Summary by Marketo

Source: Definitive Guide to Marketing Metrics and Analytics, https://cdn2.hubspot.net, © Marketo, accessed in February 2017

Marketing Communications: from Mass Market to Mass Customized

Marketing communications, according to CIM (The Charted Institute of Marketing), are the tools a firm uses to deliver a range of promotional messages to its target markets. Key examples of marketing communications which have been used across traditional medium include product brochures, mailers, advertisements, sales promotion, exhibitions, direct sales, etc. In this part of the chapter, we would lay emphasis on the various types of digital communications areas which have emerged and how communications can be managed across each of them.

Automation of Marketing Communication

During the earliest stages of the evolution of marketing communications, the marketing message was developed for a mass market and was supposed to cater to all the segments in a common fashion. In the 1960s, with the advent of computers, marketers for the first time had the power to segment their audiences on the basis of geography and zip-code, thus, giving a fillip to the concept of direct marketing. In the 1970s, the application of analytics helped further refine the audience segments to develop tailored messages for different segments. The decade of the 80s, saw the development of database marketing wherein specific individual data was available and targeted campaigns could be created through population analytics.

It was only in the 1990s that the era of relationship marketing (one-to-one marketing) emerged primarily through customer loyalty that allowed products and information to be delivered specific to individual needs and communications created accordingly. With the growth of search algorithms and the possibility to know the intent of a customer through his keywords, the decade of the 2000s provided the possibility to customize messages to each individual specifically. This was termed as mass customization, wherein customized messages could be shared with audiences based upon clusters with similar tastes and preferences. With the decade of the 2010s, the advent of real-time technologies has made it possible to even automate messages to users in a customized manner with the use of sophisticated technology.

Marketing automation typically involves using technology to aggregate contact lists, generating customized direct marketing messages using direct media channels, tracking sales leads in automated fashion, and selecting messages based on reception and multiple testing. With software systems shifting from proprietary databases to open systems, automation helps provide a coherent customer-centric view across all touchpoints, helping marketers know the exact channels they should take as a base to develop their marketing communication mix. The most recent advancements in this area include optimization of promotions and contact channels in real time to follow customer journeys across the net.

With an understanding of how technology and automation have helped support the transition from mass-based to mass-customized communications, let us look at the key benefits brought about by such a communication:

(a) **Knowledge of customer preferences**: With access to multiple customer touchpoint data collated through digital technology tools, marketers can gain tremendous insights into customer preferences for a product and the kind of communication to which they are most likely to respond positively.

(b) **Communication on preferred channels:** With knowledge of key communication platforms visited, the frequency and timing of the most profitable/loyal customers can be determined based on consumer path and attribution analysis. Communication effort and budget can then be targeted specifically to those channels for particular audience clusters.

(c) **Personalization based on prior brand interactions:** With the ability to compare multiple data points across customer interaction databases, prior interactions and experiences with the brand can be combined to provide insights which can support personalization and cross-sell/up-sell opportunities for key customer groups.

(d) **Promotions based on real-time funnel activity:** The most interesting concept of marketing communication automation is the ability to interact with each individual customer when they are visiting a brand-owned channel and share targeted promotions in real time as the customer moves across specific landing pages and multiple funnel stages to help conversion at each stage. Typical examples include:

- **Converting from mailing list to a prospect** through e-mail-automated campaigns run for the specific set of audience who have visited the site once.
- **Encouraging the prospect to become a lead** by sharing social-based recommendations of friends who have had a positive experience buying similar products on the website.
- **Converting from lead to purchase** by offering real-time discounts when a person has put a product in a cart.
- **Retargeting to customers who did not buy** by following and promoting products which a customer put in a cart but did not purchase.

Elements of Marketing Communications

Planning for communications mix starts right from the stage where the positioning strategy is being developed for the product at hand. Once marketers have conducted research on which segments they want to target and their key objectives, they decide on how they want to position their product in the mind of the target consumer, what elements they would want the customer to remember about the brand, and how would they want to develop the image and personality of the brand. To understand the key elements of marketing communication, let us study the DRIP model designed by Chris Fill.

(a) **Differentiate**: It involves differentiating a particular product from its competitors.

(b) **Reinforce**: It includes reminding people of their interactions with the brand and providing reassurance that the brand works better than any other, to resist competitor's attempts at getting 'top of the mind awareness.'

(c) **Inform**: It includes ways and means on making potential customers aware of the organization's offering.

(d) **Persuade**: It entices the customer on the desirable prospects of getting into an exchange *and buying the product*.

As an example to understand how the DRIP model can be applied, let us take the case of a juice brand coming up with a no-calories variant of its earlier launched brand which has not done that well in market. Applying the DRIP model to this case:

(a) **Differentiate**: The key differentiation which the company puts forth can be improved taste, no-calorie product, and renewed fresh packaging.

(b) **Reinforce**: The brand will develop its messaging around how customers can enjoy a juice drink with no impact on their health and reinforce the 'new and improved taste factor' available in different easy-to-carry packages.

(c) **Inform**: involves choosing key channels and promotional messaging which the brand would develop to market its new product.

(d) **Persuade**: With its messaging and brand elements, the brand will attempt to persuade customers to leave their earlier juice brand and go with this new variant which has more desirable elements.

Steps to Creating Marketing Communications Strategy

With a basic understanding of how marketing communications has evolved over the years, the concept of marketing automation, and the elements of marketing communication, we would now look to understand the basic strategy behind marketing communications development.

Steps to Developing a Communication Strategy

It is important that marketers approach the development of marketing communications in a planned and strategic manner. We are sharing the following seven key steps for developing a marketing communication strategy for a particular product or a portfolio for a firm.

(a) **Researching perceptions to present communication efforts**: As shared in the last section on technology and automation supporting marketing communication, this stage involves marketers researching and analyzing present consumer perceptions to their brands and the company's portfolio of products at large. Key steps include:
- Identifying research objectives relative to a specific advertising and marketing communications strategy
- Compiling, comparing, and evaluating the results of quantitative/qualitative research findings relative to specific marketing communications
- Selecting a relevant sampling technique and sample size to be analyzed
- Gathering qualitative and quantitative data in a variety of ways relative to the communications objective (e.g., conducting interviews, user survey software)
- Drawing valid conclusions from the analysis of data for development of an advertising and marketing communications plan

(b) **Setting the overall communication/positioning objectives**: The purpose of any form of marketing communication is to provide information to the target audience on company's specific objectives (new product launch, attracting new segment, getting present customer to buy more, rebranding–improving image of a present product, etc.). Typical objective areas could include any of the following depending upon consumers in various funnel stages and the brand's specific positioning strategy:
- **Awareness**: To make customers aware of a new or revised product
- **Preference**: Communication elements to induce preference for a product or service offering
- **Trial and repeat purchase**: Persuade customer for trial and repeat purchase
- **After image**: Improving image of the brand in consumer's mind post purchase
- **Frequency and variety of use**: Making customer visit the website frequently to buy other categories
- **Promotional incentives**: Incentivizing the customer at regular intervals with varied promotional offers to buy more

(c) **Identifying target audiences**: The primary goal in communicating with a target audience is to capture their attention. This step involves performing a market segmentation analysis, defining, and analyzing the target market/audience for specific marketing communications and selecting relevant consumer profiles with whom the communication would be shared. Target audiences should be divided into three key categories—consumer, customer, and influencer, and messages specific to each group should be created. Consumers are those who finally consume/use the product, customers are the ones who buy the product and might not necessarily use them, while influencers are the group which influence a purchase but might neither buy nor use the product.

(d) **Detailed primary and secondary communication channels**: involves the process of selecting the right media channels to deploy for communication and outlining the mix of integrated traditional and digital channels. In the previous section through the application of Digital Marketing Channel Mix Matrix, we have covered in detail the process of evaluation and selection of key communication channels which are being deployed these days for implementation across launch, growth, and established stages. Companies in this stage also need to decide on the channels which would be primary for them and the ones which are secondary based on budget availability and communication priorities. In the last part of this chapter, we would cover in greater detail, the key types of channels used for communication.

(e) **Developing the communication message/creative plan for each channel**: involves the steps and techniques towards developing the message which would be communicated across multiple chosen channels. Decisions on what aspects to communicate and the way of communication (similar or different from competition) are taken in this stage. The following are some of the key aspects of creating a communication message/creative plan (this will be discussed in more detail in the upcoming section):

- Analyzing product and brand information (for example, differentiation, positioning, brand equity, brand loyalty, product life cycle, competition)
- Preparing a creative brief and developing creative solutions
- Developing the style and tone of the message and follow-up actions required for final conversions through the message
- Deciding the imagery, design, colors, and layout for communication material
- Developing elements which reinforce the claims made through communication and back-up the messaging

(f) **Executing the communication strategy through timed campaigns**: involves setting up formal campaigns which include the best time to reach target segment, frequency, timing, and length of campaigns, budget allocation to each channel, etc. Typically, campaign implementations can be classified into three types:

- **Above the line media** characterized by their power to multiply the message many times over, but where direct feedback through the same medium is difficult, for example, radio, newspapers, magazines.
- **Below the line media** are more interpersonal, for example, conferences. These are characterized by small group communication and cannot multiply the message but direct feedback through the same medium is possible, for example, pamphlets, newsletters, brochures, special events, etc.
- **Through the line media** such as the internet is characterized by its power to multiply the message many times over and where direct feedback through the same medium is easily possible.

(g) **Evaluate and refine communication strategy on an ongoing basis**: includes establishing relevant criteria to evaluate integrated advertising and marketing communications initiatives. Key steps involve:

- Identifying and selecting appropriate tools to measure the effectiveness of integrated advertising and marketing communications initiatives

- Analyzing qualitative and quantitative data collected and determining the effectiveness of marketing communications
- Recommend alternatives for future marketing communications initiatives

Criteria for Judging Communications Strategy

Once a communication strategy has been developed, companies need a way to judge and test their strategy. CIM has shared a 4C model where each element of the media mix can be judged by the following 4C criteria

(a) **Cost**: It involves looking at the following elements:
- comparison of campaign costs overall and across media,
- wastage involved with respect to investment made, and
- evaluation of costs related to reaching out to specific segments/individuals.

(b) **Clout:** It looks at the campaign's reach quality in terms of the number of people it can impact, the campaigns that are either selective or involve mass media, and the extent of personalization provided.

(c) **Credibility**: It includes the trust factor of any specific type of promotion, both in terms of the content and the medium through which the message is shared.

(d) **Control**: It involves the kind of control marketers have to target audiences with specific needs and ability to adjust messages to suit individuals as the campaign progresses.

Apart from the elements mentioned earlier, the key criteria of success of a campaign involves measuring it in line with 'Marketing RoI Analysis' as discussed in the last section and analyzing metrics set and achieved across the funnel stages for the target audience the marketer has specified.

Developing Communications Messaging

In this section, we will study in detail the key aspects of creating a communication message and strategies that go behind it to make sure that the message yields its intended objective for the chosen channels and audience.

Developing communications message involves taking decisions on four key areas:

(a) **Message content:** What to say?
(b) **Message structure:** How to say it logically?
(c) **Message format:** How the message will be shared?
(d) **Message source:** Who would say it?

Let us discuss these areas in detail.

(a) **Message content**: Each communication is driven by some specific objectives of the firm (product). As discussed in the previous section, objectives could range from a product's presence across the marketing funnel or its present PLC (product life cycle) stage or would be driven by some specific external event (for example, a brand's reputation being questioned, a new competitor taking market share, the product being subject to compliance, etc.). In the case of large firms, it is typically the agency which does the job of getting the content created in line with the brief shared by client. This brief should typically cover details on the message objective, target audiences/personas, their buying criteria, value proposition, and how the audience should feel after the promotion.

(b) **Message structure**: The second part of message development is how to put forth the content to selected audiences. The objective of any communication would be to impact the audience in a manner which is either cognitive, affective, or behavioral. Also, various channels might be required to bring home different elements of a message in a holistic impactful manner. Key concepts which form a part of message structure include:

- **Brand voice:** One of the important objectives in developing the message structure is the ability to present a consistent experience across all channels, which means defining and developing the 'Brand Voice.' A brand voice depicts the personality elements which a marketer would want to share if the brand was taken to be like a person. The idea is that while using multiple channels, even though the message tones could be a bit different (entertainment led for a YouTube video vis-à-vis a serious tone on LinkedIn), there should be consistency in the content shared for the audience to relate to it.
- **Message tone**: The tone in which a message is put forth assumes high importance. Stephanie Schwab of Social Media Explorer breaks down a brand's voice into four categories: character/persona, tone, language, and purpose. Examples of attributes for each of these are:
  - Character/persona: friendly, warm, inspiring, playful, authoritative
  - Tone: personal, humble, clinical, honest, direct, scientific
  - Language: complex, savvy, insider, serious, simple, fun, whimsical
  - Purpose: engage, educate, inform, enable, entertain, sell, amplify
- **Message framing**: The way in which a message is framed and its tone affects its persuasiveness. Messages can be framed in a positive manner to share the product's benefits or in a negative manner to induce fear in the mind of the consumer (for example, the need to use helmets).
- **Order effects**: Typically, the order in which a message is presented affects its reception by the audience. In advertising, for example, the first and last messages are more likely to be seen and retained than those presented in between; this is known as the primacy and recent effect. Also, how the product/service attributes are listed in an advertisement matters. With customers typically having less time to scan through messages, it is crucial that important attributes/benefits are shared at the top, followed by those which are less important.
- **One-sided vs two-sided messages:** It involves a decision on whether the message should only talk about the pros or about both the pros and cons.

(c) **Message format**: It involves taking a decision on the method of presentation of the message. This is also referred to as the creative strategy and involves decision on the kind of words being used, the way the communication story is developed, the use of images, audio and video elements built for certain effects, etc.

(d) **Message source:** Source refers to the origination of the message. Source credibility is crucial as the audience is influenced by factors like the level of perceived expertise/knowledge of the source, personal motives behind the source involvement, the degree of trust that can be placed on the source, etc. Typical sources include *formal sources*—organization/firm celebrity endorsements, product experts, and *informal sources*—family, friends, peers, colleagues, and other social groups. It is widely believed that communication which comes from informal sources is perceived as being far more credible than that coming from informal sources. This is also the reason for social media channels having a big impact in terms of being the most influential vehicle for message dissemination.

Communication Mix across Digital Channels

With an understanding of communication mix, steps for strategy and message development, we would now look at how different digital channels lend the possibility to share content in multiple types/formats for differing effects as desired for an overall integrated communication mix. During our discussion on Integrated Marketing Communications (IMC), we have already laid out the key traditional and digital channels (refer Chapter 3 section titled, 'Channels for Integrated Marketing Communications') which can be used by a firm towards developing their marketing communications strategy. In this section, we would classify digital specific channels in terms of their message orientation and the type of communication they can execute which can help marketers decide on the mediums to choose for their communication depending upon their objectives.

In Fig. 6.10, we have developed the matrix with message orientation on the X axis and communication type on the Y axis. Message orientation takes into consideration the key objective of the promotion (awareness/engagement-oriented or purchase/conversion-oriented). Communication type axis involves division of the typical kind of communication that takes place on that channel which could be static or dynamic (real time) in nature of execution.

Let us study each of the matrix quadrants in more detail.

(a) **Engagement-oriented static**: This quadrant stands for channel types which typically deliver communication/messages that are static in nature (created well ahead of time and delivered in a passive format) and are more geared towards engaging target audiences rather than selling to them. Key examples include blogs, website content, webinars, social media posts, e-mail for information, and PR articles. Most of these are content types which primarily aim at creating impactful messages that drive home brand objectives and help engage the audience.

(b) **Engagement-oriented dynamic**: In this second quadrant those channels are included whose main objective is engagement again but they present content in a more dynamic (real-time) manner to audiences and can also message content in real time to share versions which connect better with a certain audience based on experience. Typical examples

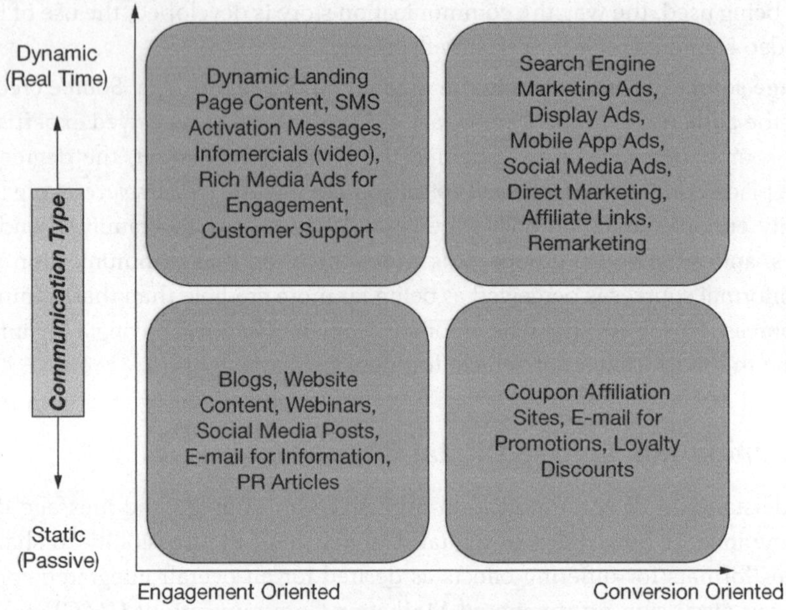

Figure 6.10 Digital Channels Communication Mix Matrix

include dynamic landing page content, SMS activation messages, infomercials (video), rich media ads for engagement, and customer support. The content development for these channels is crucial as it needs to be developed in a manner which seems non-obtrusive and is also engaging for the consumer.

(c) **Conversion-oriented static**: The third quadrant shifts to the conversion side, wherein the key role of the channel is to carry messages which result directly in a purchase, but where the messaging format is still static in nature. Key examples include coupon affiliation sites, e-mail for promotions, and loyalty discounts. The execution of communication on these channels typically should be of a guided nature in which the consumer knows of the channel of promotions or the promotions are shared on channels where he/she is most active, otherwise there could be issues of consumer not even knowing such promotions exist, hence not using them.

(d) **Conversion-oriented dynamic**: The fourth and final quadrant includes most commonly used promotional techniques along the most widely visited channels. Most of the communications in this quadrant relate to real-time advertisements which are presented to a customer at a time he/she is most vulnerable to act on them (click for conversions). Typical examples include: search engine marketing ads, display ads, mobile app ads, social media ads, direct marketing, affiliate links, remarketing, etc. The RoI for communication channels in this quadrant is based on the number of calls-to-action which are accomplished for each stage of the marketing conversion process. It needs to be established here that though the channels in this quadrant is being seen prominently as conversion vehicles, a broader objective of some of those could include engagement and brand building too, for example, display advertising.

Marketers also need to set up evaluation parameters to review the output of their communication mix across channels in all the quadrants to gauge accomplishment at each incremental stage. This would call for a strong integration with the channel partners and their dashboard/daily reports for firms to get the best view of the RoI for their investments.

INTRODUCTION TO DIGITAL MARKETING CHANNELS

As seen in the last part on designing the communication mix, a marketer can use multiple channels to communicate varied elements of their communication to share a set of integrated messages which touch consumers across all their media interactions. In this part we would study (in detail) the origin and development of each of these digital channels and how they support the digital media plans, shared earlier in the chapter.

We would classify the varied sets of digital marketing channels on the lines we shared in Chapter 1, in the section titled, 'Digital Marketing Applications and Benefits,' which includes intent-based marketing, brand marketing, content marketing, community-based marketing, partner marketing, direct marketing, and platform-based marketing. We will dedicate the first three sections to the three most important types of channels—intent-based marketing, brand marketing, and community-based marketing and would cover the rest of the four marketing channel types in the last section of this part.

Intent-Based Marketing (Search Marketing)

Widely considered as the harbinger of the field of digital marketing, intent-based marketing, (also widely known as search marketing) became one of the early ways in which marketers could use internet for digital marketing in a structured and predictable manner. In the pre-search marketing era, companies were mostly using internet as a fringe medium to put static information on their websites, develop non-targeted blogs, and be a part of random classifieds listing. But with the advent of search marketing, marketers for the first time got a definite medium which they could rely upon to deliver results in a campaign format and also measure their initiatives and investment.

Intent-based marketing, as the term suggests, includes those types of marketing which leverage the biggest strength of the digital medium—the exact knowledge of the specific intent of a particular consumer. In traditional marketing, there was never a possibility to understand consumer's intent and be able to target them on their specific needs. But with the advent of search technology and specifically the arrival of Google, there was a sort of revolution, wherein marketers could know at a mass level, the intent of a particular set of customers through the keywords they typed in a search bar and be able to bid against those keywords to place their ads in front of those who had shared that intent. That is why we call this category of search marketing in broad terms as 'Intent-based Marketing', since this is the most powerful way for marketers to know the keywords related to their specific industry, product, geographical region, and be able to choose the ones which matter, to target customers in their buying cycle (researching a product or trying to satisfy a present or a future need). Let us look at the history behind the development of search technology and concepts like Search Engine Optimization (SEO) and Pay Per Click (PPC).

Search engine marketing, by definition, involves marketing to internet users through natural search engine result page listings and paid advertisement placement next to the search results. In simplest terms, any form of search engine marketing involves:

(a) A user typing any combinations of words **(known as keywords in search terminology)**
(b) into an input space **(called a search-box)**
(c) through usage of search technologies **(crawling and indexing)**
(d) application of complex programs **(known as search algorithms)**
(e) delivering the best matched weblinks **(known as Organic Search results)**
(f) displaying paid weblinks **(known as Pay Per Click)**

In the above definition (related to point 'e'), the process by which any specific website, blog, portal, etc., applies efforts and techniques to optimize its content to be matched to a specific keyword searched is known as Search Engine Optimization (SEO).

On the other side (related to point 'f'), the structured set of marketing programs run by the specific search engine to put a price to a specific set of keywords and sell them to multiple businesses (web-marketers) is known as Search Engine Marketing (SEM) or Paid Per Click Marketing (PPC).

It is typically the application and execution of search engine marketing, which forms the base of this first category of digital marketing channels, which was popularized by Google and is now one of the most widely used marketing channels in the world.

History of Search Engine Marketing

The development of search engine marketing as a channel goes back to 1996 when the search engine *OpenText* initiated the paid search business model through a preferred listing service that aimed at highlighting businesses, services, and products, when users searched for relevant keywords. At that time, the company drew flak and did not want a commercialized version of their search results. As the market matured, post OpenText, GoTo.com pioneered the paid search business model with its Pay-for-Placement model. It also introduced an auction (bidding) process for ad placements on the search engine page. With its name changed to Overture in 2003, GoTo.com was purchased by search engine Yahoo that strengthened its paid search marketing services. In 2000, Google launched the AdWords program which saw limited success till 2003 after which it started gaining popularity. This was followed by Ask.com with its PPC services in 2005 called Ask Sponsored Listings and soon after MSN followed it in 2006. Search engine marketing programs since then have established well enough as a prime source of revenue for search engines, the biggest gainer being Google which has extended AdWords services from text ads to display, video, mobile, etc.,

How Search Engines Support Marketing

The key aim of any search engine is to help users find a specific piece of information from the billion pieces of content lying on the internet. The more powerful the search algorithms and technology, the more accurate and effective the results would be for the user. With this as the core concept, the commercial idea which search engines built was to help connect users with a specific intent for a product or service to websites, portals, blogs which could best service their need for information or a purchase. Through this, marketers who wanted to market or sell their specific products could bid against the intent of their target consumer segment (specifically bidding is done on the keywords typed in the search box and is known as search engine marketing) or optimize the content on their sites in such a way that the search engines would naturally pick up their content first and post them on the top of the search results (the activity being defined as search engine optimization). Let us have a quick look at how a search engine goes about mapping specific searched keywords to the most related content on the web.

Search engines execute two major functions which form the core of their business:

(a) **Crawling and indexing**: A search engine's main job is to crawl and index the billions of websites, their content (text, audio, video), and other unstructured files and data which typically would not be easy to locate and access by a common user.

(b) **Mapping and serving most relevant content:** includes ranking the crawled and indexed content with pre-defined parameters to filter and present the most relevant answers to a particular query put up by the user through his/her keywords.

Working of Search Engines

In Fig. 6.11, we have showcased the working of any frontline search engine which involves the following steps:

(a) The user shows his/her intent by typing a search query in any combination of words which in Search Terminology are known as 'keywords'.

(b) Once the web server receives the query, it sends the query to the index server where web pages are indexed. A typical search engine's job is to keep crawling the web regularly using software called 'spiders' which index content and save them in the index server for future use.

(c) When the user puts the query, the index server matches the most relevant pages with the help of document servers by ranking the ones which are most authoritative and have the best quality. In this stage, snippets are also generated to describe each search result to the user.

(d) Once the top results are ready to be served, they are showcased in two ways—organic results for which the website/brand does not have to pay for (Search Engine Optimized-SEO results) and those which the brand pays for visibility and which appear in the right corner and top of organic ads (which are known as search engine marketed SEM results). To make a search result appear organically, website owners have to develop the most authentic content on their owned channels (websites), at times having to look at even

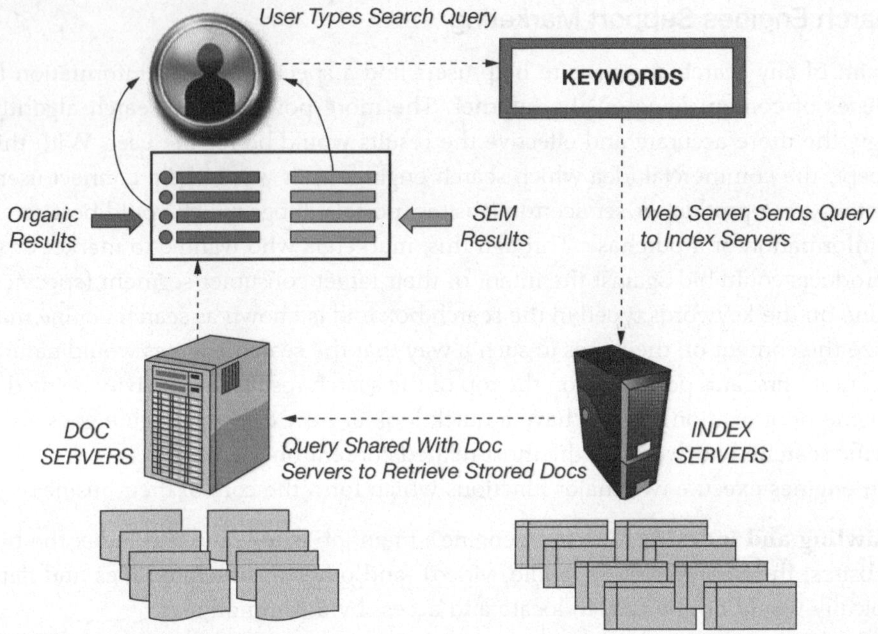

Figure 6.11 Working of Search Engines

200+ parameters. In Chapter 8, we would look at how companies can plan for better SEO and set up productive SEM campaigns. We will also discuss digital marketing campaign execution in greater detail.

Advantages of SEM, SEO as Marketing Channels

(a) SEM is generally considered to be one of the earliest approaches that digital marketers take while thinking of spending their budgets online. This is not only because of their effectiveness or low upfront cost to begin with, but also because they are one of the more non-obtrusive forms of marketing when compared to display advertising or direct marketing.

(b) The basic premise that SEM originates from is voluntary audience-driven intent and it is intrinsically a pull-marketing model rather than a push model.

(c) In the case of SEO, since brands spend a tremendous amount of time to match their content to search marketing keywords and search authority rules, what emerges is an eco-system of pure meritocracy where marketers with the most effort and ingenuity succeed. Even when compared to SEM, research shows that SEO listings yield about three-fourths of the entire traffic to websites, which goes to show how well constructed and advanced this digital medium has evolved into.

Brand-Based Marketing (Display Marketing)

The next widely deployed digital marketing channel is display marketing which takes along with it all forms of online advertising (be it across web, mobile or other emerging platforms like kiosk, surface, etc.) and is executed through graphical digital images similar to billboards, newspaper ads, and television ads. A display ad is typically embedded into a webpage and placed alongside content which is most related to the brand being advertised. We label this form of marketing as brand-based marketing, as the key objective here is to build the imagery of a brand and its elements (though it can also be used to generate leads and drive purchase through allied promotional messages).

The key elements which help develop this brand imagery (and differentiate this form of marketing from text based marketing like SEM) includes images, animation, sound, video, etc., embedded in the ad and with the development of rich media and dynamic ads (which are more graphical and interactive in nature), there is practically no limit to the kind of creativity and formats which can be generated to capture a visitor's attention to a display ad.

History of Display Marketing

The first instance of online advertising was a joint venture in the 1980s between IBM and Sears, known as Prodigy, which started displaying banners at the bottom of the screen to promote Sears (one of the top retail chains in US) products. The first clickable web ad was sold by Global Network Navigator (GNN) in 1993 to a Silicon Valley law firm. This was followed by Hotwired, which in 1994 became the first website to sell large volumes of banner ads to big businesses. One of the first ads was purchased by AT&T (480X60) pixels in size and had a 44 per cent click-through rate, which when clicked did not re-direct to AT&T's website but ironically linked it to an online tour of the world's most acclaimed art museums! But this was just the start of display marketing becoming a full-fledged industry by itself worth well over 22 Bn Dollars by 2015 (according to eMarketer—US Digital Ad Spending Statistics).

Types of Display Ads

Display marketing works on the premise that any web page in the world, which attracts decent visits, can put a section of it on sale for any brand or agency to display an advertisement (which has a context similar to the web page's content or the site itself). The chosen area on the web page is called an inventory and a standard page holds not more than three to four ad inventories which can be let out for ads. Depending on the size, placement, and orientation of the ad, there are industry-wide names that are given to standard ad sizes. A 480X60 pixel size horizontal bar ad at the top is typically known as the banner ad and is used mostly to sell premium sponsorships on the homepage of any website. Other popular types include 120X600 vertical ad called the Skyscraper, 728X90 horizontal ad at the bottom called Leaderboard, and a host of other small-sized rectangular ads (300X250, 120X60, 180X150, etc.). Also, with new types of rich media and dynamic ads emerging, the design revolution and need to reinvent ads to make them more relevant and interesting has forced the natural progression of ad making.

Delivery Method (How an Ad Is Served)

The most important aspect of display advertising is the way graphical images are served when any user visits a particular page on a website. The basic process steps for the delivery of any advertisement online are shared below.

Figure 6.12 shows the steps right from the time when the user visits a particular web page and the interactions that follow across multiple servers to publish the ad on the site. Key stages of display ad serving include:

(a) **Step A:** The user accesses the web browser to arrive at a publisher's website.

(b) **Step B**: The publishing web server sends back an HTML code which directs the browser to pick up content and also the ad tag which will help serve the ad on the page.

(c) **Step C:** The ad tag served directs the browser to the publisher's ad server which matches the most profitable and relevant ad to be served. The process of selection of the ad by the publisher is complex and we would cover the whole commercial ecosystem later.

(d) **Step D:** Publishing ad server sends the specific ad tag to redirect to marketer's ad server.

(e) **Step E:** The ad tag hits the marketing server which gets the order to serve the ad to site.

(f) **Step F:** The Content Distribution Network (CDN), finally, sends the content back to the site where it gets displayed for the user to view it as an impression or click it further.

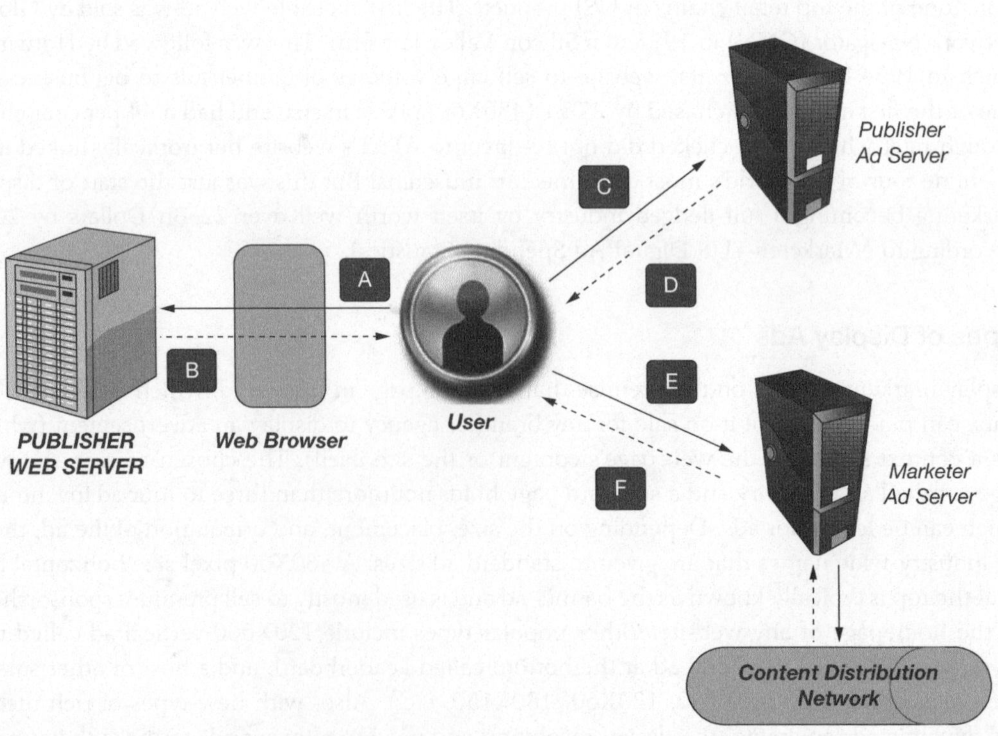

Figure 6.12 Display Ad Serving Mechanism

Key Display Ecosystem Players

To understand the commercial ecosystem of display advertising, we need to primarily understand the options through which marketers have to place different types of display ads on to their target websites. There are multiple tools and technologies which have been developed across the ecosystem to support both the buy side (advertisers) and the sell side (publishers) with their goals and profit objectives. We share a diagram below (see Fig. 6.13) which has been developed by IAB (Internet Advertising Bureau, an authority on digital advertising that develops industry standards for online advertising) and which showcases, in a simple manner, the key entities and their interactions.

In Fig. 6.13, apart from advertisers and publishers, five key entities are shown, which we would discuss along with a few other ones which have emerged lately and are making a big impact on how display advertising is being bought and sold. Let us study them below.

(a) **Ad network:** With inventory being the key currency which is bought and sold between publishers and advertisers, publishers needed support on selling the excess inventory which they were not able to sell directly with their sales force. Ad networks plug-in that need and aggregate left-over inventory of websites in their network to sell them in bulk to advertisers (generally at lower prices), which helps publishers realize money on the inventory that they otherwise could not have sold, while advertisers get access to the inventory on a mass scale on the specific type of websites and audiences they would most

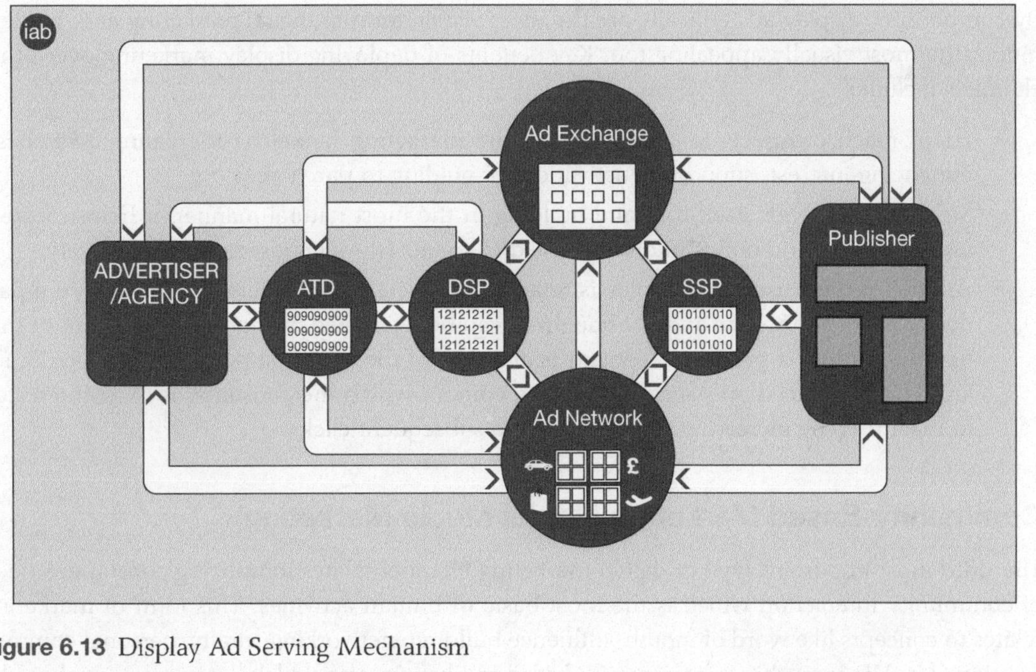

Figure 6.13 Display Ad Serving Mechanism

Adapted from: Dr. Augustine Fou, 'Slide 4, Display advertising budget allocation', https://www.slideshare.net, accessed on 27 February, 2017 at 8.54 pm.

look forward to advertise. Examples of major ad networks include Google, Microsoft, Brightroll, TribalFusion, etc.

(b) **Ad exchange**: Tools that facilitate the buying and selling of aggregated ad inventory from multiple ad networks, for example, Google Ad Exchange, OpenX, RightMedia, Advertising.com, etc.

(c) **DSP (demand side platforms)**: Tools that advertisers can control to access impressions from multiple sources, for example, DataXu, Invitemedia, Appnexus, etc.

(d) **SSP (supply side platforms)**: Tools that publishers can control to access impressions from multiple sources, for example, Pubmatic, Rubicon, Admeld, etc.

(e) **ATD (agency trading desks)**: ATDs are centralized management platforms used by ad agencies that specialize in programmatic media and audience buying. Examples include Accuen (ATD for Omnicom), Xaxis (WPP), Audience on Demand (Vivaki).

Apart from these, there are other entities too which are gaining major prominence in the display ecosystem like DMP (Data Management Platforms), retargeting tools, measurement firms, etc. The advantages of such a large, well developed, and competitive ecosystem is that it gives a chance to both the buy and sell community to wrest benefits from the launch of each new technology innovation in the market; also, firms typically keep fast-forwarding to newer products to remain competitive and not lose the edge.

Advantages of Display Marketing

By comparison, display ads typically are the most visible form of digital marketing and, by definition, the most visually appealing too. Key benefits of deploying display marketing over other channels include:

- Helps reach prospects at every stage of the marketing funnel be it creating awareness, enhancing interest, supporting activation, or guiding to purchase.
- Since display lends itself to brand building in the most natural manner, it helps create a visual connect and builds in discovery-led elements (through just a click) effectively.
- Another unique aspect of display is retargeting wherein, customers who have seen a particular product on a site and not bought it, can be retargeted with an advertisement of that brand to induce a purchase. Context is also one of the strongest points for display as ads are typically placed on pages and near to content which the consumer is most interested to read, thereby increasing the chances of a subsequent click.

Community-Based Marketing (Social Media Marketing)

The third most important type of digital marketing channel relates to utilizing consumer's need of community interaction which is the most basic of human activities. This form of marketing relates to concepts like word of mouth, influence building, networking, viralty, personal communication, etc. We term this as community-based marketing, also widely known as social media marketing.

Definition of Social Media Marketing

Social media is defined as the way people interact and communicate online utilizing platforms developed specifically for community-based networking. It refers to the process of gaining traffic or attention through social media sites.

History and Growth of Social Media Marketing

The development of social media networks started primarily with the need to share basic news, events, information, which happens between individuals and groups. The earliest form of social networks were known as Usenet systems developed in 1979 by Tom Truscott and Jim Ellis, which let users post articles or posts (referred to as news) to newsgroups. Sites such as Google and Yahoo groups use many of the conventions established by original Usenet systems.

Unlike Usenets which have no centralized server or dedicated administrator, Bulletin Board Systems (BBS) also originated in late 1970s and were hosted on personal computers which users had to dial-in through their modem. These were meeting places that allowed users to communicate with a central system where they could download files or games and post messages to other users.

Post BBSs arrived online services like Compuserve and Prodigy which introduced chat programs and affordable online services, respectively. By 1980s, home computers became more affordable and Internet Relay Chats (IRCs) started being used for file sharing and instant messaging on a much broader scale.

Social networks as we know, were built by sites like Geocities, TheGlobe.com, AOL, which allowed users to create their own sites, interact with people of similar interests through member-created communities, and also help them publish and share content. The first truly social media sites were dating sites and also niche concept sites like classmates.com, sixdegrees.com, asianavenue.com, blackplanet.com, all of which were either developed on a specific networking concept or geographic/community-based interaction idea.

The road to exponential growth of social networks started in 2002, with the launch of Friendster.com which had a concept similar to sixdegrees.com and refined it to promote a 'Circle of Friends' concept. It was the launching pad for other top websites like MySpace, Orkut, and particularly, Facebook and Twitter to emerge later on the screen. Facebook launched in 2004 to connect Harvard College students has emerged as one of the top social networking sites in the world. Similarly, Twitter, with its unique micro-blogging concept and great media marketing, has become the leader in gauging individual popularity and reputation globally. With the growth in technology and devices, firms have come up with multiple ideas to launch many other very popular social networking platforms like Youtube, Linkedin, Tumblr, Pinterest, Foursquare, WhatsApp, etc., all of them connecting communities through unique objectives with differentiated concepts.

Types of Social Media Marketing

With an understanding of the history behind social media marketing, let us study the key ways in which marketers use social media for digital marketing:

(a) **Engagement (through dedicated pages)**: Social media marketing gives a chance to marketers to create an owned media presence and engage with present customers at almost no cost.
(b) **Advertising (through native/content ads)**: The biggest advantage is to build customized content and native ads for users who are immersed in the social media site for maximum impact.
(c) **Viral platforms (through network effects)**: It is one of the few channels that supports the network effort and strong word-of-mouth.
(d) **Idea/concept testing (through crowdsourcing)**: Social media can help to get feedback on new concepts through influencer testing and also help to obtain new ideas through crowdsourcing (getting consumers to share their thoughts and provide ideas for free).
(e) **Customer feedback (through listening tools)**: Social media is a very powerful tool to gain customer feedback through listening tools like social media command center.
(f) **Learning platforms (through gamification concepts)**: It helps to propagate brand awareness and consumer connect through gamification (use of game-thinking in non-game contexts).

Advantages of Social Media Marketing

Social media marketing's unique advantages include:

(a) **Best channel to develop user following:** Social media with its networking effects provides the best opportunity to develop influencers and through them build user following.
(b) **The humanizing effect**: Social media is one of the few channels which help brands increase engagement by being more humanized across all their interactions.
(c) **Best channel to begin with a lean budget:** This channel requires minimum upfront investment to begin with and helps create an audience of thousands on a really lean budget.
(d) **Improved customer insights:** With listening tools being deployed extensively, social media helps understand what consumers are interested in and how they behave and react to marketing.

Partner, Direct, Content, and Platform-Based Marketing Channels

With an understanding of the top three marketing channels, let us look at the four other key types which are most prominently deployed:

(a) **Partner marketing** (affiliate marketing, public relations, editorial partnerships, etc.)
(b) **Direct marketing** (e-mail, sms marketing, chat, inbound calls, comments, etc.)
(c) **Content marketing** (native content, website, blog content, videos, webinars, etc.)
(d) **Platform marketing** (mobile applications, in-game marketing, kiosk marketing, etc.)

Let us understand each of these four marketing channels and their advantages.

Partner Marketing

Partner marketing is a term we have given to all types of marketing channels which involve partnering with other influencers in the same domain or area of operation (which either have their own influence or are serving similar audiences as the brand). It includes areas like affiliate marketing, online public relations, paid editorial partnerships with similar vertical sites, etc.

- **Affiliate marketing**: It is a type of performance-based marketing in which a business rewards one or more affiliates for each visitor or customer brought by the affiliate's marketing efforts. The affiliate could be an influencer, a top brand, or even a loyal customer who can get brand new customers by offering discounts and promotions (which have been shared by the brand for further promotions). Examples also include review sites, comparison, and e-commerce sites.
- **Public relations**: Public relations (PR) in traditional marketing involves all the activities a firm does to market or make available news and information on its organization, leadership, products, activities, etc. Similarly, in the online world, PR involves the brand sharing news about their initiatives on other digital sites where it knows its audience will reach or through agencies which will market this information to consumers either as feeds, articles, or regular news releases.
- **Editorial partnerships**: It involves paid articles specifically written to enhance the image of a specific product on websites which relate to the domain or vertical where the product belongs. An example would be to place a paid article on the importance of using a healthy oil brand in a site about health and wellness.

Key Advantages Partner marketing is crucial to help brands leverage the strong influence which other sites have developed with a specific target audience to utilize the sites' delivery vehicle and impact each part of the marketing funnel, be it information dissemination, brand engagement, or driving traffic to brand site for purchase.

Direct Marketing

It includes the set of channels which involve directly reaching out and marketing to consumers through direct outbound (push messages) and inbound channels (pull marketing). Key types include e-mail, SMS marketing, chat, inbound calls, user comments, etc. Let us look at each one of these in more detail.

- **Outbound Marketing (E-mail/SMS)**: It involves directly marketing a commercial message or promotion to a target audience using outbound techniques like e-mail or a mobile SMS (short messaging service). This type of marketing is considered one of the most cost-effective means and has the highest RoI as compared to other channels. It is also a powerful tool for end conversions as messages can be made highly customized
- **Inbound marketing (customer service calls/toll free numbers)**: It involves providing consumers a forum to communicate with the brand and develop a connect during that communication. Typical examples are customer service calls.
- **Response marketing (user comments)**: It includes examples where a consumer's response to brand interactions (for example, a user comment, online chat, or even a complain through mail) is responded to in a manner which improves brand connect with the customer and shows him the values of trust, care, involvement, superior service, etc.,for which the brand wants to stand.

Advantages of Direct Marketing as a Channel Direct marketing is one of the most powerful channels to develop a direct contact with consumers and respond to their queries in time to maintain brand trust and conclude a potential sale or transaction.

Content Marketing

One of the emerging channels of marketing, it includes ways and means to use "content" as a marketing channel by itself which guides consumers to purchases and end-of funnel activities. Key examples include native content, website, blog content, videos, webinars, etc. Below is provided an understanding of these areas:

- **Owned content (website/blog content/webinars)**: Content marketing is typically executed through the channels a firm owns, as these are the most trusted places which a customer visits for the first time.
- **Paid content (native content)**: The form of content marketing, which is gaining prominence, is the placement of content in a format native to the online channel (like pictures for Tumblr, tweets for Twitter, Native articles, etc.)
- **Viral content (video marketing):** Apart from text, rich media content like video, infomercials, cartoon snippets, humour-related images, etc., can be used for viral marketing which involves techniques to quickly spread self-propagating messages. Companies in present times, are looking at viral as a very important component of their online communication strategy for greater impact.

Advantages of Content Marketing as a Channel: The biggest strength of content marketing is its relevance and possibility to create an impact with messaging that is non-obtrusive, consistent, valuable, and creates traffic through a strong desire to consume quality content which has strong production values and is well curated to user's needs.

Platform Marketing

Again one of the emerging forms of marketing, it includes using new media platforms, devices, and consumer interaction media (like gaming) as vehicles for carrying marketing messages in the digital format. Examples include mobile applications, in-game marketing, kiosk marketing, wearables (watches, glasses), etc. Let us understand these areas further.

- **Device marketing (mobile/wearables)**: It involves marketing through a new set of consumer products and devices which the consumer uses as accessories to check messages multiple times a day. The best example is marketing through mobile applications or putting ads in emerging products like Google glass or wearable watch brands which are quite immersive in nature.
- **Platform marketing (kiosk marketing)**: It includes utilizing present hardware/software platforms to market through them. Best examples include ads in departmental store kiosks, or promotions through Microsoft Surface.
- **Media marketing (in-game marketing)**: With the rise of engaging media platforms like gaming or MMOW (massively multiplayer online world), which are computer-based-

simulation environments, interesting ways are emerging to share in-game placements which if contextual to the game can reap tremendous engagement and branding. The best example here is of the site Secondlife.com which became quite popular and was based on creation of avatars of real-life people to develop a commercial world wherein they could buy/sell virtual brands.

Advantages of Platform Marketing as a Channel Platform marketing is a highly engaging form of advertising which leverages a consumer's intense involvement with the device, platform, or media at hand to market in ways which target at a sub-conscious level and are in-built in the product or software applications itself.

In this last section of the chapter, we have got a good understanding of the varied types of channels marketers have at their disposal to generate desired outputs and communicate messages in a manner highly contextual to the medium and has a higher impact.

PRACTICAL EXERCISE

Establishing Earned Media Presence

Key Objective To establish presence across earned media platforms and execute partnerships and activities to garner earned influence from consumers.

Project Brief You are tasked with developing earned media presence and influence for the launch of a new B2B product by a startup firm.

Which earned media platforms will you start to develop a presence on? How would you research and decide the most effective avenues to gather word-of-mouth for your product portfolio? Which online blogs, review sites, influencers, etc., would you partner with and why? Please execute an online research and develop a custom plan.

Execution Let us look at some of the platform and partner options you could look at to establish earned presence and generate customer influence:

(a) **Social Media:** The first step in developing an earned media presence for any brand or firm is to decide on the mix of social media channels most suited for brand amplification or conversion. Based on product type, target audience, and platform specific features, marketers should decide on the top three social media platforms where they see maximum interaction for their brand. Establishing an earned media presence involves developing a page and sharing regular content on social media platforms such as Facebook, LinkedIn, Twitter, Instagram, and YouTube.

(b) **Industry Relations:** There are three key types of industry interactions most common to gathering earned media influence. Marketers should choose the best platforms or individuals for each of these three interaction areas:

- News Mentions (Media relations)
- External Blogs (Blogger relations)
- Influencer Marketing (Influencer relations)

(c) **Customer Interactions:** This involves consumer engagement to trigger interactions across multiple customer touchpoints. Marketers need to devise strategies to garner positive comments, shares, and mentions from their client community across social media channels, industry vertical sites, owned websites, consumer forums, etc.

(d) **Guest Blogs:** Another crucial way to establish earned media presence is to be involved with guest blogging, both on the brand site and on partner or affiliate sites, to cross-leverage influence across this medium.

(e) **Review Sites:** These can make or break a product's reputation. Hence, marketers need to strengthen their efforts towards having a presence on prominent vertical or technology review sites to gain maximum leverage from not only the user but also the website's admin community. This helps position the product in better light as compared to competition.

(f) **Search Engine Optimization (SEO):** SEO related efforts often provide a big boost to firms in terms of gathering stronger organic traffic (through on-page activities) and developing relevant connections with other top websites through off-page activities like back-links and social book-markings (across key vertical sites).

Deciding the most appropriate way to assess earned media platforms forms a major aspect of establishing a digital presence for any brand. Placing emphasis on developing industry partnerships and encouraging consumers to interact and share digital word-of-mouth goes a long way to support owned and paid media activities. The impact of earned media initiatives and interactions should be assessed on a regular basis and tweaks executed based on observed return on investment (ROI). Once the exercise is complete, it is advisable to discuss earned marketing plans created by other students to understand selection rationale and viewpoint on chosen platforms and partners.

CHAPTER SUMMARY

- **Part 1:** In the first section we started with developing an understanding of the basic terminologies of media planning and the impact of a shift to digital channels. This was followed by understanding the key concepts of developing web-specific media plans and the key terms involved. We then classified key promotional channels across paid, owned, and earned media, and developed the digital media planning stages to understand how firms across 6S digital implementation stages can choose the channel mix best suited for them to allocate their budget accordingly. The part also covered ways in which firms can analyze their digital marketing investments and the right metrics they should look at for planning marketing RoI.
- **Part 2:** This part covered the activities behind designing the communication mix, starting with an understanding of how marketing communications has transitioned from mass market to mass-customized mode to looking at the DRIP model for marketing communication. It was then followed by a discussion on the key steps to develop

a communication strategy along with the criteria of judging such a strategy. We then covered the four key areas of message content, structure, format, and source to understand how a particular communications message is developed. Finally, we developed the digital channels communication mix matrix to look at how different channels help firms communicate message for different end objectives (engagement or conversion) through differing message mix which could be static or dynamic (real-time).

- **Part 3**: The last part of the chapter focused on understanding the seven prominent forms of digital marketing channels, with a more in-depth look at intent-based, brand-based, and community based marketing channels which are used most widely. We looked at the history and growth behind these marketing channel types, how they operate, their ecosystem and key advantages. Apart from the three channels we also covered four other key digital marketing channels—partner, direct, content, and platform-based marketing channels, their key types, major advantages, and how each of them can specifically be applied to varied communication objectives most suited to them.

REVIEW QUESTIONS

1. What is media planning? Explain two of the six key traditional definitions which form a part of any Media Planning exercise:
   (a) Media Channel
   (b) Media Vehicle
   (c) Media Audience
   (d) Media Schedule
   (e) Media Budget
   (f) Media Delivery
2. Explain any three differences in media planning—offline versus digital platforms.
3. Share some of the key impacts of digital channels on media planning.
4. What are the two key considerations for a media planner while selecting a particular media for any type of promotion?
5. Explain four key concepts which are common to any media plan.
6. Describe any of the five key digital planning concepts as discussed in the chapter.
7. What is paid, earned, and owned media? Explain the digital media classification of promotion types.
8. What are the four key 'digital media planning' stages which marketers should follow?
9. How do we determine media planning strategy? What are the four core elements of digital media planning?
10. Group the 6S Digital Implementation stages into three buckets to chart their channel mix strategies.
11. What are the two key considerations which would help firms decide their channel mix?
12. What do you understand by the Digital Marketing Channel Mix Matrix? Explain the matrix through any of the three stages: launch, growth, or established.

13. According to Lenskold how is RoI typically calculated? Explain the three components of RoI equation which can be used to measure and plan marketing initiatives.
14. What is the three-step process to plan for marketing RoI as per the Marketo Group. Explain briefly what you understand by the Right Metrics Summary.
15. Define marketing communications? Describe the evolution to marketing communication automation.
16. What are the key benefits of marketing communication automation? Discuss key elements of marketing communication through the DRIP model.
17. What are the steps to creating marketing communications strategy? Pick up any one of the stages and discuss that in detail.
18. Describe the four key decisions to be taken into consideration while developing communications messaging.
19. Develop the Digital Channels Communication Mix Matrix and explain each of the magic quadrants in detail.
20. What do you understand by intent-based marketing (widely referred to as search marketing)? Describe in brief the working of search engines for search marketing.
21. What is brand-based marketing (widely referred to as display marketing)? Explain the display ad serving mechanism in brief.
22. What do we understand by Community-based marketing (widely referred to as social media marketing)? Describe the key types of social media marketing.
23. Describe partner, direct, content, and platform-based marketing channels? Choose any one of these four areas and detail the key types and advantages of that channel.

DIGITAL APPLICATION EXERCISES

1. Britannia has been one of the strongest traditional brands in India which has ventured into multiple categories over the years. Visit the website Britannia.co.in to study its products and through online research develop a comparison table on key media planning differences between its traditional and modern avatars.
2. Visit the media buying website themediaant.com. Pick up any newsdaily like *Times of India* or *Hindustan Times* and draw comparisons in the media planning variables between their print and digital options. What were your key observations?
3. Identify and list the paid, owned, and earned media channels for Cadbury India. Are there any key inferences to share on the differences across the three media channels?
4. Think of launching a new product digitally in any category of your liking and develop the stages involved in its digital media planning.
5. For the same product chosen in the previous question, showcase how you would develop the four digital media planning elements for launching the new product.
6. Deos as a category has picked up phenomenally in India. Pick up any three

leading Deo brands (across launch, growth and established stages) and develop the Digital Marketing Channel Mix Matrix for the three deo brands.

7. Take the case of any state government in India planning to launch a Digital India drive. What would be the key steps to the creation of its marketing communications strategy?
8. Paperboat (www.papeboatdrinks.com) has been a very good example of a brand in recent years which has broken the clutter in its category by building a unique imagery. Devise the four key elements behind its communications messaging.
9. Provide one example of an Indian brand across each of the four digital channels communication mix matrix quadrants.
10. Elucidate on the concept of affiliate networks by visiting a website and explaining one of the top affiliate networks in India (Komi, Tyroo, Vcommission, DGM, etc).

CHAPTER 7

Digital Marketing Operations Set-up

LEARNING OBJECTIVES

After studying this chapter, you will be able to:

- Explain the meaning of lead generation, lead nurturing and lead scoring for any digital marketing firm
- Understand the basics of conversion marketing and landing page optimization techniques
- Describe pre-planning activities for web development including site diagram, wireframe development, and define the basics of a web content management system
- Analyze the other key elements—user experience, usability, interaction design and service quality

CASE STUDY LinkedIn India: *Transitioning from Networking to Advertising*

Microsoft-owned LinkedIn has emerged as the largest networking platform for professionals. This is not just true for US or India, as LinkedIn undoubtedly rules the professional networking market worldwide. Since its inception, LinkedIn has focused on its Indian users, and in fact, India emerged as their largest market outside the US as evidenced by data from Statista, where LinkedIn India has 83 million users as of January 2022, only second to the U.S. In 2015, LinkedIn had much less reach in India. What was it then that made LinkedIn gain success over the next 6 years? It was the acquisition by Microsoft.

In June 2016, LinkedIn was acquired by Microsoft for US$26.2 billion. This proved to be a turning point as LinkedIn gained access to enhanced strategies, products, and services that helped this platform gain a wider user base in India and worldwide. In 2017, LinkedIn India floated their Career Advice Hub, which aimed to connect users with appropriate subject-matter experts. In the same year, they also launched the 'LinkedIn Lite' application specially for Android Users in India. As per Akshay Kothari, who was LinkedIn India's Head in 2018, the Lite app was launched to expand its reach to Tier II and Tier III towns in India. This strategy worked effectively and in 2018, LinkedIn India reached the mark of 50 million users due to the strategic push of small-town users.

In 2018, LinkedIn introduced a job-seeker toolkit that aimed to help users gain the required skills for making career changes. It also helped recruiters identify candidates that have the right skills specific to an opportunity. This was again a booster for the platform. Today, LinkedIn India is used by both job seekers and job providers. LinkedIn launched features like 'Scheduled LinkedIn Live' and 'LinkedIn Events' across LinkedIn Live Events platform for maximum reach and engagement by helping broadcasters go live spontaneously or schedule a Live Event in advance for their profile or LinkedIn Page. However, LinkedIn India's success was accelerated primarily by B2B marketers as LinkedIn is one of the very few platforms geared towards business networking (providing B2B lead generation possibility).

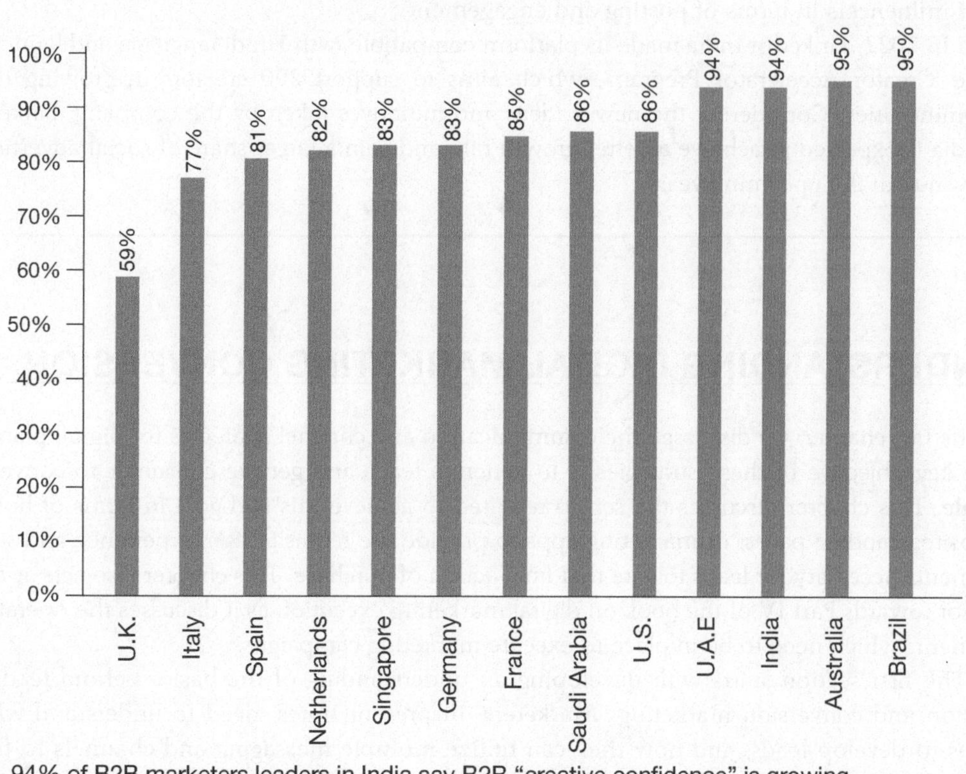

94% of B2B marketers leaders in India say B2B "creative confidence" is growing.
92% believe B2B brands are producing creative campaigns that rival consumer brands.

Figure 7.1 B2B marketing "creative confidence" soaring

Source: Data sourced from WNIP (2022). Majority of B2B leaders globally say "creative confidence" is growing: LinkedIn research. Retrieved from www.whatsnewinpublishing.com, accessed in 2022.

LinkedIn is the most trusted platform among B2B marketers for generating leads. To increase B2B marketers' user base, LinkedIn launched LinkedIn Marketing Solutions (LMS). This move was aimed at enabling marketers deepen their engagement level with target audience. Another reason for LinkedIn's growth has been the outbreak of the COVID-19 pandemic. As per Ashutosh Gupta, the India Country manager for LinkedIn in 2019, LinkedIn's app in India has experienced four times more usage than the global average in this period.

The last 5 years have been crucial for LinkedIn India. It has emerged as a professional networking platform attracting every job seeker and marketer. As per Statista figures from July 2021, LinkedIn India has a 0.25 per cent share in the social media market. While it is still getting its presence felt in the social media market, it is important to understand that the essence of LinkedIn is different from popular social media platforms such as Facebook and Instagram. However, LinkedIn is coming up with multiple strategies to increase engagement for marketers. At present, it is one of the highest growing platforms for influencers in terms of posting and engagement.

In 2022, LinkedIn India made its platform compatible with Hindi language and launched the 'Creator Accelerator Program', which aims to support 200 creators in growing their communities. Considering the newer ideas and initiatives taken by the company, LinkedIn India is expected to achieve a better growth rate and gain a larger share of social advertising revenue in the upcoming years.

UNDERSTANDING DIGITAL MARKETING CONVERSION

In the last chapter, we discussed the communication and channel strategies for digital planning. The key objective of these strategies is to generate leads and get the consumer to convert for a sale. This chapter discusses the set-up required to achieve this end goal in terms of building websites, landing pages, or marketing apps to provide the requisite user experience and service elements necessary for leads to take that final action of purchase. This chapter also acts as a precursor towards Part IV of the book on digital marketing execution as it discusses the operational elements which need to be in place to execute marketing campaigns.

The first section starts with developing an understanding of the basics behind lead generation and conversion marketing. Marketers, in present times, need to understand what it takes to develop leads, and how they can utilize multiple messaging and channels to finally help potential customers convert on to their site and fulfill their goals. Marketers need to gain an understanding of consumer needs and their journeys to help them develop the right experience and platforms for their conversion strategies. In this chapter, and particularly the next section, would look at how firms can be best prepared to lead their conversion marketing strategies to fruition.

Basics of Lead Generation and Conversion Marketing

Lead generation, by definition, is the generation of consumer attention or inquiry into products and services of a business. A lead is differentiated from a visitor or a prospect primarily in its intent, as it is more 'qualified,' thus, has higher chances of conversion. In our discussion on the REAN Marketing Funnel, we touched upon the development of a lead in the 'Engage' stage beyond which it has to be activated through what we know as 'conversion marketing.'

Conversion, according to a specialized digital marketing research firm, Marketing Sherpa, refers to "The point at which a recipient of a marketing message performs a desired action." Conversion marketing, thus, is the set of marketing activities undertaken by a firm/brand to encourage the consumer undertake specific actions that the firm wants them to take. These actions could be across any of the stages of the marketing funnel. Getting a potential consumer fill up a registration form on a website is a conversion. Having the same customer download a whitepaper is another form of conversion. Finally, buying the product on the firm's site is the most desirable of all forms of conversions.

In this chapter, we would understand how firms can set up conversion marketing activities for the set of leads they have with them at any moment in time. But first, let us look at the process of lead generation following which we will cover the ways conversion marketing is deployed to convert qualified leads to real customers, who finally make a purchase.

Lead Generation Process

The lead generation process (according to 'The Definitive Guide to Lead Generation by Marketo') involves:

(a) **Agreeing on a clear definition of the lead:** Sales and marketing teams need to discuss the elements that actually define a target as a lead.

(b) **Defining a mechanism to gather leads from all marketing channels:** Firms need to develop a mechanism to be able to gather and create a view of all their leads across multiple online and offline channels.

(c) **Classifying leads for better targeting:** Firms should classify their leads list based on demographics, budget, authority, need, time, and other such parameters.

(d) **Identifying gradation of importance and developing a list of 'quality leads':** Each company, depending on its business and nature of lead-generation process, should define a 'quality lead' for their business which they should nurture.

(e) **Developing Service Level Agreements (SLAs) between sales and marketing:** Once leads are in place and have been shared with the sales teams, SLAs should be developed between marketing and sales to ensure that sales follow through the leads in a diligent manner.

Conversion Marketing across Consumer Funnel Stages

Leads which are generated in the consumer funnel (see REAN Marketing Engagement Framework in Chapter 1) need to be gradually taken to the action level for the marketer to complete the purchase cycle. Activities performed at each of the funnel stages to take the consumer forward include 'Conversion' for that particular stage. Let us look at some of the typical conversion-marketing activities which are carried out for key funnel stages.

(a) **Conversion marketing for INTENT and AWARENESS stages**: This is the stage where the potential target segments express their needs and marketers share branding material, webinars, blog articles to convert visitors for the next stage. Key conversion stages and the marketing strategies deployed include:

- **Name**: It refers to the inclusion of the name of an individual in the database. Companies utilize techniques like an online enquiry form, a webinar registration, whitepaper download, etc., to obtain individual names for further conversion.
- **Engaged**: In this stage, individuals are engaged with the firm/brand and marketers are expected to send e-mails and communicate with them over time. Conversion techniques include direct marketing areas like sending e-mails, mobile SMS, etc.
- **Target**: Once the select group of individuals are engaged, companies can use a lead scoring system (one that helps understand quality leads through a scoring mechanism) to assess whether they are qualified potential buyers (which includes the individual fitting the brand's demographic and behavioral data).

(b) **Conversion marketing for INTEREST stage**: Once a potential visitor becomes a target or prospect for the firm and has displayed traits like making enquiries of the product or engaging with content, marketers can move forward to convert such interested targets to a lead. Marketo shares two sub-stages here:

- **Lead**: This is the stage where a potential target or prospect converts to a lead. Key conversion techniques qualifying a target as a lead include:
  - ➤ Visit to the sales web page of the company's product site
  - ➤ Selecting the product and placing it in a cart on an e-commerce site
  - ➤ Targets who have visited an affiliate site for a coupon or price comparison
  - ➤ Prospects who have initiated a direct interaction/chat to enquire more about the product
  - ➤ Targets who have taken part in a 'for-sale' promotion on the social media page of the brand
- **Sales lead**: In this stage, once the list of leads has been confirmed, sales or marketing automation tools automatically take over to convert the lead into a purchase. Leads at this stage are known as sales leads. When a lead converts to a sales lead, the account executives are given a specific period of time within which they have to convert them into customers.

(c) **Conversion marketing for ACTION and FOLLOW stages**: This stage involves conversion of sales leads to final customers who purchase a product. This is successively followed up with actions geared towards converting the loyal buyer to future follower. There are two key conversion sub-stages here:

- **Opportunity**: It involves techniques by which the sales team or automated marketing tools are deployed to convert the sales leads into real opportunities that can develop a customer. Typical conversion strategies at this stage include:

- Retargeting through branded online advertisements on products which a customer had already selected in a cart or had visited the web page
- Sending targeted e-mails for conversion with specific timed promotions
- Responding to sales queries and making outbound sales calls to help the lead move forward along purchase cycle

- **Customer**: This is the stage where leads finally purchase a product and become a customer in the database.

Along with an understanding of lead generation and conversion marketing, it is important to also go through the concepts of lead nurturing and lead scoring to appreciate the efforts marketers need to put to create desired results.

Lead Nurturing and Lead Scoring Concepts

In the last section, we understood key lead generation stages and how marketers need to handle and develop each individual who might just be a casual visitor become a serious buyer. The process of this conversion involves two major elements which need to be understood in detail—lead nurturing and lead scoring.

Lead Nurturing

It involves the series of steps marketers need to execute as a well-defined program to continually reach out to and build relationships with targets and qualified leads, and influence them throughout the consumer decision journey till they become a customer. The concept also covers present clients, who can be truned into loyal customers and subsequently influencers facilitating cross-sell and up-sell of other related products and services.

The need for lead nurturing arises from the fact that post the 'intent' and 'awareness' stages in the funnel, there are a large number of potential targets who might be interested in the product or some of its key attributes, but do not yet have either a strong emotional connect or a benefit-based understanding of product features. The job of the marketer then is to think of specific steps which would help these targets develop a regular connect with the brand and its core attributes.

Elements of Lead Nurturing

Lead nurturing as an exercise is based on the concepts of engagement or permission marketing, where the targets are not bombarded with irrelevant marketing messages, but communication is tailored specifically for different types of leads and shared in a relevant conversational manner with an implicit permission from the target to accept and act on it. Any lead-nurturing exercise should typically have the following elements built into them:

(a) **Be permission lead**: Lead nurturing should be engagement lead wherein the brand at each stage has the requisite permission from the targets to follow them.

(b) **Include educational elements**: Marketers should not only provide information but aim at educating their prospects on key brand attributes through novel educational aids.

(c) **Create moments of conversation**: Rather than trying to impinge the lead with push messages, brands should try to create multiple moments of conversation with targets.

(d) **Follow a natural progression**: There should be a logical flow to lead nurturing with each next message being in perfect natural progression of engagement as in real life.

(e) **Measure regularly**: All marketing efforts should be measured regularly on pre-decided metrics with messaging, channels and nature of communication needing to be regularly revised with new inputs.

(f) **Multi-channel interactions**: Marketers should not just look at a single channel for lead nurturing but develop a multi-channel interactions program.

(g) **Develop interactivity**: All lead-nurturing activities should have an interactive element wherein leads have an opportunity to respond back where their views can be captured.

Types of Lead-Nurturing Campaigns

Different firms depending on their needs, resources, and nature of leads for their specific products, engage in multiple types of nurturing campaigns. Marketo defines the following types of lead-nurturing campaigns that firms can deploy:

(a) **Incoming lead-processing campaigns**: It involves making the first touchpoint with the lead to create a positive impression in the mind of the individual towards the brand/product. It is important that marketers have a good understanding of the needs, intent, and present funnel stage of the various buckets of leads before developing introductory campaigns.

(b) **Stay-in-touch campaigns**: These campaigns are typically developed to regularly connect with leads who are still not open to engaging with the brand. The idea here is to share interesting, engaging, and educational material about the product to build acquaintance and trust with the company. With these efforts, the brand aims to develop top-of-the-mind recall with the lead who would have the brand image built in his/her mind whenever he/she plans to buy a similar product in the coming times.

(c) **Accelerator campaigns**: This next level of campaigns are designed for individuals who have shown a keen interest in the brand and would likely convert if pursued aggressively. It involves studying specific interactions which the prospect has with the brand and creating customized campaigns to address specific needs arising from those touch points.

(d) **Lead life cycle campaigns**: These types of campaigns are built for leads who might not be interacting at all to multiple messages and would typically be termed as stagnant or lost leads. Campaigns here are built to make sure that leads are not completely inactive. The three important stages of lead life cycle campaigns include: Lead Handoff, Lead Recycling, and New Customers.

(e) **Buying stage campaigns**: This includes campaigns which follow leads across their buying journey with targeted content developed to influence customers during each action of their buying process. These campaigns should ideally be mapped to key personas or lead buckets within the buying stages.

(f) **Interest-based campaigns:** It involves developing campaigns that build on a specific interest which the customer has responded to and sharing content or executing activities similar in nature to their interaction. Typical examples include:
- Prospects browsing specific content on the company's blog
- Responding to social media posts regularly
- Downloading marketing material/attending webinars on specific areas of interest

With some interesting examples of nurturing campaigns shared earlier, it should also be reiterated that firms need to look at their specific lead clusters, understand their interactions and buying cycles, before selecting a mix of the above or other innovative nurturing techniques.

With an understanding of the key lead-nurturing techniques, let us look at the other important area for lead generation, which is lead scoring, and which involves qualifying the importance of a lead.

Lead Scoring

It is a method used to rank prospects to understand the importance and relevance of following up with each lead in relation to the firm's investment. With the help of lead scoring, marketers are able to bucket their leads to invest time and effort in order of priority.

Advantages of Lead Scoring According to a survey by CMSwire (one of the popular web magazines on customer experience management and digital marketing), typical benefits gained by a website from their lead-scoring implementation includes:
- Measurable RoI on lead generation program
- Increased conversion rates from qualified lead to opportunity
- Increased sales productivity and effectiveness
- Shortened sales cycle
- Better forecast and pipeline visibility
- Better alignment of marketing and sales efforts

Lead Scoring Execution Following Marketo's methodology, there are three aspects to a lead scoring exercise, as defined by them:

(a) **Lead fit**: Firms should first see whether a particular lead fits in their description of who they would want to nurture. It involves looking at information shared through an online form/registration process and also gathering other demographic, psychographic, behavorial information on the lead. Scoring should also be done for negative demographic fit to exclude entries that are not authentic or worth following.

(b) **Lead interest**: The next step, which is also known as implicit lead scoring, involves measuring the level of interest the prospect has in the firm's product or service. This can be gauged by analyzing the lead's interactions with the firm/brand across various touchpoints to understand lead buckets in more depth.

(c) **Lead recycling**: Post lead-nurturing efforts, some of the leads might not be ready for the purchase stage and need to be sent back to the lead-nurturing cycle, which is also known as lead recycling. With additional information collected on the lead through previous interactions, marketers can activate a very specific lead generation program, knowing the key areas which the lead might respond to positively in future.

With an understanding of input-based lead-nurturing and lead-scoring techniques, let us now look at the outcome of digital marketing operations which is about conversions at each stage of the funnel. This would begin with looking at how conversion as a concept has evolved and is moving from websites to landing pages to the most recent marketing apps.

Setting up for Conversion: from Web-Page to Landing Page

With an understanding of the basics of lead generation, lead nurturing, and lead scoring, in this section, we would cover how these efforts culminate into action for the marketer in terms of conversion across each of the funnel stages with the final conversion being the product or service purchase.

Any marketing activity typically needs an anchor where marketers can bring in all of their targets and qualified leads for conversion. In case of traditional marketing, the place for conversion was typically a physical store where consumers would come in for a purchase after they had been exposed to marketing, or it would be a phone number which they would use to call to get in touch with a representative who would support them in accomplishing the sale.

Similarly, in the digital world, marketers need to bring in all their activated leads from different sources to a place where they can achieve the desired marketing objectives. Traditionally, that conversion point has been the homepage of the firm's website. The website has been in most cases, the primary conversion destination for digital marketing with other secondary conversion points like marketing apps also growing.

A website, which is the primary conversion tool for marketers, typically consists of web pages of which the homepage has always been the most crucial, not only because it is the first page which visitors look at but also because it is the backbone for overall page navigation on the site. In the initial days of marketing, when most of the sites were static with limited functionality, the homepage used to be the one where visitors would mostly land and from where they would navigate to other pages based on interest and need.

But as marketing started to grow more complex with multiple target consumer groups and a variety of lead-nurturing techniques, it became important that marketers use their main conversion tool (the web pages) to customize and deploy them for multiple conversion objectives. It was then that the concept of landing pages emerged.

A *landing page*, known as a 'lead-capture' page or a 'lander,' is a single web page which has been customized to receive and convert visitors on specific objectives from multiple other media channels like search campaigns, social media, e-mail campaigns, etc. Typically, a landing page should be developed as a natural extension of advertisement or link from which it is directed. The key differences between a website's homepage and its landing pages include:

(a) Homepage is proactively visited by individuals while landing pages are typically customized pages within the website where nurtured leads are redirected for specific conversion activities.
(b) Visitors to a landing page would need to be convinced and provided with some takeaway or positive experience for them to convert or visit the website again. This is not the case with regular homepage visitors who have visited the homepage out of personal discovery, through word-of-mouth, or from other sources.

With the evolution of marketing, landing pages are giving way to marketing applications (generally referred to as 'marketing apps'), which are more interactive than landing pages. Let us first understand the basics of landing pages and how they are optimized for conversion, following which we would also briefly touch upon the emerging area of marketing apps.

From our discussion on conversion marketing in the last section, we understood that each of the funnel stages have different objectives and need different kinds of conversion techniques. Landing pages are typically designed to help marketers with conversions across each of these stages. This can be achieved in multiple ways like: developing a form for registration, creating a hosting page for a webinar registration, developing a downloading page for an e-book, survey or contest, or just designing 'Contact Us' page. Each of these would be considered as stand-alone and distinct landing pages.

Landing Page Optimization

We now have an understanding of the key objectives of a landing page and how they need to be developed in a customized manner for specific desired outcomes. For a landing page to be effective, it typically needs to be regularly optimized in terms of its layout, content, images, form, length, and other elements. All the activities towards analyzing conversions and trying newer and more effective variations of landing pages include the area of landing page optimization.

Landing page optimization is crucial because of the following reasons:

(a) Some pages might be exhibiting lower conversion rates (rate of conversion of landing page visitors)
(b) Few landing pages might have high bounce rates (number of visitors bouncing off a particular landing page and not following through)
(c) Few landing pages might have visitors spending less time for them to be of any pertinent use
(d) Some pages might not be working properly, hence causing leads to slip through

Top metrics to cover landing page optimization include:

(a) Click-through rate/ratio
(b) Page views
(c) Cost per click

(d) Conversion rates

(e) Reduction in sales cycle duration for qualified leads

Landing Page Optimization (LPO) Techniques

Landing pages can be optimized based on inputs from multiple sources. Key techniques include:

LPO Based on Targeting

(a) **Associative content targeting** (also called rule-based optimization or passive targeting): Page content is modified based on information obtained from visitor's search criteria, geographic information of source traffic, and other such explicit non-research-based consumer segmentation.

(b) **Predictive content targeting** (also called active targeting): Page content is adjusted by correlating any known information about the visitor (for example, prior purchase behavior, personal demographic information, browsing patterns, etc.) to anticipate future actions based on predictive analytics.

(c) **Consumer directed targeting** (also called social targeting): Page content is created using the relevance of publicly available information through a mechanism based on reviews, ratings, tagging, referrals, etc.

LPO Based on Experimentation

(a) **Close-ended experimentation**: Consumers are exposed to several variations of landing pages, altering elements like headlines, formatting, and layout, while their behavior is observed and an optimal page is selected based on the outcome of the experiment.

(b) **Open-ended experimentation**: The approach is similar to close-ended experimentation with the difference being that the experimentation is ongoing and landing page is adjusted dynamically.

Introduction to Marketing Apps

With an understanding of the basics of landing page, let us now be familiar with the concept of marketing apps which is an emerging form of a landing page. According to Ion Interactive, one of the top 'marketing apps' firm, a *marketing app* is a browser-based digital experience designed for user interaction, which provides an experience even more engaging than the landing page. Not only does it refer to mobile apps but such a marketing app can reside within the browser regardless of the device. According to Ion, any kind of content can be converted to a marketing app to make it much more interactive and engaging for consumers. Typical examples would include:

(a) Converting a white paper into a quiz app

(b) Sharing a pricing spreadsheet as a calculator app

(c) Developing best practices into assessments, among others

Though landing page is still the holy grail of conversion, marketers can benefit immensely to create rich experiences for consumers by developing relevant and customized marketing apps.

Lead Management across Channels—Owned, Earned, and Paid

With an understanding of the basics of *lead generation to conversion*, in this section, we would spend time to understand the various ways in which leads can be generated and converted across different types of digital media channels—owned, earned, and paid. Some of the channels which we will cover in the section as examples to discuss lead management include:

- Owned channels—website, blogs
- Earned channels—social media
- Paid media—SEM, e-mail marketing

The understanding emerging from this section would form the base for a detailed coverage on digital marketing execution in Chapter 8. *Lead generation to conversion* cycle activities typically form a part of the overall campaign management process which is vital to implementing any digital marketing program on a channel.

Let us begin with the website which is the most crucial of *owned* channels for all lead management activities.

(a) **Website-based lead management**: It involves utilizing the product/brand website as the base for lead generation to conversion activities. Typically, any visitor who comes to a website (either directly or through other channels), needs to be directed to the specific action the marketer wants to accomplish. This act of getting the visitor to perform a certain intended action is termed as 'Call to Action' (CTA) in marketing. A CTA on a website, for example, could be a banner, button, graphic, text, etc., on any of the web pages which is meant to prompt a user to click it and move ahead for conversion.

Depending on the intended lead generation objective and consumer funnel stage (as discussed in the beginning of the chapter), there are multiple types of CTAs which any website could deploy. These CTAs can also be specifically built for traffic coming from various other earned and paid media channels to convert targets and leads, based on their behavior and incoming source. The most commonly used types of CTAs on a website (according to Marketo) include:

- **Website forms**: Forms are one of the most basic and yet powerful ways to capture information on visitors and to start the conversion journey.
- **Contact us**: involves developing a contact form to support visitor request for more information on the company, product, or any other specific queries.
- **Asset download**: Supporting visitors with useful content assets to share details on the product and its usage, and to also gather more information.
- **Chat**: Live chats have become a very intuitive and powerful way to connect with website visitors who have an intent and in this way marketers are able to connect on a real-time basis with prospects.

- **Surveys**: Another way to give visitors an insight into their interest area and helpful feedback is surveys. With the result of surveys, further CTAs like 'Learn More' related to the subject of the survey, can also be provided for further engagement.
- **Contests**: Quick and interesting contests with some useful freebies is also another example of using landing pages effectively to gather more information.

(b) **Blog-based lead management**: Blog opt-ins or subscriptions could be a great way to lock-in target audience, keep them engaged and offer them multiple points of conversion at regular intervals through effective use of e-mails or RSS feeds.

Next, we will move on to *earned* channels.

(c) **Social media**: Social content and CTA have become a stable and effective way not only to share engaging messages but to also generate leads without spending a lot. Also with peer-to-peer influence marketing gaining prominence, a strong social presence helps dedicated fans act as influencers for others who are willing to engage more with the brand but are still not ready for a purchase. The major social media sites which are used most extensively for lead management include:

- **Facebook:** With the largest user base among all social networks, Facebook can be a strong peer-to-peer influencer. Facebook began with giving opportunities for brands to develop free-of-cost brand pages and to share posts with a large number of fans. But with increased usage, credibility, innovation, and adoption, paid ads on Facebook (in the form of Newsfeed ads and promoted posts) are starting to become as prominent as Adwords (Google Search Advertising Program) to help convert leads to conversions.
- **Twitter:** Next to Facebook, Twitter is a popular tool to share relevant brand messages. With concepts like hashtags (grouping of similarly tagged messages) and promoted tweets gaining prominence, it is certainly a vital tool to invest in.
- **LinkedIn**: For anything related to business profiles, networking, and relationship building, LinkedIn has emerged as the premium site to market. Firms can build company pages, invest in sponsored updates and LinkedIn ads to generate traffic from those who are interested in following the company and its products.
- **Google+**: While still not as widely used as Facebook, Google+ is gaining popularity primarily through the network and integration effects of its other popular products like Google Search, Gmail, Google Maps, etc.
- **Other social media sites**: Apart from the key ones shared above, social sites like Pinterest, SlideShare, WhatsApp, Tumblr, etc., are also popular for lead generation.

Finally, we move on to the *paid* media channels which are a must for businesses to begin their lead generation and lead management programs.

(d) **SEM (Search Engine Marketing)**: With search marketing being one of the most prominent paid lead-generation techniques, firms depend on it the most to start their lead-building efforts. As discussed in the last chapter in detail, SEM utilizes the algorithmic capability of advanced search algorithms to match audience keywords to text, display, and video advertisements. SEM along with its organic counterpart SEO (which involves optimizing content, images, URL structures on web pages to rank organically for search results), accounts for a comprehensive lead management program for most of the brands. It also involves efforts towards link building like establishing link-based authority for brand sites through inclusion of quality external links to specific web pages.

(e) **E-mail marketing**: E-mail marketing has been the cornerstone for engagement building with audiences and historically has had the highest RoI of all paid programs, primarily due to the cost-effectiveness of paid e-mail programs. Vendors, typically support clients' e-mail marketing programs by helping them target on audience type and reach, topics of interest, and geo-targeting. With the development of relevant e-mail marketing metrics and strong follow-up, marketers can hope to gain a lot from their e-mail investments.

(f) **Other paid channels**: Apart from SEM and e-mail marketing, there are other types of paid marketing channels which are also the key to lead generation. These include affiliate marketing, content syndication, direct marketing, online events, among others. Apart from these, other traditional methods like inbound and outbound tele-calling are also channels wherein firms set up the infrastructure to generate new leads (through outbound calling) and grow engagement with present leads (through inbound customer care). Here, investment could be a bit higher upfront, but if firms set up an internal tele-calling unit, the results over time could reap substantial benefits as opposed to paying per call to an external vendor.

With an understanding of how varied channels can be deployed across owned, earned, and paid media towards lead generation and conversion objectives, we will move further to the next part of this chapter to look at how companies can develop the most critical instrument of lead management, that is, the whole set of activities towards website development.

Also, we need to add here that in this section, we have covered the operational part of lead generation and conversions. To execute them, marketers need to develop elaborate marketing campaigns which we would discuss at length in Chapter 8.

BASICS OF WEB DEVELOPMENT AND MANAGEMENT

Pre-Planning for Web Development

The key to any successful and integrated digital marketing program has to involve the development of a brand website which is considered to be 'THE' identity for the firm (although in the present period of mobile first, firms are constantly pushing clients to adopt mobile and other marketing apps for multiple reasons).

A website is a group of connected web pages, considered as a single entity and typically served from a single web domain. As we discussed earlier (in Chapter 1, section titled, 'Understanding Web and Wireless Technologies'), a website runs on a combination of multi-tier infrastructure stacks and helps deliver data and content in response to any request made by a user over the internet. A website is pivotal for marketing since it is the main property (similar to a retail shop or physical office) through which any firm or its brand conducts their business in the online world. A website is not just a place for conversion or sales, but also powerfully demonstrates a brand's imagery, design values, business functionality, speed of execution, product portfolio, marketing content, etc. It is the brand's address on the internet for all incoming visitors, leads, customers, and even over-lookers who may want to interact or just do an initial check on the brand and its business.

All of the above make it highly relevant for any firm to set aside a specified budget towards their website development activities. This is to make sure that they definitely match (if not exceed) competition, their web development efforts towards providing customers a web destination is admired, and at the same time, it is most effective for them to conduct business. Some other key definitions which are crucial to an understanding of website development and management include:

(a) **Web browser:** It is a software application for retrieving, presenting, and navigating information resources on the World Wide Web. A website once developed with a particular URL (Uniform Resource Locator), can be opened in any of the available web browsers with which the user has chosen to navigate the internet. The most used browsers include Microsoft Internet Explorer, Google Chrome, Mozilla Firefox among others.

(b) **Device:** It applies to a hardware instrument which hosts the web browser (software) and is used to view multiple web pages on any particular website. With a growing demand for multiple devices, an understanding of how to render web pages and content for a particular device and browser has become crucial to a consumer's overall web experience.

(c) **Platform:** includes all the aspects of a pre-built environment with which a particular device comes to support any type of computing be it web browsing, or playing a mobile game, or going through an e-book experience, rendered specifically for that platform.

What Is Web Development?

The set of activities and efforts involved with developing websites of any type constitute web development. A website can either be a single page static site with plain information or it could be a highly interactive site with thousands of web pages executing multiple transactions with high design elements and computing power. A high traffic e-commerce site, a popular gaming site, a nice social networking site, and web application running on a tablet device, all of these constitute web development effort.

Pre-Planning for Web Development Before we begin to study the website development stages in detail, firms need to pre-plan their objectives and goals from the development standpoint. Key pre-planning activities include:

(a) **Developing the purpose of the website**: The most important aspect is for firms to decide the nature of their website. Is it an information dissemination site (to support a majorly offline business)? Will the site be an integral part of the brand-building effort for a particular product? Or is the primary goal of the site to support online transactions? The purpose should guide the overall functionality, design, and transactional elements of the website.

(b) **Defining visitor segments and characteristics**: It is important to determine the kind of visitors who would frequent the site, the most important personas to target, their buying behavior and prior browsing pattern, the sections on which they spend the maximum time (predictive analytics), and the conversion types which have the highest success rate.

(c) **Researching competitive websites/elements**: To develop a successful site, it is important that the firm must have researched competing websites for the functionalities they offer, their site design, conversion techniques, etc., to differentiate and develop a unique platform.

(d) **Understanding latest computing platforms, browsers, devices**: With increased computing power and emergence of various closed and open-source platforms and browsers emerging for multiple consumption devices, firms need to develop their web architecture in a way which is compatible across emerging web technologies.

(e) **Firm's planned spend on the site**: Depending upon the type of site and the effort needed to create a differential presence, firms have to take a call on how much they need to spend to be operationally efficient and reliable as these are important factors for customers, where even a single minute downtime can earn bad reputation for even established players (of which we have seen multiple examples in recent times).

(f) **Developing in-house or vendor development teams**: Finally, firms need to take a decision on whether they want to start with a large team in-house for their web-development activities or hire an external firm and begin with a few members internally to support it. Web maintenance and frequent upgrades have made it all the more important for firms to develop certain basic set of technology capabilities in-house.

Selecting a Domain to Manage Hosting Before a firm gets into the nitty-gritties of the actual website development cycle and its key steps, they need to execute two important activities:

(a) **Obtaining a domain name:** Any website which is developed across the internet needs to have a unique identity through which people can locate it. That unique identity is known as a domain name which identifies the ownership of that website. The Internet Corporation for Assigned Names and Numbers (ICANN) manages the development and architecture of the domain name space across the internet.

A domain name typically consists of two parts, technically called labels. For example, a website by the name xyz.com has two labels 'xyz' which is the name of the website and '.com' which is a top-level domain. There are other top-level domains like '.info,' '.net,' '.org,' and other country code top-level domains like '.in' for India. A domain name is a component of the URL which is used to access websites. For example, for a URL: http://www.xyz.com/faq.html the top-level domain name is 'com,' second-level domain name is 'xyz.com,' and the host name is www.xyz.com.

Each firm should ensure that they choose a domain name that relates strongly to their business model, is differentiated from competition, and is simple enough to follow with a high recall for their target audience.

(b) **Website hosting**: It involves making the website accessible to its audience by hosting it with a service provider that provides internet services. There are multiple types of hosting services which firms can utilize for their websites, some of which include:

- **Shared web hosting**: Type of hosting where the firm's website will reside with hundreds or thousands of other sites on a shared server. It is the most common and usually the cheapest form of hosting, especially good for SMB businesses.
- **Virtual dedicated server**: A single server is divided into multiple servers each acting virtually independently for each firm, thus providing more flexibility.
- **Dedicated hosting service**: Each user gains full control over the hosting service, though they do not own the server.
- **Cloud hosting**: Hosting on cloud principles and benefits; for example, utility-based billing.
- **Reseller web hosting**: It allows clients to become web hosts themselves by getting affiliated to a reseller which provides shared hosting and support to other clients.

Each firm should look at these or any of the other options depending upon the kind of control they want for their site, the budget, key functionality, reach, security, etc.

Website Development Stages

With an understanding of the pre-planning that goes behind any web development effort, let us now understand the key stages of web development, the type of efforts which need to be put at each stage of execution, and the typical outputs.

Web Development Cycle

Any web development effort (website development being a part of it), would involve a firm going through key stages which are together known as the web development cycle. The life cycle stages follow the sequential waterfall model similar to a software development cycle, but there are multiple ways in which development can be executed and firms are not bound to follow these steps sequentially.

(a) **Analysis**: The first stage of web development begins with an analysis of the site's core users and how they would potentially interact with it. Marketers need to develop a clear idea of the website's role in helping visitors complete specific tasks and the kind of information they would look out for on various web pages.

Firms should typically have conducted prior conversions with a set of their target audience through interviews, questionnaires, surveys, and prior chat discussions to know the kind of experience they would be looking at. This exercise should help companies decide on the features to be showcased through the site and how the website would integrate best with other marketing activities happening traditionally.

Key output areas at this stage should include:

- High-level work plan for consequent stages
- High-level cost estimates for the entire effort
- Detailed technical requirements
- Vendor partnerships in place
- Content development activities

(b) **Requirements specification**: In this stage, all the research and understanding developed in the analysis stage is used to create a preliminary specification document. An overall concept understanding is put to paper, the site structure is defined, and navigation and page-flows are developed. The most important requirement at this stage is the completion of a site-map which is a list of all the main topics of the site along with the sub-topics. This exercise also helps to provide clarity on the type of content which will be put up. Key output at this stage would include requirements specification document for the website and the sign-off proposal with stakeholders.

(c) **Design and development**: Before this stage commences, the specifications developed in *the previous stage have been signed and content has been developed or acquired from* vendors. From this stage onwards, the team develops the look and feel of the website and the User Interface (UI) design development work begins. Firms need to take care of their core audience while considering the design effort for different types of web pages.

Typically, a prototype is developed that is presented and iteratively worked upon for improvements. With lean development methodologies and frameworks in vogue today, firms look for cheaper and more effective ways to test their ideas and may develop them either on paper, through power point, or tools-based prototypes to show before the management and customer focus groups. This exercise helps obtain suggestions for further revisions or to obtain final approval. These prototypes, also commonly known as 'wire-frames,' if agreed upon, can be used directly to develop real dynamic screens which look closest to the final web pages to be developed.

Once the HTML proto-site (non-design oriented) is developed, art production/GIF production begins using the proto-site as outline and structure. HTML programming is continued and the content and graphics are incorporated into the final site which is then ready for testing and deployment.

(d) **Testing**: Once the beta version of the site is available, firms proceed with quality assurance to test the complete functionality of the site. There are various types of testing which can be performed to intermediate and final versions, including usability testing, browser compatibility testing, site performance testing, etc. Once testing is complete, a testing plan should be compiled to make sure that any new changes can be documented and acted upon.

(e) **Deployment and maintenance**: Once the site is fully tested and approved, the final stage is to deploy it and upload files to the server. Key areas for successful deployment include site publishing, regular updating and monitoring, sending of website notifications to audiences, etc. Maintenance of the site post-launch is also crucial and firms need to set up a dedicated team to help with new feature additions, enhancements, and resolution of any live issue that visitors might be facing. Marketing of the site is another important area as a website is going to be the prominent vehicle for other digital marketing activities of the firm.

Apart from the firm's umbrella site, it is also important that similar elements are replicated in other marketing applications and each of the stand-alone brand websites too, as it is crucial to develop a uniform, recognizable, and trusted brand image for company's marketing communication.

Developing Site Diagrams and Wireframes

To create a useful and effective website, any web-development exercise needs to develop a robust information architecture which can successfully integrate content, site design, organization of pages, and navigation to the best support their visitor's interests. The first step towards that includes developing a master site diagram that helps plan the high-level scope of the site and also key details at each page level like navigation and information access.

According to Web Style Guide (3rd Edition) by Patrick J. Lynch and Sarah Horton, "site diagrams visualize the developing information hierarchy and help communicate organizational concepts to the team, stakeholders and project sponsors." Typically, a site diagram evolves throughout the project with multiple iterations from different teams. A site diagram could be a plain hierarchical structure laying down key pages of the site or could be developed as a complex structure geared towards the technical team, which not only shows key site areas, but also provides an overview of the site directory and file structure (see Fig. 7.2).

Jesse James Garrett, a renowned information architect, developed a widely used vocabulary for site diagrams, which has become an industry standard and is widely used for showcasing site structure, interactive relationships, and user decision points. The visual vocabulary elements of a mature site diagram, according to Web Style Guide, include:

- Content structure and organization: major site content divisions and subdivisions
- Logical functional grouping or structural relationships
- The 'click depth' of each level of the site: how many clicks are required to reach a given page?
- Page type or template (menu page, internal page, major section entry point, and so on)
- Site directory and file structure
- Dynamic data elements like databases, RSS, or applications
- Major navigation terms and controlled vocabularies
- Link relationships, internal and external to the site
- Levels of user access, log-ins required, or other restricted areas

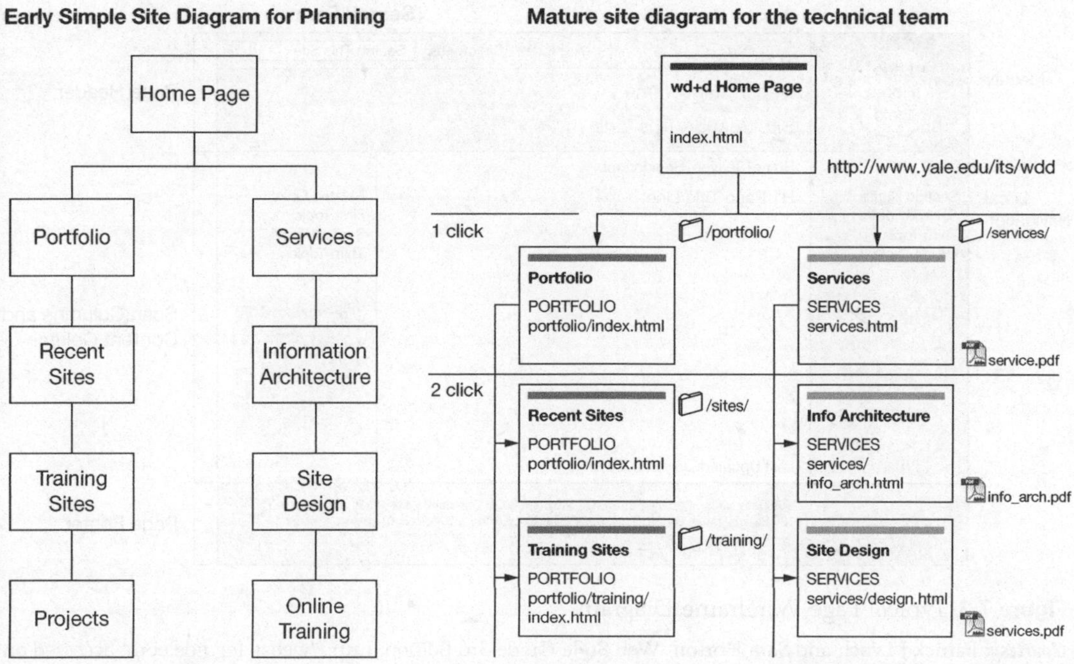

Figure 7.2 Examples of Early and Mature Site Diagrams

Courtesy: Patrick J Lynch and Sara Horton, Web Style Guide 3rd Edition, http://webstyleguide.com, accessed on 27 February 2017 at 8.55 pm.

Wireframe Development

Wireframes typically are visual sketches, an approximate representation of how the areas of a web page would be organized. Site diagrams provide an overview of the developing site while wireframes are more of a rough map which are used by graphic and interface designer teams to develop page designs for the site. Example of a typical page wireframe is depicted in Fig. 7.3.

Wireframes at the beginning could even be just hand-drawn rough diagrams but they get refined. Experts can change and improve lots of elements depending on prior experience and research on the way visitors browse content sections visually, including eye-tracking studies, which give in-depth inputs on web page components and where users are likely to search for them.

Website Content Development and Management

Along with the creation of site diagrams and wireframe development, firms have to manage collation and development of relevant content to populate various site pages. The content for any website will largely be driven by the objectives of the site and interests of the audience who would be visiting the pages. Once the content is in place, it will go hand-in-hand in selecting the sections where specific content would be placed, depending upon its impact and relevance.

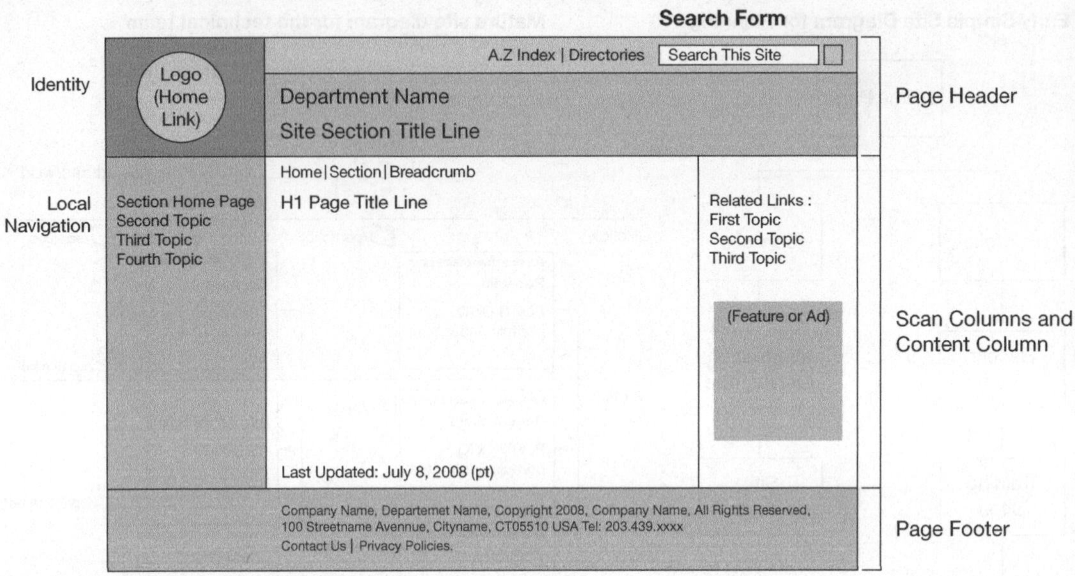

Figure 7.3 Typical Page Wireframe Diagram

Courtesy: Patrick J Lynch and Sara Horton, Web Style Guide 3rd Edition, http://webstyleguide.com, accessed on 27 February 2017, at 8.55 pm.

The key steps for defining and managing website content include:

(a) **Understanding content expectations**: The first step for developing web content includes understanding user goals and expectations from the site. Firms should pre-research the type of information which would get users most engaged and make them stay for the longest time on the site.

(b) **Defining key content areas**: As the next step, firms need to define and prioritize on key content areas to be given prime coverage and importance on the site.

(c) **Analyzing content sources:** Firms then need to dig into their archives and content across prior brochures, sales collaterals, etc., to see the content they already have and to then decide whether they need to develop their own content internally or have the website vendor develop content with inputs shared by the firm.

(d) **Revising outdated content:** An important part of content development is to identify and revise redundant content on the site and to update it with the latest product/service information.

(e) **Developing content themes**: involves bucketing different types of content across themes to be covered across the site. These themes or arrangement of similar topics, will help in site definition and navigation elements so that users see a natural flow in the website as they progress across the web pages.

(f) **Mapping content themes to sitemap**: involves developing content categories and placing content for different themes across site pages. A site page is a hierarchical diagram which shows multiple parent pages (top pages of the website) and child pages under each of them.

(g) **Outlining navigation:** The next stage, after mapping content to sitemap, involves placing each of the parent pages across their natural progression in the form of a navigation structure for users to follow.

(h) **Labeling content**: It involves providing accurate and meaningful labels to content areas. The labels should be easy to understand with simple words to avoid any confusion.

(i) **Placing content on pages**: This last stage involves placing requisite content pieces on specific web pages based on the wireframes developed earlier.

Web Content Management

To manage the wide variety of content to be shared on a website, firms typically need a web content management system. A content management system (commonly referred to as CMS) is an application or a product which supports content acquisition, creation, collaboration, editing, and publishing to multiple platforms. Systems which help develop and manage such workflows for website content are known as Web Content Management Systems (WCMS).

Historically, WCMS were developed to help non-technical teams create content for specific pages on their own with the help of an intuitive, easy-to-manage system. Earlier, technical resources used to fill-in web pages which were neither effective nor compelling as they did not have the requisite skills. The development of WCMS also provided a structure to the documents being created, thus, supporting a way in which content creators and editors can simply populate content on to a specified template and be worried only about updating content rather than its structure or code.

The key goal of a WCMS is to provide an easy-to-use platform to develop and update content at specific page levels for the website. Typical advantages of a WCMS include:

- Supports real-time creation and publishing of new content reliably and consistently
- Provides robust workflows with in-built rules and permissions for each stakeholder
- Contains standard templates which help render any new content to target site pages
- Supports re-use of content across web pages for multiple platforms and devices
- Provides customization and cost-efficiencies if open-source platforms are used
- Helps integrate and edit content collaboratively across multiple global locations

The most popular content management systems include Wordpress, Magnolia, Alfresco, Joomla, Drupal, Liferay, etc. The following considerations should be kept in mind while choosing a WCMS for a firm's specific objective and budget:

- Reputation in terms of robustness, feature updates, ease-of-use, and platform support
- Mapping of business objectives to specific features of product being compared
- Usage pattern and daily requirements of administrators, content developers, and users
- Long-term RoI across investment and ease of implementation

Typically, firms have to assess the WCMS options available, depending on the size of their site, its features, interactivity needs, presence of microsites, and support needed for complex enterprise features like multiple revenue streams, e-commerce features, multichannel publishing, global service portal, etc. In the next section, we will see how companies are managing user experience and service elements for the websites they develop.

USER EXPERIENCE, USABILITY, AND SERVICE QUALITY ELEMENTS

In the earlier two parts of this chapter, we covered the basics of lead management, from lead generation to conversion marketing, and the basics of web development and content management. In this part, we will look at user experience and related service elements, which make it worthwhile for web visitors to arrive at the firm's site again and again.

Understanding Elements of User Experience

With the growth of 'user experience' as an emerging concept in web design and development, we first need to understand how its application differentiates from and is superior to the general concepts of functionality and design itself. In his prominent book *The Elements of User Experience*, Jesse James Garrett, has shared that the fundamental difference which 'user experience' provides is the application of context of a particular design element (in relation to the other elements of the product), driven by an understanding of the psychology and behavior of users themselves rather than a stand-alone focus on design or form.

In the book, there is an interesting example about the user experience of a coffee-maker button. According to Jesse, aesthetic design is what ensures that the button on the coffee-maker has an appealing shape and texture while the functional design makes certain that it triggers the appropriate action. User experience, on the other hand, relates to how the aesthetic and functional aspects of the button work in context with other parts of the product, if the button is placed correctly, and is of the requisite size in relation to the rest of the machine, etc.

User experience thus takes into account the knowledge and understanding of visitors to the site, their motivations and attitudes, and the quality of engagement which the marketer would want the user to experience and remember once he has been on the site.

Difference between User Experience and Usability

Typically, user experience is confused with usability while both of them are different. Let us look at some key differences below.

(a) Usability is about task-based interactions. It is the ability to easily execute process and transitions on the web with certain ease, while user experience is related to the experiential elements felt by a user when they interact with the website.

(b) Usability makes a task easy and intuitive, while user experience makes it meaningful and valuable.
(c) Usability involves reducing steps and roadblocks, while user experience aims at creating an emotional connection. At the most basic level, thus, usability relates to what users do and how they accomplish it, while user experience deals with what users feel about their involvement.

Elements of User Experience

To help develop a clear understanding of the elements of user experience which influence a visitor's interaction with a website, Jesse James Garrett has shared Fig. 7.4 showing five planes as the key elements viewed in an integrated fashion. Let us study each of them below.

To provide a context to Fig. 7.4, Jesse begins with a basic duality that the web began as a place where information could be created and shared, but as technologies advanced, the web started taking on new functional capabilities. So, the whole exercise of web development can be

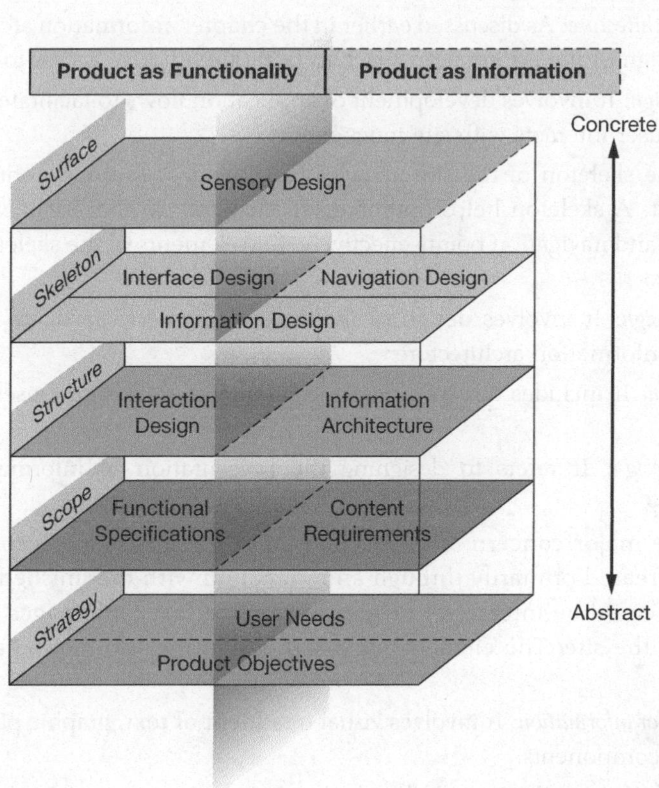

Figure 7.4 Elements of User Experience

split across five key planes (strategy, scope, structure, skeleton, and surface) to help both designers and developers identify the unique tasks they need to execute at each layer and make the web development exercise is successful.

To understand each of the five planes better, let us study them briefly. We would begin with the strategy plane and move upwards to the surface plane for sequential explanation.

- **Strategy**: It involves understanding user needs and externally derived goals for the site. These needs are typically identified through user research, ethno/techno/psychographics, etc. For this plane, the site objective should be to come up with business, creative, or other internally derived goals for the site.
- **Scope**: It involves defining the content requirement at the information side and functional specifications on the functionality side. This plane helps develop detailed descriptions of functionality and type of content that the site must include in order to meet user needs. It is not necessary that the identified functionalities or content pieces which have been opted out are finally included as there are multiple other considerations in play.
- **Structure**: Once the scope has been developed, developers need to provide a structure to the development process which is termed as 'Information Architecture' on the information side and 'Interaction Design' on the functionality side.

  Information architecture: As discussed earlier in the chapter, information architecture involves structural design of the information space to facilitate intuitive access to content.

  Interaction design: It involves development of application flows to facilitate user tasks, defining how the user interacts with site functionality.
- **Skeleton**: The skeleton of the site involves placement of buttons, controls, photos, and blocks of text. A skeleton helps optimize site elements so that users can remember the site structure and navigation points effectively. Key elements of the skeleton plane on both sides includes:

  Navigation design: It involves design of interface elements to facilitate user's movement through the information architecture.

  Interface design: It includes design of interface elements to facilitate user interaction with functionality.

  Information design: It refers to designing the presentation of information to facilitate understanding.
- **Surface**: The major concern of a web developer for this plane is to provide sensory experience created primarily through an interaction with the finished product, which, in this case, could be interactive or non-interactive text and images on multiple web pages across the site. The elements of visual design for information and functionality include:

  Visual design for information: It involves visual treatment of text, graphic page elements, and navigational components.

  Visual design for functionality: It includes graphical treatment of interface elements (also 'look and feel')

With an understanding of all the five planes, we can see how user experience can be designed in a structured manner for both information and functional elements which should ideally go hand-in-hand to provide the best visual and interactive experience to a web visitor.

Implementation of Interaction Design

With an understanding of the basics of user experience in the last section, we move ahead to study how application of interaction design concepts can help companies develop superior user experience. Interaction design as a field forms a part of the growing prominence of Human-Computer Interaction (HCI), but covers only a part of HCI.

Interaction design, according to Dan Saffer, in his widely acknowledged book Designing for Interaction involves designing for all types of possible interactions between people, machines, and systems through a prior understanding of interaction behavior. The key approaches of interaction design (as shared in the book) include:

(a) **Focusing on users**: The key premise for interaction design is that users care most about doing their tasks and achieving their goals. Designers need to be the advocates for users.

(b) **Finding alternatives**: It involves designers planning to create an improvized 'third option' rather than choosing between undesirable ones. The plan is to think out-of-the-box to create completely new ideas which have never been seen or developed before.

(c) **Using ideation and prototyping**: Brainstorming and developing multiple design prototypes rather than just a single prototype, since multiple prototypes can point to multiple solutions to create a single product.

(d) **Collaborating and addressing constraints**: This approach discusses how designers typically work together to address business goals and meet deadlines.

(e) **Creating appropriate solutions**: Designers should typically build solutions which can be used across multiple projects and replicated elsewhere (that is not just for a single context).

(f) **Drawing on a wide range of influences**: Designers should bring together influences from multiple fields like psychology, ergonomics, engineering, architecture, art, etc.

(g) **Incorporating emotion**: Emotions need to be included thoughtfully into design decisions, since without it a product would not connect with people.

Saffer shared four main approaches to interaction design:

(a) **User-centered design**: It involves designers collaborating with users through every stage of the design process to incorporate their needs, preferences, and goals while building content and awareness.

(b) **Activity centered design**: The design is focused on pre-decided tasks and actions.

(c) **System design**: It focuses on the system's inputs, outputs, processes, feedback loops, goals, etc., for developing the design.

(d) **Genius design**: It emphasizes on the skills and knowledge of subject matter experts to develop instructional content.

With multiple techniques involved in managing and developing interaction design across the overall design process, we would study three most widely used techniques here.

(a) **Use case development**: A use case is a written description of how users perform tasks on a website. The primary objective of a use case, as shared in *Writing Effective Use Cases* (one of the most popular books in this area by Alistair Cockburn), is to capture the behavior between key stakeholders.

The primary actor initiates an interaction with the system to accomplish some goal. Different sequences of behavior or scenarios unfold, depending upon the particular requests made. Use cases are typically developed in text form, although they can be written using flow charts, sequence charts, petri nets, or programming languages.

(b) **Card sorting**: It is a user-design technique which helps designers discover the best way of organizing concepts logically into categories by sharing index cards. Chosen user groups have to sort a series of cards into groups or clusters based on a logical flow of content or functionality. According to Information Architecture for the World Wide Web, card sorting "can provide insight into users' mental models, illuminating the way that they often tacitly group, sort, and label tasks and content within their own heads."

There are two primary methods for performing card sorts. In *open card sorting*, the audience is given cards to organize content across a website where there are no pre-defined categories. This type of sorting is useful in situations where new content has to be developed. The other type is the closed card sorting where audience is given cards with the initial categories already defined and they need to place cards into these pre-defined groups. This technique is useful when firms are adding new content to an already existing structure of a website.

(c) **Prototyping**: Prototyping as a concept is used across multiple industries and involves building a model (draft version) before designing the final system to test the concept or the process, understand shortcomings, and improvize to build a better final product. It is a big part of the lean development methodology, which helps entrepreneurs test and showcase ideas at a much cheaper cost to save time and investment.

The two prominent types of prototyping deployed these days are: 'Low–Fidelity Prototypes,' which are paper-based and are typically hand-drawn mock-ups to printouts which are quicker to create and change but do not allow user interactions. The second one is 'High-Fidelity Prototypes,' which are computer based and closest to the final outcome. They are typically much more effective as they can let firms gauge interaction time and realistic responses, but at the same time, can be a bit more expensive.

Understanding Web Usability and Evaluation

Apart from user design, the other aspect which is key to any web-development effort is its usability. As discussed earlier, usability is about executing web transactions effectively and making sure that users are satisfied with their interactions and find the web experience, easy, intuitive, and relevant. Usability evaluation is typically performed as an extension to the testing phase of an application software life-cycle with the aim of verifying the web application against specific usability requirements.

The definition of usability as a part of ISO 9241-11 standards is "The extent to which a product can be used by specific users to achieve specified goals with effectiveness, efficiency, and satisfaction in a specified context of use." In his book *Usability Engineering,* Jacob Nielsen suggests five qualities of a usable product.

(a) **Learnability**: It is the ease of learning functionality and behavior of the system.
(b) **Efficiency**: It refers to the level of attainable productivity once the user has learned the system.
(c) **Memorability**: It denotes the ease of remembering the system functionality on the next return.
(d) **Few errors**: It is the capability of a system to feature a low-error rate.
(e) **User's satisfaction**: It refers to the measure in which the user finds the system pleasant to use.

Apart from these, Whitney Quesenbery has shared a set of 5Es to usability as follows:

(a) **Effective**: It denotes the completeness and accuracy with which users achieve their goals.
(b) **Efficient**: It is the speed with which users complete their tasks.
(c) **Engaging**: It includes how pleasant, satisfying, or interesting an interface is to use.
(d) **Error tolerant**: It involves how well the product prevents and recovers users from errors.
(e) **Easy to learn**: It supports initial orientation and continued learning of the product.

It has to be noted here that although all five Es are important for usability, not all of them might be equally important in a particular scenario or for a specific project. The balance among the 5Es, thus, would depend on the prominence of feature and the type of stakeholder which is using that product. For example, for an e-commerce site selling products, efficiency and effectiveness could be most important, while for a site which is high on interactive educational learning, engaging and easy-to-learn attributes might be more important.

Thus, usability has to be analyzed and developed with a strong understanding of the specific situation and type of users at hand. Once firms have developed the requisite usability elements and incorporated them into the website, it is important that designers evaluate whether their final web product meets the required level of usability. We would need to develop an understanding of the concepts of usability evaluation to test if the application actually meets stated user requirements.

Usability Evaluation

It involves techniques to assess application functionality, verify the impact of the interface on users, and identify intermittent problems which might emerge. Evaluation can be performed either as formative evaluation (which takes place during design) or summative evaluation (which takes place after the product has been developed). There are typically two broad categories of evaluation methods that can be used at different stages of product development—user testing and usability inspection methods. It is to be noted that all evaluations should be conducted with the final user of the application and not with other stakeholders like developers or website owners. Let us study the two evaluation techniques—

(a) **User testing:** It involves observing and analyzing user performance of a certain set of tasks, collecting empirical data, and thereafter, improving the application. Typical areas measured are user task time, number of errors, user opinions, user satisfaction, etc.

Steps for a robust usability testing include:

- **Defining testing goals**: The objectives of testing should be clearly defined if they pertain to a larger functionality testing or just checking the landing page content.
- **Choosing sample for testing:** The sample chosen should exhaustively cover different population types in terms of user experience, age, frequency of use, etc.
- **Selecting tasks and scenarios:** The tasks for testing should be representative of the actual tasks performed on the application.
- **Defining measurement parameters:** Measures deployed should be a mix of subjective (effectiveness, user satisfaction) and objective ones (task time, errors).
- **Preparing experimental environment**: The environment should include equipment like computer/video, test audience, supporting material, etc.

(b) **Inspection methods:** It involves predicting usability problems which can typically crop up during user testing at a later stage. Key methods involve:

- **Heuristic evaluation**: It involves having a set of experts analyze the application against a list of recognized usability principles. Each evaluator goes to the interface at least twice, first to get a feel of the interaction and then to focus on specific objectives and functionality to evaluate a list of heuristics.
- **Cognitive walkthrough**: The users' problem-solving process, that is what the users will do in specific situations and why they would do so, is simulated.
- **Web usage analysis**: It refers to analyzing user-browsing patterns through data collected from user's access on application pages and collected in the web server log.

Apart from the methods shared above, designers also deploy automatic tools to support their evaluation on important areas like accessibility analysis, usability analysis, web usage analysis, etc., which help deal with the most repetitive evaluation tasks effectively, without requiring much time and investment as in user training and inspection methods.

Measuring Service Quality Elements

With an understanding of the concepts of web usability and evaluation, in this last section, we would look at key service quality elements which firms should take into consideration while developing their service quality.

With the rise of e-services, concepts like e-tailing, customer support, service delivery models, etc., have become important for firms to understand how their customers perceive their services and evaluate service quality at their end. This is where E-service Quality (e-SQ) becomes important. The first formal definition of website service quality, or e-SQ, was provided by Zeithaml, Parasuraman, and Malhotra (2000). In their terms, e-SQ can be defined as the extent to which a website facilitates efficient and effective shopping, purchasing, and delivery of products and services. According to them, there are typically four types of potential disconnects between the

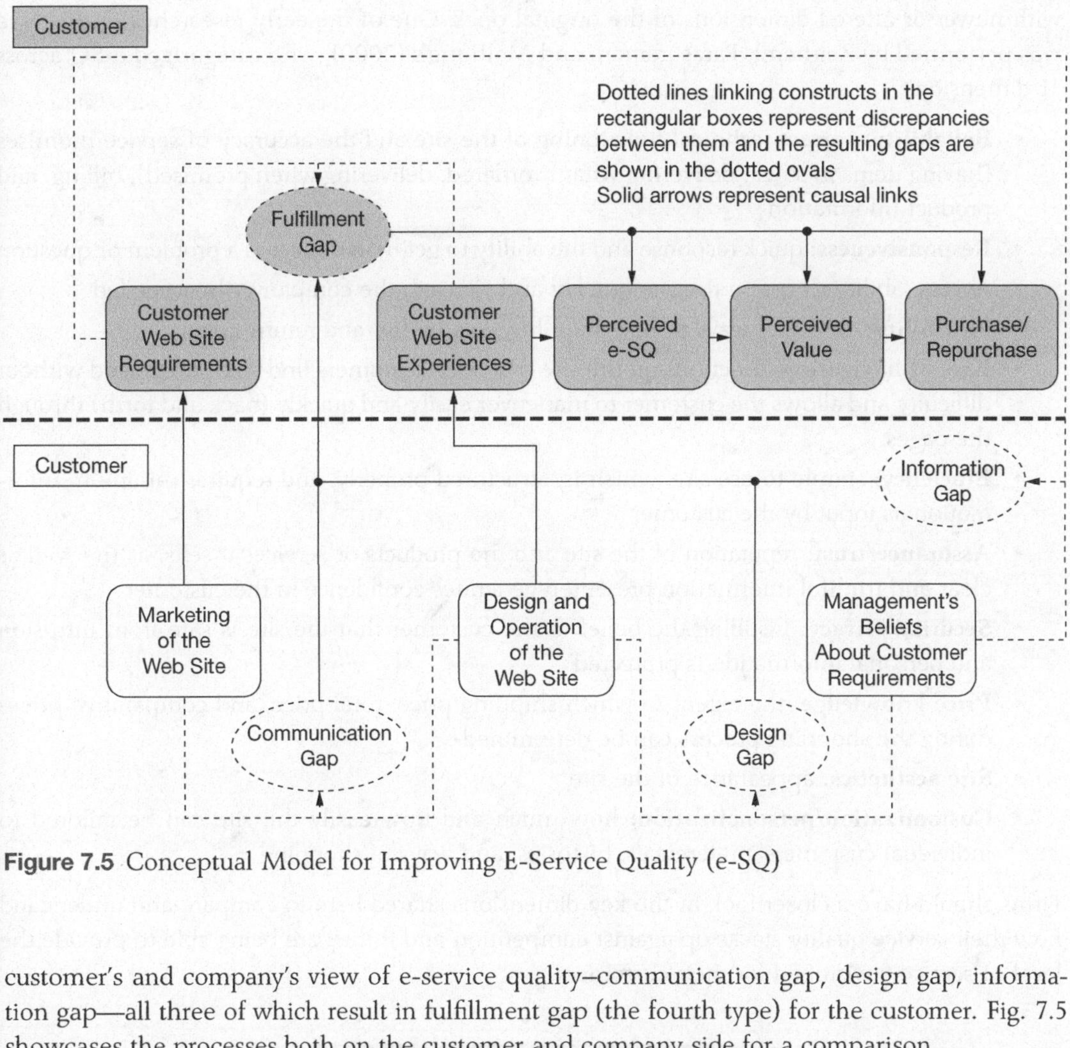

Figure 7.5 Conceptual Model for Improving E-Service Quality (e-SQ)

customer's and company's view of e-service quality–communication gap, design gap, information gap—all three of which result in fulfillment gap (the fourth type) for the customer. Fig. 7.5 showcases the processes both on the customer and company side for a comparison.

Since e-service quality measurement through websites is still a growing research concept, several businesses have developed their own methodologies to measure service quality provided by online retailers. Some examples of such methodologies are the ones provided by BizRate.com and Gomez.com. BizRate scale has 10 dimensions: ease of ordering, product selection, product information, price, website performance, on-time delivery, product representation, customer support, privacy policies, and shipping and handling. Gomez.com provides an alternative evaluation system that uses researchers rather than consumers to evaluate sites. Measurement involves direct examination of the website, performance monitoring of various pages on the site, pricing transactions, mock transactions (account opening), interaction with customer service representatives, and a questionnaire filled out by each company.

In contrast to these self-developed methodologies by firms, academic research has also laid out multiple approaches to categorizing e-SQ dimensions which, over time, have been revised with newer or altered dimensions of the original ones. One of the early researches in this area was performed by Zeithaml, Parasuraman, and Malhotra's (2000), who categorized e-SQ across 11 dimensions:

- **Reliability**: correct technical functioning of the site and the accuracy of service promises (having items in stock, delivering what is ordered, delivering when promised), billing, and product information
- **Responsiveness**: quick response and the ability to get help if there is a problem or question
- **Access**: ability to get on the site quickly and to reach the company when needed
- **Flexibility**: choice of ways to pay, ship, buy, search for, and return items
- **Ease of navigation**: functions on the site that help customers find what they need without difficulty and allows the customer to maneuver easily and quickly (back and forth) through the pages
- **Efficiency**: simple to use site, which is, structured properly, and requires minimum information as input by the customer
- **Assurance/trust**: reputation of the site and the products or services it sells, as the well as clear and truthful information presented generates confidence in the customer
- **Security/privacy**: instilling the belief in the customer that the site is safe from intrusion and personal information is protected
- **Price knowledge**: the extent to which shipping price, total price, and comparative prices during the shopping process can be determined
- **Site aesthetics:** appearance of the site
- **Customization/personalization:** how much and how easily the site can be tailored to individual customers' preferences, histories, and ways of shopping

Firms should have a closer look at the key dimensions shared here to compare and understand how their service quality stacks up against competition and if they are being able to provide the level of service envisioned for their customers.

PRACTICAL EXERCISES

Developing Owned Media Presence

Key Objective To learn the practical aspects of developing an owned media presence in the form of a website or a blog on WordPress.

Project Brief Imagine that you are volunteering at a local non-for-profit organization (of your choice) as a webmaster. Develop an owned media presence for them. You can choose one of the following ways to develop an owned media presence:

(a) Develop a WordPress Site
(b) Create a WordPress Blog

Key steps to develop a WordPress site or blog page:

(a) **Install WordPress:** Land on WordPress.Org website and install WordPress from the account dashboard. You can either buy personal hosting space or utilize pre-bought shared hosting by your organization to host your webpage or blog.

(b) **Choose a Theme (or Template) for your Website or Blog Page:** The next step involves choosing a free WordPress Theme or Template from those available. WordPress themes should be chosen based on the nature of business, product, or service for which you would develop the blog. In this case, you would choose a theme that aligns with the objective of the fictional non-for-profit organization you are developing the site for.

(c) **Add Content and Create New Pages:** Now, develop new chronological posts and add pages across categories like about page, contact page, privacy policy, etc. Posts form the core of any blog and would constitute a separate page within a website. Please create at least three posts that form the part of the blog or the webpage with the help of the page editor screen.

(d) **Add and Edit Posts:** Provide a title for each page and add different type of content through the text editor including text, links, images, videos, and audio.

(e) **Customize Titles and Taglines:** Once the content for three blogs and couple of pages have been created, you can customize the site by setting up a static front page. WordPress uses the page titled 'Home' as the site's front page and 'Blog' page to display blog posts.

(f) **Install Plugins:** Once the website or blog has been fully created, an extra exercise could be the addition of WordPress Plugins that includes addition of multiple features to the website like contact form, e-commerce features, photo galleries, etc. Plugins can also help understand areas like website optimization, improving security, adding analytics (especially Google Analytics), etc.

Once the website or blog is created, it should act as the base for other practical exercises in the upcoming chapters. This website or blog will form the basis of all digital marketing activities for your non-profit organization. Digital campaigns across channels would be directed to this home page and landing pages for specific objectives would be developed in similar templates as the host site or blog. Once developed, please have the website or blog reviewed with your faculty or instructor for any comments and feedback.

CHAPTER SUMMARY

- **Part 1:** The first section started with developing a basic understanding of lead generation and conversion marketing, which forms the core of lead management for any digital marketing firm. We studied the activities performed across each of the consumer funnel stages for conversion marketing. In the next section, we understood the concepts of lead nurturing and lead scoring. We went through the types of lead nurturing campaigns and aspects of lead scoring execution. The third section discussed the basics of landing page optimization and how various targeting techniques can help achieve desired marketing objectives. Here we also learned briefly about marketing apps. The first part ended with a look at the various ways in which leads can be generated and converted across owned, earned, and paid channels.

- **Part 2:** This part started on the basics of web development and management to help understand the pre-planning activities for web development. We then moved on to cover activities ranging from obtaining a domain name to managing site hosting, including multiple types of hosting services which firms can utilize. This was followed by getting into a detailed understanding of web development cycle (analysis, requirements specification, design and development, testing, deployment and maintenance). Next, we looked at examples of site diagram and wireframe development to build a robust information architecture. In the last section, we looked at key steps for defining and managing website content and the basics of a web content management system which supports overall content workflow.
- **Part 3**: The last part of the chapter covered other key elements (allied to web development) which include user experience, usability, and service quality, which are developing as prominent areas for customer engagement. We developed an understanding of the elements of user experience which involves integrating both information and functionality aspects. Next, we covered the techniques for managing and developing interaction design. This was followed by an understanding of the 5Es of usability along with usability evaluation types. Finally, we also became familiar with the concepts of e-service quality (e-SQ) and the 11 dimensions of e-SQ which companies can master to provide superior service quality to their website visitors.

REVIEW QUESTIONS

1. What is the definition of lead generation? Explain the steps involved in lead generation process.
2. What is conversion marketing? Take up any of the consumer funnel stages and share related conversion marketing activities.
3. What is lead nurturing? What are the elements of lead nurturing?
4. Share key types of lead nurturing campaigns and explain three of them in detail.
5. What is lead scoring? Share the typical benefits of a lead scoring exercise.
6. What is a landing page? Why is landing page optimization crucial?
7. Share key landing page optimization (LPO) techniques either on targeting or on experimentation, as explained in the chapter.
8. Explain lead management activities across any of the following: owned; earned; paid channels.

9. What is web development? Explain some of the key pre-planning activities for web development.
10. Explain the activities involved in obtaining a domain name and hosting a website.
11. What is a web development cycle? Explain the stages of a web development cycle in detail.
12. What is a site diagram? According to the *Web Style Guide*, what are the visual vocabulary elements of a mature site diagram?
13. What are the key steps for defining and managing website content?
14. What is a Web Content Management system (WCMS)? State some typical advantages of a WCMS?
15. What do you understand by user experience? Elucidate on the five key elements of user experience.
16. What is the definition of interaction design? Explain the four main approaches to interaction design.
17. Choose any one of the three key techniques involved in managing and developing interaction design and explain it in detail.
18. Explain the definition of usability. Which are the five Es of usability?
19. Describe the two key techniques of usability evaluation.
20. What do you understand by service quality elements? Explain any five of the eleven e-SQ (service quality) dimensions.

DIGITAL APPLICATION EXERCISES

1. Imagine that you are the owner of one of the finest shopping malls in any big city in India with a website by the name TheFinestMall.com. How would you define an online lead for your website? What steps would you follow for this lead definition?
2. Further to Question One (in the Digital Exercise above), choose an imaginary apparel brand on the online store and develop the set of activities that you as a marketer would pursue to lead a visitor across the REAN Consumer Funnel stages, as shared in the chapter.
3. Policybazaar.com is one of the top portals in India for buying insurance policies. Let's say as a marketing manager you have been able to get an interested offline prospect share his e-mail on the portal but he did not buy a policy from the website. What kind of lead-nurturing campaigns (as shared in the chapter) would you develop to convert the online prospect into a customer?
4. Urbanclap.com is emerging as one of the best Home and Local Services providers in India. Can you develop a plan on how such a service provider can generate new leads through owned, earned and paid media channels?
5. Let us say that your local Kirana store plans to open its local website. Develop the set of key pre-planning activities for web development.
6. For the Kirana store example in the last question share the key activities across

the five stages of the web devlopment cycle.

7. Select one of the traditional Indian banks (onlinesbi.com) and compare it with a new bank (bandhanbank.com) by developing their site diagrams with the help of any free online site diagram generator tools.

8. Visit the website g2crowd.com and choose any five top WCMS (Website Content Management Systems) to compare their key features.

9. Select any of the Indian brand websites you have liked the most and describe the elements of user experience and web usability for the website.

CHAPTER 8

UNIT IV DIGITAL MARKETING EXECUTION

Digital Marketing Campaign Management

LEARNING OBJECTIVES

After studying this chapter, you will be able to:

- Understand the seven key stages for setting up a digital marketing campaign—including campaign plan, budget, set-up, launch, monitor, fine-tune, and reconciliation
- Explain the basics of implementing intent-based campaigns, broadly known as search campaigns which include Search Engine Marketing (SEM) and Search Engine Optimization (SEO) concepts
- Describe brand-based campaigns and learn the basics of display campaign management and inventory classification along-with gaining knowledge on emerging data-driven display models (programmatic and RTB)
- Elucidate on campaign execution for emerging channels including social media, partner, communication, and platform-based marketing
- Explain basic concepts of campaign analytics and marketing RoI mapped to the refinement stage of the ASCOR digital marketing framework.

CASE STUDY MakeMyTrip India: *Recovering from the Pandemic*

The ticket booking system in India has come a long way from physical ticket counters to online websites. Launched in 2000, MakeMyTrip (MMT) has now become the most preferred platform for online travel booking. In the last 5 years, MMT has grown across all verticals, especially air ticketing, hotel packages, and bus ticketing. From major acquisitions to an IPO to the COVID-19 pandemic hit, MakeMyTrip has experienced multiple ups and downs over the past few years.

In 2016, MMT acquired Ibibo to increase penetration in the hotel booking segment. However, the acquisition closed only in January 2018 after several delays. With this acquisition, MakeMyTrip increased its dominance in the hotel segment in the Indian market. MMT also acquired RedBus to provide better product offerings, increase customer reach, and cross-sell opportunities. Apart from these two, MMT also made various other partnerships with Amazon Pay, ICICI Bank, etc. which were crucial to its growth. For example, with Amazon Pay, ICICI co-branded credit card customers will earn unlimited cash back rewards on every flight, hotel, or bus booking.

In April 2018, MMT partnered with Flipkart to grow its consumer base and drive more travel bookings through a better consumer experience. This strategic partnership provided MMT visibility to a customer base of more than 100 million users. In June 2018, another partnership with OYO helped them increase hotel bookings through their platform, strengthening the position of their prized hotel segment and benefitting them hugely. As per Statista, MMT earned US$675 million in FY2018, which was their highest ever revenue. MMT also offered a personalised experience for users through their app. Since 2018, however, MMT has experienced lesser revenues till 2022.

During the COVID-19 pandemic, MMT's travel and booking sites were highly affected. In 2020, the first wave of the pandemic hit travel booking companies hard and the situation only worsened with the second wave. Revenues of MMT plummeted by 68 per cent to US$163 million in FY21. However, as per Deep Kalra, CEO of MMT, the company has started to recover in FY'22 primarily due to their homestays offering. MMT increased its throughput by 150 per cent in leisure homestays and by 50 per cent across the entire homestay business. As of 2022, MMT is still recovering from prior losses to gain momentum again.

Table 8.1 Make My Trip Year-on-Year Revenue (FY15–22)

Financial Year	FY15	FY16	FY17	FY18	FY19	FY20	FY21	FY22
Revenue (USD mn)	299.66	336	448	675	486	512	163	303.9

Source: Annual report of MakeMyTrip for the year 2021–22

Recently, India's Tourism Ministry signed an MOU with MakeMyTrip to strengthen the hospitality industry in India. MMT has also stepped into the non-fungible-token (NFT) bandwagon with the launch of digital artwork of popular destinations in India. These NFTs are in line with MMT's overall marketing and communication objective of inspiring every Indian to discover and explore the majestic beauty of India. MMT is also going to increase their focus on premium and ultra-luxury properties, apart from the five-star hotels it already has on its platform. Another feature being worked on is Trip

Assist, a chatbot-like feature to help with various types of travel issues after a customer has made a booking.

Looking at MMT's growth trends, it is expected that this online travel agency (OTA) will surely grow at a higher clip in the upcoming years through its acquisitions, partnerships, and growth strategies.

BASIC ELEMENTS OF DIGITAL CAMPAIGNS

In the last two chapters (6 and 7), we studied the third phase of ASCOR Digital Marketing Framework to understand the concepts of digital media planning and its key stages. We also looked at the steps to develop a marketing communications strategy and a basic introduction to key digital marketing channels.

In this chapter, we will start with a detailed understanding of the key elements of campaign management which forms the base for all types of digital marketing. We will then cover the two most important types of campaign executions—intent-based campaigns (search execution) and brand-based campaigns (display execution). This will be followed by covering basic campaign execution tactics for other emerging platforms, beginning with content marketing, and moving to social media, partner, communication, and platform-based marketing. The final section of this chapter discusses campaign monitoring and refinement areas like web analytics, key performance metrics, and marketing implementation RoI (Return on Investment).

BASIC ELEMENTS OF DIGITAL CAMPAIGN MANAGEMENT

Campaign management at its most basic level involves a set of planned activities towards achieving desired marketing objectives. As discussed in Chapter 6, in the section titled, 'Digital Media Planning Stages,' for executing any digital marketing campaign a firm needs to assess its 6S digital implementation state, specific business objectives, offerings mix, and present lifestyle stage along with an understanding of the kind of channels, target audience, and communication it wants to share.

Campaign management activities follow these first three stages of assessment, strategy, communication, and channel phase mix, to get into an execution mode and decide how marketing would be run across each of the chosen channels with a specific end-purpose. The ASCOR digital marketing framework supports creation of a high-level strategy for digital marketing execution but it is the channel-wise campaigns which are actually responsible for its tactical execution. In that regard, each campaign has to be thought through and developed in detail right from developing its objectives to running, monitoring, and revising it, based on regular campaign performance inputs and the specificities of that channel.

Sharing below are the seven stages for setting up a marketing campaign for any mix of channels:

(a) **Campaign plan**: The first stage of campaign development involves planning separately for each chosen digital marketing channel. It starts with developing campaign objectives which include a high-level brief of the product, target segment types, campaign message, overall flight dates (run-time), and the desired tangible output in terms of response rates, website visits/leads, or conversions.

(b) **Campaign budget**: The second stage includes all activities leading to development of the budget for each kind of campaign and channel, based upon specific product needs and overall digital marketing budget. Discussions should also happen well in advance on the bid/quote strategy which firms would want to adopt to make sure they win against competitors and to place their ads on top inventory at prime locations where chances of viewership and conversions are the highest.

(c) **Campaign set-up**: This is the stage where actual operations work begins, first developing a campaign calendar and getting it approved internally before sharing it with the execution teams for implementation. The next step involves building and integrating target lists which are a combination of present leads, existing customers, and third-party lists. Marketers then need to plan and strategize the type of communication and messaging/creative tactics they would deploy for each specific channel campaign.

Before campaign launch, marketers also need to make sure that all business rules for campaign placements have been put in place and communicated to the publisher, and inventory has been booked and confirmed. Finally, marketers need to make sure that all conversion elements like landing pages and templates have been created and tested, and necessary authorizations and approvals from various business teams obtained before the launch.

(d) **Campaign launch**: refers to all activities towards launching the campaign across multiple channels and the campaign go-live parameters that need to be determined like bidding, geography, targeting, networks, devices, languages, ad extensions, advanced settings, etc., for effective campaign results. This stage also includes all manual activities related to campaign management (for example, keyword management and analysis for search marketing; trafficking and QA (Quality Assurance) for display marketing, etc.)

(e) **Campaign monitor**: Even before the campaign has been launched and marketers start receiving daily and weekly data points, extensive metrics need to be developed and put in place so that all captured data can be effectively analyzed and monitored. In-house or external third-party tools can be used to build reports and run dashboards which once populated with campaign data are able to monitor progress and measure RoI at regular intervals (for example, How many leads have been generated? Is it in line with the weekly targets set? How many conversions have happened? Are we lagging behind?) Essentially, this stage answers questions on the 'whats' and the 'wheres' of campaign deviance during campaign run.

(f) **Campaign fine-tune**: Involves investigating the 'whys' and the 'hows' to make each campaign successful. Campaign responses are studied, campaign variances analyzed, and accordingly, campaigns are optimized based on multiple techniques.

(g) **Campaign reconciliation**: Finally, when each campaign is executed, marketers conduct post-campaign activities to measure success and check if various channel managers have been able to deliver impressions, clicks, and leads, as promised and negotiated earlier. For discrepancies (where output does not match intended RoI), make-goods (extending campaign beyond flight-dates or giving free inventory/placements) need to be delivered or discounts need to be given against the final payment amount. All these activities form a part of 'billing and invoicing' for the campaign.

We will cover these seven stages of campaign management in detail in the next three sections of this part of the chapter, but prior to that, let us understand the five key ways in which marketing campaigns can be executed by any firm:

(a) **Agency team**: For large firms like Coke, Procter and Gamble, Samsung, etc., it is not feasible to run global and multi-channel marketing campaigns on their own. Firms have traditionally been dependent on advertising agencies (WPP, Omnicom, Ogilvy, McCaNN, Dentsu to provide a few examples) to help manage campaigns, develop creative ideas, deploy media planning, and ensure RoI, typically for a cut of the total investment spend. With digital platforms now forming an ever-increasing part of the spend, traditional advertising agencies have set up in-house teams (at the client premises, with supervision of the agency) and capabilities to manage digital campaigns in terms of final output and outcome.

(b) **Digital marketing firms**: The next set of firms which support digital marketing campaigns are specialized or niche digital marketing outfits which work specifically on the digital side and are specialists in executing digital campaigns.

(c) **In-house campaign team**: For small and medium-size companies (and those which are in new-age service businesses), it is common these days to have their own in-house design and campaign execution teams. These teams make extensive use of digital marketing products to manage and execute buys at their own level.

(d) **Product support teams**: In a few cases, firms ask product companies to provide a platform and also support campaigns on their platform through product support teams.

(e) **Outsourced teams**: Finally, a large number of firms are taking support from software and IT teams to help them manage campaigns. Key advantage is that unlike support on a single product, vendors can deploy multiple tools to run campaigns.

Campaign Planning and Budgeting

The first two stages of campaign management involve firms developing initial planning and taking decisions on overall and channel-specific budget that they would want to spend on digital campaigns. This is crucial to make sure marketers have strong insights into the kind of campaigns they want to run and the type of RoI they would expect from their spend.

Key activities for campaign planning include:

(a) **Campaign objectives**: As we saw earlier in Chapter 7 section titled, 'Basics of Lead Generation and Conversion Marketing,' the key campaign objective for any firm is to help generate leads who could then be further converted to customers to execute a sales transaction. The company needs to develop different sets of strategies and objectives for each of its campaigns depending on their specific needs and the type of channels which would best help accomplish those needs. Once the channels are chosen, firms should develop specific goals for each campaign to achieve desired actions and ensure that each channel supports the other across the marketing life cycle.

(b) **Target market**: For running any campaign it is crucial that its 'Target Market' has already been clearly identified and target personas created to help execution teams develop the right kind of message/creative without wasting spend or impressions on non-targeted audience. It is also important that the goals set above are representative of the nature of target market, and, are achievable.

(c) **Determining flight dates**: The third key activity involves deciding on flight dates (campaign run dates) as this would finally determine the impact which needs to be generated through the campaign and targets that need to be achieved at regular intervals to ensure that the campaign is successful.

(d) **Target output**: Equally important is to decide on the kind of output that is expected from the campaign and what needs to be measured to interpret its success. In case of a branding campaign, it might suffice that the population base of a specific segment is reached, while in the case of a conversion-led campaign, final sales figures are crucial. Also, specific set of metrics, data-capturing techniques and dashboards need to be created to analyze conversions and measure RoI.

(e) **Resource identification**: Finally, after all the campaign details have been resolved, firms need to look at how they would want to get campaigns delivered—through an agency, in-house, outsourced, etc—and what kind of resources need to be deployed to ensure that campaigns run smoothly and maintain the expected quality and effectiveness. There also needs to be a process defined and approved for resources and targets set for their regular performance.

Campaign Budget

The next stage *campaign budget* involves taking decisions on the type of budgets which the client would want to spend on each separate channel and also the way they would want to allocate that spend across different buying options. They would also need to do prior research on historical RoI vs spends for campaigns across similar businesses/industries to be certain that they are not over-spending or under-utilizing their budgets.

Key pointers to help decide campaign budgets include:

(a) **Deciding on spend**: Spends on digital campaigns typically vary between 5–15 per cent of the overall marketing budgets for any firm in present times. Firms mostly start with a round figure, for instance, ₹ 10 lakh, as the spend for digital campaigns. It would then be up to the hired agencies or digital marketing firms to break this pie and decide how much they would like to spend on a search-based campaign vis-à-vis a branding display campaign. As an example, for a display campaign, they would also need to decide on the amount appropriate to be spent for creating the initial buzz, amount to be deployed for product launch, and that to be put aside for future campaign sustenance. All these would be the guiding forces towards setting up measurement metrics for overall campaign too.

(b) **Bid/Quote analysis**: Once the overall spend for each channel is decided, firms also need to do research to understand the amounts they should spend on a particular campaign. Most of the search campaigns, for example, run on an auction model, wherein clients have to bid for specific keywords against which they would want to show their campaign. Similarly, for executing display campaigns, firms need to know the price they should be quoting to advertise on different types of rich-media inventories, and which advertising technology tools would help them buy relatively inexpensive inventory with a broad reach.

(c) **Expected reach/leads/conversions**: Once the budget and bid/quote amounts have been *decided, firms also need to develop an idea of the kind of reach and impact they can* expect from running campaigns across different channels. Some of the channels would be helpful in achieving impressions while others might have a cost even to acquire one visitor (specific target), convert it into a lead, and finally, ensure that he/she becomes a customer. Marketers need to determine how much investment they would like to make to convert such specific targets and the type of RoI (in terms of sales vs profitability figures) they expect to obtain.

We will cover the aspects of spend management, bidding/quote analysis and expected reach/CPM (Cost Per Mile) in broader details in the subsequent parts of this chapter where we will understand search and display campaigns in detail. In the following section, let us look at the next two aspects of campaign set-up and launch in more detail.

Campaign Set-up and Launch

Once the channels and type of campaigns have been planned, and budget has been set aside for each of them, activities towards campaign launch need to be set up. Campaign set-up includes all activities beginning with target list creation and development of target parameters thereby ensuring that the inventory has been booked, creative developed and tested, and landing pages created so that the campaign is executed successfully.

Campaign Set-up

Key activities for campaign set-up include:

(a) **Target list creation**: involves all the activities and planning behind identifying, capturing, and qualifying prospects and leads which the firm would want to nurture and develop through multiple campaigns. These include:

- **List of pre-qualified leads** integrated from firm's previous campaigns, offline sales activities, events, forms, purchased contacts, etc.
- **Present customers** if campaigns are also targeted towards them
- **New prospect type** which the firm would like to develop

(b) **Channel specific research**: Firms then need to plan for internal research to identify the best practices for different kinds of campaigns and channels. For example, in case of search marketing, firms need to do extensive research on top keywords for similar domain areas and in the case of display marketing they need to identify and analyze tools which best target and reach out to the specific audience that the firm is planning to target.

(c) **Develop targeting parameters**: Involves setting up the targeting parameters and business rules for the specific channel on which the campaign is being run. For example, typical targeting parameters include bid, budget, geography, networks, devices, languages, ad extensions, scheduling, etc. We would cover these terminologies for different channel types in detail in the following sections.

(d) **Designing communication and landing pages**: Once campaign parameters have been decided, firms need to plan for communication which includes developing the message, suitable creative and related tags for multiple channels, depending upon the type of communication each of them supports. Firms also need to develop specific landing pages, create templates, call-to-actions, etc., to ensure appropriate conversions.

(e) **Request and confirm placements**: Involves putting a request for specific keywords (in case of search marketing) or inventory (in the case of display marketing) and confirming it. It also includes review of pending placements to ensure that firms do not miss out on running campaigns on the most suited keywords/inventory.

(f) **Pre-launch testing**: Once inventory has been confirmed, immediately prior to the campaign launch, firms need to review and test all campaign elements including creative specifications, file sizes, landing pages, etc., as mentioned in the submission guidelines for each specific channel.

(g) **Developing campaign calendar**: With all campaign elements in place and tested, firms should develop a campaign calendar that includes details on campaign start/end, creative deadlines, budgets allocated, number of units/type of keywords bought, deal type (CPM/CPC numbers), intended reach, etc.

(h) **Launch approval**: Before the actual launch of campaign, all necessary approvals are to be obtained and campaigns are authorized to be launched as per decided calendar dates.

Campaign Launch

It includes all activities involved in launching the campaign which is also known as campaign go-live:

(a) **Campaign go-live activities**: Once all the elements of campaign set-up have been put in place and necessary approvals have been obtained, campaigns which have been queued with the vendors (campaign management tools) go live on specified dates and times. The go-live process could vary for each specific campaign and the channel on which it is being run. In cases of smaller campaigns (managed in-house by client), an automatic trigger on a campaign management tool can make the campaign go live across multiple sites and networks, while for larger and more complex campaigns, a series of pre-live activities are run by larger teams across multiple channels to ensure that the campaign is live and running.

Examples indicative of campaigns going live on different channels include:

- **Search campaign go-live**: Upon searching particular keyword terms (in specific geographies and for specific target audience), visitors would start witnessing the brand's search advertisement and message on the top or right side of search results listings.
- **Display campaign go-live**: For negotiated sites, visitors would start seeing display advertisements on specific inventories in which brands have invested.

(b) **Campaign trafficking**: It is a terminology often used to describe the process of going live (more common for display campaigns). It includes all activities which a trafficker (team member who runs the campaign) needs to execute from the time the campaign goes live till the time it is over. Traffickers also need to share overall campaign performance reports with the marketer and manage analytics throughout the whole period of campaign run (which includes monitoring and fine-tuning stages as well).

Campaign Monitoring to Reconciliation

Once the campaign has been initiated in the chosen platform/tool, from the first hour itself (depending upon type and automation), it needs to be continuously monitored to make sure that all the campaign elements are in place and are run to achieve the set objectives in a controlled manner. All the activities towards ensuring this effective and efficient running of the campaign include what we call as the campaign monitoring stage.

In this section, we have divided campaign monitoring into three sub-stages to help segregate and understand the concept better. These include campaign monitor, fine-tune, and reconciliation (which can also be termed as post-campaign activities).

Campaign Monitor

Key activities of campaign monitoring include:

(a) **Campaign tracking**: Once the campaign has begun, the campaign support team needs to start monitoring various elements of the campaign like-

- **Campaign delivery:** Has the campaign started delivering what it was supposed to achieve?

- **Ad unit accuracy**: Are the ad units visible to client and showing the correct message they were intended to?
- **Creative size, format, and functionality:** Is the creative unit showing up with the right size, in the desired format, and with the specific functionality it was designed to deliver?
- **Targeting QA:** Are all targeting parameters like geography, networks, devices, languages, etc., being executed as pre-decided and configured?

(b) **Data monitoring**: involves making sure that necessary tracking data to measure the campaign is being obtained from all third party tools.

(c) **Managing metrics**: Once data has been captured, pre-set metrics can be measured against available numbers to understand if the campaign is measuring up well to the intended output or is lagging behind, and needs to be fine-tuned.

(d) **Building reports/dashboards**: Regular reports and dashboards on campaign tracking activities and reported metrics are provided by campaign teams to help the marketing team assess the health of the campaign at any stage.

(e) **Performance measurement**: Finally, after obtaining all the available data and metrics, the campaign team and client need to decide campaign performance parameters like conversion analysis, channel effectiveness, closed leads, win–loss ratio, etc., to make sure whether they need to keep running the campaign as-is or make specific changes through campaign fine-tune activities, as discussed in the next stage.

Campaign Fine-Tune

It involves taking necessary steps to ensure that there are minimum variances across key campaign metrics. This includes tracking data and optimizing campaigns to put each campaign element on track and achieve desired campaign objectives.

- **Measuring campaign variance**: Campaign variance typically refers to the difference in the impressions, clicks, leads, final conversions, which the client had signed up initially and actual numbers witnessed as the output of the campaign at each stage. This variance is typically measured on a regular basis and if detected, campaigns are optimized by channel teams to bring them on track so that promised campaign output is delivered. There could be various reasons for campaign variance depending on the type of campaign, the nature of market, campaign execution methodology, the nature of targeted audience, the quality of initial planning and set-up, etc.
- **Optimizing campaigns**: Campaigns are optimized to enhance performance and bring them at par with their best possible execution values. Techniques for optimizing campaigns for each channel vary and generally resources specialized in campaign optimization execute these changes. Optimization not only includes changes which impact the outcome (for example, conversions), but also those which impact the RoI in terms of campaign cost (lowering CPC, CPA, etc.). We would discuss specific optimization techniques for the key channels in later sections.

Campaign Reconciliation

The final stage of campaign management involves activities which occur post-campaign implementation and deal mostly reconciling with unmet objectives.

(a) **Post-campaign activities**: involves measuring each aspect of final post-campaign execution to compare and ascertain if all objectives, initially discussed and agreed upon, have been met. Typically, quantitative parameters are compared and final variances are calculated and shared with the client.

(b) **Make-goods management**: If campaign execution team has not been able to meet client's cost and outcome objectives fully, the vendor team has to provide adjustments (referred to as make-goods in the media industry) to make up for the shortfall, either by providing campaign exposure for an extended period on the same channel or a discount (rerun credit) for the next set of campaigns that client would run in their upcoming campaigns with the channel.

(c) **Billing and invoicing**: involves all activities related to sharing and getting the final bills cleared for campaigns executed successfully and also managing invoicing-related activities which are critical to receive payments.

In the following sections, let us look at how campaigns are run across key channels and the specificities involved at each stage of the campaign management cycle.

IMPLEMENTING INTENT-BASED CAMPAIGNS (SEARCH EXECUTION)

In the last section, we covered the basics of campaign management and studied each of the seven stages and their sub-activities in detail. With this base, we would move further to cover the most prominent types of digital marketing campaigns, the first of them being search engine marketing campaigns, to understand how search campaigns are set up and executed.

Search Campaign Planning Basics

Before we start developing an understanding of how search-based campaigns are planned, we need to clearly understand the key difference between search engine marketing (SEM) and its often used counterpart terminology, pay-per-click (PPC) marketing (see Fig. 8.1).

SEM, as discussed earlier in Chapter 6,supports marketing in two different ways:

- Supporting a website to develop content and techniques to match with search queries and emerge at the top of the organic results' listing which is known as *search engine optimization.*
- Providing options to marketers to place their ads against related keywords by paying search engines on the basis of the number of clicks executed on the ads. This type of SEM is known as *paid search marketing.*

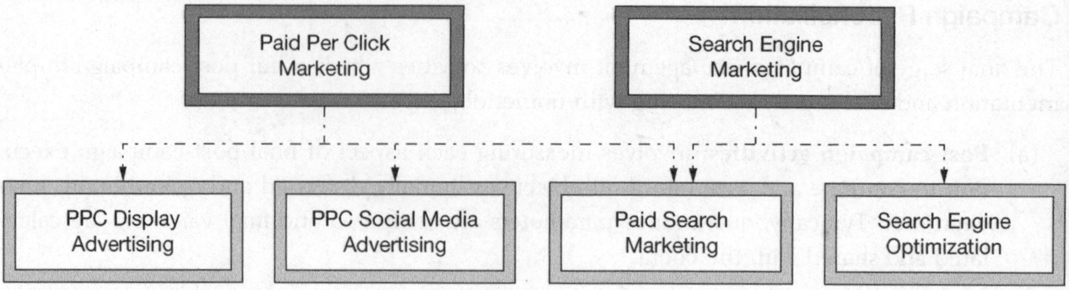

Figure 8.1 Difference between PPC and SEM

Figure 8.1 helps understand the difference between SEM and PPC marketing. Typically, PPC marketing includes all types of marketing where advertisers pay for visitors clicking their ads. SEM, on the other hand, is related to clicks against ads put next to organic search results (in its paid form) and activities to optimize for search engines (in its unpaid form). PPC marketing, thus, includes a broader set of paid marketing from search to display to social PPC, where ads can be put on search engines, advertising networks, and content websites (blogs). As we can witness in Fig. 8.1, paid search marketing (PSM) is one type of PPC marketing while Search Engine Optimization (SEO) as a concept has nothing to do with PPC since there is no bidding for SEO.

When we talk about campaign management, we typically refer to paid search marketing (PSM) and not SEO, as the concepts of campaign management and bidding apply only to PSM. For the same reason, we would first cover the concepts of PSM in this and next two sections and concepts of SEO would be discussed in the last section of this part of the chapter. Although we have clarified the difference between PSM and SEM (with PSM being a subset), we generally refer to PSM as SEM, since that is the most commonly applied terminology used for search PPC campaigns. Thus, SEM and SEO are the two acronyms we would use going forward for paid search and optimization for search.

Planning for Search Marketing Campaigns

Any discussion on SEM has to begin with a reference to the two key search engine programs which are most prominent and popular—Google AdWords and Microsoft AdCenter (representing Bing and Yahoo search engines). With Google being the market leader in SEM programs, a lot of the terminologies and concepts used in SEM industry have been derived or adapted from Google AdWords program. Microsoft's Bing which was lagging behind in SEM earlier has been able to position itself as a stable player in this market and shown good growth in recent years.

Planning for SEM campaign involves the following aspects:

(a) **Establishing the need and objectives for SEM**: Marketers typically choose SEM as one of their first options for digital marketing since SEM is one of the most credible techniques to drive regular targeted traffic to a site; is quick to learn and implement, and can be used to measure the impact cost effectively. However, each business needs to assess its product and key objectives if it plans to invest a substantial amount on this activity. Despite its advantages in some scenarios, it might not be that effective to use SEM every time. For example, if the target market is for a commodity product which people do not search online, or the product itself does not lend to higher online search by users or where the product is being targeted to a niche audience where broad SEM keywords might not be needed, it might not be wise to invest in SEM.

Also, marketers should have a fair idea of their long-term and short-term goals which could vary from brand building to lead generation for an offline product, increasing website visits for an e-commerce website, and getting visitors to convert for a specific campaign. A lot of times, SEM investment is driven as a pre-empt or counter strategy to competition, and a certain budget is allocated to it as a long-term investment.

(b) **Understanding competitor presence**: It is important for the brand to do a thorough research of the kind of competition they have for their product, category, geography, etc., to get a good idea of the investment which would be needed to compete for best placements at effective bid values. Firms can also understand the qualitative aspects of their competitor's ads, including type of language, call-to actions, and nature of landing pages, which they are using to develop differentiating elements.

(c) **Defining target audience and performing keyword research**: The next important part is to decide the type of audience marketers want to target and their typical research patterns. At this stage, brands can perform extensive keyword research using various tools provided by search channels, to know which keywords are keyed in the most by their target visitors to reach to similar products and brands, the kind of click-through rates for ads related to chosen keywords, typical conversion rates, etc. Keyword research tools also provide extensive ideas on the type of keywords matching best with the marketers' requirements and their overall cost effectiveness.

(d) **Deciding on budget and bids**: Marketers also should have developed pre-campaign strategies on the kind of budget that they would like to invest (in terms of a campaign calendar) during the various campaigns that they would execute through SEM. Also, it is advisable for firms to research on typical bids they might have to place for keywords most important to them, the kind of Ad Rank they would aim for, and the ways they would adopt to improve their Quality Score (concepts we would cover in detail in this section). Choosing a budget depends a lot on the overall brand objectives, average traffic estimates, historical CPC numbers, etc. Marketers should try to model most of this data for an effective outcome.

(e) **Defining campaign goals**: Finally, after all the research has been performed, marketers should define clear campaign execution goals like click-through rate, web traffic, conversion targets, etc., so that whichever team executes the campaign (internal or external) has clear knowhow and target on what they need to achieve for the campaign to be termed successful.

Also, if the campaigns are being run by external teams, it is crucial that qualitative insights on target audience, ad group creation, ad content development, landing page design, keyword optimization rules are shared (with as much detail as possible) for campaign teams to understand the exact nature of the campaign so that they are able to meet not only quantitative goals but also intangible objectives like brand awareness, increased product image, improved website interaction, etc.

Apart from the planning stages, it is important that marketers develop a clear governance model so that hand-offs of activities and feedback happens at regular intervals and campaigns can be best optimized for performance and investment. In the next section, we would understand key concepts of an SEM campaign set-up and execution in detail and aspects which impact its successful implementation.

SEM Campaign Set-up and Execution

With an understanding of how search campaigns are planned, we would cover the basics of setting up and executing a search campaign and also the key terminologies and concepts involved. As shared earlier, the top two search marketing programs in the world are run by Google and Microsoft, but since Google laid the foundation of a first-of-its-kind search auction model and still garners the largest share of any digital marketing channel by far, we would base our learning on the terminologies and models specific to Google AdWords program (as that would be most representative of how this particular channel works).

Basics of Search Campaign Set-Up

To understand the building blocks of a search campaign, let us take a fictitious example of a watch reseller company XYZ which wants to launch an online watch portal by the name 'Xquisite' to sell global watch brands to buyers across Indian metros. We will build the case by looking at the key aspects and decisions which the newly hired marketing manager of XYZ Digital will have to take to set up a search campaign and the parameters which need to be defined to make the launch successful.

Let us assume the marketing manager has already done all the research with regards to pre-panning of campaign launch, as mentioned in the last section, We will explain below in a sequential manner, the key concepts which he needs to know to successfully set up the campaign:

(a) **Understanding keywords**: The most basic concept we need to start with is that of 'keywords' which are core to any search marketing campaign. A keyword is typically confused and considered to be the same as a search query.

A keyword is an abstraction of multiple search queries which has been developed to support SEM bidding, while a search query is the actual set of words and phrases which any user types into the search box. During SEM what the XYZ marketer would typically bid on would be a keyword and not the actual search query. For example, if the marketing manager bids on a broad keyword like 'Watches', his ad would be served on multiple combinations of search queries related to that keyword including 'Premium watches,''Watches for gifting,' 'Watch buying websites,' etc.

(b) **Campaign and ad groups**: The next important concept which the marketing manager needs to know is how the target keywords are grouped under 'campaigns and ad groups.' The word 'campaign' has a specific meaning when we refer to AdWords search marketing. To understand what campaigns and ad groups mean, we would go back to the example of Xquisite watch portal launch. During the set-up stage, the manager will first create an account in Google AdWords search marketing tool and divide his marketing activities by grouping target keywords into logical Ad Groups, which in turn form a part of multiple types of campaigns which XYZ would want to run. So the basic set-up of an AdWords campaign involves deciding the overall marketing objectives, converting them into logical campaigns (based on service lines or products or themes, etc.), and creating multiple ad groups within each of them (which contain identified keywords).

Figure 8.2 demonstrates the relationship between campaigns, ad groups, and keywords. As represented in Fig. 8.2, a particular campaign contains ad groups and for each specific ad group, target keywords are chosen to execute search marketing campaigns. Let us first look at the definition of campaign and ad groups.

The definition of a campaign while setting up an AdWords account involves dividing the online marketing effort based on key business groups, service lines, or products, depending upon how best a company wants to focus and measure their campaigns. In case of XYZ firm, launching Xquisite online watch portal, the different ways in which XYZ can develop its campaigns could be based on:

- **Watch pricing**: premium watches, standard watches, budget watches
- **Make types**: gold watches, titanium watches, steel watches, etc.
- **Target markets**: men's watches, ladies' watches, teens' watches
- **Geography**: US watches, Europe watches, Swiss watches, Indian watches

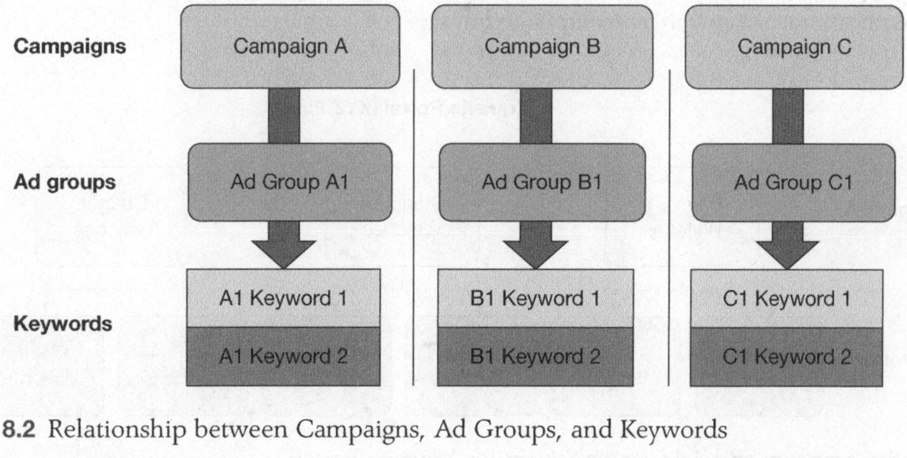

Figure 8.2 Relationship between Campaigns, Ad Groups, and Keywords

There could be many other different ways in which the firm XYZ can develop their high-level campaigns. Their selection of campaign should be based on the type which best represents how campaign investment and performance impact can be measured.

Next, we look at the *definition of ad groups*. Ad groups represent sub-groupings of ads which are run for each chosen campaign with each group containing a set of keywords chosen to execute the campaign. Well-structured campaigns typically contain two–three ad groups which basically are variations of the core campaign. To understand better how campaigns, ad groups, and keywords relate to each other, let us apply these concepts to the example of Xquisite portal launch.

Figure 8.3 is an example showing campaigns and related ad groups for Xquisite portal launch, based on pricing classification types—premium, standard, and budget. For each of these three campaign types, related ad groups have been shown including make types like gold, steel, and plastic. Campaigns are typically structured in such a way that their associated ad groups and related keywords have a consistent theme and support each other towards meeting the overall campaign objectives of the brand.

In this particular case, the Xquisite portal, typically, will have all three kinds of watches (based on pricing): premium, standard, and budget, which they would want to market using a separate set of keywords, text ads, and landing pages. Further, premium watches campaign can include ad groups with a mix of price type (premium watches) and the type of make (gold watches), so that it targets queries not only corresponding to buyers looking for premium watches but also those which are looking for other keywords like gold, platinum, palladium, etc., which also indicate an intent to buy brands which are of a premium make. Similar examples have also been showcased for other two campaign types—standard watches and budget watches. The next step involves developing a list of specific keywords which relate most to the chosen ad groups and would help achieve the objective of XYZ to specifically bid for them.

Figure 8.4 shows how keywords are developed for ad groups. We have taken examples of three ad groups out of the six showcased in Fig. 8.3 (two of them based on watch type—'gold watches' and 'plastic watches' and the third based on pricing—'standard watches'). The four basic classifications of keywords are explained in Fig. 8.4.

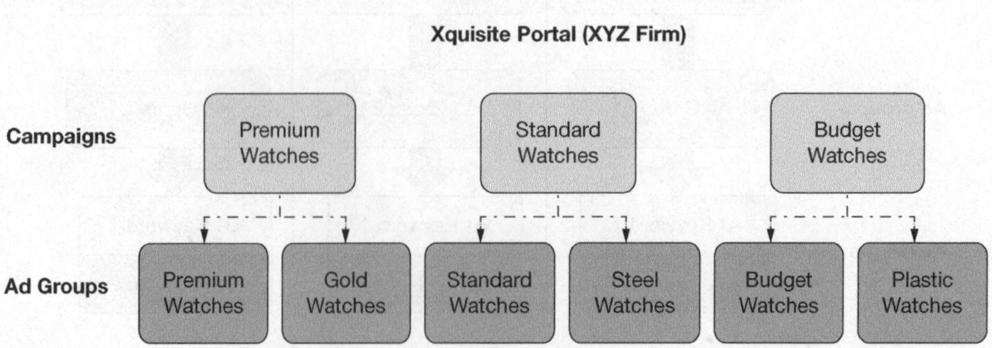

Figure 8.3 Campaign and Ad Groups Set-up for Xquisite Portal

Keywords	Gold Watches	Standard Watches	Plastic Watches
Exact Match	• [Gold Watches]	• [Standard Watches]	• [Plastic Watches]
Phrase Match	• Ladies **"Gold Watches"** • **"Gold watches"** for Gifting	• **"Standard Watches"** XYZ • Xquisite "Standard Watches"	• Discount **"Plastic Watches"** • **"Plastic Watches"** for cheap
Broad Match	• Best **Gold Watches** in India • Top Websites for buying **Gold**-Plated **Watches**	• Men's **mid-range watches** • **Standard** Pocket **watches** • **Watches** at **standard** prices	• **Plastic watches** below ₹500 • White **Plastic** Strap **Watches**
Negative Match	• Budget • Discount	• Premium • Cheap	• Premium • Mid-Range

Figure 8.4 Classification of Keyword Types for Xquisite Portal

(a) **Exact match**: If an advertiser chooses *exact match*, the keyword will display the ad only if the search term includes the exact keywords in the specific order. For example, in Fig. 8.4, if an advertiser sets the keyword [Gold Watches], an ad will be shown only if someone types the same, word by word, otherwise not. An exact match keyword is represented by [brackets] for easy reference.

(b) **Phrase match:** The next level of extension to exact match is *phrase match*, where an ad is displayed when the search query includes the exact phrase and other words are included before or after the phrase. Multiple examples shared in Fig. 8.4 include additional words like "Ladies," "For Gifting" added to the phrase "Gold Watches." An example of a query which will not be matched to this keyword would be gold-plated watches. Phrase match is represented by "inverted commas."

(c) **Broad match:** This is the default keyword match type where an ad is matched against all possible types of queries using the given keywords. The ad will show up not only in situations of different combinations but also for other variations such as singular/plural forms, synonyms, misspellings, related searches, etc. As shared in multiple instances, in Fig. 8.4, a broad match can include all types of possible combinations including:

- **Multiple words before and after phrase**—Best *gold watches* in India
- **Words inserted between a phrase**—Top websites for buying *gold-plated watches*
- **Synonyms of one of the words in a phrase**—Men's *mid-range watches*
- **Different combinations of a phrase**—*Watches* at *standard* prices

(d) **Negative match**: This option helps an advertiser select a word or a phrase for which it wants its ad to be shown when that is typed as a search term. Such words are known as negative match keywords. In the example for "Gold Watches," words like budget and discount have been chosen as negative match keywords, which means if a search term like "Budget Gold Watches" or "Discount Gold Watches" is searched, the ad.

(e) **Ad creation**: Once campaigns and ad groups have been created and keywords have been chosen for each ad group, the next step would involve developing ads for each ad group which represents multiple keywords. An ad group typically contains keywords, ads, and landing pages (the concept of landing page is explained next). For Google Ad Words, a single ad group may contains up to 50 text ads and up to 5,000 keywords. A campaign can be as extensive to contain up to 20,000 ad groups.

The text of an ad is important as it helps to attract potential customers. In the present case of Xquisite Watch Portal, the ad text should be compelling enough to get potential buyers to click on it and reach the portal for browsing, selection, and buying to happen. A text ad should contain three parts—

- **Headline,** which is 25 characters at the most
- **URL**, a 35 character URL, which acts as the landing page
- **Description of** the specific offer within 35 characters and two lines

Figure 8.5 showcases an example of a typical text ad (in this case created for the ad group "Gold Watches." As we can see, there are three key elements to the text ad—a clear eye-catching headline which relates directly to the keyword "Gold Watches," related URL, and a simple description with a compelling call to action.

To create an effective text the following guidelines should be taken care of:

- **Headline**: The best headlines are directly related to the keywords being searched, so it always benefits if one of the keywords is part of the headline.
- **URL**: There are typically two types of URLs—display and destination URL. The display URL is the one which is seen in the ad (like in this case it is www.Xquisite.in/GoldWatches), while the destination URL is actually where the ad takes the visitor once he/she clicks on it which could be different from both the display URL and the homepage of the Xquisite Portal. The most ideal destination URL would be the one which relates best to the exact product and service the visitor is searching.
- **Description**: The best way to create description text is to list the product/service for which the ad is being created, add a key benefit, and develop a strong call-to-action, which, in this example, involves getting a 10 per cent discount on all first buys of gold watches.

(f) **Landing page**: As discussed earlier, an ad group apart from keywords and ads also needs to have specific landing pages, where users who click an ad would be made to land to engage and complete a transaction. Please refer to Chapter 7, section titled, 'Setting up for

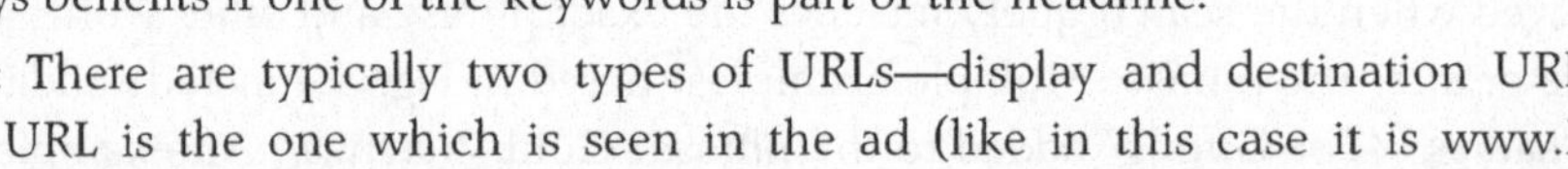

Figure 8.5 Classification of a Text Ad Example for Xquisite Portal

Conversion: from Web in Page to Landing Page,' where we have already discussed in detail the definition and basic concepts of a landing page.

(g) **Click-through rate**: The next key concept to understand is the click-through-rate or CTR (discussed earlier in Chapter 6, section titled, 'Understanding Digital Media Planning Terminology'), which is the prime barometer for a successful adwords campaign and measures the number of clicks received on a particular ad divided by the number of times it was served (impressions) for related searches. CTR is generally expressed as a percentage:

$$CTR\% = (Total\ Clicks/Total\ Impressions) \times 100$$

As an example, if the total clicks on an ad are 15 out of a total of 1000 impressions, then the CTR is calculated as:

$$CTR = 15 \times 100/1000 = 1.5\%$$

CTR is important as it not only lets the advertiser but also Google know which of the advertiser's ads are doing well and are more competitive than others. As we shall see later, this also goes in as one of the inputs to 'Quality Score' which helps Google rank the ad to determine the final price when the ad goes into an auctioning process. Advertisers on their side should also note that a higher CTR is always good for business. If the keyword set for an ad is not right for its business, then the advertiser might be spending a lot paying for ad clicks which would not yield any new sales or leads.

(h) **Quality Score**: One of the most important concepts in Adwords—'Quality Score'—is an estimate of the overall quality and relevance of ads and related keywords. The importance of Quality Score is high as it is the prime determinant of the CPC (Cost-Per-Click), which the advertiser pays for his ads and the Ad Rank in the auction process (which we would cover a bit later).Quality Score is developed by Google using multiple pre-defined parameters which are revised regularly. The key ones include:

- Expected CTR
- Keyword relevance
- Landing page quality and experience
- Ad relevance
- Historical ad words account performance

There are supposedly many other parameters which go into developing the final Quality Score which only Google knows.

(i) **Campaign bid and Ad Rank**: Campaign bid, also generally referred to as the CPC (Cost-per-Click) for the ad, is the amount an advertiser needs to spend to obtain a position higher to his next competitor on the search page where ads are shown. For determining the final CPC which the advertiser pays in the Google AdWords bidding process, Google has developed a concept known as AdRank. The concept involves ranking an ad each time it goes up for bidding, depending upon its Quality Score (in comparison to advertisers bidding for same keywords) and the CPC bid (which the advertiser is willing to place). The basic formula for AdRank calculation thus is:

$$\text{AdRank} = \text{Campaign Bid} \times \text{Quality Score}$$

To understand the concepts of AdRank better, we would take a hypothetical example of the "Gold Watches" ad for Xquisite Portal to see how the campaign bid and Quality Score impact its Ad Rank and finally, the ad position on the Google search page. In this example, Xquisite's ad is being pitched for the same keywords by four other advertisers by the names Advertiser A, B, C, and D. The key task for Xquisite is to have its ad ranked above the competitors to emerge at the top in terms of ad position on the Google page so that more visitors are able to view and potentially click it, since it is placed higher up than competition.

We look at a scenario wherein competitors have different Quality Scores and bids and Xquisite needs to take a call on how much it needs to spend to trump competition.

In Fig. 8.6, the Google auction process will first look at the Quality Score of each of the five advertisers (including Xquisite). As we can see, Advertiser C and B are higher on quality rank than Xquisite, which is placed third in this aspect. Google will also look at the bids which each of them has placed for their ad. In this case too, we see that Xquisite is in the middle with a bid of 3 dollars, while Advertiser D and A are higher at $ 5 and $ 4, respectively.

Now, as Google calculates the Ad Rank by multiplying each advertiser's Quality Score with their bids, we see that Xquisite, though it was not at top either in terms of Quality Score or bid, now, with an overall score of 24, it has the top Ad Rank which actually matters to Google while it is assigning an ad position to the advertisers. So as we can see in Fig. 8.6, that Xquisitie

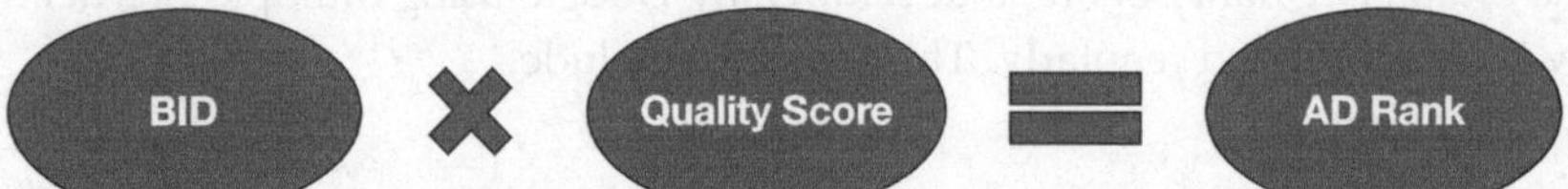

Advertiser	Bids	Quality Score*	Ad Rank	Ad Position
Advertiser A	4	5	20	3
Advertiser B	2	9	18	4
Advertiser C	1	10	10	5
Advertiser D	5	4	20	2
Xquisite	3	8	24	1

*Quality Score has 10 as Highest Value

Figure 8.6 Quality Score Calculation for Xquisite vs Competition

manages to get the first ad position in Google SEM results on the particular page for those specific set of keywords, primarily because of its relatively high Quality Score of 8 out of 10, even though its bid was just in the middle range.

Once the Google bidding process is over, we would assume that Xquisite will have to shell out \$3 for which it had bid. However, Google will actually ask the advertiser to only pay a cent above the bid of the nearest competitor which it beat, which according to the calculation below, will come out to be \$2.51 (20/8 + 0.01) instead of \$3.

Final CPC for Xquisite = Ad Rank of Competitor Below/Xquisite's Quality Score + \$0.01

Thus, we see how Google encourages a high Quality Score for ads and rewards high Ad Rank advertisers with a higher ad position and lower CPC if it is creating the best ads, having the highest quality landing pages, and ensuring top quality on all other Quality Score parameters.

Search Campaign Execution

With an in-depth understanding of the basic concepts and terminologies of a search campaign, we would now study the key steps of search campaign execution by dividing them into three key stages:

(a) **Pre-campaign launch:** involves the set of activities which need to be carried out before the search campaign begins. In the earlier section titled 'Search Campaign Planning Basics,' we laid out the key planning activities for SEM execution including needs and objectives establishment, competitive analysis, target audience definition, keyword research, bid and budget planning, and campaign goals definition. Once all these strategic elements have been decided, the following elements need to be put in place before initiating the campaign:

- **Develop base metrics for website**: Before marketers run a search marketing campaign, they should extract present reports for their website and key landing pages on the type of web traffic, visitor types, their key actions, present conversion rates, etc., to baseline present data which can then be compared with post campaign data to understand the success/RoI behind the campaigns.
- **Create account and keyword strategy**: It is crucial to have a clarified understanding and kind of account, campaign, ad groups and keyword sets, the marketer would want to develop to create a successful campaign.
- **Setting an SEM Budget**: Investors for SEM, be it corporate driven or SMBs (Small and Medium Businesses), should have a clear idea of the kind of investment they would like to put in this channel and a strategy for bidding across large sets of keywords.

(b) **Campaign launch:** This stage includes all the activities from developing an AdWords account (for Google SEM campaigns), creating targeted campaigns and ads, executing pre-decided bids and budget strategies to monitoring and optimizing campaigns. Following are the key steps for each of these activities:

- **Developing Google AdWords account**: Involves creation of Google AdWords account and understanding the key elements to be populated to initiate the first campaign

- **Creating targeted campaigns:** Google AdWords typically supports creation of two types of campaigns:
  - **Standard campaigns:** Involves selecting from the following three basic types of campaigns supported by AdWords

    Search network only: Keyword-targeted ads are shown only on Google search results.

    Display network only: Placement of ads targeted only across Google Display Network sites (earlier known as Google AdSense) where ads are matched with websites when keywords are related to a site's content or the interests of a user browsing the site. Marketers can also choose to target specific pages, topics, demographic groups, etc.

    Search network with display select: This involves targeting for search results on the search network and relevant placements within the Display Network
  - **Specialized campaigns:** Google AdWords offer additional campaign sub-types which can help marketers with advanced targeting options:

    Dynamic search ads: In this type ads use the content of marketer's website (not keywords) to target searches.

    Mobile apps: Image and text ads shown on the Google Display Network and AdMob network in mobile applications.

    Remarketing: Text, image, or video ads show people who have already visited marketer's website when they browse other sites on the Google Display Network.

    Engagement: Engagement ads are a suite of interactive, rich media ad formats that show on the Google Display Network.
- **Developing ad groups and keywords:** It involves deciding on the number and nature of ad groups to be developed for each of the varied campaigns created in the last stage and the keyword list to be developed for each of the specific ad groups finalized. Typically, an initial keyword list is generated based on advertiser's specific context and a more competent and complete list of further keywords is added with the help of tools like Google's Keyword Planner and Display Planner.
- **Deciding device type**: Next, the marketer selects the type of devices where he wants the ads to appear. Google AdWords by default targets all types of devices including desktop computers, tablets, and mobile phones. However, it provides options for optimizing specific ads or ad extensions (a feature that shows extra business information with an ad, like an address, phone number, store rating, or more webpage links) to be shown on mobile phones and tablets. It provides options to adjust bids for different device types.
- **Specifying locations**: The next selection parameter is location wherein marketers can select the geographic locations where they want their ads to be targeted. Multiple options are available for targeting Google AdWords, including countries, areas within a country, a radius around a location or location groups (helps reach customers based on the types of places they visit and demographic information based on their location).
- **Deciding target languages**: It involves deciding the language of the sites where ads will appear. Based on the language(s) selected, Google AdWords will target customers who use

Google products (Search, Gmail, etc.) or visit sites on the Google Display Network in the same language.

- **Choosing bid strategy and budget**: Marketers can choose between mainly three types of bids in AdWords—clicks-based (CPC), impressions-based (CPM), and conversions based (CPA), depending on their campaign requirements. As discussed earlier, bid amount is the most which a marketer wants to pay for a particular campaign and also influences the AdRank. Budget is the daily average amount the marketer wants to pay for all his campaigns. Typically, once the average daily budget is spent, the ads may stop showing. If traffic is higher on a particular day, AdWords allows a spend 20 per cent more than the daily amount for continuity.
- **Developing ads and campaign go-live**: Once the bids and budgets have been set up, the marketer finally creates ads specific to each ad group and can also provide ad extensions like a business address or product images for higher impact. Once all of the campaign set-up details have been furnished, marketer can set the campaign status live in the system and start monitoring each of the ad groups based on campaign objectives and daily/weekly targets.

(c) ***Post-campaign launch****: involves all activities related to making sure that AdWords SEM* campaigns are meeting the desired results within target budget spend and supporting brand and conversion objectives as per business requirements.

- **Monitoring metrics and conversion tracking**: Once Google AdWords campaign is set, it needs regular monitoring of key reporting parameters like clicks, impressions, click-through-rates, average cost per click, cost, etc., for the marketer to keep a track of under performing campaigns. Options like AdWords conversion tracking tools are also available which provide data on what a searcher does after clicking on an ad, which helps understand cost per conversion, conversion rate, total conversions, etc.
- **Optimizing under-performing campaigns**: For campaigns and ads which are under performing, there are multiple areas to scan for optimization and address-impending issues like focusing on keyword mix, changing campaign types, altering geo locations, paying attention to Quality Scores, reviewing device-type performance, evaluating landing pages, assessing remarketing options, taking advantage of ad extensions, among others. We will cover the impact of some of these options in the following section to help marketers revise their campaign strategies for optimal performance.
- **Measuring overall campaign RoI**: Finally, campaigns are also measured at an aggregate level by multinational firms across their various business divisions and countries to understand their ads and search conversion strategies across various products and derive synergies from their global campaigns.

Strategies for Successful SEM Campaigns

With an understanding of how paid search campaigns are run and managed, let us study some of the key strategies and impact factors for running successful SEM campaigns. While a lot of minor factors can impact the success of an SEM campaign, the major ones include:

(a) **Keyword management:** Google in their Google AdWords Best Practice series has shared the following guidelines for successful keyword management:

- **Align keywords with business goals** and use different keywords to cover all major kinds of business queries.
- **Delete low search volume keywords** which are not going to drive any traffic.
- **Use broad match to capture long tail queries;** reserve exact match for primary volume and value drivers.
- **Don't create close keyword variations of phrase/exact match keywords** as most of the phrase and exact match types would cover close keyword variations.
- **Make negative keyword additions a regular part of account maintenance.**

(b) **Quality Score**: According to Google, the three most important components of ad quality are ad relevance, expected CTR, and landing page experience, all three of which should be optimized for best results. Here are a few aspects which, according to Google, are more important and others which are not (while calculating Quality Score).

- **Important aspects**: Some of the more important areas include:
  - ➤ Investment in growing coverage on relevant search areas where marketer's ads have the potential to be high quality
  - ➤ Relevance of ads and landing pages to user intentions
  - ➤ Device targeting and device-specific landing page experience
- **Areas which should not be paid over-attention**:
  - ➤ Ad structuring (such as campaign names; number of ad groups) as it does not directly impact ad quality and can be restructured for internal use only
  - ➤ Targeting different networks like Google Display Network as that will not affect the the expected CTR calculation for Google.com ads
  - ➤ Though an ad's present position on the page impacts user experience, it does not affect ad quality; hence, bidding for higher positions does not help

(c) **Bidding:** Google suggests that right bidding strategies are crucial to gaining prominence in AdWords. Factors which help improve AdWords-automated bidding include:

- Dynamic bids made to user's context in real time often leads to better results
- Automate bidding based on the most accurate conversion data available
- Organizing like-performing keywords into well-defined portfolios gives more transparency and control
- Test bid strategies with targets that align to historical CPA or ROAS (Return on Advertising Spend)
- To improve automated bids, keep CPA goals, ads, and campaign daily budgets fairly steady

(d) **Ad creative:** Certain creative best practices help maximize ad relevance and RoI:

- **Place keywords back into ad creative**, making use of dynamic keyword insertion for a more automated approach

- **Include a few mobile-preferred creative per ad group**: to take advantage of the higher experience provided by mobile
- **Prioritize creative optimization efforts**, beginning with the highest-volume ad groups to maximize returns
- **Create three–four ad variations in high-volume ad groups and two ad variations in low-volume ad groups**: as multiple versions help test and optimize for best performance
- **Put automatic optimization settings to ad rotations** so that effort behind running multiple trial and error exercises is reduced
- **While testing manually, keep a tab on the time spent controlling lower performance creatives**

(e) **Ad extensions:** Managing ad extensions could be a very useful exercise to help customers interact with specific interest areas related to the ad in the following ways:

- **Managing sitelinks** which are links placed under ads to help visitors easily find information on marketers' site by just clicking single links.
- **Location extensions** provides physical location details which can attract visitors.
- **Call extensions** provides a call button which consumers can click for conversions.
- **Image extensions** helps customers see product and service images.
- **Review extensions** are extensions on positive press or awards.
- **Seller ratings** show company ratings with positive user reviews as testament.
- **Social annotations** reveal the strength of the social community following on Google+ pages.
- **Previous visit annotations** refer to the number of times a visitor last visited marketer's site.
- **Consumer ratings annotations** denote the positive ratings from Google consumer surveys

(f) **Mobile app engagement**: Since mobile is the most growing platform, increasing user engagements for a mobile app could be highly productive. Key pointers include:

- Tracking user engagement after installation
- Tailoring specific messages based on different user segments
- Setting up custom-deep links to direct visitors to specific parts of app for action
- Re-engage users with both display and search campaigns for higher interaction

Apart from strategies shared by Google, as above, there are multiple ways to impact Google AdWords parameters, about which search marketers should keep track to make their campaign successful.

SEO Basics and Management

With an understanding of the basics of search engine marketing (paid) campaigns, we would look at the other equally important aspect of search marketing known as SEO or Search Engine Optimization. By definition, SEO consists of all activities and techniques applied towards making a website (and inclusive webpages) rank at the top of any search engine's organic results listing. The prime aim of any SEO exercise for a marketer is to help generate awareness for its brand website by gaining attention through content relevance and keyword prominence rather than paying for it through SEM campaigns.

As we saw earlier in Chapter 6, section titled, 'Intent-Based Marketing (Search Marketing),' a search engine's key task is to crawl and index billions of websites (and their content), rank the crawled and indexed content, and present the most relevant answers to any particular query by matching them to searched keywords. A look-back at the history of how SEO services emerged, takes us to the time when the key activity behind SEO involved only submitting web page URLs to various search engines which used to crawl pages, index them, and show them up for relevant keywords for which they were developed. With marketers realizing the importance of new traffic generated through SEO and the need to show up in the top 10 results for keywords important to their business, they started manipulating the process first by stuffing keywords onto their titles, content, and keyword meta-tags (we shall cover this concept later). The search engines tried to outsmart by giving higher prominence to incoming links on web pages. The prominence of link management as a concept is also attributed to the emergence of Google's unique PageRank algorithm which along with incoming links, also shared a host of other parameters which would determine the overall ranking of websites (and webpages) for any keyword query.

Marketers then started newer forms of spamming (to get close to gaming Google's algorithm) by buying links from other sites, or swapping links in bulk. Search engines again had to qualify this parameter further so that link building retained the distinction of being the quality determinant of the website chosen by other top authority sites and not just developing links with any non-related sites. The above examples showcase the importance of search engine's ranking algorithms and how search engines like Google, Yahoo/Bing have to keep including newer and more relevant parameters as the online landscape changes and also to reduce spamming techniques so that users get the best results at the top, quality content creation is encouraged, and spamming malpractices are reduced.

To understand the basics behind SEO, we first need to develop an understanding of key classifications like whitehat and blackhat SEO, On-Page and Off-Page optimization, and key concept areas for website execution. Ideally for marketers, SEO should start right from the stage where any website is developed. While we discuss key SEO concepts, we would also share best practices and avoidance strategies (dos and dont's) for marketers to execute SEO successfully.

Understanding WhiteHat and BlackHat SEO

As shared in the discussion of SEO history, marketers have always tried to be one-up to prove search engines that they are better than other competitors vying for the same PageRank. Practices which are in line with how SEO companies want websites to showcase authority and superiority in their domain are known as whitehat SEO practices while those techniques which search engines find manipulative and which violate the Webmaster guidelines are known as blackhat SEO tactics.

Key examples of whitehat SEO include the website following search engine's guidelines, developing good quality, useful content, and web pages, and ensuring that the web pages are built for customers rather than search engines. Blackhat SEO (also known as spamdexing) includes practices like paying for link building, keyword stuffing, cloaked pages, including hidden texts and links, among others. Top-of-the-order companies typically make sure that they clearly understand and follow specific search engine webmaster guidelines so that they are not unnecessarily penalized and take time to again retain their rankings status. New or aggressive companies, on the other hand, might be the ones following blackhat activities since they know that developing strong organic rankings takes time, patience, and effort, which they are typically trying to bypass.

Basics of On-Page and Off-Page Optimization

Whitehat and Blackhat SEOs are typical classifications which let marketers know the do's and dont's of SEO. To understand how SEO is essentially carried out, we need to look at the definitions of On-Page and Off-Page optimization.

On-page Optimization It includes all activities which can be executed on the web pages themselves for SEO. These are parameters that typically can be controlled by coding on the page. Key activities include keyword development, meta tags management, improvement of quality content, web-page interlinking, etc.

Off-page Optimization It covers activities that take place outside web pages which cannot be controlled just through web page optimization. Key examples include link building, increasing link popularity in directories, leveraging social interactions, guest blogging, etc.

Understanding Key SEO Concepts

In this section, we would understand the key areas which form a part of on-page and off-page optimization and how they impact SEO activities:

(a) **On-page optimization impact parameters:**
- Search indexing and website navigation
- Web page tag management
- Quality content and keyword inclusion
- Content discovery and linkages
- Usability/user experience impact

(b) **Off-page optimization impact parameters:**
- Link building
- Social reputation
- Website authority and trust
- Personalization and localization

Detailing On-Page Optimization Parameters

(a) **Search indexing and website navigation:** Let us begin our understanding of SEO by taking example of the launch of the 'Xquisite' watch portal we took earlier for SEM. We start looking at each element of the website and its pages which can be optimized to support higher search engine rankings, the first of them being search engine submission.

- **Search engine submission:** For a new website like 'Xqusite.com,' it is essential to first be listed in key search engines and directories like Google and Yahoo so that when users search for watch-specific content related to this site, the website's name comes up. The first action point for Xquisite would be to submit their website and business-related details to major search engines and get them included in their list, so that next time, the search engines are able to direct user queries to the website.
- **Website navigation:** Once search engine details have been submitted and approved, next key aspect for the website is to create a robust and easy-guided navigation structure which starts from the homepage and maps the users' journeys towards discovering key products and services. Navigation structures, which have an intuitive and logical flow, are not only good for visitors but also for search engines which are able to relate to a clear flow on how the website structure flows.
- **URL structure:** Easy-to-follow filenames and URL structures are keys to support search engines in crawling better. Since URLs are individual addresses for documents on the web and are also an integral part of the search ad copy, a well-planned URL structure can also help improve search ranking if they include a descriptive use of keywords. For search engines (even if they are good at crawling complex URLs like Google), it should be made sure that enough time is spent so that there are not too many unrecognizable parameters which result in unnecessary penalization.

(b) **Web page tag management**: A title tag by definition is an HTML tag placed within the <head> tag of the HTML document. This element is meant to be the precise description of the page's content. Each page of the website should ideally have a title tag as it tells both users and search engines the specific topic covered in that particular page. Title tag of each page is also displayed as the first line of the search result. For the 'Xquisite' watch portal launch, a typical way in which a title tag would be represented in HTML code and also as a headline in the search tag is shown as below:

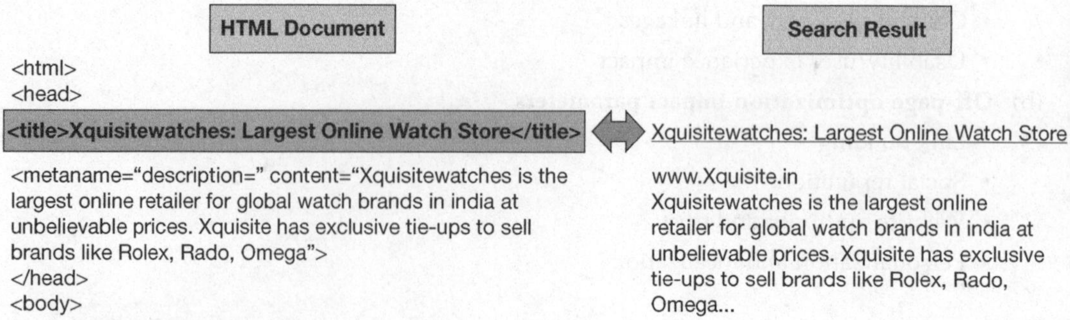

Figure 8.7 Understanding Tag Management

Figure 8.7 showcases how title tags look like in an HTML document and the same title is used as the headline for the corresponding search result. Below the title tag (in the HTML document) is also provided the meta tag (also known as 'Description Tag') which gives a brief description of the page. As can be seen in Fig. 8.7, meta tag can also be picked up by search engines as snippets for the search result.

(b) **Quality content and keyword inclusion**: Creating quality text content, which is targeted in nature, is one of the most integral aspects of SEO. Good amount of research should have gone into understanding key visitors and their needs from each web page, followed by the development of easy-to-follow and useful content refreshed regularly with structured headlines, titles, and description for each content piece. An important aspect specific to SEO which needs to be taken care is *Canonicalization,* which happens when two or more duplicate versions of a web page appear on different URLs. In this case, webmasters need to make sure that each of their content is related to one and only one URL and, if there are multiple versions present, then a canonical tag is used within the page that contains duplicate content which points to the master URL for which the company wants to rank.

- **Keyword inclusion:** A key aspect of SEO and especially quality content creation is knowledge of major keywords that visitors typically use to search for company-related topics on the web and how marketers intelligently include these keywords not only in title and description tags but across content articles. As discussed earlier, in paid search marketing sections, search engines measure the use of keywords on a page to match the relevance of a query with a particular webpage to direct traffic over there. Pages which have included user-query-relevant keywords in their content/articles wisely have a much higher chance of ranking better in search. Concepts like keyword density and keyword abuse are important because search algorithms are advanced enough to realize whether keywords have been stuffed into articles without context merely for ranking purposes or if they are actually helping visitors with more relevant and usable content. Keyword usage tactics like keyword prominence and placement are important to search marketers and the internet is abound with multiple articles and views on how to best execute and reap benefits from keyword inclusion.

(c) **Content discovery and linkages:** A search engine typically does not view a website in the same way a human does. For example, it cannot intuitively understand flash content, rich images, forms, and content embedded within such components. Key considerations for managing each type of content element include:

- **Text content**: All text content on web pages should ideally be placed in the HTML text on the page.
- **Images**: Different types of images (jpg, gif, png) should be provided with ALT text to help search engines with a text description of the images.
- **Audio/video content**: Transcripts of audio/video content should be provided to support indexing of such content by search engines.

Content linking is a crucial element of content discovery which involves managing the link tags for all text, images, audio/video so that they can click and move to other related pages as desired. A link tag would typically look like this:

<ahref="http://www.Xquisite.in">Xquisite Watches Online Store</a>

Here, the text **(http://www.Xquisite.in)** is the link referral location which is the destination site, while **(Xquisite Watches Online Store)** is the anchor text which will be visible on the webpage for the visitor (also typically referred to as Hyperlink) to click. A suitable anchor text is very useful in describing to crawlers the kind of content to which it is linked. This also helps webcrawlers understand internal and external linkages, leading to guided content discovery as the website content owners would want it.

- **Key link crawling strategies**: With an understanding of the importance of link tags, let us look at some key strategies web developers should follow for robust SEO:
  - ➤ **Managing links in JavaScript, frames or iframes**: Typically, it is difficult for search engines to find text and follow links in JavaScript, frames or iframes. As far as possible, HTML should be used so that there are least chances of crawling disruption.
  - ➤ **Effective usage of robots.txt**: There might be certain pages which web owners might not want users to discover. For those files, web developers can place robots.txt on those pages which restricts crawlers' access to them. Search engines like Google also have robot.txt generators which helps create such files.
  - ➤ **Usage of noindex/nofollow**: Usage of tags like noindex/nofollow tells the engines whether pages should be indexed/followed or not. Search engines might still go ahead and follow the links but they would not give them primary importance. Nofollow, for example, is typically used in blogs where public commenting is turned on but owners might not want negative comments to be crawled by engines, thus, damaging the reputation of the blog. Apart from these, there are also other tags that can be used by developers like noarchive, nosnippet, etc., which are evident by their names in what they indicate search engines to not follow or execute.

(d) **Usability/user experience impact**: The other important allied factors which contribute to SEO are site optimization for web design, usability, and user experience. These factors impart an indirect superiority to the site over competition, which search engines are able to judge in terms of higher incoming traffic, engagement, returns, bookmarking, sharing, etc. We have already covered the basic concepts of user experience and usability in Chapter 7. Let us look in more detail the impact of usability and user experience design on SEO.

- **Impact of usability**: Since website usability is concerned with measuring the efficiency of users completing a part task on the site, it directly impacts a search engine's objective of closing the loop on search and being able to complete the requisite task which the user searched for in the first place. Instead of just assuming that the site is usable for target users, it is suggested that web designers use specific tools for usability like Five Second Test, Feedback Army, Silverback App, etc., to accurately test, measure, and fine-tune the most prominent aspects of their sites on various operating systems and platforms.

- **Impact of user experience design**: It is important to decide the key directive to be given to a web designer. Is it to develop a search-friendly user-centric design or to develop a design which is only search-engine friendly and is aiming at getting a place in the top 10 ratings? This question itself answers the way in which web designers should be looking at developing web pages which is 'user centric,' since search engines too push for a user-experience-oriented design rather than designing the site for just higher rankings. Apart from aspects of navigation and URL structuring covered earlier, user experience design also includes looking at aspects like overall information architecture along with consistent design, layout, and labeling of web pages for maximum return on their on-page optimization efforts.

Detailing Off-Page Optimization Impact Parameters

(a) **Link building:** To understand the impact of link building we need to start with an understanding of how regular Google updates on search algorithms have resulted in this being an important parameter for sites to consider and incorporate for better rankings and higher trust:

- **Introduction of PageRank algorithm**: Google's dominance as the top search engine was established with its path-breaking PageRank algorithm, which puts link building as one of the prime factors for a page to increase its rank amongst competing pages. This was the first time search engines went beyond just keyword density and meta tags as the key-ranking parameters and brought forth the concept of choosing the best site across through web voting. This seemed like students of the same class voting for a particular student as being the brightest among them (the most credible and democratic way of knowing who the best is!).
- **Vince update (April 2009)**: This was Google's first major change to its algorithm in which it started favoring trusted brands over smaller competitors.
- **Panda update (February 2011)**: A Google update which penalized content farms like EHow, EzineArticles.com to stop websites from gaming the system.
- **Penguin update (April 2012)**: This update targeted sites that used black-hat link-building tactics, specifically over-optimized anchor text.
- **EMD update (September 2012)**: In this update, Google penalized sites that used the power of exact match domains to get an edge.

The relevance of the above information is to establish the importance of parameters like link building which have retained importance and gained prominence in the world of search engine rankings and how it is crucial for firms to invest time and effort to white-hat link-building strategies.

Link building essentially involves the set of techniques towards getting quality sites to link to a firm's site, thus affirming the quality and authority of its web pages. Links are like votes from other sites in similar business/functional areas which help increase the page rank for that site (and its specific pages).

How Link Building Happens Link building (also known as back linking) typically is a long-term activity which requires persistent efforts, managing not only content but reputation, trust, quality, and branding. There could be multiple strategies to increase link building but the most basic link acquisition types include:

- **Editorial links**: Also referred to as natural links, these are the most authoritative and sought-after links acquired through relevant well-developed content, authority blog posts, credible whitepapers, useful how-to-guides, videos, eBooks, etc.
- **Outreach links**: These are manual links requested from top sites and bloggers with a strong reasoning provided on the benefits of linking. This is also the hardest type of link-building technique which involves a lot of effort and persuasion to get links which would stand out in comparison to competition.
- **Self-created links**: This is the most undesirable type of link building which involves developing links not directly related to web content and with the sole aim of improving rankings through black-hat practices. Typical examples of self-created links include social profile creation, social bookmarking, blog/forum commenting, answer marketing (Quora/ LinkedIn Answers), Online PR. It should be noted that search engines are heavily penalizing such strategies of late.

Other link-building types which are also applied include:

- **Acquired links**: Links acquired through payment or distribution. Examples include paid linking, article distribution, directory links, etc.
- **Reciprocal links**: Links set up in a mutual reciprocation manner between two websites to ensure traffic. Such links are not given credit these days.

Link-building Strategies There could be multiple ways in which link building can be executed successfully. A few of those strategies are shared here (as mentioned in *The Beginners Guide to SEO* by SeoMoz):

- **Getting customers to link to sites**: It involves sending partnership badges to top customers and partners with graphic icons that link back to the firm's sites.
- **Developing a company blog**: Blogs, by definition, are vehicles to build and showcase unique content which is refreshed regularly on a consistent basis. They help to showcase new ideas which induce conversations, help earn listings and links from other blogs, promote sharing, all of which are strong ingredients to improve SEO.
- **Creating content that inspires viral sharing**: Also known as link-baiting in SEO, it involves using viral elements like information, usefulness, humor, entertainment, etc., to promote content through link sharing. Such content promotes editorial links which are high quality in nature and which naturally build authority and trust.
- **Being newsworthy**: Other strategies could also include developing content specifically for promotion, like releasing a new product, getting attention of media sites with unique articles, and even starting something controversial which people would want to talk about and share.

(b) **Social reputation**: With the emergence of social media and newer platforms to disseminate and share information and articles, a firm's social presence also strongly testifies how much their content is liked and shared. Social links specially to prominent sites like Facebook, Twitter, LinkedIn, Google Plus, etc., have become key parameters which tell search engines how much the site is liked by specific audiences over and above competition. Thus, it becomes important for brands to be present on such social pages and forums and have similar branding and messaging as an extension of the major websites.

Also, it is crucial that to leverage social reputation, websites should link to quality accounts rather than those which are considered fake. While social media could be easy to set up, it also has to be ensured that companies manage their online social reputation by constantly mapping social sentiment across sites and quell any negative comments or feedback that may arise time and again, and could affect rankings dramatically.

(c) **Website authority and trust**: Apart from link building and social reputation which are more of promotional in nature, it is also crucial that companies build websites which have authority in terms of being widely recognized as one of the most proficient sites in their specific field or area of operations. Thus, building authority and trust through positive reviews across the web helps a lot in positioning the company as an authentic source which the audience wants to visit as soon as they see an article being shared. Also, marketers who showcase their strong history and maintain a good track record of not violating guidelines get a preference over others in terms of rankings.

(d) **Personalization and localization**: Finally, establishing a strong identity on the web and promoting personalized and localized experiences also goes to show in a long way that a business is committed to its endeavor of keeping customer first and wooing them on a regular basis with strong, credible, and engaging content. If a site is an official site on any subject or has accreditations both from public and private bodies, it helps build a unique identity and credible relationships.

Personalization involves the site-taking efforts to develop content specific to the tastes and preferences of its audience which includes parameters like country, city, location-specific personalization. This also becomes crucial with the fast rise in mobile devices and geo-location, which can help support sharing of content in an individualized manner, which is one of the prime objectives of search engine marketing, for example, Google's Venice update placed good importance to sites physically located in visitor areas.

IMPLEMENTING BRAND-BASED CAMPAIGNS (DISPLAY EXECUTION)

In the last section, we covered the basics of search campaign planning, set-up and execution of SEM, and SEO in detail. In the present section, we would cover the second prominent type of digital marketing campaigns which relates primarily to brand-building activities and is also known as display advertising in common industry parlance.

Display Campaign Management Basics

In Chapter 6, we understood the basics of display advertising and focused on display ad servicing mechanism and key display ecosystem players. In this section, we begin with a basic understanding of key players involved in initiating and executing a display campaign and the types of display campaign inventories. Post that we will cover the key stages of display campaign management and typical stakeholder interactions that take place from the time inventory is sold and ads are delivered on multiple channels.

Understanding Key Display Advertising Players

Before we go into understanding each of the key stakeholders in detail, let us summarize what display advertising is at the most basic level. Display advertising, by definition, includes all activities involved in creating, placing, and analyzing RoI for image-based ads placed across multiple inventory types on the web, mobile, and other digital channels. There are four types of ad formats which constitute display ads:

(a) **Text ads** involve lines of text, similar to search ads.

(b) **Banner ads** involve images placed above, below, and to the side of content being viewed.

(c) **Rich media ads** which are high on interactivity and animation, usually of a larger file size than banner ads.

(d) **Video ads** include promotional video content embedded inside rich media ads which also constitutes the larger set of display ads.

With this basic understanding of major display ad types, let us now look at the key stakeholders who initiate, manage, and support overall display campaign management activities. These include the advertisers, agencies, publishers, and tech-tool providers. Here are the key roles and objectives of each of these players:

(a) **Advertisers:** They form the Buy Side of display advertising along with agencies. Advertisers can be classified on the basis of their overall spend budgets and the brand portfolios they handle in terms of large, medium, or small/local advertisers. Based on the portfolio of brands and respective marketing implementation stage for each brand, advertisers of any size could look at a mix of display marketing objectives (based on the 6S digital marketing implementation model):

- **Engagement objective (launch stage)**: Spend during this stage is primarily focused on branding. Typically, it is applied during new product launch to create buzz/awareness and establish the product in its category.
- **Conversation objective (growth stage)**: Advertisers spend more on prospecting and retargeting for higher leads primarily through CPC/CPM models.

- **Sustenance objective (established stage):** For products in their mature stage, spend has to be mixed across branding, prospecting, and retargeting to maintain brand leadership or support revitalization of a stagnating/declining brand.

(b) **Agencies:** Agencies is an industry term for a bunch of varied companies supporting advertisers with their brand and marketing objectives. The core role of agencies is to help their clients (advertisers) manage advertising budgets in the most effective manner and help them achieve desired objectives across the brands they operate. Agencies have been broadly classified as marketing agencies (those which help with media buying activities) and creative agencies (those which support creative development and deployment). But today, with a wide portfolio of digital activities to be performed across multiple channels, specialized agencies have evolved which support various parts of the advertising value chain with their revenue model being the fee-cut they obtain from owning, developing, and running these campaigns.

(c) **Publishers:** Publishers are known as the Buy side of display advertising. Also referred to as media owners, these entities sell out real estate on their web pages, known in the industry as 'inventories', which are the spaces where we see digital ads regularly. Publishers could vary from regular blog owners, to large news web pages, e-commerce sites to social media channels, mobile apps to online games, etc. Publishers typically decide the type of inventories and the price at which they would be sold to buyers.

(d) **Tech-tool providers:** As discussed in Chapter 6, section titled, 'Brand-Based Marketing (Display Marketing),' multiple tech-focused entities have developed across the ecosystem to support the ever-growing complexities of display campaign management. These tech-tool providers in the process of providing technology-based empowerment to players on both the buy side and the sell-side are also creating a niche for themselves and completely changing the landscape to compete with agencies themselves by building automated media buying and selling platforms. The most prominent of these tool providers today are Google and Facebook who are taking over a large pie of the media spend through their extensive DoubleClick and Atlas platforms, wherein they also provide campaign support services (which was earlier a core agency job). The next section on programmatic buying extensively covers how these tech-tools are taking over the display advertising process wherein more than 50 per cent of the ads, in present times, are being delivered programmatically.

Understanding Display Inventory Classification

Since inventory is the key asset which is sold by publishers to advertisers throughout the whole media buying and selling process, we will first look at how publishers forecast and classify the display inventory available to them across their websites (and web pages). Next, we will cover the display media sales process to share key interactions between advertisers and publishers during buying and selling.

Display inventory, in most basic terms, is the number of total impressions available in an aggregate manner on all web pages of a particular website, whose inventory a publisher is looking to sell. The key difference though is the nature of this inventory which is expandable in comparison to regular media vehicle inventory (like TV, radio) which is of a fixed nature. To understand this concept, we would need to begin with the basic starting point wherein the publisher forecasts and classifies its inventory at hand.

Let us (for an easy understanding) discuss the case of a single publisher group and only one of their many websites to understand how they forecast the inventory available for sales to advertisers. The general rule for this calculation involves multiplying the number of page views in a particular period (aggregate across all web pages) for the chosen website with the average number of ad inventories available on the web page (which is typically three inventories). The number arrived through this calculation is an approximation of the total ad impressions which can be garnered across the website. Apart from the data gathered from historical pageviews (across past months), publishers utilize inputs from multiple tech-based tools with sophisticated algorithms to forecast the available inventory. Key among them include:

(a) The ad server's in-built forecasting capabilities
(b) Technology solution as a feature of workflow/order management tool
(c) A stand-alone digital inventory management tool

Publishers, once they have approximately forecasted the available inventory during specific range dates, also need to provide attributes to each inventory and their related page so that they can be sold based on multiple targeting criteria which the advertisers would like to select. This refinement of inventory can be done on attributes like:

(a) **Media attributes:** contextual targeting, inventory Quality Score, rich media units
(b) **Audience attributes:** geographic, demographic, psychographic, behavorial, etc.
(c) **Page attributes**: above the fold, below the fold, section specific

With an understanding of how inventory is forecasted, let us now look at the basics of how media inventory is classified in the industry. In this section, we would explain in detail two key ways of selling inventory in the traditional (manual) fashion. The newer ways of display sales, with the use of programmatic tools and real-time technologies, would be discussed in the following section in detail.

In Fig. 8.8, we showcase the key classifying parameters for display inventory sales:

(a) **Interaction based:** Direct and indirect inventory
(b) **Sales mechanism based:** Manual and programmatic sales

As discussed earlier, we would only cover the two key ways of manual sales of inventory in this section. These include *Premium (Guaranteed)* and *Remnant (Non-Guaranteed) Inventory*. To understand the basic difference behind these two sales types, we need to go back to the prime objective of any online publisher, which is to sell maximum percentage of its inventory at a premium price. Publishers judge the pages with most profitable inventory primarily through leading indicators (like home pages and section landing pages will be the best inventory for sponsorships) and sifting through page analytics (to see which other pages are visited the most, both above and below the fold).

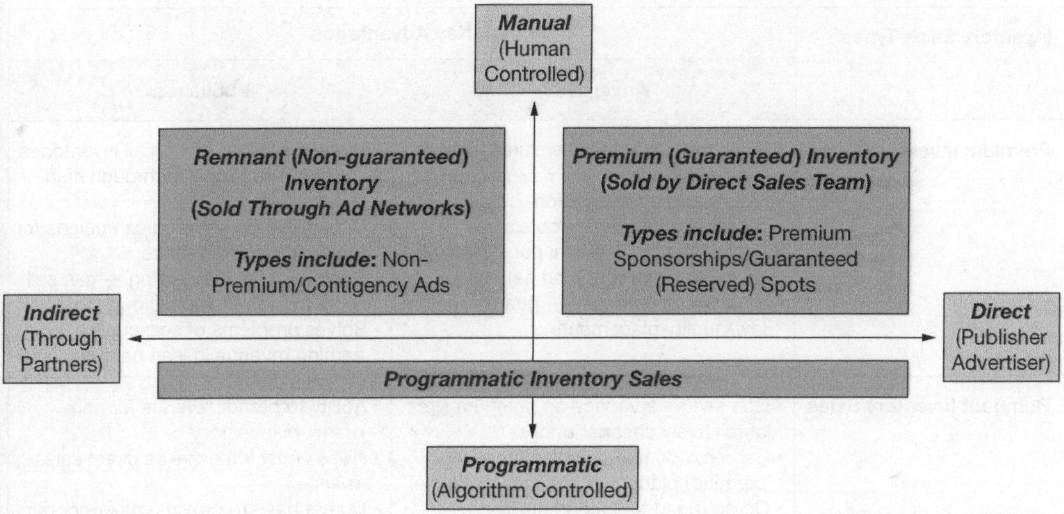

Figure 8.8 Display Inventory Sales Classification (Manual)

Based on multiple reports and tool analysis, publishers on an 80–20 principle, typically pick up the top 20 per cent of their inventory which they know would yield 80 per cent of their overall display sales revenue known as premium inventory (the first of the two types of inventory sales being discussed). Premium inventory is also termed as guaranteed inventory because while selling it to various advertiser groups, publishers make sure that the number of contracted impressions would be delivered to the advertiser at the end of the campaign. Typically, a sales team has to be set up which meets advertisers in person to confirm the booking of these slots much in advance of the actual dates when these campaigns are actually run.

The second type, known as Remnant (last minute sales) inventory, forms the rest 70–80 per cent inventory across other non-premium pages. This is the inventory which publishers have not been able to sell to advertisers directly through manual sales and depend primarily on ad networks who pick up these bulk inventories at lower prices in a non-guaranteed fashion. Ad networks, as discussed in Chapter 6 earlier, help publishers sell their excess inventory to a broad range of advertisers, which they are not able to directly sell through their salesforce. On the advertisers side, ad networks help advertisers aggregate the best possible inventory from multiple publishers based on their specific demand. From an execution standpoint, it is the agencies who typically manage the ad networks in terms of inventory selection, execution, and effectiveness of inventory buys. There are multiple categories of ad network types available for advertisers including horizontal, vertical, targeted, performance, mobile ad networks, which go to show the market maturity of this type of inventory sales.

Figure 8.9 shows the key advantages for advertisers and publishers specific to each of the manual display inventory sales channels types. With an understanding of these channels, we would now look at how a standard display campaign is run and the key steps involved.

Inventory Sales Types	Key Advantages	
	Advertisers	Publishers
Premium Inventory Sales	• Buys are guaranteed- ensures highest value for money • High branding orientation- best for reaching engagement objectives • Access to niche vertical publishers who do might sell through ad networks • Highest transparency — guards against low-quality placements	• Highest pay out among all inventories • Improved relationship through high-touch sales • Can create customized campaigns for higher impact/relevance • Reap benefits of bundling — can sell more though multiple group sites • Solves problems of seasonality-earning revenue in lean patches
Remnant Inventory Sales	• Can secure ad space on premium sites at relatively cheaper prices • Can provide real-time inventory when premium placements are not available • Do not need to spend time in negotiations/contract making • If placements are not performing, can pause or delete future bookings • Offers possibility of better targeting	• Ability to garner revenue for non-premium inventory • Not as cost intensive as direct sales channel • Do not have to provide make-goods as impressions are not guaranteed (no case of un-met impressions) • Model supports publishers with wider range of target audiences

Figure 8.9 Advantages of Manual Inventory Sales

Since premium inventory sales and campaign cycles are the most elaborate to run and also account for the maximum spends, we would take that as a base to explain display campaign stages and the key interactions between advertisers, agencies, and publishers.

Standard Display Campaign Workflow

Figure 8.10 shows the four key stages of any standard display campaign and the key interactions between the three critical stakeholders—advertiser, agency, and publisher. In a lot of cases, the activities of an agency will be divided between a creative agency (which builds the creative) and a media agency (which is involved in buying and selling inventory for advertiser). But for the sake of ease, we would treat both as a single identity (though in certain cases like smaller companies, the creative might also be developed in-house).

Let us now go into an in-depth understanding of each of the four key stages to understand key activities behind campaign run:

(a) **Stage 1: Campaign Planning**: This is the first stage of setting up a campaign and it typically starts with an advertiser developing a media plan based upon his advertising objectives and the kind of digital properties and inventories he would want to advertise (keeping in mind the budget at hand). As discussed earlier, an advertiser would typically have three kinds of advertising objectives: engagement, conversion, or sustenance. A typical media plan would consist of:

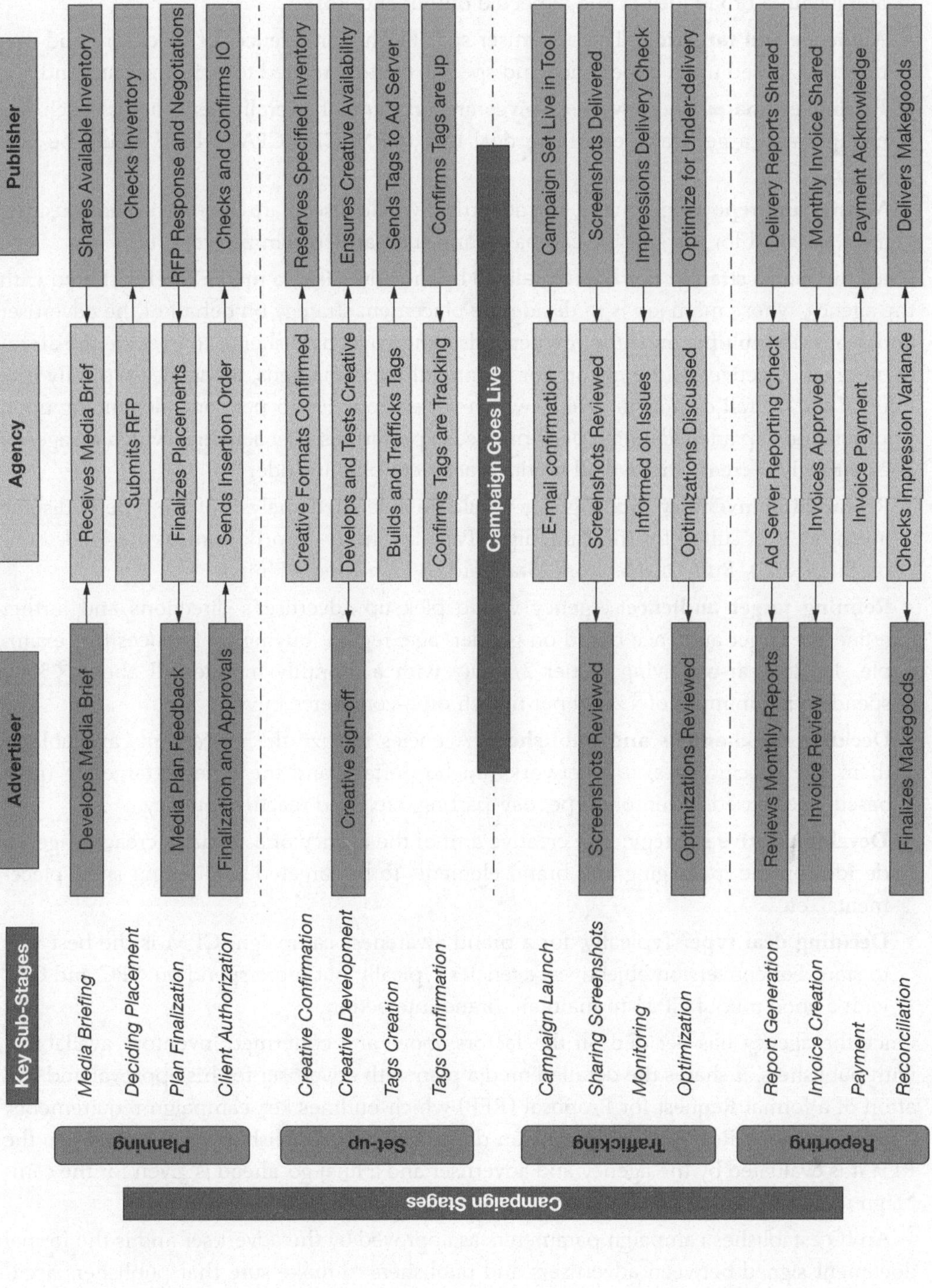

Figure 8.10 Standard Display Campaign Workflow Stages

- **Campaign objectives:** The advertiser shares high-level objectives for the campaign along with a broad idea of the expected output and RoI.
- **Audience and targeting:** The advertiser specifies his preference for inventory and user targeting, based upon experience and specific context related to objectives at hand.
- **Pricing estimate:** The advertiser gives an indicator of overall spend across each key channel and a general idea of the deal mix (CPM-CPC-CPA) which would be best suited.
- **Metrics and reporting**: Finally, the advertiser would also share the metrics he considers most essential for the specific campaign and standard/customized reports.

Once the media strategy has been finalized by the advertiser, a media brief is shared with the agency, whose main job is to decide the placement strategy on behalf of the advertiser and deal with multiple inventory owners (also known as publishers), to execute the afore-mentioned objectives of the client. For running these campaigns, an agency typically gets a fee of the overall campaign spend, which varies from 10–15 per cent, depending upon prior relationship and campaign performance expectations. Key activities which an agency goes through to create the overall media placement plan include:

- **Researching inventory mix:** Agency would do a detailed analysis of the type of display inventory best suited for the campaign (Page inventory–Top/Bottom of the Fold, Run-on-Site (ROS), Run-On-Network, Standard or Rich Media Units).
- **Refining target audience:** Agency would pick up advertiser's directions and further refine the target audience based on gender, age, region, buying preferences (for example, 18–25-year-old living in tier 2/3 city with a monthly mobile bill above ₹3000 spending a minimum of ₹2000 per month on e-commerce buys).
- **Deciding on channels and publishers**: Agencies finalize the placements available to them like specific sites, top networks, niche portals, and the type of targeting (geo-based, user-based, inventory type, day-parting, etc.) and reach/frequency.
- **Develop creative strategy**: The creative arm of the agency or a separate creative agency decides on the messaging and brand elements to be targeted to different sites, placements , etc.
- **Deciding deal type**: Typically, for a brand awareness campaign, CPM is the best way to start. For conversion objectives, agencies typically put more spend on CPC and CPA with a good mix of CPM to maintain brand interaction.

Once the agency has decided on the factors above and confirmed inventory availability with publishers, it shares the detailed media plan with advertiser for his approval and creation of a formal Request for Proposal (RFP) which outlines key campaign requirements, budget, intended RoI, and campaign run dates. Once the publishers respond back to the RFP, it is evaluated by the agency and advertiser and a final go-ahead is given for the campaign to be run through creation of an Insertion Order (IO).

An IO establishes campaign parameters as approved by the advertiser and is the formal document signed between advertisers and publishers to make sure that publishers accurately understand key specifications of the advertisers and deliver on impressions and other mutually agreed terms (which could range from billing, compliance, market goods, and competitor related clauses). Insertion orders (IOs) help define the following list of parameters (among many others) for all included parties:

- Flight dates (start and end dates)
- Target sites and networks
- Impressions to be served
- Ad unit dimensions and creative sizes
- Details on how to handle under- and over-delivery scenarios
- Monthly billing amounts and pricing structure

The publisher sales team typically uses an order management system to store all the IO details to be used by publisher's internal teams for reference and execution and even billing discussions whenever needed throughout the life of the campaign. Once the IO has been placed in the system, the agency and publishers start working towards campaign set-up which are the set of activities to be completed before Go-Live.

(b) **Stage 2: Campaign set-up**: This is the second stage of campaign management and is also generally referred to as the campaign 'pre-live' stage wherein agency and publishers perform activities which are necessary to kick-start any live campaign. Key sub-stages include:

- **Creative confirmation**: It involves agencies confirming the exact creative formats to be placed in specific sections of the publisher's sites. At their end, publishers would check internally and confirm those placements.
- **Creative development**: The agency's creative team, in the meanwhile, would develop different types of creatives (standard and rich media) and, after testing, share it with the advertiser for their approval. At the publisher's end, they communicate with the agency to make sure that creatives are available in time and do an internal quality assurance (QA) to ensure necessary standards approval are run on the website.
- **Tags creation**: Ad tags are the HTML code used by a browser to pull an ad from an ad server. For each of the creative, an ad tag has to be built and shared with the publisher's team, which in turn, places it on its ad server to call from the specific website page on which the ad has to be displayed.
- **Tags confirmation:** Once the publisher places the tags, it confirms with the agency on tags being up and, from their end, the agency confirms back that tags are being tracked. Setting up and running ad tags is important as it lets both advertisers and publishers measure and compare impressions for each creative. This is done through the implementation of conversion tags on the advertiser side and inserting landing page tags on the publisher's site.

(c) **Stage 3: Campaign trafficking**: Also known as the Campaign Go-live Stage, this is the point where the campaign is finally launched and trafficked. 'Trafficking' as a term has a specific meaning in the advertising industry and by definition refers to the process of setting up, monitoring, and optimizing an ad campaign to meet the desired objectives. Key sub-stages during trafficking include:

- **Campaign launch**: The Campaign Go-live stage starts when the trafficker sets a campaign live in ad platform which is then informed to the agency via e-mail.
- **Sharing screenshots**: Once the campaign starts delivering, agency and advertisers need to know that the campaign is running and ads are appearing on web pages. To support this, publishers typically send out campaign screenshots to agencies which review them at their end before sharing with advertisers for their confirmation.
- **Campaign monitoring:** Since a campaign typically runs for large periods (even around a month), the key job of a trafficker and the campaign manager is to regularly monitor the campaign to ensure that campaign goals are being met on a daily/weekly basis and campaigns are not under or over-delivering. If the campaign is seen as under-delivered, a publisher can also take agency's approval to re-allocate inventory so that it is able to meet the targets in specified time.
- **Campaign optimization**: Campaigns can also be optimized for under-delivery using a set of techniques which are executed in the name of campaign optimization. Optimization typically involves working with parameters like bid, pacing, frequency, targeting, etc., which we shall cover in more detail in the next section on real-time programmatic buying.

(d) **Stage 4: Campaign reporting**: As campaigns are being run, the publisher's team has to share regular delivery reports with the agency/advertiser (as agreed upon in the contract). There are different sets of reports typically created at each end (agency and publishers) which help them track their campaigns and make the payment (agency to publisher) or go through with penalties (publisher side) accordingly. Key sub-stages include:

- **Report generation**: It involves creation of standard delivery reports (impression reports) by the publishers to share them with agency/advertisers. Agencies also receive reports from their ad servers (also known as third party reports), which they compare with publisher's reports to ensure publishers have actually delivered the promised impressions for the period measured.
- **Invoice creation:** Once delivery reports have been cleared, a monthly invoice is shared by the publisher, which gets approved by the agency, and after review by the advertiser, it is put up for publisher's payment.
- **Invoice payment:** It involves activities related to invoice payment being initiated from the agency side and payment acknowledgement from publishers. In parallel, the agency also submits its campaign-run invoice (agency fee) to the advertiser who makes a separate campaign payment to the agency for its work.
- **Campaign reconciliation:** Once the campaign ends, a final report is generated by the agency which shares any discrepancies in campaign delivery and invoicing. If it is found that the campaign has over-delivered (meaning publishers have given more impressions than they signed up for), an additional payment is made to them. On the other hand, if it is seen that the campaign has under-delivered, then the publisher has to pay a penalty in the form of make goods (which involves running the campaign for a few extra days without charge or running a percentage of impressions free during the next campaign).

Only when the campaign reconciliation is complete, it is said that the campaign has finally ended. The agency at this level also shares the final campaign report with the advertiser showcasing that it has met all the key objectives stated to achieve.

Emerging Data-Driven Display Models (Programmatic and RTB)

In the previous section, we covered manual display inventory sales models in detail along with looking at the stages of a standard display campaign workflow. In this section, we shall cover the latest trends and shift towards data-driven display buying models which are essentially programmatic in nature. The key difference between manual and data-driven models involves a shift from inventory-led placement to a data-led buying model, wherein advertisers now have the possibility to target specific sets of consumers with customized messages rather than just putting money on inventories and hoping that the real target customer sees those ads.

Programmatic buying, thus, involves using technology to help display advertisers target multiple audiences through machine tools which talk to each other using complex in-built algorithms. With automated ads projected to account for nearly 50 per cent of the US display market in 2015, the programmatic ad spend is projected to exceed $20 billion in 2016, according to eMarketer. The growing importance of RTB buying within programmatic can be judged from the fact that overall ad spend through RTB increased 10X since 2010.

Figure 8.11 showcases the programmatic buying models as an extension of the Y-Axis of the diagram on Manual Display Sales Classification. To provide a better understanding, we have classified the X and Y axes and their parameters separate to the earlier-given manual classification diagram. The key classifying parameters for display sales here are:

(a) **Reservation based**: Reserved and un-reserved inventory (similar in line to the previous x-axis parameters: direct and indirect inventory)

(b) **Price mechanism based**: Fixed price and auction-based sales

For programmatic buying, publishers give Automated Guaranteed as the highest priority for sales (as it fetches the maximum price), followed by the other three. Amongst Invitation Only and Open Auction, publishers give preference to Invitation Only where they can decide the type of buyers they find to be the most lucrative to sell, as compared to Open Auction where they do not have much say.

Let us understand each of these four programmatic sales models in detail:

(a) **Automated guaranteed:** This model is most similar to a direct sale in which inventory and pricing are guaranteed with the key difference being the way in which campaign set-up and trafficking processes are automated.

(b) **Unreserved fixed rate:** Typically sold through exchange environment transactions, these types of deals help advertisers with a pre-negotiated, more predictable and fixed pricing which they typically cannot expect of transactions through exchanges.

(c) **Invitation only auction:** This is one of the two ways of an auction-led sales, wherein multiple buyers bid for specific inventory and targeting parameters, and a winner is decided within 200 microseconds with his ad being served to a profile who had just typed the URL

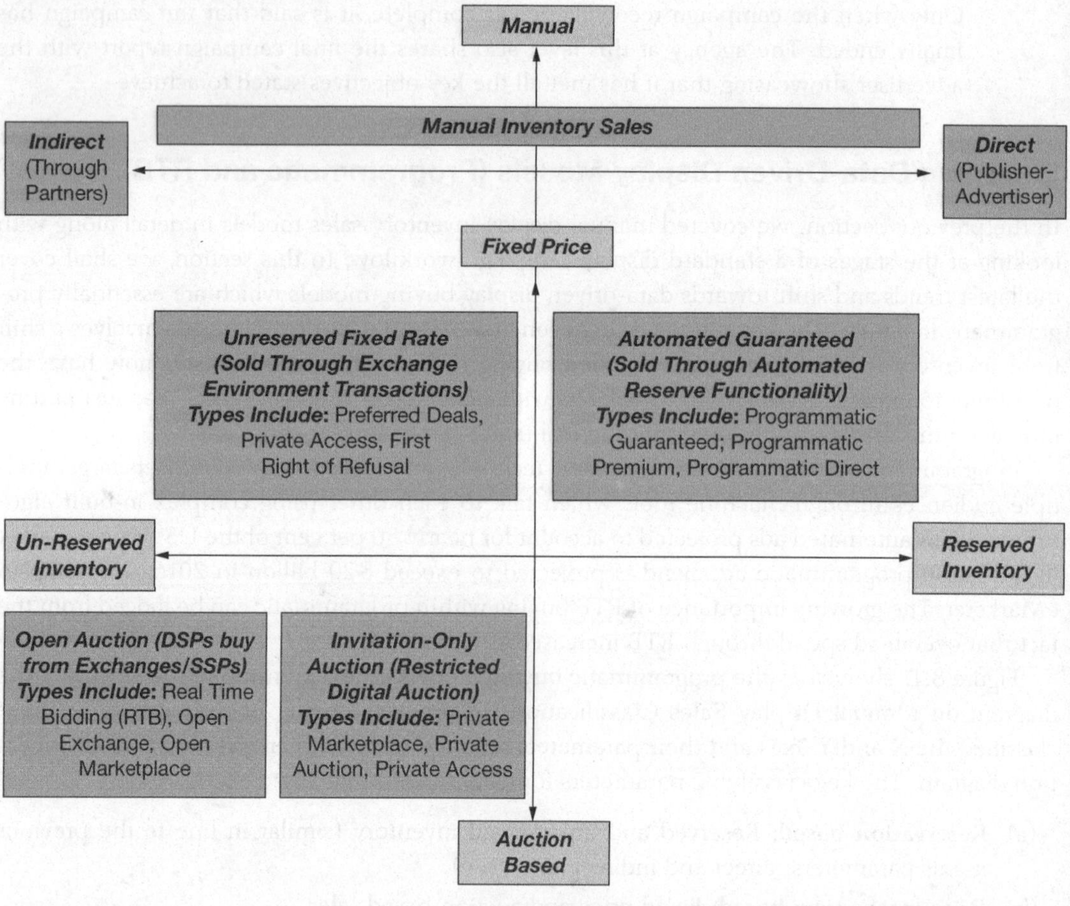

Figure 8.11 Display Inventory Sales Classification (Programmatic)

to visit the specific web page. The uniqueness of this model is that publishers have the power to select key buyers whom they want to deal with and can black-list those with whom they don't want to get involved. With this type of a model, a publisher can also offer buyers multiple levels of transparencies through the use of Deal-IDs and line items, where it can pass or mask any kind of data and sell accordingly.

(d) **Open auction:** This final type of programmatic sales model involves publishers allowing any type of buyers to buy their inventory (though publishers have the power to block certain advertisers or set a floor pricing for their inventory). The advertisers here, typically do not know the publisher with whom they are buying the inventory. Such open auction media interactions typically take place between tools on the advertiser's side—Demand Side Platforms (DSP), which automatically liaison with exchanges and Supply Side Platforms (SSPs), to get the type and price of inventory which they are looking at. The biggest example of this kind of buying is known as RTB campaigns (Real-Time-Bidding) which we would understand in more detail now.

Real-Time Bidding Campaign Workflow

Before we get into understanding the detailed steps of an RTB campaign workflow, let's look at some of the key attributes that differentiate it from the traditional types of display buying:

(a) The fundamental way in which RTB buying differs from manual buying of premium inventory is that rather than focusing on web-page placements, it looks to buy off each impression on an individual basis through an auction process.

(b) The second key difference is the way in which inventory is priced and sold. In the case of bulk impression buying, each inventory can be sold at a fixed CPM rate, since all impressions are priced the same. But in the case of RTB, since impressions are auctioned at different prices they have to be sold through a metric called eCPM (Effective CPM), which is a dynamic value derived from the individual prices paid for each impression.

(c) Advertisers based on their experiences can keep optimizing their bid strategy to get the most relevant impressions at highly competitive prices, a unique advantage which is generally not possible when they buy through fixed CPM channels.

(d) The most important difference though is the way in which advertisers can cut costs for managing the campaign process, since human effort required in the case of RTB buying is significantly lower than manual buys where time, effort, and money is spent reaching out to publishers, planning, negotiating contracts, management of tags, and many other smaller activities. RTB, thus, has clear cost benefits for advertisers. But it should also be noted here that publishers too have distinct benefits through this process wherein they can now charge a higher amount for their premium audience, which they were never able to do before and which can now result in higher revenues if handled strategically.

With an understanding of these key differentiators, let us now look at how real-time bidding campaigns are executed in detail. One important aspect we have to understand here, is that RTB is not a tool by itself but essentially a concept which can be applied to multiple ad-tech tolls to improve their efficiency or to differentiate themselves. If we take the example of Google, it has a range of products that support RTB through which they earn revenues. To provide an example, they have three key tools which they market as RTB platforms:

(a) **Google display network**: Google has incorporated RTB capabilities into its premier advertising product, which gives advertisers an option to use programmatic technology for their buys.

(b) **Double-click ad exchange:** Here RTB has been applied to their ad exchange.

(c) **Double-click invite media (DBM):** In this tool, they have integrated Invite Media (an acquired product) which they separately market as a Demand Side Platform (DSP).

We share here a base-lined version of how RTB is typically executed. As discussed earlier, there could be multiple ways of buying RTB through a mix of ad-tech tools which can perform the bidding functionality. Advertisers and Publishers typically choose the ones which suit and integrate well with their present tools ecosystem.

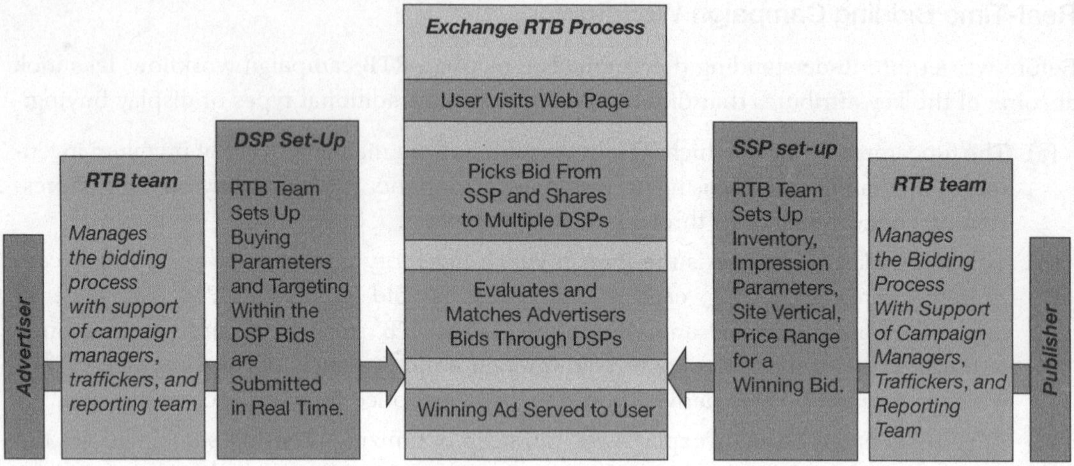

Figure 8.12 Display RTB Campaign Process

In Fig. 8.12, key interactions between the advertiser (buying) and publisher (selling) are listed for a typical case of RTB execution. Since there are multiple activities involved at each level, let us look at each of these interactions in detail:

(a) **Advertiser:** An advertiser mostly runs three types of RTB campaigns based on his campaign requirements:
- **Branding campaigns**: This is run in line with the engagement objective discussed earlier.
- **Prospecting campaigns**: key objectives include audience acquisition (lead generation) activities similar to the conversion objectives discussed earlier.
- **Remarketing campaigns**: Such campaigns are mostly executed by rising present-day e-commerce firms who would want to convert interested visitors to customers.

(b) **Publisher**: Publisher at his end would do an in-depth understanding of his first party visitor data and with the help of Data Management Platform (DMP) tools, create a list of prospective first-and third-party audience which it can sell at a premium through RTB.

(c) **Advertiser's RTB team**: The next step of action on the advertiser's side would be to set up an in-house team to execute RTB campaigns or utilize the tool-support team or outsource it to a third party for execution. The key members for RTB execution typically include a campaign manager (who manages the overall campaign), a trafficker (who sets up the campaign in the system), and a reporting team which provides standard and customized reports as per demand.

(d) **Publisher RTB team**: The publisher sets up similar teams to manage and review the RTB campaigns and optimize their inventory for maximum revenue.

(e) **DSP set-up**: This is the most crucial part of RTB campaign where we would look at key parameters set up in the system to execute RTB transactions. Let us understand how campaigns are set up and run for each of the three objectives of the advertisers:

- **Branding campaigns**: These campaigns have the highest spend and involve an initial testing across a range of publisher sites and audience. During testing, large advertisers typically keep the budget and number of target impressions as 'open' to test the percentage of target audience being touched by the brand without any fixed parameters in place. With some data gained for a particular CPM, advertisers then decide on the type of CPM to bid for specific audiences.
- **Prospecting campaigns:** The parameters for prospecting campaigns like budget and impressions are fixed from the beginning itself, as its targeting is much more defined in comparison to branding campaigns. Key variables which can be used for optimizing include:
  - **Budget capping**: Since lead-based campaigns could be pricey, RTB team should set a cap to the daily budget they want to spend.
  - **Bid capping**: It involves placing a cap on each bid so that the advertiser does not overspend on audience beyond a certain CPM.
  - **Audience targeting**: It involves analyzing the return from different audience segments and tweaking the targeting accordingly. Typical strategies for stagnant campaigns could include day-parting (targeting based on time-slots across the day) or even hourly targeting.
  - **Frequency capping**: By definition, it refers to the number of ads which are shown per day to a specific visitor. This value typically starts with three per day and seven per week. If the campaign is not doing well, it can be gradually increased to assess the optimum frequency per visitor for a week.
  - **Ad pacing**: Pacing is how fast the purchased impressions are delivered and involve managing ad deliveries so that they are not being wasted to wrong users. Advertisers need to set pacing options strategically in RTB.
- **Remarketing campaigns**: It denotes targeting visitors who have clicked on the brand or have traversed to the end stage of an e-commerce kart to target them at lower CPMs and convert them into customers. Budgets, impressions, and frequencies, in this case, are variable and the team decides how much amount they want to put into these campaigns based on the real-time return they witness from their investments.

(f) **SSP Set-up:** It involves publishers setting up their audience and inventory parameters which are made available to the exchange/DSP for them to execute RTB campaigns.

(g) **Exchange RTB process**: It relates to the key stages of RTB execution which are explained as below:

- **Stage 1: User visits webpage** The RTB process kicks in once a visitor navigates to a publisher's website. The publisher's web server in a non-RTB scenario, would send back an HTML code which would trigger rendering of content and also generate an ad tag which would point to an RTB-enabled SSP.

- **Stage 2: Picks bid from SSP and shares to multiple DSPs** Once information on publisher's ID, site ID, and other targeting parameters are set up in the SSP, exchange RTB starts the auction and shares the data with multiple DSPs, requesting bids from them on that visitor and its related data. For the SSP to track information, a visitor should typically have an SSP cookie on their machine. Once DSP looks at the attributes of the visitor, it evaluates the importance of the impression for the advertiser's specific objective and makes a decision if it wants to bid for it, mentioning the price, and also sharing an ad redirect in case their bid wins the war for that impression.
- **Stage 3: Evaluates and matches advertisers bids through DSPs** Once the exchange receives bids from multiple DSPs, it picks up the winning bid based on parameters set up by the advertiser RTB team in the DSP and passes the DSP ad redirect back to the user.
- **Stage 4: Winning ad served to user** Once the visitor receives the redirect, it calls on the DSP which sends the marketer ad server redirect. The user then, calls the marketer's ad server which serves the final advertisement to the user.

From these stages, we can gauge the complexity and targeting capabilities of a real-time bidding process, which is able to place an ad at each impression level in a matter of around 200 milliseconds.

RTB and specifically programmatic as a concept is gaining a lot of prominence in the ad-tech world with programmatic tools being developed and deployed not only for ad buying but increasingly for other digital marketing areas like content marketing, channel optimization, marketing automation, social media marketing. The concept will be given due coverage in the ensuing chapters as this is a trend which is at the heart of taking the industry to the next level, which will increasingly be more data-driven, and where we would be able to target visitors precisely for what they need in their buying cycle with offers based on their previous transactions (which hopefully they would not be willing to put down!). Next, we shall cover the third most important and growing aspect of display ad marketing—the rich media advertising and its campaign process.

Rich Media Ad Campaign Management

In the last two sections, we discussed in detail multiple types of display ad sales classification and the way campaigns are organized and run for key media buying types. One of the most crucial aspects for the success of any display campaign is undoubtedly the creative element, which as a stand-alone parameter has also gone through multiple transformations to emerge as an industry by itself similar to its traditional counterpart. The biggest contribution to this change has been the emergence of rich media ads which as a category has undergone phenomenal growth, more than three times from 2011 to 2017, as per eMarketer.

Understanding Rich Media Advertising

Before we dwell further to understand rich media advertising in more depth, let us identify how it differentiates from other digital creative categories. According to IAB, rich media includes "advertisements with which users can interact (as opposed to solely animation) in a web page format."

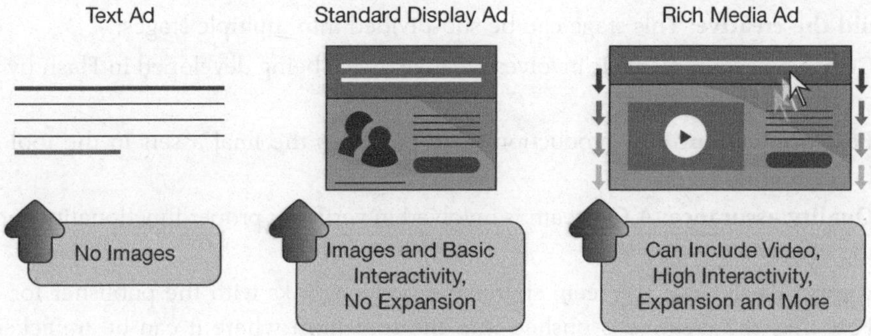

Figure 8.13 Differences between Creative Ad Types
Source: Double-Click Studio

Figure 8.13 explains the differences between different creative ad types deployed for display advertising. The most basic type is the text ad which includes basic text with no images. The second type is the one that has traditionally been used the most, the standard display ad with usually consists of text with a visual such as a logo or a graphic. Standard display ads are either static or animated with tools such as Flash and exhibit only a single interaction (means when clicked they take the visitor to a destination site).

Rich media are the next level of ads which are high on design features and interactivity. A rich media ad can have multiple actions built into its image which could support actions like expansion of ad, playing a video, making a call, and so on. Developing rich media ads involves a host of new-age programming languages like Java, JavaScript, and DHTML, which because of the popularity and rise of rich media, are also in high demand these days. Key rich media creative types include Expanding, Floating, Video, Push-down, Peel-down, Mobile In-App, among others.

Rich Media Ad Campaign Management

With a basic understanding, now let us look at how a rich media campaign is developed and executed to support any display campaign. For best illustration of the process, we are baselining the key steps on how rich media campaigns are developed using Google's Double-click Studio, which is one of the leading products for development of rich media ads. Key stages as shared by Google in their online product literature include:

(a) **Determining the team**: The media agency can either choose a creative agency or get service from the tool's support group to help develop the creative.

(b) **Collecting site specs**: Typically, a media agency develops the media plan, collects site specs, and generates a minimum requirement chart for the creative agency to follow.

(c) **Kick-off call:** A kick-off call is scheduled between the media and creative agency wherein the media agency shares the creative brief and discusses any questions which the creative team might have on execution.

(d) **Build the creative**: This stage can be sub-divided into multiple stages:
- **Creative development**: It involves creative assets being developed in Flash by the tool's creative team.
- **Post production**: Post-production team packages the final assets in the tool and publishes them.
- **Quality assurance**: A QA team is involved in verifying proper functionality and tracking the creative.
- **Approvals**: Finally, the team shares the preview links with the publisher for approval. Post this, the creative is pushed into the tool from where it can be trafficked for any related campaign.

(e) **Make an association:** An association is made by the media agency with an advertiser in the system.

(f) **Trafficking**: The units once finalized are pushed by the media agency for the trafficking stage of display campaigns which we have seen in earlier sections.

(g) **Post-launch creative changes**: It involves changes to be made to the creative after it has gone live.

(h) **Reporting:** Finally, standard and custom reporting are implemented to help review key values and metrics.

We can now appreciate why rich media development is growing in prominence and developing as an industry and how skills like JavaScript and HTML5 are gaining huge importance. The earlier three sections have helped us cover and understand the display advertising concepts and how their campaigns are developed and run. In the next part, we shall cover all the other prominent digital marketing types, including community, partner, communication, platform, and content-based marketing areas and techniques.

CAMPAIGN EXECUTION FOR EMERGING MARKETING MODELS

In this section, we shall move ahead to cover other key emerging marketing models which have contributed immensely to the growth and utility of digital marketing for practitioners. We would start with community-based digital marketing model (commonly known as Social Media Marketing) and move on to partner, communication, platform-based models, before finally covering the most crucial of them all, content marketing, which supports all the other models. Content marketing has become so crucial that in 2015, one survey has revealed "Content" to be the most used business buzzword in a list of 'Most Popular Business Words.'

Content Marketing (Cornerstone of Emerging Marketing Models)

Content, along with creative, forms the core of digital marketing, as evident from the days of Google AdWords and Google Adsense programs, which were based on placing contextual ads against web-scraped searchable content. When the ads were clicked, a visitor was taken to the firm's website or blog, which again presented a long-form content, stuffed with display ads. While this model has stood the test of time, digital content itself has grown in utility from merely providing context to actually becoming the hero and carrying digital marketing on its shoulders.

The power of content lies in the fact that with the deluge of websites and service providers which have mushroomed over the internet, the nature of marketing has changed from interruption-based marketing to a more influential engagement or conversation-based marketing for which content is the key. Also, with earned media gaining traction and marketing becoming a two-way interactive channel, content has become the core of all emerging digital marketing techniques including social media marketing, e-mail marketing, affiliate marketing, in-app marketing, etc. With its growing prominence and the way it impacts both organic and inorganic interactions, we feel this topic deserves a clear understanding before we dwell into other emerging market models.

Understanding Content Marketing

In *Content Rules*, the premier book on content marketing, Ann Hendley and C.C. Chapman have defined content as "anything your organization creates and shares to tell its story." Content Marketing Institute's (CMI) extended definition talks about content marketing as "The business process for creating and distributing relevant and valuable content to attract, acquire, and engage a clearly defined and well understood target audience—with the objective of driving profitable customer action. Content Marketing isn't a one-time campaign but a continually evolving process that follows a strategic path based on the organization's goals, assets, and unique value propositions."

Below we have classified the key stages to set up and successfully execute a content marketing plan (developed utilizing the CMI content marketing program structure):

(a) **Campaign planning**: It involves activities geared towards researching about client's major pain points and deciding on the key business objectives for content marketing. The content marketing team thinks about what the business wants to achieve in the next 6–12 months and identifies the key deliverables that marketing needs to support and achieve by that time. Depending on a firm's strategic plans, typical content objectives could include:

- Building brand awareness
- Establishing thought leadership
- Driving web traffic
- Engaging influencers
- Lead nurturing
- Generating new leads/customer retention

(b) **Content research and repurposing**: It involves collating and mapping presently available content and deciding how best it can be repurposed along with researching for content through primary and secondary sources, in-house experts, crowdsourcing, etc.

(c) **Team creation**: It involves deciding the content team mix (in-house or outsourced or mixed), key members, and each of their specific tasks and responsibilities. A firm's content team may include profiles like chief content officer, managing editor, content producers, listening officers, content creators, designers, experts, influencers, etc.

(d) **Audience definition**: It involves understanding the core audience, creation of buyer persona (roles, key traits, challenges, need–gap analysis, competitor choices available, etc.) and mapping of their journey. To create a great buyer persona, it is useful to interview stakeholders like past and present customers/account leaders (satisfied/unsatisfied), prospects, internal sales teams, customer support teams, etc.

(e) **Story development**

- **Type of content and conversion goals**: The team decides on the type of content to be developed for the present objectives. Key content type includes web pages, e-mails, infographics, blog posts, whitepapers, newsletters, webinars, slideshares, videos, etc. Also, conversion goals should be decided for all forms of content development thereby taking note of instances like opening of e-mails, time spent on the website, number of pages viewed, filling up of a contact form, etc.
- **Messaging strategy**: This includes identifying the key messages to be delivered and desired outcomes which would create the right positioning of the chosen objectives. This can be executed through internal research on trending topics, listening to social channels, mapping content keywords, developing themes, ideating with customers through interviews, surveys, developing content maps, etc. To develop a unique story we have to keep asking ourselves as to how would our messaging be relevant and why would the customer listen to our story.
- **Creation calendar**: A content calendar is important for visibility and alignment of the overall content effort, managing stakeholder accountability, and keeping teams organized. Developing the editorial guidelines is also crucial to make content creation a regular and sustainable exercise. It is always helpful if the content calendar matches with the buyer's journey across its stages and is divided across the key themes to be marketed throughout the year.
- **Content creation process:** It includes creating, hosting, flowing, editing and publishing the content. Setting up copy-style and design guidelines are important to bring out the unique voice and style of the content. The content team also needs to chalk out key support required (internal/external) to help develop and review the content.

(f) **Channel selection:** It involves selecting key channels and optimizing content specific for each channel to maximize its effectiveness. Distribution channels can be classified as:

- **Direct channels** include e-mails, phone calls, text messages, tweets, etc.

- **Indirect channels** through search engines, online forums, advertisements, social media sites, trade websites, PR articles, etc.
- **Referral channels** involve influencers like buyers, friends, colleagues, industry analysts, allied internal departments, etc.

We would also need to decide on the perfect content mix for each channel based on the type of customer, present target channels, and types of programs executed.

(g) **Promotions execution**: It involves setting of the most efficient programs to target and promote content. Content should be promoted across multiple media types:

- **Owned media**: includes website, blogs, e-mails, social pages, newsletter
- **Paid media**: involves social, content syndication, paid e-mail programs, SEM
- **Earned media**: includes earned social media shares, influencer mentions, SEO

(h) **Measurement and optimization**: Content marketing should be reviewed on a regular basis to understand impact and conversion rates. Typical measurement parameters include clicks, views, downloads, account interactions, conversations, top contributors, followers, registrations, sales, requests, coupons downloaded, shares, re-tweets, etc. If it is felt that the campaign is not running optimally as expected, firms can make use of optimization tools which impact through A/B Testing, SEO, recommendation engines, audience targeting, etc., to understand issues and improve accordingly. Finally, key learnings and failure should be documented and shared with the content team regularly.

Community-Based Campaigns (Social Media Execution)

With the rise in the types of social media marketing growing by the day, executing community-based-campaigns is getting more and more specific to the medium and type of social channels for which the campaign is to be run. A B2C campaign would differ from a B2B campaign, the objectives and activities for a Linkedin campaign are quite different from that of Twitter or Pinterest. Even on a single platform like Facebook, an 'organic posts' campaign on the main Facebook page would differ from a 'native content' advertising campaign run on customer's Newsfeed.

Given the nature, variety, and specific nuances of each platfrom, we would not be covering each of them separately and the attempt here would be to cover social media campaign activities at a broad-based level with steps that can be applied to most of the popular platforms. Key campaign stages for social media execution include:

(a) **Campaign planning**

- **Defining goals and objectives**: It involves doing an internal and external analysis (competitive assessment) to establish the need for a social media strategy and defining its key elements and objectives. Based upon the type of target customer segment and its characteristics, social media objectives could include creating buzz, generating traffic/leads, performing social listening, developing brand conversations, managing and building reputation, influencing audiences, etc.

- **Developing social media strategy**: It involves developing social strategy and implementing the brand's presence across social channels. It is important to first take stock of a firm's current social media status and the activities performed across various disparate functional units. Typically, social media activities happen across four venues:
  - **Owned media (internal)**: Firm's website, blog, application, etc.
  - **Owned media (social):** Facebook page, LinkedIn page, Twitter account
  - **Earned media:** LinkedIn group, Q&A sites, external blogs
  - **Paid media (social ads):** Facebook, Twitter, Linkedin, Redddit, etc.
- **Setting up social media internally**: It includes tackling key issues for evangelizing and setting up an internal social media team. The key activities are listed below:
  - **Identifying and overcoming cultural obstacles** demonstrating value
  - **Setting up core and distributed teams** across key divisions
  - **Creating internal policies** to have a uniform execution strategy
  - **Training on execution**, teaching how to engage with communities, conversation, and influencing techniques, crisis scenario planning, etc.
  - ***Sharing best practices*** and setting up a support structure to guide internal teams on key queries and share success stories

(b) **Content creation:** To build an execution plan, consider the following elements:

- **Understanding type of content to promote**: Based on defined objectives, the nature and type of content to be promoted should be decided (for example, posts, pools, discussion forums, contests, event videos, infographics, etc.)
- **Developing the message points**: It involves a clear understanding of the firm's space and key trending topics to offer a unique perspective to that channel's audience. Great content is articulate, targeted, involves strong imagery and messaging elements, follows key brand elements, and integrates well with SEO.
- **Choosing social media channel**: The key activities are listed below:
  - Deciding target audience type and researching about the channels they would visit and be influenced
  - Identifying opinion leaders and targeting their habits
  - Understanding the tone and spirit of each group specific to media channel
- **Creating a posting calendar:** It involves creating the publishing cycle of content for target social channel and setting timelines for overall campaign run.
- **Mapping target audience to content type:** To run the most effective social media campaign it is crucial to do a clear mapping of assets to audience types.

(c) **Campaign execution**

- **Developing promotion techniques**: Social content should be promoted according to the promotional capabilities of each platform (should be well researched).
- **Understanding key tools and technologies**: This is essential to facilitate implementation ease.

- **Link distribution strategy**: It involves building inbound links to each content piece.
- **On-site and off-site social media optimization**: Optimizing social content on website as well as external channels to encourage sharing and network expansion.

(d) **Campaign tracking and monitoring**

- **Assessing measurement tools**: Deciding on the analytics tool for social media tracking and reporting, for example, Google Analytics, Hootsuite, Adobe Social, etc.
- **Monitoring mechanisms**: Creating a custom framework which captures both quantitative and qualitative data and is able to draw meaningful inferences.
- **Campaign RoI assessment**: Establishing campaign cost and sharing RoI on social media campaign investment on a regular basis with all teams.

(e) **Campaign refinement**: The final step involves analyzing overall campaign success and key issues faced (through defined performance indicators) to refine present implementation process and make necessary changes to each of the above steps for a more effective social media RoI.

Campaigns for Partner, Communication, and Platform-Based Marketing

In Chapter 6, section titled, 'Partner, Direct, Content, and Platform-Based Marketing Channels,' we shared the definition and key types of partner, communication, and platform-based marketing to build an understanding of how digital marketers are utilizing these apart from the major four types (covered in detail in the earlier sections). In this section, we would pick up representative marketing types from each of the remaining three digital marketing areas and cover the campaign management steps involved briefly.

Starting with partner-based marketing (which covers affiliate marketing, public relations, editorial partnerships, etc.), we have chosen to explain the key campaign stages for affiliate marketing as it is being widely deployed these days along with the emerging concept of 'Performance Marketing.' Affiliate marketing is executed with a merchant on one side (who has a product/service to sell) and the affiliate partner (who runs the program) on the otherside. The key campaign stages and typical considerations taken into account by merchants to execute affiliate campaigns are listed below:

(a) **Campaign planning**: It involves strategies that need to be developed by merchants to set up affiliate marketing campaigns to attain desired objectives. Key analysis points include:

- **Understanding the costs involved:** Typically three types of costs are to be calculated for affiliate marketing—resource cost, platform cost, and creative build cost.
- **Choosing the right network:** Firms can go either with affiliate networks like share-a-sale, commission junction, or use specialized in-house software.
- **Researching keyword activity and web traffic:** For stronger visibility and reach of affiliate campaigns, it is important that firms decide on a mix of search keywords based on the type of audience visiting their websites.

(b) **Campaign set-up**: It includes the following activities prior to actual execution:

- **Affiliate recruitment:** Reaching out to affiliates through direct contact or affiliate forums to post on the benefits of affiliate program and share links to sign up page.
- **Structuring commission:** This refers to defining viable commission rates and setting up terms and conditions so that a merchant can have control over the program.
- **Choosing creative:** It involves deciding on the type of banners (file sizes, call-to-action, etc.) to be used for the affiliate program which will drive clicks and sale.
- **Affiliate landing pages:** It includes setting up of customized web pages to lead visitors (clicking on affiliate banner) to a clear and compelling conversion page.

(c) **Campaign execution**: It includes activities related to the execution of the affiliate campaign:

- **Sharing creative:** The banner/creative is shared with the affiliate partner.
- **Campaign initiation:** Communication on campaign initiation shared with partner
- **Tracking campaigns:** Involves measuring visitors converted at the end of a period
- **Rewarding affiliates:** Calculating and sharing commissions post sales validation

(d) **Campaign refinement**: It involves refinement of campaigns and affiliates post execution:

- **Tracking metrics:** Various types of campaign metrics are analyzed post execution to understand top selling affiliate products, best partners, visitor activities, etc.
- **Refining campaigns:** Campaigns are refined based on response and conversions.
- **Renewing partnerships:** New affiliates and commission structures are set for future.

Next, let us look at communication-based marketing (includes types like e-mail, SMS marketing, chat, inbound calls, user comments) wherein e-mail marketing is still considered to be the most prominent and value-for-money form of digital marketing. Key campaign stages include:

(a) **Campaign planning**: It involves researching and developing the plan for e-mail marketing.

- **Goal setting:** Defining the need, scope, budgets, frequency, and results expected from e-mail campaigns, as well as the customer value and key messages to deliver.
- **Determining audiences:** Defining the type of audiences with whom the targeted messages are to be shared, based on funnel stage, previous campaign success, and audience behavior type.
- **Content delivery plan:** Deciding on content calendar, based on varying objectives.
- **Decide distribution channels:** Identifying ways to reach out to audiences to sign-up for e-mails, web sign-ups, CRM-based mailers, partner mailers, and event-based mails.

(b) **Campaign set-up**: It includes key steps behind the setting up of a successful email campaign:

- **Developing a database:** This refers to developing segmented databases through in-house and third party data to create quality target lists for higher impact.
- **Content and design:** It involves deciding on the tone, style, messaging, and structure of content. It also includes developing design guidelines and considerations on templates, device viewers, landing pages, call-to-action settings, social integrations, etc.

- **Developing call to action:** E-mail CTAs could be web visits, promotion mails, product updates, event requests, survey forms, collateral share, coupons, etc.
- **Testing and refining:** It involves testing the design, appearance, content (at the level of subject lines, header, spam check, etc.), and refining for effectiveness.
- **Choose service provider:** It involves deciding on in-house or third party delivery.

(c) **Campaign execution**: Activities related to executing e-mail campaign delivery:

- **Email delivery:** It involves deploying custom content on multiple platforms and channels including social media, blog posts, and automated platforms.
- **Measuring quality and reputation**: For quality delivery firms check SpamScore, test links, image sizes. Reputation can be checked on senderscore.com too.
- **Goal tracking:** It refers to measuring engagement and effectiveness of campaigns through metrics like delivered, opens, clicks, unsubscribes, social activity, etc.

(d) **Campaign refinement**: Improving effectiveness during and post campaign run includes the following aspects.

- **Listening and adapting:** Regular analysis of campaigns and refining the key elements.
- **Lead nurturing:** This involves tracking lead interactions to keep offering value.

Finally, we would look at platform-based marketing (including types like mobile applications, in-game marketing, kiosk marketing) and specifically, cover mobile campaigns in detail. Since mobile as a platform is growing in prominence for all other digital marketing types, we would cover below the distinct features which render uniqueness to campaigns run on this platform.

(a) **Campaign planning**

- **Goal setting:** Analyzing present mobile traffic to site, specific campaign goals and benefits, key target groups, investment needed, desired outcomes, etc.
- **Choosing campaign types:** Marketers can use mobiles to run multiple campaign types including SMS (Short Message Service), MMS (Multimedia Messaging Service), Wi-Fi Marketing, Instant Messaging, QR codes, Voice Marketing, etc.

(b) **Campaign set-up**

- **Building audiences:** Mobile audiences can be built using CRM data, web forms data, offline events data, social media data, previous paid-campaign data, etc.
- **Creative and design:** It refers to developing the message for specific promotion type and customizing it for audience type, location, time of messaging, etc.
- **Developing CTAs:** It involves developing and promoting the right call to actions for promotion on the website and social media mobile networks of key social sites.
- **Rendering for mobile:** Benefiting from the uniqueness of mobile platforms that involves developing personalized and location-based offers.
- **Pre-launch testing:** It includes testing key mobile execution elements—user flow, carrier, customer responses, data capturing, load testing, multiple platforms, etc.

(c) **Campaign execution**

- **Campaign launch:** This denotes technically implementing the campaign and setting it live with the help of third party apps and servers and a dedicated campaign team.

- **Measuring conversions:** It involves regularly measuring multiple campaign conversions to understand and improve performance on a daily/weekly basis.
- **Reporting and analytics:** It includes generation of insights through key reports and usage of analytics to understand top keywords, referring partners, visitor interactions, etc.

(d) **Campaign refinement**

- **Tracking metrics:** It includes deriving post-campaign metrics, budget versus outcomes for RoI.
- **Refining campaigns:** It refers to identifying key areas for refinement be it messaging, CTAs, landing pages, day-parting, personalization techniques, etc.
- **Developing follow-up strategy:** Finally, marketers should develop a follow-up engagement strategy for mobile and other similar upcoming platforms to keep prospects engaged, convert leads to sales, and refer more campaigns socially.

With the growing importance of mobiles, it is clear that more rigorous planning and efforts need to be spent for running integrated campaigns on mobile platforms for stronger results.

CAMPAIGN ANALYTICS AND MARKETING ROI

In the last four parts of this chapter, we covered the campaign implementation steps for the seven key digital marketing types by taking up specific examples in detail. In this final part, we will begin with the initial understanding of the basic concepts and terminologies of web analytics. This is followed by taking a look at how digital marketing is driving analytics to shift from basic clickstream to Web Analytics 2.0 and, thus, redefining the way analytics is being measured across marketing channels. The third section would help to develop the framework for marketers to calculate overall RoI for their marketing programs by combining the analytics obtained from each of the deployed marketing channels and types. Finally, the chapter would end with a section of campaign refinement to understand how marketers can improve their next set of campaigns with key insights from previous campaign measurement and gap analysis.

Basics of Web Analytics

The fundamental goal of web analytics has been to evaluate website performance through collection and analysis of data related to web traffic and usage patterns. According to Eric Peterson, in his book, *Web Analytics Demystified*, web analytics includes assessment of the following types of data to help create a generalized experience of online visitors:

(a) **Web traffic data:** It includes data mined from web server log files and Javascript page tags

(b) **Web transactional data:** It refers to business data related to transactions like number of customers, number of orders, average size of transactions, etc.

(c) **Web server performance data:** It includes data related to usage-based characteristics of web pages, including page weight, load time, etc.

(d) **Usability studies:** It refers to data related to visitors' usage of website and key interactions.

(e) **User-submitted information:** It refers to information collated through online forms/surveys.

With this basic understanding of the types of data which have traditionally represented web analytics, let us now look at standard clickstream metrics and key performance indicators (KPIs), which are most important for measuring web analytics. According to analytics expert Avinash Kaushik, a metric is a quantitative measurement of statistics describing events or trends on a website while a KPI is a metric which helps a firm understand how it is doing against defined objectives. Key web metrics include:

(a) **Visit-related metrics:** It denotes metrics like number of visits, pages per visit, etc.
(b) **Visitor-related metrics:** It refers to metrics like new visitor, repeat visitor, etc.
(c) **Page-related metrics:** An example is Unique Page Views which is the number of visits during which a specified page was viewed once.
(d) **Time-related metrics:** Top metrics here include Bounce Rate (per cent visits where the visitor leaves the site from the entry page itself), visit duration, time on site, etc.
(e) **Engagement-related metrics:** Examples include the number of repeat metrics, customer retention related metrics, etc.
(f) **Conversion-related metrics:** Defined as outcomes divided by unique visitors, it could cover conversion types like form-filling, white-paper download, sales enquiry, etc.
(g) **Exit-related metrics:** Exit rate measures the number of visitors who exit a website from a certain page.

Understanding KPIs

KPI or key performance indicators, by definition, is a metric that helps achieve a specific company objective. The key difference between metrics and KPIs is the fact that metrics are generally measured without a specific goal at hand, while KPIs can specifically be developed based on internal-target measurement needs. For example, First time Asset Download (number of marketing assets like white papers, industry reports downloaded by unique visitors coming to the site for the first time); Share of Search (percentage of search traffic as compared to competition) etc.

Companies need to strategize and develop internal web analytics frameworks to come up with KPIs which suit their business needs best and help them achieve highest RoI.

Introduction to Google Analytics

In 2005, Google acquired Google Analytics (GA), one of the most preferred free web-analytics tools, from a web analytics firm named Urchin. This tool provides one of the best platforms to measure the success of a website and keep track of the amount of traffic coming through multiple digital sources.

Google Analytics has been the most reliable analytics tool for bloggers, SMB, and even large global firms primarily because of these three reasons:

- Ease of implementation
- Reliability that the brand Google provides
- Fact that statistics from Google Analytics can be used to compare against all other third-party analytics and advertising tools.

Google Analytics is used by the firms to: understand users' activity and the amount of time spent on their website; find out the most effective pages; the keywords that are ranking well; and much more.

The implementation of the Google Analytics includes creating an account and adding a small piece of code (Javascript) to the website's pages that helps track the activity on a website. Once operational, both webmasters and marketers can view key website statistics displayed as per the following sections:

- **Audience Overview:** The dashboard provides an overview of key parameters including total users, new users, total sessions, sessions per user, page views, pages/session, average session duration, and bounce rate. Apart from this, multiple slide and dice classifications include demographics (language, country, and city), system (browser, operating system, and service provider), and mobile (operating system, service provider, and screen resolution).
- **Real-Time Analytics:** This includes an overview of real-time user engagement statistics like active users on the website, page views (per min/sec), top referrals, top active pages, top social traffic (source and users), top keywords, and top locations (of traffic origin).
- **Acquisition Overview:** The dashboard provides a view of user acquisition with multiple options to customize acquisition data by channels, sources, and mediums. Multiple metrics are available in dashboard specific to user acquisition, behavior and conversions. Apart from these, multiple dashboards can be generated by users to analyze visitor traffic across other sources including Google Ads, Search Console, social media, and campaigns (organic and paid).
- **Behavior Dashboard:** This includes an overview of multiple user behavior analytics including behavior flow, site content, site speed, site search, events, and publisher data. A key feature in this section is 'Google Optimize' that helps marketers run analytics experiments on website data for free.
- **Conversions Dashboard:** This dashboard supports four key functions:
  - **Goals:** It includes creation of goals and combining them with Funnels to analyze user actions leading up to a Goal.
  - **Ecommerce:** It helps understand the value of a digital business through e-commerce tracking where a snippet of code is included on a site or app to collect transaction data like product sales, purchase amounts, and billing locations, which is connected back to the Google Analytics account.
  - **Multi-Channel Funnels:** These funnels show how marketing channels work together to create sales and conversions.
  - **Attribution analysis:** This is a model comparison tool to attribute visitor actions.

An understanding of Google Analytics is crucial for marketers to understand their website actions, engage better with visitors, revise goals and segments, review most prominent traffic sources and analyze website data along with campaigns. Google Analytics is often used along-with Adobe Analytics and other third-party tools to gather a complete picture of a firm's web analytics. This is often accompanied through the deployment of a custom Marketing Analytics Framework based on a company's objectives, media presence, and marketing activities.

Web Analytics 2.0: Developing a Marketing Analytics Framework

With an understanding of the basic concepts and terminologies behind web analytics, in this section, we will cover the progressive shift of web analytics to broader digital context which will include analytics from all types of owned, paid, and earned media and not just the classic definition of analytics which revolved around analyzing data only on the firm's website. The latest book *Web Analytics 2.0* by Avinash Kaushik highlights how we are at the cusp of looking at web analytics in a differentiated manner, moving from clickstream data collected by web logs and JavaScript tags to a broader set which helps answer the 'Why' behind a visitor's action and not just "What," which is the action itself.

The definition of Web Analytics 2.0, according to Kaushik, is "the analysis of qualitative and quantitative data from your website and the competition, to drive continual improvement of the online experience that your customers and potential customers have, which translates into desired outcomes (online and offline)". The key elements of Kaushik's Web Analytics 2.0 paradigm which differentiate from the earlier clickstream-only based analytics include:

(a) **Multiple outcomes analysis:** It involves measuring outcomes which means connecting customer behavior to the bottom-line of the firm.

(b) **Experimentation and testing:** It includes running multiple experiments on the site using varied testing tools to realize the features which work best for customers.

(c) **Voice of customer:** It involves getting direct feedback from customers on the site using surveys, usability testing, card sorting, and other techniques which we have covered in earlier chapters.

(d) **Competitive intelligence:** It relates to collating and comparing information on direct and indirect competitors to measure performance against competition, identify new opportunities for growth and improve present processes.

Through this framework, firms can develop a strategic view from their web analytics capture exercise rather than just work on tactical data which is not as insightful. The next step would be to look at how data can be collaborated across the three media type: owned, paid. and earned to utilize available analytics most productively.

Marketing Analytics Measurement Framework

To obtain an overall view of how marketing is progressing, it is crucial to understand the broader picture of analytics emerging not only from web (which is the focal point of all action), but also from the source side which includes data generated from all three digital media types (owned, paid, and earned). To understand and generate a coherent view of these analytics, we have developed a marketing analytics measurement framework based on REAN marketing engagement model, discussed earlier in Chapter 1, section titled, 'Digital Marketing Channels: Types and Business Models.' The model runs across key funnel stages of Reach, Engage, Activate, and Nurture, and divides the analytics gathering exercise into quantitative and qualitative areas for each of the three broader digital media classifications to provide an elaborate and in-depth measurement model.

Quantitative analytics are measured across two primary parameters:

(a) **Count:** It measures the number/ratio of a particular metric.

(b) **Return:** It measures the overall value/return on investment for related metrics.

Qualitative analytics have also been classified across two primary parameters:

(a) **Quality:** It assesses the quality/relevancy/engagement value of each metric captured.

(b) **Connect:** It develops an index to measure the connectedness of metrics to marketing objectives. This index can be developed for any variable and is context dependent.

Table 8.2 has been created to showcase how each of the qualitative and quantitative analytics are measured for the three digital media types across planning and the three funnel areas: Reach, Engage, and Activate. Nurture, the fourth part of the funnel, has not been discussed here since it represents analytics post the campaign stage.

In Table 8.2, we have divided the three digital media types into two of their most representative sub-categories (for example, Website and Content for Owned Media, Trade and Social for Earned Media, and Advertising and Partner for Paid Media). The framework begins with the planning stage which involves researching historical metrics for all the sub-categories and defining measurement processes and metrics for each of them. To take an example of how metrics are created for each of the three key funnel stages, let us pick an example of say the REACH stage metrics for the website. Key metrics devised according to the framework include:

(a) **Count:** It includes the total visitor count and unique visitors as key metrics.

(b) **Return:** It measures the value/RoI for unique and total visitors to the website.

(c) **Quality:** It includes parameters to measure the quality of visitors to the site.

(d) **Connect:** It referes to developing a visitor connect index to establish the impact of the site.

Similarly, we have showcased in Table 8.2, typical examples of key metrics for each of the sub-categories for reference and understanding. It has to be noted that the choice of final metrics would depend on each firm's specific goals and campaign objectives for a given period.

Marketing Implementation RoI

With an understanding of marketing analytics measurement framework, we would now cover the most important part of any marketing review exercise, which is to determine the final RoI (Return on Investment) from all of the marketing activities (combined together) to assess how much of this effort has resulted in actual tangible sales for the firm.

To understand how marketing RoI can be calculated, we have developed a marketing RoI model for a typical small-medium e-commerce company, on the types of marketing channel expenses such firms run and the typical marketing impact and RoI they receive from their efforts. We have based this model on one of the most widely used marketing RoI models as developed by the Lenskold group in their *CMO Guide to Marketing RoI*.

Table 8.2 Marketing Analytics Measurement Framework

REAN Funnel		Owned Media		Earned Media		Paid Media	
Plan	Count/ Return	Research on Historical Counts and Typical Return Metrics (Value, RoI, etc.) Defining Measurement Process and Targets for Count and Return Across the Three Digital Media Types					
Plan	Quality/ Connect	Research on Historical Quality and Connect Metrics Defining Measurement Process and Target Index for Quality and Connect Across the Three Digital Media Types					
		Website	**Content**	**Trade**	**Social**	**Advertising**	**Partner**
Reach Quantitative	Count	Total Visitors	Site Pages Viewed	Trade Mentions	Social Mentions	Impressions	Partnerships
		Unique Visitors	Blog Views	Article Views	Total Tweets	Target Reach	Brand Views
	Return	Unique Visitor Value	Web Content RoI	Mention Value	Social Value	Impression ROI	Partnership ROI
		Total Visitor Value	Blog RoI	Article Value	Tweets Value	Reach ROI	Brand ROI
Qualitative	Quality	Visitor Quality	Page Engagement	Mentions Quality	Social Quality	Reach Quality	Partner Quality
	Connect	Visitor Connect Index	Blog Connect Index	Trade CI	Twitter CI	Impressions CI	Brand CI
Engage Quantitative	Count	Total Leads	E-mails Opened	Analyst Listings	Channel Visits	Brand Search	Coupon Clicks
		Leads Per Category	Webinar/Video Views	Paper Downloads	Posts Clicks	Clicks	Downloads
	Return	Category Lead Value	E-mail RoI	Listings Value	Channel Value	Search RoI	Coupon RoI
		Total Leads Value	Webinar RoI	Whitepaper ROI	Posts Value	Clicks RoI	Downloads RoI
Qualitative	Quality	Lead Quality	E-mail Engagement	Listings Quality	Channel Quality	Click Quality	Coupon Quality
	Connect	Lead Connect Index	Video Connect Index	Whitepaper CI	Posts CI	Search CI	Download CI
Activate Quantitative	Count	Total Customers	Content Downloads	Visits From Trade	Social Carts	Contact Request	Redemptions
		Buys Per Category	Content Based Buys	Trade Based Buys	Hashtag Buys	Target Actions	Referrals
	Return	Customer Value	Content Download RoI	Trade Visits Value	Social Value	Actions ROI	Redemption ROI
		Buy Value	Content Based Buy RoI	Trade Buys Value	Hashtag Value	Ads RoI	Referrals ROI
Qualitative	Quality	Customer Quality	Download Quality	Visits Quality	Hashtag Quality	Ads Quality	Referral Quality
	Connect	Buy Category CI	Content buy CI	Trade Buys CI	Hashtag CI	Actions CI	Referral CI

Let us now understand each of the rows in the marketing RoI calculation table (see Table. 8.3).

The key marketing expense areas are listed on the left side of Table 8.3 and the calculations for marketing impact and RoI on the right side. The key elements of marketing channel expenses include:

- Marketing expenses have been sub-divided across owned and paid channels (earned channel expenses have been included as a part of the resource expense, as there is minimal capital expense involved for managing earned channels). Key expense areas for each of the owned and paid channels have been showcased in Table 8.3 in detail.
- Tools expenses relate to costs incurred towards buying and licensing online marketing tools (for example, automation, research, analytics).
- Resource expenses paid towards in-house and contract resources (typically calculated in terms of salaries for full-time resources and man hours for part-time effort).
- Apart from the expenses mentioned here, to calculate the total investment, we also need to add the overall costs of goods sold to each of the above categories.

Total Expense = Cost of Channels (Owned + Paid) & Expenses (Tools + Resource + COGS)

On the marketing impact calculation side, we first need to calculate the incremental revenue from all marketing activities (number of customers x sale per customer). For a typical small–medium size e-commerce company, we have taken the example in which a company has targeted a reach of 40 lakh visitors to its website. We then share typical numbers achieved across each stage of the funnel from web visit to information download, to contacting the company, asking for a product trial and, finally, getting converted to a customer.

To calculate the sale per customer, the firm needs to calculate NPV (Net Present Value) per new sale which is shown as a hypothetical number of ₹750. Once the total incremental revenue is calculated, the next step is to calculate profit from sales (which is incremental revenue × average gross margin%). Finally, net profit is calculated as Profit From Sales (Total Investment).

The overall marketing RoI is thus calculated in percentage as RETURN (NET PROFIT)/ TOTAL INVESTMENT which in this case comes out as 14.5 per cent.

This particular example calculates the overall marketing RoI for all marketing activities of the firm. We can also calculate Marketing RoI at each stage of the funnel separately and a similar exercise can be accomplished for each of the different marketing activities enlisted on the left-hand side of the table. This helps marketers keep a track of the RoI for each investment made and track the resulting marketing impact across the funnel for the best possible assessment.

Digital Marketing Refinement Phase

In the five parts of this chapter on digital marketing execution, we have discussed all stages right from planning to final execution, monitoring and refinement of key digital marketing types. Although we have covered the refinement aspect of each of the multiple types of marketing

Table 8.3 Marketing RoI Calculation Table

Expense Areas			Marketing Impact		
Marketing Channel Expenses		**Cost (in ₹)**	**Marketing Impact Calculation**		**RoI (in ₹)**
Owned Channels	Website Development (Development, Database, Hosting, etc.) and SEO			Target Reach	**40,00,000**
	Mobile Apps/External Platforms Development/ Social Landing Pages	₹ **3,70,000**	Target Reached at Each Stage	Web visit or inquiry (50%)	**20,00,000**
	Content Development Costs (Web, Blogs, Video, Webinars, etc.)			Information Downloaded (70%)	**14,00,000**
Paid Channels	Campaign Development Costs (Design, Content, Tool License, Testing, etc.)			Company Contacted (50%)	**7,00,000**
	Advertising (SEM, Display, E-mail, Platforms, Social Media, etc.)			Product/Service Trial (30%)	**2,10,000**
	Sponsorships (Online PR, Trade Sites, Vertical B2B Sites, Analyst Listings)	₹ **6,45,000**		Customer Converted (30%)	**63,000**
	Partner Marketing (Affiliates, Data Aggregators, Loyalty Sites, etc.)		Number of Customers	1.5% of Targeted Reach	**63,000**
	Direct Response Mediums (Call Center Management, Chat, Forums, etc.)		Net Present Value Per Sale	₹ 750 taken an example value	**750**
Tools Expense	Costs Incurred Towards Buying and Licensing Online Marketing Tools (e.g., Automation, Research, Analytics)	₹ **7,20,000**	Incremental Revenue	No. of Customers (63000) × Sale Per Customer (750)	₹ **4,72,50,000**
Resource Expense	All Expenses Paid Towards In-House and Contract Resource Man Hours	₹ **28,35,000**	Average Gross Margin%	Typical AGM% based on regular SG and A structure	**26%**
Cost of Goods Sold	Includes Costs of All the Goods Sold (Design, Manufacturing, Logistics, etc.)	₹ **61,53,000**	Profit From Incremental Sales	Incremental Revenue × Average Gross Margin%	₹ **1,22,85,000**
Total Investment	Total Cost of Channels (Owned + Paid) and Expenses (Tools + Resource + COGS)	₹ **1,07,23,000**	Net Profit	Profit From Sales (Total Investment)	₹ **1,22,85,000** ₹ **1,07,23,000** ₹ **15,62,000**
Overall Marketing RoI = Return (Net Profit)/Total Investment = (15,62,000/1,07,23,000)% = 14.57%					

campaigns in detail earlier, we shall close this last section by introducing the refinement process model which also forms the final stage of the 'ASCOR Digital Marketing Framework' introduced in the first chapter.

We will base our refinement process model on the Web Metrics Lifecycle Process as shared by Avinash Kaushik in his book *Web Analytics 2.0*, which essentially represents the five key steps integral to any campaign refinement process. These five steps include:

- Define
- Measure
- Analyze
- Action
- Improve or eliminate

Let us understand each of these steps in more detail:

- **Define:** It refers to defining key activities and metrics for each of the marketing campaign activities to be tracked, measured, and refined to obtain an overall picture of digital marketing campaign execution.
- **Measure:** It involves developing the marketing analytics measurement framework on the lines shared in the second section of this part to develop funnel-based quantitative and qualitative metrics for analysis.
- **Analyze:** This third step involves analyzing the overall metrics obtained to understand whether we are achieving the tactical and strategic objectives set out initially for the campaign and the typical actions involved for any recourse or changes.
- **Action:** It is the actual refinement stage wherein changes are made to key campaign targeting values and multiple optimizations and testing are conducted to improve the path taken to help deliver on finalized business objectives.
- **Improve or eliminate:** This final stage involves taking a call on the steps to move post-refinement attempts to assess whether we are witnessing necessary improvements with the refinements executed or if we need to eliminate some steps and actions.

These five refinement process steps form the part of the final digital marketing refinement stage of the ASCOR model. In the next chapter, we will focus on the elements which help support and execute these digital campaigns and the key issues involved.

PRACTICAL EXERCISE

Executing Paid Promotions

Key Objective To understand key paid media channels, platforms, and content types, along with executing multiple types of paid advertising.

Project Brief You are the marketing manager owning a portfolio of brands across major FMCG categories. You are required to develop a digital promotional spend plan.

Which paid media channels and platforms will you consider for your advertising budget? How would you ensure right channel selection? What are the major key performance indicators (KPIs) you would track to measure Return on Investment (ROI)? How would you select the right online inventory and bid price across multiple advertising tools available across the ecosystem? Execute appropriate due diligence and develop a media plan based on your research and observations.

Execution In the following discussion, we will review key channel, platform, and content options that you can review to develop the paid promotions plan:

(a) **Channel-Based Promotions:** The bulk of paid online promotions are executed via digital channels. Paid media teams should gauge their target audience to decide the impact and relevance of each channel to decide the right mix for their budget. There is a good mix of direct pay ads (where inventory is guaranteed based on the amount spent) versus auction-based ads (where the highest bidder gets to show the ad). Most important channel-based promotion types include:

- Search Advertising (Text Ads, Image Ads, Shopping Ads, etc.)
- Display Advertising (Banner, Rich Media, Retargeting, etc.)
- Social Media Advertising (Domain Ads, Lead Ads, Carousel Ads.)
- Email Advertising
- Affiliate Advertising
- Native Advertising

(b) **Platform-Based Promotions:** With the advent of strong adoption of mobile as a consumer platform, multiple advertising options have emerged across mobile platform which are quite distinct from web-only promotions. Major examples of mobile-based promotions include:

- Mobile Website Ads
- Mobile Application Ads
- In-Game Ads
- SMS/MMS Ads
- Location-Based Ads

(c) **Format-Based Promotions:** This involves promoting through multiple media types including the following formats:

- Video Ads
- Audio Ads
- Voice Ads
- Infographic Ads

(d) **Content-Specific Promotions:** Another important type of digital promotion includes those driven through content promotion. The key among them are:

- Press Release Articles
- Promoted Recommendations

- Sponsored Headlines
- Sponsored Content/articles/posts
- In-Text Promotions

While it is not difficult to gain incremental followers, leads, and conversions through multiple promotional bursts, it is far more difficult to understand overall consumer engagement patterns for ads beamed across multiple channels and platforms. It is important to identify the most appropriate channel for each strategic and tactical objective for any brand to ensure we as marketers optimize spend and turn advertising returns more effective with each campaign. With click frauds and robotic impressions becoming a common feature across digital advertising, marketers need to exercise caution and execute thorough due diligence to ensure the true impact of ad spend. Do spend some time to review and share areas of potential advertising budget leakage, which happens across your chosen promotional platforms.

CHAPTER SUMMARY

- **Part 1**: In the first part we learnt about the seven key stages of setting up a digital marketing campaign. These include campaign plan, budget, set-up, launch, monitor, fine-tune, and reconciliation. In the next three sections we delved deeper into each of the seven stages to be familiar with the key activities involved in execution.
- **Part 2**: This part covered the basics of implementing intent-based campaigns, broadly known as search campaigns. In the first section we learnt about the basic difference between pay-per-click marketing (PPC) and search engine marketing (SEM), followed by the coverage of key SEM aspects. The next section covered SEM campaign set-up and execution steps in detail, including strategies for successful SEM campaigns. The third section started with a basic understanding of Search Engine Optimization (SEO) concepts and detailed the two types of SEO: on-page and off-page optimization.
- **Part 3**: In the next part of the chapter we became acquainted with brand-based campaigns (display execution), beginning with the basics of display campaign management to understand key players, their roles and objectives. This was followed by an understanding of display inventory classification and standard display campaign workflow stages. In the next section we looked at the classification of emerging data-driven display models (programmatic and RTB), their workflow, and campaign process in detail. We also learnt about rich media campaign management and its key stages in detail.
- **Part 4**: In the fourth part of the chapter we understood the process of campaign execution for emerging marketing models, starting with an understanding of content marketing (which forms the cornerstone of other marketing types). The key emerging channels covered include social media, partner, communication, and platform-based marketing. We

became familiar with the key stages of campaign management including planning, set-up, execution, tracking, and refinement each of the emerging market types.

- **Part 5**: Finally, in the last part of the chapter we learnt about campaign analytics and marketing RoI in detail starting from how web analytics has moved to its 2.0 version to the development of a marketing analytics measurement framework that helps generate quantitative and qualitative analytics for all three digital media types (owned, earned, and paid). Next we understood how marketing RoI (Return on Investment) is typically calculated for all the marketing campaigns run by any firm. The last section of the chapter ended with discussing the five steps which showcase how campaigns are refined and mapped to the refinement stage of the ASCOR digital marketing framework.

REVIEW QUESTIONS

1. What is Campaign Management? Explain the seven stages of setting up a marketing campaign for any mix of channels.
2. What is campaign planning and budgeting? Describe the key activities for any one of these.
3. List the key activities involved in campaign set up and launch. What is meant by campaign trafficking?
4. Explain the key elements involved in the stages beginning from campaign monitoring to reconciliation.
5. What is the key difference between Pay-Per-Click Marketing and Search Engine Marketing?
6. What are the key elements of planning for any SEM campaign?
7. Explain the following terms:
   (a) Keyword
   (b) Search Query
   (c) Campaign
   (d) Ad Group
8. Explain the difference between Exact Match, Phrase Match, Broad Match, and Negative Match?
9. What are the three key parts of a text ad? What are the key guidelines to be taken care of while creating an effective text ad?
10. Explain the following terms in detail:
    (a) Click-Through Rate
    (b) Quality Score
    (c) Campaign Bid
    (d) Ad Rank
11. Explain the differences between pre campaign launch, campaign launch and post campaign launch. Pick up any one of these three stages and explain that stage in detail.
12. What are the six key stages of successful SEM campaigns? Explain any two of them in detail.
13. From the section on SEO Management, explain the difference between:
    (a) White-Hat and Black-Hat SEO
    (b) On-Page and Off-Page Optimization
14. Detail the key impact parameters of On-Page and Off-Page Optimization. Explain any one On-Page and Off-Page Optimization Impact parameter in detail.

15. Name the four types of display ad formats and four key stakeholders of display campaign management. Detail the key roles and objectives of any one of these stakeholders.
16. What are the two key classifying parameters for display inventory sales? Further, describe the two key means of manual sales: Premium (Guaranteed) and Remnant (Non-Guaranteed) Inventory.
17. Explain the key advantages of each of the two manual inventory sales types for either advertisers or publishers.
18. What are the four key stages of a standard display campaign workflow? Pick any one to elaborate in detail.
19. What are the key classification parameters for programmatic display inventory sales? Name the four programmatic sales models and explain them in brief.
20. Explain the four key attributes that differentiate a real-time bidding campaign from the traditional types of display buying.
21. Describe the key interactions and activities shared in the Display RTB Campaign Process diagram in the chapter.
22. What do you understand by rich media advertising. Explain in brief the key stages of rich media ad campaign management.
23. What is content marketing? What are the key stages to set up and successfully execute a content marketing plan? Explain any two of those stages in detail.
24. What are community-based campaigns? Explain the key campaign stages for social media execution in brief.
25. What is the difference between partner, communication and platform based marketing. Pick any one of these three campaign types to elaborate their stages in detail.
26. What is the difference between a metric and a key performance indicator (KPI)? Describe some of the key web metrics mentioned in the chapter.
27. Explain the primary parameters of quantitative and qualitative analytics as discussed in the Marketing Analytics Measurement Framework.
28. From the Marketing RoI Calculation Table, explain the key elements of marketing channel expenses.
29. Explain in brief the five steps integral to any campaign refinement process.

DIGITAL APPLICATION EXERCISES

1. Given an example of any of the five campaign marketing types (from the chapter) which you would have seen any brand utilize in India. Can you compare and contrast any two of them?
2. IPL (Indian Premier League), the T-20 cricket league in India, has been one of the hottest TV properties on TV for over a decade now. Revisit any one of the past nine years of IPL and lay down, in brief, the seven stages of setting up of campaigns (owned/paid/earned) for that year.
3. Similar to the online watch portal example *Xquisite* in the chapter, select any category and create a fictitious brand to

explain the basics of Search Campaign Set-up. You can visit any of the top keyword planner tools to generate, compare, and create your ad groups and keywords.

4. Personal insurance is supposedly a boring category to develop an advertisement. Type the keywords 'Personal Insurance' in Google and compare amongst the top two ads you see in the search results page. What differences do you observe in positioning and which one did you feel was better?
5. Pick up the website name of any two top mobile brands you like and conduct an SEO audit (with any of the freely available *audit sites*) on *key On-Page and* Off-Page impact parameters shared in the chapter. Note and present your key observations.
6. You are the marketing manager of an expensive car brand in India. Go to your Google AdWords account and through the display planner search for the top placement ideas on which you would want to run a display campaign. List the placements you decided as:
   (a) Top five websites
   (b) Top five mobile sites
   (c) Top five Youtube videos
7. Follow any latest brand campaign on TV to compare the types of content marketing it engages on multiple channels/platforms. Do you see that the messaging differs according to the media? If yes how?
8. Reliance has recently launched its 4G mobile brand Jio with much fanfare and advertising spend. Can you compare and contrast its digital marketing efforts on five key social media channels? What were your key observations on:
   (a) Social media goals
   (b) Social media strategy
   (c) Social media messaging
   (d) Campaign execution
   (e) Campaign feedback
9. Choose any one example each of partner, communication, and platform-based marketing in India. Explain the stages of campaign development for any one of the chosen examples.
10. For the chosen fictitious brand in question 3 in the Digital Exercise (above) create the Marketing Analytics Measurement Framework table (as in the chapter) based on your understanding of the brand measurement needs. Share you key observations while developing the measurement framework.

CHAPTER 9

Digital Marketing Execution Elements

LEARNING OBJECTIVES

After studying this chapter, you will be able to:

- Describe the types of revenue generation models and explain the importance and four pillars of customer loyalty management
- Understand the concepts of DRIP marketing and the five-step plan for engaging in successful advocate marketing
- Explain management of electronic payment systems and digital payment solutions along-with gaining knowledge of how firms are managing digital e-services and selling through cybermediaries
- Understand the challenges of e-commerce implementation which include internal, external and consumer specific challenges

CASE STUDY Info Edge India: *Betting on Investments for Growth*

The last half-decade has seen a tremendous rise in Internet users in India. From around 422 million internet users in 2017 to 845 million in 2021, India has been the biggest market for internet companies. This rise in users has surely helped internet companies like Info Edge India to grow rapidly. Info Edge, the parent company of Naukri (jobs portal), Jeevansathi (marriage portal), 99 acres (real estate portal), and Shiksha (education portal), has witnessed great growth since 2017, which is visible in the fact that the standalone revenues of Info Edge India were ₹8,021 million in 2017, which increased to ₹10,986 million in 2021.

Naukri.com had the highest share of revenues across Info Edge India. In the last 5 years, Naukri.com's share of Internet traffic has increased from 70 per cent in March'17 to 75 per cent in March'21. Interestingly, Naukri.com is making its highest revenues (90 per cent of the total revenue) from recruiters rather than job seekers (10 per cent of revenue). But with the COVID-19 pandemic hit, hiring activities across sectors became highly affected. However, Naukri had been the only profitable venture until the third quarter of FY21, as it saw increased demand for work from-home jobs (both from recruiters as well as job seekers) that grew four-to-five times on their platform during the pandemic.

The second platform that contributed the highest across Info Edge revenue is 99 acres. The overall traffic share of 99 acres was 39 per cent in March 2017, which remained the same in March 2021 as well. This platform was also negatively impacted by pandemic, but Info Edge focused on re-organisation of the product and opted a city-wise approach for marketing, which helped 99 acres maintain its traffic share. In terms of traffic share, 99 acres is still the market leader, but their share dropped from 50 per cent to 40 per cent due to intense competition from platforms like MagicBricks, Housing.com and NoBroker.

Even Jeevansathi (their 3rd largest platform) was majorly hit by the pandemic. However, in FY2021, this matrimonial site experienced growth with features like video profiles, video/audio calling, video-based events and AI/ML recommendations. These initiatives helped Jeevansathi grab hold of the Tier II and Tier III market with a growth of 21 per cent in profits. One of the key reasons behind the growth of matrimonial sites was that majority of the youth population were working from home and had nowhere to go due to lockdown, with ample time at hand. That time was utilised in looking for partners online and shortlisting profiles which might not have been possible earlier, due to a hectic professional life or other commitments which made them consider putting off marriage.

Apart from its business verticals, a special mention must be made of the company's investment in Zomato and Policy Bazaar. During the pandemic, the bet on Zomato proved to be a good investment for Info Edge. From a share price of ₹803 in August 2010 to ₹3,00,235 in Feb 2021, Info Edge got an amazing return on their investment. However, Info Edge sold 2.32 per cent of its stake (July 2021) and continued with a 15.23 per cent share in Zomato. Though Zomato is a jewel in Info Edge's portfolio, due to Zomato's stock price plummeting 45 per cent in the first quarter of 2022, the value of its stock went down from ₹20,190 crore to ₹11,032 crore.

As for Policy Bazaar, Info Edge holds 13.98 per cent stake (as of FY2021) in a company where it invested ₹5758 million. Info Edge has also invested in various companies including Adda, Unbox Robotics, Shop Kirana, Shipsy, Broker Network, Lumiq, Coding Ninjas, and a few more.

The overall growth of Info Edge's business verticals was slowed down with the pandemic hit having a major effect on this internet company. Regardless, the company has been able to hold on without high losses. In 2022, Info Edge is worth almost US$10 billion even while its profits have fallen for five quarters in a row. It will be interesting to see how Info Edge manages to accelerate revenue across other verticals (apart from Naukri.com) and witness increasing returns from Zomato and Policy Bazaar as they move ahead post the pandemic.

In Chapter 8, we developed an understanding of the fourth phase of ASCOR digital marketing framework to understand the key elements of digital marketing operations phase and covered campaign execution stages for all types of digital marketing, including intent, brand, content, community, partner, communication, and platform-based marketing types. The last section of the chapter covered marketing RoI and refinement which is the final phase of the ASCOR framework and showcased how marketers can make sense of their analytics and investments through a structured approach to marketing returns and refinement for future campaigns.

This chapter covers all allied execution aspects crucial to digital marketing execution but not specific to campaign management. The first section covers different digital revenue generation models, which marketers utilize to generate revenues from their digital investments, also explaining the ways by which marketers keep the revenue pipeline steady and are able to gradually transform their customers from being one-time buyers to loyalists and, finally, advocates. The next section describes the elements of managing digital delivery and services and also looks at the emerging forms of payment. The third section discusses about key internal, external, and consumer-specific implementation challenges which are becoming crucial for marketers to know and prepare for in advance.

MANAGING DIGITAL MARKETING REVENUE

Digital Revenue Generation Models

As discussed earlier in Chapter 5, section titled, 'Offering Mix for Digital,' firms deploying digital marketing typically fall in one of the five product-service states. For a company in any of these five states, it is crucial that they earn revenue on the digital platform be it a pure play offline product company which is planning to launch pure tangible goods online, or a pure services only firm which only has digital services to offer, or even a firm which has a hybrid model and is planning to generate revenue from the sale of digitized products which have a good tangible and intangible mix.

In Fig. 9.1, we have categorized digital revenue generation models into four broader categories which can be elaborated as follows:

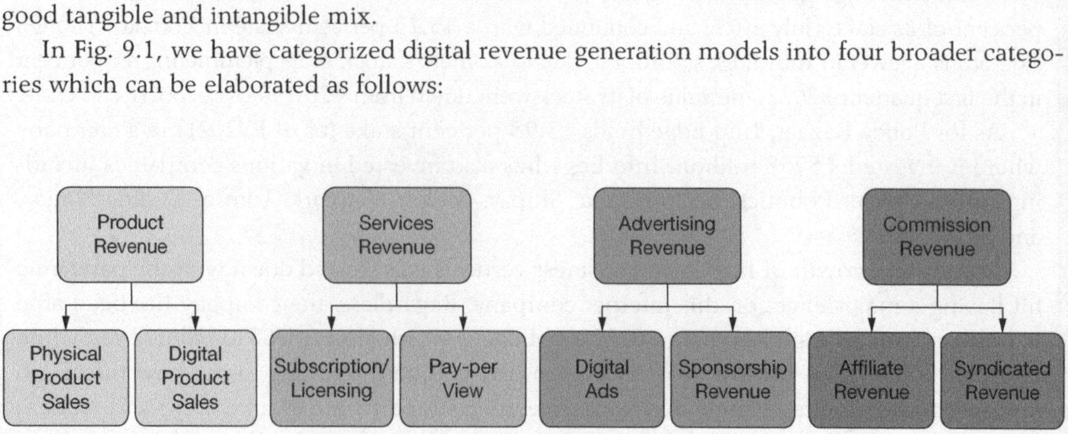

Figure 9.1 Digital Revenue Generation Models

Product Revenue Model

These models generate revenue primarily from direct sale of physical/digital products (or any related information/data) which happens more as a one-time payment exercise. Direct trade or e-commerce companies are the best examples as their proprietors use digital marketing to:

- Create a new channel to sell products for which they already have a broader market in the physical world
- Increase awareness of their products to present a set of customers already available online
- Compete against top competitors present online, in their specific categories
- Sell digital products with a direct payment model
- Sell information/data/market research as one-time-buy reports

Services Revenue Model

This model involves selling in a recurring fashion and generally includes the following two types:

- Subscription/licensing: Both the terms refer to a business model wherein consumer pays a recurring subscription to get access to a certain service for a specific period of time. In typical subscription models, the user does not own the product but is getting a period-based window to that specific service on certain pre-decided payment models. Another form of subscription is the licensing of software products. The best and most common example is the worldwide usage of Microsoft Office, whereby users have to pay for a period-based license to access online applications like Word, Excel, PowerPoint, etc.
- Pay-Per view: In this upcoming model on digital content revenue generation, certain pages/chapters of a digitized book can be accessed for an à la carte price. We have already covered aspects of such a model in detail in Chapter 2, sections titled, 'Value Chain Elaboration: Case of Journal Publishing' and 'Emergence of Digitized Value Chain,' and explained the emergence of a digitized value chain.

Advertising Revenue Model

One of the most commonly talked about and discussed online revenue models is that of advertising (which includes most of the multiple digital advertising types we have already covered in the preceding chapter) and the sponsorship revenue model (which has helped sustain a large number of small and medium digital enterprises over the past twenty years). Although not as big in terms of the revenue it generates for an enterprise moving online, it is still one of the most dependable models for any firm to start earning initial revenue.

Commission-Based Revenue Mode

This type of model is typically adopted by companies which are affiliate networks and helps provide leads to bigger online companies in lieu of specified pre-decided commissions. Another revenue model, which is also close to this type, includes examples of companies which generate revenue by syndicating content across multiple channels and gaining a cut of the revenues (earned by other companies) from utilizing that content in various forms.

With an understanding of the four major types of digital revenue generation models, we will now look at how companies create a loyal stream of customers to keep generating continual revenue and converting them into future advocates for a firm's multiple lines of products and services.

Customer Loyalty Management in the Digital Era

Managing customers and converting them into loyalists has been one of the most critical objectives for any business to earn recurring revenues. According to Stuart Evans (2007), in one of his articles, he defined *Loyalty Marketing* as an approach in which a company focuses on growing and retaining existing customers through incentives. Rajat Paharia, in his book *Loyalty 3.0,* has shared the three stages of loyalty evolution as below:

(a) **Loyalty 1.0**: It included programs that were purely transactional, completely focused on customers, and were failures at generating the kind of loyalties that businesses really wanted. The critical flaw with these programs was the long wait for any kind of loyalty program to turn into fruition.

(b) **Loyalty 2.0**: In the 1990s the concept converted into a one-to-one marketing approach, which focused on making the loyalty experience more targeted through segmentation and personalization, emphasizing largely on direct mail and e-mail campaigns. The effectiveness of this approach, however, diminished as open rates plummeted and consumers were overwhelmed by the sheer amount of noise.

(c) **Loyalty 3.0**: According to the book, there are three key enabling components which have helped the development of Loyalty 3.0:

- **Motivation**: It refers to understanding what compels and motivates human behavior to create stronger engagement and true loyalty.
- **Big data**: It denotes gathering and consuming large amounts of data generated through technology to understand, engage, and motivate consumers.
- **Gamification**: It involves utilizing gaming techniques for data-driven motivation, which can be a powerful tool to drive engagement, participation, and high-value activity for firm's customers, employees, and partners.

Mckinsey & Company, in their whitepaper titled, 'The New Era of Customer Loyalty Management' have outlined the following three key opportunities for firms to implement in the area of loyalty management:

- **Managing customer migration, not defection**: Migration is a powerful leading indicator that allows early corrective action for companies to manage customers who are increasing their spending. Its value is more than 10 times that of defection.
- **Integrating attitudes, needs, and satisfaction to understand drivers of migration**: Tracking customer satisfaction alone is not sufficient and is often misleading. But when

combined with two other factors—loyalty attitudes (that is, emotive, deliberative, or inertial) and needs and discretion—it can play an important role.

- **Tailoring investments and loyalty approaches to most critical parts of the opportunity**: Capturing the opportunity is usually based on addressing one or more of the following five levers:
  - Pursuing customers actively choosing to go or stay
  - Building 'emotiveness' into the customer base
  - Making it easier for customers to stay, harder to go
  - Reducing or eliminating sources of dissatisfaction
  - Focusing on customers' changing needs

To make the most of these new changes, driving customer loyalty management in present times, marketers (according to a whitepaper on Customer Loyalty Management by TIBCO) can look at the following as the four pillars of customer loyalty management in the digital era:

(a) **Combining traditional loyalty with new programs**: Maritz, which is the leader in loyalty programs, in its 2013 Maritz Loyalty Report has stated that "71 per cent of (loyalty program) members would join more loyalty programs, even though the average member is already enrolled in 7.4 programs." This shows that traditional loyalty programs are still the best bet across the industry to develop a first hook with the customer, be it loyalty cards or e-commerce-specific coupons fetching reward points for each consumer activity in the online cart. Traditional loyalty data, once available, can help increase data capture opportunities and connect to 'private' event streams to provide better insights into recognition and reward.

(b) **Blending wider event streams**: It refers to an ability to capture wider set of impactful events and recognize patterns which impact consumer involvement to help respond with the most engaging ideas. Gartner's Kimberly Collins in his article, 'Consider Automating These Top 12 Marketing Processes in 2013,' has shared that "By 2016, marketing organizations that leverage big data for micro-segmentation and targeting will achieve response rates of 70 per cent or higher." Typical event streams mentioned in the TIBCO whitepaper include:

- Controlled digital touchpoints like websites, e-mail, apps, messages, signage, and kiosks
- Influenced digital touchpoints like social platforms, hosted campaigns, and partnerships
- Non-digital touchpoints, because even when we engage face-to-face, our experiences are heavily influenced by digital channels and capabilities
- Social ecosystem and the way we connect to the world through our 'network of networks'
- Supply chain with its many points of demand–chain integration

(c) **Marketing-driven relationship management**: The latest trend in loyalty management (which will be covered in detail in the next section) is that of relationship marketing, which as Mari Smith claimed in her book, on *The New Relationship Marketing*, is a blend of the offline and online worlds. Relationship marketing emphasizes on the ability to continually balance the supply of offers with aligned customer demand as the best path possible for customer retention. Astute marketers can utilize relationship marketing models to form specific consumer connections for their multiple brands and products by identifying propensities, patterns, and correlations from past behaviors and marrying them with customer lifecycles and ideal purchase patterns on a segment-by-segment basis.

(d) **Test and learn (empowering creativity)**: The test and learn mechanism involves measuring analytics to determine changes in performance with small but statistically relevant sample sizes. It also involves predictive analytics, which helps measure costs relative to budget and predict impact confidently. This goes to show how scientific insights combined with marketer's creativity can help engage and create the most satisfied set of loyal customers.

Rise of Relationship Marketing: Turning Loyalists to Advocates

With an understanding of how loyalty management as a function is shifting in the digital era, in this section, we shall look at the emergence of relationship marketing and how firms need to convert loyalists into advocates to further their cause of increased revenues and customer satisfaction. Relationship marketing as a concept was shared by Christopher (et al. 1991) which, according to him, recognizes that the focus of marketing is to change from making a single transaction to moving on to the next customer, hence, building a relationship with existing customers. He proposed that the objective of relationship marketing is to turn new customers into regularly purchasing clients, and then to progressively move them to become strong supporters of the company (and its product) to finally being active and vocal advocates for the company.

The key differences between transaction marketing and relationship marketing are listed below (Jackson, 1985):

- *Transaction marketing*: Attracting customers using offensive strategies, for example, encouragement of brand switching; recruiting dissatisfied customers of competitors.
- *Relationship marketing*: Retaining customers using defensive strategies, for example, minimizing customer turnover, maximizing customer retention.

To make the concept clear, we will take up the 'Ladder of Customer Loyalty' which Christopher (et al. 2002) presented to showcase the six key stages which a relationship manager can utilize to help advance relationships up the ladder.

Figure 9.2 showcases the ascending order of the six stages of relationship marketing which can be explained as follows:

- **Prospect**: A prospect is one who pays attention to a firm's promotion and might be persuaded to buy its products.
- **Purchaser**: A purchaser is a person who has recently bought from the firm or executed any business transaction.

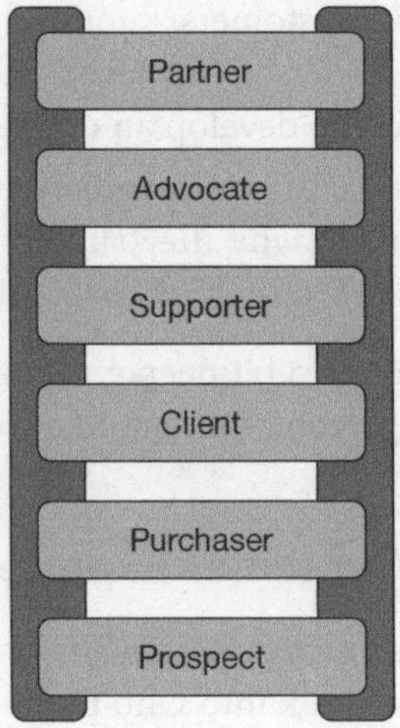

Figure 9.2 Ladder of Customer Loyalty

- **Client**: A client is one who has done business more than once with the firm but his disposition or engagement status with the firm is not necessarily positive.
- **Supporter**: A supporter is a client who has positive disposition towards the firm but might not be actively engaged with the firm's activities.
- **Advocate**: An advocate is a person who is deeply involved with an organization and also influences others through positive word-of-mouth communication.
- **Partner**: A partner is a client who is working together with the firm for mutual benefit and has a stake in its growth.

Relationship marketing essentially involves knowing each of the firm's customers, their environment, and present relationship with the brand, and most of this is not a single task. For continuous engagement and to take the prospects up the ladder to the advocate level, Chris Fill (2002) suggested a technique known as DRIP marketing, wherein with the help of four kinds of communication on a regular basis, firms can keep strengthening their relationships with clients. DRIP is an acronym for Differentiate, Reinforce, Inform, and Persuade, which also are the four communication techniques through which marketers can drive their relationship marketing agenda. Let us look at each of these in more detail:

(a) **Differentiate**: It helps channel members understand how a manufacturer or a specific product adds value and is different from the competitors and other products that they carry. The best example would be a toothpaste brand like Sensodyne, putting forth teeth 'Repair and Protect' as a differentiating theme from market leader Colgate.

(b) **Reinforce**: It involves reminding downstream members regularly about their needs, problems, and how the brand is working hard on their behalf to provide them with unique product features and benefits. For example, Bournvita, reinforces mothers regularly by telling them that their product is the best for child's overall growth.

(c) **Inform**: This includes keeping customers informed about multiple brand facets, new initiatives undertaken, market leadership achieved, etc., so that prospects themselves feel as owners of brand growth, thereby develop an urge to advocate the products proactively.

(d) **Persuade**: It involves persuading customers regularly to have a look at the features of the product or give specific reasons on why they should buy more or carry extra stock with themselves (which could include long-term benefits/discounts).

In the last section of this part, we will go a bit deeper to understand how brands can drive new digital revenues through higher engagement with brand advocates.

Driving Advocates through Customer Experience

With an understanding of the ladder of customer loyalty, in this last section on digital revenue management, we would take a deeper look into who the advocates are and how loyal customers can be turned to brand advocates whose interactions can lead to new revenues through positive word-of-mouth and proactive reach-out to communities they are a part of. Customer advocacy here should not be confused with a similar coinage which involves the latest trend of marketers helping prospects become customers by guiding their buying process and advocating for their real benefit, hence, in the process, earning their trust. Rather, it refers to utilizing the power of customers, partners, employees, and key stakeholders to gather public support, endorse, or recommend a company, its products, and its services. According to TapInfluence (It is the name of a firm), which is a marketplace of social media influencers, *advocate marketing* differs from *influencer marketing* as marketing through influencers is more around partnering with individuals who have a significant influence and audience, while advocate marketing attempts to engage advocates to support sales and marketing objectives by sharing their positive experiences.

According to Influitive, which is one of the top B2B advocate marketing software firms, any company looking to improve its lead generation process to get newer customers would need to involve dedicated advocates of all types to improve conversions and earn higher revenue. In one of the whitepapers they explained that of all the leads sources, referral leads generally generate the highest conversions. Hence, on an average, leads generated by B2B advocates are 4 to 10 times more valuable than regular leads, resulting in shorter sales cycles, increased win rates, and larger order sizes. Apart from revenue, advocates can also support a firm's intangible objectives including product design, market positioning, social media initiatives, content marketing, etc.

For any company to engage in successful advocate marketing, Influitive's advocate marketing playbook details the following five key steps:

(a) Developing a strategic plan

(b) Identifying and onboarding advocates

(c) Engaging advocates with campaigns

(d) Recognizing and rewarding advocates

(e) Analyzing and optimizing efforts

Let us closely understand all of the above five stages in more detail:

(a) **Developing a strategic plan**: Development of an advocate marketing program involves deciding on the following key elements:
   - Program objectives: This refers to thinking about key marketing objectives based on a firm's specific goals. Objectives could include increased revenue, customer engagement, brand recognition, etc. Typical end outputs could be references, case studies, testimonials, etc.
   - Developing personas: This involves defining the advocate persona to target.
   - Creating a process: This includes developing the process of running marketing campaigns.
   - Identifying people: This refers to the creation of program owners across the various divisions of the firm which would be responsible for engaging multiple stakeholders. A central marketing committee may also be set up to review the implementation of each of such campaigns.

(b) **Identifying and onboarding advocates**: It is crucial to involve the right advocates as they would be the flag-bearers of the advocacy program and their efforts would count a lot in setting up the basic tone of how engaging the activities would be. To achieve this, we can use the following tactics:
   - Using personalized outreach to invite advocates
   - Developing a program to engage advocates
   - Presenting a clearly defined set of campaigns to them
   - Gathering early feedback to fine-tune engagement
   - Scaling the program to additional advocates and campaigns

(c) **Engaging advocates with campaigns**: Once advocates have been identified and onboarded, it is important to assign the right kind of campaigns to specific advocates to make use of their expertise, experience, and interest for optimal success. Key steps for engaging advocates include:
   - Specifying high-level business and tactical objectives
   - Targeting tasks to specific target segments
   - Engaging with advocates for conversion
   - Using urgency as a tactic to complete conversions
   - Mixing high-value campaigns with the engaging ones to maintain advocate interest

(d) **Recognizing and rewarding advocates**: It is important for companies to have specific rewards and recognition programs for advocates which are not only material based but also have strong intangible components attached. Four levels of rewards and recognition include:
   - Status—Programs should help increase status of advocates. Ideas include putting up advocate names on website, at customer events, mention in content, titles, etc.
   - Access—Special accesses like new feature or version preview, opportunity to buy early event tickets, reserved seating at conferences, etc., should be provided

- Power—This denotes that advocates should have a say in building firm's products, being a peer-mentor to new customers, crafting campaign messages for firm, organizing their events, etc.
- Stuff—Tangible rewards like gift cards, merchandize, office supplies, discounts, and other giveaways of products which the company sells for a price should be shared.

(e) **Analyzing and optimizing efforts**—It refers to quantifying advocate marketing programs through pre-defined metrics that measure their efforts towards attaining objectives like revenue generated, influence created, referrals, converted leads, average revenue per campaign, etc. There are three key types of marketing metrics which can be measured and reviewed:

- Strategic metrics: It looks at business-oriented metrics related to lead generation (peer referred leads), revenue influence, renewals, and upsells.
- Tactical metrics: It includes measurement of the end results generated, for example, references, case studies, reviews, testimonials, recommendations, social shares, etc.
- Operational metrics: It studies the overall efficacy of the advocate marketing program which can be tracked as waterfall metrics, all related to each other across the campaign funnel stages. Metrics are tracked from the starting stage (total advocates signed up), to the middle stage (advocate conversion success rates), and then to the final stage (ongoing engagement rates).

MANAGING SERVICE DELIVERY AND PAYMENT

In the previous part, we studied key digital revenue generation models and how customer loyalty management is advancing to Loyalty 3.0. We then looked at the rise of relationship marketing through the stages of customer Loyalty Ladder and how we can continuously engage with customers through the DRIP model and advocate marketing. In this second part, we would look at the different types of electronic payment systems and understand how firms can set up their service delivery teams to sell through multiple online intermediaries and channels. We will also look at new forms of digital payments which are emerging in the market like Mobile, Digital P2P, Social Media, etc., forms of payments.

Understanding Electronic Payment Systems

Electronic payment systems as a field of study have become important with the recent rise in e-commerce activities taking place on the internet to help conduct faster, secure, and large-scale payments successfully. An electronic payment system, by definition, is a mode of payment that facilitates acceptance of electronic payment primarily for commercial transactions over the internet. Any electronic payment system must involve three key types of stakeholders—the payer (consumer), the payee (business or merchant), a financial network (with which both payer and payee have accounts).

Traditionally, payments used to be made through cash, cheques (using 'clearinghouse' between banks), and Giro (direct credit and debit transfers). But with the advent of internet and electronic transactions, multiple types of new payment models have emerged, the most prominent among them being credit card payments, electronic cash (also known as e-cash), electronic checks, and smart cards. Let us understand all of these four in more details.

(a) **Credit card payment**: Credit card transactions take place over large electronic networks, typically linking cardholders, merchants, card-issuing banks, merchant banks, and credit card companies.

(b) **E-cash**: Credit card transaction fees, typically, make small purchases unprofitable. Electronic cash, which is cash converted into electronic form, improves upon paper cash since the security and privacy features offer more efficient means of cash payments. E-cash, typically, have not been that popular for reasons of lack of standards and interoperable software.

(c) **E-checks**: An e-check is an electronic version of the paper check and is a payment instrument which was developed by a collaboration of several banks, government entities, technology companies, and e-commerce organizations to provide highly secure, speedy, and convenient online transactions.

(d) **Smart cards**: These are plastic cards containing an embedded microchip that contain important financial and personal information which can be periodically recharged and helped with very small transactions.

In their article 'An Analysis and Comparison of Different Types of Electronic Payment Systems,' authors Zon-Yau Lee, Hsiao-Cheng Yu, and Pei-Jen Kuo shared an elaborate comparison of these four electronic payment system types (see Fig. 9.3).

With an understanding of the four global electronic payment system types, we would now look at the key electronic payment and settlement systems in India. The RBI (Reserve Bank of India) has played a key role in making it compulsory for banks to route high value transactions through Real Time Gross Settlement (RTGS) and has also introduced NEFT (National Electronic Funds Transfer) and NECS (National Electronic Clearing Services) which has encouraged individuals and businesses to utilize electronic methods of payment. Let us understand some of these payment methods:

(a) **ECS (Electronic Clearing Service) Credit**: Known as 'Credit-push' facility or one-to-many facility, this method is used for large-value payments where the receiver's account is credited with payment from the institution making the payment.

(b) **ECS (Electronic Clearing Service) Debit**: Known as many-to-one or 'debit-pull' facility, this method is used mainly for small value payments from consumers/individuals to big organizations or companies.

(c) **RTGS (Real Time Gross Settlement)**: It is a funds transfer mechanism where transfer of money takes place from one bank to another on a 'real time' and on 'gross' basis.

Comparison Areas	Credit Card	E-Cash	E-Checks	Smart Card
Payment Time	Paid Later	Prepaid	Paid Later	Prepaid
Transaction Information Transfer	Store and Bank Checks Status	Free Transfer—no Need to Leave Parties Names	E-checks or Payments Must be Endorsed	Smart Card of Both Parties Make Transfer
Online And Offline Transactions	Online Transactions	Online Transactions	Offline Transfers are Allowed	Offline Transfers are Allowed
Bank Account Involvement	Credit Card Account Makes Payment	No Involvement	Bank Account Makes Payment	Smart Card Account Makes Payment
Users	Legitimate Credit Card Users	Anyone	Anyone with a Bank Account	Anyone with a Bank or Credit Card
Party to Which Payment is Made	Distributing Bank	Store	Store	Store
Anonymity	Partially or Entirely Anonymous	Entirely Anonymous	No Anonymity	Entirely Anonymous
Small Payments	Transaction Costs are High—not Suitable for Small Payments	Transaction Costs are Low—not Suitable for Small Payments	Suitable for Small Payments	Transaction Costs are Low—suitable for Small Payments

Figure 9.3 Comparison of Electronic Payment Systems

(d) **NEFT (National Electronic Fund Transfer)**: A nation-wide system that facilitates individuals and firms to electronically transfer funds from a bank branch to any individual or corporate having an account with any other bank branch in the country.

(e) **IMPS (Immediate Payment System)**: It is a service through which money can be transferred immediately from one account to another, within the same bank or accounts across other banks.

Emerging Digital Payments Solutions

In the last section, we understood about electronic payment systems, their key types and comparison among each of them, along with an understanding of major types of electronic payment and settlement systems in India. In this section, we shall look at the emerging forms of payments which are coming to play globally due to the digital advent and the top payment providers driving these changes.

At a fundamental level, there are three important trends which are defining the emerging payments landscape (as shared by American Bankers Association):

(a) **Consumer protection:** Numerous protections have to be offered for consumers while making electronic payments such as protection against unauthorized charges and procedures for disputing any charge.

(b) **Payment system integrity**: Overall stability, efficiency, and integrity of payments system is becoming crucial.

(c) **Competitive equity:** Government policies need to ensure that new entrants and incumbents in the payments area are treated by a similar set of rules and standards.

Let us now look at the major digital payments types which are emerging globally.

Mobile Payments Solutions

According to Juniper Research, annual retail payments on mobile handsets and tablets are expected to reach $ 707 billion by 2018. This shows the future importance and entrenchment of mobile payments. Mobile payment models include:

(a) **SMS payments**: These are text-based payments which have gained currency as one of the most popular methods of making payments through mobile phones.

(b) **NFC payments**: Near Field Communication (NFC) payments are executed through mobile phones that communicate with each other and with other NFC-enabled points of sale, utilizing radio frequency identification.

(c) **WAP payments**: It involves use of Wireless Application Protocol (WAP) facility to make payments through web pages displayed or additional applications downloaded and installed on the mobile phone. WAP payments can be executed through online payment methods such as PayPal, Google Wallet, or Yahoo Wallet, or through credit card details into the payment box of a company's WAP-enabled website.

Digital P2P Payments

P2P payments as a terminology is generally used for two kinds of payments:

(a) **Personal to personal:** It involves technologies which utilize an intermediate for customers to transfer funds from their back accounts/credit cards to another individual's account through internet or a mobile transaction.

(b) **Peer to peer:** This refers to transactions where users can transact directly without needing an intermediary. One of the most popular use of peer-to-peer technologies has been the introduction of the Bitcoin payment system which was invented by Santoshi Nakamoto in 2008. In the Bitcoin system, transactions are verified by network nodes and recorded in a public distributed ledger. The ledger uses its own unit of account, also called bitcoin.

Social Media Payments

Payments through social media platforms in the form of social coupons are rising. There are multiple applications which have come up and are utilizing the power of mobile, peer-to-peer, and other online purchase mechanisms to drive payments across social media platforms. Paypal's Venmo is one of the leaders in this area which is encouraging banks and credit unions in the US to use social engagement for digital peer-to-peer payments.

Apart from the above emerging payment solution areas, other options which are gaining currency include:

- **Digital kiosks**: Companies are setting up service kiosks which are fixed stations with phone connections, where the customer can make payments using a digital screen and keyboard to make transactions.
- **TV set-top boxes**: The future of media involves payments not only though mobile but also across the IOT (Internet of things) ecosystem where smart internet-enabled TVs are the best example.
- **Biometric payments**: These are fingerprint-based payments which have just started getting traction and could become a very secure form of payment transactions in future.

With an understanding of key emerging digital payment solutions type, let us now look at some of the major digital payment gateways in India for e-commerce ventures:

(a) **PayZippy**: Launched by Flipkart, it is a Payment Gateway Service for Indian merchants which helps with online and mobile payments without typing the card number, expiry date, name, or billing address, once the details have already been saved with PayZippy.

(b) **PayU India:** It is a part of Naspers, a $ 25 billion parent, which globally is one of the largest consumer payment processor and provides multiple payment offerings in the form of risk management system, multi-currency gateway, mobile-optimized payment page, IVR payment, store card feature, and payment analytics.

(c) **CC avenue**: It is one of the biggest payment solution providers in India as nearly 85 per cent of Indian e-commerce merchants are utilizing their services. Its key features include 100+ payment options, multiple currency processing, retry option, customization, audit and analytics, etc.

(d) **Citrus Pay**: One of the younger ventures, Citrus Pay's aim has been to simplify online payment and make it quick and effective while following all safety protocols.

(e) **DirecPay:** Part of the TimesGroup, Direcpay provides strong security features. Their security system is PCI-DSS certified and Norton Secure and they offer easy integration, registration, and flexible payment process.

Apart from these, with the recent demonetization drive by Prime Minister Narendra Modi, mobile wallets have seen a huge surge in activity and transactions. Key among them include:

(a) Paytm: By registering with Paytm service, any digital business can integrate their website with this payment gateway. It allows payments only from Paytm wallet unlike other traditional payment gateways.

(b) MobiKwik: As in the case of Paytm, merchants can accept money only through MobiKwik wallet. In 2015, over 25 million users had a MobiKwik account and 650+ merchants were using its payment gateway service.

(c) Oxigen Wallet: It is India's first RBI-approved non-bank wallet which provides instant money transfer to 60+ banks and has been in operation since 2004.

The top global emerging players include examples like Kounta (a scalable digital POS solution which works like a cash register and can be securely accessed from across a range of channels including in-store, online, and mobile), Pin Payments (which eliminates merchant accounts to help small businesses sell to international customers), Braintree (which provides next-generation payment capabilities such as one-touch purchasing, mobile payments, and foreign currency acceptance), among others. With the emergence of digital technologies and higher security demands from customers, we would see a surge in emerging payment players in the near future.

Managing Digital e-Services (Setting up Digital Services Unit)

In the previous chapters, we understood how digital marketing and campaigns are implemented. For any company to successfully execute its campaigns and get fully operational on multiple digital platforms, it first has to manage the delivery part of its online services (also known as e-services), which is what we will focus in this section. E-services as a terminology is typically used across multiple areas and had found applicability both for individual firms trying to set up their online services and also, in a broader sense, for government bodies trying to go digital with their citizen services for better governance. For our study, we are looking to confine to e-services which would help firms set up their digital marketing and sales operations, thus relating to areas like supply–chain management, customer relationship management, resource management, etc.

E-services was first defined in academic papers by Tiwana and Balasubramaniam in 2001 and, according to them, e-services are internet-based applications that fulfil service needs by seamlessly bringing together distributed, specialized resources to enable complex (often real-time) transactions. Rowley (in 2006) approached e-services as deeds, efforts, or performances, whose delivery is mediated by information technology. Such e-services include the service element of e-tailing, customer support, and service delivery. The three main components involved here are of service provider, service receiver, and the channels of service delivery (technology).

Capgemini, in their co-research with MIT, have seen that for setting up digital e-services, it is crucial that digital leaders invest in a Digital Services Unit (DSU) which can support a firm's governance initiatives around these crucial initiatives. In their whitepaper 'Accelerating Digital Transformation: Understanding and Setting Up a Digital Services Unit,' they have shared the definition of a DSU as "an organizational structure, which focuses on digital activities across an organization and plays a critical role by challenging traditional strategies and incorporating new digital initiatives."

Figure 9.4 describes a general DSU model wherein digital services are delivered by the digital marketing unit within the firm. This entity provides digital services to both the marketing and sales units and also defines a digital services catalog for all the services provided to external clients. The resources for this DSU model are basically loaned from their respective parent groups. The key advantage of this marketing DSU is that it provides autonomy to individual business units and enables dedicated service to respective clients.

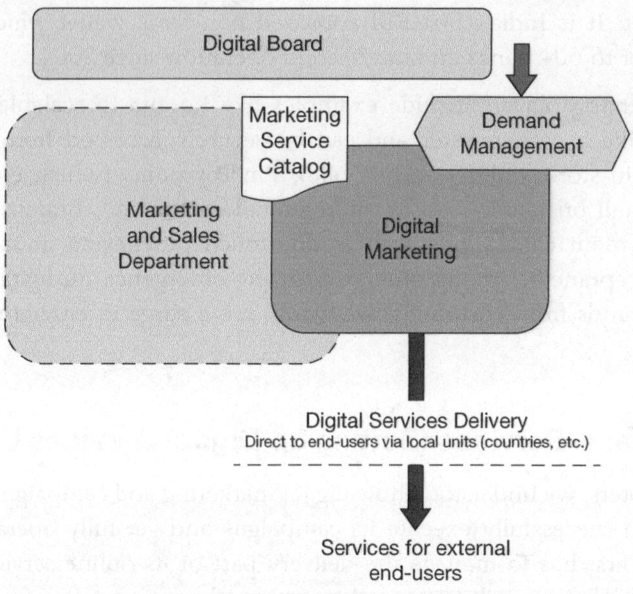

Figure 9.4 Marketing Centric DSU Governance Models (Capgemini Consulting Analysis)

Source: Accelerating Digital Transformation Understanding, https://www.capgemini.com, accessed in February 2017

Service Catalog

It is a collective definition of services that are currently being offered and those which need development. There is a digital board which takes responsibility for overlooking the coordination of actions (scope, budgets, and roadmaps) across various business units.

Figure 9.5 shows the three phases of a DSU implementation plan which involve: (a) Setting organizational principles, (b) Developing organizational and governance design, and (c) Deploying a defined governance model.

Key considerations of DSU implementation

According to the whitepaper, there are three key considerations for DSU implementation:

(a) **Evaluation of budget impacts**: DSU implementation will have an impact upon multiple organizational functions. Multiple funding models can be developed for the initial set-up cost of a new service:

- Local investments funding model: The local entities invest in their own systems.
- Central investments funding model: The central investments pay for the global part of services while local entities pay for their own local projects.
- Supplier's investment funding model: Design, build, and run of new service is outsourced to a supplier.

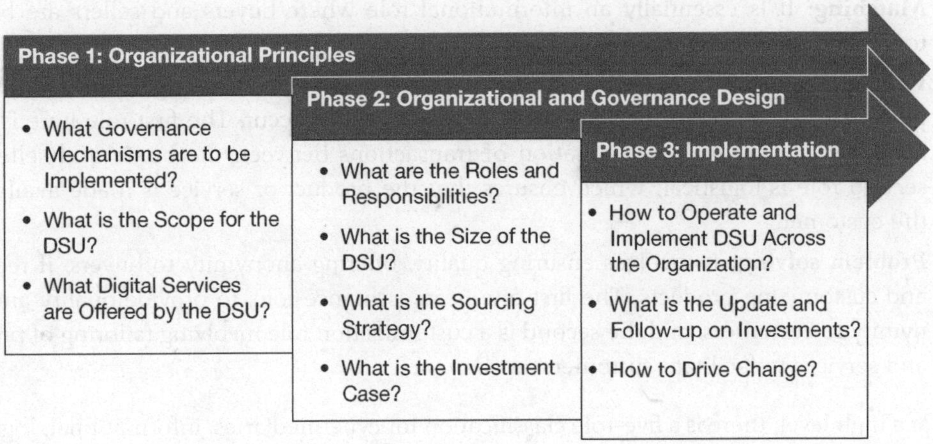

Figure 9.5 DSU Implementation Plan Development

Source: Accelerating Digital Transformation Understanding, https://www.capgemini.com, accessed in February 2017

(b) **People management and communications**: This involves managing skills and competencies both within and outside the DSU, and deciding on the investment areas.

(c) **Setting up a DSU operation on the ground**: For a DSU implementation, organizations need to carefully map hierarchy, visibility, and information access at every stage to depict interdependencies. They also need to identify and define processes to ensure clear KPIs for each entity. Firms should execute necessary changes in the current processes so that new processes can be implemented with minimal impact.

Selling through Cybermediaries

In the last section, we covered how digital e-services are managed and how companies set up internal Digital Services Unit (DSUs) to service online marketing activities. In this section, we will understand the concept of online intermediaries, their key roles, and the various types of internet intermediaries which support firms across their fulfillment value chain.

Emergence of Cybermediaries

David Barnes and Matthew Hinton observe in their whitepaper, 'Developing a Framework to Analyze the Roles and Relationships of Online Intermediaries,' explain that a cybermediary is a business organization that occupies an intermediary position in a supply chain between a buyer and seller and which has an internet-based business model. Sarkar, Butler, and Steinfeld (1996) are among the first ones who predicted the emergence of 'a new generation' of 'cyberintermediaries'. To discuss the exact role of intermediaries many researchers have shared multiple models out of which a prominent approach was attempted by Anderson and Anderson (2002) who emphasized the following three roles of cybermediaries:

(a) **Matching:** It is essentially an informational role where buyers and sellers are brought together by providing information about them and their products.
(b) **Requisitioning:** It involves bringing products to customers at the right time, in the right place, and at the right price to enable a transaction to occur. The first role here is transactional, which involves facilitation of transactions between the buyer and seller. The second role is logistical, which ensures that the product or service is made available to the customer.
(c) **Problem solving:** It involves ensuring quality, offering anonymity to buyers, if required, and customizing products. The first one is an assurance role, to provide quality and anonymity to customers, and the second is a customization role involving tailoring of products and services to facilitate customers' needs.

Thus, at a high level, there is a five-role classification for cybermediaries: informational, logistical, transactional, assurance, and customization. Sarkar et al. (1996) have identified the following 10 roles for cybermediaries within the five-role classification:

- Search and evaluation
- Need assessment and product matching
- Product information dissemination
- Purchase influence
- Provision of customer information
- Integration of consumer and producer needs
- Transaction economies of scale
- Customer risk management
- Producer risk management
- Product distribution

In one of their reports, Organization for Economic Co-operation and Development (OECD), has developed a common definition of internet intermediaries which qualifies them as entities that "give access to, host, transmit, and index content originated by third parties or provide internet-based services to third parties." Key internet intermediaries identified in the report include:

(a) **Internet access and service providers**: This includes firms whose main business model is to provide internet services to households, businesses, and governments. Key examples include: Verizon, Comcast, NTT, BT, etc.
(b) **Data processing and web hosting providers**: It denotes providing support in preparing, transforming, and storing data or content on the internet for other firms. Examples include: Akamai, Rackspace, Navisite, etc.
(c) **Internet search engines and portals**: It includes firms which develop websites and utilize search engine technology to provide internet access and easy search facility. Typical examples include companies like Google, Yahoo, MSN, Baidu, etc.

(d) **E-commerce intermediaries**: It refers to entities which enable internet transactions between buyers and sellers and includes companies like internet retailers, shopping comparison sites, electronic auction platforms, etc. Key examples include: Amazon, Ebay, Alibaba, Priceline.com

(e) **Internet payment systems**: Covered earlier in section titled, 'Emerging Digital Payments Solutions,' in detail, e-commerce payment systems support online payments to enable e-commerce transactions. Examples include: Visa, PayPal, MasterCard, etc.

(f) **Participative networked platforms**: They include services which are based on new technologies facilitating social communication and information exchange like blogs, wikis, instant messaging, podcasting, photo-sharing sites, virtual worlds, etc. Typical examples include Facebook, LinkedIn, YouTube, etc.

The two key characteristics of internet intermediaries, as discussed in the report, include:

Network Externalities

Cybermediaries typically create network externalities (also generally referred as network effects), which mean that the advantages from using the specific services increase as the diffusion spreads. Thus, as more users start using the product, the value a single user receives also starts increasing making this an underlying characteristic of internet intermediaries, and also differentiating it from other types of businesses in terms of economies of scale which can be achieved.

Two-sided Markets

By definition, these are economic networks which involve two complementary user groups that provide each other network benefits by working together. An example is internet search engines and portals which are composed of advertisers and users. According to the report, at any point in time, a market can become two-sided if:

(a) There are two distinct groups of users

(b) The value obtained by one type of user increases with the number or with the quality of other kind of users

(c) An intermediary platform is created to internalize the externalities generated by one group for the other group

MANAGING DIGITAL IMPLEMENTATION CHALLENGES

In the last part of the chapter, we started with understanding electronic payment systems and looked into the key forms of traditional and emerging digital payments. We then covered in detail the key elements of managing digital e-services and setting up a digital services unit to implement a service catalog. Finally, we looked at the emergence of Cybermediaries, their key roles, types, and characteristics, and how they help support the fulfillment part of customer's value chain. In this part, we will look at the key issues in executing digital businesses, through the example of e-commerce implementations, as most companies face multiple challenges while taking their business digital.

Understanding E-commerce Implementation Challenges

With e-commerce as one of the fastest growing areas of digital businesses, its implementation is witnessing its share of complexities in terms of transitioning offline business models online, catering to multiple consumer demands and compliances, and running operations in a highly competitive global environment. Though the advent of digital technologies has made it much easier for businesses to turn digital, they have also realized how difficult it is to deal with issues of security, trust, customer experience, payments, taxation, risk, fulfillment etc.

PWC in its report 'e-Commerce in India: Drivers and Challenges,' has divided e-commerce drivers and challenges into eight key aspects which impact the firm's internal and external implementation plan:

External elements include:

(a) **Product and market strategy**: It includes impact of emerging customer segments and their product portfolios, their go-to-market strategy, market intelligence, and customer engagement platforms

(b) **Customer/digital experience**: It includes aspects related to customer experience on multiple channels and the impact of their brand interaction and experiences.

(c) **Payments and transactions**: It involves elements like security and privacy breach and fraudulent transactions.

(d) **Fulfillment**: It includes logistics and supply chain management costs.

Internal elements consist of:

(a) **Organization scaling:** This refers to the evolution and integration of multiple functions of the firm for ensuing operations.

(b) **Tax and regulatory structuring**: It includes issues of tax planning, payment of sales tax, business license tax, franchisee fees, etc., along with management of regulatory uncertainties.

(c) **Risk, fraud, and cyber security**: It denotes management issues like internet fraud, protection of buyer's interests, ethical concerns like privacy and web tracking, etc.

(d) **Compliance framework:** This refers to ensuring legal issues like cyber laws, domain names, copyrights, etc.

For ease of understanding and to provide a simpler structure, we would group the challenges shared earlier and others into three key areas which we would study in more detail in the subsequent sections of this part of the chapter. The three key areas are:

(a) **Internal-specific—business and infrastructure challenges**: They refer to all challenges related to setting up e-commerce and underlying technology and infrastructure. Key implementation issues at a high level include:

- Lack of organizational set-up and business models
- Economic and cost justification
- Access to internet and telecom infrastructure
- Technical issues like interoperability, reliability, and integration
- Availability of skilled manpower

(b) **External specific—legal and compliance challenges**: They denote challenges which are external to the company's environment. Typical legal and compliance challenges include:

- Intellectual property rights issues
- Taxation issues
- Legal validity of transactions
- Compliance, regulatory and government policies

(c) **Consumer Specific—Security, Privacy, Ethical, and Social Challenges**: It includes challenges related to and impacting the final consumer and his/her interaction with the firm while undertaking transactions. Typical challenges included in this category are:

- Security, cybercrime, digital signature issues
- Privacy, data usage, and web tracking (client-server, data, document)
- Trust-related issues
- Ethical issues
- Societal and digital divide issues

By listing the three major types of challenge areas, we aim to see what afflicts company plans while venturing into digital implementations and why it becomes crucial for such companies to have a strategic vision.

Internal Challenges: Business and Infrastructure

The first step towards e-commerce implementation involves firms managing key business, infrastructure, and technology challenges while setting up their wares. Typically, firms overlook organizational challenges as they are busy working on scaling the technology and infrastructure issues, though ideally they should be looking into such concerns more critically since the success of an e-commerce implementation lies in its long-term sustainability. Let us look at each of the key implementation issues shared in the last section to understand them in detail.

Lack of Organizational Set-up and Business Models

Typically, companies planning to go digital and implement a commerce module, lack the knowledge of online business models, and have little or no precedence towards the best practices involved in setting them up. This lack of understanding of typical inputs and potential output is a big deterrent to digital implementations.

There are other organizational issues too which impact the successful setting up of a firm's online business model. These include:

- Internal corporate structures need to be well aligned to accommodate new business model changes.
- Strategic conflict among multiple divisions and channels, in terms of their business and sales goals, needs to be bridged.
- Firm's partners need to be integrated and geared for a full-fledged online implementation from sourcing to manufacturing to fulfillment.
- Barriers between business and information technology groups in terms of implantation models, platforms, and technologies need to be removed.
- Executive layer needs to be aligned with the overall plan and should be able to see value in going digital.

Economic and Cost Justification

Similar to organizational set-up, economic challenges are as crucial, since without assessing the overall business environment and economic viability, no digital implementation can be deemed a success. Any firm which is planning to take even a part of its overall business to a digital platform needs to develop the right estimation for its venture to have a viable RoI and should plan for such cost outlays.

Typically, the best way is to look at both the initial set-up and running costs for such implementations and then, factor them into the overall returns model. But a lot of firms do not have the foresight, prior experience, or financial modelling expertise to make these transitions. In the absence of clear justification for RoI (which is not based on tangible factors), it also becomes difficult for various divisions to carry on their initiatives in the right earnest, thus inflicting harm to the firm's expectations from such initiatives.

Access to Internet and Telecom Infrastructure

Once the business models are decided and cost factors are taken care of the next big hurdle is setting up the infrastructure for digital since accessibility to internet is still quite expensive and a lot of small firms, especially in developing countries, do not have similar access to the global infrastructure available to companies in the developed world. For most countries, it is essential that they chart out dedicated plans to make the requisite infrastructure available for emerging firms in multiple sectors to take advantage of the growing digital opportunities.

Technical Issues like Interoperability, Reliability, and Integration

Once the infrastructure is in place for the firm, the next key challenge to solve are technical issues related to interoperability, reliability, and integration with existing applications. Let us study them one by one:

- **Interoperability issues:** Interoperability as a concept involves the ability of systems running in different operating environments to communicate and work together. At an operational level, this requires the same set of rules (protocols) to be followed. This is crucial for firms looking to establish themselves in a digital environment consisting of multiple technologies and standards.

- **Reliability issues:** Reliability involves network infrastructure and application systems to be continuously upgraded, fine-tuned, and maintained to have overall systems running. This involves the systems being reliant in the face of unprecedented transactions and spikes.
- **Integration issues:** Integration between a firm's existing applications and databases with internet software is a key challenge. The typical solution for this is provided by middleware software that connects disparate systems (these middleware are mostly robust), but companies still face an issue integrating their home-grown and other commercial software for which new interfaces have to be developed, and require dedicated time and resources for execution.
- **Other technology issues:** Apart from other technical issues which firms have to face during their digital journey, there are issues including interoperability of payment instruments, development of competitive supply chain capabilities, management of multiple content and datasets, lack of standards, etc.

Availability of Skilled Manpower

Finally, we arrive at the most important aspect—availability of skilled manpower—to help a firm transition across all the above challenges. Since there are not too many digital professionals available, non-availability or inexperienced staffing results in delayed projects and revenue opportunity losses which fledgling firms/divisions cannot afford. These issues are more prominent in developed countries than in developing ones, since there is a bigger cost outlay for experts in developed nations. Companies can also look at in-house training as an option in technology areas which might not be too complex and can be managed internally.

External Challenges: Legal and Compliance

This next section will cover external challenges for e-commerce implementation which involves legal and compliance issues that have to be addressed while conducting e-commerce transactions online. Although most private companies across the world are deploying advanced technologies to deal with issues like Intellectual Property Rights (IPRs) and cybercrimes, they need tremendous support from their respective governments to implement such laws. While most governments have formulated rules for digital content on paper, it is a huge challenge for them to implement them on ground considering the complex nature of such transactions.

Key legal and compliance related challenges on which we will focus include:

(a) **Intellectual property rights issues**: According to Laudon and Laudon (1999), since digital content is different in nature to physical content (being far more amenable to replication, transmission, and alteration), it is difficult to classify, categorize, and catalogue. These elements also impact related intellectual property rights. Typical forms of intellectual property issues which are key to digital works include copyrights (related to software, arts), patents (concerned with inventions), and trademarks (represent name brands and logos).

Also as shared by Okerson (1996), the way in which information is generated and presented digitally creates a lot of complexities. An example is the creation of a web page which involves components being obtained from multiple sources, making the issue of ownership and compensation even more pertinent. There is also the contention of internet inherently being a medium which supports open transmission of information where its development is dependent on the transmission of free-flowing ideas and processes.

Globally, governments need to decide and design laws which not only help retain the essence of free information but also protect original works and contributions so that innovation does not suffer. The way laws are interpreted and enacted would also be quite different for online transactions versus their physical business models.

(b) **Taxation issues**: It involves issues related to the nature of sales tax imposed on internet-related businesses. There are multiple thoughts on taxation implementation being discussed across the world. On one hand, state and national governments are imposing taxes for their retention and the general improvement of the sector, while, on the other, there are legislators and experts who opine that imposing such taxes would actually harm the growth of this industry in its formative phase, thus hampering the overall growth of digital businesses. Complications also arise on the implementation of sales tax collection and the restrictions imposed by rules and laws of other countries.

(c) **Legal validity of transactions**: Regulating legal validity of electronic transactions was much easier for governments to implement, as for traditional businesses, each commercial transaction was paper-based (involving 'wet signatures') and was easier to conduct as it was in person. To extend the same rules to digital transactions, it is important that digital signatures and documents are granted the same legal validity as the written form. This is becoming a challenge as each geography and country might have differing rules regarding such digital validity and its implementation.

It is felt that though e-commerce transactions is a common phenomenon in the recent years, proper recognition of electronic authentication has not been established, and without such laws, the rapid expansion of this industry will be hampered. At present, even for developed countries, at times, the jurisdiction which has regulatory authority over a transaction has not been established clearly. Typically, buyers in case of any transaction-related issue have to travel to the seller's local jurisdiction for the settlement of any disputes that may arise from the electronic transaction which is clearly not the way resolutions for digital transactions should be structured.

(d) **Compliance, regulatory, and government policies:** Consultancy firm Price Waterhouse Coopers (PwC) in their report titled report titled, 'e-Commerce in India: Accelerating Growth' has identified Cyber law compliance and 'inefficient anti-corruption framework' issues as serious challenges to India's vibrant e-commerce industry that is expected to touch $22 billion in 2015.

According to the analysts who have authored the report (the research is specific to India), potential identified issues which are posing a problem include those related to cyber law compliance, inefficient anti-corruption framework, legal exposure in agreements or arrangements, indirect and direct tax compliance framework, and Foreign Exchange Management Act (FEMA) contraventions and regularization. On the regulations ad government policy side, the report also cites that the new Companies Act, policy on related-party transaction pricing, etc., could emerge as challenges for the fledgling sector in the future.

At a global level, many corporations are also concerned with sale of commodities that are restricted or deemed illegal by the laws of the country in which the product or service is being sold. In the US, there are specific regulations around e-commerce transitions for certain specific items, including the sale of pornographic material, illegal weapons, restricted chemical items, online gambling services, etc.

Once a company decides on the key products to be transitioned to digital platforms, it needs to conduct in-depth research on the specific product categories it intends to sell with regards to key compliances, cyber laws, and regulations. The firm also needs to know local rules and regulations, to assess potential sales and expected growth potential.

Consumer-Specific Security, Privacy, Ethical, and Social Challenges

In this last section, we will look at consumer-specific challenges which impact growth of e-commerce firms. While firms put in a lot of thought towards business, infrastructure, legal, and compliance challenges, consumer-specific issues like security, privacy, ethical, and social challenges might take a back seat in the quest for quick growth and customer penetration. Let us study each of these in detail.

(a) **Security, cybercrime, digital signature issues**: Issues on security can typically be related to organizational security threats as well as managing security for a firm's customers. Here, we would cover security threats which are more consumer-centric including:

- **Spamming**: It relates to unsolicited commercial e-mails targeted at individuals. Spamming is typically caused by hackers who place malicious software agents onto a third party system, thus triggering-off service attacks.
- **Cybercrimes**: Cybercrimes are propagated through self-replicating computer programs like viruses, which are designed to perform unwanted events. There are multiple categories of digital viruses, the most common of them being Worms (spread using direct internet connections) and Trojan Horses (viruses disguised as legitimate software to trick users into initiating a program).
- **Digital signatures issues**: It involves provision of legal equivalence between paper-based and electronic forms of exchange, which is the goal of e-transaction laws.

(b) **Privacy, Data Usage, and Web Tracking:** This next set of issues relates to consumer privacy areas related to online transactions:

- **Data usage:** Typically, there are multiple types of data involved while e-commerce transactions occur (client–server data, consumer data, policy data, transaction data, etc.). All this is private data which, if leaked, can be a big threat to consumers.
- **Data tracking:** There are also issues related to firms trying to track consumer usage data and patterns, much of which has been evidenced in the case of social networks and online data/service aggregation firms which have had to face consumer and anti-trust issues on how their data was being handled.

- **Theft and fraud:** More serious issues relate to those of blatant data theft and ensuing fraud when the stolen data is used or modified. There could be situations of software theft which involve illegal copying of data from the company's servers which makes it imperative for e-commerce firms to come up with measures against such occurrences. According to a US source (Risk Based Security, 2014), more than 2,100 incidents of data breaches were reported in 2013, through which some 822 million records were exposed. In one major incident, as many as 152 million names, customer identities, encrypted passwords, debit or credit card numbers, and other information related to customer orders were exposed. These statistics point to the scale of such issues.

(c) **Trust-related issues:** The issue of trust was defined by Hosmer (1995) as "the expectation that the other party will behave in accordance with commitments, negotiate honestly, and not take advantage, even when the opportunity arises." The lack of trust often results in user resistance towards buying products or services. The key components of trust include:

- **Predictability**: It relates to establishing clear expectations, for example, consistently sending e-mail notifications on order confirmation and order shipment.
- **Reliability**: It indicates to consumer that the party with which transactions are being conducted is dependable and would fulfill the commitments.
- **Technical competence**: It refers to the ability to carry out responsibilities at the technical level for each transaction.
- **Fiduciary responsibility**: It includes placing the interest of the individual who is trusting before the interests of the firm which is carrying out the transactions.

(d) **Ethical issues**: With recently funded start-ups aiming at aggressive growth, there have been multiple cases where firms have made failed ethical judgments. The rise of digital technologies not only raises ethical questions for both individuals and societies but have also impacted existing distributions of power, rights, money, and obligations. In their book *Management Information Systems: Managing the Digital Firm*, authors Kenneth C. Laudon and Jane Price Laudon have shared the following pressing ethical issues raised by information systems:

- Establishing accountability for the consequences of information systems
- Setting standards to safeguard system quality to protect individual/societal safety
- Preserving values and institutions considered essential to the quality of life

(e) **Societal and Digital Divide Issues**: Societal issues involve concerns related to cultural diversity, consumer protection issues, and shortage of labor. The digital divide issues are typically concerned with unequal access to internet technologies and acceptance of digital as a means of buying and social exclusions. Let us look at the six key issues briefly.

- **Cultural diversity**: It is typically a challenge for entrepreneurs not only to understand but also to meet local needs and preferences of many different customer groups; further, customization is expensive most of the times.
- **Consumer protection**: It involves responding to small claims, limited liabilities, and taking care of customer return policies.

- **Labor shortage**: It relates to the difficulty of filling large unfulfilled technology positions, global movement of workforce from developed to developing countries, and retention of technology workers.
- **Unequal access**: It is concerned with the digital divide between well-off and not-so-privileged sections of the society in terms of technology access.
- **Digital acceptance**: It includes medium specific limitations in terms of consumers not being able to 'touch and feel' digital products.
- **Social exclusions**: It involves public- and private-sector organizations discrimination against lower income groups. The best example here is of the recent controversies against net-neutrality and its impact on digital consumption.

PRACTICAL EXERCISE

Executing Marketing Analytics

Key Objective To develop an understanding of multiple marketing analytics techniques deployed across the digital marketing landscape.

Project Brief Imagine that you are an analytics consultant deployed by a marketing firm to execute custom marketing techniques towards a specific set of marketing analysis. Based upon the problem set, you would need to classify and decide the marketing analytics type closest to the use case and deploy accordingly.

Execution Let us look at some of the top marketing analytics classifications you can deploy towards gaining marketing insights:

(a) **STP Analytics (Segmentation, Targeting, and Positioning Analytics):** One of the most basic analytics types, it includes analytics techniques to identify most valuable market segments, target top customers within the segments, and position an offering for that target segment. The types of analytics across each of these areas include:
- **Segmentation:** Demographic, Psychographic, Behavioural Analytics
- **Targeting:** Size and Potential, Reach, Frequency Analytics
- **Positioning:** Positioning Map, Value Proposition Analytics

(b) **4Ps Analytics (Pricing Analytics, Promotion Budget Estimation, and Allocation):** It includes analytics specific to product marketing, product pricing, placement/channel selection, and promotional tactics.

(c) **Process Based Analytics (Market Research, Marketing Mix Modeling, Reach-Cost-Quality (RCQ), Attribution Based Analytics):** It involves analytics towards specific marketing processes including:
- **Market Research:** Includes complex primary and secondary analysis techniques
- **Market Mix Modeling:** Spend mix execution through what-if scenarios

- **Reach-Cost-Quality:** Quantitative method for evaluating, comparing, and selecting different media on a like-for-like basis
- **Attribution Analysis:** Identification of a set of user actions across that attribute to a particular marketing conversion

(d) **Funnel Analytics (TOFU/MOFU/BOFU/Retention Based Analytics):** It evaluates a series of events across multiple funnel stages that lead towards a marketing goal.

(e) **Operational Analytics (Revenue, Forecasting, Customer Value):** It involves measuring business related metrics for a specific period of marketing activities.

(f) **Industry Specific Analytics (Financial/Retail/CPG/E-Commerce):** It includes analysis executed for variables and parameters most common to each industry.

(g) **Channel Based Analytics (Search/Display/Social/Content/Email/Affiliate/PR):** It involves analytics across a single or mix of chosen digital marketing channels.

(h) **Owned Media Analytics (Web/App/Blog/Google Analytics):** This comprises analytics based on data integrated across owned media channels for a firm or brand.

(i) **Campaign Analytics (Landing Page/Organic and Paid Campaigns):** This deals with campaign analytics execution for organic and paid campaigns.

(j) **Integrated Marketing Analytics (Online + Offline):** It includes integrating and analyzing metrics across online and offline channels.

There are other marketing analytics use cases and techniques deployed in the industry. The above mentioned analytic types form the most representative example set.

With the rise in promotional channels and the practice of marketing data being utilized by multiple corporate stakeholders (in addition to marketing teams), marketing analytics execution is getting complex by the day. While it might not be possible for a marketer to master all analytical techniques, it is important to get a strong-hold on all bespoke analytics executed manually and through third-party analytics tools. This would enable marketers to be come data-driven and be able to measure true return on their efforts and investments. Once you have applied specific analytics for any industry's specific channels and processes, it is advised to compare the outcomes with other marketers or students to gain a strong handle on multiple ways of marketing analytics deployment.

CHAPTER SUMMARY

- **Part 1**: The first part began with an understanding of the four key types of digital revenue generation models (based on product, service, advertising, and commission) and discussed the rise of Loyalty evolution from Loyalty 1.0 to Loyalty 3.0 along with the four pillars of customer loyalty management. We then looked at how relationship marketing was rising and became familiar with the six stages of 'Ladder of Customer Loyalty,' from prospect to partner, and, learn about the importance of DRIP marketing concepts for executing relationship marketing. Finally, we studied about the five-step plan for any company to engage in successful advocate marketing.

- **Part 2**: In the second part, we started with a basic understanding of electronic payment systems and compared the four key types of traditional payments (credit card, e-cash, e-checks, smart card) across multiple parameters. We then looked at the major types of digital payments solutions emerging globally, which included mobile, digital P2P, social media payments, along with emerging ones like digital kiosks, TV set-top boxes, and biometric payments. With this understanding, we looked at how firms are managing digital e-services by setting up digital services units. We also covered DSU governance models and the three phases of DSU implementation. Finally, we also studied the emergence of cybermediaries, their key roles, and the various types of internet intermediaries which support firms across their fulfillment value chain.
- **Part 3**: In the final part, we developed the basis for understanding e-commerce implementation challenges to divide them into three key buckets (internal, external, and consumer-specific challenges). We then went deeper into understanding each of the three key areas including internal challenges which relate to firm's business and infrastructure-related implementation challenges. The external challenges covered related to legal and compliance issues while the third and final set of challenges covered consumer-specific implementation challenges including security, privacy, ethical, and social challenges.

REVIEW QUESTIONS

1. What are the four key types of digital revenue generation models? Explain any one of them in detail.
2. Describe briefly the key stages of customer loyalty evolution.
3. What is the key difference between transaction marketing and relationship marketing? Explain the six stages of relationship marketing as portrayed in the Ladder of Customer Loyalty.
4. What is advocate marketing? What are the five key steps for any company to engage in successful advocate marketing. Explain any one of them in detail.
5. What are the four key payment models which have emerged with the advent of internet and electronic transactions. Describe them briefly.
6. Name the major digital payment types which are emerging globally and explain a couple of them in detail.
7. What are e-services and what is a services catalogue in an e-services context?
8. What are cybermediaries? List any five key roles of cybermediaries.
9. What are some of the key internet intermediaries as shared in the chapter? Describe two key characteristics of internet intermediaries.
10. Describe two e-commerce implementation challenges, each for external and internal elements.
11. What are internal, external, and consumer-specific e-commerce implementation challenges? Detail their key types.

12. List five key internal challenges (business and infrastructure) and explain any two of them in detail.
13. Share four key external challenges (legal and compliance) and explain any two of them in detail.
14. Detail five key external challenges (security, privacy, ethical and social) and explain any two of them in detail.

DIGITAL APPLICATION EXERCISES

1. From your understanding of varied types of digital marketing companies, choose one top tool/platform across each of the key digital marketing types and share the key digital revenue generation models for each of them:
   (a) Search Marketing
   (b) Display Marketing
   (c) Content Marketing
   (d) Social Marketing
   (e) Affiliate Marketing
2. Visit Paytm.com, one of India's largest growing payment and commerce companies. Research and share thoughts on how Paytm might be applying the six stages of Ladder of Customer Loyalty to drive their loyalty management program.
3. Shopclues.com is one of the top online marketplaces in India. How according to you do they utilize the DRIP model to drive their relationship marketing agenda with customers?
4. Imagine that you are a local NGO fighting against tobacco consumption in India. How would you develop successful advocate marketing by incorporating the five key steps as shared in the chapter?
5. Which of the four key payment models do you typically use for your digital payments? Which of these do you feel is best suited for your needs and why?
6. Choose any two electronic payment systems and compare them across any two comparison areas as shared in the chapter.
7. Of the major digital payment types emerging globally (as shared in the chapter), which one do you feel would have more relevance for digital marketing companies going forward and why?
8. Research and provide examples of the top intermediaries in India based on the classifications shared in the chapter. What specific observations would you like to share?
9. From your understanding of the Indian e-commerce business environment, select any two Indian e-commerce companies (one large and one small) and differentiate between their implementation challenges based on the literature shared in the chapter.

UNIT V DIGITAL BUSINESS - PRESENT AND FUTURE

CHAPTER 10

Digital Business –Landscape & Emerging Areas

LEARNING OBJECTIVES

After studying this chapter, you will be able to:

- Explain global marketing spend by category as well as compare the share of global advertising spend across all traditional and digital media types
- Analyze the break up of global and digital advertising spend by format along with the ad spending share by industry
- Understand India specific digital marketing statistics with break up of media and entertainment industry segment numbers and percentage division of key digital advertising categories
- Gain exposure to India specific Digital Marketing/Advertising Tools Landscape
- Explain the impact of three major concepts that have been shaping digital marketing, namely, data technologies, business segments, and hyperlocal targeting
- Cover upcoming digital marketing concepts including Big Data and Internet of Things (IoT), Small and Medium Businesses (SMB), B2B marketing and Social, Local and Mobile (SoLoMo) concept
- Introduction to Web 3.0 concepts and in-depth coverage of key trends including Blockchain Technology, Metaverse, Artificial Intelligence and Machine Learning (AI-ML), Digital Payments and Audio-Social Marketing to review their impact on the digital marketing landscape

CASE STUDY One97 Communication: *India's Go-To Payment Partner from Starbucks to Paan walas*

One97 Communication is a fin-tech company that is best recognised by its digital payment platform, Paytm. With a vision of revolutionizing the digital payments market and reducing corruption, CEO Vijay Shekhar Sharma gained major success with Paytm. From gaining more users, to its IPO, to constant ups and downs, the current situation of Paytm is a mixed bag. In terms of its user base, merchants, and monthly active users, Paytm has experienced a steady rise. In FY 2018, Paytm had a 200 million user base, which increased to 350 million in FY21. Similarly, monthly active users also increased from 27 million in 2018 to 52 million in 2021. Despite this, Paytm has been facing a few issues over the past five years (even as it saw multiple opportunities to expand its user base during demonetisation and the COVID-19 pandemic).

Ever since Paytm got the Reserve Bank of India's approval for its Payment Bank system, it has grown a lot. As of FY21, Paytm Payments Bank claims to have issued 7 million Visa debit cards through the platform. However, One97 Communication holds only a 49 per cent stake in Paytm Payments Bank Limited.

Paytm has diversified its approach and rolled out different services through its subsidiaries. With a diversified portfolio, Paytm has tried to grab a stronger market share. Paytm launched "Digital Gold" in partnership with MMTC-PAMP (Metals and Minerals Trading Corporation of India–Produits Artistiques Métaux Précieux). This platform allowed users to buy and sell gold digitally. Paytm claimed that by 2020, 73 million customers had bought Paytm Gold from the platform. Paytm also ventured into the e-commerce vertical through Paytm Mall, although this initiative continues to incur losses with revenue declining each year. Further, the share of Paytm in the UPI payment apps market continues to gain strength in the market.

Every year, Paytm tries to reduce their losses, but the challenge is that they have been unable to accelerate their profits. Due to their crises, Paytm decided to go for an IPO in 2021. Paytm opened its IPO with a share price of ₹2150 per equity share. On the very first day of listing, the share closed 27 per cent lower than its fixed price. This continued till the 9th day, when the price reduced to almost half of the original share price (₹1051 per equity share). This setback was never expected by One97 Communication management. But by November 2021, the price increased to ₹1961. Since then, shares have continued to fall and have hit ₹546.65 per equity share. Paytm IPO was not as successful as expected.

To ensure its survival, Paytm has tried to increase its revenue through cross-selling and distribution of other products to maintain its customer base. Be it consumer lending, wealth management, insurance distribution, or mini-app platforms, Paytm is continuously striving to enhance revenues and profitability. It will be interesting to see when Paytm hits its profitability targets, given that it still has a very strong brand equity in India.

In Parts II-IV (Chapters 4–8), we covered the five phases of the ASCOR Digital Marketing Framework to understand how digital marketing strategies are developed, operations are set, and campaigns are executed. Chapter 9 covered all elements which help in executing digital marketing along, with key implementation challenges for execution.

In this last section of the book (Section V) we shall concentrate on key global and Indian trends in digital marketing and emerging areas and concepts which are impacting the digital landscape, along with covering emerging career opportunities in digital marketing (Chapter 11) for students to ensure they can utilise all the knowledge and concepts gained in the book and convert it into a successful digital marketing career. The first part of the chapter begins with an overview of global digital marketing, key trends, and tools/technology landscape. The second part focuses specifically on the Indian landscape and covers key data and trends emerging in the Indian digital marketing scene, along with a focus on e-commerce, which has been the key propeller behind this rise. Finally, we will cover the most pertinent business concepts impacting digital marketing, with a deeper focus on emerging Web 3.0 trends like Blockchain, Metaverse, Artificial Intelligence & Machine Learning (AI-ML), Digital Payments and Audio-Social marketing.

DIGITAL MARKETING LANDSCAPE

Conceptualising the Digital Marketing Landscape

With an understanding of the global marketing and advertising spends, in this section, let us look at the overall landscape for global digital marketing services which multiple vendors are delivering to clients across industries and functions. One of the best attempts at understanding and explaining this classification is by the analyst firm *Gartner*, which has developed a visually striking way of looking at these areas and services through its 'Digital Marketing Transit Map'. This map lays down almost all possible digital marketing implementation areas using a railroad styled map which lays out these services through concepts like neighbourhoods, tracks, and stations.

The map in Figure 10.1 can be better understood as being developed like a mesh of neighbourhoods, where the tracks with neighbourhoods are key digital marketing operational areas and tracks themselves being the key application domains. Gartner classifies a total of seven neighbourhoods in this map (as shown in Figure 10.1):

(a) Ad Ops
(b) Design
(c) Social Ops
(d) Mobility
(e) Web Ops
(f) Data Ops
(g) Marketing Ops

In Figure 10.2 all the seven neighbourhoods (showcased in grey) and twelve tracks have been laid out to gain a better idea of where each track runs and how it is interconnected to others. Gartner explains each of the tracks as below (from left to right):

(a) **Search:** Technology for finding relevant content on websites
(b) **Ad Tech:** Technology for managing advertisements across channels
(c) **Marketing management:** Business processes and the tools associated with the execution of marketing programs

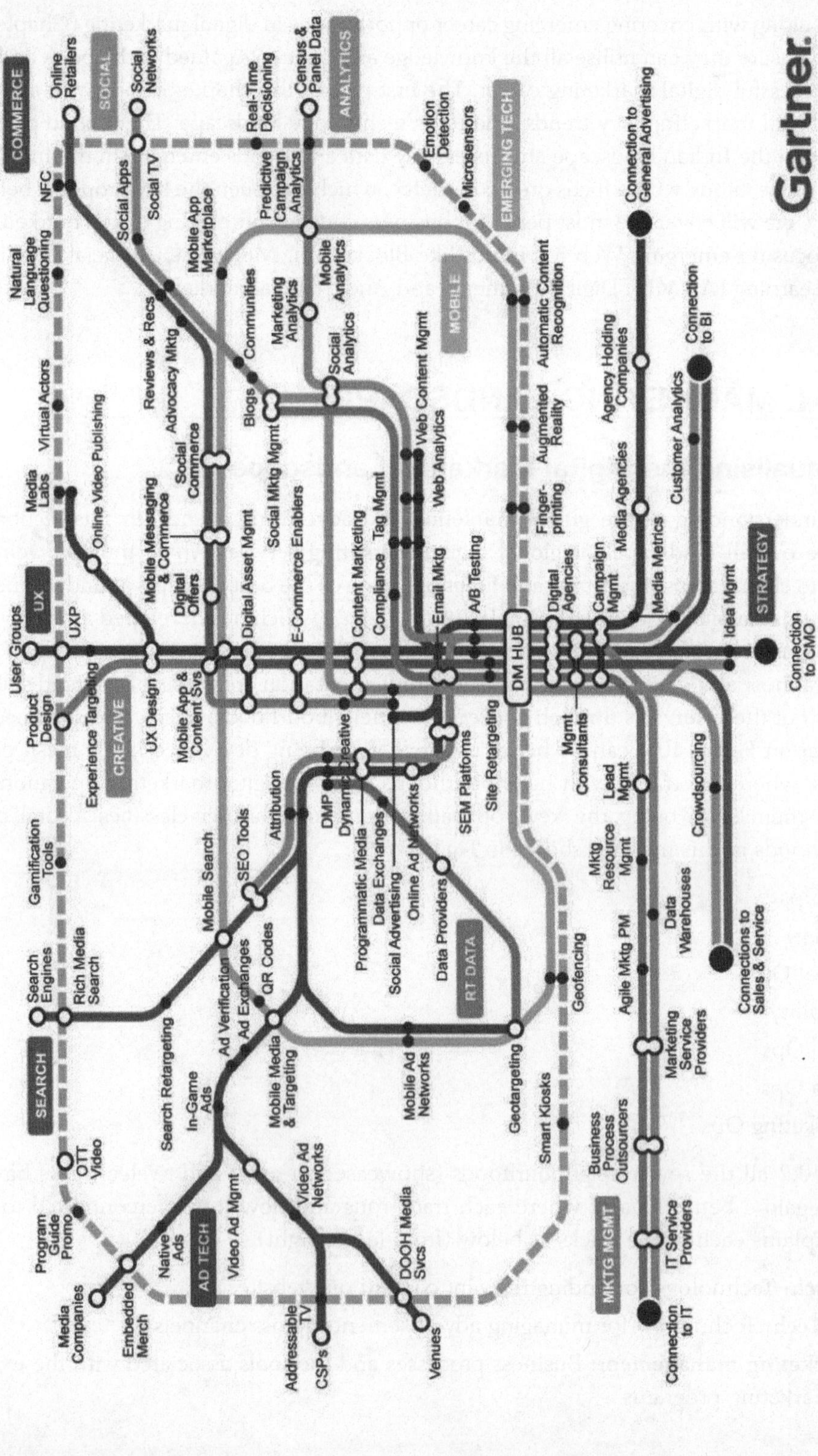

Figure 10.1 Gartner Digital Marketing Transit Map

Courtesy: Susan Hallam, Hallam Internet Ltd., UK, https://www.hallaminternet.com/, used with permission.

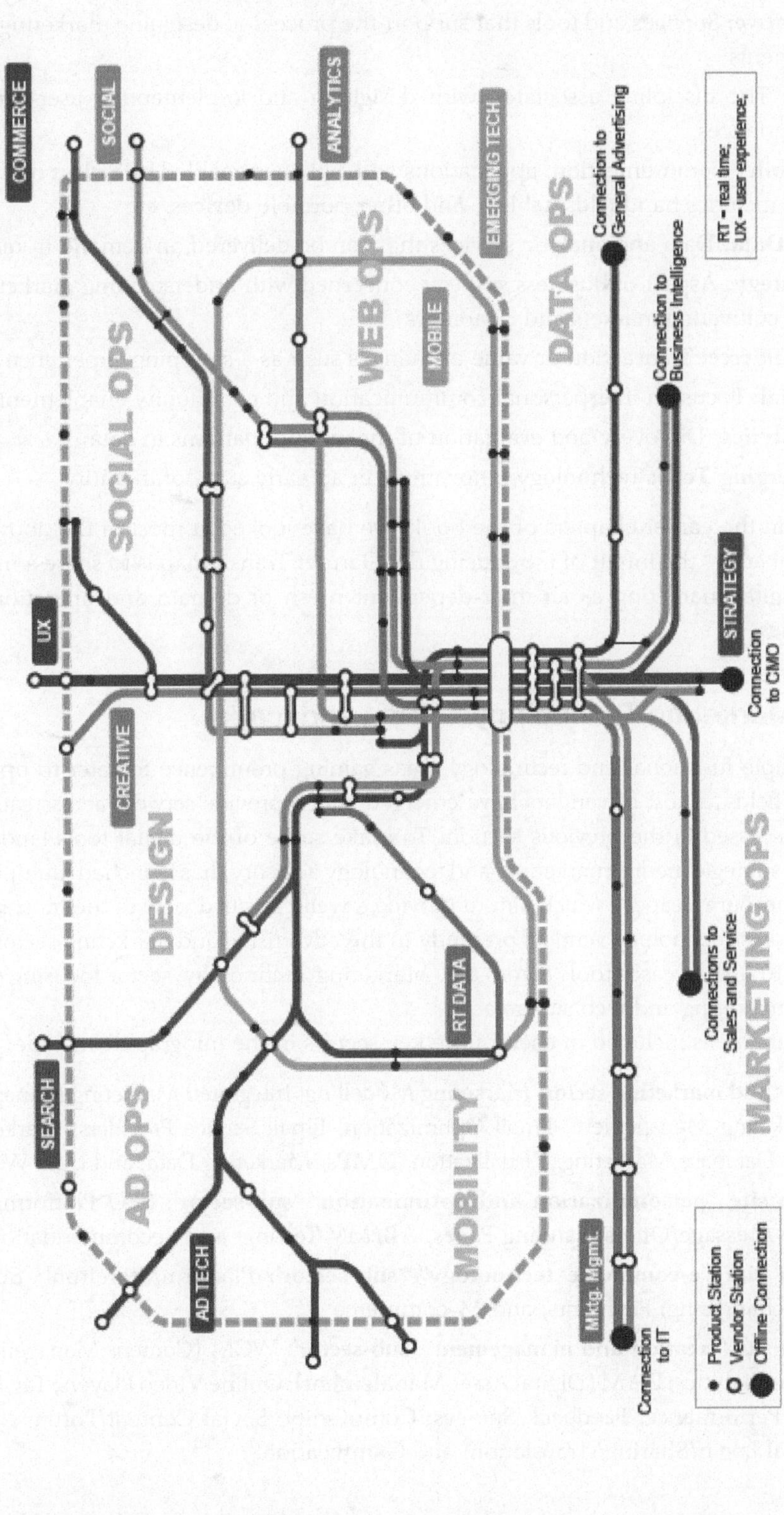

Figure 10.2 Neighbourhoods and Tracks Layout (Gartner Transit Map)

Courtesy: Susan Hallam, Hallam Internet Ltd., UK, https://www.hallaminternet.com/ , used with permission.

(d) **Creative:** Services and tools that support the process of designing marketing programs and elements
(e) **UX:** The discipline associated with designing and implementing user-centric customer experiences
(f) **Mobile:** Communication, applications and activities enabled by a class of wireless devices that includes handhelds, tablets, and other portable devices, etc
(g) **RT Data:** Data and analytic services that can be delivered on demand in real-time
(h) **Strategy:** Aspect of business strategy concerned with understanding market opportunities and cultivating markets and customers
(i) **Commerce:** Transaction or value exchanges such as a shopping experience
(j) **Social:** Focus on interpersonal communication and community enablement
(k) **Analytics:** Discovery and evaluation of meaningful patterns in data
(l) **Emerging Tech:** Technology innovations in an early stage of maturity

Although in the earlier chapters of the book, we have looked at most of the above domain and operational areas, the intent of introducing the Gartner Transit map is to share a more integrated view of digital marketing as an inter-dependent mesh of domain and operational areas, and technologies.

Digital Marketing Technology/Tools Landscape

With multiple functional and technology areas gaining prominence to cater to upcoming digital marketing fields, a host of vendors have emerged which provide services across each of the point areas as discussed in the previous section. To make sense of the digital tools landscape, LUMA Partners (a strategic media, marketing, and technology advisory) has launched multiple infographics by the name 'Lumascapes', which aim to provide a well-classified view of the most prominent and emerging tools/technology vendors presently in the advertising and marketing sectors.

Figure 10.3 showcases tools across the 'Marketing Technology' sector focusing specifically on sales and marketing and web site areas.

The main areas included in each of the key sectors in the infographic include:

(a) **Sales and marketing sector:** Marketing Modelling; Integrated Marketing Management; Social Marketing Management; Email Optimization; Email Service Providers; Marketing Automation; Database Marketing; Visualization; DMPs; Marketing Data; and Data Warehouses.
(b) **Web site "personalization and optimization" 'sub-sector':** SEO Platforms/Tools; Real-time Message/Offers; Landing Pages; AB/MV Testing; and Recommendation Systems.
(c) **Web site "e-commerce technology" 'sub-sector':** Platform/Storefront; Social Referral; Merchandising; Payments; and M-commerce
(d) **Web site "creation and management" 'sub-sector':** WCM (Content Management Systems); Web Analytics; DAM (Digital Asset Manafement); Online Video Players; Tag Management; Site Performance; Feedback/Surveys; Community; Social Content/Forums; Mobile Web; Social Login/Sharing; Translation; and Gamification.

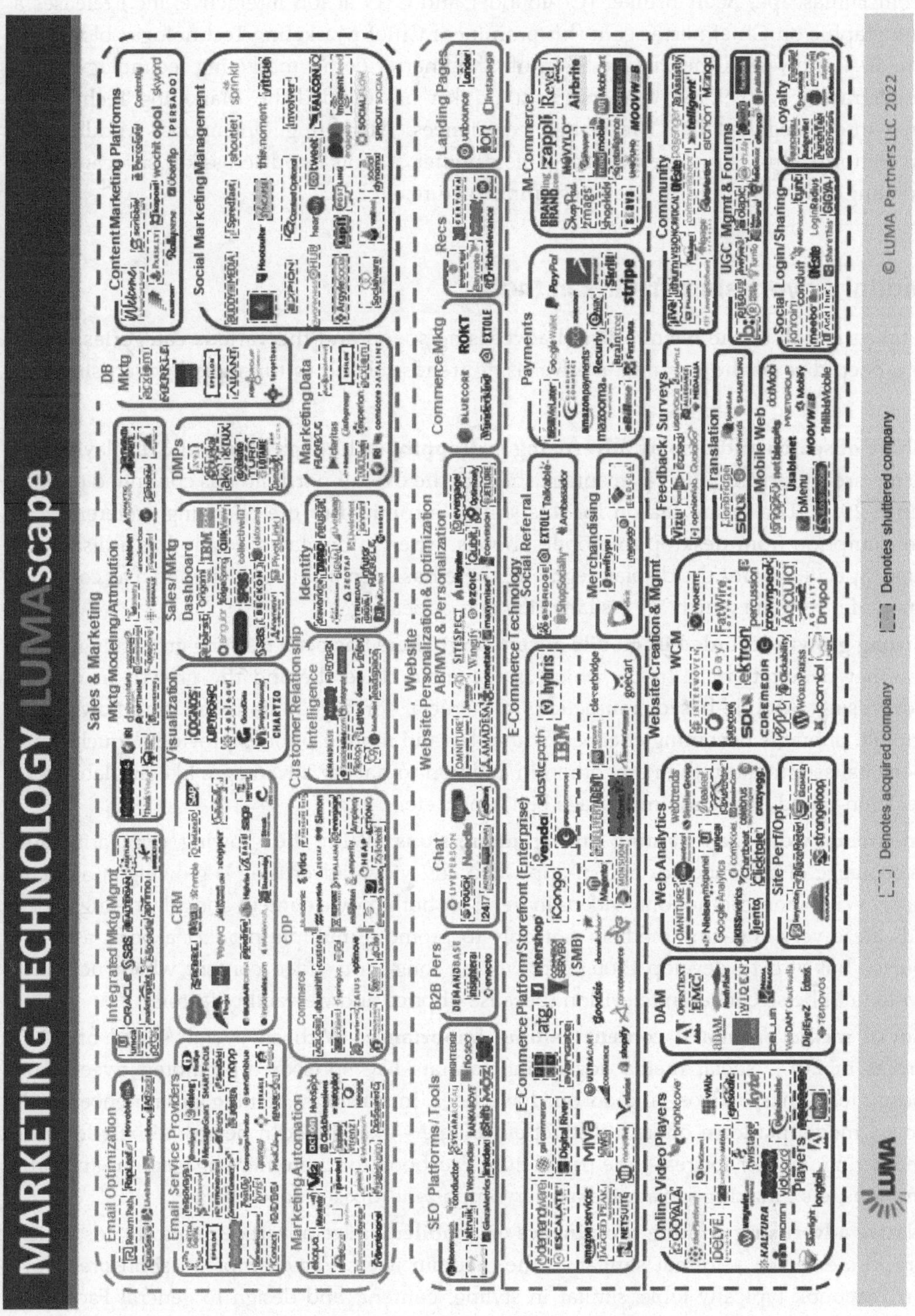

Figure 10.3 Marketing Technology 'Lumascape'

Credits: Susan Marshall & Wayne Lam on behalf of LUMA Partners LLC, MarTech LUMAscape, used with permission of LUMA Partners LLC.

Apart from Lumascape, Scott Brinker (Co-founder and CTO at ion interactive, inc.) releases a yearly infographic on Chiefmartec.com (his prominent Chief Marketing Technologist blog).

Figure 10.4 showcases the 2022 edition of Chiefmartec.com's marketing technology landscape supergraphic with 9,932 vendors. Scott Brinker has divided the Marketing Technology Landscape into categories like Marketing Experiences, Marketing Operations, Middleware, Backone Platforms, Infrastructure with the largest numer of tools listed across key sub-categories like marketing, sales, operations, analytics, infrastructure, etc.

Key Digital Advertising Trends in India

Having taken a look at the overall digital advertising spend and the various categories, let us now do a deep dive of the key digital advertising trends related to top digital advertising categories:

(a) **Share of search and display advertising is dropping:** Although search and display advertising are still strong, their percentage share in the overall portfolio has continued to drop since 2016. The prime reason for this shift is attributed to the changing preferences in consumption from desktop to mobile phones, wherein display specially has a disadvantage. Specifically for the display segment, there has been a shift to rich media as consumers prefer formats which are visually rich and appealing.

(b) **Strong growth recorded in mobile advertising:** There has been a strong growth in mobile internet penetration in India, which is the main driver behind the growth in mobile advertising. Mobile-based transactions are crucial for digital start-ups, since owning a mobile phone is becoming cheaper by the day and mobile phones provide a much more personalised medium than any other, in addition to having advantages like availability of location-based data, customer usage behaviour, etc.

(c) **In-stream video ads gaining strong impressions:** With the growing popularity and acceptance of YouTube ads and in-app video ads, video advertising is growing at a hectic pace. With short promotional videos in trend for both movie content and advertising, video ads are a very engaging medium not only to promote multiple product aspects as short bursts, but also to develop thought-provoking long-form video content which normally would not be screened on television (because of price and viewability factors).

(d) **Social media promoted content gaining importance:** With an overall spend of ₹495 crores in 2014, social media advertising formats like sponsored/promoted tweets and posts, text links, videos, and so on, have been increasingly gaining prominence. Each social media platform offers a distinct advantage - like LinkedIn being the best for B2B marketing, Twitter for real-time promotion, Facebook for customer engagement and promotions, etc., making social media a very important mix for advertisers.

(e) **Native advertising gaining prominence on mobile:** Native advertisements are ads which are in created in a format similar to the medium itself. For example, a sponsored post on Facebook typically looks similar in styling, content, and design to general Facebook posts, thus giving such an advertisement more of a chance to be discovered and read by

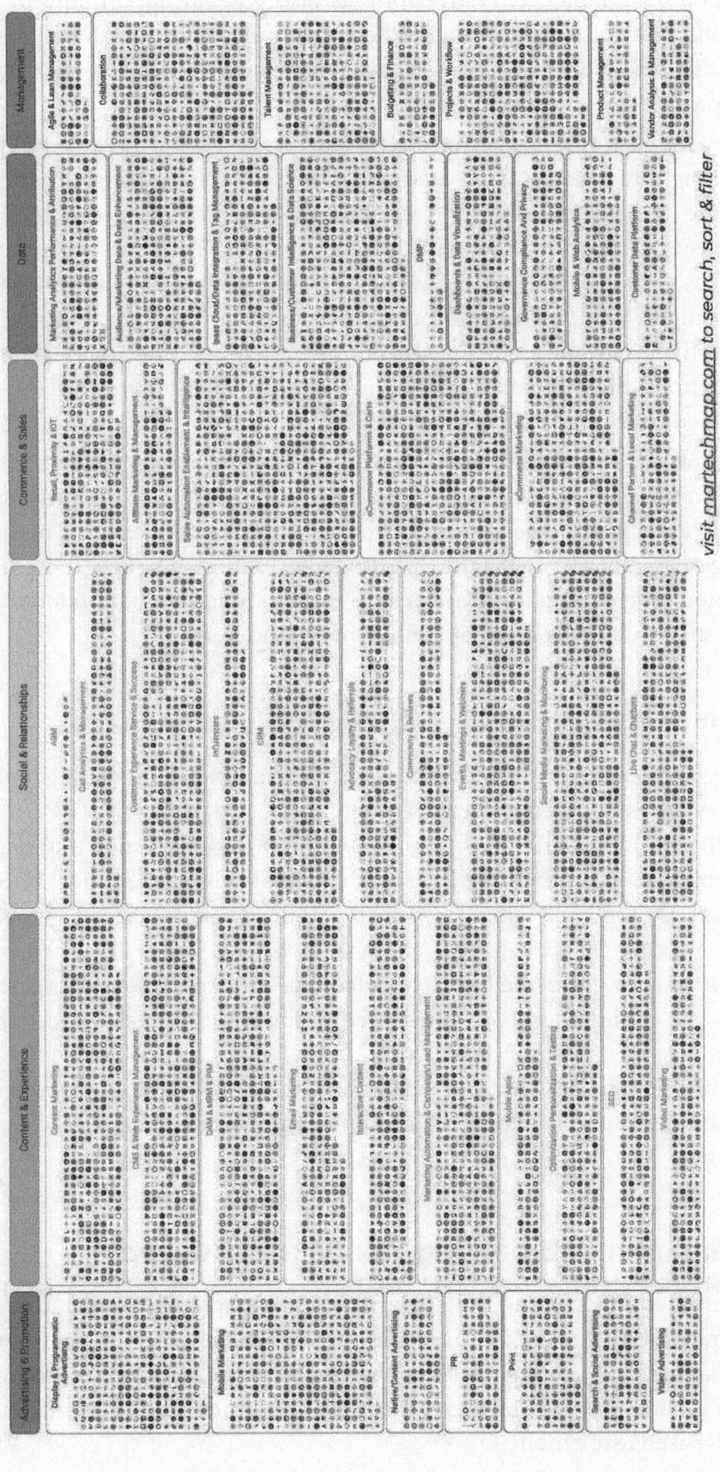

Figure 10.4 Marketing Technology Landscape (Chiefmartec.com)

Courtesy: Scott Brinker, chiefmartec.com, used with permission

the potential audience. Native formats also give an opportunity to advertisers to gather specific details for a particular audience on a platform which helps deliver real-time promotions based on the geo/user/device-specific knowledge which the mobile ecosystem can provide.

(f) **Increasing use of remarketing across platforms:** Digital marketers in India are increasingly adopting remarketing as a successful way to convert prospects which have visited firm's website, mobile website, and applications. Remarketing essentially involves targeting prospects to convert them into leads by sharing messages related to the products and services they accessed on the website earlier, and it also helps re-target products which they might have abandoned on e-commerce carts on the website. This is all possible through the advancement in algorithms which are smart enough to follow a customer throughout their buyer lifecycle on multiple platforms, and the retargeting abilities provided by multiple advertising tools.

(g) **Programmatic and real-time buying gaining traction:** The rise of algorithms is also supporting the marketing ecosystem players to buy and sell advertisements in real-time in a programmatic manner, which is not only helping reduce costs but also make the whole exercise highly targeted and RoI-driven in nature. Though Indian companies had not adopted programmatic in a major way earlier, its adoption is bound to become much more mainstream in India given global adoption and success.

India Digital Marketing/Advertising Tools Landscape

In the last section of this part, we will cover the overall digital marketing tools landscape in India across all key digital marketing areas.

Figure 10.5 showcases the most popularly used digital marketing tool brands in India in areas including email, SMS, social media, search, digital ads, and mobile VAS marketing. Details of some of these top tools are shared in the India Digital Marketing tool vendors list in the Appendix.

Figure 10.6 showcases the most popularly used display advertising tool brands in India. Details of some of these top tools are shared in the India Digital Marketing tool vendors list in the Appendix.

Figure 10.7 showcases the most popularly used mobile commerce tool brands in India. Details of some of these top tools are shared in the India Digital Marketing tool vendors list in the Appendix.

Digital Marketing—Emerging Trends and Concepts

With a round-up of global and India-specific digital marketing trends, in this section, we would cover the most pertinent digital marketing trends which are impacting both dollar spend and technology adoption. Although each of the trends is backed by quantitative data to debate the growth and influence of that area, our focus is on the most impact trends at an overall level and is not a RoI-based assessment.

Figure 10.5 India Digital Marketing Tools Landscape

Credits: Braj Mohan Chaturvedi, Understanding Digital Market Landscape/Infidirect, Digital Marketing Landscape India, used with permission

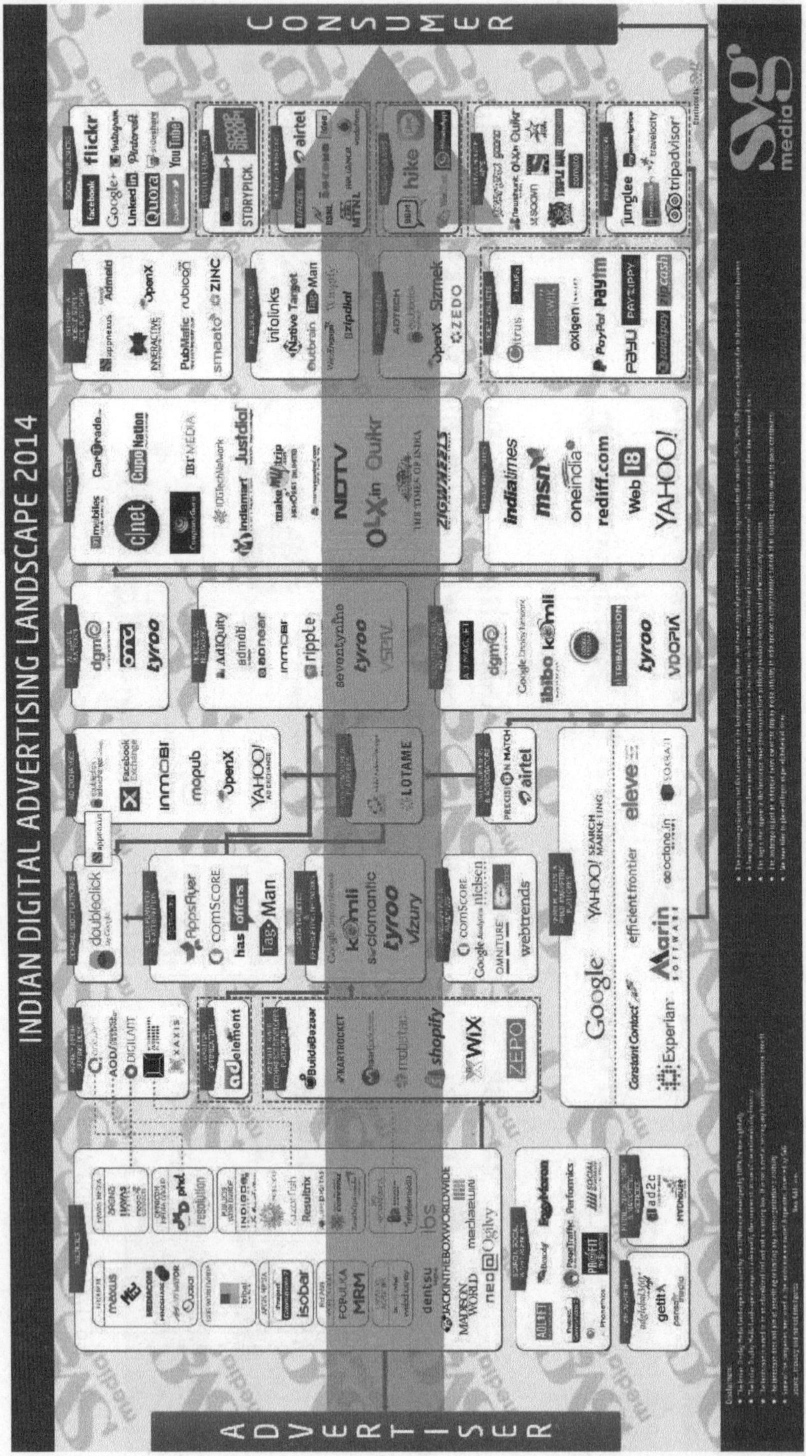

Figure 10.6 India Digital Advertising Landscape (SVG Media)

Credits: Rahul Sharma on behalf of SVG Media, used with permission of SVG Media.

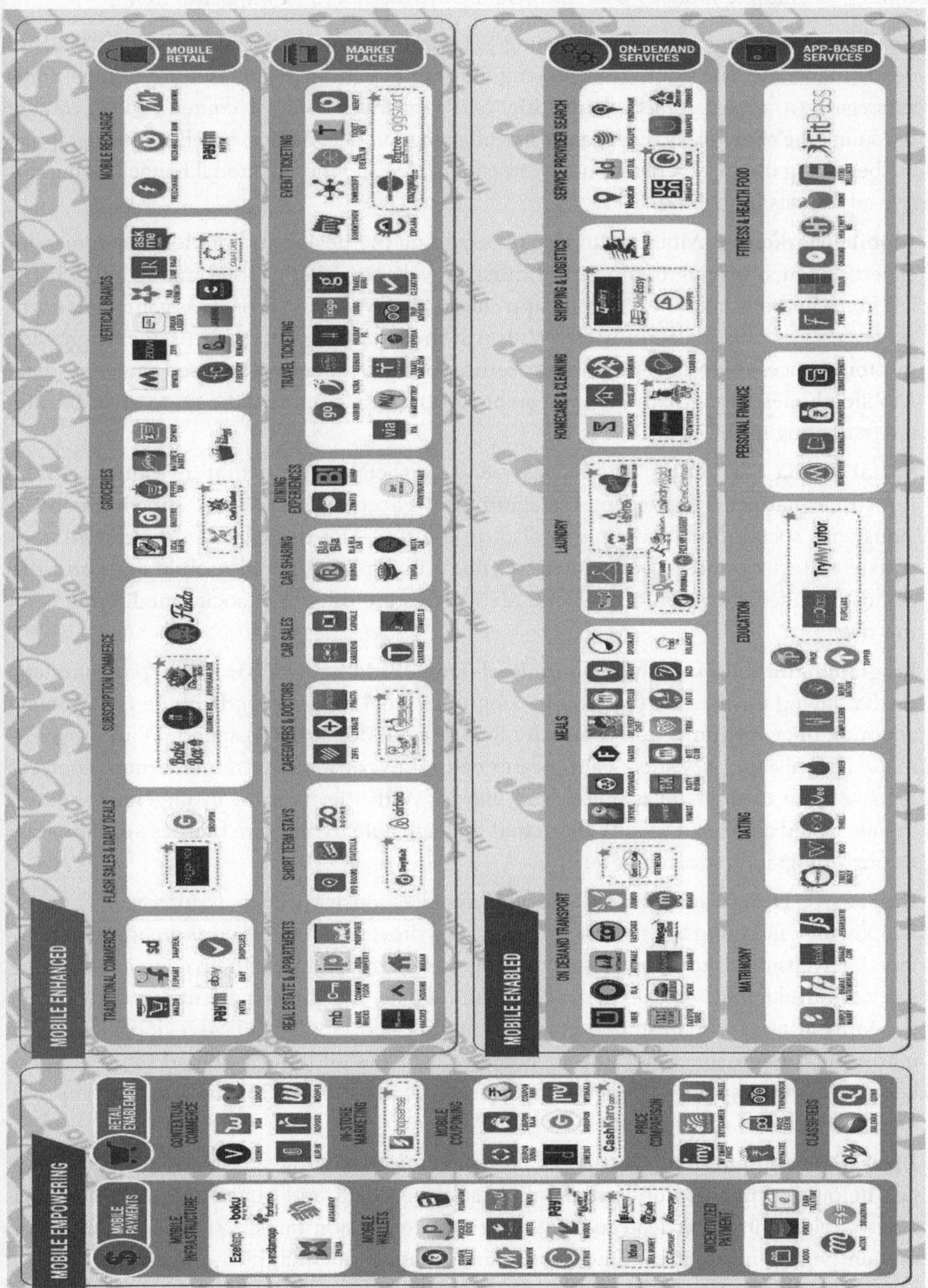

Figure 10.7 India Mobile Commerce Landscape (SVG Media)

Courtesy: Rahul Sharma on behalf of SVG Media, used with permission of SVG Media.

According to multiple industry sources, here are the top ten most impactful trends:

(a) **Content Marketing:** Content marketing is becoming crucial to propel all other kinds of digital marketing, the prime reason being the shift of consumer mindset from promotional messaging to a more practical, realistic, and fact-driven kind of content. With content becoming the erstwhile ad copy, areas like blogging, product demos, brochures, infographics are becoming the next generation advertisements, leaving the traditional banners and intrusive ad formats far behind.

(b) **Mobile Marketing:** Mobile phones are becoming the device and platform of choice for advertisements, leaving behind even desktop website visits. Mobile marketing is being led from the front by the ever-rising app culture, and video advertising is gaining its highest traction on this platform itself. With rich media and in-app advertisements growing in prominence, there is a need for advertisers to get more personalised targeting data. Mobile phones, along-with other wearable formats are definitely the go-to areas for digital marketing in the near future.

(c) **Social Media Marketing:** The biggest trend for social media is that investments in the top three platforms LinkedIn, Instagram and Facebook have start showing conversions with social media commerce also on the rise. The rise of new ad-free and non-cookie collecting social media sites, payment features on social mobile apps and rise of hosted videos in prominent social media sites are other key social media trends on the rise.

(d) **Programmatic Media Buying and Real-Time Bidding (RTB):** With programmatic media buying on the rise (even impacting traditional media spend), there is a growing adoption of algorithmic, and especially Real-Time Bidding (RTB) spend. With programmatic advertising, publishers gain greater control over their data to get a more comprehensive view of their investments and efforts. With the increase in targeting abilities, brands would also need to make sure that they are able to measure metrics appropriately through programmatic media buying.

(e) **Responsive Design and Visual Storytelling:** Responsive design is increasingly being adopted by marketing agencies since it not only provides an intuitive and engaging interface for website visitors, but also helps marketers integrate all their content including service introduction, case experiences, testimonials, insight documents, and so on, in the form of a well-orchestrated story. Increasing adoption of HTML5, focus on video marketing, design simplicity, use of dominant colours and quick upload times are also key aspects of responsive design which are a giving a boost to marketers to improve storytelling.

(f) **Marketing Automation:** The rising adoption of marketing automation tools is not just helping companies understand their audience data and buyer journey better, but is also helping improve lead management and conversion rates. With marketing automation getting more streamlined, integrating data from multiple sources and moving towards mobile optimisation will increasingly play a larger role in improving marketing effectiveness.

(g) **Personalization and Micro Targeting:** Personalised marketing involves using technology to target to individuals at scale based on key buying segments, preferences, and prior behaviours. With multiple marketing technologies now available to marketers, it is possible to identify and micro-target each customer persona with specific offers and call to actions for higher conversions. With improvements in personalisation engines and improvement in data and predictive analytics, it is becoming easier to gather actionable insights which tie online and offline information.

(h) **Localisation & Translation:** With business increasingly going global and acquiring/merging companies with multi-cultural products, it is increasingly becoming crucial to localize and translate marketing offers and messages to make them most relevant to the target market. Increasing use of machine translation (MT) tools and more local data available through mobile phones, is helping companies position their brands across multiple cultures, thus serving language and geographical alterations and providing solutions to customers in real-time and as close to their access points as possible.

(i) **Multi-Channel Marketing:** With multiple devices and platforms combining their might to provide a common brand experience to consumers across multiple-channels it is crucial that marketers devote attention to key aspects of multi-channel marketing like need for unified access to data, real-time tracking and targeting, uniform brand experience elements, etc., to ensure integrated customer interactions and help marketers reinforce their key messages in the most persuasive manner.

(j) **Big Data and Internet of Things (IoT):** With big-data and internet of things (IoT) impacting the way consumers' data is being looked at and integrated with each of their daily interactions, data and device collaboration is very crucial for marketers. Since these areas have multiple implications for marketing, we would cover them in detail in the next section.

Big Data & IoT- Data Technologies Impacting Marketing

With an understanding of emerging digital marketing trends and concepts, in this section and the ensuing three sections, we will be looking at the impact of three major concepts that have been shaping digital marketing and study them in more detail:

(a) Impact of Data Technologies: **Big Data and Internet of Things (IoT)**

(b) Impact of Business Segments: **Small & Medium Business (SMB) and B2B Marketing**

(c) Impact of Hyperlocal Targeting: **Social Local & Mobile (SoLoMo Concept)**

In the first section, we would cover the impact of emerging data technologies like big data and internet of things, and their impact on digital marketing.

Understanding Big Data

With the explosive growth in data in the past 4-5 years, the term big data has been used extensively to refer to the mix of structured and unstructured data which marketers have at their disposal to understand customer preferences, actions and behavioural patterns to target them and convert more effectively. Big Data as a concept is generally believed to include four Vs: volume, variety, velocity, and veracity, which are discussed below:

(a) **Volume:** Refers to the scale of data which is involved in any Big Data project, and which makes it viable to derive meaningful references through analytics.

(b) **Variety:** Involves looking at the kind of data which could be structured as well as unstructured, and how to best make sense from this total set. Structured data includes names, dates, addresses, credit card numbers. Examples of unstructured data would be the plethora of social data present across the internet in the form of short text, videos, pictures, etc. from which meaning needs to be derived.

(c) **Velocity:** Refers to the frequency of data which needs to be processed in a particular timeframe. Typically for big data to be applied to any practical problem, it should be dealing with a high velocity of incoming data streams which need to be managed.

(d) **Veracity:** Involves differentiation between good and bad data in terms of how trustful the source of data origination is, and how much clean-up is required before it can be usefully deployed and analysed.

The key areas where big data impacts and enhances marketing effectiveness includes:

(a) **Persona Development:** Big data can be most useful to generate more accurate buyer person as it can help track customers across their buying path.

(b) **Web Retargeting:** With the help of extended data available on each unique customer, marketers can retarget customers based on their web-visits and cookie data.

(c) **Measuring Customer Engagement:** Understanding engagement and disengagement patterns for new and loyal customers and target products/services accordingly.

(d) **Identifying Conversion Possibilities:** Through deployment of multiple parameters, marketers can judge conversion possibilities with much more accuracy than before.

(e) **Paid Campaign Analysis:** Big data can help analyse whether specific paid campaigns would be worthwhile to invest in and adjudge their expected outcomes (historical analysis).

Understanding Internet of Things (IoT)

In conjunction with Big Data, it is increasingly being realised that the internet is not standalone and if utilised to harness the power of all everyday objects, it can yield far better customer experiences and lead to a smarter world driven by analytics.

According to the Global Standards Initiative on Internet of Things (IoT-GSI), IoT has been defined as a global infrastructure for the information society, enabling advanced services by interconnecting (physical and virtual) things based on existing and evolving interoperable information and communication technologies. On the marketing side, Marketo defines the Internet of Things (IoT) as "the interconnectivity of our digital devices that provides endless opportunities for brands to listen and respond to the needs of their customers – with the right message, at the right time, on the right device".

A recap of the impact of IoT on digital marketing yields the following advantages:

(a) **IoT will provide highly actionable consumer data:** At present, most marketers are only able to access and act upon data obtained from consumer interactions with digital media and marketing technologies. With increasing amounts of data available from connected devices, consumer wearables and public-private digital platforms, marketers will be able to enrich present online-offline data sets with real-time interaction data, to influence consumers in a highly targeted fashion.

(b) **Marketers will use IoT devices to provide highly personalised consumer touch-points:** Consumers are mostly targeted through the internet, mobile phones, and other offline media. With inclusion of everyday devices like Smart TVs, interactive kitchen appliances, wearable devices, etc., marketers will be able to interact with the consumer using the digital device as an extension of its branding. For example, makers of a certain refrigerator brand are now able to gather plethora of customer information on the daily usage patterns, grocery purchases, and food intake of the consumer, which they can use to position themselves as a consumer health enhancing brand and share custom messages and experiences. A similar example is of various wearable devices (like Google Glass) which can not only provide day-day to information to consumers on multiple areas, but can also be used for digital commerce and contextual advertising whenever needed.

(c) **IoT will help refine consumer personas and buying journeys in real-time:** One of the other big challenges of marketers is to tide over the attribution issue to understand the ever-changing online-offline buying journeys of multiple consumer micro-segments. With the help of the IoT ecosystem, marketers in the near-future would be able to exactly understand and predict the real-buying points of consumers, thus utilising specific digital devices to sell closest to the consumer buying moment. The most important consideration will however, be the management of private data and how the ecosystem will support sharing of this data across brands, devices and platforms keeping in mind that customer data needs to remain permission-based.

B2B and SMB–Segments Based Digital Marketing

With digital marketing growing in stature and influence, its adoption has grown multi-fold especially across two key segments –Business to Business (B2B) and the Small and Medium Business (SMB) categories. Let us look at how each of these two segments are adopting digital marketing.

Business-to-Business (B2B) Digital Marketing

With B2B marketers planning to increase or maintain their digital marketing spend in the coming year, businesses have come a long way in terms of digital marketing adoption for their B2B interactions. B2B Marketing, which runs one of the premier portals for B2B marketing has shared the following key B2B marketing trends:

(a) Mobile phones will become significant for B2B web and brands will develop compelling and personalised experiences for their buyers on mobile platforms by investing in mobile-optimised elements, dynamic content, and fully functional mobile websites.

(b) Marketing automation will be high priority, and B2B companies would rely on these real-time automation tools to target prospects with relevant and timely messages while also saving valuable time and resources.

(c) Content marketing would become a more measurable discipline for B2B firms which would assign more resources and look at improving RoI from their content activities. Integrating content marketing throughout all communication and PR channels, focusing on quality content, and integrating visuals into content strategies would become the norm for B2B firms.

(d) Predictive analytics would gain importance and would support marketers in making the most from the behavioural and real-time data which they have gathered over time. B2B firms will rely more on predictive scoring rather than the traditional lead scoring models to predict actual buying intent.

(e) Paid digital marketing will also become crucial for B2B firms and they would spend more on paid placements like sponsored posts and targeted ads on social media.

Small & Medium Businesses (SMBs) Digital Marketing

The definition of SMBs would vary based on the region and typical revenue figures in comparison to large companies. According to Garner, companies which have either fewer than 100 employees or revenues less than US$50 million are considered SMBs in the US, while Wikipedia gives the European definition of Small and Medium Enterprises (SMEs) as those which employ fewer than 250 persons and which have an annual turnover not exceeding €50 million.

In India, according to Ministry of Micro, Small & Medium Enterprises (as shared in a Zinnov Research and Consulting Report), an SMB typically would have an employee strength up to 1000 with revenues in the range of US$0.2 to US$1.5 million. Such is the increased adoption and importance of this segment for digital marketing that Google India has recently set up a target to enable around five lakh SMBs in India. According to Google, digital advertising accounts for only 7 per cent of the total ad spend of Indian enterprises, as compared to 30 per cent in the US, thus offering tremendous potential for them in the Indian market.

Key digital marketing predictions for SMBs includes:

(a) SMBs will start incorporating technology and data in a broader manner with added advantages of cloud-based analytics tools which would help them execute digital marketing in a lean fashion to gather most accurate customer intelligence.

(b) Software with Service elements will help SMBs tide over traditional SaaS technology solutions. The do-it-yourself (DIY) model is failing organisations which actually require state-of-the art technology along-with expert service.

(c) Mobile phones will become even more crucial to respond to changing consumer behaviour patterns. The convenience of online ordering and in-app payments is going to differentiate SMBs who look to service their local clients most profitably.

(d) SMBs would need to move to the paid social model as they are seeing less impact of organic social efforts. Redirecting consumers to their owned media platform like a website, blog and email newsletter would be crucial along-with social media analytics.

(e) Another big trend would be the use of multi-channel marketing for SMBs to be able to utilise multiple platforms with a unified messaging. They would need to combine this effort with impactful content in a story-telling format for highest effectiveness.

SoLoMo-The Next level of Hyperlocal Marketing

In this last section, we shall look at the third major concept impacting digital marketing, which is that of 'Hyperlocal marketing' or the 'SoLoMo concept'. Hyperlocal marketing, by definition, involves targeting a highly specified local region based upon its cultural nuances and key concerns of its population. With advancements in technology, it has started becoming easier for marketers to keep defining narrower customer segments based on micro-regions and develop strategies and tactics to target them.

The concept of hyperlocal marketing preceded the coinage of SoLoMo (Social Local and Mobile). In terms of digital marketing, the hyperlocal concept began with Google providing the ability to marketers to target specific online audiences with advertising based on 'Geo-Tags', where a specific geographic segmentation could be chosen. With mobile phones coming of age, the next level of hyper-local segmentation came involved the use of mobile GPS technology to locate individuals within a certain area, with an ability to push messages and coupons in real-time to individuals based on proximity.

Although marketers could target local customer segments through mobile phones, they were still not able to penetrate them until the concept of social advertising fully caught on. With the emergence and wider acceptance of social media platforms like Facebook, Instagram, Foursquare, Twitter, etc., for the first time, consumers could exchange information among a known and trusted set of people to find quality restaurants, best branded items, most trusted hotels, and so on. The addition of the social angle thus completed the trio of SoLoMo, which provided the ability to mix the three elements of Geography (Location), Personalisation (Mobile) and Connections (Social) to target any individual in a trusted manner to use specific marketing messages and act upon them in real time.

To realize the power of the SoLoMo, we must first understand the technology behind it. The key difference between hyperlocal and SoLoMo technology is that hyperlocal targeting is IP based, wherein an advertisement on, say a search engine like Google, would target users based on their IP address. But this approach was not useful as IP addresses could not be trusted for accuracy and could not target a client in real-time. Instead, the Geofencing technology available on mobile phones is far more advanced as it uses geo-location technology to target customers.

A geofencing technology is a virtual parameter for a particular area, which picks up a signal from a mobile device in any particular location and targets promotions and ads in real-time.

With consumers hooked onto mobile apps, this technology supports customer privacy concerns too as it can be developed with permissions built-in to ask the consumers if they want to opt-in for offers from certain brands and retailers, thereby making the technology a pull-based rather than a push-based intrusive model. Companies like Groupon, Yelp, and Starbucks have successfully implemented geo-fencing technologies in the form of apps.

Implementation of SoLoMo Marketing

With an understanding of the differences between Hyperlocal and its next level SoLoMo, let us look at the key elements involved in the implementation of each of the three concepts: Social, Local and Mobile, and the impact they generate towards making SoLoMo relevant and usable.

Social: With consumers trusting their social circles and gathering advice from their networks on everything – from the cat food they should buy to the next apartment they should invest in, social technology has become crucial for most purchase decisions across the world. With social commerce gathering steam, social media now accounts for almost 8 per cent of all traffic to retail websites (according to Experian), and brands are taking the help of social sites to enable social sharing of their product and content to drive in-store sales through online social interactions.

With platforms like Facebook introducing tools like Facebook's Graph Search (semantic search engine), marketers are able to gain a view into customer actions and interests, which is helping them design more intuitive experiences that can lead to an offline sale. Marketers can now use social media APIs to gather more information on their most popular posts, articles, pins, etc., thereby giving them the ability to target specific products through branded apps in real-time as soon as a customer steps inside their offline showroom.

Mobile: According to the Vibes Mobile Consumer Report, 82 per cent of smartphone owners said they always have their phones with them when they are in-store. Consumers use a mix of online-offline data to make a final decision on a purchase even inside a store. With smartphone usage increasing by the day, and mobile users being present on the internet almost all the time, mobile phones provide the perfect platform for data exploration.

Marketers who have developed interactive apps have the highest chance of gathering deeper product interaction and consumer engagement insights to use them later for targeting. With in-app advertising gaining traction and the rise of wearables in different forms, new iterations and placement of mobile receptors is enabling marketers to push data to customers in ways not imagined before.

Local: Finally, with localisation being the key differentiator for the SoLoMo concept, the rise of location-based services offer convenience to an individual to get a particular product or brand with the best offers in a nearby location, which is the ultimate experience a consumer looks for.

With consumers utilising their smartphones extensively during the buying cycle by looking for reviews on a particular product, checking availability, asking a friend about their experiences of a particular store, localisation will undoubtedly drive commerce in a huge way in the coming years. In a country like India where most of the population still prefers shopping offline but want to check for the best offers online, SoLoMo needs to be perfected by most upcoming digital marketers and brands to offer not only convenience, variety, and availability, but also combining them in forms most preferred by consumers.

Emerging Web 3.0 Trends

In Chapter 1, we discussed the rise of Web 3.0, key differentiators and highlighted the areas which will be impacted. In this section, let us deep-dive into the most relevant trends and their implications in the coming times.

(a) **New opportunities in metaverse space:** With the rebranding of Facebook, opportunities for digital marketers have risen. Facebook is planning to create its own Metaverse space, which is an essential part of Web 3.0. This space will not be limited to a screen but will be highly interactive. Metaverse will open several digital marketing opportunities for brand marketers to provide the best user experience and generate leads from the Metaverse space.

(b) **Use of digital currency:** With the Web 3.0 version, the use of digital currency and blockchain networks will become prominent. Today, users usually receive loyalty points and vouchers, but in Web 3.0, tokens awarded to users will act as a payment mode by themselves. Businesses will also benefit from this value creation brought about by Web3.0.

(c) **NFTs will reshape marketing:** Non fungible tokens will be an essential part of digital marketers in Web 3.0 version. NFTs are used to assign custody to digital assets, and they will provide an opportunity for digital marketers to create brand awareness and increase audience reach.

(d) **Limited access to user's data:** As mentioned above, the use of blockchain technology will be persistent in Web 3.0. Users will have more control over how their data is used and with whom it is shared. This will also become a challenge for digital marketers because of limited access to user data in coming times.

(e) **Shift to community-focused approach:** In Web 3.0, users will decide how to promote their ideas. This will impose another challenge for the digital marketers on how to manage strong communities driven more by users.

(f) **Content creation with autonomy:** With Web 3.0, content creators who were earlier dependent on their platforms for flexibility of content rules would have more autonomy due to newer revenue models.

Blockchain Technology

As per IBM, 'Blockchain is a shared, immutable ledger that facilitates the process of recording transactions and tracking assets in a business network. An asset can be tangible (a house, car, cash, land) or intangible (intellectual property, patents, copyrights, branding). Virtually anything of value can be tracked and traded on a blockchain network, reducing risk and cutting costs for all involved.' Blockchain works across three key steps:

(a) ***Each transaction is recorded as a 'block' of data:*** Transactions show the movement of an asset. The data block can record the information of your choice: who, what, when, where, how much, and even the condition—such as the temperature of a food shipment.

(b) ***Each block is connected to the ones before and after it:*** These blocks form a chain of data as an asset moves from place to place or ownership changes hands. The blocks confirm the exact time and sequence of transactions, and the blocks link securely together to prevent any block from being altered or a block being inserted between two existing blocks.

(c) ***Transactions are blocked together in an irreversible chain (a blockchain):*** Each additional block strengthens the verification of the previous block and hence the entire blockchain. This renders the blockchain tamper-evident, delivering the key strength of immutability.

Blockchain Technology is an anti-tampering structure that stores the transaction records (known as blocks) in a network of databases connected through peer-to-peer nodes (also known as a chain). This whole structure is typically known as a digital ledger. All the transactions that are recorded in this digital ledger are protected with the digital signature of the owner which authenticates and safeguards it from tampering. No one can change or update the records and in case of any mistake, a new record should be entered for reversing the effect of the former record.

The recent trend of blockchain technology can be seen in the fact that brands like Amazon, PayPal, Visa, Microsoft, Walmart, Walt Disney, Accenture, and other successful brands are actively building their blockchain network. Blockchain technology has often been connected with finance systems, but it is bringing revolutionary changes across marketing systems too.

Multiple concepts have emerged from blockchain technology as can be seen in the growing demand for cryptocurrency and Non-fungible Tokens (NFT). Cryptocurrency is a digital currency or asset that is based on blockchain technology, which can be traded as a medium of monetary exchange and possesses the same value as a currency. In the case of NFTs, each token has its unique valuation and is secured with a blockchain. This differs from fungible tokens like cryptocurrencies, which are identical to each other and, therefore, can serve as a medium for commercial transactions (can be traded or exchanged at equivalency). NFTs allows tokenise things like real estate, art, computers, or things that have unique properties.

One of the examples of blockchain technology adoption in digital marketing is Taco Bell, which has adopted this technology to receive great success. Taco Bell is a fast-food chain outlet known for its digital marketing stunts, one of those being the release of 25 NFTs on the occasion of returning potatoes to their menus. The NFT craze is evident since all the NFTs were claimed within 30 minutes of being released. Among these, one NFT was claimed for US$3,646 and was recently sold for 10ETH. The success of this campaign showed how blockchain technology can work wonders for digital campaigns.

Blockchain technology acts as an ultimate solution for the shortcomings that digital marketing strategies may usually face. Blockchain is transforming digital marketing through following ways:

(a) **Improving Campaigns:** Blockchain technology allows marketers to have a link with merchants and eliminate the middleman. It is possible for every digital marketer to monitor their marketing campaigns in real-time to derive trustworthy metrics.

(b) **Authentication and Transparency:** With blockchain technology, it becomes easy for marketers to get transparent and encrypted data stored in a digital ledger system. Finding out accurate online statistics can be difficult due to site clicks and bots. The adoption of blockchain technology in digital marketing campaigns offers transparency as marketers can analyse whether their targeted audience is viewing their ads or not. This allows the marketers to reduce their ad spend and work on the elements which are not working.

(c) **Content Monetisation:** Blockchain technology makes the content management process more efficient by providing a decentralised ledger to protects copyrights. Companies can even compensate consumers for the value of their data. This will provide more freedom to the readers on how they pay or consume content. For instance, a browser called 'Brave' allows users to make decisions about the advertisements that they will see and who can receive their personal information. In exchange for it, consumers are given tokens called BATs to users who opt to view the ads.

Metaverse

The Metaverse was the most talked about emerging trend amongst all others in 2021. Mark Zuckerberg gave impetus to the Metaverse wave by changing the brand name of his entire company from Facebook to Meta. It was done in view of building a Metaverse space for its users to experience every interaction on this platform. As per Wikipedia, 'Metaverse is a hypothetical iteration of the Internet as a single, universal and immersive virtual world that is facilitated by the use of virtual reality (VR) and augmented reality (AR) headsets. In colloquial use, a metaverse is a network of 3D virtual worlds focused on social connection.'

Key characteristics of the Metaverse include:

(a) **Combination of virtual and physical worlds:** The Metaverse is the convergence of the 3D virtual world and the physical world that offers persistent and real-time experiences which allow a total sense of presence to the point where it embodies us. This virtual world is based on a timeline that synchronises with real-world timing. Therefore, in essence it does exist in real-time.

(b) **Individual identities:** The elements of Metaverse include avatars and technical infrastructure platforms. Avatars are the digital representation of a user's physical self that enters the Metaverse space.

(c) **Virtual economies:** It means that users can create, own, sell, and invest in the land of the universe. Users can also get rewarded for the labour they may put in the Metaverse world. The use of cryptocurrencies and non-fungible tokens prevails in the Metaverse world. However, companies may incorporate their own virtual currencies in the future.

(d) **Content generation:** Users can generate content for entertaining other users. For instance, marketers can use the Metaverse space for providing brand experiences to users.

Metaverse technology is already being used across virtual reality, eCommerce, video gaming industry, digital marketing, and other use cases are extending across multiple industries by the day. There are real-world examples where brands have used Metaverse for better marketing. Famous instances include:

- **Nike:** Nike created a virtual world called 'NIKELAND' on the Roblox platform which enables users to play sports games. Nike filed for digital trademarks of its main logos for the creation of Nike sneakers and gear. All such sneakers and gear can be used by users while playing on the Nikeland platform.
- **Dimension Studio:** One of the other successful examples of Metaverse is the virtual world created by Dimension Studio. This company made US$6.5 million in revenue by setting up a virtual platform that allows users to test garments - from AR try-ons to VR show-rooms and fashion games.

The Metaverse will enable digital marketers to communicate the same things that they are doing today, but in a three-dimensional mode. All text, graphics, and videos as part of a digital marketing strategy can be easily communicated in this virtual 3D world. With the growth of this trend, digital marketers need to adapt to this technology and utilise it to fit their marketing needs. It is difficult to predict how marketing strategies would get affected by this trend, but here are some expected changes in the digital marketing world:

- **Social media marketing:** Facebook is developing its own Metaverse space to offer a better experience for the users with their social connections. More users will get added to this

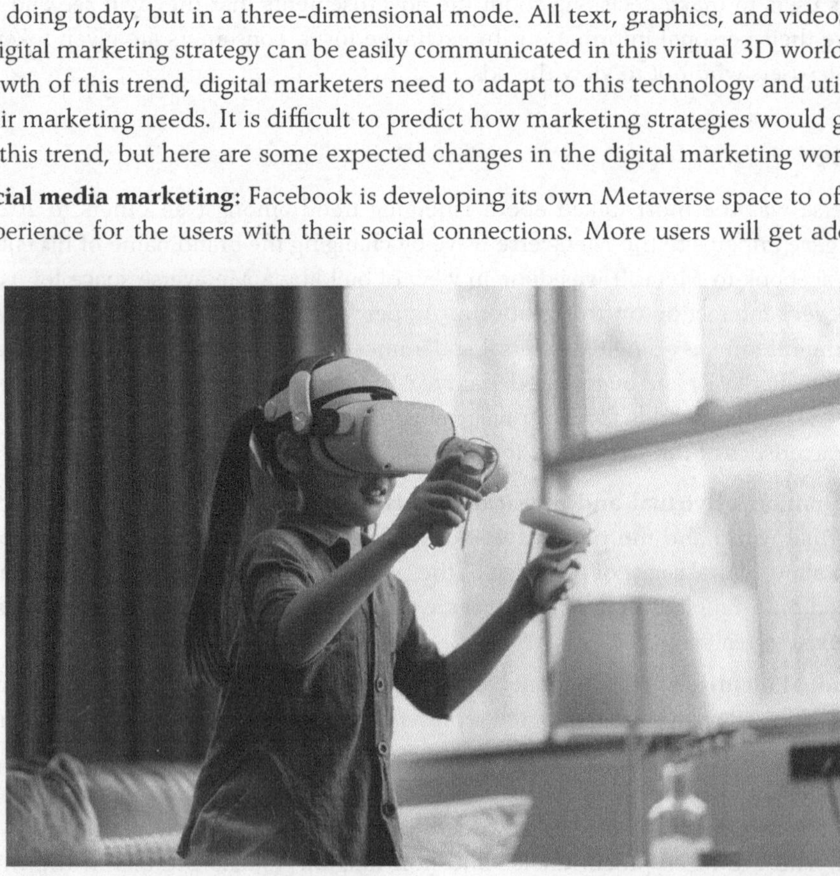

Figure 10.8 Child enjoying metaverse gaming with wearable VR headset and control handle

Source: WHYFRAME / Shutterstock

platform, offering better reach to digital marketers. Social media marketing can become easy for brands with the Metaverse platform. Users will have 3D avatars which they can also use while visiting websites and making purchases.

- **Content marketing:** Content Marketing through the Metaverse will be more interactive with 3D interactive graphics. With the help of interactive media, digital marketers can easily allow users to visit websites in a fun and engaging way. The connection between the real world and virtual world will help marketers to have lasting relationships with customers.
- **Search Engine Optimization (SEO):** The overall principles of SEO will stay the same, but with this trend, Google may go for an immersive approach towards search marketing. Google might offer a mixed reality search engine that will guide users to visit websites leveraging VR technology.
- **Virtual marketing:** The Metaverse will see a rise in adoption and effectiveness of virtual conferences, events, product tours, etc., which would help increase brand awareness and virtual conversions.
- **Influencer marketing:** The biggest impact of the Metaverse will be to aid influencers through virtual avatars, which will help integrate and enhance their persona and brand value even further.

There can be some challenges pertaining to security and privacy in the Metaverse, but they can be resolved with time. The digital marketing scope for brands in the Metaverse is high, as the space also includes the usage of digital currency for buying and selling. Although it can be a risky deal for brands, it may offer better results due to its growth.

Artificial Intelligence & Machine Learning (AIML)

Artificial Intelligence and Machine Learning technologies have been designed to respond to and perform the tasks of humans. While both terms are used interchangeably at times, there is a key difference between AI and ML. Artificial Intelligence involves an algorithm thinking like a human and perform tasks on its own. Machine Learning, on the other hand, deals with how a computer system can develop its own intelligence over a period of time by analysing multiple historical datasets available across repositories.

Many technical tasks such as robotics, speech, and image recognition are performed through AI/ML algorithms and models. The use of AI in marketing is not new, but it has risen over the last few years. Artificial Intelligence is helping digital marketers communicate easily with their customers. Digital marketing today highly relies heavily on AI/ML techniques for better productivity, efficiency, RoI, and insights. The implementation of AI/ML in digital marketing can be seen in the following instances:

(a) **AI-powered content marketing:** Brands can generate content with the help of AI/ML, based on data fed to them. In addition to content generation, AI helps brands draw the attention of users and deliver material through better segmentation and targeting. AI/ML can provide details of preferences and interactions of each individual that can be highly efficient to select most appropriate content across multiple campaign types.

(b) **Automated marketing:** The use of AI in digital marketing helps marketers to automate their SEM, PPC ads, Display Ads, Keyword Research, SEO, and SMM.

(c) **Targeted marketing:** AI/ML use-cases across virtual assistants, smart design, and predictive segmentation are helping marketers develop targeted campaigns and individualised customer experiences. Customised data can be utilised to estimate whether buyers are interested in buying the product or not, and at what time/channel a particular promotion should be shared.

(d) **Better understanding of customers:** AI helps marketers to analyse huge volumes of data and predict a customer's purchase behaviour, thus enabling effective engagement.

The proliferation of Web3.0 technologies is directing the future of digital marketing towards highly reliable AI/ML use-cases. With AI, users will be able to easily search for a product and its recommendations with the highest accuracy, whereas for digital marketers, AI acts as an incredible tool to make better use of data and offer targeted campaigns.

Digital Payments

Another emerging trend (which also relates to Web3.0) is digital payments through which payment modes like wallets, internet banking, credit/debit cards, UPI, AEPS, or USSD will receive better adoption and security. Usage of digital payments has increased in recent years and has impacted digital marketing adoption and sales tremendously.

Digital payment platforms allow digital marketers to improve brand awareness and customer engagement. Marketers are hopping on this trend, with mobile wallet marketing

Figure 10.9 Digital Payment Trends

Source: Kaspars Grinvalds / Shutterstock

being one of the latest trending strategies. A good example is the #AbHarDinHuaAasan campaign by Amazon India. Amazon Pay India's CEO & VP Mahendra Nerurkar said that Amazon's endeavour was to "demonstrate how digital payments simplify daily lives for these stakeholders. Through this campaign, we have captured various perspectives and stories that further strengthen the sense of trust around digital payments and drive adoption."

Mobile wallet marketing includes personalised loyalty cards, tickets, and passes that are used to engage customers on a mobile platform. From personalisation to updates and notifications, digital payment platforms have become easier to operate and more ubiquitous for users. Digital platforms benefit digital marketers in following ways:

(a) **D2C brand activation:** Digital payment platforms serve as an effective digital marketing tactic for D2C brands seeking to boost their presence in marketspace. Vouchers, cash-back, and discount offers across payment platforms help boost brands in their specific markets.

(b) **Customer engagement & website traffic:** Drawing customer engagement through digital payment platforms can be done through advertising and offering best deals to users. Each offer and deal will ultimately drive new users to the website.

(c) **App selling:** Brands owning mobile applications increase their chances of a sale by offering digital payment systems to users. For instance, Amazon introduced Amazon Pay to offer ease of payment for its users. Even with other digital payment platforms, it becomes easy for brands to advertise and increase adoption through local-based and integrated in-store, online, and in-app offers.

(d) **Tracking consumer behaviour:** Brand offers on digital payment platforms can help digital marketers track consumer behaviour and reduce ad spending. It becomes easier to receive details about clicks and traffic directed from the link mentioned on the payment platform. Personalised offers and discounts can be given to the users who are showing positive behaviour.

Audio-Social Marketing

Audio-social marketing is a type of conversational marketing that works better for personalising customer experience. It is an experiential form of marketing, which utilises the combination of voice and social-networking rooms to induce topical discussions, bring experts as influencers and leverage audio-interactions for brand engagement. With audio-social marketing, digital marketers can offer a unique experience which is more socially engaging and leverages users' latest inclination to the audio format.

Key examples of audio-social marketing include Clubhouse, Twitter Spaces, Spotify Greenroom, Live Audio Rooms by Facebook, among others. Brands have started leveraging this trend across multiple digital marketing use-cases including product launches, guest appearances, press conferences, live entertainment, branded Q&A, etc.

Clubhouse is one of biggest audio-social applications that allows users to launch or activate audio-only chat rooms. The application launched recently in 2020 and had over 10 million users (as of February 2021). This high number of users has made this platform an additional channel to reach out to a new audience through conversational marketing. The Clubhouse platform can be used by brands to share their experiences across audiences through audio. For digital marketers,

Clubhouse can be a good platform for holding discussions, sharing insights, and carrying live Q&A sessions.

Audio-Social marketing has already started to make its impact and brands have received a positive response for their efforts. Key examples being NBA hosting talks on Twitter Spaces around the 2021 playoffs, and Sotheby's celebrating 50 years of photograph auctions through hosted conversations on Clubhouse. Clubhouse marketing can be done in following ways:

(a) **Native advertisement:** Marketers can mention an advertisement or product link in the comment section of the platform. Generally, on audio-social platforms, such kinds of advertisements are read out by the host personally.

(b) **Brand awareness:** Digital marketers can collaborate with creators for sponsored rooms who develop voice-based content for the brand. It can be highly impactful for users who get attracted to voice-based content easily.

(c) **Get instant product feedback:** With live audio social marketing, marketers can interact with a live audience and get feedback about their products. It helps improve customer experience and engagement levels for any brand.

Clubhouse has established audio-social marketing as one of the future channels of digital marketing. The platform is growing and has already touched the milestone of 10 million users, which makes it an effective medium for digital marketers to further invest in.

CHAPTER SUMMARY

- **Part 1:** The first part began with an overview of the global digital marketing landscape, wherein we gained a conceptual understanding of the digital marketing landscape through the Gartner Digital Marketing Transit Map, which showcases key digital marketing areas as a complex mesh of neighbourhoods and tracks which interact with each other. In the last section, we looked at the Lumascapes and Chiefmartec's Marketing Technology infographics, which provide a well-classified view of the most prominent and emerging technology vendors presently in the advertising and marketing sectors.
- **Part 2:** In the second part, we studied key digital advertising trends in India, which was followed by the last section on the digital marketing, advertising and mobile tools that are most used by Indian marketers.
- **Part 3:** In the final part, we started by having a look at top ten most impactful emerging trends and concepts in digital marketing which are impacting both dollar spend and technology adoption. We then covered the impact of three major concepts that have been shaping digital marketing which included the impact of data technologies, business segments, and hyperlocal targeting. Finally, we took a look at how major Web 3.0 trends like Blockchain, Metaverse, Artificial Intelligence & Machine Learning (AI/ML), Digital Payments, and Audio-Social marketing are impacting the digital landscape.

CHAPTER 11

A Career in Digital Marketing

LEARNING OBJECTIVES

After studying this chapter, you will be able to:

- Understand the changing role of CMOs in organizations through the five core areas that impact marketing transformation—strategy, customer, operations, organization, and technology
- Explain the concept of the T-shaped Web Marketer for digital marketing and how aspiring marketers should follow the model to build a digital marketing career
- Understand the top digital marketing areas as career tracks
- Explain how digital marketers should approach a career in digital marketing

In the last chapter, we had an overview of global and India-specific digital marketing and advertising trends, and key digital marketing technology/tools landscape. We also covered the emerging trends and concepts in digital marketing by looking at the impact of data technologies (Big Data and Internet of Things), business segments (SMB and B2B marketing), and hyperlocal targeting (SoLoMo concept).

With an overall understanding of digital marketing concepts, frameworks, and an in-depth knowledge on prominent digital marketing areas, we will end the book with a final chapter on how the reader can build a career in digital marketing and the emerging career opportunities provided by this field of study. We will first look at how a CMO's role is changing in the organization, thus providing new opportunities to those who want to rise higher in the field of marketing with relevant digital marketing skills at hand. This is followed by a section on understanding major career tracks for digital marketing professionals followed by the key steps to building a career in each of the top digital marketing areas. Finally, the last section will cover key pointers to be kept in mind while approaching a career in digital marketing.

EMERGING OPPORTUNITIES FOR DIGITAL MARKETING PROFESSIONALS

Digital marketing is gradually spreading its tentacles and developing a critical space for itself across the marketing ecosystem. Be it the traditional corporate marketing division and marketing agencies or the newly growing tribe of internal digital marketing teams and outsourced cloud-based marketing platforms, all of them are now leaning to digital marketing experts to propel an organization-wide change. In the following sections, we will look at the impact of these changing digital imperatives from a people perspective and the type of opportunities it is opening up for students and professionals across India.

The Changing Role of CMOs in Organizations

Marketing as a corporate function is witnessing big changes which are not only impacting the core skills marketers need to possess, but also necessitating future CMOs to primarily be digital natives rather than retain their erstwhile traditional avatar. With the coming of age of digital, marketing has changed its face forever with customers demanding 24×7 product availability, product life cycles shrinking drastically, and traditionally entrenched products losing to new age service-oriented products. All these changes necessitate a change in the overall skills of the marketing function much of which will be increasingly attributed to the knowledge of digital marketing and its implementation.

Vivaldi Partners Group, a brand consulting firm in NewYork, in their recent study on 'The Changing Role of the CMO' have shared five core areas which are impacting marketing transformation, creating newer opportunities and changing the marketing landscape. These include:

(a) **Strategy**: As per the report, marketing has moved far ahead of traditional push-based communications and is now more about co-creating products with customers. CMO's key role involves shaping the strategy and identifying newer opportunities to integrate with functions like sales, innovation, customer service, and experience to develop experiences across platforms which are unbeatable. Marketing needs to orchestrate these company-wide changes by integrating traditional offerings with digital in a seamless fashion.

(b) **Customer**: Engaging the customer through social listening and new digital technologies is becoming crucial as traditional ways of assessing marketing needs with just a round-table discussion in the office does not suffice in today's time. Since consumers have taken control of the brand, it is important to know that the integrated customer path is becoming crucial to share the right customer story at the right moment. In a multi-channel world, it is becoming crucial to design consistent positive experiences for customers across the value chain to increase revenue and product adoption.

(c) **Operations**: According to the report, CMOs are developing digital command centers to collect near real-time insights and data to manage highly advanced and efficient decision making. This can only happen through access to data-driven insights and use of digital analytics to identify who the actual customer is and what are the potential new customer profiles. Marketers might try to catch-up with all platforms and customer touchpoints but it is becoming increasingly important to deploy advanced statistical models and attribution analysis to decide which channels are more crucial and which investments would yield optimal rewards.

(d) **Organization**: With rapid decision making becoming more and more crucial for the marketing function, cost is not as important as the ability to get various groups across the organization work together with the marketing team on multiple digital platforms to generate the impact a CMO is envisaging.

Marketing needs to be much more integrated with customer care, innovation, R&D, CRM and experience management groups to deliver the right experiences. CMOs are being increasingly judged on the way they are able to integrate people, processes, and data across the organization to make an impact on the customer in a holistic manner.

(e) **Technology**: Technology, which is the basis of differentiation for marketers strengthening their hold on digital platforms, is impacting the way CMOs are allocating their costs across all marketing functions. With a plethora of marketing tools available in the market including automation, analytics, social, inbound, customer experience management, etc., CMOs have to decipher the right outlay of technology which will bring desired output and impact. Digital platforms increasingly will have a large role to play in these decisions.

With a look at the above five key impact areas for CMOs, we now understand the impact digital marketing and related technologies will have on the marketing landscape going forward. In the subsequent sections, we shall look at the career opportunities emerging in the market through these shifts for which an aspiring digital marketer can develop skills to make a digital career. Though most of these skills look simple to grasp, the complex part for budding marketers will be to understand how to create the right impact with these digital skills.

Building a Career in Digital Marketing

According to the McKinsey Global Institute (MGI) report, Executive Summary March 2019 (see Bibliography for details), the digital marketing industry has more potential to unlock 60-65 million new jobs by 2025. As per Randstad India estimates, the starting salary for digital marketing professionals is in the range of ₹4.5–5.5 lakhs.

The T-Shaped Web Marketer

Though there are lots of job opportunities across multiple digital marketing areas, building a career in digital marketing needs a lot of focus in a particular digital marketing field with a broad knowledge of how all the key areas work in unison, to help achieve a marketer's objectives. This thought was first propagated by the team at Moz (which is one of the top SEO and digital marketing consulting blogs in the world), which shared the concept of a 'T-shaped web marketer', referring to the quality of possessing general skills in a broad set of areas and deep knowledge in a single area.

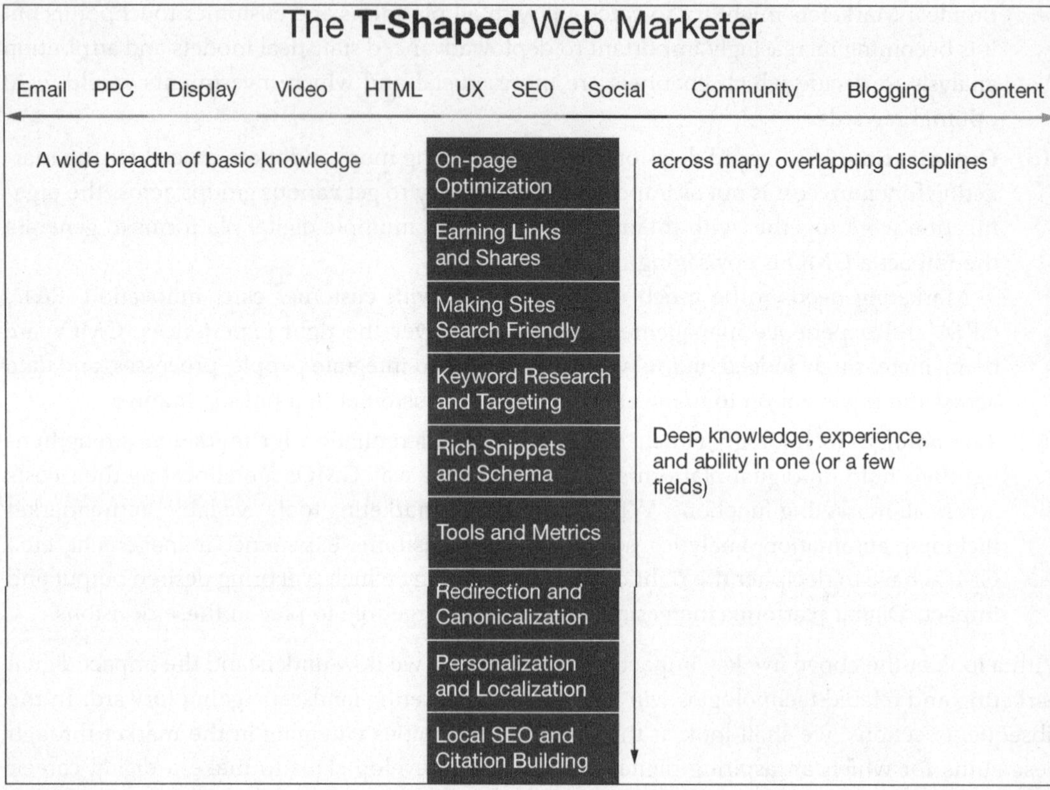

Figure 11.1 The T-Shaped Web Marketer by Moz

Source: Moz

Figure 11.1 shows the key areas which any digital marketing executive should know at a general level, and specific examples of depth areas (like SEO) and its major sub-areas which the digital marketer should know in depth, to become a balanced web marketer. According to Moz, following are the key advantages of such a model:

- **Breadth showcases knowledge:** With the kind of dependencies each digital marketing area and channel have on each other, it is crucial that digital marketers have a basic knowledge of all key areas to be able to gauge the impact of multiple outcomes on each other.
- **Depth provides expertise:** The real competence of a digital marketer will be assessed from their knowledge of specific deep-down experience in a particular area (for example, SEO as showcased in the diagram). The more knowledge professionals gain in any specific area, the greater are the chances of a brilliant career in that discipline.
- **T-joint provides cross-innovation:** The T-model provides a structure whereby professionals can develop multiple overlapping T-shapes by mixing their expertise area with a general area which is gaining importance to showcase innovation. For example, a

Figure 11.2 The T-Shaped Web Marketer by Volume Nine

Source: Volume Nine

marketer with strong knowledge of programmatic advertising can use that knowledge for mobile/video ad buying.

- **T-model reduces people dependencies:** Every firm can benefit from the T-model to nurture professionals with all-round experience, who can not only complement skills of other professionals but also be available in case an employee with a critical skill is unavailable or leaves the firm.

Figure 11.2 depicts another version of the T-shaped model as developed by Volume Nine, a Denver-based SEO firm. According to them, to become a T-shaped marketer, any digital marketing professional has to first accurately access their skill gaps to understand which general areas they need to know as generalists and which learnings will complete their specialist role.

The team at Volume Nine believes that while their team has SEO specialists who are specialists in areas like Conversion Rate Optimization, Content Marketing, Social Media Marketing, Local Optimization, they also need to learn general skills in other related areas like website development, creative advertising, or marketing automation. By getting their team to develop these varied skills that complement SEO knowledge, they can service their clients with unique skillsets, which is a key differentiator. This example proves the validity and relevance of the T-shaped model and its applicability to digital marketers all over the world and especially in India, where it is necessary to gather both vertical and horizontal skillsets for market relevance.

The demand for growth hackers is high among startups and young professionals are increasingly choosing this career option to a remarkable extent. However, being a growth hacker requires a strong understanding of digital marketing skills, which equips freshers with the necessary skills to be off to a good start in this field.

With the T-shaped model, the required growth hacking skills are categorized into three categories, including Fundamental, Generalist, and Specialist skills. These three skills signify the level and depth of knowledge that a growth hacker is expected to develop. As per this model, these are the growth hacking skills required:

Fundamental Skills: As the name suggests, fundamental skills include the basic and primary knowledge of growth hacking. Key fundamental skills of growth hacking include:

- **Data Tracking & Analytics:** A growth hacker needs to have a basic knowledge of Google Analytics, Google Tag Manager, Excel, Google Spreadsheet, and CRM software.
- **Behavioural Psychology:** Growth hacking is successful when a customer gets rightly influenced in an intended manner. The growth hacker must have knowledge about consumer psychology and how to convince consumers.
- **Learnability:** Every growth hacker needs to have the ability to learn new things to stay effective.
- **Growth Hacking Mindset:** Growth Hacking Mindset refers to the fact that a growth hacker does not take decisions based on their understanding but tries to explores alternatives before taking any decision.
- **Technical Skills:** The growth hacker needs to have technical skills like developing landing pages, web scrapping, front-end coding, and the use of growth hacking tools.

Generalist Skills: Generalist skills pertaining to the next level of growth hacking include skills that are necessary to carry out daily tasks. Generalist skills broadly include:

- **Customer Development:** When a lead funnel is leaking, it becomes important to evaluate the reason behind that leakage. Customer interviews are the way to find out the reason behind such leakages. A growth hacker should know how to ask questions to customers.
- **UI & UX:** The knowledge and practical application of UI and UX are important for growth hackers. These two elements are useful for creating a better customer experience. Initially, knowing the basic applications of UI and UX can work, but at an advanced level, a growth hacker should be efficient in making an excellent interface for customers.
- **Copywriting:** For developing landing pages and advertisements, a growth hacker needs to possess copywriting skills. Copywriting is not an easy skill and every growth hacker may not be good at it. Growth hackers must use catchy texts to engage customers.
- **Visual Design:** Visual design is the basic skill a growth hacker needs to have because it is required more often. Designing landing pages, ads, whitepapers, or lead magnets is the job of a growth hacker.
- **Customer Retention:** Retaining customers is another skill that a growth hacker needs to possess because a leaking funnel is not a good sign of being a growth hacker. A professional needs to know the necessary tactics for customer retention.

Specialist Skills: Specialist skills is the highest level of abilities that a growth hacker needs to possess. These skills are not necessarily possessed by growth hackers at the beginning of their careers, but over time, they should gain specialist skills that differentiate their abilities. These specialist skills include:

- **Conversion Rate Optimization:** Conversion Rate Optimization is a part of specialist skills which means that a growth hacker needs to have a good knowledge of A/B testing techniques and software. At the initial level, it is not expected from a growth hacker but at the senior level, a growth hacker needs to know all A/B testing techniques.
- **Marketing Automation:** Marketing automation is a skill that is generally possessed by all growth hackers. Marketing automation can help marketers deploy marketing tactics in an easier manner.
- **Acquisition Marketing:** Acquisition Marketing or Channel Marketing is the trunk of the T-shaped growth hacking structure. Acquisition Marketing includes marketing skills like SEO, SEM, PR, Influencer Marketing, social media marketing, email marketing, and B2B outreach. These skills are necessary for a growth hacker to possess but expecting a fresher to master these skills is not possible.
- **Referral Programs & Viral Marketing:** Referral programs (setting up affiliates to resell products and services) and viral marketing (utilizing techniques to rapidly spread information) are other effective skills that growth hackers possess. But this skill is less expected of a fresher. A growth hacker can master this skill over a period of time.
- **Activation & Onboarding:** Activation and user onboarding are specialist skills that a growth marketer needs to possess. The knowledge of customer journey mapping is necessary to provide the right user onboarding services.

CHAPTER SUMMARY

- In this chapter, we began with an understanding of the changing role of CMOs in organizations which involves having a look into the five core areas which are impacting marketing transformation: strategy, customer, operations, organization, and technology. We then understood the concept of the T-shaped career model for digital marketing and how aspiring marketers should follow the model for a rewarding future career. Further, we shared the top ten emerging digital marketing areas which are opening up multiple career options for marketing professionals. Finally, key tips were shared on how digital marketers should approach a career in digital marketing and the personal and professional traits that go along with it.

Bibliography 1
Source Links on Chapters

CHAPTER 1

1.1(a)

- Impact of Internet on Business. Retrieved from www.bqwireless.com, as accessed on 22 September, 2014 at 7pm
- The Evolution of Marketing. Retrieved from http://dstevenwhite.com, as accessed on 22 September, 2014 at 7pm
- History of Marketing. Retrieved from http://en.wikipedia.org, as accessed on 22 September, 2014 at 7pm
- Evolution eras. Retrieved from http://www.marketingmri.net, as accessed on 22 September, 2014 at 7pm
- Evolution of Marketing. Retrieved from http://www.gktoday.in, as accessed on 22 September, 2014 at 7pm
- Marketing Definition. Retrieved from http://heidicohen.com, as accessed on 22 September, 2014 at 7pm
- Definition of Marketing. Retrieved from https://www.ama.org/AboutAMA, as accessed on 22 September, 2014 at 7pm
- The Evolution of Marketing from Traditional to Modern Marketing. Retrieved from http://www.wordgurus.com, as accessed on 22 September, 2014 at 7pm
- Lyquist, M. (2019, Oct 27). Traditional vs. Internet Marketing. Retrieved from http://thebalancemoney.com, as accessed on 22 September, 2014 at 7pm
- Traditional Marketing (2020, Nov 30). Retrieved from http://www.marketing-schools.org
- Stroll, H. Marketing Challenge: Traditional vs. New Marketing. Retrieved from http://www.marketingprofs.com, as accessed on 22 September, 2014 at 7pm
- History Marketing. Retrieved from http://www.mediabistro.com, as accessed on 22 September, 2014 at 7pm

1.1(b)

- The Dot-com Bubble. Retrieved from http://www.thebubblebubble.com, as accessed on 22 September, 2014 at 7pm
- Basic Wikipedia Definitions of – Dotcom. Retrieved from https://en.wikipedia.org, accessed on 22 September, 2014 at 7pm
- Evolution of the web. http://www.evolutionoftheweb.com, as accessed on 22 September, 2014 at 7pm
- Internet World Stats. Retrieved from http://www.internetworldstats.com, as accessed on 22 September, 2014 at 7pm
- Dot-com bubble. Retrieved from http://en.wikipedia.org, as accessed on 22 September, 2014 at 7pm

1.1(c)

- Web history. Retrieved from http://www2.uncp.edu, as accessed on 22 September, 2014 at 7pm
- Cormode, G., & Krishnamurthy, B. (2008). Key differences between Web 1.0 and Web 2.0. First Monday, 13(6). https://doi.org/10.5210/fm.v13i6.2125
- Sharma, Madhurkant. "Comparison Between Web 1.0, Web 2.0 and Web 3.0". Retrieved from https://www.geeksforgeeks.org, accessed 19 Jan, 2023

1.1(d)

- Retrieved from workshop04_kromkryp.pdf at http://mngdep.teipir.gr, as accessed on 22 September, 2014 at 7pm
- e-Commerce and e-Business: Concepts and Definitions. Retrieved from http://en.wikibooks.org, as accessed on 22 September, 2014 at 7pm
- Relationship between e-Marketing, e-Commerce, e-Business and Internet Marketing. Retrieved from http://narimanhb.com, as accessed on 22 September, 2014 at 7pm
- The Difference Between E-business and E-commerce. Retrieved from http://www.computerworld.com, as accessed on 22 September, 2014 at 7pm
- Porter's Value Chain. Design Support Tools. Retrieved from http://www.ifm.eng.cam.ac.uk, as accessed on 22 September, 2014 at 7pm
- E-commerce. Retrieved from http://en.wikipedia.org/wiki/E-commerce, as accessed on 22 September, 2014 at 7pm

1.1(e)

- Jargon Buster. Retrieved from http://www.theidm.com, as accessed on 22 September, 2014 at 7pm
- E-commerce Navigation. Retrieved from http://www.bruceclay.com, as accessed on 22 September, 2014 at 7pm

1.2(d)

- Digital Media. Retrieved from http://en.wikipedia.org, as accessed on 22 September, 2014 at 7pm
- AIDA (Marketing). Retrieved from http://en.wikipedia.org, as accessed on 22 September, 2014 at 7pm
- Inbound Marketing: Funnell and Scape. Retrieved from http://www.smartinsights.com, as accessed on 22 September, 2014 at 7pm
- ImaginativePRO. Retrieved from http://tommytoy.typepad.com, as accessed on 22 September, 2014 at 7pm

1.3(a)

- Difference between Internet, Intranet and Extranet. Retrieved from http://www.differencebetween.info, as accessed on 22 September, 2014 at 7pm
- http://www.hcidata.info/inet.html, as accessed on 22 September, 2014, at 7pm
- Joan, B. Difference between Intranet and Portal. Retrieved from http://www.differencebetween.net, as accessed on 22 September, 2014 at 7pm
- Web Portal. Retrieved from http://en.wikipedia.org, as accessed on 22 September, 2014 at 7pm
- Dincer, N. (2020). Evolution of Web from 1.0 to 5.0. Retrieved from http://myeltcafe.com, accessed in March, 2023.
- Odigwe, E. (2021). The Evolution of Web 3.0 and the return of data privacy. Retrieved from https://mozartcultures.com, accessed in March, 2023.
- Verma, P. (2021). Evolution of web: From Web 1.0 to 3.0. Retrieved from https://dev.to/pragativerma18, accessed in March, 2023.

1.3(b)

- Geller, T. (2021). Getting Started as a Full-Stack Web Developer. Retrieved from http://www.lynda.com, as accessed on 22 September, 2014 at 7pm
- Tao, L. Introduction to Web Technologies. Retrieved from http://fi.ge.pgstatic.net, as accessed on 22 September, 2014 at 7pm
- Web Architectures. Retrieved from http://queens.db.toronto.edu, as accessed on 22 September, 2014 at 7pm
- Webopedia Staff (2021, May 24). How Wireless Networks Work. Retrieved from http://www.webopedia.com, as accessed on 22 September, 2014 at 7pm
- Wireless. Retrieved from http://en.wikipedia.org, as accessed on 22 September, 2014 at 7pm
- Mobile Marketing. Retrieved from http://en.wikipedia.org, as accessed on 22 September, 2014 at 7pm
- Wireless Mobile Devices Applications Solutions. Retrieved from http://finance.yahoo.com, as accessed on 22 September, 2014 at 7pm

- What is Mobile? 20 Facts and Figures. Retrieved from http://www.knowtebook.com, as accessed on 22 September, 2014 at 7pm

CHAPTER 2

2.1(a)

- Brick and Mortar. Retrieved from http://en.wikipedia.org, Retrieved from as accessed on 22 September, 2014 at 8pm
- Bricks and Clicks. Retrieved from http://en.wikipedia.org, Retrieved from as accessed on 22 September, 2014 at 8pm
- Travelportals-yepme-dressberry. Retrieved from http://articles.economictimes.indiatimes.com, Retrieved from as accessed on 22 September, 2014 at 8pm
- 2012 Industry Digitization Index. Retrieved from http://www.strategyand.pwc.com, as accessed on 22 September, 2014 at 8pm
- Baby Products Portal FirstCry to Open more Offline Stores in India. Retrieved from http://www.medianama.com, as accessed on 22 September, 2014 at 8pm

2.1(b)

- Interactive meaning. Retrieved from http://dictionary.reference.com, as accessed on 22 September, 2014 at 8pm

2.1(c)

- Network Effects. Retrieved from http://oz.stern.nyu.edu, as accessed on 22 September, 2014 at 8pm
- Network Effect. Retrieved from http://en.wikipedia.org, as accessed on 22 September, 2014 at 8pm
- Liebowitz, S. J. and Margolis, S. E. Network Externalities (Effects). Retrieved from https://www.utdallas.edu, as accessed on 22 September, 2014 at 8pm
- WhatsApp and the Erosion of the Network Effect. Retrieved from http://www.theatlantic.com, as accessed on 22 September, 2014 at 8pm
- Building the next WhatsApp Instagram network effect playbook. Retrieved from http://www.wired.com, as accessed on 22 September, 2014 at 8pm
- What to do if you are a platform with two-sided network effects. Retrieved from http://lsvp.com, as accessed on 22 September, 2014 at 8pm
- Managing in the Marketspace. PDF Retrieved from http://itu.dk, as accessed on 22 September, 2014 at 8pm
- Blischok_Market_POVR3.pdf. Retrieved from http://www.iriworldwide.com, as accessed on 22 September, 2014 at 8pm

2.1(d)

- Market (place). Retrieved from http://en.wikipedia.org, as accessed on 22 September, 2014 at 8pm
- Marketspace. Retrieved from http://en.wikipedia.org, as accessed on 22 September, 2014 at 8pm
- Managing in the Marketspace. PDF Retrieved from http://itu.dk, as accessed on 22 September, 2014 at 8pm
- Blischok_Market_POVR3.pdf. Retrieved from http://www.iriworldwide.com, as accessed on 22 September, 2014 at 8pm

2.1(e)

- James, G. (2013, Feb 26). Selling in the Post Internet Age. Retrieved from http://www.inc.com, as accessed on 22 September, 2014 at 8pm
- These New Rules of Sales and Service Change Everything. Retrieved from https://www.linkedin.com, as accessed on 22 September, 2014 at 8pm
- Sales Training for the Internet Age. Retrieved from http://www.dealermarketing.com, as accessed on 22 September, 2014 at 8pm
- Customer Service. Retrieved from http://en.wikipedia.org, as accessed on 22 September, 2014 at 8pm

CHAPTER 3

3.1(a)

- Module-1-1.pdf. Retrieved from http://nptel.ac.in, as accessed on 22 September, 2014 at 8pm
- Consumer_Behaviour_Theory_-_Approaches_%26_Models.pdf. Retrieved from http://eprints.bournemouth.ac.uk, as accessed on 22 September, 2014 at 8pm
- Vikram, gb (2013). Models of consumer behaviour. Retrieved from http://www.slideshare.net, as accessed on 22 September, 2014 at 8pm
- CB_Intro_Models.doc. Retrieved from www.geocities.ws, as accessed on 22 September, 2014 at 8pm

3.1(b)

- Persona (user experience). Retrieved from ttp://en.wikipedia.org, as accessed on 22 September, 2014 at 8pm

3.1 (c)

- EliaMiranda.pdf. Retrieved from http://studentnet.cs.manchester.ac.uk, as accessed on 22 September, 2014 at 8pm
- Hasslinger, A. Hodzic, S. & Opazo, C. (2007). Consumer behaviour in online shopping. Retrieved from http://hkr.diva-portal.org, as accessed on 22 September, 2014 at 8pm
- Lau, K. M. (2017). What Is Data-Driven Marketing? – Definition, Examples and Case Studies. Retrieved from https://www.makethunder.com, accessed on 3 March, 2022
- 5 Winning Data-Driven Marketing Strategies. Retrieved from https://online.maryville.edu, accessed on 3 March, 2022
- Bernazzani, S. (2022). A Basic Definition of First Party, Second Party, & Third Party Data. Retrieved from https://blog.hubspot.com, accessed on 3 March, 2022
- What are 1st, 2nd and 3rd party data? Retrieved from https://blog.relevant-digital.com, accessed on 3 March, 2022
- What is Data Analytics? Retrieved from https://www.oracle.com, accessed on 3 March, 2022
- 6 Step Guide to Creating a Successful Data-Driven Marketing Campaign. Retrieved from https://www.lotame.com, accessed on 3 March, 2022
- Gaikwad, M. 4 Effective Strategies to Run Data-Driven Marketing Campaigns. Retrieved from https://blog.processology.net, accessed on 3 March, 2022
- 7 Amazing Examples of Data-Driven Marketing. Retrieved from https://triggerbee.com, accessed on 3 March, 2022

3.1(d)

- EliaMiranda.pdf. Retrieved from http://studentnet.cs.manchester.ac.uk, as accessed on 22 September, 2014 at 8pm

3.2(a)

- Demand. Retrieved from http://en.wikipedia.org, as accessed on 22 September, 2014 at 8pm
- Types of Demand. Retrieved from http://www.marketing91.com, as accessed on 22 September, 2014 at 8pm

3.2(b)

- Online demand analysis through user queries keywords research. Retrieved from http://www.slideshare.net/jorgeserranocobos, as accessed on 22 September, 2014 at 8pm

3.2(c)

- Choosing brand elements. Retrieved from http://www.slideshare.net/guest98aa8c, as accessed on 22 September, 2014 at 8pm
- Brand equity. Retrieved from http://en.wikipedia.org, as accessed on 22 September, 2014 at 8pm
- Mind Tools Content Team. Keller's Brand Equity Model. Retrieved from http://www.mindtools.com, as accessed on 22 September, 2014 at 8pm
- Branding 101. Retrieved from http://www.slideshare.net/monoxid, as accessed on 22 September, 2014 at 8pm
- How to build a brand on the Internet Infographic. Retrieved from http://contently.com, as accessed on 22 September, 2014 at 8pm
- Brogen, C. (2008). Building your online brand. Retrieved from http://mashable.com, as accessed on 22 September, 2014 at 8pm
- Ward, T. Building a web brand. Retrieved from http://www.prescientdigital.com, as accessed on 22 September, 2014 at 8pm
- What is Customer Identity? Retrieved from https://signal.co, accessed on 3 March, 2022
- Data Privacy (2019). Meeting Data Compliance with a Wave of New Privacy Regulations: GDPR, CCPA, PIPEDA, POPI, LGPD, HIPAA, PCI-DSS, and More. Retrieved from https://cloud.netapp.com, accessed on 3 March, 2022
- HP TECH TAKES (2018). Exploring today's technology for tomorrow's possibilities. Retrieved from https://www.hp.com, accessed on 3 March, 2022
- What are Cookies? Retrieved from https://www.kaspersky.com, accessed on 3 March, 2022
- Epsilon Marketing (2020). 1st-party vs 3rd-party cookies: What's the difference? Retrieved from https://www.epsilon.com, accessed on 3 March, 2022
- Rivero, N. (2021). The digital ad industry is rewriting the bargain at the center of the internet. Retrieved from https://qz.com, accessed on 3 March, 2022
- Cooper, S. (2022). 6 Best Cookie Consent Tools for 2023. Retrieved from https://www.comparitech.com, accessed on 3 March, 2022
- Books. Retrieved from https://secureprivacy.ai/books, accessed on 3 March, 2022
- What is a web session? Hazelcast. Retrieved from https://hazelcast.com, accessed on 3 March, 2022
- What Do Cookies Do for Digital Marketers? MNI Targeted Media. Retrieved from https://www.mni.com, accessed on 3 March, 2022

3.2(d)

- Website visitor tracking. Retrieved from http://en.wikipedia.org, as accessed on 22 September, 2014 at 8pm

- 10-Step-Google-Analytics-Audit. Retrieved from http://www.slideshare.net, as accessed on 22 September, 2014 at 8pm
- Geary, J. (2012). Tracking the trackers: What are cookies? An introduction to web tracking Retrieved from http://www.theguardian.com, as accessed on 22 September, 2014 at 8pm
- If they are watching should you watch too. Retrieved from https://www.newfangled.com, as accessed on 22 September, 2014, at 8pm
- Website monitoring service. Retrieved from http://www.truste.com, as accessed on 22 September, 2014 at 8pm

3.3

- Integrated marketing communications. Retrieved from http://en.wikipedia.org, as accessed on 22 September, 2014 at 8pm
- Decreasing message impact and credibility. Integrated Communication: Synergy of Persuasive Voices. Book retrieved from http://books.google.co.in, as accessed on 22 September, 2014 at 8pm
- http://ac.els-cdn.com, as accessed on 22 September, 2014 at 8pm
- kliatchko-revisiting-the-imc-construct.pdf. Retrieved from http://www.soundwater.com, as accessed on 22 September, 2014 at 8pm
- Communication Society. Retrieved from http://www.unav.es/fcom, as accessed on 22 September, 2014 at 8pm

CHAPTER 4

4.1(a)

- Marketing strategy, http://en.wikipedia.org, as accessed on 03 November, 2014 at 12pm

4.1(c)

- https://ujdigispace.uj.ac.za, as accessed on 03 November, 2014 at 12pm
- Marketing Environment. Retrieved from http://www.slideshare.net/mustafvi786, as accessed on 03 November, 2014 at 12pm

4.1(d)

- Market research. Retrieved from http://en.wikipedia.org, as accessed on 03 November, 2014 at 12pm
- Competitor analysis. Retrieved from http://en.wikipedia.org, as accessed on 03 November, 2014 at 12pm
- Brand audit. Retrieved from http://www.milesdesign.com, as accessed on 03 November, 2014 at 12pm

4.2(a)

- SWOT analysis. Retrieved from http://en.wikipedia.org, as accessed on 03 November, 2014 at 12pm
- SWOT analysis. Retrieved from http://ctb.ku.edu, as accessed on 03 November, 2014 at 12pm

4.2(b)

- Marketing mix. Retrieved from http://en.wikipedia.org, as accessed on 03 November, 2014 at 12pm
- Marketing Management -14th Edition, by Philip Kotler
- What is the STP process. Retrieved from http://www.segmentationstudyguide.com, as accessed on 03 November, 2014 at 12pm
- Segmentation / Targeting / Positioning. Retrieved from http://www.slideshare.net/crisanthony, as accessed on 03 November, 2014 at 12pm

4.2(c)

- Resource. Retrieved from http://en.wikipedia.org, as accessed on 03 November, 2014 at 12pm
- Resource Based View - The VRIN Characteristics. Retrieved from http://www.managementstudyguide.com, as accessed on 03 November, 2014 at 12pm

4.2(d)

- Core competency. Retrieved from http://en.wikipedia.org, as accessed on 03 November, 2014 at 12pm
- Corecompetence.pdf. Retrieved from http://km.camt.cmu.ac.th, as accessed on 03 November, 2014 at 12pm
- Core competencies cafe. Retrieved from www.rockford.edu, as accessed on 03 November, 2014 at 12pm
- Core_competence_for_sustainable_competitive_advantage_a_structured_methodology_for_identifying_core_-W9A.pdf. Retrieved from http://web.iaincirebon.ac.id, as accessed on 03 November, 2014 at 12pm

4.3(c)

- SMART criteria. Retrieved from http://en.wikipedia.org, as accessed on 03 November, 2014 at 12pm
- Marketing plan. Retrieved from http://en.wikipedia.org, as accessed on 03 November, 2014 at 12pm
- Philip Kotler (Marketing Management, Millennium Edition)

CHAPTER 5

5.1(a)

- Strategic Management. Retrieved from http://en.wikipedia.org, as accessed on 03 November, 2014 at 12pm
- Contemporary strategy analysis. Retrieved from https://www.inkling.com, as accessed on 03 November, 2014 at 12pm
- 9780198289883-chapter-21. Retrieved from http://www.oxfordscholarship.com, as accessed on 03 November, 2014 at 12pm

5.1(c)

- 36-150-1-PB.pdf. Retrieved from http://jgbc.fiu.edu, as accessed on 03 November, 2014 at 12pm
- The 2013 value shift index. Retrieved from http://www.strategyand.pwc.com, as accessed on 03 November, 2014 at 12pm
- Management tools - Core competencies. Retrieved from http://www.bain.com, as accessed on 03 November, 2014 at 12pm
- hse_ethesis_12638.pdf. Retrieved from http://epub.lib.aalto.fi, as accessed on 03 November, 2014 at 12pm

5.1(d)

- Marketing personas beginners guide. Retrieved from http://blog.bufferapp.com, as accessed on 03 November, 2014 at 12pm
- Personas: Understanding the person behind the visit. Retrieved from http://moz.com/blog, as accessed on 03 November, 2014 at 12pm
- Olsen_persona_toolkit.pdf. Retrieved from http://www.interactionbydesign.com, as accessed on 03 November, 2014 at 12pm
- Datasheet_segmentation_guide.pdf. Retrieved from http://assets.omniture.com, as accessed on 03 November, 2014 at 12pm
- 30MM-Customer-Personas-Updated.pdf. Retrieved from http://www.marketingsherpa.com, as accessed on 03 November, 2014 at 12pm
- Handout_persona.pdf. Retrieved from http://www.winthropinteractive.org, as accessed on 03 November, 2014 at 12pm
- Personas. Retrieved from http://www.usability.gov, as accessed on 03 November, 2014 at 12pm
- Haydon, J. (2012). How To Create User Personas for Your Website. Retrieved from http://www.huffingtonpost.com, as accessed on 03 November, 2014 at 12pm

- 4 lecture segmentation positioning and targeting. Retrieved from http://www.slideshare.net/monikaskarzauskaite, as accessed on 03 November, 2014 at 12pm
- Create a Persona to Identify who your online Customer is. Retrieved from http://www.dummies.com, as accessed on 03 November, 2014 at 12pm
- My Best Segments. Retrieved from http://www.claritas.com, as accessed on 03 November, 2014 at 12pm
- The house of marketing online-segmentation approach. Retrieved from http://www.slideshare.net/pieterlievyns, as accessed on 03 November, 2014 at 12pm
- Segmentation and Targeting in Marketing. Retrieved from http://www.slideshare.net/ProfessorMathur, as accessed on 03 November, 2014 at 12pm
- Building a data-backed persona. Retrieved from http://boxesandarrows.com, as accessed on 03 November, 2014 at 12pm
- Creating_Quality_Personas.pdf. Retrieved from https://www.msu.edu, as accessed on 03 November, 2014 at 12pm
- Mapping customer journey. Retrieved from http://www.thecustomersshoes.com, as accessed on 03 November, 2014 at 12pm

5.2(a)

- Philip Kotler (Marketing Management–14th Edition)
- How to create a personal learning plan. Retrieved from http://www.mindtools.com, as accessed on 03 November, 2014 at 12pm

5.2(b)

- Philip Kotler (Marketing Management–14th Edition)

5.2(c)

- The 4 Ps of E-marketing. Retrieved from http://www.hudsonhorizons.com, as accessed on 03 November, 2014, at 12pm
- Marketing: Channels of Distribution. Retrieved from https://www.youtube.com, as accessed on 03 November, 2014 at 12pm
- Should you be building indirect sales channels. Retrieved from http://labs.openviewpartners.com, as accessed on 03 November, 2014 at 12pm
- Make your first ecommerce sale. Retrieved from https://ecommerce.shopify.com, as accessed on 03 November, 2014 at 12pm
- Selling online. Retrieved from http://northcarolinadeportal.com, as accessed on 03 November, 2014 at 12pm

5.2(e)

- Philip Kotler (Marketing Management–14th Edition)

5.3(c)

- Product lifecycle. Retrieved from http://en.wikipedia.org, as accessed on 03 November, 2014 at 12pm

CHAPTER 6

6.1(a)

- Milano, S. How to Develop a Marketing Plan Budget. Retrieved from http://smallbusiness.chron.com, as accessed on 16 December, 2014 at 1pm
- 7 Essential Best Practices for Digital Media Planning. Retrieved from http://www.*slideshare.net/jameswindrow, as accessed on 16 December, 2014 at 1pm*

6.1(b)

- Media planning. Retrieved from http://en.wikipedia.org, as accessed on 16 December, 2014 at 1pm
- realize-the-power-of-multimedia--7-steps.pdf. Retrieved from https://citycms.s3.amazonaws.com, as accessed on 16 December, 2014 at 1pm
- Media Planning 101. Retrieved from http://www.slideshare.net, as accessed on 16 December, 2014 at 1pm

6.1(c)

- Budget allocation within and across ppc seo and content. Retrieved from http://www.clickz.com, as accessed on 16 December, 2014 at 1pm
- Econsultancy-Marketing-Budgets-2014-Report.pdf. Retrieved from http://www.responsys.com, as accessed on 16 December, 2014 at 1pm
- How much budget for online marketing in 2014. Retrieved from http://www.webstrategiesinc.com, as accessed on 16 December, 2014 at 1pm
- Allocation online marketing dollars. Retrieved from http://www.marketingsherpa.com, as accessed on 16 December, 2014 at 1pm
- http://digitalmarketingcalculator.com, as accessed on 16 December, 2014 at 1pm

6.1(d)

- Mkt_mgmt_may2002.pdf. Retrieved from http://www.lenskold.com, as accessed on 16 December, 2014 at 1pm
- Roi_for_marketing_balancing_accountability3-29.pdf. Retrieved from http://www.hawkpartners.com, as accessed on 16 December, 2014 at 1pm

6.2(a)

- Marketing automation with 20SAS.pdf. Retrieved from http://www.csb.uncw.edu, as accessed on 16 December, 2014 at 1pm
- H17mm-bktaster.pdf. Retrieved from http://www.internationalmba.eu, as accessed on 16 December, 2014 at 1pm
- Kosela, J. Mass Customisation and Personalisation: One-to-one Customer Approach on a Mass Scale. Retrieved from http://kosela.info, as accessed on 16 December, 2014 at 1pm
- Rangaswamy, A. (2001). Mass Customisation and Personalisation. Journal of Interactive Marketing. Retrieved from http:// www.academia.edu/, as accessed on 16 December, 2014 at 1pm
- Roumeliotis, J. D. (2013). Mass Customization & Personalization: The Pinnacle of Differentiation and Brand Loyalty. Retrieved from http://jdrazure.wordpress.com, as accessed on 16 December, 2014 at 1pm

6.2(b)

- Marketing communications planning framework. Retrieved from http://en.wikipedia.org, as accessed on 16 December, 2014 at 1pm
- Fill_IM.pdf. Retrieved from http://wps.prenhall.com, as accessed on 16 December, 2014 at 1pm

6.2(c)

- Module.6-31.pdf. Retrieved from http://nptel.ac.in, as accessed on 16 December, 2014 at 1pm
- Integrating digital channels into your communication-mix. Retrieved from http://www.slideshare.net/kateelphick, as accessed on 16 December, 2014 at 1pm
- Digital Media Plan. Retrieved from http://www.slideshare.net/RanjanaPawar1, as accessed on 16 December, 2014 at 1pm
- Fill, C. (2009). Marketing communications: interactivity, communities and content. Retrieved from https://researchportal.port.ac.uk, as accessed on 16 December, 2014 at 1pm

- Content Planning.pdf. Retrieved from http://www.luminpdf.com, as accessed on 16 December, 2014 at 1pm
- Smith ,P. R. & Taylor, J. Marketing Communications: An Integrated Approach. Retrieved from http://books.google.co.in, as accessed on 16 December, 2014 at 1pm
- Integrating digital channels into your communication mix. Retrieved from http://www.slideshare.net/kateelphick, as accessed on 16 December, 2014 at 1pm

6.3(a)

- Search engine marketing: A brief history and a promising future. Retrieved from http://www.clickz.com, as accessed on 16 December, 2014 at 1pm
- How SEO works. Retrieved from http://boomient.com, as accessed on 16 December, 2014 at 1pm
- How search engines operate. Retrieved from http://moz.com, as accessed on 16 December, 2014 at 1pm
- What is sem? Retrieved from http://searchengineland.com, as accessed on 16 December, 2014 at 1pm
- How search works - The story. Retrieved from http://www.google.co.in, as accessed on 16 December, 2014 at 1pm
- Intro to Sem. Retrieved from http://www.sempo.org, as accessed on 16 December, 2014 at 1pm
- Benefits of sem. Retrieved from http://www.relevant1.com, as accessed on 16 December, 2014 at 1pm
- How does search engine marketing really work. Retrieved from http://blogsuccessjournal.com, as accessed on 16 December, 2014 at 1pm

6.3(b)

- Online advertising. Retrieved from http://en.wikipedia.org, as accessed on 16 December, 2014 at 1pm
- Whitepaperdisplayadvertising.pdf. Retrieved from http://www.wsimarketbuilders.com, as accessed on 16 December, 2014 at 1pm
- History of online display advertising. Retrieved from http://www.vantagelocal.com, as accessed on 16 December, 2014 at 1pm
- How does ad-serving work. Retrieved from http://www.adopsinsider.com, as accessed on 16 December, 2014 at 1pm
- The evolution of online display advertising. Retrieved from http://www.iabuk.net, as accessed on 16 December, 2014 at 1pm
- Benefits of display advertising. Retrieved from http://www.slideshare.net/CecilieBurleson, as accessed on 16 December, 2014 at 1pm

- 4 common display advertising mistakes. Retrieved from http://www.marketingexperiments.com, as accessed on 16 December, 2014 at 1pm

6.3(c)

- Beginners guide to social media. Retrieved from http://moz.com, as accessed on 16 December, 2014 at 1pm
- Social media marketing. Retrieved from http://en.wikipedia.org, as accessed on 16 December, 2014 at 1pm
- Social networking service. Retrieved from http://en.wikipedia.org, as accessed on 16 December, 2014 at 1pm
- What is social media marketing? Retrieved from http://searchengineland.com, as accessed on 16 December, 2014 at 1pm
- The history of social networking. Retrieved from http://www.digitaltrends.com, as accessed on 16 December, 2014 at 1pm
- The history and evolution of social media. Retrieved from http://www.webdesignerdepot.com, as accessed on 16 December, 2014 at 1pm
- The complete history of social media. Retrieved from http://smallbiztrends.com, as accessed on 16 December, 2014 at 1pm
- The top 10 benefits of social media marketing. Retrieved from http://www.forbes.com, as accessed on 16 December, 2014 at 1pm

6.3(d)

- Public relations. Retrieved from http://en.wikipedia.org, as accessed on 16 December, 2014 at 1pm
- Affiliate marketing. Retrieved from http://en.wikipedia.org, as accessed on 16 December, 2014 at 1pm
- Email marketing. Retrieved from http://en.wikipedia.org, as accessed on 16 December, 2014 at 1pm
- What is content marketing? Retrieved from http://contentmarketinginstitute.com, as accessed on 16 December, 2014 at 1pm
- Viral marketing. Retrieved from http://en.wikipedia.org, as accessed on 16 December, 2014 at pm
- Virtual world. Retrieved from http://en.wikipedia.org, as accessed on 16 December, 2014 at 1pm
- Second life. Retrieved from http://en.wikipedia.org, as accessed on 16 December, 2014 at 1pm

CHAPTER 7

7.1(a)

- Lead management. Retrieved from http://en.wikipedia.org, as accessed on 16 December, 2014 at 2pm
- Lead generation. Retrieved from http://en.wikipedia.org, as accessed on 16 December, 2014 at 2pm
- Kirkpatrick, D. (2012). Marketing 101: What is conversion? Retrieved from http://sherpablog.marketingsherpa.com, as accessed on 16 December, 2014 at 2pm
- 30 lead conversion strategies. Retrieved from http://marketingwizdom.com, as accessed on 16 December, 2014 at 2pm

7.1(b)

- 5 Best Practices for Lead Nurturing Emails. Retrieved from http://blog.hubspot.com, as accessed on 16 December, 2014 at 2pm
- How does lead scoring really benefit businesses. Retrieved from http://www.cmswire.com, as accessed on 16 December, 2014 at 2pm
- Predictive lead scoring. Retrieved from http://www.lattice-engines.com, as accessed on 16 December, 2014 at 2pm

7.1(c)

- The evolution of the landing page. Retrieved from https://prezi.com, as accessed on 16 December, 2014 at 2pm
- Landing page. Retrieved from http://en.wikipedia.org, as accessed on 16 December, 2014 at 2pm
- Landing page optimization. Retrieved from http://en.wikipedia.org, as accessed on 16 December, 2014 at 2pm
- LandingPage-cheatsheet2-10.pdf. Retrieved from http://www.marketo.com, as accessed on 16 December, 2014 at 2pm
- Most entertaining guide to landing page optimization. Retrieved from http://moz.com, as accessed on 16 December, 2014 at 2pm
- Alex Gofman, Howard Moskowitz, and Tonis Mets. 2009. Integrating Science into Web Design: Consumer Driven Website Optimization.
- The Journal of Consumer Marketing
- Landing Page Optimization: The Definitive Guide to Testing and Tuning for Conversions. E-book retrieved from http://www.amazon.in, as accessed on 16 December, 2014 at 2pm

7.1(d)

- The Definitive Guide to Lead Generation by Marketo

7.2(a)

- Web hosting service. Retrieved from http://en.wikipedia.org, as accessed on 16 December, 2014 at 2pm

7.2(b)

- Web development. Retrieved from http://en.wikipedia.org, as accessed on 16 December, 2014 at 2pm
- Website development process the life cycle steps. Retrieved from http://1080design.co.nz, as accessed on 16 December, 2014 at 2pm
- Goto_stage.pdf. Retrieved from http://www.gotomedia.com, as accessed on 16 December, 2014 at 2pm
- Six Phases of the Website Design and Development Process. Retrieved from http://www.idesignstudios.com, as accessed on 16 December, 2014 at 2pm

7.2(c)

- Presenting Information Architecture. Retrieved from http://webstyleguide.com, as accessed on 16 December, 2014 at 2pm
- IAguide2.pdf. Retrieved from http://www.princeton.edu, as accessed on 16 December, 2014 at 2pm
- Site Structure. Retrieved from http://webstyleguide.com, as accessed on 16 December, 2014 at 2pm

7.2(d)

- IAguide2.pdf. Retrieved from http://www.princeton.edu, as accessed on 16 December, 2014 at 2pm
- Web content management system. Retrieved from http://en.wikipedia.org, as accessed on 16 December, 2014 at 2pm
- What is Web Content Management (WCMS). Retrieved from http://www.contentmanager.eu.com, as accessed on 16 December, 2014 at 2pm
- Choose website content management system. Retrieved from http://www.inc.com, as accessed on 16 December, 2014 at 2pm

7.3(a)

- Retrieved from Jesse James Garrett- Book on "The Elements of User Experience"
- What is user experience? Retrieved from http://www.slideshare.net/chuckmallott, as accessed on 16 December, 2014 at 2pm
- Guidelines_book.pdf. Retrieved from http://www.usability.gov, as accessed on 16 December, 2014 at 2pm

7.3(b)

- Löwgren, J. Interaction Design. The Encyclopaedia of Human-Computer Interaction, 2nd Ed. Retrieved from https://www.interaction-design.org, as accessed on 16 December, 2014 at 2pm
- Designingforinteraction2_sample.pdf. Retrieved from http://www.designingforinteraction.com, as accessed on 16 December, 2014 at 2pm
- Methods. Retrieved from http://www.usability.gov, as accessed on 16 December, 2014 at 2pm
- Design Process Diagram. Retrieved from http://www-boxesandarrows-com, as accessed on 16 December, 2014 at 2pm
- User centered design. Retrieved from http://en.wikipedia.org, as accessed on 16 December, 2014 at 2pm
- Second life. Retrieved from http://en.wikipedia.org, as accessed on 16 December, 2014 at 2pm
- Myth#31: UX design is a step in a project. Retrieved from http://uxmyths.com, as accessed on 16 December, 2014 at 2pm
- Tools. Retrieved from http://iainstitute.org, as accessed on 16 December, 2014 at 2pm
- User-Centered Design Process Map. Retrieved from http://www.usability.gov, as accessed on 16 December, 2014 at 2pm
- Card Sorting: Designing Usable Categories By Donna Spencer
- Card sorting: A definitive guide. Retrieved from http://boxesandarrows.com, as accessed on 16 December, 2014 at 2pm
- PDF Files/5.pdf. Retrieved from http://www.rose-hulman.edu, as accessed on 16 December, 2014 at 2pm
- Retrieved from http://areas.kenan, as accessed on 16 December, 2014 at 2pm
- Prototyping: A Practitioners Guide By Todd Zaki Warfel
- Prototyping. Retrieved from http://www.usability.gov, as accessed on 16 December, 2014 at 2pm
- Prototype. Retrieved from http://en.wikipedia.org, as accessed on 16 December, 2014 at 2pm

7.3(c)

- 5es-citj0204.pdf. Retrieved from http://www.wqusability.com, as accessed on 16 December, 2014 at 2pm
- Ch02 Usability.pdf Retrieved from http://www.comp.nus.edu.sg, as accessed on 16 December, 2014 at 2pm

7.3(d)

- e-SERVQUAL-A Multiple Item Scale for Assessing Electronic Service Quality.pdf. Retrieved from http://areas.kenan-flagler.unc.edu, as accessed on 16 December, 2014 at 2pm
- 1.pdf. IJUNESST, vol2_no1. Retrieved from http://www.sersc.org, as accessed on 16 December, 2014 at 2pm

CHAPTER 8

8.1(a)

- Best practice campaign management for marketing, Retrieved from http://www.slideshare.net/Shelly38, as accessed on 20 October, 2015 at 9pm
- Marketo services. Retrieved from https://launchpoint.marketo.com, as accessed on 20 October, 2015 at 9pm

8.1(b)

- BP_MrktngMngrs.pdf. Retrieved from http://www.salesforce.com, as accessed on 20 October, 2015 at 9pm
- Marketing Campaign Management. Retrieved from http://www.slideshare.net/lampereg, as accessed on 20 October, 2015 at 9pm

8.1(c)

- Setting Up Execution Options for Campaigns. Retrieved from http://docs.oracle.com, as accessed on 20 October, 2015 at 9pm
- Marketing Campaign Management. Retrieved from http://www.slideshare.net/lampereg, as accessed on 20 October, 2015 at 9pm

8.1(d)

- Marketo campaign execution services. Retrieved from https://launchpoint.marketo.com, as accessed on 20 October, 2015 at 9pm

8.2(a)

- What is paid search. Retrieved from http://searchengineland.com, as accessed on 20 October, 2015 at 9pm
- About campaign settings. Retrieved from https://support.google.com/adwords, as accessed on 20 October, 2015 at 9pm

8.2(b)

- Google adwords best practices. Retrieved from http://searchengineland.com, as accessed on 20 October, 2015 at 9pm
- Online Marketing 201: Running a campaign. Retrieved from https://support.google.com, as accessed on 20 October, 2015 at 9pm
- PPC University. Retrieved from http://www.wordstream.com, as accessed on 20 October, 2015 at 9pm
- The beginners guide to google adwords. Retrieved from http://wpcurve.com, as accessed on 20 October, 2015 at 9pm
- Powerpoint arcsi final presentation. Retrieved from http://www.slideshare.net/HawkEyePPC/, as accessed on 20 October, 2015 at 9pm
- Learn PPC Marketing. Retrieved from http://www.wikihow.com/, as accessed on 20 October, 2015 at 9pm
- Blogs. Retrieved from http://services.google.com, as accessed on 20 October, 2015 at 9pm
- Google partners. Retrieved from https://www.google.com, as accessed on 20 October, 2015 at 9pm
- Learning the world of pay-per-click advertising Retrieved from http://www.slideshare.net/sageisland, as accessed on 20 October, 2015 at 9pm
- Sem benefits. Retrieved from http://www.thepamediagroup.com, as accessed on 20 October, 2015 at 9pm

8.2(c)

- SEOmoz-The-Beginners-Guide-To-SEO-2012.pdf. Retrieved from http://static.seomoz.org, as accessed on 20 October, 2015 at 9pm
- The changing face of seo. Retrieved from http://www.stonetemple.com, as accessed on 20 October, 2015 at 9pm
- Seo101.pdf. Retrieved from https://web.stanford.edu, as accessed on 20 October, 2015 at 9pm
- SEO-101-The-Basics-Act-On.pdf. Retrieved from http://www.musselwhitemarketing.com, as accessed on 20 October, 2015 at 9pm

- Search Engine Optimization (SEO) Starter Guide. Retrieved from https://support.google.com, as accessed on 20 October, 2015 at 9pm
- Search-engine-optimization-starter-guide.pdf. Retrieved from http://static.googleusercontent.com, as accessed on 20 October, 2015 at 9pm
- On-page vs off-page optimization what's the difference. Retrieved from https://www.betaout.com, as accessed on 20 October, 2015 at 9pm
- Web_SEO_Factors.pdf. Retrieved from http://nmis.isti.cnr.it, as accessed on 20 October, 2015 at 9pm
- Book- Search Engine Optimization for Dummies
- Tips. Retrieved from http://www.search-usability.com, as accessed on 20 October, 2015 at 9pm
- Anchor text. Searched from https://www.google.co.in, as accessed on 20 October, 2015 at 9pm
- Link building. Retrieved from http://en.wikipedia.org, as accessed on 20 October, 2015 at 9pm
- Understanding three types link building. Retrieved from http://www.stryde.com, as accessed on 20 October, 2015 at 9pm
- What is link building. Retrieved from http://searchenginewatch.com, as accessed on 20 October, 2015 at 9pm
- Link building. Retrieved from http://backlinko.com, as accessed on 20 October, 2015 at 9pm
- Link building strategy. Retrieved from http://www.wordstream.com/, as accessed on 20 October, 2015 at 9pm

8.3(a)

- Display advertising. Retrieved from http://en.wikipedia.org, as accessed on 20 October, 2015 at 9pm
- Campaign improvement – adjusting postlaunch. Retrieved from https://www.advertising.com, as accessed on 20 October, 2015 at 9pm
- Additional resources. Retrieved from https://optimizingadsense.withgoogle.com, as accessed on 20 October, 2015 at 9pm
- Aluge, P. Display Advertising Basics (DSPs, RTB, Ad Exchanges, DMPs) - Pete Kluge, Adobe. Retrieved from https://www.youtube.com, as accessed on 20 October, 2015 at 9pm
- http://www.imediaconnection.com, as accessed on 20 October, 2015 at 9pm
- Planner. Retrieved from http://www.bionic-ads.com, as accessed on 20 October, 2015 at 9pm
- http://directory.iab.net, as accessed on 20 October, 2015 at 9pm

- Bionic media planner advertising flowcharts. Retrieved from http://www.bionic-ads.com, as accessed on 20 October, 2015 at 9pm
- How do Ad Agencies charge their clients. Retrieved from http://www.quora.com, as accessed on 20 October, 2015 at 9pm
- Rich media. Retrieved from https://support.google.com, as accessed on 20 October, 2015 at 9pm
- Google Ad Manager Help. Retrieved from https://support.google.com, as accessed on 20 October, 2015 at 9pm
- Mix and match. Retrieved from https://publisheruniversity.withgoogle.com, as accessed on 20 October, 2015 at 9pm
- https://www.youtube.com, as accessed on 20 October, 2015 at 9pm
- What publishers should ask from an inventory forecasting system part-1. Retrieved from http://www.adservingblog.com, as accessed on 20 October, 2015 at 9pm
- Blog. Retrieved from http://www.yieldex.com, as accessed on 20 October, 2015 at 9pm
- Increase confidence in inventory forecasting and ad revenue growth is sure to follow. Retrieved from http://www.yieldex.com, as accessed on 20 October, 2015 at 9pm
- Revenue_maximization_090210.pdf. Retrieved from http://static.googleusercontent.com, as accessed on 20 October, 2015 at 9pm

8.3(b)

- Online media planning buying remnant vs guaranteed display ads. Retrieved from http://certifiedknowledge.org, as accessed on 20 October, 2015 at 9pm
- Online advertising – Define programmatic buying. Retrieved from http://adexchanger.com, as accessed on 20 October, 2015 at 9pm
- How to read double click ad-tags and ad-tag variables. Retrieved from http://www.adopsinsider.com, as accessed on 20 October, 2015 at 9pm
- Authorized buyers help. Retrieved from https://support.google.com
- Automated guaranteed. Retrieved from http://www.isocket.com, as accessed on 20 October, 2015 at 9pm
- Data-driven thinking – programmatic direct. Retrieved from http://adexchanger.com, as accessed on 20 October, 2015 at 9pm
- Shift programmatic picking speed. Retrieved from http://blogs.adobe.com, as accessed on 20 October, 2015 at 9pm
- Kantar Media SRDS. How to Access and Buy Programmatic Guaranteed Direct Inventory in SRDS.com. Retrieved from https://www.youtube.com, as accessed on 20 October, 2015 at 9pm
- IAB_Digital_Simplified_Programmatic_Sept_2013.pdf. Retrieved from http://www.iab.net, as accessed on 20 October, 2015 at 9pm

- Barbell. Retrieved from http://www.614group.com, as accessed on 20 October, 2015 at 9pm
- Programmatic-Buying-of-Online-Display-Inventory.pdf. Retrieved from http://aforetheherd.com, as accessed on 20 October, 2015 at 9pm
- Programmatic direct - data-driven thinking. Retrieved from http://adexchanger.com, as accessed on 20 October, 2015 at 9pm
- Diagramming the ssp dsp and rtb redirect path. Retrieved from http://www.adopsinsider.com, as accessed on 20 October, 2015 at 9pm
- Real time bidding. Retrieved from http://en.wikipedia.org, as accessed on 20 October, 2015 at 9pm
- Basics–Support. Retrieved from http://www.sitescout.com, as accessed on 20 October, 2015 at 9pm
- Google White Paper The Arrival of Real Time Bidding. Retrieved from http://static.googleusercontent.com, as accessed on 20 October, 2015 at 9pm
- 5 ways real-time bidding differs from direct buys. Retrieved from http://marketingland.com, as accessed on 20 October, 2015 at 9pm
- Real-time bidding. Retrieved from http://www.periscopix.co.uk, as accessed on 20 October, 2015 at 9pm

8.3(c)

- What's rich media ad anyway. Retrieved from http://googleblog.blogspot.in, as accessed on 20 October, 2015 at 9pm
- IAB_Rich_Media_Measurement_11_12_07.pdf. Retrieved from http://www.iab.net, as accessed on 20 October, 2015 at 9pm
- What is rich media? Retrieved from https://support.google.com, as accessed on 20 October, 2015 at 9pm
- Rich media. Retrieved from https://support.google.com, as accessed on 20 October, 2015 at 9pm

8.4(a)

- What is content marketing. Retrieved from http://contentmarketinginstitute.com, as accessed on 20 October, 2015 at 9pm
- Definitive guide to engaging content marketing. Retrieved from http://www.marketo.com, as accessed on 20 October, 2015 at 9pm
- How to create a content marketing-strategy. Retrieved from http://www.convinceandconvert.com, as accessed on 20 October, 2015 at 9pm
- The advanced guide to content marketing. Retrieved from http://www.quicksprout.com, as accessed on 20 October, 2015 at 9pm

8.4(b)

- How to build a social media campaign. Retrieved from http://www.slideshare.net/ArtilleryMarketing, as accessed on 20 October, 2015 at 9pm
- ebook_SocialMediaBlueprint2_SalesforceRadian6.pdf. Retrieved from http://igo2group.com, as accessed on 20 October, 2015 at 9pm
- Best practices for social media wp 1588491.pdf. Retrieved from http://www.oracle.com, as accessed on 20 October, 2015 at 9pm
- Social media campaign elements. Retrieved from http://www.socialmediaexaminer.com, as accessed on 20 October, 2015 at 9pm
- Run a Successful Social Media Marketing Campaign. Retrieved from http://www.wikihow.com, as accessed on 20 October, 2015 at 9pm
- Socialbakers Acquires Edgerank Checker. Retrieved from http://techcrunch.com, as accessed on 20 October, 2015 at 9pm
- The complete guide to global social media marketing.pdf. Retrieved from http://www.ciccorporate.com, as accessed on 20 October, 2015 at 9pm
- Social-Media-Strategy-Guide.pdf. Retrieved from http://socialbusiness.hootsuite.com, as accessed on 20 October, 2015 at 9pm
- Run-a-Successful Social Media Marketing Campaign. Retrieved from http://www.wikihow.com, as accessed on 20 October, 2015 at 9pm
- Personal branding tips. Retrieved from http://www.navidmoazzez.com, as accessed on 20 October, 2015 at 9pm
- Beginners guide to social media>best-practices. Retrieved from http://moz.com, as accessed on 20 October, 2015 at 9pm
- Social-Media-Strategy-Guide.pdf. Retrieved from http://socialbusiness.hootsuite.com, as accessed on 20 October, 2015 at 9pm
- 7 steps in creating and implementing a social media marketing campaign. Retrieved from http://www.jeffbullas.com, as accessed on 20 October, 2015 at 9pm
- Eight basic rules for running a social media campaign. Retrieved from https://econsultancy.com, as accessed on 20 October, 2015 at 9pm
- https://partnersallstars.withgoogle.com, as accessed on 20 October, 2015 at 9pm

8.4(c)

- Affiliate marketing. Retrieved from http://en.wikipedia.org, as accessed on 20 October, 2015 at 9pm
- 7 tips for success in your affiliate marketing campaigns. Retrieved from http://www.blurgroup.com, as accessed on 20 October, 2015 at 9pm

- Affiliate. Retrieved from http://conversionxl.com, as accessed on 20 October, 2015 at 9pm
- Launching your First Affiliate Marketing Campaign. Retrieved from http://www.impactradius.com, as accessed on 20 October, 2015 at 9pm
- Resources. Retrieved from http://www.emailaudience.com, as accessed on 20 October, 2015 at 9pm
- Successful marketing campaigns step-by-step. Retrieved from http://unbounce.com, as accessed on 20 October, 2015 at 9pm
- The ultimate guide for a successful email campaign. Retrieved from http://www.tintup.com, as accessed on 20 October, 2015 at 9pm
- 18 tips on running successful email marketing campaigns. Retrieved from https://www.jonnyross.com, as accessed on 20 October, 2015 at 9pm
- Marketing automation statistics overview. Retrieved from http://www.emailmonday.com, as accessed on 20 October, 2015 at 9pm
- Conversion economics the cpa sweet spot. Retrieved from http://unbounce.com, as accessed on 20 October, 2015 at 9pm
- What Is a Landing Page? Retrieved from http://thelandingpagecourse.com, as accessed on 20 October, 2015 at 9pm
- A step-by-step guide to setting up a mobile-marketing campaign. Retrieved from http://www.convinceandconvert.com, as accessed on 20 October, 2015 at 9pm
- 6 steps: Create successful messaging campaign. Retrieved from http://www.waterfall.com, as accessed on 20 October, 2015 at 9pm
- Mobile campaign management. Retrieved from http://www.urbanshuffle.com, as accessed on 20 October, 2015 at 9pm
- 3 Steps for a Successful Start to Your Mobile Campaign. Retrieved from https://mobilecommons.zendesk.com, as accessed on 20 October, 2015 at 9pm
- 5 steps to the ultimate ppc mobile campaign. Retrieved from http://www.clickz.com, as accessed on 20 October, 2015 at 9pm
- 6 steps to set up a successful mobile marketing campaign. Retrieved from http://solamaragency.com, as accessed on 20 October, 2015 at 9pm
- 5 steps successful mobile marketing campaign. Retrieved from http://evvnt.com, as accessed on 20 October, 2015 at 9pm
- Mobile Marketing Handbook Step-Step. Retrieved from http://www.amazon.com, as accessed on 20 October, 2015 at 9pm
- https://support.google.com, as accessed on 20 October, 2015 at 9pm
- Your first mobile adwords campaign. Retrieved from http://www.sparkpage.com, as accessed on 20 October, 2015 at 9pm

CHAPTER 9

9.1(a)

- Subscription business model. Retrieved from https://en.wikipedia.org, as accessed on 20 October, 2015 at 9pm

9.1(b)

- Customer_retention_loyalty_r_fludgate.pdf. Retrieved from http://www.kiahdesign.co.uk, as accessed on 20 October, 2015 at 9pm
- Loyalty business model. Retrieved from https://en.wikipedia.org, as accessed on 20 October, 2015 at 9pm
- Loyalty_30_Chapter_1.pdf. Retrieved from http://www.loyalty30.com, as accessed on 20 October, 2015 at 9pm
- The new era of customer loyalty management. Retrieved from http://www.customerlifecycle.us, as accessed on 20 October, 2015 at 9pm
- Loyalty marketing finding the holy grail.pdf, Retrieved from http://www.hachiko.com.au, as accessed on 20 October, 2015 at 9pm

9.1(c)

- Baron, S., Conway, T. & Warnaby, G. Relationship Marketing: A Consumer Experience Approach (SAGE Advanced Marketing Series), Retrieved from http://www.amazon.in, as accessed on 20 October, 2015 at 9pm
- Baron et al. Relationship marketing themes from Relationship Marketing: The State of the Art. Retrieved from http://www.sagepub.com, as accessed on 20 October, 2015 at 9pm
- Smith, M. The New Relationship Marketing: How to Build a Large, Loyal, Profitable Network Using the Social Web. Retrieved from http://www.amazon.in, as accessed on 20 October, 2015 at 9pm

9.1(d)

- Fill, C., Hughes, G. Marketing Communications. Retrieved from https://books.google.co.in, as accessed on 20 October, 2015 at 9pm
- Influencers-vs.-Advocates-Whats-the-Difference-eBook-Final-v2-1.pdf. Retrieved from http://www.tapinfluence.com, as accessed on 20 October, 2015 at 9pm
- AdvocateMarketingPlaybookParts1to5.pdf. Retrieved from http://info.influitive.com, as accessed on 20 October, 2015 at 9pm
- Building Customer Loyalty. Retrieved from http://www.smartinsights.com, as accessed on 20 October, 2015 at 9pm

- How-Technology-Marketers-Can-Better-Engage-Customers.pdf. Retrieved from http://www.rosetta.com, as accessed on 20 October, 2015 at 9pm
- Social cem moving beyond customer loyalty to customer advocacy part 5. Retrieved from http://www.drnatalienews.com, as accessed on 20 October, 2015 at 9pm

9.2(a)

- E-commerce payment system. Retrieved from https://en.wikipedia.org,as accessed on 20 October, 2015 at 9pm
- The e-payment systems. Retrieved from http://www.slideshare.net/Vishalchd11, as accessed on 20 October, 2015 at 9pm
- Payment and settlement systems in India. Retrieved from https://en.wikipedia.org, as accessed on 20 October, 2015 at 9pm

9.2(b)

- Emerging Payments 2013. Retrieved from http://www.aba.com, as accessed on 20 October, 2015 at 9pm
- Payments digital physical goods pr, Retrieved from http://www.juniperresearch.com, as accessed on 20 October, 2015 at 9pm
- ACI's Emerging Payment Systems (West Coast-2013) brochure.pdf. Retrieved from http://www.dwt.com, as accessed on 20 October, 2015 at 9pm
- Mobile payment. Retrieved from https://en.wikipedia.org, as accessed on 20 October, 2015 at 9pm
- Different types of mobile payments. Retrieved from http://www.mobiletransaction.org, as accessed on 20 October, 2015 at 9pm
- Bitcoin. Retrieved from https://en.wikipedia.org, as accessed on 20 October, 2015 at 9pm
- Payment-Card-Institute-Emerging-Payments-Technologies-3.pdf. Retrieved from http://www.paymentlawadvisor.com, as accessed on 20 October, 2015 at 9pm
- Person-person payments. Retrieved from http://www.investinganswers.com, as accessed on 20 October, 2015 at 9pm
- e-Payment. Retrieved from http://www1.american.edu, as accessed on 20 October, 2015 at 9pm
- The future of payment technology new systems which could help your business. Retrieved from http://www.smartcompany.com.au, as accessed on 20 October, 2015 at 9pm

9.2(c)

- Retrieved from https://en.wikipedia.org/wiki/E-services, as accessed on 20 October, 2015 at 9pm

- Scupola, A. Cases on Managing E-Services. Retrieved from https://books.google.co.in, as accessed on 20 October, 2015 at 9pm
- Accelerating_digital_transformation_understanding_and_setting_up_a_digital_services_unit.pdf. Retrieved from https://www.capgemini-consulting.com, as accessed on 20 October, 2015 at 9pm

9.2(d)

- Online intermediaries. Retrieved from http://www.slideshare.net/m9821735856, as accessed on 20 October, 2015 at 9pm
- The economic and social role of internet intermediaries. Retrieved from http://www.oecd.org, as accessed on 20 October, 2015 at 9pm

9.3(a)

- Understanding_and_implementing_internet_e-commerce.pdf. Retrieved from http://*www.imanet.org, as accessed on 20 October, 2015 at 9pm*
- ChallengesToGlobalEC.PDF. Retrieved from http://users.ipfw.edu, as accessed on 20 October, 2015 at 9pm
- Ciiem5d2_en.pdf. Retrieved from http://unctad.org, as accessed on 20 October, 2015 at 9pm
- E-Commerce_talk.pdf. Retrieved from http://cpe.ku.ac.th, as accessed on 20 October, 2015 at 9pm
- E-commerce in India: Drivers and Challenges. PDF retrieved from http://www.pwc.in, as accessed on 20 October, 2015 at 9pm

CHAPTER 10

Digital Marketing Landscape

- Marketing Charts. Last Year's Global Ad Spend Said to Have Outperformed Pre-Pandemic Total by Almost 20%. Retrieved from https://www.marketingcharts.com, accessed on June 21, 2022
- Internet Policy Research Initiative – Massachusetts Institute of Technology. The Future of the Ad-Supported Internet Ecosystem. Retrieved from https://www.internetpolicy.mit.edu, accessed on June 21, 2022
- Milestone Internet. Guide to Pay-Per-Click Marketing, PPC and Paid Search Marketing Retrieved from https://blog.milestoneinternet.com, accessed on June 21, 2022
- Emarketer. US Mobile Ad Spending Will Manage to Grow in 2020. Retrieved from https://www.emarketer.com, accessed on June 21, 2022

- Luma Partners. Marketing Technology LUMAscape. Retrieved from https://www.lumapartners.com, accessed on June 22, 2022
- ChiefMartec. Marketing Technology Landscape 2022". Retrieved from https://www.chiefmartec.com, accessed on June 22, 2022
- Kantar. Internet Adoption in India – ICUBE 2020". Retrieved from https://images.assettype.com, accessed on June 22, 2022
- Ministry of Electronics and Information Technology – Government of India. India's Trillion-Dollar Digital Opportunity. Retrieved from https://www.digitalindia.gov.in, accessed on June 23, 2022
- Media-and-Entertainment-April-2021.pdf. Retrieved from https://www.ibef.org, accessed on June 23, 2022
- Dentsu. Digital Advertising in India – 2021. Retrieved from https://www.e4media.net, accessed on June 23, 2022

Blockchain Technology

- IBM. What is blockchain technology? Retrieved from https://www.ibm.com, accessed on June 23, 2022
- Investopedia. What is a blockchain? Retrieved from https://www.investopedia.com, accessed on June 23, 2022
- Investopedia. Non-fungible token". Retrieved from https://www.investopedia.com, accessed on June 23, 2022
- Medium. Blockchain for Dummies. Retrieved from https://www.medium.com, accessed on June 23, 2022
- UpGrad. Blockchain in Digital Marketing [And Why It is the Future]. Retrieved from https://www.upgrad.com, accessed on June 23, 2022
- 2Stallions. What is Blockchain and How Can It Benefit Digital Marketing. Retrieved from https://www.2stallions.com, accessed on June 23, 2022
- Marketing Tech. Blockchain in digital marketing: More consumer trust – and new ways of advertising. Retrieved from https://www.marketingtechnews.net, accessed on June 23, 2022
- Big Wave Marketing. An Introduction to Blockchain and Cryptocurrency in Marketing. Retrieved from https://www.bigwave.co.uk, accessed on June 23, 2022
- AdGully. Blockchain: The Future of Digital Marketing. Retrieved from https://www.adgully.com, accessed on June 23, 2022
- FirstPage. How Can NFTs be used for Digital Marketing? Retrieved from https://www.firstpage.hk, accessed on June 23, 2022
- BrandWatch. How Are Brands Using NFTs, and What Does This Mean for the Future? Retrieved from https://www.brandwatch.com, accessed on June 23, 2022
- Simplilearn. What is blockchain technology? How does blockchain work?. Retrieved from https://www.simplilearn.com, accessed on June 23, 2022

- ReadWrite. How Blockchain is Impacting the Digital Marketing Industry. Retrieved from https://www.readwrite.com, accessed on June 23, 2022
- Forkast. 81 of top 100 companies use blockchain technology, Blockdata research shows. Retrieved from https://www.forkast.news, accessed on June 23, 2022

Metaverse

- Wikipedia. Metaverse. Retrieved from https://www.en.wikipedia.org, accessed on June 24, 2022
- Hypebeast. Nike announces details for its immersive NIKELAND 3D space on Roblox. Retrieved from https://www.hypebeast.com, accessed on June 24, 2022
- Salespanel Blog. How the Metaverse will change digital marketing. Retrieved from https://www.salespanel.io, accessed on June 24, 2022
- Star 2.0. What does the metaverse mean for the future of digital marketing? Retrieved from https://www.star-digital.co.uk, accessed on June 24, 2022
- Clearwater Agency. How will the 'Metaverse' change the future of digital marketing? Retrieved from https://www.clearwateragency.com.au accessed on June 24, 2022
- Popupsmart. Ultimate Guide To The Future of Marketing On The Metaverse. Retrieved from https://www.popupsmart.com, accessed on June 24, 2022
- Jefferies LLC. Going Outside is Highly Overrated: Metaverse Primer. Retrieved from https://assets.website-files.com, accessed on June 24, 2022

Artificial Intelligence

- NIHT. Artificial Intelligence in Digital Marketing. Retrieved from https://www.nihtdigitalmarketing.com, accessed on June 25, 2022
- Adtext AI. 9 Applications of Artificial Intelligence in Digital Marketing That Will Revolutionize Your Business. Retrieved from https://blog.adtext.com, accessed on June 25, 2022
- Institute of Entrepreneurship Development. How AI is transforming the future of digital marketing. Retrieved from https://www.ied.eu, accessed on June 25, 2022
- Marketing Insider Group. Top Benefits & Uses of AI in Digital Marketing. Retrieved from https://www.marketinginsidergroup.com, accessed on June 26, 2022
- Forbes. How AI is transforming the future of digital marketing. Retrieved from https://www.forbes.com, accessed on June 25, 2022

Digital Payments

- AdGully. "Amazon Pay's #AbHarDinHuaAasan showcases the power of digital payments". Retrieved from https://www.adgully.com, accessed on June 26, 2022

- Clevertap. "What is Mobile Wallet Marketing? More Than Just a Digital Payment Approach". Retrieved from https://www.clevertap.com, accessed on June 26, 2022
- Retail Dive. Mobile wallets are more marketing channel than payments topic: Forrester. Retrieved from https://www.retaildive.com, accessed on June 26, 2022
- iBrand Studio. Mobile Wallet Marketing: The New Digital Marketing Trend. Retrieved from https://www.ibrandstudio.com, accessed on June 26, 2022
- 6 ways to integrate mobile payment into your consumer marketing strategy. Retrieved from https://blog.marketo.com, accessed on June 26, 2022
- ETA – Transcation Trends. Guest Past: 6 Steps to Launching a Digital Marketing Campaign in Payments. Retrieved from https://www.electran.org, accessed on June 26, 2022

Audio-Social Marketing

- BrandWatch. The Complete Social Marketing Guide. Retrieved from https://www.brandwatch.com, accessed on June 26, 2022
- Social Samosa. Guide: How to leverage Live Audio for marketing. Retrieved from https://www.socialsamosa.com, accessed on June 27, 2022
- Your Target. How to use Clubhouse for marketing. Retrieved on https://blog.yourtarget.ch/en, accessed on June 27, 2022
- Business2Community. How You Can Use Clubhouse as a Marketer. Retrieved from https://www.business2community.com, accessed on June 27, 2022
- AdCore. Why Marketers Need Clubhouse (And How to Use it)? Retrieved from https://www.adcore.com, accessed on June 27, 2022
- Zoho Social. Why audio-based social media is the future. Retrieved from https://www.zoho.com, accessed on June 27, 2022

CHAPTER 11

11.1(a)

- The evolving role of the CMO. Retrieved from http://www.mckinsey.com, as accessed on 15 November, 2015 at 4pm
- The Rebirth of the CMO. Retrieved from https://hbr.org, as accessed on 15 November, 2015 at 4pm

11.1(b)

- McKinsey Global Institute. Executive Summary- March 2019. Retrieved from https://www.mckinsey.com, accessed on June 21, 2022

- Sparktoro. The T-Shaped Web Marketer. Retrieved from https://www.sparktoro.com, accessed on June 21, 2022
- Aikens, C. Building A T-Shaped Marketing Skill Set. Retrieved from https://www.v9digital.com, accessed June 21, 2022.
- Grow With Ward. Growth Hacker Skills in 2021: Technical, Analytical and Marketing Skills. Retrieved from https://www.growwithward.com/ (Accessed on June 21, 2022)
- Building a T-shaped Skillset. Retrieved from https://www.distilled.net, as accessed on 15 November, 2015 at 4pm

11.1(c)

- SEO as a Career Choice – Salary Career Growth. Retrieved from http://blog.learnpact.com, as accessed on 15 November, 2015 at 4pm
- SEO Career. Retrieved from http://www.link-assistant.com, as accessed on 15 November, 2015 at 4pm
- Start Career SEO. Retrieved from http://www.stateofdigital.com, as accessed on 15 November, 2015 at 4pm
- How to get a job in SEO. Retrieved from https://builtvisible.com, as accessed on 15 November, 2015 at 4pm
- SEO Career Article. Retrieved from http://www.webconfs.com, as accessed on 15 November, 2015 at 4pm
- Social Media Jobs that will be big in 2014. Retrieved from http://jobs.aol.com, as accessed on 15 November, 2015 at 4pm
- Swallow, E. (2010, June 24). 5 Tips for Aspiring Social Media Marketers. Retrieved from http://mashable.com, as accessed on 15 November, 2015 at 4pm
- What a Content Career in Marketing Looks Like. Retrieved from http://blog.hubspot.com, as accessed on 15 November, 2015 at 4pm
- Frey, C. (2015, July 8). Is Your Content Marketing Career on Autopilot? Retrieved from http://contentmarketinginstitute.com, as accessed on 15 November, 2015 at 4pm
- What is the Career Path Development for a UX Designer. Retrieved from https://www.quora.com, as accessed on 15 November, 2015 at 4pm
- Parke, T. (2013, Dec 1). Beyond UX Design: Finding Your Path. Retrieved from http://uxmas.com, as accessed on 15 November, 2015 at 4pm
- Malecek, P. (2011, Mar 16). UX Career Paths and Job Satisfaction Retrieved from http://uxmag.com, as accessed on 15 November, 2015 at 4pm
- CRM Marketing. Retrieved from http://www.totaljobs.com, as accessed on 15 November, 2015 at 4pm
- Majid K. Top 5 Career Options in Mobile Marketing. Retrieved from http://www.digitalvidya.com, as accessed on 15 November, 2015 at 4pm

11.1(d)

- Swallow, E. (2010, Oct 2). 10 Tips for Aspiring Digital Marketers. Retrieved from http://mashable.com, as accessed on 15 November, 2015 at 4pm
- Simply Hired Staff. (2017, Sep 13). What You Need to Know About a Career in Digital Marketing Retrieved from http://www.simplyhired.com, as accessed on 15 November, 2015 at 4pm
- Dreller, J. (2015, Aug 10). Where Do You Go From Here? 7 Career Paths For The Search Engine Marketer http://searchengineland.com, as accessed on 15 November, 2015 at 4pm

Bibliography 2
Source Links on Case Studies

CASE STUDY 1

1. India Brand Equity Foundation. "E-commerce Industry in India". Retrieved from www.ibef.org (Accessed Jan 5, 2023).
2. The Economic Times. "Reliance, Tata to join Amazon and Flipkart in dominating Indian e-commerce: Forrester". Retrieved from https://economictimes.indiatimes.com (Accessed on June 03, 2022).
3. The Economic Times. "Ten years on, here's what flipped the fate of Flipkart". Retrieved from https://economictimes.indiatimes.com (Accessed on Jan 06, 2023).
4. BBC. "Why did Walmart buy India's Flipkart?" Retrieved from https://www.bbc.com (Accessed on Jan 06, 2023).
5. Dayalani, V. (2021). "Amazon Vs Flipkart: Who Led The Indian Ecommerce War In 2021?" ©Inc42 (December 21, 2021). Retrieved from https://inc42.com (Accessed on June 04, 2022).
6. Insider. "Flipkart is poised to overtake Amazon in India by 2023". Retrieved from https://www.businessinsider.com/ (Accessed on Jan 05, 2023).
7. Inc42. "Amazon Vs Flipkart: Who Led The Indian Ecommerce War In 2021?" Retrieved from https://inc42.com (Accessed on Jan 06, 2023).
8. Modern Retail. "How the pandemic strengthened Walmart-owned Flipkart's marketshare". Retrieved from https://modernretail.co, accessed on June 04, 2022.
9. Bloomberg (2021). Walmart Plans Massive India Warehouse With Billionaire Adani. Retrieved from www.bloomsberg.com, accessed 20 March, 2023.
10. Business Standard. "Flipkart India unit's FY18 losses zoom 742% in spite of 39% rise in revenue". Retrieved from www.business-standard.com (Accessed on Jan 06, 2023).
11. COTW (2020). Hagglebot with Flipkart. www.campaignsoftheworld.com, accessed 20 March, 2020.
12. Financial Express (2020). After listing 50k kiranas, Flipkart to hire 70k delivery executives, packers, sorters this festive season. www.financialexpress.com, accessed 20 March, 2020.

13. The New Indian Express (2022). E-commerce firms clock Rs 40,000 crore sale in festive season, Flipkart tops order volume. https://www.newindianexpress.com, accessed 20 March, 2023.

CASE STUDY 2

1. Inc 42. "Amazon vs Flipkart: Who Led the Indian Ecommerce War In 2021?". Retrieved from https://www.inc42.com (Accessed on June 04, 2022)(Accessed on June 04, 2022).
2. Forbes. "7 ways that Amazon is winning by acting glocally in India". Retrieved from https://www.forbes.com (Accessed on June 04, 2022).
3. Business Standard. "Amazon crosses 10 lakh sellers milestone across India". Retrieved from https://www.business-standard.com (Accessed on June 04, 2022).
4. Business Insider. "Flipkart is poised to overtake Amazon in India by 2023". Retrieved from https://www.businessinsider.com (Accessed on June 05, 2022).
5. Nagpur Today. "Amazon vs Flipkart: Who Dominates the Indian Race of E-Commerce". Retrieved from https://www.nagpurtoday.in (Accessed on June 05, 2022).
6. Modern Retail. "How the pandemic strengthened Walmart-owned Flipkart's market share". Retrieved from https://www.modernretail.co (Accessed on June 05, 2022) .
7. Economic Times. "Amazon acquires reseller platform Glowroad in social commerce push". Retrieved from https://www.economictimes.indiatimes.com(Accessed on June 05, 2022).
8. Economic Times. "Amazon India marketplace clocks 49% revenue growth in FY21". Retrieved from https://www.economictimes.indiatimes.com (Accessed on June 05, 2022).

CASE STUDY 3

1. Statista. "Revenue of Google India from financial year 2015- 2021 (in billion Indian rupees". Retrieved from https://www.statista.com/ (Accessed on June 06, 2022).
2. Financial Express. "India is on the forefront of cloud adoption: Bikram Singh Bedi, managing director, Google Cloud India". Retrieved from https://www.financialexpress.com/ (Accessed on June 06, 2022).
3. Inc42. "PhonePe, Google Pay led UPI Txn With Total 83% Market Share in 2021". Retrieved from https://www.inc42.com/ (Accessed on June 06, 2022).
4. Mantraa. "Amazon's ad business to overtake Google and Facebook ads". Retrieved from https://www.mantraa.com/ (Accessed on June 06, 2022).
5. Inc42. "Meet the 20 Indian Start-ups That Are Part of Google Accelerator's 6th Cohort ". Retrieved from https://www.inc42.com/ (Accessed on June 06, 2022).

6. Digital News Publishers ... vs Alphabet Inc. And Others on 7 January, 2022. Retrieved from https://indiankanoon.org, accessed March 20, 2023.
7. India Today (2021). Google committed to India's new IT rules, assures CEO Sundar Pichai. Retrieved from https://www.indiatoday.in, accessed March 20, 2023.

CASE STUDY 4

1. Financial Express. "Meta's India revenue up 16% to Rs 1,485 crore in FY21". Retrieved from https://www.financialexpress.com/ (Accessed on June 06, 2022).
2. Business Standard. "Facebook India launches loans programme for small businesses in 200 places". Retrieved from https://www.business-standard.com/ (Accessed on June 06, 2022).
3. Statista. "Number of WhatsApp users in selected countries worldwide as of June 2021 (in millions)". Retrieved from https://www.statista.com/ (Accessed on June 06, 2022).
4. Fortune India. "Facebook's new game plan for India". Retrieved from https://www.fortuneindia.com/ (Accessed on June 06, 2022).
5. World Population Review. "Facebook users by country – 2022". Retrieved from https://www.worldpopulationreview.com/ (Accessed on June 06, 2022).
6. The Drum. "Facebook India's Avinash Pant on finding the winning strategy for its biggest audience". Retrieved from https://www.thedrum.com/ (Accessed on June 07, 2022).
7. Statista. "Number of Facebook users in India from 2017 to 2020, with estimates until 2040". Retrieved from https://www.statista.com/ (Accessed on June 06, 2022).
8. The Hindu Business Line. "Facebook's new five-pronged growth strategy for India". Retrieved from https://www.thehindubusinessline.com/ (Accessed on June 07, 2022).
9. Financial Express. "Ajit Mohan defines Meta India's key focus in 2022; and why is it an important market". Retrieved from https://www.financialexpress.com/ (Accessed on June 07, 2022).
10. Business Today. "Facebook 2.0 – Meta's India Play". Retrieved from https://www.businesstoday.in/ (Accessed on June 07, 2022).

CASE STUDY 5

1. Economic Times. "India became our number one market in daily users: Twitter's new India director Taranjeet Singh". Retrieved from https://www.economictimes.indiatimes.com/ (Accessed on June 08, 2022).
2. CNN Business. "Twitter is a mess in India. Here's how it got there". Retrieved from https://www.edition.cnn.com/ (Accessed on June 08, 2022).
3. Timesnext. "Why Twitter has shifted its focus to India with a sharp eye for international growth". Retrieved from https://www.timesnext.com/ (Accessed on June 08, 2022).

4. Statista. "Share of Twitter in social media market across India from April 2019 to July 2021". Retrieved from https://www.statista.com/ (Accessed on June 08, 2022).
5. Statista. "Forecast of the number of Twitter users in India from 2017 to 2025 (in millions). Retrieved from https://www.statista.com/ (Accessed on June 08, 2022).
6. Social Samosa. "Twitter marketing solutions and audience insights from India". Retrieved from https://www.socialsamosa.com/ (Accessed on June 08, 2022).

CASE STUDY 6

1. Exchange4Media. "Times Internet FY21 online advertising income surges 26% to ₹621.27 crore". Retrieved from https://www.exchange4media.com, accessed on June 09, 2022
2. Times Internet. "Times Internet Today – 2019". Retrieved from https://www.timesinternet.in, accessed on June 09, 2022
3. Times Internet. "Times Internet Today – 2020". Retrieved from https://www.*timesinternet.in, accessed on June 09, 2022*
4. Inc42. "Times Internet posts 24% jump in FY2020 revenue, crosses 557 Mn MAU". Retrieved from https://www.inc42.com, accessed on June 09, 2022

CASE STUDY 7

1. Statista. "Leading countries based on LinkedIn audience size as of April 2022 (in millions)". Retrieved from https://www.statista.com, accessed on June 10, 2022
2. Times of India. "LinkedIn hits 50m on small town push". Retrieved from https://www.timesofindia.indiatimes.com, accessed on June 10, 2022
3. Money Control. "India becomes LinkedIn fastest-growing market in terms of engagement: Report". Retrieved from https://www.moneycontrol.com, accessed on June 10, 2022
4. BusinessWorld. "LinkedIn to be available in Hindi, seeks to expand reach in India". Retrieved from https://www.businessworld.in, accessed on June 10, 2022
5. BusinessInsider. "LinkedIn launches new features for marketers to grow and deepen community engagement". Retrieved from https://www.businessinsider.in, accessed on June 11, 2022
6. Maps of India – My India. "What makes LinkedIn so popular in India?". Retrieved from https://www.mapsofindia.com, accessed on June 11, 2022
7. The Global Statistics. "India Social Media Statistics 2022". Retrieved from https://www.theglobalstatistics.com, accessed on June 11, 2022
8. Best Media Info. "Majority of B2B marketing leaders in India say B2B 'creative confidence' is growing: LinkedIn". Retrieved from https://www.bestmediainfo.com, accessed on June 11, 2022

CASE STUDY 8

1. Inc42. "MakeMyTrip Revenue plummets by 68% in FY21; Second COVID wave threatens further slowdown". Retrieved from https://www.inc42.com, accessed on June 12, 2022
2. LiveMint. "Homestays have been a silver lining of the pandemic cloud". Retrieved from https://www.livemint.com, accessed on June 12, 2022
3. The Hindu Business Line. "Tourism Ministry signs MOU with MakeMyTrip, Ibibo to strengthen hospitality industry". Retrieved from https://www.thehindubusinessline.com, accessed on June 12, 2022
4. Skift. "India's MakeMyTrip sees strong recovery in domestic business travel". Retrieved from https://www.skift.com, accessed on June 12, 2022
5. Seeking Alpha. "MakeMyTrip: Dominant Market Share, Fastest growing major economy, South Asia tourism boom – 12% upside opportunity". Retrieved from https://www.seekingalpha.com, accessed on June 12, 2022
6. Statista. "Revenue of MakeMyTrip Limited from financial year 2015 to 2021 (in million US dollars)". Retrieved from https://www.statista.com, accessed on June 12, 2022
7. Startup Talky. "MakeMyTrip Success Story – How the company is making travels hassle-free". Retrieved from https://www.startuptalky.com, accessed on June 12, 2022

CASE STUDY 9

1. Statista. "Number of internet users in India from 2010 to 2020, with estimates until 2040". Retrieved from https://www.statista.com, accessed on June 13, 2022
2. Info Edge. "Annual Report 2020-21". Retrieved from https://www.infoedge.in, accessed on June 13, 2022
3. Economic Times. "Info Edge clocks a return of 1,050 times on Zomato investment". Retrieved from https://www.economictimes.indiatimes.com, accessed on June 13, 2022
4. Business Insider. "Info Edge is now worth almost 10 billion even with its profits falling for five quarters in a row". Retrieved from https://www.businessinsider.in, accessed on June 13, 2022

CASE STUDY 10

1. Das, U. R. & Das, D. (2016). Paytm Founder, Vijay Shekhar Sharma's incredible life story! Retrieved from http://www.businessinsider.in, as accessed on 05 May, 2016 at 8pm
2. Paytm registers 122 million active users. Retrieved from http://www.moneycontrol.com, as accessed on 05 May, 2016 at 8pm

3. Pani, P. (2016). Paytm's next big bet — online-to-offline model. Retrieved from http://www.thehindubusinessline.com, as accessed on 05 May, 2016 at 8pm
4. Nair, S. (2015). I bought a TV after I sold my first company: The many struggles of Paytm's Vijay Sharma. Retrieved from http://www.firstpost.com, as accessed on 05 May, 2016 at 8pm
5. Rags to riches story of the man behind Paytm Vijay Shekhar Sharma. Retrieved from https://mindbatteries.com, as accessed on 05 May, 2016 at 8pm
6. Choudhury, K. (2016). Paytm eyes education sector to hit high revenue. Retrieved from http://www.business-standard.com, as accessed on 05 May, 2016 at 8pm
7. Guest (2016). Paytm Financials: One97'S Revenue At INR 337 Cr, Loss At INR 372 Cr In FY 14-15. Retrieved from http://trak.in, as accessed on 05 May, 2016 at 8pm

Index

3D graphics, 10
4Ps of marketing, 203, 206
6i model, 48
6S digital marketing implementation framework, 43
6S digital marketing implementation strategy, 207
6S framework, 207
8Ps of marketing mix, 147–148

A

Accelerator campaigns, 266
Access point (AP), 33
Acquire content, 68
Acquired links, 326
Acquisition marketing, 431
Actionable reporting, 20
Active digital influences, 92
Active engagement, 109
Active influences, 90
Active targeting, 270
Activity/promotions-based interactions, 58
Ad creation, 312
Ad exchange, 250
Ad extensions, 319
Ad network, 249
Ad pacing, 341
Ad rank, 313
Ad supported model, 198
Ad unit accuracy, 304
Advertisers, 328, 340
Advertising, 119
Advertising exposure, 102
Advertising revenue model, 369
Affiliate marketing, 253
Affiliates, 225
Affordable method, 230
Agencies, 329
Agency team, 299
Agency trading desks (ATD), 250
Aggressive market leader, 177
AI-powered content marketing, 421
Alfresco, 281
American association of advertising agencies (4As), 117
American marketing association (AMA), 5
Annual plan control, 164
App selling, 423
App server, 32
Application of digital marketing, 44
Artificial intelligence & machine learning (AIML), 421
Artificial intelligence, 10
ASCOR digital marketing framework, 41, 38, 132
Assessment phase elements, 134
Assessment phase, 41
Asset download, 271
Associative content targeting, 270
Attitudinal attachment, 109
Attributes of online buying behavior, 92
Auction type, 198
Audience attributes, 330
Audience targeting, 20, 341

Audio-social marketing, 423
Augmented reality (AR), 419
Automated marketing, 422
Automation, 18
Automation of marketing communication, 234
Autoridade nacional de proteção de dados (ANPD), 112

B

Banner ads, 328
Bargain hunters, 92
Behavioral loyalty, 109
Bid capping, 341
Big data, 411
Billing and invoicing, 305
Biometric payments, 380
BlackHat SEO, 320
Blockchain technology, 417
Blockchain, 11
Blog-based lead management, 272
Brand, 107
Brand audit, 141
Brand awareness, 424
Brand building on the web, 107
Brand elements, 107
Brand equity, 107
Brand marketing, 27, 123
Brand voice, 240
Brand-based campaigns, 327
Brand-based marketing, 247
Branding campaigns, 341
Brazilian general data protection act (LGPD), 112
Breadth showcases knowledge, 428
Brick and mortar, 55
Bricks and clicks, 54, 55
Broad match, 311
Broadcasting, 5
Budget allocation for channel mix, 43
Budget capping, 341
Building a career in digital marketing, 427
Building blocks of web experience, 95
Building reports/dashboards, 304
Bulletin board systems (BBS), 251
Business strategy for digital, 204, 205
Business to business (B2B), 33
Business to consumer (B2C), 33
Business-to-business (B2B) digital marketing, 413
Buying stage campaigns, 266

C

California consumer protection act (CCPA), 111
Call to action (CTA), 271
Campaign analytics and marketing RoI, 352
Campaign bid, 313
Campaign budget, 298, 300
Campaign delivery, 303
Campaign execution, 44
Campaign execution for emerging marketing models, 344–352
Campaign fine-tune, 299, 304
Campaign go-live activities, 303
Campaign intelligence, 102
Campaign launch, 298, 302, 315
Campaign monitor, 298, 303
Campaign monitoring and tracking, 44
Campaign plan, 298
Campaign planning, 332–335
Campaign planning and budgeting, 299
Campaign reconciliation, 299, 305
Campaign reporting, 336–337
Campaign set-up, 298, 301, 335–336
Campaign tracking, 303
Campaign trafficking, 303
Career in digital marketing, 425–431
Cart-based pricing, 199

Cases
  Amazon India: with the metros in its pocket, 'Apni dukan' amazon to wow the heartland, 52–54
  Facebook (META): Indians don't text, they 'WhatsApp', 128–130
  Flipkart India: Walmart acquired flip, grows at top clip, 1–4
  Google India: your voice can command everything, 83–85
  Info edge India: betting on investments for growth, 366–367
  LinkedIn India: transitioning from networking to advertising, 260–262
  MakeMyTrip India: recovering from the pandemic, 295–297
  One97 Communication: India's go-To payment partner from Starbucks to Paan Walas, 397–398
  Times Internet: the voice of Indian news, 216–217
  Twitter India: working towards zero rifts and monetization, 169–170
Category analysis, 140
CC avenue, 380
Changing role of CMOs in organizations, 426
Changing sales and customer service patterns, 62
Channel, 122
Channel and communication plan, 41, 43
Channel mix, 226
Channel mix development, 43
Channel specific research, 302
Channels, 225
Channels for integrated marketing communications, 119
Channels of purchase, 199
Chat, 271
Citrus pay, 380
Clicks, 223
Click-through, 223
Click-through rate, 313
Client layer, 32
Client–server model, 31
Close-ended experimentation, 270
Cloud hosting, 276
Cognitive walkthrough, 288
Collaboration, 18
Commerce-based revenue models, 28
Commission-based revenue model, 369
Communication channel marketing, 27, 124
Communication mix, 233
Communication mix across digital channels, 241
Communication program design, 43
Communications messaging, 239
Community interactions, 58
Community-based campaigns, 347
Community-based marketing, 27, 123, 250
Comparative pricing, 198
Competition analysis, 138, 140
Competition-based objectives, 161
Competitive advantage and core competencies, 151
Competitive parity method, 230
Competitor-driven factors, 174
Competitor-driven needs, 155
Consent management platforms (CMP), 114
Consumer behavior, 89
Consumer behavior models, 86
  evolution of, 86
Consumer behavior on the internet, 85
Consumer data repository creation, 100
Consumer decision process (CDP), 90
  model, 88
Consumer demand, 102
  factors impacting, 103
  managing, 102
Consumer directed targeting, 270
Consumer factors, 103
Consumer for digital marketing, 83–125
Consumer funnel stages, 191

Consumer protection, 392
Consumer segments development, 101
Consumer to consumer (C2C), 33
Consumer-initiated contact, 21
Consumer-specific security, privacy, ethical, and social challenges, 391
Consumption function, 17
Content, 122
 owned, 254
 paid, 254
 viral, 254
Content aggregators, 79
Content creators, 225
Content discovery and linkages, 323
Content factors, 95
Content licensing, 80
Content management system (CMS), 281
Content marketing institute's (CMI), 345
Content marketing, 27, 123, 252, 254, 345, 410
Contests, 272
Convenience, 93
Conversation objective, 328
Conversion marketing, 263
Conversion rate optimization, 431
Conversion-oriented dynamic, 242
Conversion-oriented static, 242
Conversion-related metrics, 353
Cookies
 first-party, 113
 HTTP, 112
 persistent, 113
 session, 113
 third-party, 113
 website, 112
Core competencies analysis, 151
Core competency, 151
Core competency alignment (CCA), 180
Core competency alignment, 205
Correlating food data with political leanings by GrubHub, 99
Cost justification, 388
Cost leverage, 20
Cost per action (CPA), 223
Cost per click (CPC), 223
Cost-per-thousand (CPM), 223
Crawling, 244, 245
Critical success factors for digital marketing, 48
Cross-channel advertising, 98
Cultural diversity, 392
Customer data privacy, 111
Customer development strategy, 43, 184, 204, 205
Customer engagement & website traffic, 423
Customer feedback, 252
Customer funnel, 23
Customer identity, 110
 and privacy management, 110–112
 developing, 112
Customer interaction, 20
Customer lifetime value (CLV), 231
Customer loyalty management in the digital era, 370
Customer relationship management (CRM), 56, 101
Customer service patterns, 63–64
Customer value, 38
Customer-based brand equity (CBBE) model, 107
Customer-based objectives, 161
Customer-driven needs, 155
Customers, 225
Customized messaging, 102
Customized pricing, 199
Cybercrimes, 391

D

D2C brand activation, 423
Data
 earned media, 100
 owned media, 100
 paid media, 100
 web server performance, 352
 web traffic, 352
 web transactional, 352

Data management platform (DMP), 98
Data monitoring, 304
Data protection officer (DPO), 112
Data segmentation matrix, 187
Data server, 32
Data tracking, 391
Data types, 96
Data usage, 391
Data-driven
  analytics, 97
  campaigns, 98
  digital marketing, 95
  digital marketing strategy, 97
  display models, 337
  marketing implementation, 99
  promotions, 102
Decision process stage, 88
Decline phase, 211
Declining demand, 103
Dedicated hosting service, 276
Delivering enhanced customer value, 38
Delivery function, 17, 65, 69
Delivery function processes, 67
Demand
  declining, 103
  full, 103
  irregular, 103
  latent, 103
  negative, 103
  non-existent, 103
  overfull, 103
  unwholesome, 103
Demand side platforms (DSP), 250
Demand-led product development process, 105
Demographic data usage by GreenPal, 99
Descriptive data analytics, 97
Design communications program, 226
Designing the communication mix, 233
Developing campaign calendar, 302
Developing communications messaging, 239
Developing customer identity, 112
Developing site diagrams, 278
Development phase, 211
Device marketing, 254
Device, 274
Diagnostic data analytics, 97
Digital advertising, 123
Digital asset management (DAM), 402
Digital business strategy, 171
Digital business structures, 175
Digital campaign management, 297
Digital campaign planning, 43
Digital campaigns, 297
  basic elements of, 297
Digital core competency alignment, 179
Digital era, 5
Digital e-Services, 381
Digital factors impacting business strategy, 172
Digital implementation challenges, 385
Digital kiosks, 380
Digital ladder, 158, 162
Digital laggard, 158, 162
Digital launch, 158, 163
Digital leader, 158, 163
Digital leverage, 158, 163
Digital marketing, 17, 19, 120
  application of, 44
  assessment phase, 128–166
  business models, 27
  campaign management, 295–362
  career in, 425–431
  channels, 23
  communications and channel mix, 216–256
  consumer for, 83–125
  critical success factors for, 48
  emerging trends and concepts, 407
  evolution of, 4–5
  execution elements, 366–394
  framework, 37
  impact of networks on, 60
  implementation strategy, 207
  internal assessment, 141
  introduction, 19
  mix strategy, 205
  models creation, 52–81

Digital marketing, (*Continued*)
objectives development, 158
objectives planning, 153
objectives review, 164
operations set-up, 260–291
planning development, 217–233
strategy groundwork, 171–192
strategy roadmap, 204
strategy, 169–213
types, 23, 27
Digital marketing applications and benefits, 28–30
Digital marketing assessment phase, 128–166
Digital marketing business models, 71–80
Digital marketing channels, 23, 243
Digital marketing conversion, 262
Digital marketing firms, 299
Digital marketing framework, 37
Digital marketing implementation strategy, 205
Digital marketing internal assessment, 141
Digital marketing landscape, 399–424
Digital marketing mix, 43, 192
Digital marketing mix strategy, 204
Digital marketing models
application of, 78
creation, 75
Digital marketing objectives development, 158
Digital marketing objectives planning, 153
Digital marketing operations, 41, 43
Digital marketing refinement, 44
Digital marketing refinement phase, 358
Digital marketing revenue, 368
Digital marketing technology/Tools landscape, 402
Digital media planning, 43
Digital media planning stages, 223
Digital media planning terminology, 220
Digital on traditional mediums, 7
Digital payments, 422
Digital payments solutions, 378
Digital presence, 156
Digital presence analysis (DPA), 42, 135, 153, 157
matrix, 156, 207
Digital pricing models, 196
Digital revenue generation models, 368
Digital scale-up, 208
Digital scoping, 208
Digital services development, 38, 40
Digital services unit (DSU), 381
Digital set-up, 208
Digital shadow, 208
Digital signatures issues, 391
Digital spectrum, 208
Digital stability, 208
Digital strategy, 43, 133
Digital SWOT, 143
Digital value-Led marketing approach, 74
Digitization, 18
Digitized value chain, 69
Dimension studio, 420
DirecPay, 380
Direct marketing, 120, 252, 253
Direct network effects, 60
Direct pull channels, 201
Direct push channels, 201
Direct sales, 28
Directed buyers, 92
Directed information-seekers, 92
Display ads, 247
Display advertising, 22, 123
Display advertising model, 79
Display campaign go-live, 303
Display campaign management basics, 328
Display inventory classification, 329
Display marketing, 247
advantages of, 250
history of, 247
Do-it-yourself (DIY) model, 414
Dotcom era, 7

Double-click ad exchange, 339
Double-click invite media (DBM), 339
Driving advocates through customer
experience, 374
Drupal, 281
D-SWOT analysis, 143

E

Earned media data, 100
E-commerce, 7, 14
E-commerce implementation challenges, 386
Economic and cost justification, 388
Economic resources, 149
Editing, 68
Editorial links, 326
Editorial partnerships, 253
Efficiency control, 165
Electronic data interchange (EDI), 12
Electronic payment systems, 376
Elements of marketing communications, 236
Elements of user experience, 282, 283
E-mail marketing, 6, 273
EMD update, 325
Emergence of cybermediaries, 383
Emergence of digital marketing as a tool, 20
Emergence of digitized value chain, 69
Emerging data-driven display models, 337
Emerging digital business structures, 175
Emerging opportunities for digital marketing
professionals, 426
Engagement objective, 328
Engagement-oriented dynamic, 241
Engagement-oriented static, 241
Engagement-related metrics, 353
Engel, Blackwell and miniard (EBM)
model, 87
Enhancement phase, 211
Enterprise resource planning (ERP), 56
Entertainment seekers, 92
Established stage, 227, 230
Ethical issues, 392
Evolution of digital marketing, 4–5
Evolution of network effects, 59
Exact match, 311
Exit-related metrics, 353
Expert function, 65, 67
transaction cost concept for, 67
Expert opinion interactions, 58
Expert partners, 65
External analysis, 41, 135
Extranet, 31

F

Facebook, 272
Factors impacting
consumer demand, 103
digital marketplace, 54
digital strategy, 205
Federated learning of cohorts (FLoC), 115
Feedback eliciting interactions, 58
Feeling dimension, 108
Firms strategic intent, 205
First-party cookies, 113
First-party data, 96
Frequency capping, 341
Full demand, 103
Functionality factors, 95

G

General data protection
regulation (GDPR), 111
Going rate, 198
Google, 272
Google analytics (GA), 353
Google display network, 339
Growth and impact of search technologies, 9
Growth stage, 227, 228

H

Heuristic evaluation, 288
Home marketing, 5
Howard Sheth model of buying behavior, 86

HTTP cookies, 112
Human resources, 149
Hyperlocal marketing, 415
Hypertext transfer protocol (HTTP), 7

I

Identity-Based tracking, 115
Imagery dimension, 108
Impact of digital channels on IMC, 123
Impact of digital on customer service patterns, 63–64
Impact of digital technology on consumer behavior, 89
Impact of networks on digital marketing, 60
Impact of user experience design, 325
Impact on consumption function, 14
Impact on delivery function, 14
Impact on procurement function, 13
Impact on production function, 13
Implementation of interaction design, 285
Implementing brand-based campaigns, 327
Implementing intent-based campaigns, 305
Implicit lead scoring, 267
Inbound logistics, 11
Inbound marketing, 253
Incoming lead-processing campaigns, 266
Indexing, 244, 245
India digital marketing/Advertising tools landscape, 406
Indirect network effects, 60
Indirect pull channels, 201
Indirect push channels, 201
Individual business owner, 179
Industry analysis, 138, 139
Influence of the web experience, 94
Influencer marketing, 374, 421
Information and communication technologies (ICT), 13
Information input stage, 88
Information processing stage, 88
Information-seeking interactions, 57
In-game marketing, 254
In-house campaign team, 299
Initial public offerings (IPOs), 8
Inner digitized value chain, 69
Input-driven resources, 149
Inspection methods, 288
Instant customer interaction, 20
Institute of direct and digital marketing (IDM), 19
Integrated marketing communications (IMC), 117
  basics of, 117
  channels for, 119
  four pillars of, 121
  impact of digital channels on, 123
Integrated marketing communications (IMC), 241
Intellectual resources, 149
Intent-based campaigns, 27, 123, 243, 305
Interaction functions, 65
Interactions
  activity/promotions-based, 58
  community, 58
  expert opinion, 58
  feedback eliciting, 58
  information-seeking, 57
  problem-solving, 57
Interactive platforms, 56
  growth of, 56
  impact of, 57
  importance of, 57
Interest-based campaigns, 267
Intermediary resources, 149
Internal analysis, 42, 135
Internal resource mapping, 149
Internet, 31
  consumer behavior on, 85
Internet basics, 31
Internet corporation for assigned names and numbers (ICANN), 275
Internet layer, 32

Internet marketing, 30–37, 120
  challenges to, 36
  opportunities to, 36
Internet of things (IoT), 411, 412
Internet relay chats (IRCs), 251
Investment analysis and planning for marketing RoI, 231
Irregular demand, 103

J

Joomla, 281
Journal publishing value chain, 68
Judgment dimension, 108

K

Keller's CBBE brand equity model, 108
Key digital advertising trends in India, 404
Key digital planning concepts, 222
Key display advertising players, 328
Key display ecosystem players, 249
Key value chain process, 66
Keyword inclusion, 323
Keyword management, 318
Keywords, 244, 245
Kiosk marketing, 254

L

Labor shortage, 393
Landing page optimization (LPO), 269
  based on experimentation, 270
  based on targeting, 270
  techniques, 270
Landing page, 268
Last minute pricing, 198
Latent demand, 103
Launch approval, 302
Launch stage, 226, 228
Lead fit, 267
Lead generation process, 263
Lead generation, 263
Lead interest, 267
Lead life cycle campaigns, 266
Lead management across channels, 271
Lead nurturing, 265
  campaigns, 266
  elements of, 265
Lead recycling, 268
Lead scoring, 267
  advantages of, 267
  concepts, 265
  execution, 267
Lead-capture, 268
Learning platforms, 252
Legal validity of transactions, 390
Leveraging first-party cookies, 115
Liferay, 281
Link building, 325
Link-building strategies, 326
LinkedIn, 272
Local area opportunist, 179
Local network effects, 60
Localisation & translation, 411
Location-based messaging, 20
Loyalty management, 370

M

Macro-factors, 104
Macro-micro environments, 136
Macro-micro environment analysis, 136
Magnolia, 281
Make-goods management, 305
Managing metrics, 304
Manuscript authoring, 68
Manuscript review, 68
Market opportunity analysis, 38, 40
Market research, 68, 66, 139
Market segment analysis, 139
Market-based objectives, 161
Market-driven factors, 174
Market-driven needs, 155

Marketing, 4
  affiliate, 253
  AI-powered content, 421
  applications, 80
  audio-Social, 423
  automated, 422
  brand, 27, 123
  brand-based, 247
  communication channel, 27, 124
  community-based, 27, 123, 250
  content, 27, 123, 252, 254, 345
  conversion, 263
  device, 254
  digital, 120
  direct, 120, 252, 253
  display, 247
  e-mail, 6, 273
  evolution of digital, 4–5
  home, 5
  inbound, 253
  influencer, 421
  in-game, 254
  intent-based, 27, 123, 243
  internet, 120
  kiosk, 254
  media, 254
  modern, 4
  objectives review, 164
  one-to-one, 5
  outbound, 253
  partner, 27, 123, 252
  platform, 254, 252
  platform-based, 27¸124
  print, 5
  relationship, 372
  response, 253
  search, 6, 123, 243
  search engine, 272
  social media, 6, 250
  SoLoMo, 416
  strategy, 131
  targeted, 422
  traditional, 5
  video, 254
  virtual, 421
Marketing analytics measurement framework, 355
Marketing apps, 270
Marketing automation, 410, 431
Marketing communication, 234
  automation of, 234
  criteria for judging, 239
  elements of, 236
Marketing era, 4, 5
Marketing implementation RoI, 356
Marketing intelligence from user's online data, 100
Marketing measurement framework, 44
Marketing mix, 142
Marketing mix analysis, 146
Marketing mix and the 8Ps, 146
Marketing objectives review, 164
Marketing shift, 219
Marketing situation analysis, 138
Marketplace to marketspace model, 60–62
Marketplace, 61
Mark-up pricing, 198
McKinsey global institute (MGI) report, 427
Measuring campaign variance, 304
Measuring service quality elements, 288
Media attributes, 330
Media audience, 218
Media budget, 218
Media channel, 218
Media consumption drivers for new marketing environment, 22
Media delivery, 219
Media marketing, 254
Media planning strategy, 224
Media schedule, 218
Media types, 121
Media vehicle, 218
Medium-initiated contact, 21
Message content, 239
Message format, 240
Message framing, 240
Message source, 241

Message structure, 240
Message tone, 240
Metaverse, 419
Micro-factors, 104
Minimum viable product (MVP), 40
MobiKwik, 380
Mobile app engagement, 319
Mobile marketing, 410
Mobile payments solutions, 379
Modern marketing, 4
Modern portfolio theory, 172
Multi-channel campaign set-up, 44
Multi-channel marketing, 411
Multi-channel reach, 20

N

Native advertisement, 424
Need for digital strategy, 133–134
Need recognition, 88
Negative demand, 103
Negative match, 311
Network economy phenomenon, 59
Network effect, 59
  direct, 60
  evolution of, 59
  indirect, 60
  local, 60
  two-sided, 60
  types of, 59
Network externalities, 385
New browser tracking techniques, 115
New network economy, 59
Nicosia model, 86
Nielsen's PRIZM segmentation framework, 188
Non-existent demand, 103

O

Objective and task method, 230
Objectives development and review, 42, 135
Offerings and marketing mix, 142
Off-page optimization impact parameters, 325
Off-page optimization, 321
One-to-one marketing, 5
Online advertising, 6
Online audience, 109
Online buying behavior, 92
Online data collation, 100
Online prospector firm, 178
Online value proposition (OVP), 38, 103, 171
Online/Internet marketing, 17
On-page optimization, 321
Open auction, 338
Open-ended experimentation, 270
Opportunity analysis, 139
Optimizing campaigns, 304
Organic search results, 244
Other equipment manufacturers (OEMs), 201
Outbound logistics, 11
Outbound marketing, 253
Outreach links, 326
Outsourced teams, 299
Oval layer, 69
Overfull demand, 103
Owned content, 254
Owned media data, 100
Oxigen wallet, 381

P

P2P payments, 379
Page attributes, 330
Page views, 223
Page visits, 222
PageRank algorithm, 325
Page-related metrics, 353
Paid content, 254
Paid media data, 100
Paid per click marketing, 244

Paid search marketing (PSM), 306
Panda update, 325
Partner marketing, 27, 123, 252
Partner/intermediary resources, 149
Passive digital influences, 91
Passive influences, 90
Passive targeting, 270
Pay per click, 244
Pay-per content/use model, 198
Paytm, 380
PayU India, 380
PayZippy, 380
Peer to peer (P2P), 33, 35
Penguin update, 325
Perceived value, 198
Percentage of sales method, 230
Performance dimension, 108
Performance measurement, 304
Persistent cookies, 113
Personalization and micro targeting, 411
Personalization strategy, 97
Phrase match, 311
Platform, 274
Platform marketing, 252, 254
Platform-based marketing, 27, 124
Porter's
  five force analysis, 172
  generic strategies, 172
Positioning, 148
Positive externalities, 59
Post-campaign activities, 305
Post-purchase evaluation, 88
Pre-campaign launch, 315
Predictive content targeting, 270
Predictive data analytics, 97
Pre-launch testing, 302
Pre-planning for web development, 273, 274
Pre-purchase alternative evaluation, 88
Prescriptive data analytics, 97
Price, 93
Pricing methods, 198
Pricing shift, 219
Primary research, 139
Print marketing, 5
Printing, 68
Problem-solving interactions, 57
Procure supplies, 66
Procurement function, 65, 68
Procurement function processes, 66
Product assembly, 67
Product creation, 67
Product delivery, 67
Product era, 4
Product factors, 104
Product growth/enhancement phase, 210
Product launch/development phase, 210
Product life cycle (PLC), 209
Product maturity phase/decline phase, 210
Product optimization, 102
Product package, 67
Product purchase analysis, 106
Product quality, 67
Product revenue model, 369
Product storage, 67
Product sunset phase/termination phase, 210
Product support teams, 299
Production, 68
Production era, 4
Production function, 65, 68
Production function processes, 67
Profitability control, 164
Programatic marketing, 220
Programmatic media buying, 410
Promotion investment type, 228
Promotion outcome type, 228
Promotional channels, 201
Proofing, 68
Prospecting campaigns, 341
Psychological factors, 95
Public relations, 120, 253
Publishers, 329, 340

Pull marketing, 21
Purchase funnel, 23
Push marketing, 21

Q

Quality content and keyword inclusion, 323
Quality score, 313, 318
Quicker funnel fulfillment, 20

R

Radio frequency (RF), 33
Reach engage activate nurture (REAN) model, 23
Real-time bidding (RTB), 410
Real-time bidding campaign workflow, 339
REAN model stages, 24
Reciprocal links, 326
Referral programs, 431
Refinement phase, 41, 44
Relationship era, 5
Relationship marketing, 372
Request and confirm placements, 302
Reseller web hosting, 276
Resonance dimension, 108
Resource identification, 300
Response marketing, 253
Rich media ad campaign management, 342, 343
Rich media ads, 328
Rich media advertising, 342
Rise of the internet, 7
RoI model, 44
Role of the expert function, 69
Rule-based optimization, 270

S

SaaS technology solutions, 414
Sales era, 4
Sales funnel, 23
Sales promotion, 120
Salience dimension, 108
Search algorithms, 244
Search campaign execution, 315
Search campaign go-live, 303
Search campaign planning, 305
Search engine marketing (SEM), 105, 244¸272
 history of, 244
Search engine optimization (SEO), 244, 319, 421
 basics, 319
 management, 319
Search engine submission, 322
Search engines, 78, 245
Search execution, 305
Search indexing and website navigation, 321
Search marketing, 6, 22, 123
Search marketing campaigns, 306
Search marketing concept, 78
Search technologies, 9
Search-box, 244
Second party data, 96
Secondary research, 139
Segmentation, 148
Segmentation, targeting, and positioning (STP), 142
Self-created links, 326
Self-Esteem data usage by activia, 99
Selling through cybermediaries, 383
SEM campaign set-up and execution, 308
Semantic web, 10
Sense of community, 109
Sentiment analysis, 102
SEO basics and management, 319
Server layer, 32
Service catalog, 382
Service delivery and payment, 376
Service quality elements, 288
Services revenue model, 369
Session cookies, 113

Shared web hosting, 276
Skilled manpower, 389
Small & medium businesses (SMBs)
digital marketing, 414
Small and medium businesses (SMB), 44
Small and medium business groups (SMBs), 35
SMART criteria, 159, 160
SMART objectives creation, 159
Social collaboration based revenue models, 28
Social local and mobile (SoLoMo), 415
Social media marketing, 6, 22, 250
advantages of, 252
definition, 251
growth of, 251
history of, 251
types of, 251
Social media payments, 379
Social media, 272
Social targeting, 270
Societal and digital divide issues, 392
SoLoMo concept, 415
SoLoMo marketing, 416
Spamdexing, 320
Spamming, 391
Specialized campaigns, 316
Stakeholder-based objectives, 160
Stakeholder-driven factors, 173
Stakeholder-driven needs, 154
Stakeholders, 122
Standard campaigns, 316
Standard display campaign workflow, 332
Status quo disruptor, 178
Stay-in-touch campaigns, 266
Steps to creating marketing communications strategy, 236
Steps to developing a communication strategy, 237
Stock keeping units (SKUs), 72, 105
Strategic control, 165
Strategic management, 171
Strategies for successful SEM campaigns, 317
Strategy phase, 41, 42
Strengths, weaknesses, opportunities, and threats (SWOT), 143
Strong national player, 178
Subscription model, 198
Subscription-based revenue models, 28
Supplies conversion, 67
Supply side platforms (SSP), 250
Surveys, 272
Sustenance objective, 329

T

Target list creation, 301
Target market, 300
Target return, 198
Targeted marketing, 422
Targeting, 148
active, 270
associative content, 270
consumer directed, 270
passive, 270
predictive content, 270
social, 270
Taxation issues, 390
Technology resources, 149
Tech-tool providers, 329
Termination phase, 211
Text ads, 328
Theft and fraud, 391
Third party data, 96
Third-party cookies, 113
Time-related metrics, 353
Tracking consumer behaviour, 423
Trade era, 4
Traditional marketing, 5
Transaction cost concept for expert function, 67
Transaction cost, 67

Transaction fee/affiliate/market-pace based revenue models, 28
Trust, 93
Trust-related issues, 392
T-Shaped web marketer, 427
TV set-top boxes, 380
Twitter, 272
Two-sided markets, 385
Two-sided network effects, 60
Types of network effects, 59

U

Understanding
customer data privacy, 111
digital marketing business models, 27
digital marketing conversion, 262
elements of user experience, 282
problem-value mapping, 38
web usability and evaluation, 286
WhiteHat and BlackHat SEO, 320
Undirected information-seekers, 92
Unique visitors, 222
Unreserved fixed rate, 337
Unwholesome demand, 103
URL structure, 322
Usability evaluation, 287
Usability studies, 352
Usability/user experience impact, 324
User interface (UI) technologies, 9
User testing, 288
User-submitted information, 352

V

Value chain, 65
Value chain digitization, 64–71
Value chain elaboration, 67
Value elements, 71
Value pricing, 198
Value shift functions (VSF), 180
Vertical portals, 79
Video ads, 328
Video marketing, 254
Vince update, 325
Viral content, 254
Viral marketing, 431
Viral platforms, 252
Virtual dedicated server, 276
Virtual economies, 419
Virtual marketing, 421
Virtual reality (VR), 419
Visitor-related metrics, 353
Visit-related metrics, 353
Visual storytelling, 410
VRIN framework, 149
VRIN model, 150

W

Warehouse supplies, 66
Web, 31
Web 3.0 trends, 417
Web analytics, 44, 352, 355
Web browser, 274
Web content management systems (WCMS), 281
Web content management, 281
Web development, 274
Web development cycle, 276
Web experience, 94
Web page tag management, 322
Web server, 32
Web server performance data, 352
Web style guide, 278
Web traffic data, 352
Web transactional data, 352
Web usability and evaluation, 286
Web usage analysis, 288
Web visits, 222
Website, 31
Website content development and management, 279
Website cookies, 112
Website development stages, 276
Website forms, 271

Website hosting, 276
Website navigation, 322
Website-based lead management, 271
Web-tracking audits, 116
  and forecasting, 115
  need for, 116
Web-tracking system, 116
WhiteHat SEO, 320
Wireframe development, 279
Wireless local area network (WLAN), 33
Wireless networks, 33
Wireless technologies, 31
WordPress, 281
Working of search engines, 245
World wide web, 7